# TESTING COMPUTER SOFTWARE

## Second Edition

**CEM KANER**

Ph.D., ASQC-CQE

**JACK FALK**

**HUNG QUOC NGUYEN**

ASQC-CQE

INTERNATIONAL THOMSON COMPUTER PRESS

I(T)P™    An International Thomson Publishing Company

London • Bonn • Boston • Johannesburg • Madrid • Melbourne • Mexico City • New York • Paris
Singapore • Tokyo • Toronto • Albany, NY • Belmont, CA • Cincinnati, OH • Detroit, MI

Library Congress Catalog Card Number 92-42366
ISBN 1-85032-847-1

For more information, contact:

International Thomson Computer Press
20 Park Plaza, Suite 1001
Boston, MA 02116
USA

International Thomson Publishing GmbH
Königswinterer Strasse 418
53227 Bonn
Germany

International Thomson Publishing Europe
Berkshire House 168-173
High Holborn
London WCIV 7AA
England

International Thomson Publishing Asia
221 Henderson Road #05-10
Henderson Building
Singapore 0315

Thomas Nelson Australia
102 Dodds Street
South Melbourne, 3205
Victoria, Australia

International Thomson Publishing Japan
Hirakawacho Kyowa Building, 3F
2-2-1 Hirakawacho
Chiyoda-ku, 102 Tokyo
Japan

Nelson Canada
1120 Birchmount Road
Scarborough, Ontario
Canada M1K 5G4

International Thomson Editores
Campos Eliseos 385, Piso 7
Col. Polanco
11560 Mexico D.F. Mexico

International Thomson Publishing Southern Africa
Bldg. 19, Constantia Park
239 Old Pretoria Road, P.O. Box 2459
Halfway House, 1685 South Africa

International Thomson Publishing France
1, rue st. Georges
75 009 Paris France

QEBFF 16 15 14 13 12 11 10 9 8 7 6
Library of Congress Cataloging-in-Publication Data
Kaner, Cem.

Testing computer software / Cem Kaner, Jack Falk, Hung Quoc
Nguyen.
    p. cm.
Includes bibliographical references and index.
1. Computer software—Testing. I. Falk, Jack L., 1950–
II. Nguyen, Hung Quoc.  III. Title.
QA76.76.T48K36  1993
005.1'4—dc20                          92-42366
                          CIP

Publisher/Vice President:  Jim DeWolf, ITCP/Boston
Project Director:  Chris Grisonich, ITCP/Boston

# CONTENTS

## SECTION 1—FUNDAMENTALS

## SECTION 2—SPECIFIC TESTING SKILLS

## SECTION 3—MANAGING TESTING PROJECTS AND GROUPS

# PREFACE

*Testing Computer Software* provides a realistic, pragmatic introduction to testing consumer and business software under normal business conditions. We've tested software and managed testers for well known, fast-paced Silicon Valley software publishers. We wrote this book as a training and survival guide for our staffs.

Many good books teach testing of software products that must be ultra-reliable. Life-critical and financial-industry-critical applications are specified and designed in detail, well in advance. These quality assurance and testing efforts are well funded. The testing staff has full access to the product's source code and the time to read it. Starting from these assumptions, these books explain how to do a thorough job of testing.

Much of the computing community, including most of the personal computer industry, strives to develop useful, reliable software, but not ultra-reliable software. Just as you can buy excellent economy cars and excellent mid-priced cars, most programs don't have to be Rolls Royces. (Nor can most people afford Rolls Royces.) Developers of consumer, general business, academic, and personal software have more modest test budgets, tighter schedules, and smaller staffs. Yet many of their programs are of very satisfactory quality. How do they do it? *Testing Computer Software* explains the testing part of it.

## IT'S NOT DONE BY THE BOOK

Some books say that if our projects are not "properly" controlled, if our written specifications are not always complete and up to date, if our code is not properly organized according to whatever methodology is fashionable, then, well, they should be. These books talk about testing when everyone else plays "by the rules."

> *This book is about doing testing when your coworkers don't, won't and don't have to follow the rules.*

Consumer software projects are often characterized by a budget that is too small, a staff that is too small, a deadline that is too soon and which can't be postponed for as long as it should be, and by a shared vision and a shared commitment among the developers.

The quality of a great product lies in the hands of the individuals designing, programming, testing, and documenting it, each of whom counts. Standards, specifications, committees, and change controls will not assure quality, nor do software houses rely on them to play that role. It is the commitment of the individuals to excellence, their mastery of the tools of their crafts, and their ability to work together that makes the product, not the rules.

The development team has a vision of what they want to create, a commitment to getting as close to the dream as they can, and a recognition that they'll have to flesh out details by trial and error. By the time they've worked out the final details of one aspect of the product, they have a working version that one or two key people understand fully. That version is the "specification." It is not engraved in stone: it will be reviewed and polished later, to achieve consistency with other parts of the system. Much of the polishing may be at your suggestion, as the tester.

In the real world, product changes are made late in development. When you're developing a product for public sale, your customers—your *potential* customers—did not agree to any specification. If a competitor creates something more appealing, you have to respond quickly.

Desirable features are frequently dropped because there is no time to implement them. Code rewrites are also set aside, even if they're needed to bring a fragile first working version to a level the programmer considers professional. A conscientious programmer might take the initiative and do the job anyway, "on the sly." Late in the project, he may drop a significant change into the package without warning. These efforts go beyond the call of duty and the 40-hour week. They may improve the product tremendously or destabilize it badly, probably both for a time. Whatever the result, people take personal initiative to improve the product.

There are always late changes. The goal is to cope with them—they are needed—as painlessly as possible. The goal is not to create a bureaucracy to inhibit them. If you can't keep up with them as a tester, you have a problem. But the solution won't come from complaining about them or in trying to stop them.

## WHO THIS BOOK IS FOR

This book speaks to the person *doing* the testing, usually of someone else's code. The topics and discussion levels reflect what we think this person will find interesting or useful. This leads us away from certain academically interesting topics, such as proofs of program correctness. It leads us to include material not normally stressed in testing texts. For example, we often comment on interpersonal and corporate political issues. Even the most junior tester has to judge other people's work—this is the essence of testing. In the course of communicating their judgments, testers are subject to abuse. (Sometimes they deserve it.) Their work's visibility is way out of proportion to their status, which can make them political targets or easy scapegoats. We don't have solutions to the status problems. We do have suggestions for improving effectiveness and avoiding certain traps.

We also discuss project management issues. Estimating, planning, and scheduling software testing is hard because there's no true end point. There are always more tests and risks associated with skipping them. Individual testers need to understand these tradeoffs. They need to be able to plan their time to take them into account. For example, a tester may postpone important tests in order to do other tasks excellently, then find that she can never run the postponed tests because she has run out of time. Trying to do a better job, she has accomplished a worse one. This is a common and dismaying situation. Priorities and efficiency are major concerns in this book.

Testers also have to deal with design errors. A program that perfectly meets a lousy specification is a lousy program. Most books on software reliability and testing set aside the user interface. They treat it as the sole province of the human factors analyst. We disagree. (Even the one of us who *is* a human factors analyst disagrees.) A system's reliability is determined by how well *all* its parts, *including* the people who use it, work together.

Your task as a tester is to find and flag problems in a product, in the service of improving its quality. Your reports of unreliability in the human-computer system are appropriate and important, whatever the problems' root causes. *You are one of few who will examine the full product in detail* before it is shipped. Where else will this feedback come from?

Our discussions of user interface issues won't make you an expert. You will still miss significant problems. Some of your design suggestions will be silly. You should still submit these reports. They are important. Some will lead to improvements that wouldn't otherwise have been made.

## LIFE-CRITICAL SOFTWARE

In some environments, it is *not acceptable* for programmers or their managers to deviate from standardized methodologies. Control programs for nuclear reactors must be well documented and thoroughly specified. They should change only after careful calculation. If they fail, test documentation will be important legal evidence. Very large Quality Assurance staffs and huge testing budgets are affordable for projects like this. For QA workers on such projects, other books on testing are more appropriate than this one.

Even on these projects, though, there is often an acceptance test process at the end. These testers aren't insiders in the development effort. Their budget is tiny. Their deadlines are impossible. The Quality Assurance organization looks down its collective nose at them. They never have a product long enough to do "real" testing the "right" way. If you do test under these circumstances, we think this book is more appropriate for you than the traditional textbooks.

## SO THIS IS A TEXTBOOK?

We've interviewed and hired a lot of testers. We have yet to meet a computer science graduate who learned anything useful about testing at a university.

The Association for Computing Machinery and the IEEE Computer Society just published *Computing Curricula 1991*, which will heavily influence the design of university computing degree programs for the next decade. The amount of required study of testing techniques is trivial—a few hours over the course of four years. The curriculum guide suggests one optional course, *Advanced Software Engineering*, that includes testing topics among many others, but the guide doesn't mention the idea of a course focused on testing.

Over the next decade, we don't expect to meet many computer science graduates who learned anything useful about testing at a university.

There is no reason why a college couldn't fill this gap. We'd expect an Associate of Sciences who'd taken a couple of courses in testing, supplemented by introductory courses in programming and project management, to be quite employable. The starting pay rates for testers are pretty good, too. This is the kind of job we think colleges were designed to train people for.

Many of the revisions that we made for this edition were with the college student, who's probably never been near a software test lab, in mind. For colleges that don't yet offer a course on testing general business software, we hope this book will help them develop one.

If you are taking an A.S. degree, thinking of a job in testing, one caution. An A.S. and a few testing courses might get you in the door, but they leave you in a weak position for advancement. We strongly recommend that you start taking university night courses almost immediately—as soon as you're competent in your basic job.

# NOTES ON THE BOOK'S STRUCTURE AND LAYOUT

## FIRST, SOME NOTES ON THE STRUCTURE

This is a training book. Many readers will be new to the field. Others will be experienced testers who've learned their trade through on-the-job training: this is their first book on testing. Its organization reflects our interest in serving these readers.

The book presents information in layers. We cover the same issues at different levels of sophistication, detail, or depth in different places in the book. For example, Chapters 1 and 7 both discuss boundary conditions. Chapters 3 and 13 both describe project time lines and lay out testing tasks along the lines. Rather than trying to cover all aspects of a topic in one place, we present additional information about the field's core problems as readers develop additional background and sophistication.

### SECTION 1—FUNDAMENTALS

The first five chapters discuss the fundamentals of the field at a level appropriate to the new tester. Everyone should read these chapters.

### To the new tester:

You'll enjoy this book most if you read Chapters 1, 2, 4, and 5 carefully and just skim Chapter 3. Then, if you can, do some testing for a few weeks, report some bugs, and get some feedback before pressing on with Chapter 6 and beyond.

### To the teacher:

If your students don't have on-the-job experience, consider assigning a small testing project (perhaps 10 to 20 hours work) before progressing to Chapter 6. For example, look for bugs in shipping products (there are plenty in every shipping product). Don't force an analytic approach yet. Just get those bugs and design comments written up, and write simulated responses to some of them. At the end of the exercise, go over the coverage achieved so far and point out significant areas of weakness or missing tests.

### SECTION 2—SPECIFIC TESTING SKILLS

Chapters 5 through 12 focus on specific skills or issues. You can read these chapters independently of each other and in almost any order (read 5 before 6). They are useful to all testers. We wrote these chapters at a slightly more sophisticated level, to a reader who already writes test plans and leads small teams of testers or is training for these roles. However, a new tester who has read Chapters 1 through 5 should be able to work through this material.

**To the new tester:**

Chapter 6 describes the handling of Problem Reports by the product's development and marketing team and the design of a problem reporting database to facilitate this handling. Readers find Chapter 6 more interesting after they've repeatedly experienced the frustration of working hard to track down and describe serious errors, only to have these reports dismissed, ignored, misunderstood, or set aside. That's when they get motivated to understand how error reports are processed and how it could be done better. If Chapter 6 seems dull to you, just skim the first sections and skip everything from "Mechanics of the Database" onward.

Chapter 8, on printer testing, is written at the level of detail that we'd expect one of our staff to master if she was designing printer tests for a program that does a lot of printing. If this is too much detail for you, or if you don't work much with printers, try to understand the overall strategy that this chapter illustrates. Study the difference between device-independent errors, printer (or modem, or terminal, or video card, etc.) class-specific errors, driver-specific errors, and device-specific errors. If you understand why we test for these types of errors in the order that we do, you understand the core concepts of the chapter.

**To the teacher:**

As tester interviewers, we gladly look at samples of work (code or test plans or reports) done by the person we're interviewing. Trade secret rules prohibit most testers from showing the work they did on their previous job, so good work samples may be useful for a few years after graduation. Here are some possible projects that a student could do for credit, and keep for her portfolio:

- Create a Boundary Chart (see Chapters 7 and 12) for a highly structured data entry screen used in a commercially available program. Many check-writing programs, address books, and contact managers are good examples of suitable, inexpensive database applications. How many tests are necessary to check each boundary condition in isolation? Approximately how many tests are possible if we check combinations of boundary conditions? Identify any special combinations that must be tested. For the rest, write a short program that uses a random number generator (Chapter 7) to generate test case combinations of the boundaries. Is this approach better or worse than hand-selecting each combination for boundaries?

- A student who understands how software interacts with some other device can write an adaptation of Chapter 8 to modems, mice, video cards, sound cards, or whatever. Include examples of tests that could be run in specific, commercially available programs.

- Test a commercially available program against its manual (Chapter 10). The project report is the marked up manual, plus bug reports for each discrepancy between the program and the manual that might plausibly reflect an error in the software rather than the book.

- Apply a test automation tool (see Chapter 11) to a commercially available program. How long did different types of test cases take to create? How does this compare to the amount of time required to run the test by hand? How much could the program change without invalidating each test case? Based on this information, how would this student use this test tool—under what circumstances, and for what types of tests?

The final chapters, 12 to 15, talk to senior testers and test managers. Chapters 12 and 13 put the preceding material into a test-plan-wide (Chapter 12) or project-wide (Chapter 13) perspective. Chapter 14 considers the legal consequences of inadequate testing, and Chapter 15 discusses test group management.

## A FEW NOTES ON THE BOOK'S LAYOUT

This book is organized hierarchically, and we've done a few things to try to make this structure readily apparent. For example, different levels of heading are in different fonts:

## THIS IS A MAIN HEADING.

### THIS IS A SECOND-LEVEL HEADING, I.E. A SUBHEADING.

#### This is a third-level heading, a subheading of a subheading.

##### *Here is a fourth-level heading, a subheading of a subheading of a subheading.*

For the rest of the book, we will show you where you are in the chapter in a box at the top of the left-side page. The box looks like this:

---

**THE MAIN HEADING IN EFFECT AT THE START OF THIS PAGE**
  THE CURRENT SECOND-LEVEL HEADING (IF THERE IS ONE)
    The current third-level heading (if there is one)
      *The fourth-level heading (if there is one)*

---

We also try to signal some information using typefaces or special characters:

- `Courier text` indicates text that you type on the computer's keyboard or, when useful to avoid confusion with surrounding material, text displayed on the computer's screen or printed by the computer in a database report.

- `COURIER TEXT IN SMALL CAPS` is used for database field names or program variable names

- *Italics* often indicate the first significant use of a term. The surrounding paragraph defines this term.

- `<Key>` is the name of a key on the computer's keyboard, such as `<Enter>` and `<Ctrl>`.

Finally, when we refer to another section of the book, we use colons to separate headings. For example:

See Chapter 12, "Main heading: Second-level heading: Third-level heading."

# ACKNOWLEDGMENTS

Work started on this book in 1983. Over the years, several people have helped us with this book, criticizing manuscripts and the first edition (published by Kaner in 1988).

We particularly want to thank the following people (listed in alphabetical order): Professor Elaine Andersson, Dr. Boris Beizer, Jim Brooks, Randy Delucchi, Mel Doweary, David Farmer, Professor Larry Jones, Sharon Hafner, Mahmood Kahn, Ginny Kaner, Dr. Sam Kaner, John Lavelle, Dr. Larry Malcus, Ted Matsumara, Dr. Don Maxwell, Bruce Miller, Derick Miller, Rachel Miller, Peter Morse, Jane Stepak, and Emmanuel Uren.


Of course, any errors remaining in the book are the responsibility of the authors.

# AN EXAMPLE TEST SERIES

## THE REASON FOR THIS CHAPTER

Software testing is partly intuitive but largely systematic. Good testing involves much more than just running the program a few times to see whether it works. Thorough analysis of the program lets you test more systematically and more effectively.

This chapter introduces this book by illustrating how an experienced tester could approach the early testing of a simple program. To keep the example easy to understand, we made the program almost ridiculously simple. But we did give it some errors that you'll see often in real programs.

## THE FIRST CYCLE OF TESTING

You've been given the program and the following description of it:

The program is designed to add two numbers, which you enter. Each number should be one or two digits. The program will echo your entries, then print the sum. Press <Enter> after each number. To start the program, type ADDER.

### Figure 1.1  A first test of the program

| *What you do* | *What happens* |
|---|---|
| Type ADDER and press the <Enter> key | The screen blanks.  You see a question mark at the top of screen. |
| Press 2 | A 2 appears after the question mark. |
| Press <Enter> | A question mark appears on the next line. |
| Press 3 | 3 appears after the second question mark. |
| Press <Enter> | A 5 appears on the third line.  A couple lines below it is another question mark. |

## STEP 1: START WITH AN OBVIOUS AND SIMPLE TEST

Take time to familiarize yourself with the program. Check whether the program is stable enough to be tested. Programs submitted for formal testing often crash right away. Waste as little time on them as possible.

The first test just adds 2 and 3. Figure 1.1 describes the sequence of events and results. Figure 1.2 shows what the screen looks like at the end of the test.

The cursor (the flashing underline character beside the question mark at the bottom of the screen) shows you where the next number will be displayed.

**Figure 1.2   How the screen looks after the first test**

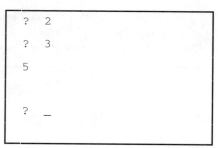

The cursor (beside the question mark at the bottom of the screen) shows you where the next number will be displayed.

## PROBLEM REPORTS ARISING FROM THE FIRST TEST

The program worked, in the sense that it accepted 2 and 3, and returned 5. But it still has problems. These are described on Problem Report forms, like the one shown in Figure 1.3.

1. *Design Error:* Nothing shows you what program this is. How do you know you're in the right program?

2. *Design Error:* There are no onscreen instructions. How do you know what to do? What if you enter a wrong number? Instructions could easily be displayed on the screen where they won't be lost, as short printed instructions typically are.

3. *Design Error:* How do you stop the program? These instructions should appear onscreen too.

4. *Coding Error:* The sum (5) isn't lined up with the other displayed numbers.

---

### *Submit one Problem Report for each error.*

---

All four errors could fit on the same report, but that's not a good idea. Problems that are grouped together might not be fixed at the same time. The unfixed ones will be lost. If the programmer wants to group them, she can sort the reports herself. To draw attention to related problems, cross-reference their reports.

YOUR COMPANY'S NAME        *CONFIDENTIAL*        PROBLEM REPORT # _____

PROGRAM _____   RELEASE _____        VERSION \_\_\_\_

REPORT TYPE (*1-6*) \_\_          SEVERITY (*1-3*) \_\_          ATTACHMENTS (*Y/N*) \_\_\_
*1 - Coding error  4 - Documentation*    *1 - Fatal*          *If yes, describe:*
*2 - Design issue  5 - Hardware*      *2 - Serious*          _____
*3 - Suggestion    6 - Query*        *3 - Minor*          _____

PROBLEM SUMMARY _____

CAN YOU REPRODUCE THE PROBLEM? (*Y/N*) \_\_

PROBLEM AND HOW TO REPRODUCE IT_____
_____
_____
_____

SUGGESTED FIX (optional) _____
_____
_____
_____

REPORTED BY _____        DATE \_\_/\_\_/\_\_

*ITEMS BELOW ARE FOR USE ONLY BY THE DEVELOPMENT TEAM*

FUNCTIONAL AREA _____        ASSIGNED TO_____

COMMENTS _____
_____
_____
_____

STATUS (*1-2*) \_\_          PRIORITY (*1-5*) \_\_\_\_
*1 - Open        2 - Closed*

RESOLUTION (*1-9*) \_\_\_          RESOLUTION  VERSION _____
*1 - Pending        4 - Deferred      7 - Withdrawn by reporter*
*2 - Fixed          5 - As designed    8 - Need more info*
*3 - Irreproducible  6 - Can't be fixed  9 - Disagree with suggestion*

RESOLVED BY        _____        DATE \_\_/\_\_/\_\_

RESOLUTION TESTED BY    _____        DATE \_\_/\_\_/\_\_

TREAT AS DEFERRED (*Y/N*) \_\_\_\_\_

**Figure 1.3  The Problem Report form**

## STEP 2: MAKE SOME NOTES ABOUT WHAT ELSE NEEDS TESTING

After your first burst of obvious tests, make notes about what else needs testing. Some of your notes will turn into formal *test series*: well-documented groups of tests that you will probably use each time you test a new version of the program. Figure 1.4 is a test series that covers the valid inputs to the program—pairs of numbers that the program should add correctly.

**Figure 1.4  Tests of "Valid" Input**

| Test case | Expected results | Notes |
|---|---|---|
| 99 + 99 | 198 | Largest pair of numbers the program can add. |
| -99 + -99 | -198 | The spec didn't say you couldn't use negative numbers. |
| 99 + -14 | 85 | A large first number might affect the program's interpretation of the second. |
| -38 + 99 | 61 | Check addition of a negative to a positive number. |
| 56 + 99 | 155 | Large second number's effect on first. |
| 9 + 9 | 18 | 9 is the largest one-digit number. |
| 0 + 0 | 0 | Programs often fail on 0. |
| 0 + 23 | 23 | The program may treat 0 as a special case.  It should be tested in the first and second entry position. |
| -78 + 0 | -78 | |

In the first test, you entered two numbers, didn't try to change them, and examined the result. Another 39,600 tests are similar to this.[1] It would be crazy to run them all. Figure 1.4 includes only eight of them. How did we narrow it down to these eight? A minor factor in determining specific values was that we wanted to use each digit at least once. Beyond that, we restricted the choices to the tests that we considered most likely to reveal problems. A powerful technique for finding problem cases is to look for boundary conditions.

---

[1] To confirm that there are 39,601 possible tests, consider this. There are 199 valid numbers ranging from -99 to 99. You can enter any of these as the first number. Similarly, you can enter any of these 199 as the second number. There are thus $199^2 = 39,601$ pairs of numbers you could use to test the program. Note that this is before we even start thinking about what happens if you do something complicated, like pressing <Backspace>. Once editing keys are allowed, the sky is the limit on the number of possible tests.

Calculating the number of possible test cases is an application of a branch of mathematics called combinatorial analysis. It's often a simple application. You can get the formulas you need from almost any introductory probability textbook, such as Winkler and Hays (1975). For an excellent introduction, read the first 100 or so pages of Feller's *An Introduction to Probability Theory and Its Applications* (1950).

## LOOKING FOR BOUNDARY CONDITIONS

If you test $2 + 3$, and then $3 + 4$, your tests aren't *exact* repetitions of each other, but they're close. Both ask what happens when you feed the program two one-digit positive numbers. If the program passes either test, you'd expect it to pass the other. Since there are too many possible tests to run, you have to pick test cases that are significant.

---

*If you expect the same result from two tests, use only one of them.*

---

If you expect the same result from two tests, they belong to the same class. Eighty-one test cases are in the class of "pairs of one-digit positive numbers." Once you realize that you're dealing with a class of test cases, test a few representatives and ignore the rest. There's an important trick to this:

---

*When you choose representatives of a class for testing, always pick the ones you think the program is most likely to fail.*

---

The best test cases are at the *boundaries* of a class. Just beyond the boundary, the program's behavior will change. For example, since the program is supposed to handle two-digit numbers, 99 and any number smaller should be OK, but 100 and anything larger are not. The boundary cases for these two classes are 99 and 100.

All members of a *class* of test cases cause the program to behave in essentially the same way. Anything that makes the program change its behavior marks the boundary between two classes.

Not every boundary in a program is intentional, and not all intended boundaries are set correctly. This is what most bugs are—most bugs cause a program to change its behavior when the programmer didn't want or expect it to, or cause the program not to change its behavior when the programmer did expect it to. Not surprisingly, some of the best places to find errors are near boundaries the programmer did intend. When programming a boundary it doesn't take much to accidentally create an incorrect boundary condition.

There are no magic formulas for grouping tests into classes or for finding boundaries. You get better at it with experience. If you looked for boundary conditions by reading the code, you'd find some that aren't obvious in normal program use. However, the programmer should have tested anything obvious in the program listing. It's your task to analyze the program from a different point of view than the programmer's. This will help you find classes, boundary conditions, critical tests, and thus errors that she missed. You should classify possible tests according to what you see in the visible behavior of the program. This may lead to a set of tests very different from those suggested by the listings, and that's what you want.

A final point to stress is that you shouldn't just test at one side of a boundary. Programmers usually make sure that their code handles values they expect it to handle, but they often forget to look at its treatment of unexpected values (ones outside the boundaries). They miss errors here, that you should not miss.

## STEP 3: CHECK THE VALID CASES AND SEE WHAT HAPPENS

The test series in Figure 1.4 only covers valid values. In your next planning steps, create series like this for invalid values. Another important series would cover edited numbers—numbers you entered, then changed before pressing <Enter>. But first, check Figure 1.4's easy cases.

---

*The reason the program is in testing is that it probably doesn't work.*

---

You can waste a lot of time on fancy tests when the real problem is that the program can't add 2 + 3.

Here are the test results:

- Positive numbers worked fine; so did zero.

- None of the tests with negative numbers worked. The computer locked when you entered the second digit. (*Locked* means that the computer ignores keyboard input; you have to reset the machine to keep working.) You tried -9 + -9 to see if it accepts single-digit negative numbers, but it locked when you pressed <Enter> after -9. Evidently, the program does not expect negative numbers.

## STEP 4: DO SOME TESTING "ON THE FLY"

No matter how many test cases of how many types you've created, you will run out of formally planned tests. At some later point, you'll stop formally planning and documenting new tests until the next test cycle. You *can* keep testing. Run new tests as you think of them, without spending much time preparing or explaining the tests. Trust your instincts. Try any test that feels promising, even if it's similar to others that have already been run.

In this example, you quickly reached the switch point from formal to informal testing because the program crashed so soon. Something may be fundamentally wrong. If so, the program will be redesigned. Creating new test series now is risky. They may become obsolete with the next version of the program. Rather than gambling away the planning time, try some exploratory tests—whatever comes to mind. Figure 1.5 shows the tests that we would run, the notes we would take in the process, and the results.

---

*Always write down what you do and what happens when you run exploratory tests.*

---

As you can see in Figure 1.5, the program is unsound—it locks the computer at the slightest provocation. You are spending more time restarting the computer than you are testing.

As you ran into each problem, you wrote a Problem Report. Hand these in and perhaps write a summary memo about them. Your testing of this version of the program may not be "complete," but for now it is finished.

## STEP 5: SUMMARIZE WHAT YOU KNOW ABOUT THE PROGRAM AND ITS PROBLEMS

This is strictly for your own use. It isn't always necessary but it is often useful.

To this point, your thinking has been focused. You've concentrated on specific issues, such as coming up with boundary conditions for valid input. Keeping focused will be more difficult later, when you spend more time executing old test series than you spend thinking. You need time to step back from the specific tasks to think generally about the program, its problems, and your testing strategy.

You benefit from spending this time by noticing things that you missed before—new boundary conditions, for example.

### Figure 1.5 Further Exploratory Tests

| Test | Why is this of interest | Notes |
|------|------------------------|-------|
| 100 + 100 | Boundary condition: Just greater than the largest valid value (99) | The program accepted 10. When you entered the second 0, to make 100, the program behaved as if you had typed <Enter>. The same for the second 100, so at the end of the test the screen looked like this:<br><br>? 10<br><br>? 10<br><br>20 |
| <Enter> + <Enter> | What happens when there is no input? | When you pressed <Enter>, the program printed a 10 -- the last number you had entered. Same thing when you pressed <Enter> again, and it printed 20 as the sum. |
| 123456 + 0 | Enter the maximum number of digits | The program accepted the first two digits and ignored the rest, just like it did with 100. In later tests, however, these will be distinct cases. How many digits will the program take and how will it respond to more than that number? |
| 1.2 + 5 | Try a decimal number | Treated the decimal point the same as a <Enter> |
| A + b | Invalid characters | Program locked up when you pressed <Enter> after an A. To continue testing you had to restart the computer. |
| <Ctrl-A> + <Ctrl-B><br><Ctrl-C> + <Ctrl-D><br><F1>    + <Esc> | Control characters and function keys are often good for a crash. | For everything but <Ctrl-C>, the program displayed graphics symbols, then locked when you pressed <Enter>. When you entered <Ctrl-C>, the program exited to the operating system. |

A good starting activity is to write down a list of points that summarize your thoughts about the program. Here's our list:

- The communication style of the program is *extremely* terse.

- The program doesn't deal with negative numbers. The largest sum that it can handle is 198 and the smallest is 0.

- The program treats the third character you type (such as the third digit in `100`) as if it were an `<Enter>`.

- The program accepts any character as a valid input, until you press `<Enter>`.

- The program doesn't check whether a number was entered before `<Enter>`. If you don't enter anything, the program uses the last number entered.

Assuming that the programmer isn't hopelessly incompetent, there must be a reason for this ugliness. Possibilities that come to mind right away are that she might be trying to make the program very small or very fast.

Error handling code takes memory space. So do titles, error messages, and instructions. There isn't much room for these in a program that *must* fit into extremely few bytes. Similarly, it takes time to check characters to see if they're valid, it takes time to check the third character to make sure that it really is an `<Enter>`, it takes time to print messages on the screen, and it takes time to clear a variable before putting a new value (if there is one) into it.

You can't tell, from looking at this list of problems, whether the program was stripped to (or past) its barest essentials in the interest of speed or in the interest of space. You certainly can't tell from the program whether the extreme measures are justified. To find that out, you have to talk with the programmer.

Suppose the programmer is coding with space efficiency as a major goal. How might she save space in the program? Most of the visible "tricks" are already in evidence—no error handling code, no error messages, no instructions onscreen, and no code to test the third character entered. Is there any other way to save space in a program? Yes, of course. She can minimize the room needed to store the data. The "data" in this program are the sum and the entered characters.

### Storage of the sum

The valid sums range from -198 to 198. But the program doesn't handle them all. It only handles positive numbers, so its sums run from 0 to 198.

If she stores positive numbers only, the programmer can store anything from 0 to 255 in a *byte* (8 bits). This is a common and convenient unit of storage in computers. If the programmer thought only about positive numbers and wanted to store the sum in the smallest possible space, a byte would be her unit of choice.

A problem will arise if the program is changed to handle negative numbers. The programmer *can* use a byte to hold both positive and negative numbers but she must use one of its eight bits as a *sign bit*, to signal whether the number is positive or negative. A byte holds numbers between -127 and 127. The program will fail with sums greater than 127.

Most programs that try to store too large a number in a byte fail in a specific way: any number larger than 127 is interpreted as a negative number. Maybe that will happen with this program. You should pay attention to large sums in the next cycle of tests; 127 and 128 are the boundary values. The test series in Figure 1.4 already includes a large sum (99 + 99), so no new test is needed if the program handles this correctly. You should make a note beside this case to watch for weird results.

This boundary condition is interesting because it depends on how the programmer or the programming language defines the memory storage requirements for a piece of data. *Data types* are usually defined at the start of the program or in a separate file. You could look at a listing of the part of the program that adds two numbers and never see anything wrong. The program will appear to collect two numbers, add them, put the result somewhere, and everything will look perfect. The problem is that sometimes the sum doesn't fit in the place it's being put. It's easy to miss this type of problem when you're looking at the part of the program that does the addition.

**Storage of the input**

Having considered storage of the sum, let's move on to classification of characters that the user types at the keyboard.

This section illustrates how you can translate knowledge about program internals into further test cases. Here, we look at a *hidden boundary*—a boundary condition that isn't apparent to the user, but would be apparent to someone reading the code. In this case, you can plan these tests without reading the code, as long as you understand the basics of character classification (ASCII codes). In general, the more you know about programming, the more internal boundaries you can anticipate and test for, even without reading the code.

This example confuses new testers and testers who lack programming experience. Feel free to skip to the next section.

Keyboard input is usually collected and encoded by a special control program supplied with the computer. That program assigns a numeric code to each key on the keyboard and sends that code to your program when the key is pressed. Most computers use the ASCII code. Figure 1.6 gives the relevant values for digits.

When you press a key, the programmer has to check the key's ASCII code to find out whether you typed a digit. Her routine works something like this:

```
IF ASCII_CODE_OF_ENTERED_CHAR is less than 48    (48 is ASCII for 0)
    THEN reject it as a bad character.
    ELSE IF ASCII_CODE_OF_ENTERED_CHAR
    is greater than 57                            (57 is ASCII code for 9)
       THEN reject it as a bad character
       ELSE it is a digit, so accept it.
```

Consider how this code could fail. Here are six simple programming errors that are very common:

- Suppose the programmer said `less than or equals` instead of `less than`. The program would reject 0 as a bad character.

The only way to catch this error is by testing with 0, the digit with the smallest ASCII code (48).

**Figure 1.6  ASCII codes for digits (and other values of interest)**

| Character | ASCII code |
|-----------|------------|
| / | 47 |
| 0 | 48 |
| 1 | 49 |
| 2 | 50 |
| 3 | 51 |
| 4 | 52 |
| 5 | 53 |
| 6 | 54 |
| 7 | 55 |
| 8 | 56 |
| 9 | 57 |
| : | 58 |
| A | 65 |
| b | 98 |

- If she said `less than 47` instead of `less than 48`, the program would accept / as a digit.

  The only way to catch this error is by testing with /, the non-digit with the ASCII code one less than 0's. Every other character will be classified correctly as a digit or a non-digit.

- If she said `less than 38` (a typing error, 38 instead of 48), the program would accept / and nine other non-numeric characters (&, ', (, ), *, +, ,, -, and .) as digits.

  You can catch this error with any of the non-number characters whose ASCII codes fall between 38 and 47. This range includes the boundary value, ASCII 47, character /.

- Now consider the test for the largest digit, 9 (ASCII code 57). The most common error substitutes `greater than or equal to 57` for `greater than 57`. If you type a 9, the code received by the program is equal to 57, so the program will erroneously reject the 9 as a non-digit.

  The only misclassified character is the largest digit, 9, so you must test with this character to catch this error.

- If the programmer said `greater than 58` instead of `greater than or equal to 58` (same thing as `greater than 57`), the program will misclassify one character only, the colon : (ASCII code 58).

- If the programmer made a typing error, for example reversing the digits in 57 to get 75, the program would accept as digits all characters with ASCII codes between 48 and 75.

  A test with any character whose ASCII code was between 58 and 75 would reveal this error, but since this includes the boundary character, :, whose ASCII code is 1 greater than 9's, you don't have to test with anything else.

*Testing with just the four boundary characters, /, 0, 9, and :, will reveal every classification error that the programmer could make by getting an inequality wrong or by mistyping an ASCII code.*

In Figure 1.5, we used A (ASCII code 65) and b (ASCII code 98) to check the program's response to non-digits. The test worked—the program crashed. But what about the six types of errors we worked through here? If you had tested with A, you would only have discovered an error in the last case. You would have found no errors with b. Using the boundary non-digits, / and :, you would have caught four errors. As usual, the boundary tests are the most powerful.

## THE FIRST CYCLE OF TESTING: SUMMARY

You started with the simplest possible test. The program passed it, so you constructed a formal series of tests to see how well the program works with other valid values. You'll use these tests again next time. The program failed some of these tests badly, so you decided not to formally plan your next series. Instead, you conducted a quick series of tests to see if the program was hopelessly unstable. It was. You kept notes on your tests, and you'll refer to these next time.

If the program had performed better with the quick tests, you'd have gone back to constructing formal test series, covering the same ground that you skimmed with the quick tests, but more thoroughly, with more carefully thought-out test cases. As long as the program continued to look reasonably solid, you would have kept making series of tough tests, until you ran out of ideas or time. Just before running out of testing time, you probably would have run a few quick tests of areas that weren't covered by the various series developed to that point, and kept your notes for later.

After finishing testing and test reporting paperwork, you took some time to gather your thoughts. You started by listing the salient problems with the program, but this was just a vehicle to get started. You had no fixed agenda. You followed whatever lines of thought seemed interesting or promising. In the process, you found two new lines of attack. You have to *decide* to make time to mull over the program. It's important to do this, even if the project is behind schedule.

## THE SECOND CYCLE OF TESTING

The programmer has told you that speed is critically important. How much code space is taken is irrelevant. Her responses to the Problem Reports are in Figure 1.7.

### STEP 1: BEFORE DOING ANY TESTING, REVIEW THE RESPONSES TO THE PROBLEM REPORTS CAREFULLY TO SEE WHAT NEEDS TO BE DONE, AND WHAT DOESN'T

It's just as well that you didn't spend much time designing tests for error handling, because the programmer didn't add any error handling. Further, even though the program will now handle negative numbers, it won't handle any from -10 to -99; these are three characters long and the program still treats the third as if it were <Enter>. Looking back at your planned test series in Figure 1.4, you see that you can't run the tests that use -99, -78, and -14. Don't just skip these tests: you still have to test addition of negative numbers. Use -9 + -9 instead of -99 + -99. Use single digit negative numbers instead of -78 and -14.

It is common and reasonable for a programmer to ask you to test the rest of the program while she keeps trying to fix a difficult bug. You probably can't run some tests in your planned series until that error is fixed. Don't give up on tests similar to them. Create new ones that can be run, even if they aren't as good as the originals. If you wait until you can run the "best" tests, you'll postpone testing whole areas of the program,

**THE SECOND CYCLE OF TESTING**

STEP 1: BEFORE DOING ANY TESTING, REVIEW THE RESPONSES TO THE PROBLEM REPORTS CAREFULLY TO SEE WHAT NEEDS TO BE DONE, AND WHAT DOESN'T

often until it's too late to fix any but the most serious problems. In this example, using numbers between -1 and -9 isn't as good as using the ones planned, but it does test addition of negative numbers. It is far better than skipping all tests of negative numbers.

This takes care of the tests you no longer have to run, and the ones you have to replace with others. Do the responses to the Problem Reports lead to any new tests? Yes.

### Figure 1.7 Responses to the First Round of Testing Reports

| | | |
|---|---|---|
| 1. Design Issue: | No program title onscreen. | |
| Resolution: | Won't be fixed. | |
| 2. Design issue: | No instruction onscreen. | |
| Resolution: | Won't be fixed. Comment:"Good point but slows program." | |
| 3. Design issue: | How do you stop the program? | |
| Resolution: | Fixed: "Press Ctrl-C to Exit" displayed onscreen. | |
| 4. Bug: | The sum (5) isn't lined up with the other displayed numbers. | |
| Resolution: | Fixed. | |
| 5. Bug: | Crashes on negative numbers. | |
| Resolution: | Fixed. Will add negative numbers. | |
| 6. Bug: | Assumes 3rd character is <Enter> without checking. | |
| Resolution: | Pending (not yet fixed). | |
| 7. Bug: | Crashes when you enter non-numbers. | |
| Resolution: | Not a problem. Comment: "Don't do that." | |
| 8. Bug: | Crashes when you enter control characters. | |
| Resolution: | Not a problem. Comment: "See report 7." | |
| 9. Bug: | Crashes when you press function keys. | |
| Resolution: | Not a problem. Comment: "See report 7." | |

## STEP 2: REVIEW COMMENTS ON PROBLEMS THAT WON'T BE FIXED. THEY MAY SUGGEST FURTHER TESTS.

The most serious problem in the program is terrible error handling. The programmer does not intend to fix it. What can you do about it?

> *The single most effective tactic for getting a bug fixed is to find test cases that make it appear so likely to occur under such innocent circumstances that absolutely no one would be willing to tolerate it.*

A good way to find the worst (best) examples of a bug's misbehavior is to boil it down to its simplest, barest essentials. As you try to do this, you'll often find simpler, nastier looking manifestations of the same error.

In the present case, the program crashes when you press certain keys. You tried alphabetic keys, control keys, and function keys. The program locks the computer whenever you enter any invalid (non-numeric) character. The programmer says that you shouldn't enter these characters anyway. Your point is that it should reject them gracefully, rather than forcing you to restart the computer. Work backwards. The program rejects some keys ungracefully. The programmer doesn't think it matters because no one would expect the program to accept these keys anyway.

What if the program crashes with characters that people *would* expect it to accept? If you can find enough of them, the programmer will have to write so much special code to deal with them that she may as well deal with the whole keyboard.

Think about what keys people might expect to be able to press in an arithmetic program. Your best bet is to **brainstorm**. Write down any key that you think someone *might* argue should be usable, and why. Don't worry about whether the programmer will agree that a given key should be usable. You can edit your list later. Figure 1.8 shows the list that we came up with.

Some of the ideas in Figure 1.8 are poor. For example, if you tell the programmer that 4/3 + 2 doesn't work, you can bet she'll say "tough." But, again, for the first draft of the list, that doesn't matter. You want a good starting point, a list that doesn't miss anything. You can decide later which cases to report, after you find out what halts the computer.

## STEP 3: PULL OUT YOUR NOTES FROM LAST TIME, ADD YOUR NEW NOTES TO THEM, AND START TESTING

It's tempting to start with the complicated, brilliant new test cases you just thought of. Don't. Start with those drudge tests that confirm that the program can still add 2 and 2 and not get 5. About one in three attempts to fix a program doesn't work or causes a new problem. Test the basics first.

You try everything in the "formal" series (Figure 1.4's tests of "Valid Inputs") as modified to only include one-digit negative numbers. It all works.

One thing you notice in the process is that the program says `Press Ctrl-C to quit` after each addition. Figure 1.9 shows the screen after the first two pairs of numbers.

The programmer told you that the speed of the program is an issue. Anything that wastes time in the program is a bug. Submit the following Problem Report:

10. *Design Error*: Writing "Press Ctrl-C to Quit" on the screen after each result wastes a lot of machine time. One of the design goals for this program is speed, so this is a problem. When the program starts, why not just write "Press Ctrl-C to Quit" at the bottom of the screen and never let that line be overwritten? (If this is possible, can you put a title and some instructions at the top of the screen in the same way?)

**Figure 1.8 Brainstorm: What keys would you expect to be allowed to enter as part of a number or while entering number?**

- Digits, of course.

- And the minus sign.

- But if the minus sign is OK, the plus sign should be too.

- Spaces. People type spaces in front of numbers to line them up neatly in columns.

- If spaces are OK before a number, they should be OK after it.

- What about arithmetic operators, like * and / (e.g. 4/3)?

- Dollar sign?

- Percent sign?

- Parentheses -- sometimes a negative number is written in parentheses, like (1000) for -1000.

- Backspace -- what if you type the wrong number?

- Delete key.

- Insert key. You enter 1 and want to back up to insert a 2 in front of it to make 21.

- Cursor movement keys in general.

Your notes include a reminder to check single-byte sums. These range from -127 through 127 or from 0 to 255. You can't enter two-digit negative numbers, so -127 is out of range. However, 99 + 99 yields the right answer, so this isn't a problem. Oh, well.

***If the programmer is reasonably careful, most of your tests won't find errors, including many of the ones you took the most time thinking about.***

Don't stop thinking. Some of your tests *will* find problems, and the more care you put into crafty thinking, the more you'll find.

The last tests check error handling. You can't enter three-digit numbers because of the known and to-be-fixed bug. That leaves the invalid characters, and you've cut this group down to the special characters, like <Backspace>, <Space>, <Delete>, and <+>, that you listed in Figure 1.8.

The program crashed in response to every one of these keys, except the minus sign. Here's the Problem Report.

**Figure 1.9 The screen during second cycle tests**

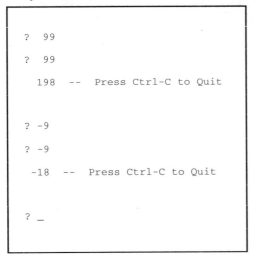

```
?  99

?  99

   198  --  Press Ctrl-C to Quit


?  -9

?  -9

   -18  --  Press Ctrl-C to Quit


?  _
```

11.  *Coding Error*

*Problem Summary*: Editing keys and other "normal" inputs lock the computer.

*Problem and How to Reproduce It*: The problems with non-numeric keys are worse than they appeared in Problem Reports 7, 8, and 9. In those cases, characters you wouldn't expect to be entered when adding digits locked the computer. Later tests showed that editing keys (<Backspace>, <Delete>) also lock the computer. So does <Space>, which a user might reasonably enter to align digits in a sum. Plus sign (<+>) also crashes the program. This may be a common error condition because some users might type <+> reflexively between numbers they add. (Example for reproducing the problem: enter an A, then press <Enter> and the program will lock.)

*Suggested Fix:* Test each character on entry. Ignore all invalid input or give error messages.

Note how you start this report: you explicitly state that the problem is worse than you made it seem in your last reports. This gives the programmer a chance to save face. She can say that she refused to fix it last time because she didn't realize (you didn't tell her) how serious the problem is.

***The best tester isn't the one who finds the most bugs or who embarrasses the most programmers. The best tester is the one who gets the most bugs fixed.***

## WHAT WILL HAPPEN IN LATER CYCLES OF TESTING

As development progresses, you will create more formal test series, and will follow them each time the program returns to you. Once a few versions of the program have consistently passed every test in a series, you'll probably use only a few of these tests in later cycles. To be safe, try to rerun every test in what you think is the final cycle. Before that, why run tests that a program can pass?

As the program gets closer to being finished, you'll use stricter tests. You'd rather run the toughest tests first, but you won't think of many of them until you've tested the program for a while and learned its quirks.

Along with using tests to expose new errors, you'll look for ways to reopen consideration of problems that you've been told won't be fixed, but that you feel are important. You will not win every battle, nor should that be your goal. Attempts to fix a program can do much more harm than good. Near the release date, some problems are best left alone. Your objective is to make sure that a problem's severity is clearly understood by everyone who has a say in how it should be addressed.

# THE OBJECTIVES AND LIMITS OF TESTING

## THE REASON FOR THIS CHAPTER

Realistic test planning is dominated by the need to select a few test cases from a huge set of possibilities. No matter how hard you try, you will miss important tests. No matter how careful and thorough a job you do, you will never find the last bug in a program, or if you do, you won't know it.

Many new testers come into the field with the beliefs that:

- they can fully test each program, and

- with this complete testing, they can ensure that the program works correctly, and

- their mission as testers is to assure program correctness by doing complete testing.

On realizing that they cannot achieve this mission, many testers become demoralized. They wonder about the integrity of the company they work for (since it won't fund a complete testing effort) and about their own professional standards. After learning that they can't do the job "right," it takes some testers a while to learn how to do the job "well."

This chapter debunks some popular testing myths. With them out of the way, we can consider some of the difficult questions that testers continue to face throughout their career, such as:

- What *is* the point of testing?

- What distinguishes good testing from poor testing?

- How much testing is enough?

- How can you tell when you've done enough?

As we see it, testing is the process of searching for errors. Good test cases are more likely to find errors, or more likely to find serious errors, than poor test cases. In future chapters (especially 7, 8, and 13) we discuss good testing strategies.

## INTERESTING READING

In an influential book on the philosophy of science, Karl Popper (1965) argues that the correct approach to testing a scientific theory is not to try to verify it, but to seek to refute the theory—that is, to prove that it has errors. The harsher the testing, the more confidence we can have in a theory that passes it. Much of Popper's reasoning applies directly to software testing.

## YOU CAN'T TEST A PROGRAM COMPLETELY

What does it mean to test a program completely? It must mean that at the end of testing, there are no undiscovered software errors. Whether they've been fixed is a different issue, but all problems must be known and understood.

## YOU CAN'T TEST A PROGRAM COMPLETELY

There is a popular belief that you *can* test a program completely:

- Some junior-level programming texts even claim to tell you how to do it: test the program's response to all possible inputs, or test all possible paths through the program. We'll soon see that neither of these tasks is adequate for complete testing, and both tasks are usually impossible.

- Many managers also believe in the possibility of complete testing. They order their staffs to do it, and assure each other that it's being done.

- Sales brochures from some software testing companies promise they'll fully test your code.

- Test coverage analyzers are sometimes marketed with the promise of telling you whether you've fully tested the code, and what further testing you must do to achieve complete testing.

- Many salespeople believe their software products are fully tested and error-free, and pass on this claim to customers.

Some testers also believe in the myth of complete testing. They suffer for it. They feel insecure, frustrated, and guilty because no matter how hard they try, how cleverly they plan, how much time they spend, and how many staff and computers they use, they still can't do enough testing. They still miss bugs.

Here are three reasons that complete testing is impossible:

- The domain of possible inputs is too large to test.
- There are too many possible paths through the program to test.
- The user interface issues (and thus the design issues) are too complex to completely test.

### YOU CAN'T TEST THE PROGRAM'S RESPONSE TO EVERY POSSIBLE INPUT

The previous chapter described a trivial program that added a pair of one- or two-digit numbers. The number of test inputs, even for this simple a program, is huge. Here's a breakdown of the types of tests you'd have to run:

#### You'd have to test all valid inputs

Even this simple program treats 39,601 different pairs of numbers as valid input data. If we made it accept four-digit numbers, we'd have to test 399,960,001 different pairs of numbers. Most addition programs accept 8 or 10 digits, or more. How could you possibly test all these?

#### You'd have to test all invalid inputs

You have to check everything you can enter at the keyboard. This includes letters, control characters, combinations of numbers and letters, numbers that are too long, question marks, the works. If you can type it, you have to check what the program does with it.

## You'd have to test all edited inputs

If the program lets you edit (change) numbers, you have to make sure editing works. Make sure you can change every number, letter, or whatever into any other number (or whatever). Next, check repeated editing: enter a number, change it, change it again. How many times should you do this? Well, consider the following bug:

> A person is interrupted while working at an intelligent terminal. He fidgets. He keeps pressing a number key, then <Backspace>, then the number, then <Backspace>, and so on. The terminal echoes and erases the numbers onscreen, but also saves them in its input buffer. When he finally gets back to work, enters a number and presses <Enter>, the terminal sends everything to a main computer. It sends all the digits, all the <Backspace>s, plus the final entry. The computer doesn't expect so much input at once from a terminal. Its input buffer overflows, and the system crashes.

This is a real bug. Variants of it have cropped up in many systems. It's triggered by an unexpected input event. You could keep testing input editing forever to make sure there's nothing like it in the system you're testing.

## You'd have to test all variations on input timing

You have to test the effect of entering data at every temporal point in the program. Don't wait to enter numbers until the computer has printed a question mark and started flashing its cursor at you. Enter numbers when it's trying to display others, when it's adding them up, when it's printing a message, whenever it's busy.

In many systems, pressing a key, or pressing a special key like <Enter>, generates an interrupt. These interrupts tell the computer to stop what it's doing and read the input stream. The computer can pick up where it left off after reading the new input. You can interrupt the computer at any time (just press a key), and so at any place in the program. To fully test the program's vulnerability to inputs at unexpected times, you'd have to interrupt it at each line of code, sometimes in more than one place in a line.

Chapter 4 and the Appendix talk about timing issues, usually under the heading of *race conditions*. Many programs show some timing vulnerability. They may respond to inputs or other events that happen at unexpected times by ignoring or discarding them, by misreading or misclassifying them, or by running amok or crashing. Timing vulnerability is a serious issue. You must test for it.

## What if you don't test all possible inputs?

There are so many possible tests that you can't run them all, so don't. Test inputs of each of the four types (valid, invalid, edited, entered at different times). Pick their values with care. But realize that as soon as you skip any input value, you have abandoned "complete testing."

> *If you think you can fully test a program without testing its response to every possible input, fine. Give us a list of your test cases. We can write a program that will pass all your tests but still fail spectacularly on an input you missed. If we can do this deliberately, our contention is that we or other programmers can do it accidentally.*

Here are two examples of failures under circumstances you might consider too complex or too specialized to check:

- One database management program trashed data files that were an exact multiple of 512 bytes long. Another couldn't work with files that were exactly 16,384 bytes long, or exact multiples of that length, even if it had created them.

- One word processor used to get lost in text files that were long (100,000 bytes) and physically fragmented (pieces stored in many nonadjacent places on the disk). After editing with no problems, moving the cursor one more time would cause a paragraph to suddenly disappear.

You might not include cases like these in tests of all "plausible" inputs to a program. But these were real problems, complained about bitterly by real customers who paid lots of real money for the privilege of having the computer make a real mess of their work.

To test a program completely, you must test its reaction to all combinations of valid and invalid inputs. Moreover, you must test these at every point at which you can enter data, under every state the program can be in at that point. This is just not possible.

## YOU CAN'T TEST EVERY PATH THE PROGRAM CAN TAKE

A program path can be traced through the code from the start of the program to program termination. Two paths differ if the program executes different statements in each, or executes the same statements but in a different order. For examples, consider Chapter 1's program. You can start the program, then press <Ctrl-C> immediately to stop it. That's a path. Or you can start it, enter two numbers, look at the sum, then press <Ctrl-C>. In another path, you would enter a digit, then press <Backspace> before continuing.

To illustrate the problem, here's one example, oversimplified, of a system that has very few state transitions but is horribly complex to test. This is based on a real bug, found during field testing.

- The system starts in State 1. This is its normal state, and it returns to State 1 as quickly as possible.
- From State 1, it always goes to State 2.
- From State 2, it can go to State 3 or State 5.
- From State 3, it can go to State 4 or State 5.
- From State 4, it can go to States 3, 5, or 6.
- From State 5, it can go to States 1, 4, or 6.
- From State 6, it can go to State 3 or State 5.

With only six states, this might seem easy to test. In fact, it did seem easy to test until the test team discovered that if the system went from State 4 to State 5 thirty times before getting back to State 6, it failed. If you didn't suspect that error, but were just mapping out the different possible tests of transitions between states, how many other paths would you expect to test before you bothered with this case?

This bug was found in a telephone (PBX) system. In State 1 the phone is idle. It rings (State 2) and either the person answers it (State 3, connected) or she doesn't and the caller hangs up (State 5, hung up—disconnect). Once the called person answers the phone, she can put the caller on hold (State 4) or hang up (State 5). When the caller's on hold or when a caller has just hung up, the called person can answer a waiting call (State 6 is an alert that a waiting call can be picked up.) When the caller has hung up and there are no waiting or holding calls, the phone returns to idle.

The PBX operator will often have a busy phone, and will often answer and place calls on hold before transferring them or before dealing with them. Whenever she puts a caller on hold, the PBX-controlling computer puts some information into a temporary area called a stack. It clears the call information from the stack when the call is retrieved from hold. When the phone reaches idle state, no calls can be on hold, and no other stack-using activity can be happening, so the software clears the entire stack just in case a routine forgot to tidy up after itself.

When a caller on hold hangs up, the stack is left with the call data. If the operator's phone goes idle before 30 callers hang up, no harm is done because the computer clears the phone's stack when it hits idle state. But if 30 callers hang up before before the phone next goes idle, the stack overflows and the operator's phone goes out of service.

Most programs are tremendously more complex than this six-state simpleton with a stack. And our inability to exercise all of the paths through a program is just one of the inabilities we have in analyzing the design and test of a program. As a result, we rely on heuristics, strategies that we think are more likely to minimize the number of errors made in the first place, more likely to make errors be obvious if they're made, or more likely to detect them. We are just beginning to figure out how much "more likely" is "more likely," or how to figure out, over time, what the differences are.

Myers has delighted in demonstrating that even simple programs can have huge numbers of paths. In 1976 he described a 100-line program that had $10^{18}$ unique paths. For comparative purposes, he noted that the universe is only about $4 \times 10^{17}$ seconds old.

> *Myers described a much simpler program in 1979. It was just a loop and a few IF statements. In most languages, you could write it in 20 lines of code. This program has 100 trillion paths; a fast tester could test them all in a billion years.*

Myers' programs are *simple*. Yes, they were "cooked," designed to have many paths to make a point, but if he can write a 20-line program with 100 trillion paths, how many paths go through a 5,000-line text editor, a 20,000-line basic spreadsheet, or a 400,000-line desktop publishing program? Plenty. More than anyone can test. Many more than a fancy automated testing program could run through before the computer died.

As with testing input data, it is important to realize that you haven't completely tested the program unless you've exercised every path. If you can think of a set of paths that should be safe to skip, we can make a problem that will show up only in those paths.

Also, note that you can't make a serious try at path testing without a listing of the program. Without looking at the code, you can't know whether you missed a path. As a tester working with the program from the outside, without a listing, you can't test all paths in a simple program—or you couldn't be sure you'd tested all paths— even if you had a billion years to test it.

By the way, suppose you could fully test a program (all inputs, all paths) in only a few hundred or thousand hours. Would this solve your problem? No. In the process of running the test you would find errors. After they were fixed, you'd have to run the tests again. Then you'd find more bugs. You'll probably have to test a program ten times or more before it's ready to ship.

---

*If you think you can completely test a program once, great. Can you completely test it ten times?*

---

## YOU CAN'T FIND EVERY DESIGN ERROR

If the program does exactly what a specification says it should, and doesn't do anything else, it meets the specification. Some people want to declare a program correct if it meets the specification, but is this reasonable? What if the specification says that 2 + 2 should be 5? Is it a bug if the program meets a specification that probably has a typo in it, or is it a bug if the program deviates from the specification?

Specifications often contain errors. Some are accidents (2+2=5). Some are deliberate—the designer thought he had a better idea, but didn't. Many user interface failings are design errors. Being in the specification doesn't make them right. If the program follows a bad specification, we say that it's wrong.

We don't know anyone who claims that she can find all the errors in the user interface. We don't know how to either. You can't completely test a program if you can't find all of its design errors.

## YOU CAN'T PROVE PROGRAMS CORRECT USING LOGIC

The computer operates on logical principles. The programs are expressed in a precise language. If the program is organized well, you should be able to make assertions about the state of the program under various conditions and then prove, by tracking through the logic of the program, that these assertions are correct.

Ignoring the issues of time and number of conditions, realize that this method can only validate the internal consistency of the program. It might prove that the program performs according to specification, but is the specification good?

How do you prove the proof procedure is correct? Even if the procedure is correct in principle, how do you know that a proof was done correctly? If a program did it, what proved the proof-generating capabilities of the program? If the proof was done by a human, since when should we believe that a program prover is more accurate than a program writer?

There are more problems than this. See Beizer (1984) or Dunn (1984). The bottom line is that it takes more time than you have to prove less than you'd like.

## THE TESTER'S OBJECTIVE: PROGRAM VERIFICATION?

Testing is often described as a process of verifying that the program works correctly:

- *This description doesn't make sense:* you can't test the program thoroughly enough to verify that it works correctly.

- *It's also mistaken:* the program doesn't work correctly, so you can't verify that it does.

- *It sets testers up for failure:* if your goal is to show that the program works correctly, you fail every time you find an error.

- *It fosters an ineffective attitude:* if you set your mind to showing that the program works correctly, you'll be more likely to miss problems than if you want and expect the program to fail.

Consider these claims in turn:

### YOU CAN'T VERIFY THAT THE PROGRAM WORKS CORRECTLY

Earlier in this chapter, the section, "You can't test a program completely," explains why it is impossible to fully test any nontrivial program. But if you can't fully test the program, you *can't* verify that it works correctly. It might fail under any of the billions of conditions that you don't test.

### THE PROGRAM *DOESN'T* WORK CORRECTLY

It is easy, *very easy*, to spend $100,000 testing a program. If you have the money, spending a million is only a little harder. Common estimates of the cost of finding and fixing errors in programs range from 40% to 80% of the total development cost. Companies don't spend this kind of money to "verify that a program works." They spend it because the program *doesn't* work—it has bugs and they want them found. No matter what development methodology they follow, their programs still end up with bugs.

#### How many bugs?

Beizer's (1990) review estimates the average number of errors in programs released to Testing at 1 to 3 bugs per 100 executable statements. There are big differences between programmers, but no one's work is error-free.

#### Public and private bugs

One error per 100 statements is an estimate of public bugs, the ones still left in a program after the programmer declares it error-free. Beizer (1984) reported his private bug rate—how many mistakes he made in designing and coding a program—as *1.5 errors per executable statement*. This includes all mistakes, including typing errors.

---

*At this rate, if your programming language allows one executable state-ment per line, you make 150 errors while writing a 100 line program.*

---

Most programmers catch and fix more than 99% of their mistakes before releasing a program for testing. Having found so many, no wonder they think they must have found the lot. But they haven't. Your job is to find the remaining 1%.

## IS TESTING A FAILURE IF THE PROGRAM DOESN'T WORK CORRECTLY?

Is the tester doing a good job or a bad job when she proves that the program is full of bugs? If the purpose of testing is to verify that the program works correctly, then this tester is failing to achieve her purpose. This should sound ridiculous. Obviously, this is very successful testing.

Ridiculous as it seems, we have seen project managers berate testers for continuing to find errors in a program that's behind schedule. Some blame the testers for the bugs. Others just complain, often in a joking tone: "the testers are too tough on the program. Testers aren't supposed to find bugs—they're supposed to prove the program is OK, so the company can ship it." This is a terrible attitude, but it comes out under pressure. Don't be confused when you encounter it. Verification of goodness is a mediocre project manager's fantasy, not your task.

## TESTERS SHOULDN'T WANT TO VERIFY THAT A PROGRAM RUNS CORRECTLY

If you think your task is to find problems, you will look harder for them than if you think your task is to verify that the program has none (Myers, 1979). It is a standard finding in psychological research that people tend to see what they expect to see. For example, proofreading is so hard because you expect to see words spelled correctly. Your mind makes the corrections automatically.

Even in making judgments as basic as whether you *saw* something, your expectations and motivation influence what you see and what you report seeing. For example, imagine participating in the following experiment, which is typical of signal detectability research (Green & Swets, 1966). Watch a radar screen and look for a certain blip. Report the blip whenever you see it. Practice hard. Make sure you know what to look for. Pay attention. Try to be as accurate as possible. If you expect to see many blips, or if you get a big reward for reporting blips when you see them, you'll see and report more of them—including blips that weren't there ("false alarms"). If you believe there won't be many blips, or if you're punished for false alarms, you'll miss blips that did appear on the screen ("misses").

It took experimental psychologists about 80 years of bitter experience to stop blaming experimental subjects for making mistakes in these types of experiments and realize that the researcher's own attitude and experimental setup had a big effect on the proportions of false alarms and misses.

---

If you expect to find many bugs, and you're praised or rewarded for finding them, you'll find plenty. A few will be false alarms. If you expect the program to work correctly, or if people complain when you find problems and punish you for false alarms, you'll miss many real problems.

Another distressing finding is that trained, *conscientious*, intelligent experimenters unconsciously bias their tests, avoid running experiments that might cause trouble for their theories, misanalyze, misinterpret, and ignore test results that show their ideas are wrong (Rosenthal, 1966).

---

*If you want and expect a program to work, you will be more likely to see a working program—you will miss failures. If you expect it to fail, you'll be more likely to see the problems. If you are punished for reporting failures, you will miss failures. You won't only fail to report them—you will not notice them.*

---

You will do your best work if you think of your task as proving that the program is no good. You are well advised to adopt a thoroughly destructive attitude toward the program. You should want it to fail, you should expect it to fail, and you should concentrate on finding test cases that show its failures.

This is a harsh attitude. It is essential.

## SO, WHY TEST?

You can't find all the bugs. You can't prove the program correct, and you don't want to. It's expensive, frustrating, and it doesn't win you any popularity contests. So, why bother testing?

### THE PURPOSE OF TESTING A PROGRAM IS TO FIND PROBLEMS IN IT

Finding problems is the core of your work. You should want to find as many as possible; the more serious the problem, the better.

Since you will run out of time before running out of test cases, it is essential to use the time available as efficiently as possible. Chapters 7, 8, 12, and 13 consider priorities in detail. The guiding principle can be put simply:

---

*A test that reveals a problem is a success. A test that did not reveal a problem was a waste of time.*

---

Consider the following analogy, from Myers (1979). Suppose that something's wrong with you. You go to a doctor. He's supposed to run tests, find out what's wrong, and recommend corrective action. He runs test after test after test. At the end of it all, he can't find anything wrong. Is he a great tester or an incompetent diagnostician? If you really are sick, he's incompetent, and all those expensive tests were a waste of time, money, and effort. In software, you're the diagnostician. The program is the (assuredly) sick patient.

## THE PURPOSE OF FINDING PROBLEMS IS TO GET THEM FIXED

The prime benefit of testing is that it results in improved quality. Bugs get fixed. You take a destructive attitude toward the program when you test, but in a larger context your work is constructive. You are beating up the program in the service of making it stronger.

# TEST TYPES AND THEIR PLACE IN THE SOFTWARE DEVELOPMENT PROCESS

## THE REASON FOR THIS CHAPTER

This chapter is a general overview of the field of testing. It provides four types of information:

1. *Terminology:* Testing terminology includes names of dozens of development methods, risks, tests, problems. As a working tester, you must be fluent with most of them.

2. *Overview of the software development process:* A software product develops over time. Testers often complain that they join a project too late to do much good: though they can report all the errors they find, the critical decisions about usability and reliability-affecting technology and design have already been made.

   You probably *can* have an effect earlier in development, but only if you offer the quality improvement services appropriate to the level of progress of the team. For example, if they've just drafted the program's specification, don't expect to test much code—there probably isn't much code written. But you *could* lead a technical review that evaluates the logical consistency of the specification, and the feasibility, usability, and testability of the product specified.

3. *Description of the key types of tests:* This chapter describes the main types of software tests, in context. It describes the intent of each test, the appropriate time to use it, and perhaps also a critical issue involved in conducting this type of test successfully.

   This chapter describes much that we will not discuss again, such as many glass box testing techniques. We have to cover these, and you must learn something about them: otherwise, an experienced coworker or prospective employer will consider you testing-illiterate. We often spend a bit more space on tests and issues that we describe only in this chapter.

4. *Guide to references in the field:* There are many useful books and papers on testing and software development. Throughout this book we try to point out good material for extra reading. We do this particularly intensely in this chapter because we can readily fit the material into a context of development process and testing issues.

   Writers generally use references to back up a point they're making, to give credit to someone else's insight, or to show that they've considered other points of view. We use references for this too but, especially in this chapter, our focus is outward (to steer you to additional reading) rather than inward (to support our text). We only point to a reading when we have a particularly good one in mind, so some sections have many references and others have few. If you read this chapter as a research essay, you'll find its use of references very unbalanced. But that's the wrong reading: this chapter is more like a topically annotated bibliography, more like a guided tour, than an essay.

Later chapters will supplement much of the technical detail of this chapter. After them, we return to broad overviews in Chapters 12 and 13. Especially in Chapter 13, we again consider a product's development and testing issues from project start to finish. Chapter 3 is a useful reference for Chapter 13, but the purposes of the chapters are different. Chapter 3 introduces you to the notion of an ongoing, changing, process of testing as part of the ongoing progress of a project. Chapter 13 assumes that you have learned the basics. Along with Chapter 12, its focus is on strategy: with a limited budget, how can testing and test planning be organized to maximize improvement in the program's quality?

## NOTE

This chapter is superficial. Some readers are overwhelmed by the number of new topics that seem to fly by. Some readers have identified this as the most boring chapter of the book. People who stopped reading this book tell us they stopped here.

Here is our advice:

- First, don't worry about fine distinctions between software development terms. Our goal is to make you just familiar enough with the terminology to be able to ask programmers basic questions about the program's internal design and understand the main thrust of their answer. We're trying to provide a basis for learning on the job (or from our supplementary references), not a general book on software engineering.

- Next, treat this chapter as a reference section. Skim it the first time through—don't try to learn all the details. Look for a general overview of development and associated testing processes. Mentally note where to find more detailed information when you need it. As you go further in the book, come back here for background or context information. We indexed this material extensively to help you use the chapter when you need it, even if you completely skipped large sections on your first reading.

- If you are a student trying to master this material for a test, we suggest creating a chart that summarizes this chapter. Use a structure similar to Figure 13.3. Don't spend a lot of time on software development (as opposed to testing) terminology, except for terms that your professor explained in class. In a course that emphasizes Chapter 13, we recommend making a study aid for your final exam that expands the chart in Figure 13.4 by including the material in this chapter.

## OVERVIEW

We describe software development in this chapter as if it proceeds in stages, and we describe the test techniques that are useful at each stage. The chapter proceeds as follows:

- Overview of the development stages
- Planning stages
- Testing during the planning stages
- Design stages
- Testing the design
- Glass box testing as part of the coding stage
- Regression testing
- Black box testing
- Maintenance

In business, software development is usually done by a group of people working together. We call that group the *development team*. Perhaps you write all your own code, or work in a two person company. You will still play all the roles we identify in the development team; one person will just wear more than one hat. For clarity, we describe a development team that includes separate people for separable roles. In practice, most small companies combine these roles in fewer people:

- The *project manager* (also known as *software development manager* or *producer*) is responsible for the quality level, schedule, and development budget of the product. While many other structures are possible, we assume that the designers and programmers report directly to the project manager.

- The *designers* of the product might include:

  - An *architect* specifies the overall internal design of the code and data structures, the approach to data communication or data sharing between this and related programs, and the strategy for developing sharable or reusable modules if this product is one of a series that will use many of the same routines. The architect might also write the high level glass box test plan, supervise technical reviews of all specifications, and design an acceptance test that checks the code against the product requirements.

  **3**

  TEST TYPES &
  SOFTWARE
  DEVELOPMENT

  - A *subject matter expert* or a *software analyst* who understands what customers want and how to specify this in terms that a programmer or other designer can understand.

  - A *human factors analyst* (or *ergonomist*) typically has extensive training in psychology and understands what makes software designs usable and how to test a product's (or prototype's) usability. A few of these (fewer than the number who think they do) also know enough about internal software design and implementation to be effective primary designers of the software user interface. The others share this role with a user interface programmer.

  - A *user interface programmer* specializes in creating user interfaces. This person is typically a professional programmer who understands a fair bit about windowing architectures and computer graphics, and who may also have some knowledge of cognitive psychology.

    Think of the user interface as a layer of the program that presents information to the user (graphically or textually, onscreen, on-printer, etc.) and collects information from the user (by keyboard, mouse, etc.) which it passes back to the main program for processing. The user interface programmer writes this layer of the program, which is sometimes also called the presentation and data collection layer.

    A broader conception of user interface includes the content of the information going back and forth between the user and the program. For example, a user interface designer must decide what options to present to the customer, and how to describe them in a way that the customer will understand, not just how to display them. Many user interface programmers feel fully capable of designing as well as implementing user interfaces, and some of them are. The others work best in conjunction with a human factors analyst.

  - The *lead programmer(s)* often write the internal design specifications. In many consensus-based programming teams, programmers do the architecture as a group rather than delegating this to a separate architect.

- The *product manager* (or *product marketing manager*) is accountable for delivering a product that fits within the company's long term strategy and image and for marketing activities (such as advertising, PR, sales force training) after release. In most companies, she is accountable for product profitability. Product managers generally define *market requirements*, critical features or capabilities that the product must have to be competitive. Many product managers play an active role in feature set selection and also list the equipment that the program must be compatible with (and be tested for compatibility with).

- The *technical support* representative is a member of (or manager of) a group of people who handle customers' complaints and requests for information. During product development, they will try to influence the design of the program and the content of the manual in ways that increase clarity and reduce customer calls.

- The *writers* (members of the *documentation group*) create the user manuals and online help. They, along with you (the tester) and technical support, are often advocates of making the software simpler and more consistent.

- The *testers* are also members of the development team.

- Specific projects will include other team members, such as graphic artists, reliability analysts, hazard (safety) analysts, hardware engineers, attorneys, accountants, and so forth.

With the players in mind, let's consider the software development process.

## OVERVIEW OF THE SOFTWARE DEVELOPMENT STAGES

Software goes through a cycle of development stages. A product is envisioned, created, evaluated, fixed, put to serious use, and found wanting. Changes are envisioned and made, the changed product is evaluated, fixed, etc. The product may be revised and redistributed dozens of times until it is eventually replaced. The full business, from initial thinking to final use, is called the product's *life cycle*.

The product's life cycle involves many tasks, or stages. These are often described sequentially—as if one finishes before the other begins—but they usually overlap substantially. It's easier to envision the tasks if we describe them sequentially. We'll discuss parallel development in Chapters 12 and 14.

This chapter is organized around five basic stages:

- Planning
- Design
- Coding and Documentation
- Testing and Fixing
- Post-Release Maintenance and Enhancement

In their book, *Software Maintenance*, Martin & McClure (1983, p. 24) summarized the relative costs of each stage, as follows:

Development Phases:                          Production Phase:

| | | | |
|---|---|---|---|
| Requirements Analysis | 3% | Operations and Maintenance | 67% |
| Specification | 3% | | |
| Design | 5% | | |
| Coding | 7% | | |
| Testing | 15% | | |

These numbers were originally reported by Zelkowitz, Shaw & Gannon (1979). According to their study and others cited by Martin & McClure (1983), maintenance is the main cost component of software. Testing is the second most expensive activity, accounting for 45% (15/33) of the cost of initial development of a product. Testing also accounts for much of the maintenance cost—code changes during maintenance have to be tested too.

Testing and fixing can be done at any stage in the life cycle. However, the cost of finding and fixing errors increases dramatically as development progresses.

- Changing a requirements document during its first review is inexpensive. It costs more when requirements change after code has been written: the code must be rewritten.

- Bug fixes are much cheaper when programmers find their own errors. There is no communication cost. They don't have to explain an error to anyone else. They don't have to enter it into a bug tracking database. Testers and managers don't have to review the bug's status, as they would if it were in the database. And the error doesn't block or corrupt anyone else's work with the program.

- Fixing an error before releasing a program is much cheaper than sending new disks, or even a technician, to each customer's site to fix it later.

Boehm (1976) summarized cost studies from IBM, GTE, and TRW that show that the later an error is found, the more it costs to fix. The cost increases exponentially, as shown in Figure 3.1. Errors detected during the planning stages are cheap to fix. They become increasingly expensive as the product moves through design, coding, testing, and to the field. For one Air Force computer, software development costs were about $75 per instruction. Maintenance cost $4000 per instruction.

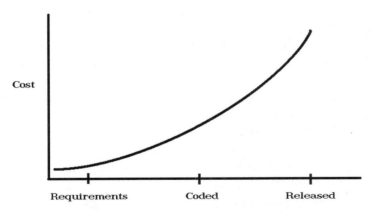

Figure 3.1  Cost of finding and fixing software errors

---

*The sooner a bug is found and fixed, the cheaper.*

---

See DeGrace & Stahl (1990), Evans & Marciniak (1987), Myers (1976), and Roetzheim (1991) for detailed discussions of the development stages. For further analyses of development costs, see Boehm (1981), Jones (1991), and Wolverton (1974).

## PLANNING STAGES

A product planning team should include senior engineers, sales and marketing staff, and product managers. They define the product but do not write its code. They might make mock-ups (on paper or onscreen) to clarify their thinking. The planners produce one or a few documents to guide future development.

### OBJECTIVES STATEMENT

The planners start by describing their vision of the product—what it should do and why. This document may not be very detailed or specific. It may tentatively describe the user interface and goals for reliability or performance. It will probably state cost objectives (cost to develop and cost to the customer). The finished product probably won't meet all the objectives, especially not in the first released version. The point of the objectives statement is to provide the development team with a shared goal.

### REQUIREMENTS ANALYSIS

A requirement is an objective that *must* be met. Planners cast most requirements in functional terms, leaving design and implementation details to the developers. They may specify price, performance, and reliability objectives in fine detail, along with some aspects of the user interface. Sometimes, they describe their objectives more precisely than realistically.

The requirements, or some other early document, also express fundamental hardware decisions. To avoid further complexity in this chapter, we do not consider joint development of hardware and software or progressive refinement of hardware compatibility decisions over time. Instead, we assume that we know from the start what processor and input/output devices will be used with the product.

### FUNCTIONAL DEFINITION

The functional definition bridges the requirements analysis and the engineering design documents. The requirements analysis is written for a marketing-oriented reader. To an engineer, some parts may seem vague, incomplete, or confusing.

---

The functional definition translates the market or product requirements into a list of features, functions, and reports. It includes only enough detail for the programmer to understand what's being described. Unless absolutely necessary, it does not specify how features will be implemented, internally or externally. The document might outline *possible* implementations, to make definitions easier to understand, but the final internal and external designs will probably differ from these illustrations.

The *IEEE Guide to Software Requirements Specifications* (ANSI/IEEE Standard 830-1984) is a good model for developing what we call a functional definition.

## TESTING DURING THE PLANNING STAGES

Ideas are tested now, not code. The "testers" (reviewers) include marketers, product managers, senior designers, and human factors analysts. Members of the Testing Group are rarely involved at this stage. (See Chapter 13 for useful planning-stage tasks for testers.)

**3**

TEST TYPES &
SOFTWARE
DEVELOPMENT

The reviewers read drafts of the planning documents. Then they gather data, using comparative product evaluations, focus groups, or task analyses. These are commonly described as planning and design tools, but they are also testing procedures: each can lead to a major overhaul of existing plans.

The reviewers should evaluate the requirements document (and the functional definition based on it) in terms of at least six issues:

- *Are these the "right" requirements?* Is this the product that *should* be built?

- *Are they complete?* Does Release 1 need more functions? Can some of the listed requirements be dropped?

- *Are they compatible?* Requirements can be logically incompatible (i.e., contradictory) or psychologically incompatible. Some features spring from such different conceptualizations of the product that if the user understands one of them, she probably won't understand the other(s).

- *Are they achievable?* Do they assume that the hardware works more quickly than it does? Do they require too much memory, too many I/O devices, too fine a resolution of input or output devices?

- *Are they reasonable?* There are tradeoffs between development speed, development cost, product performance, reliability, and memory usage. Are these recognized or do the requirements ask for lightning speed, zero defects, 6 bytes of storage, and completion by tomorrow afternoon? Any of these might be individually achievable, but not all at once, for the same product. Is the need for a priority scheme recognized?

- *Are they testable?* How easy will it be to tell whether the design documents match the requirements?

If you go to a requirements review, evaluate the document in advance in terms of the questions above. Dunn (1984), Gause & Weinberg (1989), and ANSI/IEEE Standard 830 describe other problems to consider and questions to ask when reviewing requirements.

Having considered the general issues of interest to reviewers, consider the data collection tools: comparative product evaluations, focus groups, and task analyses.

## COMPARATIVE PRODUCT EVALUATIONS

In the comparative product evaluation, the reviewer asks what will make this product different from others already on the market. What does the competition do better? Which of their features must be built into this product?

The reviewer uses working copies of competing products, demonstration versions, or published descriptions if that's all he can get. He lists their features, their strengths and weaknesses, and anything about them noticed (praised or panned) in product reviews. He may categorize them in terms of the market segment to which they appeal, or the specific application for which they're best suited. He derives detailed profiles of competing products' capabilities, adding obvious "next steps" since these will probably come to market soon. He writes a similar profile for the planned product. How does it compare? Why would anyone want to buy it?

Initially, this evaluation leads to expansion of the requirements document and functional definition. The reviewer is tempted to design the ultimate product, packing into it the hundreds of good ideas gleaned from the competition. Unfortunately, it costs too much to include them all. Further, it's impossible to put them all into one cohesive product. Many features reflect fundamentally different conceptions of a product's task. They just don't work well together. Even with compatible features, as the feature set grows, so does the product's complexity. At some point the product is so feature-laden that it's too hard to use, even though each feature is a good one in its own right. (Read Rubenstein & Hersh, 1984, and Norman, 1988.)

Some reviewers ignore problems of feature compatibility and complexity. They just generate a long list of competitors' good ideas. This can be a useful reference. However, before these are all tossed in as requirements, someone must prune the list. The reviewer may draft a much shorter list for this purpose, or he might submit the full list for review. Focus groups and task analyses can provide bases for much of the pruning from this list.

## FOCUS GROUPS

A product is targeted toward specific market segments. The reviewer wants to know how they'll respond to it.

The reviewer chooses a small group he considers representative of a market segment. Group members don't know each other. He asks them to discuss one or very few topics. He decides the topics, the scope, and focus of the discussion. He may moderate the discussion or he may hire a moderator. He does not participate as a discussant except, possibly, to ask the occasional question. His goal is to gauge current market reaction to an idea, not to convince these people of anything.

Focus groups can give feedback at many levels of generality. The reviewer might want an overview of what the group wants from this type of product, how they'll use it, and what features are most important. Or, he might focus on only one feature or one product application. He might use the group to generate ideas, before much detailed planning of the product has been done, or he may use it later, to test their reactions to details of the product plan.

## TASK ANALYSES

The product automates or partially automates some task, probably a complex task. The analyst observes people doing their work, interviews them, tries to figure out all aspects of the task that the product will help them do. The analyst asks, what exactly is this task? How do people do it now, without the product? What order are subtasks done in? Why? When is what information needed and why? What are the bottlenecks in the work flow and why haven't they been solved? A task analysis is a design tool, vital for designing the user interface.

The task analysis might not be done until after the requirements seem settled. However, the results often challenge product requirements. They lead the analyst to simplify, combine, or eliminate features. New ones are born of the analyst's conceptualization of the job actually done by the users.

For more information on task analyses, see Bailey (1989), Card, Moran, & Newell (1983), Helander (1991, especially Chapter 38), Norman & Draper (1986, Section IV), and Rubenstein & Hersh (1984). See Baecker & Buxton (1987, e.g., Chapter 6) for interesting examples.

**3**

TEST TYPES &
SOFTWARE
DEVELOPMENT

## DESIGN STAGES

The designers figure out how to provide the planned capabilities of the product. There are external and internal designs. The *external design* describes the product from the user's point of view. The *internal design* describes the internal workings of the product. These are developed in parallel; each forces constraints and requirements on the other.

Design depends on a requirements document that lists the planned capabilities of the product. If that document is absent, incomplete, or in a constant state of flux, the designers have to make their own decisions about product capabilities.

According to the traditional model of software development, coding doesn't start until the design is complete. Prototyping doesn't count as coding because the prototype is developed only to explore how part of the product could work. In practice, however, much prototype code might be used in the final product. The designers might also code some low level routines early, to check their assumptions that these routines can meet critical time and space constraints. We discuss alternatives to the traditional model in Chapters 12 and 14.

Myers (1976), Jones (1979), and Yourdon (1975) are good sources for general reading on software design.

## EXTERNAL DESIGN

The external design includes a complete description of the user interface. It describes all screens and other outputs. It describes the commands available, the command syntax, all interactions between commands or features, and the responses to all possible inputs. A careful task analysis is vital to the development of a good external design.

The external specification is one document that can be produced during external design. The user manual is another. In some projects, such as custom jobs, people who will use the system are given responsibility for its external design. They write the user manual and so specify the design in concrete terms they understand, before any coding begins.

The external design is subject to many late changes because it's a flop if people can't work with the program. Design errors show up in even the most carefully considered user interfaces when users start working with the product. It doesn't matter that the underlying code is flawless—any part of the user interface is bad if it leads reasonable people into errors, confuses them, irritates them, or provides them with too little flexibility or functionality to do a task they reasonably expect to be able to do with the product.

Martin (1973) is a dated but still interesting introduction to the external design process. Helander (1991) is a more recent survey of user interface design. Baecker & Buxton (1987), Card, Moran, & Newell (1983), and Rubenstein & Hersh (1984) are classic works or collections of classic works.

## INTERNAL DESIGN

Internal design specifies how tasks will be subdivided among different pieces of code (*structural design*), what data the code will work with (*data design*), and how the code will work (*logic design*).

### Structural design

Nontrivial tasks can be broken into distinguishable subtasks. The subtasks can probably be broken into simpler pieces. The simplest pieces should be designed and coded as separate units. The analysis of a task into component pieces is called *decomposition*.

A complex software product is developed as a *system*, a collection of self-contained but related programs rather than a single program. Especially if they can run concurrently, these programs are called processes. Even though processes can work independently, many must communicate. For example, if two processes use the same data, one has to find out about updates made by the other. Also, one process might do tasks at the request of another.

*Protocol documents* specify the rules governing communications between processes. A system's *software architecture* divides it into separate components, and specifies the communication protocols between them.

Processes (and most other programs) are themselves subdivided. *Modular decomposition* involves breaking a program into *modules*. A module is a distinct section of code that can be treated as one unit. In many languages, a module can be compiled independently of the rest of the program. It has a name, it should have one entry point and one exit point. It should do only one type of task or a clearly related group of them. If it does a group of tasks, it should itself be decomposed into modules, which do the individual tasks. No other module should do the same task as this one. To perform this task, all parts of the program *call* (use) this module. Modules are often named *procedures, subroutines* and *functions*, and we'll use these terms interchangeably in this book.[1]

---

[1] We ignore here a trend among some compiler vendors to call any independently compilable code file a "module," but be aware that this diluted meaning is out there. For a review of the modular programming movement of the 1970's, read Yourdon (1975) Chapter 3.

A module *passes* (sends) data to another module and then that module *returns* data. For example, a program may pass numbers to a subroutine that will return their sum. *Interface specifications* describe the variables passed to and from modules.

Yourdon (1975) is a good introduction to logic design and structural design. After Yourdon, read Yourdon & Constantine (1979).

**Data design**

The designer asks the following questions:

- *What are the data and what data structures are appropriate to hold them?* Related data should be organized in a way that leaves the relationships clear. Different types of relationships are best expressed by different data structures. Examples of data structures are simple variables, arrays, records, stacks, queues, linked lists, and trees. Elson's (1975) introduction to these is quite readable.

- *Which routines need access to a given set of data?* Should these data be stored globally, in memory or on disk, accessible to any routine that asks for it, or should one routine own the data and pass copies to others on request? Which routines are allowed to change these data? How is it ensured that only these routines can change them? How are these restrictions made obvious to someone reading or modifying the code?

- *How should the data be named?* Are there naming conventions? Can a maintenance programmer understand the function of each variable from the name?

- *What about data storage?* Some data will be stored (e.g., on disk) and retrieved later. How should they be stored? How should they be organized on disk? How should they be retrieved? (See Part II of Martin & McClure (1983) for a good introductory discussion of these issues.)

Implicit in the discussion of structural design was the view that a product should be primarily analyzed in terms of its functions. Under this perspective, a module is characterized by what it does; analysis of its data is secondary.

Realize, though, that two modules that operate on the same data are closely related, even if they do different things to the data for different purposes. For example, if the data structure changes, both modules must be recoded.

It's useful to stand the function-oriented approach on its head, conceptualizing the program from the point of view of the data. From this perspective, a program is something that transforms data, in stages, from initial input, through various intermediate results, to final output (such as a report). Modules are considered incidentally, and only in terms of their effect on the data: this module needs that information as input, expects that these data were entered or calculated already, and will produce these outputs. A module is characterized by a description of its inputs and outputs; its "function" is implicit in this description. Such an analysis can expose a variety of natural, and sometimes inescapable, relationships between what might otherwise be considered different pieces of a program. Overall design and decomposition might take advantage of these relationships, defend against consequences of them, or passively reflect them as a natural approach to decomposition of the program's tasks.

For a good introductory comparison of different design approaches, see Bergland (1981). Gane & Sarson (1979) is an excellent introduction to data design. For further discussion of data flow and relationships between modules, begin with DeMarco (1979), then read Yourdon & Constantine (1979). To follow up on data-oriented testing approaches, read Beizer (1990).

## Logic design

Design doesn't end with the specification of a module's task and data. Someone (usually the programmer) still has to figure out how to do the task. This may include choosing an "optimal" algorithm. It includes outlining the logical steps involved in the task, often in progressively greater detail.

Yourdon (1975) is a good source on the process of translating a high level design and into working code.

## PROTOTYPING

A *prototype* is a *model* of the system or of part of it. The prototype is built as quickly and cheaply as possible. It should be easy and cheap to change. It does *not* have to do any "real" work. Its function is to give the people who work with it an inexpensive, direct experience of one way that the product can work.

Some prototyping is done in the service of internal design. In a *top-down* design process, the system is broken into a few higher order processes or modules, which are in turn broken into modules, which are then broken down further. Each higher order module is coded before the modules it calls are coded. Sometimes, though, the design depends on assumptions about the lowest level routines. Suppose the design of a module requires a particular low level interrupt handling routine to execute and exit within 60 microseconds. It is only prudent to model this routine early, and make sure it can meet its requirements. Otherwise the other modules (in some real cases, the whole system) will have to be redesigned.

Prototyping is most often done to explore and evaluate the functionality and user interface of the system. This is essential: once people get a chance to play with the system, or with a model of it, their requirements change. Ideas that seemed reasonable or even good when they were written in a specification look less good in a working model (Martin & McClure, 1983; Wasserman & Shewmake, 1985).

Martin & McClure (1983) strongly recommend that functionality and user interface prototypes be written in the language of the final product. If the prototype works well, they say it should become the final product. With rare exceptions, we think this is bad advice because:

- Many development languages are not suited to rapid, cheap prototyping.

- This notion flies in the face of good advice from Brooks (1975) and Kernighan & Plauger (1974). They recommend throwing away the first draft of any program. Their recommendation is especially applicable to prototypes. A prototype doesn't have to be well designed internally. It needn't always work. It can be slow and inefficient. As long as it gives the user a feel for the product, it's OK. We don't want this as production code. Designers need the freedom to write bad code quickly that models a system well, and then throw that code away.

DeGrace & Stahl (1990), Helander (1991, Chapter 39), Rubenstein & Hersh (1984), Ould (1990), and Schneiderman (1987) discuss user interface prototyping, evaluation strategies, and techniques.

## TESTING DURING THE DESIGN STAGES

No code has been written yet, so we're still testing ideas. These ideas are more formally expressed and more detailed than the original plans. Examining the design documents, reviewers should develop a clear picture of how the system will work if it's built according to the design. Testers may not be included in these reviews, but they will be valuable for your test planning, so try to find time for them. (But don't speak in review meetings unless you have something valuable to say.) The reviewers should explore the following issues:

- *Is the design good?* Will it lead to an efficient, compact, testable, maintainable, product?

- *Does the design meet the requirements?* If the planning documents are informal, changeable, and ambiguous, the design will be the first formal statement of the product requirements. Management and marketing staff should review the design as such, not just as a design.

- *Is the design complete?* Does it specify all relationships between modules, how they pass data, what happens in exceptional circumstances, what starting state should be assumed for each module, and how that state will be guaranteed?

- *Is the design possible?* Can the machine run this quickly? Is there enough memory? Are there enough I/O devices? Can data be retrieved this quickly from a database? Can this version of the development language *do* the things you're trying to do?

- *How well does the design cover error handling?* Especially when doing top-down design, it's easy to think of error paths as "details," to be dealt with "later." All too often, by the time "later" rolls around, these "details" have been forgotten. Along with checking that all remotely plausible error conditions are dealt with in the design, it is also important to ask whether a given error is handled at the right level. For example, if an error detected in one module forces backtracking and cancellation or correction of work done in other(s), the error should probably be handled in the higher-level module that calls all the affected modules.

Dunn (1984) and Freedman & Weinberg (1982) list many other possible design errors and provide extensive checklists for evaluating a design document. Read Beizer (1990) on design testability.

## REVIEW MEETINGS

The objective for any review meeting is to *identify* problems with the design. It is not to solve them.

Review meetings should be small (about seven people). They should include people who did not work on the design. Reviewers should read design documents in advance and challenge or question them in the meeting. Many companies don't consider a design complete until it is approved in a formal review. A design is reworked and re-reviewed until it is finally abandoned or accepted. Three common types of review meetings are walkthroughs, inspections, and technical reviews:

- *Walkthrough:* The designer simulates the program. She shows, step by step, what the program will do with test data supplied by the reviewers. The simulation shows how different pieces of the system interact and can expose awkwardness, redundancy, and many missed details.

- *Inspection:* Reviewers check every line of the design against each item in a checklist. An inspection might focus on error handling, conformity with standards, or some other single, tightly defined area. If time permits, an inspection checklist might cover a second area of concern.

- *Technical review:* Reviewers bring a list of issues to the meeting. During the meeting, they describe their objections and point out things that are ambiguous or confusing. The purpose of the review is to generate a list of problems and make sure that the designer understands each one. Deciding what changes to make, and designing them, are not part of this meeting.

The ideal review meeting is administered by a meeting manager (or facilitator) and a recorder. Neither comments on the design. The meeting manager runs the meeting. This includes finding the room, recognizing speakers, stopping interruptions, keeping the discussion focused, and preparing a summary report. It is the meeting manager's job to make sure that the meeting does not bog down into discussions of possible solutions of particular problems. These must be done later, by a smaller group, outside the meeting.

The recorder writes all significant comments on flip chart sheets, transparencies, or other surfaces that can be kept and that everyone in the room can see. Anyone who thinks the recorder has missed something important can ask her to put this on the record. The record includes every agreement. When an issue is left open for later discussion, the record should list the questions that must be answered next time (if these have been identified). This process can yield much more productive meetings, especially when the design is controversial.

Some Testing Groups train their staff to be meeting managers and recorders for design reviews. This is a valuable service: few software development companies have access to meeting managers or recorders, and their review meetings (if there are review meetings) aren't always very satisfying. To learn more about meeting management techniques, read Doyle & Straus (1976). For excellently written applications of these techniques to review meetings, read Freedman & Weinberg (1982) and Gause & Weinberg (1989).

## PSEUDOCODE ANALYZERS

*Pseudocode* (*structured English*) is an artificial language that combines coding language constructs with English (or another natural language). For example, the following description, from Chapter 1, is pseudocode:

```
IF ASCII_CODE_OF_ENTERED_CHAR is less than 48
   THEN reject it
     ELSE IF ASCII_CODE_OF_ENTERED_CHAR is greater than 57
        THEN reject it
        ELSE it's a digit, so accept it
```

As designers develop more detailed documents, they find it convenient to describe the design in a language almost as formal as a programming language, with many of the same constructs. Many designers find pseudocode natural for this.

If designers use a formally specified version of pseudocode, they may be able to use a program (a *pseudocode analyzer*) that looks for flaws in their design. For example, it might find modules that are never called, or modules that are called but haven't been designed. It can list all modules called by any one, and all callers of any module. The pseudocode analyzer depends on entry of a complete, low level (logic) design of all the code that will soon be written.

If your company designs to this level of detail, read Dunn (1984) for more details on this type of tool.

## GLASS BOX CODE TESTING IS PART OF THE CODING STAGE

During the coding stage, the programmer writes the programs and tests them. We assume that you understand what coding is, so we won't describe it here. But we will describe *glass box testing* (sometimes called *white box testing*), because this is the kind of testing the programmer is especially well equipped to do during coding.

**3**

TEST TYPES &
SOFTWARE
DEVELOPMENT

Glass box testing is distinguished from *black box testing*, in which the program is treated as a black box. You can't see into it. The tester (or programmer) feeds it input data, observes output data, but does not know, or pretends not to know, how the program works. The test designer looks for interesting input data and conditions that might lead to interesting outputs. Input data are "interesting" representatives of a class of possible inputs if they are the ones most likely to expose an error in the program.

In contrast, in glass box testing, the programmer uses her understanding and access to the source code to develop test cases. This provides benefits:

- *Focused testing:* The programmer can test the program in pieces. She can write special test code that feeds interesting values to an isolated module, and reports intermediate results obtained from the module. It's much easier to give an individual suspect module a thorough workout in glass box testing than in black box testing.

- *Testing coverage:* The programmer can also find out which parts of the program are exercised by any test. She can find out which lines of code, which branches, or which paths haven't yet been tested, and she can add tests that she knows will cover the areas not yet touched. We briefly discuss *coverage monitors*, which track and report the degree of testing coverage, in this chapter and in Chapter 11.

- *Control flow:* The programmer knows what the program is supposed to do next, as a function of its current state. She can modify the program so that it constantly reports what it's doing, or she can use a special program called a *debugger* to run the program and track the order in which lines of code are executed. (Debuggers track many other things too, such as the values of key variables and reads from or writes to identified areas of memory.) When the program goes astray, she can tell immediately.

- *Data integrity:* The programmer knows which parts of the program modify (or should modify) any item of data. By tracking a data item through the system, she can spot data manipulation by inappropriate modules. She might also write special code that calculates the value that a test variable should have at a given point in the program, compares this with the value the variable actually has, and reports an error. This is an example of automated testing using an *oracle*, which we further discuss, briefly, in Chapter 11.

- *Internal boundaries:* The programmer can see internal boundaries in the code that are completely invisible to the outside tester. For example, a program might use different calculation methods to estimate values of the chi-square function depending on whether its shape parameter (degrees of freedom) is smaller or larger than 100 (recommended by Abramowitz & Stegun, 1964, p. 941). Other programs will put input data into temporary storage if too much comes too quickly. The programmer is in a much better position than a black box tester to force a memory or processing time overflow and see how well the program handles temporary storage.

- *Algorithm-specific testing:* For example, there are many ways to invert a matrix, and well understood ways to miscalculate the result. The programmer can apply standard numerical analysis techniques to predict (and thus check) the results. We'll mention Carnahan, Luther, & Wilkes (1969) as an old but instructive general sourcebook of numerical analysis. If your program uses traditional algorithms to perform complicated calculations, and you know the algorithms, check the most technical university library in your area. You might find a book with directly relevant test cases and expected results.

We think of glass box testing as part of the programming process because so many programmers routinely run glass box tests of their modules just before and just after integrating them with other parts of the system. This is common good practice, taught to all programming students. However, you should know that most testing textbooks spend most of their pages describing glass box techniques. These authors expect testers, as well as programmers, to run glass box tests.

This book is about black box testing, which is what most of the testers that we know spend most of their time doing. (The exceptions test mainframe data processing applications, which are better analyzed by authors like Beizer, Hetzel, and Myers than by us.) Black box testers don't invest the time learning the source code; instead they study the program from the outside, which is how the customer will work with it. And, just as the glass box approach makes it easy to run certain types of tests, black box thinking exposes errors that will elude glass box testers (see Chapter 12, "What types of tests to cover in test planning documents: What glass box testing misses").

In the next few sections we describe basic glass box concepts that you must be familiar with or traditionally trained testers will consider you an ignoramus. We briefly return to glass box methods in Chapters 7 and 11. In the Appendix we describe many software errors in terms of the internal problem, letting you imagine black box tests that could expose the symptoms of one of these problems, in the particular type of program you're testing.

## STRUCTURAL VERSUS FUNCTIONAL TESTING

*Structural testing* is glass box testing. The main concern is proper selection of program or subprogram paths to exercise during the battery of tests.

*Functional testing* is one type of black box testing. Functions are tested by feeding them input and examining the output. Internal program structure is rarely considered.

For more detailed descriptions of these two terms, see Beizer (1984).

Dunn (1984) notes that although structural testing has been the subject of more extensive theoretical analysis and there are better tools to do it, most tests performed are functional. As he notes, part of the reason for the greater theoretical concentration on structural testing is that path testing is more amenable to mathematical treatment. However, "easier to model" does not imply "better." Each can find errors not usually detectable by the other. In his experience, neither is more effective at finding errors than the other.

## PATH TESTING: COVERAGE CRITERIA

Earlier, we defined a *path* as a sequence of operations that runs from the start of the program to an exit point. This is also called an *end-to-end* path. A *subpath* is a sequence of statements from one place in the program to another. *Subpaths are also called paths*. The smallest "path" is a single line of code.

The programmer can't test all the paths (see "You Can't Test Every Path The Program Can Take" in Chapter 2). *Coverage criteria* specify a class of paths she should test. In contrast to absolutely complete path testing, these criteria define achievable (if possibly expensive) amounts of testing. Coverage criteria are also called *logic coverage criteria* and *completeness criteria*. This section describes three criteria in common use: line coverage, branch (or complete) coverage, and condition coverage. Testing done according to these criteria is called *path testing*.

*Line coverage* is the weakest coverage criterion. It requires execution of every line of code at least once. Although line coverage is more than some programmers do, it is not nearly enough. Many lines check the value(s) of some variable(s) and make decisions based on this. To check each of the decision-making functions of the line, the programmer has to supply different values, to trigger different decisions. As an example, consider the following:

```
IF ( A > B and C = 5 )
     THEN do SOMETHING
SET D = 5
```

To test these lines she should explore the following cases:

```
(a) A < B and C = 5      (SOMETHING is done, then D is set to 5)
(b) A < B and C ≠ 5      (SOMETHING is not done, D is set to 5)
(c) A ≥ B and C = 5      (SOMETHING is not done, D is set to 5)
(d) A ≥ B and C ≠ 5      (SOMETHING is not done, D is set to 5)
```

The programmer can execute all three lines of code by testing case (a).

For *branch coverage,* the programmer can use case (a) and any one of the other three. At a branching point, a program does one thing if a condition (such as A < B and C = 5) is true, and something else if the condition is false. To test a branch, the programmer must test once when the condition is true and once when it's false. The branch coverage criterion requires testing of all lines and all branches.

Branch coverage is sometimes called *complete coverage* of the code. Beizer (1984) argues forcefully that complete coverage does not constitute complete testing. He estimates that testing to the level of "complete" coverage will find, at best, half the bugs.

A stronger level of coverage, *condition coverage*, checks each of the ways that the condition can be made true or false. This requires all four cases above.

A key notion of organized path testing is that once a coverage criterion has been met, path testing is complete. Special programs called *execution coverage monitors* calculate how many paths must be tested to meet the completeness criterion and count how many of these have been tested. From the two measures, the programmer can calculate how close she is to complete coverage.

In path testing, no credit is given for repeated testing of the same path using different data. Even though cases (b), (c), and (d) above might all be important, most coverage monitors would treat execution of the three of them as wasteful (Dunn, 1984). All three start at the same statement and run through the same statements thereafter. To test each case is to test the same path three times.

No matter what completeness criterion is used, path testing alone is not complete testing. Even if every path is executed once, the program can still have bugs. Goodenough & Gerhart (1975) point out a classic example: division by zero. Imagine executing the line:

```
SET A = B/C
```

This works if C is nonzero. But what if C is 0? In many languages, the program will halt. The difference between the two cases is a difference in data, not in paths.

DeMillo *et al.* (1987) define a path as *error-sensitive* if an error in it *can be* detected when it is exercised. A path is *error-revealing* if the error always appears when the path is taken. Any path that includes the division B/C is error-sensitive. The error only shows when C is zero. A critical problem in path testing is how to find the error conditions (such as C = 0) in the error-sensitive paths. While some progress is being made (see, for example, Rapps & Weyuker, 1985), to a large degree it is black box rather than glass box tests that find the value-dependent errors in error-sensitive paths.

Rapps & Weyuker's (1985) description of paths is formal, very concise, but readable. Beizer (1984, 1990) spends more pages on paths, and discusses testing techniques for specific control structures such as loops. For a particularly clear discussion of coverage criteria, read Myers (1979).

## INCREMENTAL VERSUS BIG BANG TESTING

A system is developed piecemeal, as a collection of processes and modules. The distinction between incremental and big bang testing boils down to a choice between testing the product piecemeal or in one big lump.

Under an *incremental testing strategy,* each piece is first tested separately. The testing of individual pieces of a process or program is called *module testing, unit testing,* or *element testing.*

Once the individual parts work, a few are tested together. They may not work together. For example, reversed variables in a function call won't be discovered until the code that calls the function and the function itself are tested together. Testing combinations of pieces of the product is called *integration testing*. As integration testing proceeds, groups of modules are tested with other groups until, eventually, all of a process' modules are tested together. If there are many processes, they'll be tested in pairs before being tested en masse.

Incremental testing makes it easy to pin down the cause of an error. When the programmer tests only one module, any errors are either in that module or in a simple program she wrote to test it. She doesn't have to look through much code to find the problem. If a new problem shows up when separately tested modules are tested together, the error is almost certainly in the interface between them. Another benefit of incremental testing is that the programmer focuses on each module individually, which probably yields better test coverage.

The main problem with incremental testing is that it requires special test code. To test a function, the programmer has to write a *driver*, which calls the function and passes it test data. If that function calls another, the programmer must either test both together or write a *stub* to take the called function's place. A stub might always return the same value or it might return different values, including bad ones to check the calling function's error handling. A stub's code should always be simpler than the function it replaces.

Stubs and drivers are often seen as throwaway code. It is true that they aren't in the final version of the product. However, once written they can be reused to retest the program whenever it changes. A good collection of stubs and drivers is a powerful testing tool.

In contrast to incremental testing, under a *big bang testing strategy* the modules and processes are not thoroughly tested until full system integration. Everything is tested with everything else and, usually, it all blows up together.

The only apparent advantage of big bang testing is that stub and driver code don't have to be written. Some project managers suggest the big bang by pointing to all the time they can "save" by running only one large set of tests. This is such transparently bad thinking, though, that we can't believe that most of them mean it. Here are some of the disadvantages:

- ***It's too hard to figure out what caused a failure.*** This is the main problem. Since no module has been thoroughly checked, most of them probably have bugs. The question isn't which module has a bug, but which bug in which module is the one causing this failure. And when bugs in different modules are triggered together, they cause even more confusion and make the failure much harder to isolate or replicate.

  Errors in one module can also block testing of another. If the only module that calls a function doesn't work, how does the programmer test the function? Unless she writes a test driver (not done in big bang testing), she has to wait until the module works. Will this leave time for testing and fixing?

- ***Bad feelings:*** When it's unclear which module has the bug, one programmer may point her finger at another's code. If the other points back, we get a big argument but ineffective debugging.

- ***Weak automation:*** The "advantage" of big bang testing—no need for stubs and drivers—is a mixed benefit. A program under development changes daily. It must be constantly retested. Stubs and drivers would help automate these tests.

Since (most) project managers aren't stupid, when one tells us that he's going for a big bang approach to save the stub and driver writing time, we have to assume that he sees advantages that he doesn't care to verbalize. Some project managers believe that they and the project will be better off if the testers are a little less efficient. Others don't care about test efficiency; they just want to be able to report to management that "Coding is complete" as soon as possible, even if nothing works. If the project schedule falls behind from this point forward, they can blame it on Murphy's Law, or the testers, or bad luck, but they got what they see as their part (code complete) done on time. We don't understand these attitudes, but we have each been project managers and we have each known other project managers who operate in these ways.

## TOP-DOWN VERSUS BOTTOM-UP TESTING

Both top-down and bottom-up strategies are incremental. The product has been designed hierarchically. A main module calls sub-modules (lower level modules) which in turn call even lower level modules until finally some module calls the one that does the work. The question is, which level of module should be tested first.

In *bottom-up testing*, the lowest level modules are tested first. Test drivers are written to call them and pass them test data. Then the next higher level modules are tested. The tested low level routines are used during testing of the higher modules, rather than stubs. In *top-down testing*, the highest level modules are tested first. Drivers aren't needed. Stubs are used, then replaced by the next highest level modules once the toplevel module is pronounced good.

Yourdon (1975) argues that top-down testing is a decidedly better strategy. Myers (1979) argues that there are advantages and disadvantages to each approach but that on balance bottom-up is better than top-down. Dunn (1984) argues that some of each should be done. In practice, it's common to test a module soon after writing it; sometimes this is bottom-up, sometimes top-down.

## STATIC VERSUS DYNAMIC TESTING

In *static testing,* the code is examined. It is tested without being executed. In *dynamic testing,* the code is executed. It is tested without, necessarily, being examined.

As described to this point, both glass box and black box tests are dynamic. Data are fed to the program, then the programmer or tester examines the result. The distinction between them is the information used for choosing the data.

Many tools do static analysis. An obvious first example is a compiler. The compiler delivers error messages instead of object code when it discovers syntax errors or other invalid operations. Similarly, a linking loader refuses to organize compiled modules into an executable program if it can't find every variable and function referred to. Chapter 11 discusses automated testing tools for static and dynamic testing.

Static analysis can also be done by people. They read a listing of the code, perhaps discuss it, and usually find many errors. Examples are:

- **Walkthroughs**, **code inspections**, and **code reviews.** These are the same types of meetings discussed previously (see "Review Meetings" earlier in this chapter). Myers (1979) provides a useful checklist for inspections. Fagan (1976) is a classic discussion of inspections. Myers (1978) found that walkthroughs were as effective in finding errors as dynamic testing by someone who didn't write the code.

- **Desk checking** means that someone reads the program carefully and analyzes its behavior without running test cases at the computer. In practice, if the reader can't understand what the program will do at a certain point, he may run a test to find out. The desk checker may or may not be the author of the program. It's useful either way. The desk checker probably spends more time than the length of a technical review meeting and often reads a much longer collection of code.

Reading your own code or someone else's can be boring, and some people object to others reading their code. Weinberg (1971) is credited with repopularizing code reading. Beizer (1984, 1990) suggests that desk checkers ignore syntax, standards adherence, and anything else the computer can check.

One of the most important things a code reader does is determine whether the code makes sense to a reader. If it is confusing to read, it probably reflects confused thinking about the problem. If it doesn't contain an error yet, it will after a maintenance programmer makes any change to it.

## STANDARDS COMPLIANCE

Automated tests can check whether coding practices meet company standards. For example, one test might count comments per 100 lines of code and another might count the lines in each module. Some contracts require such measurements.

## SOFTWARE METRICS

It is fashionable to calculate some statistics describing the structure or content of a program, call them "metrics," and treat these numbers as if they had a theoretical basis and predictive value. This is another type of static glass box testing. Rather than scanning the code for errors, a program scans the code in order to tabulate characteristics of interest. We are skeptical of much (though not all) of the work in this area.

We are concerned about the application of this work. Testers calculate "measures" of software complexity, then management insists that the programmers revise the code to achieve a better "complexity" number. This absolutely does *not* mean that the programmers have made the program less complex (and thus more reliable, more testable, and more maintainable). It means they reworked the code to get a better number. To achieve this, they may have made the code much more difficult to understand and maintain (which is what we think of when we think of "complex").

How can this be? Well, suppose you measure the length of a line by measuring the weight of the ink used to draw the line. This works, usually: longer lines use more ink, so the pages are heavier. But if you measure a particularly heavy line one day, we could make it "shorter" by making the line narrower, or by using a lighter weight of ink or paper. You could make the line "shorter" (less ink weight) even while making it longer (as measured by a ruler). Before you tell someone to reduce their complexity number, be sure that you're using something more like a ruler than like ink weight (or worse), or their changes may have no effect on the real, underlying complexity of the program.

47

Before you adopt a metric as a measure that you will treat seriously in your company, ask a few questions:

- A *metric* is a system of measurement. What does this metric purport to measure?

- What is the theoretical relationship between the characteristic being measured (such as length or complexity) and the measurements being taken (as ink weight, ruler length, lines of code, number of operators, number of links and nodes in a graph of the program)? Do you *have* a theory relating the measurements to the characteristic? Are you taking these particular measurements because you think they're the *right* ones, the ones that bear some fundamental relationship to the characteristic (as a ruler measurement does to length) or because they're convenient? Can you vary your measurement without affecting the underlying characteristic (as we did with ink weight and length)?

- How convincing is the empirical relationship between the characteristic being measured and the measurements? For example, how much more reliable, testable, readable, maintainable, or otherwise wonderful are programs with lower complexity numbers? How big a difference does a small change in complexity number make? How statistically reliable is this relationship between complexity number and testability or reliability or whatever? How procedurally reliable are the experiments that establish this relationship?

- When you instruct programmers to reduce their (e.g., complexity) number, is the revised program more or less reliable, maintainable, testable, or readable than the original?

Consider lines of code as a measure of reliability, for example. Professional programmers normally leave one to three errors per hundred lines of code. More hundreds of lines of code means more errors. But after a programmer finishes writing a program, should you require her to reduce the program's length? You *might* get a carefully restructured program that is shorter, clearer, and faster, but if it was already well structured, you're in for a short surprise, riddled with tricks and GOTO's, slower, and with many more bugs. This is so obvious that no one (we hope) expects to improve reliability by insisting on fewer lines of code. As Beizer (1990, p. 119) puts it "Don't squeeze the code. *Don't squeeze the code!* **DON'T SQUEEZE THE CODE!**"

---

*If you make programmers reduce their code's complexity numbers, are you telling them to do the equivalent of squeezing the code? How do you know?*

---

Beizer (1990) provides a sympathetic introduction to software metrics. We strongly recommend Jones (1991) as a general survey of software measures. For the mathematically capable reader who wants to evaluate software metrics as metrics, we recommend reading some books on theory of measurement, such as Krantz, Luce, Suppes, and Tversy (1971), and Pfanzagl (1971). For a simpler introduction, read Churchman & Ratoosh (1959) or the first chapters of Torgerson (1958).

---

## DELIBERATE ERRORS: BEBUGGING AND MUTATION

In *bebugging* a program, someone deliberately introduces bugs into it *before* the person who will test it starts testing. Weinberg (1971) suggested this as a way of increasing programmers' motivation to find bugs. If they *know* there are errors in the program, they know their tests should find some. They will keep building better tests until they do.

Mills (1970) suggested using bebugging to estimate the number of errors left in the program. If 100 bugs are inserted into the program, and testers find 20 of these, along with 200 others, the odds are that another 880 bugs (counting the 80 inserts) exist in the program. This is superficially plausible, but it is not as well based in probability theory as some people think. If the 100 seeded bugs are striking (e.g., system crashers) and easy to trigger, testers will find them quickly. If they are subtle, they might be among the last errors found. For good estimation, the 100 seeded bugs would have to be somewhat similar to the "real" bugs in range of subtlety and types of problems. This is difficult, maybe impossible.

*Mutations* are introduced into a program to test the adequacy of the test data. A mutation is a *small* change made to the program. The effects of that change should show up in some test. If it doesn't, the test set is probably inadequate.

DeMillo *et al.* (1987) discuss mutation in detail and review the literature.

After bebugging or mutation errors are put in the code, testing can be static, black box or glass box. The error introduction is "glass box" in the obvious sense that the person changing the code must see how the code works.

## PERFORMANCE TESTING

Performance can be tested using glass box or black box techniques. Glass box testing allows a finer analysis because you can use profilers or hardware-based execution monitors to study the time the program spends in specific modules, along specific paths, or working with specific types of data.

One objective of performance testing is performance enhancement. The tests might determine which modules execute most often or use the most computer time. Those modules are re-examined and recoded to run more quickly.

Testing groups do black box performance tests. They use *benchmark* tests to compare the latest version's performance to previous versions'. Poor performance can reflect bugs, especially when a part of the program that used to run quickly is now slow.

Performance benchmark tests against the competition are also useful for evaluating the salability of the product and determining the need for time-consuming performance enhancements.

Beizer (1984) discusses many aspects of performance testing in detail.

## REGRESSION TESTING

Regression testing is fundamental work done by glass box and black box testers. The term *regression testing* is used in two different ways. Common to both is the idea of reusing old tests:

- Imagine finding an error, fixing it, then repeating the test that exposed the problem in the first place. This is a regression test. Added variations on the initial test, to make sure that the fix works, are also considered part of the regression test series. Under this usage, regression testing is done to make sure that a fix does what it's supposed to do.

  Some programming groups create a set of regression tests that includes every fixed bug ever reported by any customer. Every time the program is changed in any way, all old fixes are retested. This reflects the vulnerability of code fixes (which, unless they're well documented, often don't look "right" when you read the code) to later changes, especially by new programmers.

- Imagine making the same fix, and testing it, but then executing a standard series of tests to make sure that the change *didn't disturb anything else*. This too is called regression testing, but it tests the overall integrity of the program, not the success of software fixes.

  Stub and driver programs developed during incremental testing can be the basis of an automated regression test battery. Or you can create an automated regression suite of black box tests using a capture/replay program (discussed in Chapter 11, "Automated acceptance and regression Tests").

Both types of tests should be executed whenever errors are fixed. Someone talking about regression testing after bug fixing often means both.

## BLACK BOX TESTING

When coding is finished, the program goes to the Testing Group for further testing. You will find and report errors and get a new version for testing. It will have old errors that you didn't find before and it will have new errors. Martin & McClure (1983) summarize data collected by Boehm on the probability of bug fixes working:

- The probability of changing the program correctly on the first try is only 50% if the change involves ten or fewer source statements.

- The probability of changing the program correctly on the first try is only 20% if the change involves around 50 statements.

Not only can fixes fail; they can also have *side effects*. A change that corrects one error may produce another. Further, one bug can hide (or *mask*) another. The second doesn't show up until you get past the first one. Programmers often catch their initial failures to fix a problem. They miss side effects and masked bugs because they often skip regression testing.

Because you will not catch all the errors in your first wave(s) of tests, and because the bug fixes will cause new bugs, you should expect to test the program many times. While early in testing you *might* accept revised versions every few hours or days, it's common to test one version thoroughly before accepting the next for testing. A *cycle of testing* includes a thorough test of one version of the program, a summary report describing the problems found in that version, and a summary of all known problems.

Project managers often try to schedule two cycles of testing: one to find all the bugs, the second to verify the fixes. Eight cycles is more likely. If you do less thorough testing per version, expect 20 or 30 (or more) cycles.

## THE USUAL BLACK BOX SEQUENCE OF EVENTS

This section describes a sequence of events that is "usual" in the microcomputer community, once black box testing starts. The mainframe culture is different. Friends who work in banks tell us that they start designing and writing tests well before they start testing. They tell us this earlier start is typical of mainframe testing even when the test effort is otherwise mediocre.

### Test planning

The testing effort starts when you begin test planning and test case design. Depending on the thoroughness of the specifications and your schedule, you can start planning as soon as the requirements document is circulated. More likely, you will begin detailed planning and designing tests in the first cycle of testing. Chapter 7 discusses the design of individual tests and Chapter 12 discusses the overall test plan.

### Acceptance testing

Each time you receive a new version of the program, check whether it's stable enough to be tested. If it crashes at the slightest provocation, don't waste your time on it. This first bit of testing is called acceptance or qualification testing.

Try to standardize the acceptance test. Distribute copies of it to the programmers so they can run the test before submitting the program to you, avoiding embarrassing rejections. The acceptance test should be short. It should test mainstream functions with mainstream data. You should be able to easily defend the claim that a version of the program that fails this test is in miserable shape.

Many companies partially automate their acceptance tests using black box automation software. Several packages are commercially available.

### Initial stability assessment

How reliable is the program? Will it take 4 cycles of testing or 24? You might be asked to assess stability for scheduling, to estimate the cost of sending it to an outside testing agency, or to estimate the publishability or supportability of a program your company is considering acquiring and distributing.

You are not trying to find bugs per se at this point. You are trying to decide which areas of the program you trust least. If the program looks weak in an area that's hard to test, expect testing to take a long time. Checking the existing manual against the program is a good start. This covers the full range of the program's functions with easy examples. Try a few other tests that you might expect the program to fail. At the end of this initial evaluation, you should have a feel for how hard the program will be to test and how bug-ridden it is. We can't tell you how to translate this feeling into a numerical estimate of required person-hours, but a qualitative gauge is much better than nothing.

You should rarely spend more than a week on an initial stability estimate. If you can't test the manual in a week, use part of it. Make sure to include a review of each section of the manual.

If the program is not trivial, and if it is not a new version of an old program that you've tested many times before, don't expect to be able to say much about the program in less than a week.

### Function test, system test, verification, and validation

You *verify* a program by checking it against the most closely related design document(s) or specification(s). If there is an external specification, the *function test* verifies the program against it.

You *validate* a program by checking it against the published user or system requirements. *System testing and integrity testing* (see below) are validation tests.

*Independent Verification and Validation* (IV&V) is a popular buzzphrase referring to verification and validation testing done by an independent test agency.

The testing phase includes both function and system testing. If you have an external specification, testing the program against it is only part of your task. We discuss the questions you will raise during testing in the next major section of this chapter, "Some tests run during function and system testing."

For a more complete discussion of verification and validation, see Andriole (1986) or the *IEEE Standard for Software Verification and Validation Plans* (ANSI/IEEE Standard 1012-1986).

### Beta testing

When the program and documentation seem stable, it's time to get user feedback. In a *beta test*, people who represent your market use the product in the same way(s) that they would if they bought the finished version and give you their comments.

Prudent beta testers will not rely on your product because you will warn them that this unfinished version may still have horrible bugs. Since they're not working full time with your product, they will not test it as thoroughly or as quickly as you would like. Expect a beta tester to take three weeks to work with the product for 20 hours.

> *The 20 hours work from a beta tester are not free. You or another tester will probably spend 4 to 8 hours recruiting, managing, nagging, and supporting each outside tester, plus additional time writing the beta test instructions and questionnaire.*

Some people will use the beta test version of the product much more thoroughly. They will use it more extensively if:

- This is the only product of its type; they need it even if it is unreliable.

- You pay them enough. Typical payment is a free or deeply price-reduced copy of the product. This is enough if the purchase price is high for that tester. If you're testing a $500 database manager, many users would not consider a free copy of the program to be enough. If they use the program to keep important records and it crashes (as it probably will) it will cost them a lot more to re-enter the data.

- You give them a service guarantee. For example, you might promise that if the program crashes, *you* (someone in your company) will re-enter their data for free.

In Chapter 13, the section "Beta: Outside beta tests" discusses beta testing in much more detail.

## Integrity and release testing

Even after you decide that the product is finished, problems are still possible. For example, many companies have sent out blank or virus-infected disks for duplication.

In the *release test*, you gather all the things that will go to the customer or to a manufacturer, check that these are all the right things, copy them, and archive the copies. Then you release them.

A release test of a set of disks might be as simple as a binary comparison between all files on these disks and those on the version you declared "good" during the final round of testing. Even if you make the release disks from the tested disks, do the file comparisons. It's cheap compared with the cost of shipping thousands of copies of the wrong disk.

We strongly recommend that you test the product for viruses as part of the release test. If you send out software in compressed format, test the compressed disks but also install the program, run the program, reboot, and check if your computer got a virus from the decompressed program. It's not yet clear whether your customers can sue your company, or for how much, if your software carries a virus, but it's not unlikely that your company would be dragged into court (see Chapter 14).

*Integrity testing* is a more thorough release test. It provides a last chance to rethink things before the product goes out the door. The integrity tester tries to anticipate every major criticism that will appear in product reviews, or, for contract work, every major complaint the customer will raise for the next few months. The integrity tester should be a senior tester who wasn't involved in the development or testing of this product. He may work for an independent test agency. The integrity tester assumes that function and system testing were thorough. He does *not* deliberately set out to find errors. He may carefully compare the program, the user documentation, and the early requirements documents. He may also make comparisons with competing products.

An integrity test should also include all marketing support materials. The product must live up to all claims made in the advertisements. Test the ad copy and sales materials before they are published.

The test is best conducted by one person, not by a team. Budget two weeks for an integrity test of a moderately complex single-user program.

## Final acceptance testing and certification

If your company developed the program on contract, the customer will run an *acceptance test* when you deliver it. In small projects, this test may be informal. For most projects, however, test details are agreed to in advance, in writing. Make sure the program passes the test before trying to deliver it to the customer. An acceptance test usually lasts less than a day. It is not a thorough system test. Beizer (1984) describes the preparation and execution of formal customer acceptance tests. Perry (1986) is, in effect, a *customer's guide* to creating acceptance tests. Consider using Perry (1986) to structure your negotiations with the customer when you jointly design the acceptance test.

*Certification* is done by a third party. The certifier might be an agent of the user or an independent test agency. A certification test can be brief, at the level of an acceptance test, or more thorough. Development contracts may require certification in place of acceptance testing. The contract should spell out the level of testing or inspection involved and any standards that must be met by the program, the development process or the testing process. If your company is seeking some form of certification voluntarily, probably for marketing purposes, the amount of testing involved is negotiable.

## SOME TESTS RUN DURING FUNCTION AND SYSTEM TESTING

Having defined function and system testing above, here are examples of tests that are run during the function or system testing phases.

### Specification verification

Compare the program's behavior against every word in the external specification.

### Correctness

Are the program's computations and its reports of them correct?

### Usability

You can hire people who are like those who will use the product, and study how they work with it. A beta test is an attempt to run a usability test cheaply. However, since you don't see the problems as they arise, and you can't set the people's tasks, you won't learn as much from beta testing as you could from studying representative users in your laboratory.

### Boundary conditions

Check the program's response to all extreme input values. Feed it data that force it to output extreme values.

## Performance

This is black box performance testing. Identify tasks and measure how long it takes to do each. Get a good stopwatch.

## State transitions

Does the program switch correctly from state to state? For example, if you can tell it to sort data, print them, then display a data entry screen, will it do these things in the correct order? Can you make it do them out of sequence? Can you make the program lose track of its current state? Finally, what does the program do with input while it's switching between states? If you start typing just as it stops printing and prepares to display the data entry screen, does the program crash?

## Mainstream usage tests

Use the program the way you expect customers to use it. Do some real work with it. It's surprising how many errors show up in this type of test that didn't come up, or didn't seem important, when you did the more formal (e.g., boundary) tests.

## Load: volume, stress, and storage tests

*Load tests* study the behavior of the program when it is working at its limits:

- *Volume tests* study the largest tasks the program can deal with. You might feed huge programs to a compiler and huge text files to a word processing program. Or you might feed an interactive program input quickly but steadily, to try to overflow the amount of data it can receive and hold in temporary storage. (Interactive programs often minimize their response times to keystrokes and mouse strokes by putting input in temporary storage until a break between bursts of input. Then they process and interpret the input until the next input event.) You should also feed programs with no executable code to the compiler and empty files to the word processor. (For some reason these are not called volume tests).

- *Stress tests* study the program's response to peak bursts of activity. For example, you might check a word processor's response when a person types 120 words per minute. If the amount of activity that the program should be able to handle has been specified, the stress test attempts to prove that the program fails at or below that level.

- *Storage tests* study how memory and space is used by the program, either in resident memory or on disk. If there are limits on these amounts, storage tests attempt to prove that the program will exceed them.

## Background

In a multi-processing system, how well does the product do many tasks? The objective is to prove that the program fails when it tries to handle more than one task. For example, if it is a multi-user database have many people use it at the same time, or write a program to simulate the inputs from many people. This is the background activity. Now start testing. What happens when two users try to work with the same data? What if you both try to write to the printer or disk simultaneously? See Beizer (1984) for further discussion.

## Error recovery

Make as many different types of errors as you can. Try to get the program to issue every error message listed in the documentation's Error Messages appendix. (Also generate any messages that aren't listed in the documentation.) Error handling code is among the least tested so these should be among your most fruitful tests.

## Security

How easy would it be for an unauthorized user to gain access to this program? What could she do to your data if she did? See Beizer (1984) for thoughts on security testing and Fernandez *et al.* (1981) for a much broader discussion of security issues.

## Compatibility and conversion

*Compatibility testing* checks that one product works with another. Two products might be called compatible if they can share the same data files or if they can simultaneously reside in the same computer's memory. Since there are many types of "compatibility," you must know which one is claimed before you can test for it.

If they are not directly compatible, your program might still be able to read another's data files by using a two step process. First, run a *conversion program* that rewrites the files in your program's format. Then your program reads those new files.

The most common conversion problem is between two versions of the same program. An updated program must detect that the data are in the old version's format and either read and rewrite them or call a conversion utility to do this. Your program might also be able to rewrite files from its format into one compatible with another program.

## Configuration

The program must work on a range of computers. Even if it only has to operate on one model of computer, two machines of that model will differ in their printers, other peripherals, memory, and internal logic cards. The goal of the configuration test is finding a hardware combination that should be, but is not, compatible with the program.

## Installability and serviceability

An installation utility lets you customize the product to match your system configuration. Does the installation program work? Is it easy to use? How long does the average user take to install the product? How long does an expert take?

If the program is installed by a service person or by any third party, installation is an issue within the larger scope of serviceability. The serviceability question is this: if the program does fail, how easily can a trained technician fix it or patch around it?

### Quickies

The *quicky* is a show tool. Its goal is to cause a program to fail almost immediately. Quickies are "pulled" in front of an audience, such as visiting executives. If the test is successful, the people watching you will be impressed with how good a tester you are and how unstable the program is.

You have no planning time for a quicky. When you get the program, you have to guess what might be wrong with it based on your experience with other programs written by the authors of this one, with other programs that run under the same operating system, etc. For example, try pressing <Enter> or moving and clicking the mouse while a program is loading from the hard disk. In general, try to provoke race conditions (see "Race conditions" in Chapter 4) or error recovery failures.

Your tests should be unobtrusive. Ideally, no one looking over your shoulder would realize that you tried a test unless the program fails it.

## MAINTENANCE

A large share of the money your company spends on this program will be spent changing it after it's completed. According to Martin & McClure's (1984) textbook:

- Maintenance accounts for almost 67% of the total cost of the software.
- 20% of the maintenance budget is spent fixing errors.
- 25% is spent adapting the program so that it works with new hardware or with new co-resident software.
- 6% is spent fixing the documentation.
- 4% is spent on performance improvements.
- 42% is spent making changes (*enhancements*) requested by users.

Most of the testing you will do during the maintenance phases should be similar to what you did during function and system testing. Ideally, you will have a battery of regression tests, many of them automated, that you can run every time the program changes. Remember that maintenance changes are likely to have side effects. It is necessary to verify that the code as a whole works.

## PORT TESTING

The *port test* is unique to maintenance. Use it when the program is modified to run on another (similar) operating system or computer. The product might be ported to many different types of computers; you have to check that it works on each. Here is our strategy for port testing (assuming that the port required relatively few and minor modifications):

- ***Overall functionality:*** Use your regression series. If you don't have one, create one that exercises each of the main functions using mainstream data or a few boundary data values. If a function doesn't port successfully, it will usually not work at all, so these tests don't have to be subtle. Ported software doesn't usually fail tests of general functionality, so don't waste your time executing lots of them.

- ***Keyboard handling:*** Two computers with proprietary keyboards probably use them slightly differently. Many errors are found here. Test the effect of pressing every key (shifted, altered, etc.) in many places.

- ***Terminal handling:*** The program may not work with terminals that are commonly used with the new computer. You must test the popular terminals even if the program works with ANSI Standard terminals because the Standard doesn't include all the characters displayed on many "ANSI Standard" screens. Along with incompatible characters, look for problems in color, highlighting, underlining, cursor addressing including horizontal and vertical scrolling, and the speed of screen updating.

- *Sign-on screen, version and system identification:* The program's version ID has changed. Is the new ID everywhere? Also, if the program names the computer or operating system at startup, does it name the right one?

- *Disks:* Disk capacities and formats differ across machines, and formats might be different. Make sure the program works with files that are exactly 128, 256, 512, 1024, 2048, 4096, 8192, and 16,384 bytes long. Try it with a huge drive too, if that is supported on the new system but wasn't available (or tested) in the original environment.

- *Operating system error handling:* If you fill the disk, does the operating system let your program handle the problem or does it halt your program and report a system-level error? If the old machine handled errors one way, the new one may handle them the other. How does your product insulate the user from bad operating system error handling and other system quirks?

- *Installation:* When you install the product, you tell it how much memory it can use, the type of printer and terminal, and other information about peripherals. The installation routines were probably the most heavily modified part of the product, so spend some time on them. Check their responses to all keystrokes, and their transitions across menus. Set up a few peripheral configurations to see if the product, after proper installation, works with them. Be particularly wary of configurations that were impossible (and so untestable) on the old system, such as huge amounts of available memory, huge hard drives, multi-tasking, or new types of printers.

- *Compatibility:* Suppose that on the original computer, your program was compatible with PROGRAM_X. If PROGRAM_X has also been ported to the new computer, is your ported program compatible with ported PROGRAM_X? Don't bet on it.

- *Interface style:* When you take a program from one graphical environment to another (Windows, Mac, AmigaDOS, Motif, etc.), different user interface conventions apply. Some people are adamant that the program behave as though it was designed for their computer from the start, without carrying in rules from some other environment.

- *Other changes:* Ask the programmers what other changes were made during porting, and why. Test to make sure that the changes are correct.

Expect the first port to a new platform to require a lot of testing time, maybe a quarter as long as the original testing, while you figure out what must be tested and what can be skipped. Tests to later platforms will probably go more quickly, now that you understand how the program will usually change.

# SOFTWARE ERRORS

## INTRODUCTION: THE REASON FOR THIS CHAPTER

Your primary task as a tester is to find and report errors. The purpose of your work is improvement of product quality. This brief chapter defines "quality" and "software error." Then, because it helps to know what you're looking for before hunting for it, we describe thirteen categories of software errors.

The Appendix describes the error categories in more detail, and illustrates them with over 400 specific types of errors.

## USEFUL READING

Deming (1982), Feigenbaum (1991), Ishikawa (1985), and Juran (1989) are well respected, well written books with thoughtful discussions of the meaning of quality.

**4**

SOFTWARE

ERRORS

## QUALITY

Some businesses make customer-designed products on order. The customer brings a detailed specification that describes exactly what he wants and the company agrees to make it. In this case, *quality* means matching the customer's specification.

> *Most software developers don't have such knowledgeable and precise customers. For them, the measure of their products' and services' quality is the satisfaction of their customers, not the match to a specification.*

If the customer doesn't like the end result, it doesn't matter if the product meets a specification, even if the customer agreed to the specification. For that customer, it's not good quality if he's not happy with it.

One aspect of quality is *reliability*. The more reliable the program, the less often it fails while the customer is trying to use it, and the less serious the consequences of any failures. This is very important, but testers who say that quality *is* reliability are mistaken. If the program can't do what the customer wants to do with it, the customer is unhappy. If the customer is not happy, the quality is not high.

A program's quality depends on:
- the features that make the customer want to use the program, and
- the flaws that make the customer wish he'd bought something else.

Your main contribution as a tester is to improve customer satisfaction by reducing the number of flaws in the program. But a project manager who forces a particularly useful feature into the program at the last minute may also be improving the product's quality, even if the changed program is less reliable. Features and flaws both determine quality, not just one or the other. (For more discussion, read Juran, 1989.)

The rest of this chapter is about the flaws. How will we know one when we find it?

## WHAT IS A SOFTWARE ERROR?

One common definition of a software error is a mismatch between the program and its specification. Don't use this definition.

---

*A mismatch between the program and its specification is an error in the program if and only if the specification exists and is correct.*

---

A program that follows a terrible specification perfectly is terrible, not perfect. Here are two better definitions:

- A software error is present when the program does not do what its end user reasonably expects it to do (Myers, 1976, p. 6).

- There can never be an absolute definition for bugs, nor an absolute determination of their existence. The extent to which a program has bugs is measured by the extent to which it fails to be useful. This is a fundamentally human measure (Beizer, 1984, p. 12).

Myers (1976) explicitly excluded "human factors errors" from his definition of software errors. We see these as just another group of errors and you should too. It may be harder to convince a programmer that a user interface error is an error, or that it's important, or that testers have any right to tell him about it, but customers complain about serious human factors errors every bit as much as they complain about crashes.

## CATEGORIES OF SOFTWARE ERRORS

We describe 13 major categories. Nothing is sacred about this categorization. Beizer's (1990), for example, is useful and quite different.

### USER INTERFACE ERRORS

There are many ways to make a program a misery to work with. We lump them under the heading of "user interface." Here are some subcategories:

#### Functionality

A program has a functionality problem if it doesn't do something it should do, or does it awkwardly or incompletely. Specifications define a program's functionality for an implementation team, but the final definition of what a program is "supposed to" do lives in the mind of the user.

---

A program has a *functionality problem* if something that a user expects the program to do is hard, awkward, confusing, or impossible. This problem is a *functionality error* if the user's expectation is reasonable.

## Communication

How do you find out how to use the program? What information is readily available onscreen? Is there enough? Is it intelligible? Is it insulting? What are you told when you make a mistake or press <Help>? Is it useful? Is it accurate? Is anything irritating, misleading, confusing or poorly presented?

**4**

## Command structure

SOFTWARE
ERRORS

Is it easy to get lost in the program? Are any commands confusing or easy to confuse with others? What errors do you make, what costs you time, and why?

## Missing commands

What's missing? Does the program force you to think in a rigid, unnatural, or inefficient way? Can you customize it to suit your working style or needs? How important is customizability for a program like this?

## Performance

Speed is of the essence in interactive software. Anything that makes the user *feel* that the program is working slowly is a problem. (Especially if the competition's program feels faster.)

## Output

Most programs display, print, graph, or save information. You use most programs to get these results. Are you getting what you want? Do the printouts make sense? Can you read the graphs? Will the program save data in a format that another program can read? Can you tailor the output to suit your needs? Can you redirect output to your choice of terminal, printer, or file?

## ERROR HANDLING

Errors in dealing with errors are common. *Error handling errors* include failure to anticipate the possibility of errors and protect against them, failure to notice error conditions, and failure to deal with a detected error in a reasonable way. Many programs correctly detect errors but then branch into untested error recovery routines. These routines' bugs can cause more damage than the original problem.

## BOUNDARY-RELATED ERRORS

The simplest boundaries are numeric, like the ones discussed in the first example in Chapter 1. But the first use of a program is also a boundary condition. The largest and smallest amounts of memory that a program can cope with are *boundaries*. (Yes, some programs do die horrible deaths if you allow them too much memory.)

If any aspect of a program's use or functioning can be described as running from more to less, biggest to smallest, soonest to latest, first to last, briefest to longest, you can check boundaries at the edges of these ranges of values. Within the boundaries, the program works fine. At or outside the boundaries, the program may croak.

## CALCULATION ERRORS

Simple arithmetic is difficult and error-prone in some languages. More likely, the program will misinterpret complicated formulas. It may also lose precision as it calculates, due to rounding and truncation errors. After many intermediate calculations it may claim that $2 + 2$ is -1, even though none of the intermediate steps contains a logical error.

This category also includes computational errors due to incorrect algorithms. These include using incorrect formulas, formulas inapplicable to the data at hand, and breaking down a complex expression into components using incorrect rules. In algorithmic errors, the code correctly does what the programmer had in mind—it's just that his conception of what the code *should* do was a little batty.

## INITIAL AND LATER STATES

A function might only fail the first time you use it. That first time, you may get odd displays, wrong calculations, infinite loops, or out-of-memory error messages. Some of these come back each time you restart the program. The most insidious programs save initializing information to disk and only fail the first time they're used—before they create the initialization file. After you use the program once, you can't find these bugs without a fresh copy of the program. This seems harmless until you realize that every one of your customers will start with a fresh copy of the program.

Programmers also sometimes forget that you might back up in the middle of a routine, to try to change something you did before. If everything is set to zero the first time you use part of a program, what happens if you return to that part? Does it reset everything to zero? Did you just lose all your data?

## CONTROL FLOW ERRORS

The *control flow* of a program describes what it will do next, under what circumstances. A control flow error occurs when the program does the wrong thing next. Extreme control flow errors halt the program or cause it to run amok. Very simple errors can lead programs to spectacular misbehavior.

## ERRORS IN HANDLING OR INTERPRETING DATA

One module can pass data to another module or to another program. A set of data might be passed back and forth many times. In the process, it might be corrupted or misinterpreted. The latest changes to the data might be lost, or might reach some parts of the system but not others.

## RACE CONDITIONS

The classic *race* is between two events, call them A and B. Either A or B can happen next. If A comes first, the program works. If B happens before A, the program fails because it expected A to always occur before B. The programmer did not realize that B could win the race, and B will come first only under special conditions.

Race conditions are among the least tested. Expect race conditions in multi-processing systems and interactive systems (systems that respond to user input almost immediately). They are hard to replicate, especially if the tester isn't sensitive to timing issues. They lead to many reports of "irreproducible" bugs.

## LOAD CONDITIONS

The program may misbehave when overloaded. It may fail under a high *volume* (much work over a long period) or high *stress* (maximum load at one time). It may fail when it runs out of memory, printers, or other resources, or when it tries to share memory or CPU time with other programs or between two of its own routines. All programs have limits. The issues are whether the program can meet its stated limits and how horribly it dies when the limits are exceeded.

**4**

SOFTWARE
ERRORS

## HARDWARE

Programs send bad data to devices, ignore error codes coming back, and try to use devices that are busy or aren't there. Even if the hardware is broken, the software is also broken if it doesn't recognize and recover from hardware failure.

## SOURCE AND VERSION CONTROL

Old problems reappear if the programmer links an old version of one subroutine with the latest version of the rest of the program. You have to know (someone has to know) the version of every piece of a program being used or shipped to customers.

Somebody also has to make sure the program has the right copyright messages, sign-on screens, and version numbers. Dozens of small details must be checked.

Enforcement of source and version control "standards" (i.e., nagging everybody) is often delegated to Quality Assurance groups. In our view, identification of source and version control problems is a Testing function; enforcement is not. Expanding a Testing Empire to encompass source and version control is asking for a license to get on people's nerves.

## DOCUMENTATION

The documentation is not software but it is part of the software product. Poor documentation can lead users to believe that the software is not working correctly. Detailed discussion of documentation errors is beyond the scope of this book, but documentation testing is discussed in Chapter 10.

## TESTING ERRORS

Last, but definitely not least: if a programmer makes one and a half mistakes per line of code, how many mistakes will you make per test? Errors made by the tester are among the most common errors discovered during testing. You don't want them to be the most common errors reported—you'd lose credibility quickly. But don't forget that some of your errors reflect problems in the program's user interface. If the program leads you to make mistakes, it has design problems. Your errors are test data too.

# REPORTING AND ANALYZING BUGS

**5**

REPORTING &
ANALYZING BUGS

If your reports are not clear and understandable, bugs won't get fixed. You should spend the minimum time needed to describe a problem in a way that maximizes the probability that it will be fixed. The content and tone of your reports affect that probability.

*The point of writing Problem Reports is to get bugs fixed.*

To write a fully effective report you must:

- *Explain how to reproduce the problem*. Programmers dismiss reports of problems that they can't see for themselves.

- *Analyze the error so you can describe it in a minimum number of steps*. Reports that contain unnecessary steps make the problem look less general than it is. They also confuse and intimidate the reader. A programmer is more likely to postpone dealing with a report that looks long and involved.

- *Write a report that is complete, easy to understand, and non-antagonistic*. A report that confuses or irritates the programmer doesn't motivate her to fix it.

## WRITE PROBLEM REPORTS IMMEDIATELY

The Problem Report form includes sections for each type of information. Fill in as much of the report as soon as you can, while you have the problem in front of you. If you just jot down notes and write the reports later, without verifying each report at the computer, you may never realize how complex some problems are. Your report will only describe the steps you *think* are necessary to repeat the bug. When you are wrong, the programmer will reject the report as irreproducible. This does your credibility no good, and it can hurt morale. All too often, testers complain about programmers who "habitually" dismiss bugs as irreproducible, when the real problem is that the testers "habitually" write inaccurate or incomplete reports.

> *As soon as you run into a problem in the software, fill out a
> Problem Report form.*

## CONTENT OF THE PROBLEM REPORT

The type of information requested on Problem Report forms is much the same across companies; the organization and labeling varies. Figure 5.1 shows the layout of the form that we refer to throughout this book. The rest of this section examines the individual fields on the form.

### PROBLEM REPORT NUMBER

Ideally, the computer fills this in. It's unique—no two reports have the same number.

### PROGRAM

If there is more than one program in the product, or if your company makes more than one program, you have to say which one has the problem.

### VERSION IDENTIFICATION: RELEASE AND VERSION

These identify the code under test. For example, the VERSION identifier might be 1.01m. The product will be advertised as RELEASE 1.01. The VERSION LETTER, m, indicates that this is the thirteenth draft of 1.01 created or released for testing.

YOUR COMPANY'S NAME          *CONFIDENTIAL*          PROBLEM REPORT # _____

PROGRAM _____ RELEASE _____          VERSION _____

REPORT TYPE (*1-6*) ___                SEVERITY (*1-3*) ___          ATTACHMENTS (*Y/N*) ___
  *1 - Coding error  4 - Documentation*          *1 - Fatal*          *If yes, describe:*
  *2 - Design issue   5 - Hardware*          *2 - Serious*          _____
  *3 - Suggestion    6 - Query*          *3 - Minor*          _____

PROBLEM SUMMARY _____

CAN YOU REPRODUCE THE PROBLEM? (*Y/N*) ___

PROBLEM AND HOW TO REPRODUCE IT_____
_____
_____
_____

SUGGESTED FIX (optional) _____
_____
_____
_____

REPORTED BY _____          DATE __/__/__

          *ITEMS BELOW ARE FOR USE ONLY BY THE DEVELOPMENT TEAM*

FUNCTIONAL AREA _____          ASSIGNED TO_____

COMMENTS _____
_____
_____

STATUS (*1-2*) ___                                        PRIORITY (*1-5*) _____
  *1 - Open          2 - Closed*

RESOLUTION (*1-9*) ___                    RESOLUTION  VERSION _____
  *1 - Pending        4 - Deferred*        *7 - Withdrawn by reporter*
  *2 - Fixed          5 - As designed*        *8 - Need more info*
  *3 - Irreproducible  6 - Can't be fixed*    *9 - Disagree with suggestion*

RESOLVED BY          _____          DATE __/__/__

RESOLUTION TESTED BY          _____          DATE __/__/__

TREAT AS DEFERRED (*Y/N*) _____

**Figure 5.1  The Problem Report form**

When the programmer can't reproduce a problem in the current version of the code, the VERSION identifier tells her what version the problem was found in. She can then go to this exact version of the code and try to recreate it there.

Version identification prevents confusion about reports of errors that have already been fixed. Suppose the programmer sees a report of a problem after she has fixed it. Is this problem from an old version of the program, before the fix, or did the fix fail? If she assumes that the report is from an old version, she will ignore it. VERSION shows the problem remains in the new version.

## REPORT TYPE

REPORT TYPE describes the type of problem found.

- **Coding error**: The program behaves in a way that you think was not intended. A program that claims that $2 + 2 = 3$ probably has a Coding error. It is fair for the programmer to respond to a Coding error report by saying that the program works As designed.

- **Design issue**: You think the program works as intended, but you disagree with the design. You will report many user interface errors as design issues. The programmer should not resolve this report As designed because you claim the design itself is wrong. If the programmer considers the design correct, she should resolve the report as Disagree with suggestion.

- **Suggestion**: You are making a Suggestion if you are not claiming that anything is wrong, but you believe that your idea can improve the program.

- **Documentation**: The program doesn't behave as described in a manual or online help. Identify the document and page. You aren't necessarily saying whether the change should be in the code or the document. You're asking for a resolution. Be sure both the programmer and the writer get to see this. Features not described anywhere are also noted as Documentation errors.

- **Hardware**: Choose this to report faulty interactions between the program and some type of hardware. Don't use this to report problems due to a broken card or some other type of hardware. Use it to report when the program will fail on all cards or machines or machine models.

- **Query**: The program does something you don't understand or don't expect. Though you doubt that the program should work this way, if you aren't sure, choose Query. If you've found a problem, the programmer will still fix it. If she doesn't, or if you don't like her rationale for keeping the program this way, you can always submit a Design issue report later. In adversarial environments, Query is useful in forcing the programmer to state, in writing, that she has made a certain decision.

## SEVERITY

The reporter uses SEVERITY to indicate his rating of the seriousness of the problem.

How serious is the problem? There are no hard and fast answers. Beizer (1984, p. 20) presents a rating scale from 1 (Mild, such as spelling errors) to 10 (Infectious: causes failures in other systems, starts wars, kills, etc.). But Beizer rates errors that annoy the user or waste his time as Minor. This is a common bias, but the cost to the customer of these "annoyances" can be high. Annoyances often appear in magazine reviews. How costly is a bad review? In practice, different companies use different scales, reflecting what they think is important for quality.

As a final caution on SEVERITY ratings, bugs rated Minor tend not to be fixed. While spelling mistakes and misaligned printouts are individually minor, the program's credibility suffers if there are many of them. People can *see* these errors. We've seen salespeople crucify fundamentally sound products by demonstrating minor errors in them. If there are *lots* of minor errors, write a follow-up report (rated Serious) drawing attention to their quantity.

We find it hard to reliably rate problems on more than a three-point scale, so we use Minor, Serious, and Fatal. If you must work with more categories, develop written definitions for each and be sure the rest of the company accepts your definitions of relative severities.

## ATTACHMENTS

When you report a bug, you might attach a disk containing test data, a keystroke capture or a set of macros that will generate the test case, a printout from the program, a memory dump, or a memo describing what you did in more detail or why you think this problem is important. Each of these is an ATTACHMENT. Any time you think an ATTACHMENT would be useful, include it with the Problem Report.

**5**

In the report itself, note what item(s) you are including so the programmer who gets the report will realize what she's missing if she doesn't get all the attachments.

## PROBLEM SUMMARY

Writing a one- or two-line report summary is an art. You must master it. Summaries help everyone quickly review outstanding problems and find individual reports. Most reports that circulate to management list only the REPORT NUMBER, SEVERITY, some type of categorization, and PROBLEM SUMMARY. The summary line is the most carefully read part of the report.

When a summary makes a problem sound less severe than it is, managers are more likely to defer it. Alternatively, if your summaries make problems sound more severe than they are, you will gain a reputation for alarmism.

*Don't use the same summary for two different reports, even if they
are similar.*

The summary line should describe only the problem, not the replication steps. "Program crashes when saving using an invalid file name" is an example of a good summary.

*Note:* You *must* treat the summary and the description as *separate*. You will print them independently of each other. Don't run the summary into the description, or these printed reports will be useless.

## CAN YOU REPRODUCE THE PROBLEM?

The answer should be Yes, No, or Sometimes. If you have trouble reproducing the problem, keep at it until you either know that you can't get it to repeat at all (No), or you can repeat it only sporadically (Sometimes). If you say Sometimes, be extra-careful describing what you tried, what you think might be triggering the bug, and what you checked that is not triggering the bug. Remember: if you say Yes or Sometimes, the programmer may ask you to demonstrate the problem. If you can't reproduce a bug when the programmer asks for a demonstration, you will waste everyone's time and lose credibility. On the other hand, if you say No, some programmers will ignore the report unless more reports relating to this problem follow.

## PROBLEM AND HOW TO REPRODUCE IT

What *is* the problem? And, unless it's obvious, explain why you think this is a problem. Step by step, from a clear starting state, tell what to do to see the problem. Describe all the steps and symptoms, including error messages. It is *much* better to spoonfeed the programmer in this section than to say too little.

Programmers dismiss many legitimate bugs because they don't know how to reproduce them. They postpone dealing with bugs they can't immediately reproduce. And they waste a lot of time trying to reproduce bugs that aren't fully described. If you habitually write irreproducible reports, your reports will be ignored.

Another important reason for completing this section carefully is that you will often discover that you *don't know* exactly how to recreate the conditions that led to the error. You should find this out now, not later when the programmer comes to you unable to reproduce the bug.

If you can't reproduce a bug, and try and try and still can't reproduce it, admit it and write the report anyway. A good programmer can often track down an irreproducible problem from a careful description. Say what you tried. Describe all error messages as fully as possible. These may fully identify the problem. Never toss out a report because you can't reproduce the problem, unless you think you were hallucinating (in which case, take the rest of the day off).

## SUGGESTED FIX

This section is optional. Leave it blank if the answer is obvious or if you don't have a good fix to suggest.

Programmers neglect many design and user interface errors because they can't quickly imagine what a good fix would be. (This goes especially for wording and screen layout changes.) If you have an excellent suggestion, offer it here. Someone might follow it immediately.

## REPORTED BY

The reporter's name is essential because the programmer must know who to call if she doesn't understand the report. Many people resent or ignore anonymous reports.

## DATE

This is the DATE you (or the reporter) discovered the problem, not the day you wrote the report or the day you entered the report into the computer. Discovery Date is important because it helps to identify the program version. VERSION information isn't always enough because some programmers neglect to change version numbers in the code.

*Note:* **The following report items are used solely by the development team. Outside reporters, such as Beta testers and in-house users, do not comment in these areas.**

## FUNCTIONAL AREA

FUNCTIONAL AREA allows you to roughly categorize the problem. We urge you to keep the number of functional areas to a minimum to keep their distinctions clear. Ten is not too few. Everyone should use the same list of functional areas because this categorization is used in many reports and queries.

## ASSIGNED TO

ASSIGNED TO names the group or manager responsible for addressing the problem. The project manager will assign the report to a particular programmer. The reporter does not assign work to individuals (not even the lead tester).

## COMMENTS

In paper-based bug tracking systems, COMMENTS is a field reserved for the programmer and her manager. Here the programmer *briefly* notes why she is deferring a problem or how she fixed it.

Multi-user tracking systems use this field *much* more effectively. In these systems, COMMENTS can be arbitrarily long. Anyone who has access to the report can add a comment. Difficult bugs often develop long comment discussions. These include feedback from the programmer, one or more testers, technical support, the writer, product manager, etc. This is a fast, effective way to add information about the bug, and it is much less likely to be lost than a string of email messages. Some test groups consider this the most important field in the database.

## STATUS

All reports start out with the STATUS as Open. After fixes are confirmed as fixed, or when all agree that this report is no longer an issue for this release, change STATUS to Closed. In many projects only the lead tester can change STATUS to Closed.

(Some companies use three STATUS codes, Open, Closed, and Resolved. Programmers search the database for Open bugs, and testers search for Resolved bugs. (RESOLUTION CODE contains the resolution of Resolved and Closed bugs.) In our system, programmers search for bugs with a RESOLUTION CODE of Pending. Testers search for Open, non-Pending reports. The systems are logically equivalent, but we've seen people with strong preferences on both sides.)

## PRIORITY

PRIORITY is assigned by the project manager, who typically uses a 5- or 10-item scale. The project manager asks programmers to fix bugs in priority order. The definition for each PRIORITY varies between companies. Here's a sample scale:

(1) Fix immediately—this is holding up other work

(2) Fix as soon as possible

(3) Must fix before the next milestone (alpha, beta, etc.)

(4) Must fix before final

(5) Fix if possible

(6) Optional — use your own judgment

In practice, some project managers want 3-point scales and some want 15-point scales. And different managers word the priority scale names differently. We recommend that you treat this as the project manager's personal field. Design the database to make it easy for each manager to define her own scale.

*Only* the project manager should change PRIORITY and *only* the reporter (or lead tester) should ever change SEVERITY. The project manager and the reporter may strongly disagree about the importance of a bug but neither should change the other's classification. Sometimes a tester marks a bug Fatal and the project manager treats it as low priority. Because both fields (SEVERITY and PRIORITY) are in the system, the tester and project manager have their own places to rate the bug's importance.

## RESOLUTION AND RESOLUTION VERSION

RESOLUTION defines the current status of the problem. If software was changed in response to this report, RESOLUTION VERSION indicates what version of the program contains the change. Here are the different types of resolutions:

- **Pending**: Reports start out as Pending. Pending tells the project manager to look at this report; he has to classify and assign it. Change RESOLUTION back to Pending whenever new information contradicts the current RESOLUTION. For example, change RESOLUTION from Fixed to Pending if you can recreate a problem that the programmer claims is fixed.

- **Fixed**: Programmers mark bugs Fixed. Along with marking them Fixed, they indicate which version the fix was made in.

- **Irreproducible**: The programmer cannot make the problem happen. Check the bug in the current version and make sure every necessary step is clearly stated. If you add new steps, reset the STATUS to Pending and explain what you did in the COMMENTS field.

- **Deferred**: The project manager acknowledges that there is a problem, but chooses not to fix it in this release. Deferred is appropriate whether the bug reflects an error in coding or design.

- **As designed**: The problem reported is not an error. The behavior reported reflects the intended operation of the program.

- **Withdrawn by reporter**: If the person who wrote this report feels that he should never have written it, he can withdraw it. No one else can ever withdraw the report, only the original reporter.

- **Need more info**: The programmer has a question that the reporter must address.

- **Disagree with suggestion**: No change to the design will be made.

- **Duplicate**: Many groups include this RESOLUTION CODE and close duplicate bugs. This is risky if you close bugs that are similar rather than identical. Similar-looking bugs might have different causes. If you report them as duplicates, the programmer might fix only one without realizing there are others. Also, the different reports may contain usefully different descriptions. Always cross-reference Duplicate bugs.

## SIGNATURES

Some companies use a manual problem tracking system and have people sign actual reports. We use *sign* when people sign forms and also when they enter their names in an online system. Each company has its own rules about who has to sign the forms. We think RESOLVED BY should always be signed by the person who resolved (e.g., fixed) the problem or by her manager. Some companies add SW MANAGER APPROVAL here. RESOLUTION TESTED BY is signed by a tester to show that he's tested the fix and is satisfied that the report can be Closed.

## TREAT AS DEFERRED

A bug is Deferred if the project manager agrees that it's a software error but has decided that it won't be fixed in this release. Both coding errors and design errors can be deferred.

Good problem tracking systems print summary reports that list every Deferred bug, for higher management review.

---

*Some programmers deliberately bury reproducible, fixable bugs under codes other than Deferred to hide shoddy or schedule-threatening work from management.*

---

How should you deal with honest classification errors, disagreements over classification, and deliberate bug-hiding?

- Some Testing Groups change the RESOLUTION CODE. We don't recommend this. It can cause loud arguments.

- Some Testing Groups reject Problem Reports that should be marked as Deferred but are marked As designed. They send the report back to the project manager and insist that he reclassify the RESOLUTION. Don't try this without solid management support.

- Many Testing Groups ignore this issue. Many problems are buried as a result.

We created TREAT AS DEFERRED to address this issue. As with the PRIORITY field and the extended COMMENTS, this field reflects our belief that disagreements between project managers and testers are healthy and normal. The tracking system should *reflect* the differences, letting both sides put their judgment on record.

If you dispute a RESOLUTION of As designed, leave it alone. But answer Yes to TREAT AS DEFERRED. Thereafter this report will be included with the Deferred bugs in all reports. This is *almost* the same as changing the programmer's resolution, but not quite. The difference is that the Testing Group is saying, "Fine, that's your opinion and we'll leave it on record. But we get to choose what problems we show to senior management and this one's on our list." This is much more sensible than changing the Resolution Code.

## CHARACTERISTICS OF THE PROBLEM REPORT

A good report is *written, numbered, simple, understandable, reproducible, legible,* and *non-judgmental*.

### WRITTEN

Some project managers encourage testers to report bugs verbally, by email notes, or in some other informal, untrackable way. Don't do this. Unless the programmer will fix the error the instant you describe it to her, you must describe it in writing. Otherwise, some details (or the whole problem) will be forgotten. Even if the programmer does fix it immediately, you need a report for testing the fix later.

Realize too that you and the programmer aren't the only people who need to know about these problems. The next tester to work with this program will scan old reports to get a feel for the prior release's problems. A maintenance programmer may review the reports to see if an odd-looking piece of code was a bug fix. Finally, if the bug is not fixed it is essential to have a record of this, open to examination by management, marketing, and product support staff.

There is one exception to the principle that all Problem Reports must be reported. On occasion, you may be loaned to a programming team during their first stages of testing, well before official release of the code to the Testing Group. Many of the problems you'll find wouldn't survive into formal testing whether you were helping test or not. Normally, few bugs found at this stage of development are entered into the problem tracking database. The programming team may ask you to refrain from entering your discoveries. In this case, you are working as part of a different group and should conform to their practices. We recommend that you agree to this (after getting management approval), but you should still report your findings using standard Problem Report forms. Number them, track them yourself, but keep them out of the corporate database. Eventually, discard the Resolved reports. When the product is submitted for formal testing, enter reports of bugs that remain.

## NUMBERED

Track Problem Reports numerically. Assign a unique number to each report. If you use a computerized database, the report number will serve as a *key field*. This is the one piece of information that always distinguishes one report from all the rest. It's best to have the computer assign report numbers.

## SIMPLE

By simple, we mean not compound. Only describe one problem on one report. If you find five problems that appear related, describe them on five reports. If you have five different suggestions about a part of the program, write them on five reports. Cross-reference related reports (if you can do so conveniently).

Multiple bugs on a single report are always a problem because the programmer will only fix some of them. She will pass the report back, as `Fixed`, even though some bugs have not been fixed. This wastes time and can lead to bad feelings. Remaining problems often stay unfixed because no one notices that they weren't fixed.

Multiple bugs in one report are also confusing when they arise from different underlying problems.

Finally, five problems crammed onto one report will look like a significant task. The programmer may set them aside. She is more likely to deal quickly with five individual problems, if each looks clear and easy to fix.

## UNDERSTANDABLE

The more understandable a report, the more likely that the programmer will deal with it. You must describe the program's problematic behavior clearly. Keep all unnecessary steps out of your list of the steps required to reproduce the problem. This requires analysis on your part, (See "Analysis of a Reproducible Bug" later in this chapter.)

## REPRODUCIBLE

We stress reproducibility. Untrained reporters, such as customers and many product support staff, don't write reports that are reproducible. Many programmers habitually dismiss reports from the field, because these reports are so rarely reproducible.

Many project managers tell the programming staff to ignore irreproducible reports and not to work on problems that are not exactly described in the report. If you know how to reproduce a bug, your report must state clearly, step by step, what the programmer should do to see it. If you don't know how to reproduce it, use the techniques discussed below: "Making a Bug Reproducible". Then if you can't reproduce the bug, say so directly in your report.

## LEGIBLE

If your company's problem tracking system is a manual one, this should be obvious. Too many testers submit Grade A Chickenscratch. Think of the person reading it. Unless you are reporting a disaster, the programmer will toss an illegible report onto her pile of things to look at next year.

Spacing improves legibility. The less you say in the report the more blank space you can leave between lines on the form. Reports with more than one problem on the same form are usually illegible: they try to pack too much onto one page.

Our strongest recommendation for improving legibility is to use a computerized problem tracking system (see Chapter 6). Make the computer type your reports.

## NON-JUDGMENTAL

Nobody likes being told that what they did was wrong, wrong, wrong. As a tester, that's what you tell people every day. You can ensure your unpopularity by describing problems in a way that tells the programmer you think she is sloppy, stupid, or unprofessional. Even if you think she is, keep it out of the report. If the programmer considers you a jerk and your reports vindictive, she will want to ignore your reports and complain about you to her management.

Complaints about maliciously written Problem Reports can have serious consequences. First, they reduce your chances of raises and promotions, and may cost you your job. Some testers think their "straight" (nasty) reporting style is more courageous than foolish. But malice leads to a justifiable movement to censor Problem Reports. Because of censorship, only some reports reach the programmers, and censors don't just reject inappropriate wording. They also suppress reports of problems they consider too minor or that they decide will have political repercussions they don't care to face. Once censorship starts, some testers will stop reporting some classes of problems because they "know" that these reports will never make it past review anyway. Under these conditions, many fixable problems are never reported and never fixed.

Think twice, and twice again, before declaring war on programmers by expressing personal judgments in your reports. You will almost certainly lose that war. Even if you keep your job, you will create an adversarial relationship that will cost you reporting freedom. It will not improve product quality even if every judgment you express is correct.

We are not saying *never* express a judgment. Occasionally, you may have to write a powerful, bluntly worded report to alert management to a serious problem that a programmer will not acknowledge or fix. Fine. Use your most effective tactics. But choose your battles carefully. Don't do this more than twice per year. If you feel that you have to engage in more mudslinging than that, circulate your resume. Either the company has no standards or your unhappiness in your environment is expressing itself in a very unhealthy way.

## ANALYSIS OF A REPRODUCIBLE BUG

The rest of this chapter concentrates on reporting of coding errors rather than design issues. In this section, and the next, we assume that each bug is reproducible. We explain tactics for reproducing non-reproducible bugs shortly, in the section, "Making a Bug Reproducible."

Reproducibility implies the following:

- You can describe how to get the program into a known state. Anyone familiar with the program can follow your description and get the program into that state.
- From that state, you can specify an exact series of steps that expose the problem.

To make your report more effective you should analyze it further. If the problem is complicated either because it takes many steps to recreate or because the consequences are hard to describe, spend time with it. Simplify the report or break it into a series of many reports. The objectives of your analysis are:

- Find the most serious consequences of the problem.
- Find the simplest, shortest, and most general conditions that will trigger the bug.
- Find alternate paths to the same problem.
- Find related problems.

## FINDING THE MOST SERIOUS CONSEQUENCES

Look for the most serious consequences of a bug in order to boost everyone's interest in fixing it. A problem that looks minor will more often be deferred.

For example, suppose a bug displays a little garbage text in a corner of the screen. This is minor but reportable. It will probably be fixed, but against a deadline, this bug would not stop shipment of the program. Sometimes, onscreen garbage is merely an isolated problem (and the decision to leave it alone might be wise, especially just before release). Often though, it is the first symptom of a more serious underlying problem. If you keep working with the program, you might discover that it crashes almost immediately after displaying the garbage. This is the consequence you're looking for; it will get the screen garbage fixed.

REPORTING &
ANALYZING BUGS

When a program fails, it either:

- falls into a state the programmer didn't expect, or
- falls into error recovery routines.

If the state is unexpected, subsequent code makes incorrect assumptions about what has happened. Further errors are likely. As to error recovery routines, these are often the least tested parts of the program. They often have errors and are poorly designed. Typically, error routines contain more serious bugs than the one that led there.

When the program logs an error, displays garbage onscreen, or does anything else that the programmer didn't intend, always look for a follow-up bug.

## FINDING THE SIMPLEST AND MOST GENERAL CONDITIONS

Some bugs show up at midnight every leap year, but never appear any other time. Some bugs won't show up unless you make a complex series of erroneous or unlikely responses. Bug fixing involves tradeoffs:

- If it takes minimal effort to understand and fix a problem, someone will fix it.

- If the fix requires (or looks like it will require) lots of time and effort, the programmers will be less willing to fix it.

- If the problem will arise during routine use of the program, management interest in the problem will increase.

- If it appears that almost no one will see the problem, interest will be low.

Finding simpler ways to reproduce a bug also makes the debugging programmer's task much easier and faster. The fewer steps that it takes to reproduce a bug, the fewer places the programmer has to look (usually) in the code, and the more focused her search for the internal cause of the bug can be. The effort involved in fixing a bug includes finding the internal cause, changing the code to eliminate the cause, and testing the change. If you make it easier to find the cause and test the change, you reduce the effort required to fix the problem. Easy bugs get fixed even if they are minor.

## FINDING ALTERNATE PATHS TO THE SAME PROBLEM

Sometimes it takes a lot to trigger a bug. No matter how deeply you analyze a problem, you still need many steps to reproduce it. Even if every step is likely in normal use of the program, a casual observer might believe that the problem is so complicated that few customers will see it.

You can counter this impression by showing that you can trigger the error in more than one way. Two different paths to the same bug are a more powerful danger signal than one. Two paths suggest that something is deeply wrong in the code even if each path involves a complicated series of steps.

Further, if you describe two paths to a bug, they probably have something in common. You might not see the commonality from the outside, but the programmer can look for code they both pass through.

It takes practice to develop judgment here. You must present different enough paths that the programmer won't dismiss them as alternative descriptions of the same bug, but the paths don't have differ in every detail. Each path is valuable to the degree that it provides extra information.

## FINDING RELATED PROBLEMS

Look for other places in the program where you can do something similar to what you did to expose this bug. You've got a reasonable chance of finding a similar error in this new code. Next, follow up that error and see what other trouble you can get into. A bug is an opportunity. It puts the program into an unusual state, and runs it through error recovery code that you would otherwise find hard to reach and test. Most bugs that you find under these conditions are worthwhile because some customers will find another way to reach the same error handling routines. Your investigation can avert a disaster.

Again you must develop judgment. You don't want to spend too much time looking for related problems. You may invest time in this most heavily after deferral of a bug that you know in your heart is going to cause customer grief.

## TACTICS FOR ANALYZING A REPRODUCIBLE BUG

Here are a few tips for achieving the objectives laid out in the previous section:

### LOOK FOR THE CRITICAL STEP

When you find a bug, you're looking at a symptom, not a cause. Program misbehavior is the result of an error in the code. You don't see the error because you don't read the code; you just see misbehavior. The underlying error (the mistake in the code) may have happened many steps ago: any of the steps involved in a bug could be the one that triggers the error. If you can isolate the triggering step, you can reproduce the bug more easily and the programmer can fix it more easily.

Look carefully for any hint of an error as you take each step. Often minor indicators are easily missed or ignored. Minor bugs might be the first symptoms of an error that will eventually manifest itself as the problem you're interested in. If they occur on the path to the problem you're analyzing, the odds are reasonable that they're related to it. Look for:

- *Error messages*: Check error messages against a list of the program's error messages and the events the programmer claims trigger them. Read the message, try to understand why it appears and when (what step or substep).

- *Processing delays*: If the program takes an unusually long time to display the next bit of text or to finish a calculation, it may be wildly executing totally unrelated routines. The program may break out of this with inappropriately changed data or it may never return to its old state. When you type the next character, the program may think you're answering a different question (asked in an entirely different section of code) from the one showing onscreen. An unusual delay may be the only indicator that a program has just started to run amok.

- *Blinking screen*: You may be looking at error recovery when the screen is repainted or part of it flashes then reverts to normal. As part of its response to an error, the program makes sure that what shows on the screen accurately reflects its state and data. The repainting might work, but the rest of the error recovery code may foul up later.

- *Jumping cursor*: The cursor jumps to an unexpected place. Maybe it comes back (error recovery?) or maybe it stays there. If it stays, the program may have lost track of the cursor's location. Even if the cursor returns, if the program maintains internally distinct input and output cursors (many do), it may have lost one of them.

- *Multiple cursors*: There are two cursors on the screen when there only should be one. The program may be in a weird state or in a transition between states. (However, this may not be state-dependent. The program may just be misdriving the video hardware, perhaps because it's not updating redundant variables it uses to track the register status of the video card.)

- *Misaligned text*: Lines of text that are normally printed or displayed in a consistent pattern (e.g., all of them start in the leftmost column) are slightly misprinted. Maybe only one line is indented by one character. Maybe all the text is shifted, evenly or unevenly.

- *Characters doubled or omitted*: The computer prints out the word `error` as `errrro`. Maybe you've found a spelling mistake or maybe the program is having problems reading the data (the string "error") or communicating with the printer. Some race conditions cause character skipping along with other less immediately visible problems.

- *In-use light on when the device is not in use*: Many disk drives and other peripherals have in-use lights. These show when the computer is reading or writing data to them. When a peripheral's light goes on unexpectedly, the program might be incorrectly reading or writing to memory locations allocated to these peripherals instead of the correct area in memory. Some languages (C, for example) make it especially easy to inadvertently address the wrong area of memory. The program may "save" data to locations reserved for disk control or have previously overwritten control code with data it thought it was saving elsewhere. When this happens you don't see the internal program being overwritten (which will result in horrible bugs when you try to use that part of the program), but you can see the I/O lights blink. This is a classic "wild pointer" bug.

## MAXIMIZE THE VISIBILITY OF THE BEHAVIOR OF THE PROGRAM

The more aspects of program behavior you can make visible, the more things you can see going wrong and the more likely you'll be able to nail down the critical step.

If you know how to use a source code debugger, and have access to one, consider using it. Along with tracing the code path, some debuggers will report which process is active, how much memory or other resources it's using, how much of the stack is in use, and other internal information. The debugger can tell you that:

- A routine always exits leaving more data on the stack (a temporary, size-limited data storage area) than was there when it began. If this routine is called enough times, the stack will fill up and terrible things will happen.

- When one process receives a message from another, an operating system utility that controls message transfer gives the receiving process access to a new area of memory. The message is the data stored in this memory area. When the process finishes with the message, it tells the operating system to take the memory area back. If the process never releases message memory, then as it receives more messages, eventually it gains control of all available memory. No more messages can be sent. The system grinds to a halt. The debugger can show you which process is accumulating memory, before the system crashes.

You can find much more with debuggers. The more you know about programming and the internals of the program you're testing, the more useful the debugger will be. But beware of spending too much time with the debugger: your task is black box testing, not looking at the code.

Another way to increase visibility is to print everything the computer displays onscreen and all changes to disk files. You can analyze these at your leisure.

If the screen display changes too rapidly for you to catch all the details, test on a slower computer. You'll be able to see more of the display as it changes. You have other ways to slow down the program. For example, on a multi-user system, get lots of activity going on other terminals.

## ONCE YOU'VE FOUND THE CRITICAL STEP, VARY YOUR BEHAVIOR

You know that if you do A then B then C, the computer does something bad at C. You know the error is in B. Try A then B then D. How does the program foul up in D? Keep varying the next steps until you get sick of it or until you find at least one case that is serious (such as a system crash).

## LOOK FOR FOLLOW-UP ERRORS

Even if you don't know the critical step, once you've found the bug, keep using the program for a bit. Do any other errors show up? Do this guardedly. All further problems may be consequences of the first one. They may not be reproducible after this one is fixed. On the other hand, once you find one error, don't assume that later ones are necessarily consequences of the first. You have to test them separately from a known clean state and through a path that doesn't trigger the initial problem.

**5**

## PROGRESSIVELY OMIT OR VARY YOUR STEPS

If the problem is complex and involves many steps, what happens if you skip some or change them just a little? Does the bug stay there? Does it go away or turn into something else?

The more steps you can get rid of, the better. Test each to see if it is essential to reproducing the bug.

As to varying the steps, look for boundary conditions within a step. If the program displays three names per line, and you know it fails when it has exactly six, what happens if it has exactly three?

## CHECK FOR THIS ERROR IN PREVIOUS PROGRAM VERSIONS

If the error isn't in the last version of the program you tested, the error was introduced as part of a change. This information can substantially narrow the programmer's search for the cause of the error. If possible, reload the old version and check for it. This will be most important at the end of a project.

## LOOK FOR CONFIGURATION DEPENDENCE

Suppose your computer has two megabytes of memory. Can you reproduce the bug on one that has 640K or four megabytes? What if you add a network or window environment or TSR programs? If you've configured the program to work with two terminals, what happens if you change this to one or four? If the problem appears on a color monitor, what happens on a monochrome monitor? If program options are stored in a data file, what if you change some values? Chapter 8 discusses configuration issues.

## MAKING A BUG REPRODUCIBLE

A bug is *reproducible* only if someone else can do what you say and get what you got. You must be able to explain how to put the computer into a known state, do a few steps that trigger the bug, and recognize it when it appears. Many bugs corrupt unexpected areas of memory, or change device states. To be sure that you aren't looking at a side effect of some previous bug, as part of your reproduction drill you will generally reboot the computer and reload the program before trying the steps you think are necessary to trigger the bug.

Suppose you don't know how to reproduce a bug. You try to reproduce it and fail. You're not sure how you triggered the bug. What do you do?

First, write down *everything* you remember about what you did the first time. Note which things you're sure of, and which are good guesses. Note what else you did before starting on the series of steps that led to this bug. Include trivia. Now ask the question, "Why is this bug hard to reproduce?"

Many testers find it useful to videotape their steps. Many computers or video and sound cards provide output that can be recorded on video tape. This can save many hours of trying to remember individual steps, or it can be a serious time sink: approach it with caution. With a program prone to irreproducible problems, a record of last resort may be essential for tracing back through a particularly complex path. And a recording of a bug proves that the bug exists, even if you cannot reproduce it. Other testers use capture programs to record all their keystrokes and mouse movements. These are also good tools to help you identify the things you did before running into the bug.

If retracing your steps still doesn't work, keep at it. There are no intermittent software errors. The problem may appear rarely, but each time the exact conditions are met, the same behavior will repeat. All bugs should be reproducible. There are many reasons that you might not be able to reproduce a bug immediately. Here are a few hypotheses to consider:

### RACE CONDITIONS

Once you're used to conducting a test, you might run through its steps quickly. It's common (and good practice) to slow down when you find a bug. You did it fast the first time, now watch what you're doing carefully while you try it again. If you can't repeat the error, your problem may be timing: race conditions show up when you're trying to push the program to work faster than it can. Run the test again quickly, with the same rhythm you used the first time. Try this a few times before giving up. Try slowing the computer down or testing on a slower machine.

### FORGOTTEN DETAILS

If you're testing on the fly (i.e., without a test plan) and you find a problem that you can't repeat, you've probably forgotten something about what you did. It's easy to forget under these circumstances because you don't have a step-by-step plan of what you were going to do. Sometimes you may be pressing keys almost randomly.

If you are interrupted during a test, you may do something twice, or something apparently extraneous that should be harmless (for example, turn a terminal or printer on or off, or press a key then press <Delete>). Try to remember exactly what you did just before the interruption, what fidgeting you did during the interruption, and what you did just after you got back to work.

## USER ERROR: YOU DIDN'T DO WHAT YOU THOUGHT YOU DID

This will often be the explanation for a "bug." As long as you don't repeat your error, you won't be able to recreate the bug. Even though this is a likely guess, accept it only when you run out of alternatives.

If you think that people will make this error frequently, and the program's response to it is unacceptable, report a problem with the program's error handling. Don't ignore your errors. Carefully examine what the computer does with them.

## AN EFFECT OF THE BUG MAKES REPLICATION IMPOSSIBLE

Bugs can destroy files, write into invalid memory areas, disable interrupts, or close down I/O ports. When this occurs you can't reproduce a problem until you recover the files or restore the computer to its proper (or previous) state.

Here's an example of this type of problem. One of your customers sends you a letter of complaint and a floppy disk. To replicate the problem you start the program, load the disk, run the test and OOPS, the bug trashes the data files on the customer's disk. You've reproduced the problem once, but now until you get another copy of the disk from the customer, you'll never reproduce it again.

**5**

To avoid problems like this, make sure to back up data files before attempting to replicate a bug.

*Never, never, never use the original source of the data. Always use copies.*

## THE BUG IS MEMORY-DEPENDENT

The program may fail only when a specific amount or type of memory is available. Another memory-specific condition may be that the total amount of available memory appears adequate, but it turns out to be too fragmented (spread across smaller blocks that are not contiguous).

A message box that displays the amount of free memory, perhaps also showing the sizes of the five largest blocks, can be extremely handy. You see how much memory is available at the start of a test, and so, how far to reduce available memory to truly reproduce a problem. Further, this helps you understand how much memory each operation uses, making it much easier to get the program back into the original memory state. (These memory dialogs are often put in for debugging purposes, accessed by a special key, but they are often left in programs for product support use later. They are very handy.)

## THIS IS A FIRST-TIME-ONLY (INITIAL STATE) BUG

In the classic case, when you run the program for its first time, one of its first tasks is to initialize its configuration data file on disk. If you can get the program to do anything else before initialization, it will misbehave. As soon as initialization of the data file is complete, however, the program will work fine. This error will only be seen the very first time the program is run. Unfortunately, it might be seen by every person who buys the program when it is run for the first time.

As a variant of this problem, a program might not clean out the right parts of the computer's memory until after running for a while. Rather than finding 0's, the program might find what it thinks is data. What it has really found is junk left over from the last program that was running. Once the program initializes this area of memory, you won't see the problem again until you reload the other programs into memory, then reload this on top of them.

The question to ask is how to get the computer, the program, and the data files into the state they were in before the program misbehaved. To answer this question perfectly you have to know all the changes the program makes and when it makes them. You probably don't know this (if you did, you could reproduce the bug), so returning everything to initial states won't be easy. If you suspect initialization problems test from its initial state, turn off the computer and start over with a never-used copy of the program (make a supply of them.)

## BUG PREDICATED ON CORRUPTED DATA

The program might corrupt its own data, on disk or in memory, or you may have fed the program bad data. The program chokes on the data, or detects the error but stumbles in the error handler. In either case, the error you're seeing is one of error detection and recovery. To reproduce the error, you must give the program the same data again. This sounds obvious, but every tester misses this point sometime.

## BUG IS A SIDE-EFFECT OF SOME OTHER PROBLEM

This is an error recovery failure. The program fails, then, in handling the error, the program fails again. Often the second failure is much worse than the first. In watching the spectacular crash caused by the second bug, you may not notice that tiny first glitch. Your objective, after you realize that there is a first bug, is to reproduce the first one. The second one reproduces easily after that.

## INTERMITTENT HARDWARE FAILURE

Hardware failures are usually complete. Usually, for example, a memory chip will work or it won't. But heat build-up or power fluctuations may cause intermittent memory failures or memory chips may work loose and make intermittent connection. Data or code in memory are only occasionally corrupted. If you think this is happening check the power supply first. Be reluctant to blame a bug on hardware. The problem is rarely in the hardware.

## TIME DEPENDENCY

If the program keeps track of the time, it probably does special processing at midnight. A program that tracks the day may do special processing on New Year's and at the end of February in a leap year.

The switch from December 31, 1999 to January 1, 2000, is being anticipated with dread because range checks, default date searches, and other assumptions built into many programs will fail.

Check the effect of crossing a day, week, month, year, leap year, or century boundary. Bugs that happen once a day or once a week may be due to this kind of problem.

## RESOURCE DEPENDENCY

In a *multi-processing system*, two or more processes (programs) share the CPU, resources, and memory. While one process uses the printer, the other must wait. If one uses 90% of available memory, the other is restricted to the remaining 10%. The process must be able to recover from denial of resources. To replicate a failure of recovery, you have to replicate denial of the resource (memory, printer, video, communication link, etc.)

## LONG FUSE

An error may not have an immediate impact. The error may have to be repeated dozens of times before the program is on the brink of collapse. At this point, almost anything will crash it. A totally unrelated bug-free subroutine might do the magic thing that crashes the program. You'll be tempted to blame this latecomer, not the routines that slowly corrupted the system.

REPORTING &

ANALYZING BUGS

As an example, many programs use a *stack*. A stack is an area of memory reserved for transient data. The program puts data onto the "top" of the stack and takes data off the top. The stack may be small. You can fill it up. Suppose the stack can handle 256 bytes of data and Subroutine A always puts 10 bytes of data onto it and leaves them there instead of cleaning up when it's done. If no other routine takes those 10 bytes off the stack, then after you call Subroutine A 25 times, it has put 250 bytes of data onto the stack. There is only room for 6 more bytes. If Subroutine B, which has nothing to do with Subroutine A, tries to put 7 bytes of data onto the stack, the stack will *overflow*. Stack overflows often crash programs.

You can call Subroutine B from now until the computer wears out; you will not repeat this error until you call A 25 times. When the routine you think is the culprit doesn't cause the system to fail, ask what routines preceded it.

## SPECIAL CASES IN THE CODE

You don't know what the critical conditions are in the code. A cooperative programmer can save you hours or days of work trying to reproduce difficult bugs by suggesting follow-up tests. We list this last because you can alienate a good programmer by constantly pestering her about bugs you can't repeat. If you go to her with irreproducible bugs too often, she may well conclude that you are a sloppy tester and are wasting her time.

## S<small>OMEONE</small> (<small>ELVES</small>) <small>TINKERED WITH YOUR MACHINE</small>

This happens. You do some testing, go to the washroom, and while you're away someone enters new data, tinkers with the program itself, or turns off the printer. Maybe this is a practical joke. Or maybe your manager just *has* to demonstrate this new program to a visitor and forgets to leave you a note. Whenever you leave your computer or terminal logged on you risk returning to a changed situation.

# THE PROBLEM TRACKING SYSTEM

## THE REASON FOR THIS CHAPTER

In Chapter 5, we described how a bug is reported. Here we describe what happens to the Problem Report after you report it. This chapter provides the basic design of a problem tracking database and puts it in perspective. It describes the system in terms of the flow of information (bug reports) through it and the needs of the people who use it. We provide sample forms and reports to illustrate one possible implementation of the system. You could build many other, different, systems that would support the functional goals we lay out for the database.

## NOTE

Up to now, the "you" that we've written to has been a novice tester. This chapter marks a shift in position. From this point onward, we're writing to a tester who's ready to lead her own project. We write to you here assuming that you are a project's test team leader, and that you have a significant say in the design of the tracking system. If you aren't there yet, read on anyway. This chapter will put the tracking system in perspective, whatever your experience level.

## ALSO NOTE

In our analysis of the issues involved in reporting information about people, we assume that you work in a typically managed software company. In this environment, your group is the primary user of the tracking system and the primary decision maker about what types of summary and statistical reports are circulated. Under these circumstances, some types of reports that you can generate can be taken badly, as overreaching by a low level department in the company. Others will be counter-productive for other reasons, discussed below.

But the analysis runs differently if you work for a company that follows an executive-driven quality improvement program. In these companies, senior managers play a much more active role in setting quality standards, and they make broader use of quality reporting systems, including bug tracking information. The tracking system is much more of a management tool than the primarily project-level quality control tool that we discuss in this chapter. These companies also pay attention to the problems inherent in statistical monitoring of employee behavior and to the risk of distracting a Quality improvement group by forcing it to collect too much data. Deming (1982) discusses the human dynamics of information reporting in these companies and the steps executives must take to make these systems work.

**6**

PROBLEM

TRACKING

## OVERVIEW

The first sections analyze how an effective tracking system is used:

- We start with a general overview of benefits and organizational risks created by the system.

- Then we consider the prime objective of the system, its core underlying purpose. As we see it, the prime objective is getting those bugs that should be fixed, fixed.

- To achieve its objective, the system must be capable of certain tasks. We identify four requirements.

- Now look at the system in practice. Once you submit the report, what happens to it? How does it get resolved? How does the tracking system itself help this process?

- Finally, we consider the system's users. Many different people in your company use this system, for different reasons. We ask here, what do they get from the system, what other information do they want, and what should you provide? There are traps here for the unwary.

The next sections of the chapter consider the details of the system.

- We start with a detailed description of key forms and reports that most tracking systems provide.

- Now you understand problem reporting and the overall tracking system design. We suggest some fine points—ways to structure the system to increase report effectiveness and minimize interpersonal conflicts.

- The last section in this group passes on a few very specific tips on setting up the online version of the report form.

Problem Reports are a tester's primary work product. The problem tracking system and procedures will have more impact on testers reports' effectiveness than any other system or procedure.

You use a problem tracking system to report bugs, file them, retrieve files, and write summary reports about them. A good system fosters accountability and communication about the bugs. Unless the number of reports is trivial, you need an organized system. Too many software groups still use pen-and-paper tracking procedures or computer-based systems that they consider awkward and primitive. It's not so hard to build a good tracking system and it's worth it, even for small projects.

This chapter assumes your company is big enough to have a test manager, marketing manager, project manager, technical support staff, etc. It's easier for us to identify roles and bring out some fine points this way. Be aware, though, that we've seen the same interactions in two-person research projects and development partnerships. Each person wears many hats, but as long as one tests the work of the other, they face the same issues. If you work in a small team, even a significant two person class project in school (such as a full year, senior year project), we recommend that you apply as much of this system and the thinking behind it as you can.

This chapter describes a problem tracking system that we've found successful. We include the main data entry form, standard reports, and special implementation notes—enough for you to code your own system using any good database program. Beyond these technical notes, we consider the system objectives, its place in your company, and the effect of the system on the quality of your products.

The key issues in a problem tracking system are political, not technical. The tracking system is an organizational intervention, every bit as much as it is a technical tool. Here are some examples of the system's political power and the organizational issues it raises:

1. ***The system introduces project accountability.*** A good tracking system takes information that has traditionally been privately held by the project manager, a few programmers, and (maybe) the product manager, and makes it public (i.e., available to many people at different levels in the company). Throughout the last third of the project, the system provides an independent reality check on the project's status and schedule. It provides a list of key tasks that must be completed (bugs that must be fixed) before the product is finished. The list reflects the current quality of the product. And anyone can monitor progress against the list over a few weeks for a further check on the pace of project progress.

2. ***As the system is used, significant personal and control issues surface.*** These issues are standard ones between testing, programming, and other groups in the company, but a good tracking system often highlights and focuses them. Especially on a network, a good system captures most of the communication between the testers and the programmers over individual bugs. The result is a revealing record that can highlight abusive, offensive, or time-wasting behavior by individual programmers or testers or by groups.

   Here are some of the common issues:

   - Who is allowed to report problems? Who decides whether a report makes it into the database? Who controls the report's wording, categorization, and severity?

   - Who is allowed to query the database or to see the problem summaries or statistics?

   - Who controls the final presentation of quality-related data and other progress statistics available from the database?

   - Who is allowed to hurt whose feelings? Why?

   - Who is allowed to waste whose time? Do programmers demand excessive documentation and support for each bug? Do testers provide so little information with Problem Reports that the programmers have to spend most of their time recreating and narrowing test cases?

   - How much disagreement over quality issues is tolerable?

   - Who makes the decisions about the product's quality? Is there an appeal process? Who gets to raise the appeal, arguing that a particular bug or design issue should not be set aside? Who makes the final decision?

**PROBLEM**

**TRACKING**

3. ***The system can monitor individual performance.*** It's easy to crank out personal statistics from the tracking system, such as the average number of bugs reported per day for each tester, or the average number of bugs per programmer per week, or each programmer's average delay before fixing a bug, etc. These numbers look meaningful. Senior managers often *love* them. They're often handy for highlighting personnel problems or even for building a case to fire someone. However, if the system is used this way, some very good people will find it oppressive, and some not necessarily good people will find ways to manipulate the system to appear more productive.

4. ***The system provides ammunition for cross-group wars.*** Suppose that Project X is further behind schedule than its manager cares to admit. The test group manager, or managers of other projects that compete with Project X for resources, can use tracking system statistics to prove that X will

consume much more time, staff and money than anticipated. To a point, this is healthy accountability. Beyond that point, someone is trying to embarrass X's manager, to aggrandize themselves, or to get the project cancelled unfairly—a skilled corporate politician can use statistics to make a project appear much worse off than it is.

The key benefits of a good bug tracking system are the improvements in communication and accountability that get more bugs fixed. Many of the personnel-related and political uses of the database interfere with these benefits by making people more cautious about what information they put on record, what reports they make or allow others to make, and so on. We'll discuss some of these risks in more detail later. First, though, consider the approach that we believe works well.

## THE PRIME OBJECTIVE OF A PROBLEM TRACKING SYSTEM

*A problem tracking system exists in the service of getting the bugs that should be fixed, fixed. Anything that doesn't directly support this purpose is a side issue.*

Some other objectives, including some management reporting, are fully compatible with the system's prime objective. But each time a new task or objective is proposed for the system, evaluate it against this one. Anything that detracts from the system's prime objective should be excluded.

## THE TASKS OF THE SYSTEM

To achieve the system objective, the designer and her management must ensure that:

1. Anyone who needs to know about a problem should learn of it soon after it's reported.

2. No error will go unfixed merely because someone forgot about it.

3. No error will go unfixed on the whim of a single programmer.

4. A minimum of errors will go unfixed merely because of poor communication.

The minimalism of this task list is not accidental. These *are* the key tasks of the system. Be cautious about adding further tasks.

## PROBLEM TRACKING OVERVIEW

Having defined the overall objective and tasks of the system, our next step is to look at how Problem Reports are handled in practice, including common handling problems. The challenge is how to structure a system that copes well with these difficulties.

## THE PROBLEM GETS REPORTED

This starting point was discussed in Chapter 5. A problem is found, investigated in enough detail to write a clear description, and a Problem Report is entered.

The next step is to enter the report into the tracking system. In many companies, submitting the report and entering it into the tracking system are the same thing—a report is submitted by keying it into the database. In other companies, however, the original Problem Report is handwritten on a standard form, then entered into the tracking database by someone else. Many companies that allow testers to enter bug reports directly into the database still require other staff, such as technical or customer support, administrative support, or sales staff, to submit each report to someone (perhaps a tester, systems analyst, or project manager) who decides whether to enter it into the database or not. There's a difficult tradeoff here. On the one side is the risk of wasted time. Reports from non-technical staff are often unusably incomplete or reflect the reporter's ignorance of the product design rather than any problem with the product. On the other side, many important issues have been accidentally lost or deliberately filtered out, only to surface again in customer complaints or magazine reviews.

The tracking system might be single-user or multi-user. The typical single-user database sits on one computer in the Testing offices. Everyone enters reports at this computer and runs reports from it. Only testers have direct access to the computer, perhaps only some testers. Problem Reports and summary status reports for each project are printed and circulated by one of the testers assigned to the project. The typical multi-user system is on the company network or mainframe. All testers and project managers have access to it. Programmers and tech writers probably have access to it. Marketing and tech support staff may or may not have access rights (we think they should). In the multi-user system, anyone with access rights can enter her own reports, query the database, and print summary reports.

## THE REPORT GOES TO THE PROJECT MANAGER

Once the report is in the database, a copy goes to the project manager. In a multi-user system this is automatic; the project manager has direct access to the database and can see the reports as soon as they're entered. In the single-user system, Testing gives the project manager the new reports every few days.

**PROBLEM**

**TRACKING**

The project manager will normally either prioritize the problem and pass it to the programmers, or she'll respond to it:

- In the majority of cases, the project manager will evaluate the report, add some comments, prioritize it, and pass it on to the programmers. A report given a low priority might not be looked at again until higher priority problems are fixed. In some companies, low-priority problems might be looked at out of turn if the programmer is already working on a higher priority problem in the same area of the code. It's easier, faster, and usually sounder to evaluate a group of problems in the same area together, then fix them together. (Note that the companies that do this rely on good categorization of reports, either by testers or programmers.)

- She might try to reproduce the problem. If she is unsuccessful, she will send it back to the reporter for more detail.

- She might send the report back for more detail without even trying to reproduce it, asking for configuration information, clarification, or for a test file that illustrates the problem. The best system makes it easy to add the project manager's and programmer's questions and the reporter's responses to the original report, so that all the information is in one place. The report can't (in most databases) include test files, but it should include references to them.

There's a balance to strike between the amount of investigation done by testing staff and the amount done by programmers. Some project managers or programmers will demand tremendous amounts of data, or will insist on test files even for perfectly obvious problems. Others will try to make do with impossibly sketchy reports and will spend hours recreating a test situation themselves rather than asking for more materials. There is no "right" balance. Here are some factors to consider:

- *Tester time is usually cheaper, per hour, than programmer time.* However, a skilled debugging programmer can often track down a problem and fix it much faster than a tester can gather further relevant information after coming up with an initial well written report.

- *The programmers' tasks are often on the critical path at the end of the project*—the faster they can fix the problems, the faster the product ships. The more information they get from testers, at whatever cost in testing time, the faster they fix the problems. Since it's also easier to productively add more testers than more programmers late in the project, it might be best to demand debugging information from the testers that the programmers could generate themselves. However, all debugging time spent by the testers is time not spent finding new bugs. The test group must have enough time to execute all tests that it considers critical, or the product won't be ready to ship when the programmers think they're finished. A rebalancing of debugging responsibilities from programming to testing might also require an increase in testing staff, if the project is going to succeed.

- *In some projects the testers are more skilled debuggers than the programmers* or are more motivated to gather whatever information is necessary to demonstrate that a problem can be fixed. It may be appropriate to drain testing resources in these cases, especially if the programmers are irreplaceable and obstinate, or are operating under a poorly drafted development contract that provides no incentives or disincentives for them to clean up their work. Again, a wise test manager will demand that rebalancing the workload be made explicit, and may demand additional staff to get the testing job done on time.

- *It is never appropriate to deliberately waste someone else's time*, such as by not bothering to include relevant information on the report that is known or easily collected or by demanding unnecessary follow-up investigation.

- Finally, the project manager might respond by deferring the report or marking it `As designed`. Or she might ask the reporter to reclassify the problem as a documentation issue, or otherwise route the report to the writers to make sure that it's covered in the manual, perhaps in a troubleshooting section.

Eventually, the requests for more detail are resolved and the project manager passes reports in one direction (to the programmers to be fixed) or the other (deferred, left as designed, or confirmed by Testing as not reproducible). Some project managers absentmindedly or deliberately keep a few reports in limbo for a while, neither prioritizing them nor responding to them, but a good summary reporting system exposes these and encourages their resolution.

## THE PROJECT MANAGER SENDS THE REPORT TO THE PROGRAMMERS

When a report goes to a programmer, the project manager is asking for a fix or for investigation and explanation of why the problem shouldn't be fixed. Usually, the bug gets fixed.

Instead of fixing a problem, a programmer might ask for more information or (sometimes justifiably) argue that a bug is impossible to replicate, too hard to fix, not a bug, something only an absolute idiot would run into, the product of an unfair test case, or is otherwise unworthy of consideration. Some programmers love to evade bugs. They may ignore specific reports, hoping that no one will notice until it's too late. Or they may make following up on a bug painful, hoping the reporter will give up on it. Every time they see the bug report, they'll argue it, then demand follow-up information such as new test files, or user research data proving that real customers would object to this problem, or verification that the problem still exists in the latest version (even though they didn't deliberately fix it, because maybe they accidentally fixed it while working on some other problem). Another tactic is the technical sandstorm—in jargon that a non-programmer will not understand, they explain that altering this particular area could undermine the delicate underpinnings of the program's structure and jeopardize the prospective reliability of the whole system.

Testers can only progress so far against determined programmer resistance. The COMMENTS section of the Problem Report is a powerful tool for dealing with resistance. You (or another tester on the project) should enter every comment, every explanation, every denial or rationalization in the COMMENTS section. In a multi-user system, programmers enter their comments directly. Otherwise, enter their comments yourself, including your notes from discussions with programmers about individual reports. (Make sure entries are neutral in tone and fair summaries of what was said.) A good project manager reviewing these comments will see the difficulties and deal with them, often without needing any prompting from you.

By the way, at some point in almost every project, testers become convinced that they are facing unreasonable programmer resistance. They're often wrong. A detailed comment history in each Problem Report provides data that the project manager or test manager can use to clear up misunderstandings and reduce friction between testers and programmers.

**PROBLEM**

**TRACKING**

## WHEN THE PROBLEM IS (ALLEGEDLY) FIXED

When a programmer has fixed a problem, he marks the problem as fixed in the database and, perhaps, adds some comments. (Things are less direct in the single-user system, but somehow, you find out that the bug has been fixed.) This is not the end of the report. The programmer is often wrong. Either the problem has not been fixed or the code change has caused some new problem. In our experience with development of microcomputer software packages written for retail sale, fix failure rates of 10% are very good. That is, we are pleased with the attentiveness of the programmers we work with if we discover problems in only 10% of the bugs they send back to us as "fixed." We are annoyed but not outraged with failure rates as high as 25%. As we noted in Chapter 3 ("Black box testing"), much larger fix failure rates, up to 80%, have been reported in larger systems.

The ideal person to retest a `Fixed` problem is the tester who reported it. If a non-tester reported it, and you are retesting a problem, make sure you can recreate the problem in an earlier (unfixed) version of the program. (Try to keep the latest three versions of the program handy, so that you can easily recreate old bugs or otherwise check current program behavior against recent behavior.)

When the Problem Report comes back to you, start by executing the exact test case reported. Surprisingly often, the you'll find that the fix didn't work.

If the fix passes the initial test (as most do), try some variations. Read the programmer's notes and any other comments recorded on the report. What areas of the program might have been affected by this fix? What could have been broken by this change? Try a few tests for obvious side effects. Also, try variations on the initial test case. Where there was one error, there are likely to be more. Look for a more general problem than the one reported, or for related problems. Testers more often spend too little rather than too much time analyzing "fixed" bugs and trying test variations.

If the program fails the same test that it used to fail, note this on the original Problem Report, change the report's RESOLUTION back to `Pending` from `Fixed`, and send it back to the project manager or programmer.

If the program passes the original test, it's generally better to close the original report as `Fixed` and open a new report. Most programmers and project managers prefer this. These reports are simpler and easier to understand than reports that trace fix after fix of related problems.

## IRREPRODUCIBLE PROBLEMS

If the programmer and project manager can't recreate a problem, they can't fix it. They'll mark the report `Can't reproduce` and return the report to you. Try to recreate the problem. If necessary, try to recreate it in the version of the program that you were testing when you initially reported the problem. If necessary, use the replication tactics suggested in Chapter 5.

If you can recreate the problem, say so on the report (in the COMMENTS section) and add further details that will help the programmer recreate it himself. If necessary, go to the programmer or project manager and demonstrate it to them. Or give them a test file or a video recording. Note what you've shown or given in the COMMENTS section.

If you can't recreate the problem in this version, but you can recreate it in previous versions, it's often best to mark the problem `Fixed` and close it, especially if recent changes to related code might have fixed this problem. (Always check with the programmer or project manager before marking any bug `Fixed`.) Add a note to your test plan and retest for this problem one or two code versions from now, just to be sure.

If you can't recreate the problem in any version, confirm that it's irreproducible but hold the report open for a few versions, perhaps until the next major development milestone. Look for it in each new version. If you can't replicate it in a few versions (or by the milestone), close the report.

## DEFERRALS AND THE APPEAL PROCESS

A deferral acknowledges that there is a problem, but the project manager is choosing not to fix it in this version of the product. (Some development groups use a third related response, Can't be fixed, meaning permanently deferred.) Many coding errors and design issues are deferred in every well-tested product of good commercial quality. Near the end of every project, the risk of side effects far outweighs the benefit of fixing minor coding errors. Similarly, design polishing can go on forever, but it must taper off and then stop at least a few weeks before the product goes into final test. One of the project manager's key responsibilities is deciding which problems should be deferred.

Many project managers briefly explain the reasoning behind a deferral in the COMMENTS section of the Problem Report. This is very useful during the appeal meeting and, especially, during development of the next release of the product. At the start of the new project (next release), all problems deferred in the previous release are re-opened for reconsideration. A deferred report may be a year or three old before work starts on the next release of a product. The deferral notes are tremendously valuable to the (often new) project manager.

When a project manager marks a Problem Report As designed, she means that the program is supposed to behave this way. If she makes this comment on a Design issue report, check her comments to make sure that she understands that you know the program is supposed to work this way, but you're challenging the design. If you're not sure, ask.

Some project managers take each deferral as an admission of failure, and deal with this by marking many real errors As designed rather than Deferred. (Maybe the failure is still there, but they're not going to admit it.) When summary reports break deferred bugs out separately, classifying bugs As designed rather than Deferred makes the statistics look better. Also, many deferral review meetings (below) consider only deferred bugs, so classifying a bug As designed is an effective way of sweeping it under the carpet. Finally, in some cases there is merely an honest difference of opinion between the tester and the project manager as to whether a problem should be marked Deferred or As designed.

When there is a difference of opinion (honest or otherwise) between testers and the project manager as to whether a particular problem should be marked Deferred or As designed, some test groups change the resolution to Deferred and some project managers aren't angered by this. We think it's better for the tester to leave the project manager's response alone. Instead, say Yes in the TREAT AS DEFERRED field. Circulate these reports with the deferred bugs for review in the deferral bug meetings. Reopen the reports with all the deferred reports when work begins on the next release of this product. But leave the RESOLUTION set to As designed to leave the project manager's opinion on the record.

Every few weeks, and more often near the project's end, the project manager or the lead tester should call a deferred bug review meeting. In some companies, As designed reports are reviewed in the same meeting. We think these meetings should include the marketing manager, the technical support manager or staffer who will do or supervise most of the customer support for this product, the documentation manager or the manual writer, the project manager, the lead tester, and possibly the project manager's boss and the test manager.

In the review meeting, the final decision to defer a bug is made. This is the forum for appeals. Before the meeting, circulate copies of all problems deferred since the last meeting. (Circulate the full reports, with all the accumulated comments made on each, not just summaries.) Anyone invited to the meeting can object to

**6**

PROBLEM

TRACKING

the deferral of any bug. The group as a whole argues it out and ultimately accepts the deferral or asks the project manager to try harder to fix the problem. If this group agrees to defer a problem, the issue is closed. Drop it until work begins on the next release of the program, after this release has shipped.

Regular review meetings that make final decisions about bug deferrals are important to the success of the project. First, if there's no recognized appeal process, disgruntled testers and technical support staff create informal channels for appeal. They demonstrate their pet deferred bug to marketing managers, directors, vice-presidents, the company president, newspapers, etc. These bugs can turn into big political issues. A clear review process that invites comments from all affected groups in the companies almost eliminates deferrals as political issues. Second, when the review meeting agrees with the project manager's decision to defer a bug, the decision has been made. Except in very rare circumstances (presidential temper tantrums will do), the decision is final and no further development time need be spent on it. This gives the project manager more schedule and workload predictability. In contrast, imagine that there is only one deferral review meeting, scheduled late in the project, perhaps just as the product is entering the final test phase (last two weeks of testing). If the group sends more than one or two bugs back to the project manager, it sets back the schedule. This makes the deferral review group more reluctant to challenge deferrals (resulting in lower quality and more informal appeals earlier in the project, i.e., more politics) and it increases schedule uncertainty. Early decisions about the deferrals as they're made are much better than later, even if slightly better informed, decisions.

## PROBLEMS THAT AREN'T BEING ADDRESSED

Some Problem Reports get lost, others are deliberately set aside, some are assigned a low priority and forgotten. They must all be resolved (fixed or otherwise dealt with) before the product ships. This is an important rule. Any other rule encourages sloppiness.

To make sure that no one has forgotten about not-yet-resolved problems, it pays to circulate a summary report every week or two that lists all pending reports.

It's also very effective to review these reports in detail with the project manager a few weeks before each project milestone. The goal of the review meeting should be to decide, for each open bug, whether it must be fixed or otherwise resolved before the milestone can be considered met. If you are fortunate enough to be working with a project manager who will join such negotiations, be reasonable or that manager won't join them next time. This review not only guarantees that certain problems will be addressed soon (including many that have been trying to hide under the carpet). It also reminds the manager of less urgent problems that must be scheduled and firmly but inoffensively makes the point that none of these problems will be forgotten. Seeing all the unfixed problems together may also help the manager spot a personnel or workload problem.

## PROJECT STATUS REPORTS

These handy reports state how many bugs have been found through the project and how many are still outstanding, how many have been deferred compared to how many fixed, how many were found by testers and how many by others. They reports show progress each week as well as cumulative totals.

Status reports help managers evaluate the quality of the programming effort, the current reliability of the product, the effectiveness of the testing effort, the rate of discovery of new bugs compared to the rate of progress of fixing bugs (and so the likely project completion date).

## THE USERS OF THE TRACKING SYSTEM

In the last section, we looked at the progress of Problem Reports through the system, what gets done to them, who reads them, how they can be lost and found, etc. In this section, we look at the same process through the eyes of the people who read and act on the reports. What do they want or need from the tracking system?

You are a user of the tracking system if you report a problem, read or respond to a Problem Report, or generate or review a summary report about the problems. Clearly, testers are not the only users of the tracking system. The Testing Group maintains the system, but it belongs to the company as a whole, not to the Testing Group or to any individual tester.

### THE LEAD TESTER

The lead tester heads the testing effort for this project and is accountable for the quality of testing and problem reporting. She may be the only tester allowed to close Problem Reports. She reviews all questionable reports, including reports sent back as irreproducible or for more information. She reviews all reports marked `Deferred` or `As designed` and decides which ones to challenge at the review meeting. She prepares and circulates the summary reports. She may periodically scan each report looking for indications of poor communication, low tester productivity (few problems reported or an excess of reports of trivia), or issues of friction or bug-fixing productivity that might benefit from a private chat with the project manager. She will also look for clusters of problems, especially clusters of irreproducible problems, for hints on what areas of the program might need the most follow-up testing.

### THE OTHER TESTERS

The other testers report problems and monitor resolutions to the problems they reported. They retest all "fixed" problems. They reconsider all deferred problems and rejected design issues, and revise the old reports or submit a new one if they can come up with a significantly more compelling way to explain or illustrate a problem.

**6**

PROBLEM

TRACKING

### THE PROJECT MANAGER

The project manager is accountable for releasing a high quality product on time. The manager is constantly balancing cost, reliability, product capability (features), and schedule. The database is a powerful source of data about the product's current reliability and progress relative to the schedule.

The project manager decides which problems will be fixed, in what priority order, and which will not (subject to an appeal process).

Many project managers review every pending bug in the database every week, looking for communication problems, staff problems, clusters of bugs that suggest a weak area of code, and individual bugs that just won't go away no matter how often people try to fix them. Bug persistence often suggests that the fixing programmer(s) needs consulting help or a reference book or some piece of debugging equipment. An important part of the manager's job is recognizing from bug report progress and comments that someone needs technical help, and getting that help for them. Minor but persistent bugs get deferred near the end of the project.

Project managers get frustrated by the database or by the bug handling process:

- *When they don't get answers in a timely manner.* When they return problems as irreproducible or needing more information, these reports are in limbo. Maybe they refer to real problems that must be fixed and maybe not. A big stack of maybes threatens the accuracy of any scheduling effort. And what should the project manager do with all the maybe bugs when negotiating with the programmers over what bugs must be fixed right away in order to meet an impending milestone?

- *When bug fixes aren't tested for days or weeks.* Since many of these "fixed" problems are not fixed, or will yield new bugs, untested fixes are a stack of added uncertainty. The project manager needs the bad news now, in time to react to it, not later.

- *When they see the same deferred problems coming back time after time,* having been re-marked `Pending` by one of the testers who attached yet another weak argument to the report to justify keeping the bug open. As a rule of thumb, most project managers are happy to be challenged on up to half of their deferrals the first time they defer a bug. But the challenge must be good, the new argument or explanation must feel like it was worth reading at least a third or half of the time. If the project manager reads the tester's argument and defers the problem again, she will probably not respond well to a tester who undefers the bug again without an excellent reason. If you feel strongly about the bug, talk to the project manager directly or save it for the appeal meeting, but don't mark a deferred bug `Pending` more than once.

- *When the database is stuffed with trivia or repetitious reports,* especially late in the schedule, especially if there is a hint of deliberateness, to inflate a tester's apparent productivity or to demonstrate that the program is still full of open bugs. Even if motives are good, stacks of new reports arguing about the design are dismaying. A good project manager will encourage design commentary even past the User Interface Freeze milestone (no further changes to the UI are allowed) because this is good feedback for the next release of the software. But you are pushing your luck if you let late-joining testers write report after report demanding that an Amiga, Windows, or DeskMate product adopt Macintosh user interface standards.

- *When published summary statistics showing the number of outstanding bugs include many that are fixed* and waiting for retesting or are irreproducible or otherwise out of the programmers' and project manager's hands. This unfairly underestimates the programmers' progress.

- *When inaccurate summaries of the bug status are published.* For example, if 40 bugs are fixed and 40 new ones are reported, including 35 unrelated minor design issues, and the summary report notes say that most of the fixes appear to be generating new bugs, this is wrong. The fixes are working fine and the project is progressing well. This inaccurate summary (a common one when the number of new bugs approximates or exceeds the number of fixes) completely misrepresents the progress of the project to management.

- **When overly simplistic summary reports circulate to senior management**, especially reports that only track the number of remaining open bugs at the end of each week. As we'll discuss in more detail below, once these reports gain credibility with management, project managers are under much pressure to make the numbers look good, even if that means taking actions that weaken the quality of the bug discovery and reporting process.

- **Whenever any information from the database is used to attack** the project manager personally or any member her staff or used to attack the project itself or its progress.

## THE PROGRAMMER

The programmer reads the Problem Reports and responds to them. He gets grumpy about them:

- When the reports are not clear, simple, or otherwise helpful for tracking down the bug.

- When it's not clear what the tester objects to, or what the programmer is supposed to do about it. Some Problem Reports seem like general essays on the behavior of the program. At the end, the reader asks, "Yes, but what's the problem?"

- When the reported problems are irreproducible.

- When a report sent back for more information comes back without information.

- When the test case is very complex, but the tester is not making her test materials available.

- When the report wording could be taken as personal criticism.

- When summary statistics from the database are used by managers to track personal productivity.

**6**

## THE PRODUCT MANAGER

The product manager is concerned by every problem that affects product salability or technical support costs. A product manager is sometimes a powerful quality advocate. Other times he is much more attentive to the product's schedule, but he will still refuse to release a product that he feels has commercially unacceptable problems.

The product manager is usually too busy to read through all the deferred bugs, and may be unwilling or unable to use the database effectively. In many companies it is worth the time to print special summary reports for him, using a highlighting pen to draw attention to problems of special interest.

## TECHNICAL SUPPORT

Technical support is accountable to customers who call for information, and to management to keep support costs down and to keep product reviews good when they include technical support quality in their ratings. Technical support has a stake in every deferred and missed bug, in every rejected design issue, and in every error or ambiguity in the manual. These generate customer calls, costing support staff time, and requiring the staff to get information to give to the callers.

Before release, usually when the program is fairly stable, technical support staff often want to review the program and manual and enter bug reports. These reports will identify problem areas that will yield calls from confused or unhappy customers. Customer calls are an important indicator of quality (fewer is better). They are also expensive to handle. To address the strongest technical support concerns, it might be profitable to delay release or to schedule work on a maintenance release to begin immediately after this product ships.

Technical support often attends bug deferral review meetings and argues against deferring problems that will increase customer call rates. In many companies, objections from technical support account for more bugs being undeferred in review meetings than objections from any other group, including testing.

Technical support departments often ask, for every deferred problem and rejected design issue, for an explanation on the bug report of what to say to a customer who calls with this problem. Adding this information to the database is very time consuming. Project managers don't want programmers doing it because they're too busy finishing the code, so testers often end up with the job (resulting in less testing and more missed bugs). Many companies won't do this. Some companies instead include a thorough trouble-shooting section in the manual. This usually documents every error message and explains workarounds to some (definitely not all) bugs. New issues are added to the manual at each reprinting, to answer the most common customer questions. In other companies, technical support staff administer the beta test phase (pre-release testing involving customers and product reviewers), learn the product and its idiosyncrasies, and write the materials that the support department will use after the product is released.

Technical support staff also want to use the database after release. When customers report newly discovered problems, support staff write Problem Reports and then want to know who's going to fix the problem and when the fix will be ready for release. Because customers with defective product are waiting, turnaround time is very important to technical support staff. Statistics showing average turnaround times and other measures of development staff responsiveness are very important to technical support management.

## THE WRITER

The writer is accountable for the user manuals and perhaps technical support materials and other technical or marketing documentation. He must know of design changes, including deferral of bugs that affect the visible behavior of the program. The bug tracking system provides useful update information. The writer is also interested in project status information: is the programming on time or should further writing be postponed until the programmers catch up? When will the user interface *really* be frozen?

The writer also runs into bugs while trying to write the manual. Like a tester, he might use the tracking system to enter Problem Reports on the reliability and design.

Testers also write some Problem Reports pointing out errors in the user manual. Usually they write notes on review copies of the manuscript, but they often file bug reports when the problem is an unresolved discrepancy between the manual and the program behavior, especially if a specification agrees with the manual. If the design has changed, the manual must be corrected. Other Problem Reports covering program misbehavior are also eventually routed to the writer, for inclusion in a troubleshooting section or to flag a design change. In this case, the writer might play much the same role in the system as the programmer. He might retrieve Problem Reports, fix the manual, mark the report fixed, and send the report back on its way.

The relationship between the tracking system and the writer varies across companies. In some, the relationship is recognized as being so close that writers and testers are in the same department. In others, the writers have nothing to do with the database.

## THE TEST MANAGER

The test manager is accountable for the quality of the testing effort and for supervising the testing staff. He reviews Problem Reports asking whether they suggest that a tester needs further training. He also looks for communication or work-balancing problems between the test group and other departments.

Some test managers are tempted to collect individual productivity statistics from the database. How many bugs did each tester report per week? We've found that it's useful to study trends in number of bugs reported. Here are some questions to consider:

- *Who's reporting more bugs, the testers, writers, technical support staff, or the project manager?* Normally the testers report the most bugs, but many problems are often raised by the project manager or someone working with her. This person often tests the program differently from the testers, using it to do the kinds of things customers will do rather than testing features individually or in controlled combinations. This is healthy if it lasts for a few weeks, but if testers are frequently outperformed by someone else, review your testing strategy. It seems ineffective.

- *Does the pattern in the number of problems reported per week by each tester make sense?* Usually a tester reports many design problems at the start of testing, then flurries of bugs around the alpha milestone, because the code isn't very stable, and then it depends on the project. On very unstable products, you may see a continuing high rate mixed with weeks of only five Problem Reports, but each involving extensive investigation of an important intermittent problem. On other projects you might see increasing reports for a while, reflecting the tester's increased familiarity with the product and its probable weak spots, followed by a gradual decline as the program stabilizes. The patterns vary, but they make sense in the context of the program being tested. Look at the types of problems being reported, not just at the numbers. One pattern that warrants scrutiny is a fairly steady, not very high rate of bugs reported. You often get this from people who are juggling many tasks—they report a few bugs each day, then move to the next task. Be especially concerned if this person's reports include a high percentage of easy to spot design issues and other obvious errors. A flat bug rate might also point out a tester who has not worked out a good test plan and is not testing more areas or in new and different ways as the project progresses.

**6**

PROBLEM

TRACKING

We find it misleading to consider bug counts per tester without carefully reading the individual reports. For example, some testers investigate more thoroughly than others, spend more time tackling harder-to-reproduce problems or harder areas to test. Their bug counts are often much lower than the group average. We usually call these people "senior testers" not "less productive."

We are extremely reluctant to quote any bug counts per tester to anyone, including the tester, in private or in public. Some people react very badly to having their performance monitored this closely (and they may perceive that you are monitoring their performance much more closely than you are). Emotions will run especially high if the numbers are quoted as productivity measures, either in public or in any private meeting that could be taken as a performance appraisal. Even staff who aren't intimidated or offended will vary their behavior if they believe that you measure their performance with simplistic bug count statistics. Some boost their numbers by reporting more easier bugs and spending less time on valuable investigation. Some go further and clog the database with trivia or with endless variations on the same problem. The numbers look great but productivity has declined.

We occasionally look at bug counts (not each week), but we don't quote them. We privately note the numbers, read the reports, and, if there is a problem, we act accordingly.

## SENIOR MANAGERS

Senior managers don't care about individual bugs, except for very serious ones being deferred. The managers learn about these from the lead tester, the test manager, the project manager, or someone else who draws their attention to a problem that seems to require management attention. Management-worthy bugs include the following:

- *Program behavior that will embarrass the company.* This includes seriously rude error messages, pornographic (or even mildly indecent) art, and expletives embedded in the code. Even if the program won't display these words, many enthusiasts examine the text strings in commercial software and would gladly quote racy language in user group newsletters, magazine letters, or product reviews.

- *Failure of the program to provide a core benefit that is either being advertised or that a reasonable customer would always expect.* If the word processor won't print and the project manager defers it, someone higher up might want to reconsider. Similarly, for less fundamental features that management counts on to distinguish this program from the competition.

- *Program behavior that will seriously anger a reasonable person.* If your copy protection scheme responds to unauthorized copying by erasing the customer's hard disk, mention it to the president or the company lawyer before shipping the program.

It's unwise to push less serious problems at senior management, or to push any problem up that hasn't yet been deferred. You'll lose credibility.

Executives want to know the status of projects, they want information that feels objective, and they don't want to spend much time thinking about it. They are suckers for counts of the number of outstanding bugs and charts of the number of bugs reported and fixed each week. Be wary of treating these numbers as meaningful and important without further interpretation. This late in the schedule, executives will believe you (or act as if they believe you, when it suits their purposes) if you treat these numbers as important. These become a means of putting pressure on the project manager, and they will drive her crazy when the numbers convey false impressions. The result will often be lower product quality, exactly the opposite of the expectations of most test managers who publish these numbers. Here are some examples:

- *These statistics can create a disincentive to adding testers late in a project.* When new contractors submit the customary stack of first-time-through design issues and rediscovered deferred problems, they inflate the just-found and still-open bug counts. The numbers suggest a big, scary drop in reliability, even though they really mean "new testers on board." A project manager who must repeat this explanation for two or three weeks after you add each new tester will ask you to quit adding testers.

- *These statistics can create a disincentive to collecting one last round of design criticism just before User Interface Freeze.* Shortly before UI Freeze, some project managers circulate screen shots, design notes, and software beta copies to a wider audience, and ask for one last design review from the writers, testers, marketers, and customer service staff who've been on the project team all along. The goal is to collect the last of the user interface design feedback, reach agreement on changes that will and will not be made, and freeze the user interface design. All design criticisms should go into the database, to track now and to preserve for reconsideration in the next release. The bug counts go up dramatically. The product reliability hasn't changed a bit, but because of these despised numbers, the project manager has more explaining (excuse-making) to make to management. The system tempts her to skip the final review, or to insist that the criticisms not go into the database. In most companies, a project manager can get away without doing either, even though both contribute to the quality of the project.

- *These statistics oversensitize project managers to multiple reports of similar problems.* If four testers report the same problem, the bug count goes up by four, not by one. A project manager under pressure from management will notice every time the same problem is reported more than once. She will ask you to screen reports and check whether they are or might be duplicates. In some companies, management will require you to do this, to improve the integrity of your statistics. Now you're doing useless paperwork instead of finding bugs or training testers to be more effective.

- *These statistics pressure the project manager to ask testers to quit reporting design issues.* If a tester raises a design issue, the bug count goes up. A tester who raises many design issues gets noticed by a project manager who's constantly asked why the bug counts are so high. She pressures you to cut down on the design issues. From the viewpoint of these statistics, which management incorrectly interprets as direct measures of reliability and status, the project manager is right. Design issues raised late in testing don't often get fixed and don't imply any reliability problems. So maybe they shouldn't be reported. Of course, any coding errors that are misinterpreted as design errors also don't get reported. And none of the design issues are in the database when the next release of the program is being specified and redesigned.

- *Reliance on bug statistics pressures the project manager to defer deferrable bugs early, reducing product polish.* Some project managers are quick to defer any problem that doesn't have to be fixed. The individual decisions are all justifiable, and the overall effect looks good in the statistics— problems are being addressed and closed at a fast pace. Other project managers give such problems a low priority but keep them open in case the programmers find time to fix them. In our experience, programmers often fix low priority problems when they're already working in that area of the code.

Many more cosmetic issues and minor nuisances get fixed if the project manager keeps them open, without affecting the schedule a bit. No one of these problems affects the overall impression of product quality, but when an extra 50 or 100 minor problems get fixed, the product feels much more polished.

Executives also need objective-sounding means of measuring individual performance, especially when they want to fire someone or put pressure on them. The database provides ready-made, detailed performance information on each tester, programmer, and project manager. You can report the number of Problem Reports found per tester, in comparison to all other testers. You can compare the number of bugs per programmer. You can compare the number of bugs per project, across project managers, and the ratio of bugs fixed to the number she defers or rejects.

You should flatly refuse to provide personal performance data in support of employee disciplinary actions, no matter who asks for it, how persistently they beg for it, no matter how much a troublesome person deserves to be monitored this way, and no matter how much management will bribe you to provide it. You are not using the system for bug tracking when you use it to provide information about individual performance. You're using it to monitor and evaluate people. As soon as the tracking system is used to attack any individual, its credibility is shot. (See Irving, Higgins, & Safayeni, 1986, for a recent review of the computerized performance monitoring literature.) Resistance to your system will make your life miserable and, we predict, ultimately cost you (as test manager) your effectiveness and your job. We think this is the most tempting and most serious tactical error you can make.

We've noted some of the problems with using the tracking system for performance monitoring of testers. Your problems are worse if your victims are programmers or project managers, because they don't report to you. Every time you allow anything in the database that might unfairly inflate their bug counts, you will be asked to retract it. If you refuse, expect the programmer and project manager to bring in their managers, the head of Human Resources, and who knows who else. And it's only fair. If the system provides personnel evaluation information to management, affecting raises and job security, the personnel get to defend themselves. Here are the battles you will constantly fight:

- *You will be asked to retract every duplicate Problem Report.* For true duplicates this is no problem, just a waste of time. What about reports of similar program misbehavior? Often these refer to the same underlying error, but sometimes they are due to different bugs. If you retract all similar reports but one, you lose all the other similar bugs.

- *You will be asked to retract dissimilar-looking reports of behavior allegedly caused by the same underlying problem.* Many different program symptoms can stem from the same underlying coding error (a wild pointer for example). Shouldn't you retract all but one of the relevant Problem Reports? How will you determine whether ten dissimilar reports came from the same underlying error? Inspect the code? Trust the programmer? Refuse to trust the programmer and use your own judgment? (Are you calling the programmer or project manager a liar?)

- *You will be asked to retract every query* because these are not error reports. Don't expect to get answers to the queries either.

- *You will be asked to retract all design suggestions and most design issues.* After all, if the program's behavior matches a reviewed specification, it would hardly be fair to count it as a bug. Our impression is that, over a few releases, perhaps 15% of the design changes suggested by testers are implemented. In practice, this contributes strongly to the polish and usability of the program. Do you really want to lose this information from your database?

- *Plan to spend days arguing whether reports point to true bugs or just to design errors.* This is especially likely if you try to keep design issues in the database by agreeing to count only coding errors in the employee performance monitoring statistics. If you're already sick of arguing with people who say "but it's supposed to crash," just wait until their raise depends on whether you class reports as coding errors or design issues.

- *Expect your staff to be criticized every time they report a "bug" that turns out to be a user error.*

- *Expect to be asked to retract every irreproducible Problem Report.* It shouldn't count against the programmer if the problem is truly irreproducible. There are lots of non-programming-error reasons for these problems (user error, power wobbles, hardware wobbles, etc.). If the programmer does track down the coding error underlying an "irreproducible" problem, this report now counts against his statistics. If he can convince you that it's irreproducible, it won't count against his statistics. How hard should he look for coding errors underlying these reports?

- *Don't expect any programmer or project manager to report any bugs* they find in any product under development.

- *And someday, you'll be sued.* Many people who are fired or who quit under pressure sue their former employer for wrongful dismissal. If you're the test manager, and your database provided performance monitoring that contributed to the departure of an employee who sues the company, you may be sued along with the company. This tactic lets the lawyer ask you more questions before trial more easily than if you're just a witness. Sound like fun? Who's going to pay your legal bills? Think before you say, "The Company." Probably they'll be glad to let you use the company's lawyer, but if you and the company are both defendants in the same trial, and the company's lawyer sees a way to help the company that hurts you, what do you think will happen? Maybe it depends on the company and the lawyer.

> *The objective of the database is to get bugs fixed, not to generate nice management statistics.*

## LAWYERS

Everything in the problem tracking database is open to investigation in any relevant lawsuit by or against your company (also see Chapter 14):

- Problem Reports that include tester comments raging against programmer unprofessionalism can be very damaging evidence, even if the comments are entirely unjustified.

- The company might gain credibility if the database gives evidence of thorough testing and thorough, customer-sensitive consideration of each problem.

- It is illegal to erase Problem Reports from the database in order to prevent them from being used as evidence.

## MECHANICS OF THE DATABASE

At some point you get to design your own system or to suggest extensive revisions to someone else's. From here, we'll assume that the design is yours to change. These are our implementation suggestions for a problem tracking system. Many other systems will satisfy your needs just as well, but variants on this one have worked well for us.

### REPORTING NEW PROBLEMS

The Problem Report (Figure 5.1) is the standard form for reporting bugs. Chapter 5 describes it in detail.

We recommend that anyone in the company can file a Problem Report. Your group allows some people to enter problems into the computer directly. Others write reports on paper (as in Figure 1.1), which you enter into the computer.

**Figure 6.1  Weekly Summary of New Problem Reports sorted by Functional Area**

```
                         New Problem Reports                    07/08/92

Program   CalcDog                                   Release      2.10

Functional Area = Spreadsheet layout

Minor        9900   Can't make column width 17. 1-16 and 18-32 are OK.

Minor       10000   Want to boldface by column

Functional Area = Spreadsheet recalculation

Fatal        9998   Infinite loop for spreadsheets longer than 100 lines

Fatal       10001   Crash when calculation makes # longer than 5 digits

Serious      9996   Wrong number displays on bottom right corner
```

**Figure 6.2  Weekly Summary of New Problem Reports sorted by Severity**

```
                            New Problem Reports                    07/08/92

Program      CalcDog                                    Release      2.10

Severity = Fatal

Spreadsheet  recalc     9998   Infinite loop for spreadsheets longer than 100 lines

Spreadsheet  recalc    10001   Crash when calculation makes # longer than 5 digits

Severity = Serious

Spreadsheet  recalc     9996   Wrong number displays on bottom right corner

Severity = Minor

Spreadsheet  layout     9900   Can't make column width 17. 1-16 and 18-32 are OK.

Spreadsheet  layout    10000   Want to boldface by column
```

The system checks some aspects of the report as it's entered. It does not accept reports that it classifies as incomplete or incorrect. If someone doesn't know how to fill in all the required fields, ask her to report the problem on paper. The Testing Group (you) will replicate the problem, flesh out the report, and enter it into the computer.

On a single-user system, and in some multi-user systems, when you enter a new Problem Report, the computer prints at least 3 copies of it. One goes to the person who reported the problem. The second goes to the programmer, perhaps via his manager. The third copy is the Testing Group's file copy. (If your disk ever crashes, you'll be glad you kept a copy of each report on paper. Your paper files don't have to be elaborate, but they must include each Problem Report.)

**6**

PROBLEM

TRACKING

## WEEKLY STATUS REPORTS

At the end of each week, issue status reports. Be consistent: circulate the reports to the same people, week in, week out.

The *Weekly Summary of New Problem Reports* tells everyone on the project what new problems were found this week. Figure 6.1 shows the new problems sorted by FUNCTIONAL AREA. Figure 6.2 shows the same problem sorted by SEVERITY. Some project managers have strong preferences for one order over the other. Be flexible.

The *Weekly Status Report* (Figure 6.3) shows the state of the project, and how this has changed since last week. These is a popular and useful report, but don't present the numbers without careful commentary explaining unusual jumps in the counts.

## END OF A TESTING CYCLE

At the end of each cycle of testing, issue the *Testing Cycle Complete* report (Figure 6.4). A testing cycle includes all tests of one version of the product. For example, if you are testing CalcDog 2.10, one cycle of testing covers VERSION 2.10g and another covers VERSION 2.10h.

The Test Cycle Complete report summarizes the state of the project, in much the same way as the weekly summary. The weekly report is convenient because it comes out every week, but comparing different weeks' data can be difficult because more testing is done in some weeks than others. Test Cycle Complete reports are more comparable because each covers one full cycle of testing.

## RESOLVED AND UNRESOLVED PROBLEMS

Problem Reports come back to you when they're resolved. Some problems are fixed, others set aside (deferred), and others are rejected. Try to recreate problems marked Fixed, before accepting them as fixed.

**Figure 6.3 Weekly Status**

```
                    Problem Report Status

Program CalcDog                               Release  2.10

This report was generated on 07/08/92. The last report is dated 07/01/92.

        Outstanding Bugs          Now            Last Report

            Fatal                 113                100

            Serious               265                220

            Minor                 333                300

            Total                 711                620

How many found since last report:         182

How many fixed since last report:          85

How many deferred since last report:        7

Total number of deferred bugs:            118
```

**Figure 6.4 Testing Cycle Complete**

**This report describes the results of the latest cycle of testing.**

```
                          Test Cycle Complete

Program CalcDog                        Release 2.10 Version  g

               Unresolved    New Problems  Resolved   Remaining Problems
               Problems Before
               this Version

Fatal              8             10           9              9

Serious           48             12          16             44

Minor             80             15          14             81

Total            136             37          39            134

Resolution in this Version:

Fixed             22          Deferred        6

Irreproducible     5          Other           6
```

If the problem is only partially fixed, close this report, then write a new one that cross-references this one. If the problem wasn't fixed at all, re-open the report with a polite note.

For each unfixed problem (Can't be fixed, As designed, and Disagree with suggestion), decide whether to say Yes to TREAT AS DEFERRED (see Chapter 5, "Content of the problem report: Treat as deferred").

Distribute copies of all resolved reports to the people who reported the problems. They may respond to unfixed problems with follow-up reports.

Some Problem Reports are misplaced or ignored. Periodically—perhaps every two weeks—distribute a *Summary of Unresolved Problems* (Figure 6.5). Your goal is to keep these problems visible, but in a way that looks routine, impersonal, and impartial. Figure 6.5 organizes the problems by severity, without mentioning who's responsible for them.

Figure 6.6 is a more personal variation on the Summary of Unresolved Problems. It organizes everything around who's supposed to fix each problem. Don't circulate this report publicly. Use it during private discussions with individual managers.

## DEFERRED PROBLEMS

If your company doesn't hold regular review meetings for deferred Problem Reports, distribute the *Summary of Deferred Problems* (Figure 6.7) biweekly. This report describes every problem that the programmers

**6**

PROBLEM

TRACKING

**Figure 6.5 Summary of Unresolved Problem Reports**

```
                  Unresolved Problem Reports            07/08/92

Program    CalcDog                              Release     2.10

Severity Level = Fatal

07/02/92    10001   Crash when calculation makes # longer than 5 digits

07/07/92     9998   Infinite loop for spreadsheets longer than 100 lines

Severity Level = Serious

07/06/92     9996   Wrong number displays on bottom right corner

Severity Level = Minor

02/22/92     9900   Can't make column width 17. 1-16 and 18-32 are OK.

07/07/92    10000   Want to boldface by column
```

This report includes all Problem Reports that have a Resolution Code of 0. It doesn't include deferred bugs, rejected suggestions, etc.

**Figure 6.6 Summary of Unresolved Problem Reports**

```
                  Unresolved Problem Reports            07/08/92

Program    CalcDog                              Release     2.10

Development Group: User Interface

07/06/92    Serious   Wrong number displays on bottom right corner

02/22/92    Minor     Can't make column width 17. 1-16 and 18-32 are OK.

07/07/92    Minor     Want to boldface by column

Development Group: Computation

07/02/92    Fatal     Crash when calculation makes # longer than 5 digits

07/07/92    Fatal     Infinite loop for spreadsheet longer than 100 lines
```

This represents the same information as Figure 6.5 but emphasizes the Development Group's responsibility for fixing the problems.

**Figure 6.7 Summary of Deferred Problem Reports**

```
                    Deferred Problem Reports                    07/08/92

Program     CalcDog                                  Release       2.10

Severity Level = Fatal

Recalc          9998    Infinite loop for spreadsheets longer than 100 lines

Recalc          10001   Crash when calculation makes # longer than 5 digits

Severity Level = Serious

Recalc          9996    Wrong number displays on bottom right corner

Severity Level = Minor

Layout          9900    Can't make column width 17. 1-16 and 18-32 are OK.

Layout          10000   Want to boldface by column
```

deferred or that you said should be treated as deferred. Senior managers see these reports and sometimes insist that certain deferred bugs be fixed. Also, this report keeps deferred problems visible. Programmers who see that these problems are still of concern sometimes find simple solutions to them.

If you do have regular review meetings, this summary is still useful for the meetings, but only show the problems that were deferred since the last meeting. Also, add the PROBLEM AND HOW TO REPRODUCE IT field and the COMMENTS field, or print this summary but append full copies of each summarized report. Distribute the report a few days in advance of each meeting.

## PROGRESS SUMMARIES

The *Weekly Totals* (Figure 6.8) summarize the project's progress over time. A similar report shows one line per cycle of testing instead of one line per week. A third useful report shows how many minor, serious, and fatal problems were reported each week. A fourth tracks reports of problems within each functional area.

Each of these reports gives you a base of historical data. Summaries from old projects are handy for comparison to today's project. For example, you can use them to demonstrate that:

- *The project requires months of further testing.* The number of new Problem Reports (per week or per cycle) usually increases, peaks, then declines. It is unwise to ship the product before reaching a stable, low rate of discovery of new problems.

**6**

PROBLEM

TRACKING

- *It doesn't pay to cut off testing a week or two early* or without notice. Testers often make an extra effort during the last cycle(s) of testing. Summary reports reflect this by showing a jump in the number of serious problems found and fixed at the end of the project.

- *A sea of reports of user interface errors is normal* at the current (e.g., early) stage of the project.

Always generate one of these reports at the end of a project, for future use. Beyond that, the report is discretionary—generate it when you need it, and give a copy to whoever wants one.

Many project groups like to see these data in a graph, distributed with the Weekly Status report.

## WHEN DEVELOPMENT IS COMPLETE

When the product is almost ready for release to customers, tie up loose ends. Get unresolved Problem Reports fixed or signed off as deferred. Once the paperwork is tidy, and the product is ready to ship, circulate the *Final Release Report* (Figure 6.9).

The report shows the number of deferrals. Attach a copy of the *Summary of Deferred Problems* (Figure 6.7). Because this is a last-chance-for-changes report, consider adding the PROBLEM AND HOW TO REPRODUCE IT field from the Problem Reports to the description of each deferred problem.

The report goes to everyone who has to sign it. Circulate a draft copy, with XXXs through the signature areas, a day in advance. Give readers the day to review the deferrals and scream if they should. The next day, visit each person and have them sign the final copy of the report (all signatures on the same copy).

**Figure 6.8 Weekly Totals**

| | | | | |
|---|---|---|---|---|
| | **Weekly Totals** | | | 07/07/92 |
| **Program** CalcDog | | | **Release** | 2.10 |
| Week Ending | New Problems | Fixes | Other Resolutions | Total Unresolved |
| 06/19/92 | 7 | 2 | 3 | 24 |
| 06/26/92 | 6 | 4 | 4 | 22 |
| 07/03/92 | 5 | 8 | 2 | 17 |
| 07/08/92 | 3 | 4 | 7 | 9 |

**Figure 6.9 Release Report**

---

**Release Report form**

‾‾‾‾‾‾‾‾‾‾‾‾‾‾‾‾‾‾‾‾‾‾‾‾‾   ‾‾‾‾‾‾‾

The Testing Group reports that all Problem Reports for this product have been resolved. Summary of ___ deferred problems are attached to this report.

We instruct the Manager of the Testing Group to release this product for manufacturing.

‾‾‾‾‾‾‾‾‾‾‾‾‾‾‾‾‾‾‾‾                      ‾‾‾‾‾‾‾‾‾‾‾‾‾‾‾‾‾‾‾‾

Title of person who's          Title of person who's
supposed to sign here          supposed to sign here

‾‾‾‾‾‾‾‾‾‾‾‾‾‾‾‾‾‾‾‾                      ‾‾‾‾‾‾‾‾‾‾‾‾‾‾‾‾‾‾‾‾

Title of person who's          Title of person who's
supposed to sign here          supposed to sign here

Report prepared by _____ for the Testing Group.

---

Senior management, not you, decides who signs this report. Anyone who must approve the release of the product before it goes to manufacturing (and thence to the customer) should sign this release. Don't ask anyone who can't veto the release for their signature.

Note that a tester's (your) signature appears at the bottom of the report, beside PREPARED BY. The Testing Group prepares this report but does not approve a product for release. You provide technical input. Management decides to hold or release the product. If you feel that testing was inadequate, say so, and say why, in an attached memo.

## REOPEN DEFERRED BUGS FOR THE NEXT RELEASE

You finally close the books on Release 2.10 and ship it. the company begins planning Release 3. As part of the planning or early development process, you should reopen the bugs that were marked Deferred, Treat as deferred, and, perhaps As designed too.

6

PROBLEM

TRACKING

113

This is one of the system's most important functions. `Deferred` bugs are just that, *deferred*, *set aside until later*. The normal expectation is that they will be fixed in the next release. The tracking system must ensure that they are not forgotten.

Your database management software should be able to copy these reports to a temporary file, modify them as listed below, move them to the main data file for the next release, and print copies of each report. Modify each report as follows:

- Reset the RESOLUTION CODE to `Pending`.
- Change RELEASE and VERSION ID (for example, to `3.00a`).
- Assign a new PROBLEM REPORT #.
- Clear any signatures (except for the report's author) and the associated dates.
- Clear the COMMENTS.

Leave the rest of the report as it was. After entering them into the database, circulate these reports in the usual way.

In practice, some companies review the bugs before reopening them, and carry only a selection of the deferred bugs forward. The three of us are split on this issue, reflecting our different situations. Company practices vary widely.

## TRACKING PATCHES

Some companies respond to customer complaints with patches. A patch is a small change made to fix a specific error. It's easy to miss side effects because the rest of the code isn't thoroughly retested. The patched

### Figure 6.10 Summary of Current Patches

```
                       Summary of Current Patches              07/08/92

Program    CalcDog                                   Release      2.10

SW Manager = Jane X

Serious      9996    Wrong number displays on bottom right corner

Minor       10000    Want to boldface by column

SW Manager = Joe Y

Fatal        9998    Infinite loop for spreadsheets longer than 100 lines
```

version is sent to the customer and kept on file. New customers are still sold the original version, with the error still there. If they complain, they get the patch too.

Patches are supposed to be integrated with the software in the next major release of the product, after thorough testing. However, they are often forgotten. It's up to you to check that old patches are incorporated in the product.

If your company sends patches to customers, create a new resolution code, `Patched`, to the Problem Report form. This indicates a temporary resolution of the problem. Reclassify the problem as `Fixed` when you're satisfied that the patch is in the code to stay. Until then, whenever you feel that it's appropriate, remind people to integrate patches into the code by circulating the *Summary of Current Patches* (Figure 6.10).

## FURTHER THOUGHTS ON PROBLEM REPORTING

Our system's key operating principle is to focus on bugs. Not politics. Not measurement. Not management. Just bugs. Capture all the problems you can find, report them as well as you can, make it easy to question and add detail to individual reports, and help get the right bugs fixed. We've learned a few lessons along the way. We noted some in the first sections of this chapter. Here are a few others that stand best on their own.

### EXERCISING JUDGMENT

Every tester and Testing Group is criticized for missed bugs and for unnecessary reports. Project managers complain about wasteful reports during development and about missed bugs when customers discover them. Dealing with these complaints is an integral part of problem tracking. A test manager can improve tester performance by reviewing the reports and training the staff, but these problems and complaints don't vanish when all testers are well trained. Every tester will see program behavior that she is not sure whether to report or not. If she reports it, she might be wasting everyone's time. If she ignores it, she might be failing to report a genuine error. Good testers, and a well run Testing Group, spend time thinking at a policy level about these cases. The errors are related—miss more legitimate bugs or add more junk to the database. Which should the tester more strenuously try to avoid?

Every time you file a Problem Report, you're making a judgment that this is information worth having in the database. You're asking for a change in the product, or at least consideration of a change, and your judgment is that the change is worth considering:

- When do you report something that you think is program misbehavior? Some testers say that *any* misbehavior is worth reporting. At the other extreme, some people won't report a bug unless it trashes their data or keeps them from using the program. If they can find a workaround, they don't report the bug. No matter where you fit between these extremes, whenever you report a problem, it's because you have decided that the misbehavior is serious enough to be worth reporting.

- If you don't like something about the program, or if you don't mind it but you think someone else might object, you'll report it if you think the design is objectionable enough or if you think that some other design will make a big enough improvement.

- If you see misbehavior that is similar to a problem already reported, you won't write a new Problem Report unless you think this is dissimilar enough to the other bug that it might be a different one.

- If you can't reproduce a problem, you'll report it anyway if you think you remember enough of what you did and saw to make the report at least potentially useful.

- If you make an unusual number of mistakes using the program, should you complain about the design even though the results are your mistakes?

- If the specification is frozen, should you complain about the design at all?

Your standard of judgment probably changes over time. Very early in development, when the program crashes every few minutes, you might report only the most serious problems. When the program is a bit more stable you'll probably report everything you find. Very near the end of the project, you might stop reporting minor design issues and report only serious coding errors.

Your standard of judgment is something you learn. It changes as you adapt to each new project manager, each new test manager, and each new company. The test management philosophy associated with the problem tracking system has a major effect on the standard of judgment of every person who reports problems.

The problem with any standard of judgment is that it sets you up for mistakes. The problem of duplicated bug reports is the clearest example of this. Suppose you've read every report in the database. You're now testing the program and you see something similar to a problem already reported. It's not exactly the same, but it is quite similar:

- ***There's no value in adding duplicates to the database,*** so if you decide that the new bug and the old bug are similar enough, you won't report the new one.

  - If you are correct, if you are looking at the same bug, you save everyone's time by not reporting it.

  - ***Consumer Risk:*** But if you're wrong, the programmer will fix the problem in the database but will never fix (because he never found out about) the problem you decided not to report. (In Quality Control terminology, *Consumer Risk* is the probability that the customer will receive a

### Figure 6.11 The problem of similar bugs

|  | *You file a bug report* | *You ignore it* |
|---|---|---|
| ***It is a new bug*** | It gets fixed | *Never fixed* <br> *(Consumer risk)* |
| ***Same old bug*** | *Waste of time* <br> *(Producer risk)* | Gets fixed anyway |

defective lot of goods because the defects were not detected during testing. Similarly here, the customer receives defective goods because of testing failure. Feigenbaum, 1991.)

- If you decide that the old bug and the new bug are probably different, you'll report the new one:

  - If you're right, both bugs get fixed.

  - *Producer's Risk:* If you're wrong, you report a duplicate bug, and you waste everyone's time. The waste includes the time to report the problem, the time for the project manager to read and assign it, the time for the programmer to investigate and determine that it's the same problem, the time to retest or to review it if it's deferred, and the time to close it. (In QC terminology, *Producer's Risk* is the probability that a tester will misclassify an acceptable lot of goods as defective.)

Your problem is to strike the right balance between consumer and producer risk. Which error is worse? Failing to report the bug because you incorrectly decided it was too similar to another one? Or reporting a duplicate?

Psychologists have analyzed peoples' classification errors using *Signal Detection Theory* (Green & Swets, 1974), which we've already mentioned in Chapter 2. Here are some important lessons that Kaner draws from that research:

1. When you're dealing with an experienced, well-trained tester, don't expect to be able to improve her ability to tell whether two similar program behaviors stem from the same underlying bug or two different underlying bugs. If the behaviors look different enough, she'll report two bugs, sometimes reporting what turns out to be the same bug twice. If they're similar enough, she'll report one bug, sometimes failing to report a real second error. To catch more errors, she must lower her standard of dissimilarity and file two reports for slightly more similar pairs of behaviors than she did before. As a result, she will also file more reports that turn out to be duplicates. If she tries to reduce duplicates, she will also increase the number of unreported bugs.

2. You can directly influence a tester's performance. If you ask her to cut down on duplicates, she will. But more similar-but-different bugs will go unreported too. Very few project managers understand this tradeoff.

3. You can indirectly influence a tester's performance by leading her to believe that similar behaviors are more likely, in this particular program, to stem from the same underlying bug. She'll file fewer duplicate reports (and miss more similar-but-different bugs).

4. You can also indirectly influence tester performance by attaching different consequences to different errors. If the project manager doesn't complain about missed bugs, but whines or throws tantrums every time two reports turn out to refer to the same underlying problem, most testers will file fewer duplicates (and miss more similar-but-different bugs).

For illustration purposes, we've concentrated on the problem of similar bugs, but the same point applies to all the other judgments testers have to make. Every tester will make mistakes and you have to decide (as a tester, test manager, or project manager) which mistakes you prefer. Would you rather have more legitimate bugs going unreported or more chaff in the database? For example, is it worse to fail to report a serious bug that didn't seem worth reporting, or to report one so trivial that no one would fix it? Is it worse

**6**

PROBLEM

TRACKING

to fail to note a serious design error in an approved specification, or to waste everyone's time on an issue raised too late? For all these judgments, you have thinking about policy to do.

## SIMILAR REPORTS

So what should you do about similar program misbehaviors?

Dealing with ten reports of the same problem *is* a time-wasting nuisance for the programmers and the project manager. If you can safely avoid filing duplicate reports, do so.

Here are the arguments in favor of allowing reports of similar misbehaviors in the database:

- Two similar reports might describe different bugs. If you discard one report, its bug won't be fixed.

- The same error can occur in two places in the code. If you report only one instance, will the programmer find the other?

- Two reports of the same problem can provide different clues about the underlying problem. It's much better to give all the information to the programmer, instead of trying to second-guess what he'll find useful.

- How will the second person to report a problem react if you return her report with a note saying the problem is already on file? Next time she sees a problem, will she report it? (Perhaps this shouldn't be a concern when collecting reports from testers, but it should be a strong consideration when you receive a report from someone outside the Testing Group.)

Here are some tester responsibilities that we recommend:

- Every tester should be familiar with the problems currently pending in the area of the code that she's testing. No tester should deliberately report a problem if she believes it's already in the database. If she has more detail to add to an existing report (whether filed by her or by someone else), she should add it to the COMMENTS section of that report rather than writing a new report. Test managers differ on how much time testers new to the project should spend reviewing the already-filed bugs. Some insist that new testers review the bugs before filing their first report. Many expect the new testers to gradually become familiar with the database and they accept a high rate of duplicate reports from new testers as a consequence.

- Testers regularly scan the currently pending reports and will note problems that appear similar. They should cross-reference them, noting report numbers of similar problems in the COMMENTS field.

- Testers should not close out similar reports as duplicates unless they are certain that both reports refer to exactly the same problem. Cross-referencing reports is much safer than discarding them. We also recommend against merging reports that look similar into one big report. Unless you're sure that two reports refer to exactly the same problem, we think you should let them be.

## ALLOWING FOR DIVERGENT VIEWS

Testers, project managers, and other members of the project team often have different opinions about individual Problem Reports. This often causes tremendous friction. You can design the problem tracking and reporting forms and system to accept divergent views and minimize the friction. Here are some specific aspects of our system that are designed to let people have their say:

- **SEVERITY** *versus* **PRIORITY:** The tester enters a SEVERITY level but the project manager assigns PRIORITY. Systems which contain only one of these fields create disputes between tester and project manager. For example, what happens when a tester says a bug is fatal but the project manager resets the bug to minor because she considers it low priority. Who should win? Why should either have to win? Note that reports can be sorted by priority just as well as by severity.

- **TREAT AS DEFERRED:** The project manager can enter a non-fixed resolution code that is not Deferred (for example, As designed and Can't reproduce) and the tester can treat the report as if it were deferred, including it in all the deferred bug summaries, by marking a separate field, TREAT AS DEFERRED. This preserves the project manager's statement while allowing the tester to have the problem reviewed if she thinks it's necessary.

- **COMMENTS:** The COMMENTS field allows for a free flowing discussion among the programmers, project manager, and tester(s). This field is awkward in single-user systems. In our experience, it is the biggest advantage multi-user systems have over single-user bug tracking systems. The running commentary in individual Problem Reports resolves many communication problems and information needs quickly and effectively. It also provides a forum for a tester to explain why she thinks a problem is important, for a programmer to explain the risks of fixing this problem, and for a project manager to explain why she thinks the problem is or is not deferrable. If this discussion doesn't end in consensus, it provides a clear statement of the tradeoffs and opinions during the appeal process.

- *The appeal process:* We recommend regular review meetings to consider Problem Reports marked Deferred or TREAT AS DEFERRED. No deferred bug can be closed until it has passed review. This provides a forum for identifying and resolving the remaining differences between the project manager, and the tester, technical support representative, writer, or marketing manager about the deferrals. The group discusses the problem, the risks of leaving it alone and the costs of fixing it, and makes a decision.

- **Resolved** *versus* **Closed:** The project manager marks a Problem Report as resolved (e.g., Deferred, Fixed, etc.), but the report isn't closed until Testing says it's closed. In the interim, the tester runs regression tests if the problem is fixed or waits until closure is approved in a deferred bug review meeting.

- *Never reword a report:* Many people are offended when someone (even another tester) rewords their Problem Reports. Even apart from offensiveness, rewording can introduce misunderstandings or mischief. Therefore never reword someone else's report and protest loudly if the programmer or project manager tries to. You can add comments, or ask the person to reword her own report, including changing its severity level. But she isn't required to make the change (unless her boss says so, of course), and no one else can make the change if she won't. We recognize an exception for incomprehensible reports submitted by non-technical staff who expect rewording.

**6**

PROBLEM

TRACKING

- ***Don't filter reports that you disagree with:*** Some lead testers refuse to allow design issue reports into the database unless they agree with the issue or the recommended change. This filtering is often done at the request of the project manager or with her enthusiastic consent. We disagree with the practice. In our experience, technical support staff, writers, and other reasonable people in the company sometimes have very useful things to say that don't meet the lead tester's biases. The lead tester is not the product designer and should not step into the designer's shoes to decide which of these criticisms or suggestions is worthy of the design.

## INTERNAL DETAILS

Programming groups may ask you to record which module an error is in, or to classify problems by type or functional area. FUNCTIONAL AREA is easy if there are 10 to 30 areas, but not if you have to choose the right one from a list of 50 or 500. For this, you must look at the code.

This information is useful. For example, the more problems you've already found in a module, the more you'll probably find (Myers, 1979). Particularly bad modules should be recoded. Also, if you find that programmers keep making errors of the same type, management may organize appropriate retraining classes.

Unfortunately, it's not easy to collect this information. Only the debugging programmer sees the error in the code. Only she knows what module it's in, and only she can accurately classify it by type or functional area. Many programmers don't want to report these details as part of the problem tracking process.

> *Some Testing Groups make intelligent guesses about the module and type when they report a problem. Some of these guesses don't look the least bit intelligent to the debugging programmer. In our experience, this guess-work takes more time than it saves. We don't recommend it.*

We don't think you should track anything about the insides of the program that you don't get from the debugging programmer. What is the payoff for pestering programmers for this information? Many programming teams want it only sporadically. They can collect what they need without your help.

## A FEW NOTES ON THE PROBLEM REPORT FORM

Chapter 5 provided a detailed description of the Problem Report form. This section adds a few details that are useful if you're creating a tracking system. If you aren't designing your own system, you can safely skip this section.

- Store lists of names or other valid responses in separate data files. When you enter data into a field, have the computer check your entry against the list. You can do this for the PROGRAM, all names, and the FUNCTIONAL AREA. Allow Unknown (or ?) as a valid entry in some fields. For example, you have to enter a question mark into VERSION if someone can't tell you what version of the program they were using when they had a problem. Also, along with Y and N, S (for "Sometimes") should be a valid response to CAN YOU REPRODUCE THE PROBLEM?

- The form has two fields for each name, for FUNCTIONAL AREA and for ASSIGNED TO. The first field is 3 to 5 characters long. Enter initials or some other abbreviation into it. The computer looks for the abbreviation in a reference file. If the abbreviation is there, the system fills the second field with the full name. This is a big time saver when you enter many reports at once. You should also be able to skip the abbreviation field and enter the full name into the long field beside it.

- When you first enter a report, the system should mark RESOLUTION CODE as Pending (unresolved).

- Only the tester should be able to enter Closed in the STATUS field. The system should default the value to Open.

## GLOSSARY

This section defines some key terms in database design. For more, we recommend Gane and Sarson (1979)

***Database Management System (DBMS):*** a collection of computer programs that help you define the database, enter and edit data, and generate reports about the information. You will probably use a commercially available DBMS (such as DB2, Oracle, Paradox or R:BASE). These provide tools for creating a database about almost anything. Makers of these products would call the problem tracking system an *application*. Users (including you) might refer to the full tracking system as a DBMS.

***File:*** a set of information that the operating system keeps together under one name. A database can have many files. For example:

- The main data file includes all Problem Reports. If there are many problems, you may have to split this file, perhaps by type or date.

- An index file keeps track of where each report is within the main data file(s). One index might list Problem Reports by date, another by problem area, etc.

- A reference file holds a list of valid responses. The computer checks entries made into some fields, and rejects entries that don't have a match in the reference file. The abbreviations for the Problem Report's names and Functional Area are stored in reference files.

***Field:*** a single item of data within a record. For example, DATE, PROBLEM SUMMARY, and SUGGESTED FIX are all fields in the Problem Report.

***Form*** (or ***Data Entry Form***): used to enter records into the database. It shows what information should be entered and where to enter it. A form might be on paper or it might be displayed on the computer screen. Online forms are also called Entry Screens. Many problem tracking systems use the same form both ways: people can fill out reports on paper or they can enter them directly into the computer.

***Record:*** a single complete entry in the database. For example, each Problem Report is a record in the tracking system.

**6**

**PROBLEM**

**TRACKING**

***Report:*** a description or summary of information in the database. Usually you create a Report Definition once, using a programming language or a Report Generator. You can then run the report many times (e.g., once per week). Many Report Generators let you specify formatting details (margins, boldfacing, underlining, skipped lines, etc.). This is useful for reports that you copy and distribute.

Report also refers to the Report Definition. Creating a report means programming the definition. Running a report means running the reporting program which will print the summary. The reporting program that generates an actual report (does the calculations and prints the numbers) is called the Report Writer.

Unfortunately, in problem tracking systems there are also Problem Reports. Thus we have reports (of bugs), reports (summary reports about reports of bugs), and reports (definition files or programs used to generate reports that summarize reports of bugs). Such is the jargon of the field. We try to distinguish them by capitalizing "Problem Reports" and by referring to "summary reports."

# TEST CASE DESIGN

## THE REASON FOR THIS CHAPTER

This chapter is about creating good black box test cases.

- Black Box versus Glass Box: Even though we mention glass box methods in other chapters, this book is primarily about black box testing. This chapter describes what good black box tests look like, and how to analyze the program to develop great tests.

- Test Cases versus Test Plans: Our focus is on individual tests and small groups of related tests. We broaden this analysis in Chapter 12, which looks at the process of creating a test plan—a collection of tests that cover the entire program. You'll appreciate Chapter 12 much more if you apply this chapter's techniques to at least one program before trying to tackle the overall test planning function.

## READER'S EXERCISE (NOT JUST FOR STUDENTS)

Select a program to test, probably a commercially available (allegedly fully tested) program. Choose five data entry fields to test. There are data entry fields in every program. They're more obvious in databases, but word processors and paint programs probably take numbers to set margins and character (or other object) sizes, or to specify the page size. You're in luck if you can enter configuration information, such as how much memory to allocate for a special function. Configuration and preference settings may not be as thoroughly debugged as other parts of the program, so if you test these you may be rewarded with a crash. (Back up your hard disk before playing with I/O port settings or any disk configuration variables.)

Here are your tasks. For each data entry field:

1. Analyze the values you can enter into the field. Group them into equivalence classes.

2. Analyze the possible values again for boundary conditions. You'll get many of these directly from your class definitions, but you'll probably also discover new classes when you focus your attention on boundaries.

3. Create a chart that shows all the classes for each data entry field, and all the interesting test cases (boundaries and any other special values) within each class. Figure 7.1 will give you a good start on the organization of this chart. If you don't come up with a satisfactory chart design of your own, read the subsection "Boundary Chart" of Chapter 12, "Components of test planning documents."

7

TEST CASE

DESIGN

4. Test the program using these values (or some selection of them if there are too many to test). Running the program doesn't just mean booting the program and seeing if it crashes. *Ask when the program will use the data you are entering.* When it prints? When it calculates the amount of taxes due? Create a test procedure that will force the program to use the data you entered and to display or print something that will tell you whether it used your value correctly.

## OVERVIEW

The chapter starts by considering the characteristics of good test case.

Next it asks how to come up with powerful test cases. It discusses five techniques:

- Equivalence class analysis
- Boundary analysis
- Testing state transitions
- Testing race conditions and other time dependencies
- Doing error guessing

It considers a class of automation techniques called function equivalence testing.

It describes an absolutely required testing technique, regression testing. Regression test cases may or may not be as efficient as the rest, but they are indispensable.

Finally, there are a few notes on executing test cases. Sometimes testers have great testing ideas but they miss the bugs because they don't conduct their tests effectively. Here are some traps to avoid.

## USEFUL READING

Myers (1979) presents the issues discussed in this chapter, especially boundaries and equivalence classes, extraordinarily well. For discussions of glass box techniques, read just about any book by Myers, Dunn, Hetzel, Beizer, or Evans. Yourdon (1975) also makes some good points in a readable way.

If you had the time, you could develop billions or even trillions of different tests of the program. Unfortunately, you only have time for a few hundred or a few thousand tests. You must choose well.

## CHARACTERISTICS OF A GOOD TEST

An excellent test case satisfies the following criteria:

- It has a reasonable probability of catching an error.
- It is not redundant.
- It's the best of its breed.
- It is neither too simple nor too complex.

### IT HAS A REASONABLE PROBABILITY OF CATCHING AN ERROR

You test to find errors. When searching for ideas for test cases, try working backwards from an idea of how the program might fail. If the program *could* fail in this way, how could you catch it? Use the Appendix as one source of ideas on how a program can fail.

### IT IS NOT REDUNDANT

If two tests look for the same error, why run both?

### IT'S THE BEST OF ITS BREED

In a group of similar tests, one can be more effective than the others. You want the best of the breed, the one most likely to find the error.

Chapter 1 illustrated that boundary value inputs are better test inputs than non-boundary values because they are more likely to demonstrate an error.

### IT IS NEITHER TOO SIMPLE NOR TOO COMPLEX

You can save testing time by combining two or more tests into one test case. But don't create a monster that's too complicated to execute or understand or that takes too much time to create. It's often more efficient to run simpler tests.

Be cautious when combining invalid inputs. After rejecting the first invalid value, the program might ignore all other further input, valid or not. At some point, you might *want* to combine error cases to see what the program does when confronted with many disasters at once. However, you should start with simple tests to check each of the program's error-handling capabilities on its own.

### IT MAKES PROGRAM FAILURES OBVIOUS

How will you know whether the program passed or failed the test? This is a big consideration. Testers miss many failures because they don't read the output carefully enough or don't recognize a problem that's staring them in the face.

- Write down the expected output or result of each test, as you create it. Refer to these notes while testing.

- Make any printout or file that you'll have to inspect as short as possible. Don't let failures hide in a mass of boring print.

- Program the computer to scan for errors in large output files. This might be as simple as comparing the test output with a known good file.

## EQUIVALENCE CLASSES AND BOUNDARY VALUES

It is essential to understand equivalence classes and their boundaries. Classical boundary tests are critical for checking the program's response to input and output data. But further, thinking about boundary conditions teaches you a way of analyzing programs that will strengthen all of your other types of test planning.

## EQUIVALENCE CLASSES

If you expect the same result from two tests, you consider them equivalent. A group of tests forms an equivalence class if you believe that:

- They all test the same thing.
- If one test catches a bug, the others probably will too.
- If one test doesn't catch a bug, the others probably won't either.

Naturally, you should have reason to believe that test cases are equivalent. Tests are often lumped into the same equivalence class when:

- They involve the same input variables.
- They result in similar operations in the program.
- They affect the same output variables.
- None force the program to do error handling or all of them do.

## FINDING EQUIVALENCE CLASSES

Two people analyzing a program will come up with a different list of equivalence classes. This is a subjective process. It pays to look for all the classes you can find. This will help you select tests and avoid wasting time repeating what is virtually the same test. You should run one or a few of the test cases that belong to an equivalence class. Leave the rest aside.

Here are a few recommendations for looking for equivalence classes:

- Don't forget equivalence classes for invalid inputs.
- Organize your classifications into a table or an outline.
- Look for ranges of numbers.
- Look for membership in a group.
- Analyze responses to lists and menus.
- Look for variables that must be equal.
- Create time-determined equivalence classes.
- Look for variable groups that must calculate to a certain value or range.
- Look for equivalent output events.
- Look for equivalent operating environments.

### Don't forget equivalence classes for invalid inputs

This is often your best source of bugs. Few programmers thoroughly test the program's responses to invalid or unexpected inputs. Therefore, the more types of invalid input you check, the more errors you will find. As

**Figure 7.1 A tabular format for listing equivalence classes.**

| *Input or Output Event* | *Valid Equivalence Classes* | *Invalid Equivalence Classes* |
|---|---|---|
| Enter a number | Numbers between 1 and 99 | 0<br><br>> 99<br><br>An expression that yields an invalid number, such as 5-5, which yields 0.<br><br>Negative numbers<br><br>Letters and other non-numeric characters |
| Enter the first letter of a name | First character is a capital character<br><br>First character is a lower case letter | First character is not a letter |
| Draw a line | From 1 dot-width to 4 inches long | No line<br><br>Longer than 4 inches<br><br>Not a line (a curve) |

**This layout is taken from Myers (1979).**

an example, for a program that is supposed to accept any number between 1 and 99, there are at least *four* equivalence classes:

- Any number between 1 and 99 is valid input.
- Any number less than 1 is too small. This includes 0 and all negative numbers.
- Any number greater than 99 is too big.
- If it's not a number, it's not accepted. (Is this true for *all* non-numbers?)

**TEST CASE**

**DESIGN**

### Organize your classifications in a table or an outline

You will find so many input and output conditions and equivalence classes associated with them, that you'll need a way to organize them. We use two approaches. Sometimes we put everything into a big table, like Figure 7.1. Sometimes we use an outline format, as in Figure 7.2. Note that in both cases, for every input and output event, you should leave room for invalid equivalence classes as well as valid ones.

Both approaches, table and outline, are good. There are advantages and drawbacks to each.

**Figure 7.2 An outline format for listing equivalence classes**

1.  Enter a number
1.1     Valid Case
1.1.1       Between 1 and 99
1.2     Invalid Cases
1.2.1       0
1.2.2       > 99
1.2.3       A calculation whose result is invalid, such as 5-5 yielding 0
1.2.4       Negative numbers
1.2.5       Letters and other non-numeric cases
1.2.5.1         Letters
1.2.5.2         Arithmetic operators such as +, *, -
1.2.5.3         The rest of the non-numeric characters
1.2.5.3.1           Characters with ASCII codes below the ASCII code for 0
1.2.5.3.2           Characters with ASCII codes above the ASCII code for 9
2.  Enter first letter of a name
2.1     Valid Cases
2.1.1       First character is a capital character
2.1.2       First character is a lower case character
2.2     Invalid Cases
2.2.1       First character is not a character
2.2.1.1         First character's ASCII code below that for "A"
2.2.1.2         First character's ASCII code between the codes for "Z" and "a"
2.2.1.3         First character's ASCII code greater than the code for "z"
3.  Draw a line
3.1     Valid Case
3.1.1       From 1 dot-width to 4 inches long
3.2     Invalid Cases
3.2.1       No line
3.2.2       Longer than 4 inches
3.2.3       Not a line
3.2.3.1         What's possible??? Curve? Circle?

The tabular format is easier to read than an outline. You can digest more information at once. It's easier to distinguish between equivalence classes for valid and invalid inputs. We think it's easier to evaluate the coverage of invalid equivalence classes.

Unfortunately, these tables are often bulky. There are often many more columns than in Figure 7.1, there to reflect interactions between different pieces of data, expand an event into sub-events ("Enter a name" might break down into "Enter the first letter" and "Enter the rest of the name"), or expand an equivalence class into subclasses.

You can start with big charts for rough work, then make final drafts with three columns by using a new line for every variation on the same theme. However, this hides much of the thinking that went into the chart. All the logical interrelationships that were so interesting in the wide table are no longer apparent.

One of us makes these charts on large desk pads or flipchart paper, then tapes them on the wall for future reference. It's hard to add new lines to these handwritten tables, and it's hard to photocopy them. Spreadsheet programs are a good alternative. Tape the printouts of the spreadsheet together to make your wallchart.

We also make outlines at the computer. Good outline processing programs make it easy to add to, change, reorganize, reformat, and print the outline. (Mediocre outliners don't make reorganization so easy. Don't give up; try a different one.)

We break conditions and classes down much more finely when we use an outline processor. We've shown this in Figure 7.2. This is usually (but not always) a good thing. However, we also repeat things more often with an outline processor and the initial outline organization is often not as good as the organization of the tables.

We don't recommend one approach over the other. Both are quite powerful.

This outline also illustrates a practical problem. Look at outline section 1.2.5.2 dealing with arithmetic operators. Conceptually "arithmetic operators" is an equivalence class of its own and the programmer might in fact treat this group *as* an equivalence class by testing inputs against a list of every arithmetic operator. Now consider 1.2.5.3.1 and 1.2.5.3.2. These *also* include all the arithmetic operators.

How should you deal with overlapping equivalence classes? You don't know how the programmer checks these inputs, and it probably changes from variable to variable, so there's no reliable rule based on what the programmer is "really" doing.

The simplest way is often best. A note on your chart that points out the overlap will steer a tester away from repeating the same tests. Don't drive yourself crazy trying to figure out elegant ways to define non-overlapping equivalence classes.

**7**

## Look for ranges of numbers

Every time you find a range (like 1–99), you've found several equivalence classes. There are usually three invalid equivalence classes: everything below the smallest number in the range, everything above the largest number, and non-numbers.

Sometimes one of these classes disappears. Perhaps no number is too large. Make sure that the class is gone. Try outrageously large numbers and see what happens.

Also, look for multiple ranges (like tax brackets). Each subrange is an equivalence class. There is an invalid class below the bottom of the lowest range and another above the top of the highest range.

## Look for membership in a group

If an input must belong to a group, one equivalence class includes all members of the group. Another includes everything else. It might be possible to subdivide both classes further.

For example, if you have to enter the name of a country, the valid equivalence class includes all countries' names. The invalid class includes all inputs that aren't country names.

But what of abbreviations, almost correct spellings, native language spellings, or names that are now out of date but were country names? Should you test these separately? The odds are good that the specification won't anticipate all of these issues, and that you'll find errors in test cases like these.

While you enter the name, the program might scan characters. The first character must belong to one of two groups: capital letters or lowercase letters. These are the valid equivalence classes. All non-letters are in the invalid equivalence class. These can in turn be subcategorized, as in Figure 7.2. (Note: A more complete chart would also consider accented letters. This is lots of fun because different language groups use different character sets, with different accented letters and different codes for some of the same letters.)

## Analyze responses to lists and menus

You must enter one of a list of possible inputs. The program responds differently to each. Each input is, in effect, its own equivalence class. The invalid equivalence class includes any inputs not on the list.

As one example, if a program asks `Are you sure? (Y/N)`, one equivalence class contains `Y` (and should contain `y` too). Another contains `N` (and `n`). Anything else is invalid (or *everything* else should be taken as equivalent to `N`).

As another example, American taxpayers file as single, married filing a joint return, married filing separate returns, head of household, or qualifying widow(er) with dependent child. Some refuse to describe their marital status, which is also legal. There is an invalid equivalence class: some people claim not to fit into any of these categories. They write notes on the tax return explaining why. How does the program deal with these?

## Look for variables that must be equal

You can enter any color you want as long as it's black. Not-black is the invalid equivalence class. Sometimes this restriction arises unexpectedly in the field—everything but black is sold out. Choices that used to be valid, but no longer are, belong in their own equivalence class.

## Create time-determined equivalence classes

Suppose you press the space bar just before, during, and just after the computer finishes reading a program from the disk. Tests like this crash some systems. What are the equivalence classes here? Well, everything you do *long before* the task is done is probably one equivalence class. Everything you do within some short time interval before the program finishes is another class. Everything you do just before the program starts reading is another class.

Similarly, you can direct a file to the printer when it's idle, when it's already printing something else, and as soon as it stops printing that document. Try this with a twist in a multi-user system: what if your user priority is higher than the person using the printer?

### Look for variable groups that must calculate to a certain value or range

Enter the three angles of a triangle. In the class of valid inputs, they sum to 180 degrees. In one invalid equivalence class, they sum to less than 180 degrees. In another they sum to more.

### Look for equivalent output events

So far, we've stressed input events, because they're simpler to think about. The third event in Figures 7.1 and 7.2 is an example of an output event. A program drives a plotter that can draw lines up to four inches long. A line might be within the valid range (one dot's width to four inches), there might be no line, the program might try to plot a line longer than four inches, or it might try to plot something else altogether, like a circle.

The difficulty lies in determining what inputs to feed the program to generate these different outputs. Sometimes many different classes of inputs should have the same effect. Unless you know that the differences don't matter by the time the program is at the output stage, you should treat them all as distinct equivalence classes, even though they lead to the same type of output event. This is especially important for inputs that will force error handling at the output stage.

As another output example, imagine that a program's specification says that after a series of computations, it will print a number between 1 and 45. Work backwards. What input could make it print something bigger than 45 or less than 1? Create test cases to try them.

### Look for equivalent operating environments

The program is specified to work if the computer has between 64 and 256K of available memory. That's an equivalence class. Another class includes RAM configurations of less than 64K. A third includes more than 256K. Some well-known programs fail on machines that have more than the expected maximum amount of memory.

**TEST CASE**

**DESIGN**

Some programs are affected by the number of terminals, monitors, printers, telephones, or disk drives attached to the system. Some are affected by the computer's clock speed. You can subject each of these quantities to boundary condition analysis.

## BOUNDARIES OF EQUIVALENCE CLASSES

Use only one or two test cases from each equivalence class. The best ones are at the class boundaries. The boundary values are the biggest, smallest, soonest, shortest, loudest, fastest, ugliest members of the class, i.e., the most extreme values. Incorrect inequalities (such as > instead of ≥) cause failures only at the boundaries. Programs that fail with non-boundary values usually fail at the boundaries too.

You have to test each edge of an equivalence class, on all sides of each edge. A program that passes these tests will probably pass any other test drawn from that class. Examples:

- If the valid input range is 1 to 99, the valid test cases are 1 and 99. Use 0 and 100 as tests of invalid input.

- If a program writes checks from $1 to $99, can you make it write a check for a negative amount, for $0 or for $100? Maybe you can't, but try.

- If the program expects an uppercase letter, give it A and Z. Test @ because its ASCII code is just below the code for A, and [, the character just beyond Z. Try a and z too.

- If the program prints lines from one dot to four inches long, try one-dot lines and four-inch lines. Try to make it print a line that's four inches and one dot-width long. Try to make it attempt a zero-dot line.

- If the inputs must sum to 180, feed the program values that sum to 179, 180, and 181.

- If the program needs a specific number of inputs, give it that many, one more, and one fewer.

- If the program gives you menu options B, C, and D, test each of them, and test A and E too.

- Try sending your file to the printer *just* before and *just* after someone else sends his.

- When reading from or writing to a disk file, check the first and last characters in the file. (Can you read past the file's end?)

In analyzing program boundaries, it is important to consider all outputs. Look at every piece of data the program prints: what's the biggest legitimate value and what's the smallest? How can you make the program print a barely bigger or barely smaller one?

Realize that input boundary values might not generate output boundary values. For example, the relationship between input and output values might look like a sine wave.

Many testers include a mid-range value in their boundary tests. Time permitting, this is good practice.

## VISIBLE STATE TRANSITIONS

Every interactive program moves from one visible state to another. If you do something that changes the range of available choices or makes the program display something different on the screen, you've changed the program's state. (For a more formal discussion of state transitions, see Beizer, 1983.)

A menu system is a simple example. The program starts with an introductory menu. When you select an option, the program changes state and displays a new menu. Eventually, you get some information, a data input screen, or some other non-menu.

You must test each option in each menu. You should make sure that each selection you make takes you to the state (e.g., to the menu) that you should reach next.

Ideally, you will also check every pathway to every option in every menu. You might be able to reach Menu 15 from a choice on Menu 14 and from another on Menu 27. If so, you should test every choice in Menu 15 twice—once after reaching the menu from Menu 14, again after reaching it from Menu 27. If there are ten ways to get to Menu 14, there are at least ten ways to get to menu 15, each a different route that takes you through Menu 14. If you can, test them all. Unfortunately, if there are many menu choices or levels, you'll wear out your keyboard and your fingers before finishing all the possible tests.

For testing interactions between paths, we recommend that you select paths through the program as follows:

- Test all paths that you think people are particularly likely to follow.

- If you have any reason to suspect that choices at one menu level or data entry screen can affect the presentation of choices elsewhere, test the effects of those choices or entries.

- Along with conducting the most urgent types of tests, as described above, try a few random paths through the program. Randomly select different paths in each test cycle.

State transitions can be much more complex than menu-to-menu. In some data entry systems, the form you get next depends on the numbers you entered into the present form. Numbers you enter into one field might also affect the range of choices available in another, or trigger the program to ask a series of further questions. Ranges of inputs might be treated equivalently. For example, a number between 1 and 99 gets you Form A; otherwise you get Form B. In these cases, you should do equivalence class and boundary value analysis, along with following the paths.

Some testers find it useful to create *menu maps*. A menu map shows where you go from each menu choice in the program. If tools or keyboard commands take you to different dialogs or states than do menu commands, the map shows these too. For example, a map might show a path from a File menu to a File Open command to a File Open dialog and then back to the main program state. A map is particularly handy for spaghetti designs. If you can reach a dialog in several ways, and go from the dialog to several places, the map lets you trace transitions between states on paper and check the program against them. It's often easier to spot relations between states on these diagrams than when working directly with the program.

## RACE CONDITIONS AND OTHER TIME DEPENDENCIES

Can the program be executed too quickly or too slowly? You can vary this directly by switching clock chips, by running the program on fast and slow models from the same line of computers or by flipping a speed switch on the machine.

Try to disrupt the program when it's in a state of transition. Press keys or send it other I/O requests while it's switching menus or servicing I/O.

Try to confuse the program when it's about to change state because of a time-out. In a *time-out* situation, the program waits for input for a limited period. If it hasn't received input by the end of the interval, it

**7**

TEST CASE
DESIGN

changes state, perhaps beeping and waiting for some other input. Press keys or get interrupts generated just as (just before, just after) the program times out.

Test the system under heavy load. In a multi-processing system, run other programs while you test this one. In a single-user system, send files from a buffer to the printer. Use a machine with a slower clock and less memory, attach more I/O devices and have them generate interrupts as often as plausible. Slow the computer down however you can. Relative to this slower program, you can respond more quickly, perhaps more quickly than it can accept. Even if you can't get the program to fail when it's running at normal load, you may confuse it during state transitions once you've slowed it down.

Do a fair bit of "normal" testing when the system is under load (or slowed however you can slow it). In many programs, you'll find race conditions you had never imagined possible. In a system that has shown itself vulnerable to races, execute a full cycle of testing under load. Don't be dissuaded by project managers who whine that you're testing the program unfairly. People *will* run the program concurrently with others, even on supposedly non-concurrent computers. People *will* use cheaper versions of the computer that have slower clocks, slower memory, and less memory. Your task is to make sure the program works under these adverse conditions, or to find out which conditions make it fail.

(By the way, if program performance is unacceptable under a configuration you think some customers *will* use, report this separately—maybe even on another day. Make sure to report bad performance, but make sure not to confuse the marketing issue of performance acceptability with the engineering issue of code failures that *will* arise on faster machines, that you've simply made easier to find by testing under slow conditions.)

## LOAD TESTING

Test every limit on the program's behavior that any of the product's documents asserts. Check the size of files it can work with, the number of printers it can drive, and the number of terminals, modems, bytes of memory that it can manage. Open the maximum number of files the program allows. Check how much (of anything) the program is supposed to handle at once, and how much over a long period. When no limit is stated, but you think there must be one, test an outrageously large (or small) value and see if the program can cope with it. If not, report a bug. If the program survives the test, maybe it is limitless in this respect.

Make sure to test the program as it pushes its devices to their limits too. Test with a full disk (and test with an almost-full disk because you'll find different bugs). Test with the printer out of paper (or about to run out of paper). Test under low memory conditions. Test with slow modems and fast modems. Push the machinery and see how the program responds when you've pushed the machinery too hard.

Load testing is boundary condition testing. Run a test that the program should be able to pass (such as maximum number of terminals) and another test that the program should fail (one too many terminals). Test many limits in combination. It may not be able to cope with more than one limiting case at once. Also, do enough general testing while you've got the program operating under this load to be sure it can continue to cope.

## ERROR GUESSING

For reasons that you can't logically describe, you may suspect that a certain class of tests will crash the program. Trust your judgment and include the test. Some special cases (such as input values of 0) aren't boundary values but are mishandled by many programs. Don't bother trying to justify a hunch that a special case might be mishandled here. Just test it and find out.

In complex situations, your intuition will often point you toward a tactic that was successful (you found bugs with it) under similar circumstances. Sometimes you won't be aware of this comparison—you might not even consciously remember the previous situations. This is the stuff of expertise (Brooks, 1978). Use it. Trust your instincts.

## FUNCTION EQUIVALENCE TESTING: AUTOMATION, SENSITIVITY ANALYSIS AND RANDOM INPUT

*Function equivalence* tests compare two programs' evaluation of the same mathematical function. This has nothing to do with "equivalence classes." If both programs always arrive at the same values for the function, the methods they use for computing the function are equivalent.

Suppose you're testing a program that evaluates a mathematical function and prints the result. This could be a simple trigonometric function or a complicated one that inverts a matrix or returns coefficients of the best fitting curve to a set of data. You can usually find another program that does the same job, that's been around for a long time, and that you consider reliable. The function in the program being tested is called the *test function*. The function in the reliable old program is the *reference function*. If the test and reference functions consistently agree across different inputs, the two programs use equivalent implementations of the underlying function.

### AUTOMATION OF FUNCTION EQUIVALENCE TESTING

Function equivalence testing is your method of choice whenever possible because:

- You don't have to calculate any values by hand, or look anything up in printed tables. You get all answers from the reference function. This saves you minutes or weeks depending on the complexity of the function.

- You can probably automate the comparison process. The most primitive automation strategy has both programs print to disk the function values for the same series of input values. Then the computer compares the files. Are the values the same or (taking roundoff errors into account) almost the same? The computer will compare the two lists more quickly and accurately than you.

TEST CASE

DESIGN

- You might be able to automate the entire process, from selection of input data through feeding it to the programs, collecting the output on disks, and comparing the files. If so, you can compare an enormous number of values of the two functions at virtually no cost. The comparisons can use a lot of computer time, but they don't take any of your time.

Automating these tests is straightforward, but it takes preparation. If the programs read data from disk, all you need do is prepare the right input files for each, and write short control and comparison programs.

Automation is harder when one or both of the programs demands keyboard input. However, you can send input remotely to most programs on most computers. Computers usually pass input they receive through a modem to application programs in a way that makes the modem input look just like keyboard input. To simulate keyboard input, program a second computer to send data to the first by modem. It's a little clumsy, but it works.

There are costs here. You need tools, including that old, reliable reference program which might not be cheap. You also have to do some programming, or get someone else to do it. You might have to buy or tie up a second computer. There are limits on how much you should spend, but we urge you to challenge an arbitrarily low tools budget that prohibits efficient function equivalence testing.

- Estimate how many days it will take you to test the function manually. Include time for planning, calculating, and running the tests. Don't forget that you'll have to run each test more than once, because you'll find bugs and have to redo testing in the next test cycle. Estimate five to eight cycles of testing. (Or use the average number of cycles needed by your company in the past.)

- Estimate how much time the tools will save you. Allow for planning, programming, and debugging the automated tests. Be realistic. If you are allowed to automate testing, this estimate will be quoted back to you.

- Multiply the number of days the tools save by *twice* your daily salary. The doubling takes benefits and overhead into account. If your estimates are correct, the company will save at least this much by buying you the tools. If the tools cost less than this, any rational manager should approve the purchase.

- Prepare a proposal and a presentation that explain your need for the tools and the basis for your cost estimates. If short term savings won't pay for the tools, be prepared to explain how the tools will pay for themselves over a period of no more than three years.

## SENSITIVITY ANALYSIS

Suppose that you automate function equivalence testing. You can now execute many more tests than you could by hand. However, you still have to select test cases with care: the number of values that can be passed to the function under test is probably too large (maybe infinite) for complete testing.

Naturally you should test boundary values, but now you have the luxury of testing the function more thoroughly. How do you select good test cases? *Sensitivity analysis* provides one approach. The general notions are:

- Check the function at points selected from across its range to get an overview of the function's behavior.

- Look for cases in which small differences between inputs cause large differences in the function's value. (For example, if X is near 90 degrees, the value of `tan(X)` changes a lot with small changes in X.) *These regions are the most likely to reveal errors.*

- The values reported by the test and reference functions may not agree exactly. If they use floating point arithmetic, different roundoff and truncation errors can make the outputs differ slightly. These minor differences are rarely a problem. However, you want to know if any part of the input space triggers larger than usual differences between the test and reference functions.

The approach we recommend is to divide the input range into a series of equally spaced subranges (perhaps 100 of them). Create one test case for each subrange. If a function accepts any value between -1 and 1, feed it a value between -1 and -0.98, another that's between -0.98 and -0.96, and so on. Check that the function gives the right values in each case before proceeding.

Next, look at the function's values across the different inputs. Look at the difference between the test and reference functions' values. Are there any big changes or do these values seem to rise and fall at about the same rate everywhere? If there aren't any interesting differences, stop.

Suppose the function (or the difference between test and reference) rises sharply in the region from 0.4 to 0.46. Divide this into 100 equal subranges and use a test case from each. If necessary, divide a group of these subranges into another 100 pieces. Ultimately, you will either be convinced that the test and reference functions are equivalent over this range or you will find an error.

If you have a lot of functions to test, and if you have some background in statistical theory, you can use more efficient approaches to find areas in which a small difference in input makes a maximal difference in the function's value, or in the difference between the test and reference functions' values. We recommend Bard's (1974), Beck & Arnold's (1977), and Chambers' (1977) discussions of sensitivity and optimization. Start with Beck and Arnold.

## RANDOM INPUTS

Rather than explicitly subdividing the input range into a series of equal subranges, you could use a series of randomly selected input values. Since random selection ensures that any input value is as likely as any other, any two equal subranges should be about equally represented in your tests. If you test with a sequence like 0.02, 0.04, 0.06, you'll never know how the program works with odd inputs (0.03) or inputs with more significant digits (0.1415).

Whenever you can't decide what values to use in test cases, choose them randomly. Consider random input selection whenever you can automate testing and evaluation of the results.

Because you don't have a clearly developed rationale for each test case, testing with random inputs is not efficient. You must make up for a lack of rationale with quantity. The goal is to run enough tests that, if there are different underlying equivalence classes, you will probably select at least one test from each class. There's no rigid rule for quantity. We run *at least* 1000 test cases under fully automated testing with randomly chosen test cases.

### What is a random number generator?

"Random" input does *not* mean "whatever input comes to your mind." Most people's selections of test cases are too patterned. Use a table of random numbers or (better yet) use a random number generating (RNG) function on the computer.

RNG functions on large systems (Knuth, 1981) and microcomputers are often poor. The worst don't even use the basic algorithm correctly; they use floating point routines to do what should be strictly integer arithmetic. Others only work with numbers between 0 and 65,535 and repeat their sequence every 65,536th number. These are unacceptable.

We can't go into the subtleties of creating and testing RNGs in this book. Kaner & Vokey (1984) overview the problems and testing techniques. Knuth (1981) is the authoritative text. Here are some suggestions:

- Read up on random number generators before you do any testing using random inputs. Don't trust someone else's generator just because it's there, even if it's provided as part of a respectable language on a respectable machine.

  Keep reading about generators until you understand the suggestions that follow. You don't have to take the suggestions, but if you don't understand them, you know little enough that you risk wasting lots of time generating oops-they-weren't-so-random test cases.

- If you're going to use a generator supplied with your programming language, sample many (100–1000) numbers from it and shuffle them. That is, use further random numbers to reorder them. This is slow, but it brings many poor RNGs up to a level of acceptability.

- If you use a language that allows high precision *integer* (not floating point) arithmetic, consider writing your own function to use one of the following generators. Define the RNG by:

```
R[N+1] = (A * R[N] + C) modulo M
```

That is, generate the N+1st number by multiplying the Nth by A, adding C and taking the result modulo M. The larger M is, the better, but slower. Figure 7.3 lists good values for the parameters.

The value of C is not critical (as long as it's odd), but careful selection can reduce serial correlations. The values for $M = 2^{40}$ are from Kaner & Vokey (1984). The rest are from Knuth (1981). To give you an idea of the care that goes into selecting these parameters, Kaner and Vokey tested over 30,000 candidate values for A, and perhaps a hundred values for C.

**Figure 7.3 Parameters of some published random number generators:**

| M | A | C |
|---|---|---|
| $2^{32}$ | 69069 | odd number |
| $2^{32}$ | 1664525 | odd number |
| $2^{35}$ | 17059465 | odd number |
| $2^{40}$ | 27182819621 | 3 |
| $2^{40}$ | 8413453205 | 99991 |
| $2^{48}$ | 31167285 | odd number |
| $2^{64}$ | 636413622384679300 | odd number |

$R[N+1] = (A * R[N] + C)$ modulo M

## GENERALIZED EQUIVALENCE TESTING

Mathematical functions are no longer the only reference functions available. You can use output from other products to test quite a few aspects of your product's behavior. For example:

- If your program licenses the same underlying spell-checking code as another program, run the same word list through both programs.

- To test the adequacy of your hyphenation algorithm (especially a variant of the algorithm that you're trying to apply to another language), test against a respected program sold in your target market (e.g., Germany). Create narrow columns of text to force hyphenation, and feed both programs the same word lists.

- Test your program's inter-character and inter-line spacing by laying out the same text, with the same fonts, in your desktop publisher and in a competitor's.

- Check the control codes you send to a printer (redirect output to a file) against codes from another program that is printing an identically formatted document.

If you can capture output from another program, you can test yours against it. It might take more work than it's worth to set these tests up, and you always run the risk that the other program has bugs, but keep the option in mind.

Remember to include comparison output from the other program with your bug reports. This is the first step in reverse engineering the other program, and it might be enough in itself to tell the programmer how the bug should be fixed.

## REGRESSION TESTING: CHECKING WHETHER A BUG FIX WORKED

When you report a problem, you tell the programmer exactly what you did to find it. Some programmers examine the code thoroughly, find the cause of the problem, fix it, and test the fix. Some address only the symptoms you reported. They write special-case "fixes" which don't solve the underlying problem but do keep it from appearing under precisely the circumstances you reported. Some misunderstand your report, and find, fix, and test the wrong problem. A few change code blindly, don't check their work, and give back code with the same bug plus whatever they broke making their "fix." There is a continuum of thoroughness and you have to be ready for it.

It's often claimed that one third of the "fixes" either don't fix the problem or break something else in the process. Martin & McClure (1983) summarized data showing that fewer than half of the fixes work the first time they are tested by the programmer (if he tests them).

When you test a bug fix, you have three objectives:

- ***Check that the bug was actually addressed.*** Run exactly the same test that you ran when you found the problem, the one you described in your report. If the program fails this test, you don't have to do any further regression testing. On the other hand, if the program passes this test, take a second to ask whether you're running the right test. *Are you sure* that you know how to demonstrate the bug? If you have any doubt, load the old version of the program, the one you know has the bug in it, then follow the bug report's steps and make sure you can bring up the bug on command. How can you tell if the bug's been addressed if you don't know how to find it?

- ***Try to find related bugs.*** Make the assumption that the programmer fixed only the symptoms you reported without fixing the underlying bug. How could you reach this bug in different ways? Could there be similar errors in other parts of the code? Take your time with this—if you think you need to, give it an hour or even a few hours. Run plenty of tests just this once.

- ***Check the rest of the program.*** Did this fix have unwanted consequences on anything else? Again, this involves informal planning and test cases that you won't keep forever. Ask yourself what parts of the program might have been affected by the change and look at them.

## REGRESSION TESTING: THE STANDARD BATTERY OF TESTS

Over time you'll develop a library of test cases. The idea behind this *regression test library* is that whenever a new version of the program is submitted for testing, you should run every test in the library.

If the tests are fully automated, do run them all each time. You've got nothing to lose except some computer time. It's harder if the tests aren't automated, because it costs your labor. How big is this library? How did the tests get here? Do you really want to run them *all* again and again?

It's hard to decide in advance which tests belong in the regression test library. Probably all the boundary condition and timing tests, belong there. But run them *every time*?

Regression tests (as a standardized battery) are frustrating to work with because they are among the least likely to expose a new bug in the program. They might have exposed an error once—some companies' test libraries only have tests that found bugs—but that bug was found and fixed months ago. It's gone. You probably won't find it again (though it is good to make sure).

Rather than agonizing over which tests to introduce into a standard series, we recommend that you cast a wide net. Review the series later, perhaps every third cycle of testing. Your overriding objective is to reduce the time needed for regression testing without sacrificing the assurance that you will probably detect new failures in old, already tested code. Here are some tactics:

- ***Drop tests that are virtual repetitions of another.*** These shouldn't have reached the test library in the first place, but it's common when more than one person creates tests.

- ***Reduce the concentration of tests on a bug that has now been fixed***. If a bug and variants of it persist across many cycles of testing, many tests to check for it will be added to the regression library. This is appropriate. You want to keep examining that bug, thoroughly, until all traces of it are purged from the program. Once the bug is gone, select a few of that mass of tests. Get the rest out of the library.

- **Combine test cases.** If you can combine 15 tests that you expect the program to pass into one big test case, do it. Streamline test cases so you spend as little on each as possible.

- **Automate if you can.** If you're sure that a test will be used across the next five or ten cycles of testing, it will probably pay to spend the time to automate the running of it. (See the discussion of automated testing in Chapter 11.)

- **Designate some tests for periodic testing.** Rather than running these every time the program changes, run them every second or third cycle of testing. Try to run the lot during what you think is the final cycle of testing, just to make sure that the program is ready to ship. Before then, just run half or a third of the tests in each cycle.

The regression test library might include all of your best-designed tests, but if it includes too many you won't have time to design new tests. Your newest tests are the ones most likely to find new errors. Don't lock yourself into a system that discourages you from developing them.

## EXECUTING THE TESTS

Now that you've created a great test case, it is absolutely essential that you test the program with it in an appropriate way. Here are some examples:

- If you can choose different options when you install the program onto your computer, don't just run the install program and see if it takes the different options. Run the program itself after each different installation and take it to a place that uses or displays the option you chose. Make sure the program works with this option.

- If your test case has the computer sending special configuration codes to a printer, don't forget to print a test document that uses the formatting feature you've defined. (Similarly when the program configures any other device.)

- If you enter a special paper size in your program, don't just smile when the dimensions look right onscreen. Make sure the program and the paper don't jointly jam the printer when you try to use this size paper.

- If you create a test document with special high ASCII characters, don't stop when you see them onscreen. Print them (if your program prints) or send them out the modem (if your program does telecommunications) or do whatever your program does with them. Your program's device driver might not work with these characters, or the import algorithm might not have set up the data in a way that lets the printer driver recognize these characters, even if the video driver can recognize them.

**7**

TEST CASE
DESIGN

The general rule is that you must always create a test procedure that will force the program to use the data you've entered and to prove that it is using your data correctly.

# TESTING PRINTERS (AND OTHER DEVICES)

## THE REASON FOR THIS CHAPTER

This chapter is about configuration testing in general and about printer testing in particular. The chapter starts with a general discussion of configuration testing and presents a generic (device-independent) strategy for doing configuration testing. It then illustrates the strategy with printers, as a carefully worked example.

Printer testing is interesting in its own right because most programs print. And, unless they're designed to use only the printer's basic, default fixed width font, programs have many printer compatibility problems.

In every software test lab that we've worked in, we've had to train testers how to plan, create, and execute printer tests. It takes a lot of training. This chapter covers most of that training.

- One reason that this chapter's printer coverage is so detailed is that we actually do train printer testers to this level of understanding. Otherwise they miss bugs and waste far too much testing time.

- Another important reason for this chapter's level of detail is to clearly illustrate how much you need to know to do effective configuration test planning. For example, if you're going to test modems, you should learn as much about modem control codes, modem device classes, modem driver classes, and typical modem-specific incompatibilities as we discuss here about printer control codes, device classes, etc.

## OVERVIEW

The chapter covers the following material:

- General issues in configuration testing.

- How printers work and how programs control them.

- The overall strategy for testing printers (and many other machines):
    1. Look for device-independent, functionality errors first.
    2. Then test for device-class-specific errors.
    3. Then test for driver-specific errors.
    4. Finally, test for errors that arise only with a specific printer model.

- How to organize feature testing across the different types of printers.

- How (and why) to collect historical information about your tests.

- How to automate much printer testing.

- How to set up and equip a printer test lab.

**PRINTERS &**

**OTHER DEVICES**

## NOTE

Configuration testing is much more complex in multi-user, multiprocessing environments. Many principles that we raise here will probably apply, but if you start working in this type of environment, get advice from an experienced coworker on how to apply them most effectively (and on the other essential principles that we miss.)

## SOME GENERAL ISSUES IN CONFIGURATION TESTING

Most programs work under a wide range of hardware configurations and operating environments. Here are typical configuration questions:

- Which printers is the program that you're testing compatible with?

- Which video cards or chipsets, what video modes (resolution, number of colors, etc.), and which types of monitors?

- Which mice (manufacturer, release version) and which mouse drivers?

- What range (minimum and maximum) does the program work in? Does it require a special type of memory (such as chip RAM rather than fast RAM, or base RAM rather than extended or expanded)?

- Which models of a given manufacturer's computer does the program work with (e.g., which version of Macintosh), or which brands and models of allegedly compatible computers (e.g., IBM vs. Tandy)?

- Which versions of the core system software (e.g., which versions of the operating system, windowing software, memory management software, or application support routines embedded in ROM)?

These all yield different *configurations*—when you change any aspect of the hardware or system software, you have a new configuration. *Configuration testing* is concerned with checking the program's compatibility with the many possible configurations of hardware and system software.

Configuration testing can be a black hole. For example, suppose you're testing a graphics program on an MS-DOS computer. Consider tests of video display capability. There are a few hundred different video cards, most claiming compatibility with a "standard," such as CGA, EGA, HMGA, MCGA, MDA, VGA, Super VGA, TCGA, or XGA. Many cards are only almost-compatible.

- A program that works with many EGA cards may fail with many others. How do you decide which cards to test? And don't forget mice when you test EGA. Programs can lose track of the mouse cursor when running on a computer with EGA. The problem is that you can't read certain memory locations (registers) when working with most EGA cards, but you can read them on others, including VGA cards when they emulate EGA cards. Programmers can easily miss such a bug because it depends on the card, the program, and the mouse driver (the utility program that directly controls the mouse. For details, see Microsoft (1991), Chapter 10). Mouse vendors update their drivers frequently—a given type of mouse may have been sold with a dozen different drivers. So what do you test? If you test the 10 best selling cards with the 5 best selling mice, that's 10 x 5 = 50 tests, and if you check each mouse with each of the 3 most common (most different, most something-or-other—how do you choose?) versions of the mouse driver, you'll run 50 x 3 = 150 configuration tests just to check a few EGA cards with a few mice and a few mouse drivers.

**Figure 8.1 Seven steps to good Configuration Testing**

1.  *Analyze the market*

    Which of these devices (which printers, which video cards, etc.) must the program work with? How can you get them? (You may get this information from marketing or the project manager. Often, though, you will be more aware of critical-to-test, almost-compatible devices.)

2.  *Analyze the device*

    How does it work? How will this affect your testing? Which of its features does the program use?

3.  *Analyze the ways the software can drive the device*

    How can you subdivide the world into groups of devices that share the same errors?

4.  *Save time*

    Test only one device per group until you eliminate the errors that are common to the group. Then test each device in the group.

5.  *Improve efficiency*

    Look for ways to improve efficiency and save time on this repetitious and boring task. Consider automation. Organize the lab effectively. Create a precise planning and recordkeeping system to make it easy to communicate to helpers what must be done, and to track exactly what has been done.

6.  *Share your experience*

    Organize and share your research and test results so the next project will research, plan and test more efficiently.

7.  *Does this type of device interact with other devices?*

    If necessary, select a small sample and test them with some of the other devices.

- Now consider VGA cards: these behave differently (you'll find different bugs in the program) depending on whether you test the program with a color monitor, a gray-scale monitor, or a simple monochrome monitor. There are over a hundred different VGA cards, not fully compatible with each other. Should you test each with each of the three types of monitor (300 tests)? What about testing these with different mice?

**8**

PRINTERS &
OTHER DEVICES

Even if you could find the time for all these card and mouse and monitor tests, you couldn't afford all the cards and mice and monitors (and RGB adaptors and terminals and two monitors connected simultaneously and printers and font cartridges and printer memory and plotters and paper trays and cables and switch boxes and printer buffers and modems and fax cards and keyboards and joysticks and trackballs and light pens and bar code readers and voice synthesizers and music synthesizers and music keyboards and digitizers and scanners and genlock cards and film recorders and disk drives and optical drives and tape drives and drive controllers and network cards and television receiver boards and A/D+D/A converters and serial or parallel expansion ports and clock chips and memory configurations and ROMs and main processors and accelerator cards and coprocessors and computers) and the lab space to keep them. You must learn how to configuration test efficiently, or the task will swallow you.

To plan and conduct configuration tests effectively and efficiently, you have to learn a lot about the hardware you're testing. You have to learn what features of a device the program uses, and how to test whether the program successfully controls the device to use those features. You have to learn how compatible or incompatible similar devices (like VGA cards) can be, and how differences between them might affect the program you're testing. You have to learn which devices emulate each other perfectly, so you can save time and money by testing just one representative of a group, but you need a nose for imperfect emulations. Manufacturers may stretch the truth when they say their card works "just like" some other card. Some companies' credibility (and emulation skill) is better than others'. Some technologies are harder to emulate than others. Before you class 20 different cards as equivalent (and then test one representative, leaving the others untested), you should have some basis, independent of manufacturer claims, that those cards emulate each other well. Otherwise you risk program failure when customers use it with those untested cards. The trade press *loves* to write up programs that don't work with popular hardware. These articles can cost your program market share, and can cost you your job.

Figure 8.1 summarizes our approach to configuration testing. The rest of the chapter shows how we apply it to the paradigmatic device, printers. Printers are what testers usually think of first when they think of configuration testing and they're what customer support staff usually curse about first when they complain about a lack of configuration testing.

## PRINTER TESTING

Over 1000 different printers have been released for use with microcomputers. The market is fragmented. To cover 80% of the MS-DOS retail customer base, you might have to support as many as 20% of these printers (200 printers). Similarly for the Amiga, Apple //, and Commodore 64 printer markets. The Macintosh market was very concentrated but has broadened considerably.

Some programs take no advantage of any printer features: no graphics, no boldface, no underline, no support for proportional fonts (or any other particular fonts), no color, nothing but 79 characters per line of standard ASCII text. These are compatible with almost all printers and they require almost no configuration testing.

As to programs that do take advantage of printer features, no one tries to support 1000 printers. A very few programs try to support 500 printers and the cost of this support (including testing) is one reason these programs list for hundreds of dollars.

Try to test every printer listed in the program and key compatible models that have significant market share, or that you suspect aren't 100% compatible with the machine they claim compatibility with, or that historically have highlighted program problems unusually well, or that have generated more than their market share worth of support calls with this or other products. If you're lucky, the product manager or project manager will list the most popular printers and the others most important for marketing reasons (special features, joint promotions, etc.) If you must do your own market research (don't be surprised), *Computer Reseller News*, *PC Magazine* (especially the annual printer issue), and *MacWorld* are among many quick and useful sources of information.

## OVERVIEW OF PRINTERS

It's useful to start with an overview. Printers vary along a few basic dimensions: mechanism, control codes or languages, color capabilities, and interface type. We explore these dimensions first.

### Printer mechanisms

Here are a few classes of print technologies:

- *Typewriter-like* printers get ink onto paper in much the same way that typewriters do. This includes the old teletypes that could only print uppercase letters and couldn't even form feed, plus daisy wheel printers and electronic typewriters. The best of these, like the Xerox Diablos and the Qumes, are very rugged and produce high-quality type, including proportional fonts with microspacing. However, these printers are slow and not good for graphics. Many current programs do not support these printers. New versions of some older programs have dropped support for these printers.

- *Dot matrix* printers have one or more columns of thin wires (pins). The pins point outward, from the printhead to the printer ribbon and the paper behind the ribbon. When a pin is pushed out and hits the ribbon, it makes a dot on the paper. When all the pins in a column are pushed forward at the same time, the result is a column of dots that looks like a vertical line, about an eighth of an inch tall. The printer makes letters by pushing a few pins forward (printing the leftmost section of a letter), then moving the printhead very slightly to the left, then pushing out the pins needed to print the next bit of the letter. Dot matrix printers typically have 9 or 24 pins. Older models had 8 pins. Some have 18 pins. Some line printers have a printhead that's a full line wide, with many columns of pins. They print the entire line at the same time, rather than printing part of a letter at a time. Text from dot matrix printers may look grainy, especially from older printers and from current 9-pin printers when printing in "draft mode" (at their fastest speed). As technology has advanced, printer manufacturers have learned how to move the printhead more finely, letting them pack dots tighter together. The result is better looking print and higher resolution graphics. Most dot matrix printers provide graphics capabilities. Common graphics resolutions are 60 dots per inch (dpi) and 72 dpi (these are grainy, ugly, and fast to print), 120 and 144 dpi (pretty good), and 240 and 360 dpi. In comparison, typical laser printer output is at 300 dpi. A dot matrix machine that prints 360 dots or blanks in each inch of each row of a page is printing a slightly sharper picture than a typical laser printer.

  **8**

  PRINTERS &
  OTHER DEVICES

  Dot matrix printers are very popular in MS-DOS, Amiga, and 8-bit computer environments. They are much less popular on Macintoshes and UNIX machines. Many Mac programs don't work with dot matrix printers or work with them only halfheartedly (72 dpi).

- *Impact* printers include the typewriter-like and dot matrix printers. They make their mark by hitting the page.

- *Ink jet* printers squirt a dot of ink onto the page. Their main advantage used to be quietness, but the better current models are more respected for the print quality they provide at a reasonable price. Some emulate laser printers. Others print in color.

- *Page* printers operate on a full page at a time. The underlying technologies include laser, lcd, and thermal transfer printing.

### Printer control codes and languages

A printer's physical printing mechanism is interesting, but from the software's point of view, the key issue is the set of commands that it can send to the printer. This is what differentiates printers as far as the program is concerned.

Most dot matrix and typewriter-like printers are controlled with very simple codes. To turn boldfacing on, you might send an <Escape> code (ASCII code 27) followed by one other character. To select a font or to change line height or graphics resolution, you might send an <Escape> followed by four or five characters. The collection of all the control codes that you can send to a printer is its *control code set*. The most common sets of control codes today were invented by Epson and IBM. (There are many variants of each.) Historically, several other sets of control codes were popular, including some from Centronics, Diablo, C. Itoh, Dataproducts, NEC, Okidata, Qume, and Tandy.

Page printers and some inkjets are controlled using much more complex (and longer) commands; the collected command sets are often called *languages*. The main languages are PostScript and Hewlett Packard's Printer Control Language (PCL). Credible PostScript alternatives are underway. Canon and IBM sell popular printers, competitive with HP's, that use their own proprietary language, but the IBM also has built-in HP emulation. It's not yet clear whether either Canon's or IBM's language will gain significant acceptance.

### Color capabilities

Color dot matrix printers use a color ribbon. The top of the ribbon is one color, then there's a row of another color, etc. The same printer pins hit black parts of the ribbon, yellow parts, green parts, etc. Over time the ribbon will smudge. Color inkjet printers squirt dots of different colors, from separate reservoirs of color ink. A well maintained color inkjet printer gives a very nice color printout.

### Interface type

The printer either connects directly to the computer through a standard parallel or serial port, or through a hardware company's proprietary type of port, or indirectly through a network. The network link raises many interesting problems to be discussed later. Here, we'll just note that different protocols, diagnostics, and error states are involved with parallel and serial printers.

In the MS-DOS and Amiga worlds, parallel printers are more standard. In a parallel connection an entire character is sent to the printer at once. The character is encoded in eight bits, and each bit is sent down its own wire, at the same time as the others. Other wires carry information about the readiness state of the printer, making hardware error conditions fairly easy to detect and deal with.

Serial printers add some complexity. In a serial connection, each bit of a character is sent one bit at a time. You can vary the transfer rate the printer is expecting (how many bits per second), along with protocol details such as how to tell whether the connected printer is ready, or how to mark the beginning and end of a series of character bits. Serial printers have become more adaptable, so serial printer testing is less complex than it used to be. We won't cover it here. If you need to investigate serial problems in any detail, you might find the terms and concepts as well or better explained in books on modems or terminals.

The key point of note is this: if your program supports both parallel and serial printing, you must test all of your program's printer error handling with parallel and serial printers. It might respond entirely differently to an off-line serial printer or to a serial printer that runs out of paper.

## STRATEGIES FOR DRIVING PRINTERS

First, consider a programming style that is completely printer-specific. Back in the bad old days, a programmer might write a program that was perfectly tailored to one printer. Then another printer would come along and she'd copy the first printer's code, change it for the second printer, and put both versions of the print routine into the program. The program would run through the original code to print to the first printer, and through the changed code to print to the second. This is the quickest and easiest way to add support for a second printer, but it is so disreputable that no one admits to coding this way (even Kaner insists he only did it once or twice). It is disreputable because it becomes a maintenance nightmare so quickly. Imagine adding support for *another* three printers by making three more copies of the print code, changing them to make one for each printer, and adding *them* back. If you find a bug in one, will you remember to fix all five? What if you add a new printing feature, such as boldfacing. Will you get it right all five times? All five times for the main text? For headers? Footers? Title page? Footnotes? What if you add another 20 printers?

At the other extreme is the *virtual printer*. This is an abstract, fictitious device. Associated with it is a list of capabilities and commands to invoke them. There is also a translation table. For each printing command, the table lists the control code required to execute the command on each supported printer. When the program sends a given command to the virtual printer, a translator uses the translation table to substitute the command codes appropriate to the customer's printer.

For example, suppose you have an Epson FX-85 printer. The translator knows you have this printer because you said so at some point (see below). The code for turning boldfacing (emphasized mode) on is <Esc-E>. To turn on boldfacing, the program "prints" _boldface_on to the virtual printer. The translator looks up _boldface_on in the translation table, finds <Esc-E> in your printer's column, and sends out <Esc-E> to make your printer boldface.

**8**

PRINTERS &
OTHER DEVICES

In many environments, such as Amiga, Macintosh, and Windows, you name your printer as part of a general system setup. Every program can access this information. The translation table is also part of the environment, not of any application program that runs within the environment. At run time, the environment reads what printer is installed, reads the command set for that printer, and sends out the correct printer command (such as `<Esc-E>`) whenever the application program issues the more general virtual code (such as `_boldface_on`).

In practice, the translation table is a collection of tables. There might be one per printer or one for each group of printers. Support a new printer by adding a new table and telling the environment that it's there. These tables are often called *printer drivers.*[1]

The beauty of this approach is that the program knows nothing about any particular printer, and its promise is that what works for one printer works for them all. The program writes to only one printer, the virtual printer. There is no special code for individual printers. When drivers are system level, the translator is a developer's tool supplied with the environment. The drivers come standard with the environment or are supplied later, often by the printer manufacturers. Presumably, the translation tables and translator were well tested, against many programs, before being added to the system. Presumably, if a program prints correctly to any printer, the translator must correctly understand the commands the program is issuing to the virtual printer, and it can reliably translate the commands to any one of the supported physical printers.

The virtual printer's promise is realized by many programs that don't do anything fancy with the printer. Beyond that, well, anyone who believes these translators are bug free should contact us about a virtual bridge we'd like to sell. Similarly for driver files (yes, even on Macintoshes). Also, these files often don't support all the features available on the individual printers. Given a choice between writing to a printer "safely" through a driver or printing faster with a better looking font or higher graphic resolution by writing custom code, what should a programmer do? Sometimes the answer is direct printer control, or a mix of driver-based control of most print functions plus direct control for a few others.

Between the extremes of custom code for every printer and system-level support for a virtual printer is program-specific support for a virtual printer. In this case, the programmer writes the translator and develops the translation tables (drivers). The customer names her printer when she installs the program. Implementations vary widely but the idea, however implemented, is to separate the printer-specific decisions from the rest of the code, just as in the virtual printer model.

For the sake of speed or conceptual simplicity, this type of program might treat different classes of printers separately. It might have, in effect, a virtual dot matrix printer and a very different virtual page printer, and two sets of translators and tables, one for each type of virtual printer. There is nothing disreputable about this approach, even if there are more than two classes of printer. It's harder to maintain and test, but when output

---

[1] The term *printer driver* is also used to describe a special subprogram or system-level program written to control individual printers or groups of similar printers, and some people get fussy about the distinction (the programs can send data to the printer, whereas the tables just hold control data that gets sent). When we say printer driver, we mean any table, file, subprogram, or program that makes a program capable of controlling a specific printer.

**Figure 8.2 An illustration of printer categorization**

| Class of printer | Representative drivers | Representative printers |
|---|---|---|
| Simple control codes | Epson 24 pin | Epson LQ-510 |
| | | Panasonic KXP-1124 |
| | IBM Graphics | IBM Graphics printer |
| | | Tandy DMP-106 |
| | Okidata native codes | Okidata ML-82 |
| | | Okidata ML-92 |
| Hewlett Packard PCL | HP LaserJet II | HP LaserJet II |
| | | HP LaserJet IID |
| | HP PCL5 | HP LaserJet III |
| Postscript | Postscript | Apple LaserWriter NT |
| | | QMS 810 |

Note that this organization, while common, is not at all necessarily the one you'll find in your program.

quality and printing performance are important issues, maintenance and testing ease are less important than customer satisfaction.

## THE OVERALL STRATEGY FOR TESTING PRINTERS

Individual programs structure their printing in their own ways. As a general practical rule, you can always think of printing being organized at different levels. The last section provided some theoretical insight into the levels you'll find in many programs. Whether the program you're testing conforms to that theory or not, you'll find it useful to think in terms of four classes of errors: device-independent functional errors, class-specific errors, driver-specific errors, and printer-specific errors.

Suppose you are testing a word processing program. Have it print some words in boldface.

- The *device-independent error:* Perhaps the program doesn't recognize your input as requesting boldfacing, or it doesn't send a boldface command to the (virtual) printer. It doesn't print any text, or it prints in italics. It prints to the modem instead of the printer. It doesn't matter what printer is connected—the program will fail in the same way in each case. You want to catch these errors first, before you start testing lots of different printers.

**8**

PRINTERS &
OTHER DEVICES

- The *printer class-specific error:* There is an intermediate level in the program: the program is organized to analyze printing tasks differently depending on the general class of printer attached. Perhaps the program works correctly with dot matrix command sets and PostScript printers, but fails with LaserJet compatibles.

  Figure 8.2 illustrates the difference between classes of printers, drivers, and individual printer models.

- The *driver-specific error:* The program has a special section of code, or a special table of printer commands, set aside for the type of printer you're connected to. This special code or table is the driver for your printer. The program might use the same driver for many different printers. For example, it might use an Epson FX whenever it prints to any Epson FX printer, whether the printer is an FX-80, FX-85, FX-86e, FX-100, FX-286e, FX-1050, or FX-something-else. The driver might contain an error, such as the wrong control code to turn boldfacing on or off. It will fail on each of these different printers.

- Finally, the *printer-specific error:* Perhaps the program uses the wrong driver for your printer. Or perhaps this printer is almost compatible with the other printers covered by the driver, but its boldface command is different. The error is that this printer shouldn't be included with the others in the same driver. This is a common problem when the manufacturer of Printer A advertises that its printer is 100% compatible with another company's Printer X.

Your strategy should be to proceed, in testing, from the general to the particular. Start by testing with one printer. Look for printer-independent bugs. Then add a few more, fundamentally different, printers and look for class-specific errors. Then test with one printer for each driver, to find driver-specific errors. Finally, test with one of every printer that you list in your program, to find printer-specific errors.

There are two aspects to this strategy. First, you avoid redundant testing. There's no point tripping across the same bug on 48 different printers. Get rid of the general errors before testing on many printers. Second, you will change your testing focus as your tests become more printer-specific.

### Testing for functional errors (printing)

Pick one printer to test with. Choose a reasonably high end printer that will support most of the printing features the program supports.

Make a list of all the printing features the program supports. The list might include italics, boldface, switching fonts, and underlining. Make another list of all the places in the program that might be coded independently that support different printer features. For example, a list might include the main body of text on a page, the header, the footer, end of chapter footnotes, and title pages.

**Figure 8.3 Progression of printer tests**

1.  Test for device independent, functional errors. These will occur on any printer.

2.  Test for class specific errors. Repeat essentially the same tests on a few printers, one from each class.

3.  Test for driver specific errors. Check each function supported by a given driver.

4.  Test for printer specific errors. Check each printer controlled within a driver group.

Combine the lists: test italics in the main body, the header, the footer, the end of chapter footnotes and on the title page. Similarly for boldface, switching fonts, and underlining. Turn each feature on and off and on again in each section. Look for inappropriate carryover of features from one section to another, such as carrying over the header's font into the main body. Try combined features, like boldface and italic together.

As much as is reasonably possible, with this one printer, you are testing everything everywhere. At the end of testing you will have found some bugs unique to this printer, some unique to its driver, some unique to its class (e.g., the class of simple control code controlled dot matrix printers), and some common to all printers. Ideally, all of these will be fixed before you progress to the next level of testing.

### Testing for class-specific errors

Pick the three or four printers that are the most different from each other that you can find. If the programmer does write special code for each class of printer, your printers are probably in different classes. (Accurate information on printer classification from the programmer is always helpful but not always available.)

This level of testing is useful even if the program doesn't distinguish between broad classes of printers. If there are printing bugs, you're more likely to find them by testing printers that are very different from each other than by testing similar printers.

The level of testing is thorough, much the same as the initial tests with the first printer. Test all features in all areas of the program and test combinations of features.

### Testing for driver-specific errors

Think of two questions. First, if you ask the program to boldface, will it try to boldface? Second, given that it's going to try to boldface, will it know how to do it on your printer?

By the time you start looking for driver-specific errors, you should be convinced of the answer to the first question. The program will normally boldface when you tell it to. Therefore you don't have to check whether it boldfaces in every area (main body, headers, footers, etc.). If it knows the correct command to turn on boldfacing on your printer, it will use it everywhere.

Consult your list of printing features (italics, boldface, switching fonts, underlining, etc.) Make sure you can turn each feature on, each feature off, and each feature back on again. You might check some combinations. Perhaps you'll discover a printer that wildly smashes its

**8**

**PRINTERS &
OTHER DEVICES**

printhead against the right limit of its range of travel if you ask it to doublestrike proportionally printed characters. Perhaps you'll find something less dramatic.

Finally, fiddle with the front panel switches or the DIP switches of the printer you're using to test the driver. Does the driver assume that the printer's default font is a fixed-width draft font at 10 characters per inch? Check text output when it's trying to print in some other typeface or character size. Also, check graphic output from the program, especially graphics that involve lots of white space to the left, right, or between images. Depending on the printer driver's whitespace algorithm, adjusting the printer's cpi might affect horizontal positioning. Look at vertical spacing too. A driver for an IBM-emulating printer may have trouble (in text or graphics) with the Alternate Graphics Mode (check what happens when you switch from six lines vertical spacing per inch)? Check the printer manual to see how you can use switches to vary the basic behavior of the printer.

### Testing for printer-specific errors

Run the same tests that you used to test the driver.

This level of testing is controversial because it is perceived as unnecessary. If you've tested Printer A, and you know Printer B is compatible with A, why bother testing B? Much of the time, you shouldn't test B. However, there are circumstances that bear consideration:

- *Printers listed on the program's installation menu:* You should always select and try every option on every menu in every program you test.

  Some programs list hundreds of printers and you can't test them all, if only because you can't get to all the printers. You can still do *some* testing here. If Printer A and Printer B are supposed to be compatible, but you don't have Printer B, select B from your menu anyway, and print to Printer A. At least you'll know that the menu choice points to the right driver, and that making the selection won't crash the program.

- *Printers that should be listed on the menu:* How much does the average Technical Support call cost your company? $10? $20? Suppose that Printers A and B are compatible, and that Printer A is in your menu but B isn't. Some customers who have Printer B will call to ask what printer to choose from the installation menu, given that B isn't there. Or they'll call to complain because they think their printer's compatible with Printer C, so they chose that one and it doesn't work. You can reduce this expense by improving the documentation, but it doesn't drop to 0. How many calls does it take before it would be cheaper to list, buy, and test the printer than to answer all the calls?

- *Popular compatibles that aren't compatible:* A few years ago, some DOS and Amiga developers were surprised by the HP DeskJet. They believed the DeskJet was LaserJet compatible, but in many critical ways it wasn't. The DeskJets became bestsellers that were, for a time, inadequately supported by many popular programs. The technical support call volumes for those programs were dismaying and expensive. Many of these programs could have avoided this problem if only their test group had tested with a DeskJet instead of assuming it was LaserJet compatible. The DeskJet is far from being the only example. If you know that a printer is very popular, or it's going to be, try to test with it. You usually won't find a problem, but each test is like a payment on an insurance premium. Occasionally you'll avoid a very embarrassing and expensive mistake.

- ***Indistinguishable bad member of a popular class:*** We talk about the Epson LQ as if it were one printer, but there are many different Epson LQ models. Suppose your driver works well for every Epson LQ but one. A customer who has this (hypothetical) printer but chooses the Epson LQ driver will be grumpy. If you want to support a class of printers, and you have no good way of teaching customers not to think of this as a member of the class ("What do you mean it's not really an Epson LQ? It's made by Epson and it says LQ on the front!"), then you should consider checking your program against every member of the class. Again, this type of problem is rare. However, it's expensive when it hits. We know of perhaps 10 examples (spread across different manufacturers) arising over the last 13 years.

The less use your program makes of special printer features, the less likely it is to have printer-specific problems, and the less printer-specific testing is needed. The fancier your program's output, the more printers you should test it on.

## THE PRINTER TEST MATRIX

Printer testing is very detail-oriented, even in comparison to other testing tasks. It is too easy to forget to check something and too much of a nuisance to find the printer again, check its switch settings, connect it to your test computer, run the test, then put it back in the right place in the lab or bring it back to whoever you borrowed it from. Setup and teardown time is often the most expensive part of printer testing. Without a checklist you almost guarantee that you'll have to redo some tests, and waste the setup time that goes with them.

If you test enough printers, it's worth the investment of time to create a group of standard printer test files. Try to combine features tested to reduce the number of files you need. It is *much* faster to test with these standard files than to recreate a test case for each feature on each printer each time you test.

### Test matrix layout

Use your spreadsheet to create a test matrix something like the one in Figure 8.4. (A spreadsheet is much more suited to these columnar organizations than a word processor).

If you use a standard set of test files, your test matrix will be simpler than Figure 8.4. Instead of listing features and program areas, you can just list the test files, and check them off as you run them.

This matrix stretches on, with one column for each printer to be tested. In practice, you should create at least two different matrices. The one shown lists every feature (or combination of features) to be tested within each area of the program—you'd use this to test the first printer, and one of each of the main printer classes. A second matrix would list the printer features without repeating feature tests in each program area. Use this for tests of individual printers or printer drivers.

**8**

Across the top of the matrix, list the printer name and its driver. Somewhere in the column, make it easy to record switch settings, cartridges loaded, amount of memory installed in the printer, and any other configuration information that seems relevant. You'll find that this information is more pressing for some programs than others.

## A few feature test notes

You'll find a good list of printer features in any printer manual. We aren't going to list most of them here. However, some raise interesting test questions, so we'll note the questions here.

- *Native fonts:* Does the printer have built-in fonts and does the program support them? If so, does the program support the printer's best looking fonts? If not, are you risking a customer support problem with this printer? Does the program switch smoothly between fonts? Can you print in two different

**Figure 8.4 Printer test matrix**

| Program area | Print feature | Epson LQ-510 (Epson LQ) | Panasonic 1124 (Epson LQ) | IBM Graphics (IBM Graphics) | Tandy DMP-106 (IBM Graphics) |
|---|---|---|---|---|---|
| Headers | Boldface on | | | | |
| | Bold off | | | | |
| | Italics on | | | | |
| | Italics off | | | | |
| | Normal font | | | | |
| | Compressed on | | | | |
| | Back to normal | | | | |
| Main Body | Boldface on | | | | |
| | Bold off | | | | |
| | Italics on | | | | |
| | Italics off | | | | |
| | Normal font | | | | |
| | Compressed on | | | | |
| | Back to normal | | | | |

fonts on the same line? (Same question for boldfacing, italics, etc. You might need or get a carriage return when changing the font or style).

- ***Downloaded fonts:*** A program might download its own custom defined character set to the printer and print with those characters. Many dot matrix and laser printers accept downloaded fonts. What if one of the characters is not perfectly defined? On the HP LaserJet II, inconsistencies in the description of a character will cause the printer to reject that character at downloading time. The printer will print the other downloaded characters, but prints a blank in place of the rejected character. This problem is easy to miss, especially if the program can download characters of many different sizes. Select many different character sizes and print the *entire* character set at each size. Otherwise you risk missing individual character downloading errors, and these are more common than you might wish. Download to the worst-case printer in a class—for example, the LaserJet II (not the IID or the IIP) is the least forgiving of the class of LaserJet II series printers.

- ***Special characters:*** If the program prints upper ASCII graphic or non-English characters, make sure the printer will print them. Perhaps the printer must be switched to a different character set, or the program must download special characters and switch to this alternate character set, or the program must switch into a graphics mode to print these special characters. What happens to line spacing or to vertical lines if the program switches fonts or switches to graphics?

- ***Graphics:*** Bidirectional printing on impact and inkjet printers can be a problem. Print a vertical line: does it waver? If so, the program should disable bidirectional printing. Also, vertical spacing depends on graphic resolution. If you set your printer into a graphic mode (such as AGM on the IBM Proprinters), what happens to vertical line spacing when you print text. The typical line spacing is six lines per inch, and this usually works well. But what happens if you switch to eight or ten lines per inch? Does the program get these values, or something else?

- ***Graphic resolution:*** If the program can drive the printer at three different graphic resolutions (e.g., 60, 120, and 240 dots per inch), test it at all three resolutions. The program might run out of memory at the highest resolution. It might fail to print at the other resolutions for many other reasons. Or it might fail to switch to the other resolutions. Especially at the highest density, print complex documents, large pages with lots of complex graphics that contain lots of transitions between black and white. (Complex graphics can challenge some internal optimization routines in printers and in drivers communicating with some laser printers.)

- ***Error handling:*** With complex graphics or a many-character document in a tiny downloaded font, you can run a laser printer out of memory or overdrive its dot positioning software so severely that it gives an Image Too Complex error. If your program can do this, does the manual's troubleshooting section deal with it? How does the program cope with this? Can you make the printer fail with reasonable use of the program or do you have to do something particularly unlikely? What if you test the printer at its lowest shipping memory configuration? Or if you test earlier models in a line of printers, which probably have less advanced error handling? (Just like programs get more fault-tolerant in each new release, expect printer error handling to improve with each new model.) One last, important test—after you make the printer fail, reset it (with the reset key, not by turning off the printer) and try to print another test document. If you get a mess, is it the software or the hardware?

**8**

PRINTERS &
OTHER DEVICES

- *Proportional spacing width tables:* If your program supports proportionally spaced characters, look for width table errors. The width table stores the width of each character, i.e., how many dots across it takes to print the character. A WYSIWYG (what you see is what you get) program spaces the characters according to the width tables and might overlap characters or space them too far apart onscreen if the table has an error. Non-WYSIWYG programs figure out where to break lines by estimating the combined widths of the characters printed so far. Width table errors can cause uneven, and sometimes very odd, line breaks. Width tables are different for every font. Width tables may differ across printers for fonts with the same name. If one dot matrix printer claims to be the clone of another, don't bet that the width tables of their proportional character sets match.

- *Graphic formats:* If your program can print graphics stored in different formats, test each, in portrait (standard vertical) and landscape (sideways printing) modes. Check these for each class of printer, since different classes will probably have different routines for translating the imported images into an internal printable format that looks good.

- *Color:* The mapping of screen color to printer color might be terrible. Report this. Programmers may alter a standard system level driver to improve the color mapping, or they may send special color values to the driver that depend on which printer the program knows is installed. Thereafter, you must test this printer driver as a separate class. It has been altered from the standard.

- *Output formats:* The program might have to work with different sizes of paper, such as letter, legal, A3, and A4, and possibly custom sizes. It might have to print onto specific forms or print data into specific places on the page. For each paper size or print layout, you have two classes of paper to consider: cut sheet (single pages for laser and other printers) and continuous, tractor-feed paper. The two types of paper have different issues relating to horizontal and vertical margins preset by the printer. Test the layouts in the different fonts supported by the program. Beyond that, it's probably not necessary to test all paper sizes or layouts on all printers. Test each paper or layout carefully on one printer from each class. If these work, tests on the other printers will probably (not always, but probably) pass too.

- *Expensive forms and paper:* If the program must print on special, expensive forms, don't test on those forms until you're fairly sure that the program works. Until then, test on blank paper and compare the print positions to the form, or print on a photocopy of the form.

- *Text and graphic positioning:* Page printers have an unprintable zone around the top and sides of the paper. Many inkjets have a big dead zone along the sides of the page. (The unprintable zones of compatible printers are not always the same.) Does the program let you place text or graphics where they can't be printed?

- *Streaking, banding, odd unintended fill patterns:* Your program's and the printer's graphic algorithms may interact to produce occasional very odd results. If a filled object (like a big, grey square) looks odd when printed (typically on a page printer), don't assume that the problem is with the printer, such as a bad toner cartridge. Not even if the programmers tell you that must be the problem. Check it by generating and printing the same image with a different program.

## SAVING, SHARING, AND REUSING YOUR PRINTER KNOWLEDGE

Individual testers build up private knowledge about specific printers. They discover that some printers are fully compatible, that others claimed to be compatible are not, that one model in a line of printers has weaker error handling than the rest, that particular bugs are commonly found when testing with particular printers. Technical support staff also build up printer knowledge, from their own reading and from the many customers who call to complain about the program's compatibility with their printer. Programmers, project managers, and other members of the development team also learn very specific, useful things about individual printers.

Tester after tester relearns the same information the hard way, by wasting time testing fully compatible printers or by missing bugs in many ways.

It's important to make it easy to share this information. We suggest a central printer database, available to developers, testers, marketers, and support staff. Each record describes an individual printer, or a group of compatible printers normally supported by a single driver. Fixed fields might contain printer capability information such as the printer type, the fonts supported by the printer, etc. (Be cautious about making too many fixed fields or no one will fill in the record.) Then there are long, free form fields, as many as needed, for people to record their experiences with the printer. They might summarize a magazine review's comments about the printer, or their test results, or the results of research they made in response to a customer call, or compatibility information or testing tips provided to a developer by the printer manufacturer. Insist that each entry have a name and date.

---

*Over time, a printer (or other configuration) database can become a significant corporate resource.*

---

It is very important to make it easy for many different people to enter and look up this information. It is foolish to hoard the information in a database that is private to the Testing Group or to one individual printer expert. Maybe knowledge is power, but few people will contribute much to a database that they have limited access to, nor will many people benefit much from it.

## SOME TIPS ON AUTOMATED TESTING

The printer testing strategy limits the testing investment, but often at the expense of the product schedule. At some point you finally test all those drivers and compatible printers and find lots of bugs. The earlier you do this testing, the more program changes (e.g., bug fixes) get made after your tests. Since late changes have an annoying habit of screwing up the printer you'd least expect to be affected, you end up having to retest the printers, perhaps many times. From the viewpoint of testing efficiency, the later you do the printer testing, the better.

**8**

PRINTERS &
OTHER DEVICES

Unfortunately, when you finally do the first wave(s) of printer testing, you spring dozens of bugs on the programmers. If you save printer testing for the last minute, you probably destroy the product schedule. The threat of a blown schedule gives the project manager an ulcer from waiting for you to start testing printers. So from the viewpoint of the project manager and the project schedule, the sooner you start printer testing, the better.

You should start testing all those printers sooner rather than later, so plan for retesting the printers a few times. (You should still test printers in the order we suggest. Otherwise you'll retest them even more times.)

To avoid wasting too much time on printer testing, you should try to automate, and we provide some tips. However, be warned of four risks:

### Four risks of automated print testing

- *Beware of spending so much time automating* everything that you could have done all the testing faster by not automating anything. Don't fall in love with technology.

- *Beware of generating output that you don't properly review.* Don't generate tons of output that you don't have time to review. Keep tests simple and to the point to reduce the amount of output. Don't expect an untrained contractor to be able or motivated to run the tests and review the output properly.

  Don't let passing test results look like failing test results or you'll miss bugs when you review the output, no matter how motivated you are.

- *Beware of missing bugs associated with printing.* Look for bugs on the screen when the print-related commands are issued. Look for bugs during printing (what if you click the mouse or fool with the keyboard?). If the program can format or update data while it prints, look for data corruption. Look at program functioning after printing is complete. Remember, printing often involves swapping in a printer overlay, or allocating a big data buffer. It's easy to overwrite the wrong part of the program, or to write past the edge of the buffer, or to lay the buffer over top of some key data. Some effects of printing might not be seen until later, when the program finally tries to execute the corrupted code, or use the corrupted data.

- *Beware of rigidity.* Don't just run the same old printer tests time after time. The programmers will eventually fix all the bugs that you can find with these tests. To find new bugs, you'll need new tests. On a regular basis, use the program in a useful or fun way and print the results. It's amazing how many new bugs appear when you use the program to achieve something that you want. This doesn't replace formal, planned testing, but it is a powerful and necessary supplement.

### Where to save time and improve test reliability

Printer testing involves four time-consuming tasks. First, there is planning and developing the test. Second, you have to find the printer, (perhaps you have to borrow it from a friend or coworker), then check its DIP switches and front panel settings, and connect it to the test machine. After you run the test, you have to put the printer away. If you borrowed it, you must reset the switches before you give it back. This setup and teardown time may take as much as ten times as long as the actual test. The third task is running the test. The fourth task is evaluating the output. This section considers ways to save time in each of the four tasks. They all work, but they're not all compatible. You will make choices.

### The test files

Our main suggestion for test file design is to make everything obvious.

- *Make text attributes obvious.* If text should be in boldface, print something like:

  **This is boldface.** This is not boldface. **This is boldface.** This is not boldface.
  **This is boldface.** This is not boldface. **This is boldface.** This is not boldface.
  **This is boldface.** This is not boldface. **This is boldface.** This is not boldface.

  Normal. *Italics.* **Bold.** ***Bold italics.*** Normal. *Italics.* **Bold.** ***Bold italics***
  Normal. *Italics.* **Bold.** ***Bold italics.*** Normal. *Italics.* **Bold.** ***Bold italics***
  Normal. *Italics.* **Bold.** ***Bold italics.*** Normal. *Italics.* **Bold.** ***Bold italics***

  The repeating patterns make the output easier for a person to analyze quickly.

- *Make margins obvious.* If you can print a border on a page to show where the margins are, do it. If you can't print a graphic box to show the margins, fill the page with text. Make the text useful:

  ```
  123456789a123456789b123456789c123456789d123456789e
  223456789a123456789b123456789c123456789d123456789e
  323456789a123456789b123456789c123456  89d123456789e
  423456789a123456789b123456789c123456789d123456789e
  ```

  Because everything is numbered, you can tell that the blank is on the third line, in the 37th position and that the lines all end after 50 characters. This is *so* much easier than counting characters. *Never* make yourself count characters.

- *Fill data fields with numbers, with real data, and with boundary data.* Use numbers (e.g., `123456789a123`) to show the length of the field. You see where printing starts and ends; if it prints `456789a123`, you know that the first three characters were lost. If you see `123456789a`, you know that the last three characters were lost. If you see `1a23987456`, you know that something is weird.

You might print `A23456789a123` in the first field and `B23456789a123` in the second, using first letters (or put letters in the middle) to check whether the right number string is printed into the right field.

You might use a standard end-of-field character to show at a glance that the whole field was printed: `A23456789a12X`, `B23456789a12X`. Or use the same letter that you used at the start of the field, perhaps in lowercase to catch wraparound bugs: `A23456789a12a`, `B23456789a12b`.

Use real data (names, phone numbers, poetry, whatever is normally supposed to appear in the field) so you can see how output will normally look. This is your best gauge of attractiveness and readability of the output.

**8**

PRINTERS &
OTHER DEVICES

## PRINTER TESTING
### SOME TIPS ON AUTOMATED TESTING
#### Where to save time and improve test reliability
##### *The test files*

When testing proportional fonts, print short text and long text. Here are 20 proportionally spaced *i*'s and *W*'s:

iiiiiiiiiiiiiiiiiiii

WWWWWWWWWWWWWWWWWWWW

Occasionally someone asks how they can possibly fill the same field with numbers, normal output, narrow output (like *i*'s), and wide output (like *W*'s). Easy. Print four records. Each one has different data. Or print four pictures or four files.

### Reducing setup and teardown time

You can reduce setup and teardown time by having all the printers handy in the lab, connected to switch boxes,which are in turn connected to test computers. This is how the big kids do it. Turn the switch, turn on the power, and you're ready to test. We'll talk more about the laboratory later.

If you aren't one of the big kids, your best way to reduce setup time is to print to each printer as few times as possible. Obviously, one way to achieve this is to test the printers at the very end of the project after all the non-printer bugs in the program have been fixed, but the project manager won't (or shouldn't) let you get away with this. And so, the question is, since you're going to have to test a printer five times over the course of the project, how do you do it without having to connect and disconnect the printer five times?

- *Print to disk:* Early in development, ask the programmer to include a print to disk function. This is a simple redirection of the output to a disk file. The file must include all printer control codes. If you redirect output from an Okidata 82 to a disk file, you must be able to copy this file to the Okidata and get the same printout that you would have gotten by printing from the program directly to the printer.

  When you do your first round of printer testing, print to the disk as well as to the printer. Next time, print the same files to the disk and compare the first output files with the second. If the files match, tests that were passed before have been passed again, and bugs that were found before have not yet been fixed. If the files differ, something has changed. Now it's worth connecting the printer to see what happened. (By the way, you don't have to rerun the program. Just copy the output file to the printer. This is often much faster than regenerating the output.)

- *Test many printer selections on one compatible printer*. Suppose the Epson FX-86e and the Panasonic 1191 are perfectly compatible printers. Don't reconnect each one each time you retest printing. Connect one of the two, then select the Epson FX-86e from your printer menu and run your tests. Then select the Panasonic 1191 from your printer menu and run the tests again. You print to the same printer both times, but since one printer is essentially the same as the other, you'll see bad output as well on one as on the other.

Sometime during testing, you are well advised to test both printers. Heaven help you if the two printers aren't as compatible as you thought, but you don't discover it in testing because of a shortcut. Your printer compatibility database (see "Saving, sharing, and reusing your printer knowledge" earlier in this chapter) will be invaluable here, as a summary of the compatibility knowledge of everyone in your group and everyone in customer support.

- *Evaluate test output as it comes out of the printer.* If you evaluate the output while the printer is connected, you can run followup tests when you find a bug. You can check the DIP switch settings if you haven't already done so. You can answer whatever questions the anomalous printout leads you to ask. On the other hand, if you evaluate a big stack of test output that you generated last week, for every followup test you'll have to reconnect the printer. Either your followup testing suffers or you waste time.

- *Test printers on the network.* Programmers, testers, and tech support staff often have oddball printers connected locally to their networked computer. You save setup and teardown time by running test cases on these computers. Install the program on the network server and you can run it on any compatible computer connected to the network.

### Reducing test execution time

If you print less, it takes less time, but you shouldn't make a strong test weaker by shortening it just for the sake of shortening it. When you have good tests that you don't wish to shorten, you can still limit the time you spend babysitting the printer.

First, test on more than one printer at once. Test on as many printers as you can effectively control. Effective control means that you have time to walk from printer to printer (computer to computer) inspecting results or starting the next test, without missing an error or making a mistake setting up, recording, or running the test.

Second, have the programmer build in command line control for test automation. The program will probably need the following parameters: name of the input file that the program is to print, name of the output file if printing is to be redirected to a file, name of the printer (possibly including the printer driver) and setup information such as the initial font or printer output resolution. The program should exit after printing. Given this facility, you can build a batch file that does the following:

- feeds a file to the program, selects the printer, and tells it to print the file to disk
- compares the file to one saved previously
- if there's a difference between the files, prints the new one
- feeds the next file to the program, prints, compares, etc.

With this capability, you can easily set up a set of test files that will keep the computer busy all night (after go home). You can print many test files to the same printer or to many different printers by redirecting output to them to the disk. If ten printers on the program's menu are fully compatible, connect one of these printers to the computer, then use the batch file to print to this printer, telling the program that it's printing to each of the ten compatible printers in turn. The menu selections are all compatible if they all make the same printer print the same things the same way. All of this kind of tedious work you can set up to run automatically.

**8**

PRINTERS &
OTHER DEVICES

**PRINTER TESTING**
  SOME TIPS ON AUTOMATED TESTING
    **Where to save time and improve test reliability**
      *Improving test evaluation*

### Improving test evaluation

Print tests aren't worth much if they miss bugs or if they reveal bugs but you miss them while scanning the output. It is too easy to miss bugs when scanning a big stack of output. You must plan carefully to catch the problems your tests reveal.

- *Make everything obvious.* We covered this while describing test file design.

- *Don't print anything you don't need.* For example, if you compare last week's test output file with this week's and the files match, don't print the test documents again. There's no point; you analyzed them last week. Nothing has changed. Instead, just print a comment that File X and File Y were compared and they match. Don't print extra pages, extra sentences, extra fields, extra anything. The bugs can't hide in the crowd if there's no crowd to hide in.

- *Print comparison pass results on the left, failures on the right* or do *something* to make obvious any errors that the batch file or program detects

- *When two test files don't match,* print the old one and the new one (and label them). Make it easy to compare the files and see the difference.

- *Evaluate output as it comes out of the printer.* Don't wait till this afternoon or next month to evaluate the printout. Be prepared to look at the output, decide whether it's any good, then do followup tests on the spot if you see a problem.

- *Run some tests interactively just to see them interactively.* Don't rely exclusively on automated tests or you'll never notice that the screen flashes obscenities in pink and purple halfway through each print job.

- *Make sure that some data are meaningful.* Output looks different when you print normal text or graphics instead of test patterns. Usually it looks better. If it looks worse (as it sometimes does), figure out what looks wrong and submit some Design Issue reports. Apart from aesthetics, you might not notice some problems, such as transposed lines, until you print some text and read it.

### Keep your output

Keep interim printouts until you ship the product. Keep final printouts (the last set of printouts you obtained from each printer you tested) for years. Some companies keep many interim printouts for years too. These document the actual compatibilities of the shipping product and they will be handy in many different ways. For example, tech support groups often find these printouts useful for comparing a customer's printouts with the results you got from a specific printer in the lab. Also, you can use them when you develop the next release of the program—printer by printer you can check whether specific output imperfections are new to the latest version.

## SETTING UP A PRINTER TEST LAB

You can spend a fortune setting up a printer test lab. We assume that you have some money to spend, but not a fortune. We assume that you're interested in efficiency, and will spend some money to reduce labor costs, but that you would rather spend your money on a trip to Hawaii than on more printers, shelving, and lab equipment.

### Getting printers on loan

No one buys all the printers they test. They buy the models they will constantly need to test. For the others, they get loaners for 30, 45, or 90 days from the printer manufacturers. (If you own a perfectly good printer that never appears in any program's menus, it's probably because the printer company won't send out loaners. No one will list a printer in their program that they can't test, and no one sane will buy a printer for testing unless adding that printer to the menu will generate at least enough added profit to pay for the purchase and warehousing of the machine.)

Many printer manufacturers have ISV (Independent Software Vendor) programs. If you're developing software for mass market resale or non-profit distribution, call your favorite printer manufacturers, tell them you're developing software for publication, and that you want to test your product's compatibility with some of their printers. Can you borrow these printers (be prepared to list the model names) for testing? Expect to repeat yourself to a few different people. Explain politely that you can't afford to buy one of every printer from every manufacturer, not even these wonderful printers from this delightful company. Eventually, if there is an ISV contact or administrator (usually in Sales or Marketing), you'll finally reach the right person.

Call many weeks in advance, so that you have time to receive, fill out, and return paperwork that proves that you are who you say you are and not just some smart college kid who's figured out a way to get free printers. Expect the company to lose the first copy of your paperwork and to take a while to read the second copy, before (finally) sending (some of) the requested printers.

Many printer companies also publish books or looseleaf notebooks showing all the switch settings and every command for every printer they make. You can get these free or for a modest fee once you've proved you're a development house. Ask for them. Some companies forget to mention them until you ask.

On a 90-day loan, it is wise and courteous to send test output from the printer to the lending company no later than 60 days after you receive the printer. Just write a note to the ISV administrator that thanks him for the loan of the printer, names the program being tested, and says here's some sample output from the printer. Don't forget to include the printout. This letter will make the administrator *much* more willing to extend your loan for another 90 days if you haven't finished testing on time.

A wise and courteous test group sends a free copy of the published program and a note of thanks to printer manufacturers who loaned printers as soon as the program is published. These letters and sample products have a big effect on the lending company—a few of them from different developers can make the difference between continuing and discontinuing the ISV program. These letters with product also sometimes result in joint marketing offers.

We wish we could list the main printer companies with ISV programs and their contacts, but the research that has generated our lists is proprietary—it belongs to our employers and we cannot print it here. Get a copy of Juliussen and Juliussen's annual *Computer Industry Almanac*. It lists lots of printer manufacturers. So does *PC Magazine*'s annual printer issue. Spilker and Strudwick (1992) and Churilla (1991) are also useful.

**8**

PRINTERS &

OTHER DEVICES

Don't suppose that only printers can be borrowed. Whether something is hardware or software, if proven compatibility with your product could boost its sales, call its manufacturer to arrange a loan.

### Organizing the lab

If you have a few (or many) test computers and printers, organize them efficiently. Make it easy to run a test on any printer, with a minimum of setup time. If you've never seen a well organized print lab, you might not realize how big a difference it makes. To convince yourself (or to convince an executive), tour some of the stereo stores in your area. They have the same needs in their listening rooms, connecting receivers, tape decks, amplifiers, etc. to each other and to speakers. Watch how smoothly salespeople and technicians can work in the well organized stores and how long it takes to get the right sound out of the right speakers in the poorly organized stores.

- *Put printers on sturdy shelves*. This gets you much more room per square foot of floor space. Space shelves enough apart vertically to make it easy to work with each printer. Leave enough room to the left and right of each printer and between its back and the wall that no printer overheats from poor air circulation for its fan. Also, leave enough room to make it easy to turn on the printer, to reach its switches or cables, and to feed paper.

- *Space racks a safe distance apart. Avoid clutter on the floor.* You *will* have power failures in the building. There are no windows in the printer lab. Make absolutely sure that you can always walk safely to the door in the dark, from any place in the lab, without any chance of tripping over anything. There's probably a governmental safety code that specifies how far apart shelves have to be for a safe walkway. You company's facilities manager can probably tell you the minimum legal value. If you don't have a facilities manager, ask your human resources manager. She might not know the answer, but because this is an employee safety issue, she should know how to find out.

- *The printers should be ready to print.* They should be loaded with paper. For dot matrix printers, trays make it easier to load paper and catch output. Good ones cost as little as $10. Each printer should be cabled (serial or parallel, plus electric power), plugged in, and ready to run. (We strongly recommend surge protected power strips.)

- Use *switch boxes*. Connect four or more printers to each computer through a switch box. With a switch box, you plug the box's cable into the computer, where you would normally plug the printer. Then plug cables from many printers into the box. Turn the switch to a different position to select a different printer. When the computer prints, it prints through the selected printer. If you pick four fairly different printers per computer, you can probably keep each computer occupied throughout most of your printer testing.

  Some programs have problems when connected to a printer through a switch box. They expect return signals from the printer that don't make it back through the box. This is a problem, but it's one that many customers will have too. Lots of people use switch boxes. Make the program work with the boxes and you'll not only test more efficiently, you'll also save all those customer support calls.

- *If you can't connect all your printers to computers,* connect the most commonly tested ones and put the others in a safe, easy to reach place. Leave open space on shelves near the computers to make it easy to swap these less used printers in and out. Don't store printers in stacks, one printer stacked on top of another, because you'll break the machines this way. Store them safely or get rid of them.

- *Invest in some roll-around carts or tables.* Testers and programmers will want to take a few printers or a printer and test computer out of the lab, to do prolonged testing at their own desks. These carts make it easy to move the equipment, and provide a place to keep the equipment when it's in the person's office or cubicle.

- *Fix what breaks.* It takes an amazingly long time to fix a printer. The repair shop never has the right parts and the manufacturer's local warehouse just ran out of the parts you need. The technician trained to fix this type of printer just quit. The new technician will break something else trying to fix the original problem, and those parts are out of stock too. Too many products have shipped without testing on a particular printer because the test lab didn't send the printer out for repairs until a month before alpha testing started and the printer came back two weeks after final testing ended.

- *Keep reasonable supplies on hand.* Keep a small supply of spare ribbons, toner, ink cartridges, paper, etc. The last thing you need is printer that won't work until you add paper or ink, especially since this always happens on a weekend you set aside for printer testing, just after the stores close. Spare ribbons are handy even if the printers will work with the old ribbon, because heavy testing wears out ribbons quickly. Unreadably faint output is wasted work. Hard to read output causes missed bugs.

- *Photocopy your manuals and archive the originals.* Printer manuals disappear at an alarming rate. They are hard to replace. They are absolutely essential. Don't work with the originals. Copy the originals, lock them up, and work with the copies.

- *Label the printers.* Show the standard switch settings for all of the key emulation modes that you test.

- *Protect your ears.* Impact printers, like dot matrix printers, are often loud. When many of them print at the same time, the noise is louder. Prolonged exposure to loud noise causes permanent hearing damage (Miller, 1978). The hearing loss is usually gradual; by the time you realize you have a problem, you're stuck with it for the rest of your life.

For advice on measuring sound levels in your lab and on the laws requiring your company to help you protect your hearing, call OSHA or your state's equivalent department of occupational safety and health.

**8**

PRINTERS &
OTHER DEVICES

# LOCALIZATION TESTING

## THE REASON FOR THIS CHAPTER

Translation and export of software is becoming more common; you'll probably be involved with at least one translation over the next few years. Unfortunately, Americans are still naive about translating software. There is a whole lot more to localizing a product than changing the words from one language to another.

This chapter describes many of the changes that must be made to the program in the process of localization. The most common error in localizing products is to miss necessary changes, so your first task is to check that everything actually got done. This list of localization requirements should also be a springboard for your test planning: given that the program changed in the following ways, what bugs might have crept in? The chapter also includes some specific testing recommendations.

Our discussion implicitly assumes translation to West European languages, but the same issues (and more) arise with other languages. The references discuss localization to many other countries. We also cast the discussion in terms of the IBM DOS environment because we know localization issues on this one best.

## USEFUL REFERENCES

Most systems companies are releasing guides for localization *development.* For example, read:

- IBM's *National Language Information and Design Guide* (1987, 1990)

- Apple's (1992) *Guide to Macintosh Software Localization,* and *Software Development for International Markets* and *Macintosh Worldwide Development: Guide to System Software.*

- Digital Equipment Corp.'s *Developing International User Information* (Jones, Kennelly, Mueller, Sweezy, Thomas, & Velez, 1992) and *Digital Guide to Developing International Software* (1991).

- Microsoft's *Microsoft Windows International Handbook for Software Design.*

- The *OSF/Motif Style Guide* (1990) contains some information on localizing Motif.

Several books on localization are just being published. Carter (1990) is a good nuts and bolts source on localizing Macintosh products. We've benefited from drafts of Uren, Howard & Perinotti (*in press*, 1993).

The best discussion of *localization testing* that we've seen is in Microsoft's *Microsoft Windows International Handbook for Software Design.*

Finally, international software design and development are the topics of various ISO (International Standards Organization) standards. For example, ISO's Technical Committee 159, Sub-Committee 4, Working Group 5 is developing software ergonomics standards. These include standards for help systems, menus, dialogs, and many other aspects of user interface design. Once these standards are approved, nonconforming products probably won't be importable into the European Community. Read Pat Billingsley's column, *The Standards Factor,* in Association for Computing Machinery's magazine *SIGCHI Bulletin* for updates on the development of this and many other standards. The 88open Consortium (1991) has also published an outline of the key UNIX-relevant standards and how to get them.

Localization is the process of adapting software for a new place. It might involve a change of language, but it doesn't have to. There's often a lot of work to do to make an American product suitable to a British market, for example. Along with changing the language, you have to adapt to the culture too. The localizer is the person who does or manages the translation and other adaptation of the program to the new market.

## WAS THE BASE CODE CHANGED?

This is the first question you need to have answered when you plan testing of a localized product. Some products are made easily localizable in their English version. To translate the text, change the units of measurement, etc., all the localizer must do is reset options in the program and change data (such as text) in external files. The program itself is never recompiled or relinked. It's safest to do a fairly thorough functionality test during translation to the first new language, but for subsequent translations (if the first test results found bugs only in localization areas) you can probably focus testing to the international issues and test other parts of the code lightly and briefly.

Other programs require recoding during localization. Localized versions of these are new versions, with many new features added. Anything can break when you add new features to a program. Expect more bugs and plan for a full functionality test. Each new translation will require new code. The programmers will get practiced at localizing a program after the first or second time and make far fewer bugs, but they are still adding and changing code, recompiling and relinking code. You should check overall functionality of each new localized version.

It is fashionable to criticize products that are not originally created with built-in easy localizability. Think twice before joining this criticism. Choosing whether to add localizability features to the original American version or to add them as needed to any translation is a tough business decision. During the localization phase it is more expensive to develop and test a localized version of strictly American code. However, an American version that doesn't worry about offshore compatibility features can come to the American market sooner, at a lower initial development and testing cost, and the American code will probably be smaller and faster because it doesn't have all the non-American baggage coded in.

## WORK WITH SOMEONE FLUENT IN THE LANGUAGE.

You can tell when something was translated from Japanese or Korean into English by someone who is not perfectly fluent in the language. Translations from English to other languages are just as obviously bad. Of course (?) your product's translator will be perfectly fluent in both languages and in the technical terminology. The point here is that someone involved in the testing must also be fluent, preferably a native of the country you're localizing the program for, and a native speaker of that country's language.

## IS THE TEXT INDEPENDENT FROM THE CODE?

If the product will be translated into more than one language, its text has probably been separated from the code. Don't take the programmer's word that this has been done. Look inside the file, or use a utility that strips text strings out of a binary file. You may well find that critical error messages remain—it's a bit difficult to read "Disk I/O failure" from a resource file when you need it.

It is not impossible to translate critical error messages, even if it is impossible or unwise to pull them out to a resource file. All the programmer or translator has to do is patch the object code (the executable program file). You need some elegance? Get the programmer to write a short editing tool that finds strings in the object code, lets the translator overwrite them but stops him from entering a string longer than the original, and null terminates the string if necessary.

## TRANSLATED TEXT EXPANDS

Several languages, especially German, require more space for brief messages and command names than English. Figure 9.1 shows IBM's estimates of normal growths during translation, assuming there are no abbreviations in the English text.

Text can overflow menus or dialog boxes. Abbreviations to fit text in the boxes might be unacceptable. Text strings might overflow internal storage, overwriting other code or data. Text strings might overwrite each other onscreen. Menus may grow so wide that you can't fit them all onscreen.

**Figure 9.1 How much a typical message grows during translation**

| English Length | Additional space |
|---|---|
| up to 10 characters | 101-200% |
| 11-20 characters | 81-100% |
| 21-30 characters | 61-100% |
| 31-50 characters | 41-60% |
| 51-70 characters | 31-40% |
| over 70 characters | 30% |

## CHARACTER SETS

We aren't going to try to fully explain code pages here, but you should probably learn something about them. MS-DOS testers will find the Microsoft MS-DOS 5 manual very useful.

In brief, a typical character set contains 254 characters, numbered from 1 through 254. *ASCII* (American Standard Code for Information Interchange) defines which characters are numbered from 32 through 127. Most character sets include the ASCII characters and define the symbols that will be numbered from 0 through 31 (*low ASCII*) and from 128 to 255 (*high ASCII*). Calling these extended ranges "ASCII" is common but it is incorrect because there is no single standard character set from 1 to 254.

Some character sets are well known and in common use. Of these, a few are called code pages and are numbered. Technically, any symbol set that associates symbols for each number from 1 to 254 is a code page. We mean something more narrow than this. The numbered code pages are particular, well known symbol sets in use across many countries and computers. For example, code page 437 is the standard character set in ROM on American and German machines. Code page 850 is an ISO standard international set, in use in most European countries.

The *National Language Information and Design Guide* and MS-DOS manuals provide tables of common code pages. Microsoft Windows uses its own ANSI character set. (The *OEM character sets* referred to in Windows books are the MS-DOS code pages.) Apple machines also come with their own character set.

Be sure that the character set used by your program is commonly used where you plan to sell the program. IBM assigns *primary* and *secondary* code pages to each country. Does this mean that both are in common use in some countries? What if the customer's computer is set up to use one but not the other? Will your high ASCII characters (such as accented letters) display correctly in both character sets? (Not necessarily— compare the code page tables.)

You might ask whether a pair of code pages numbered and defined by IBM are the main code pages in use in a given country. There are European computer manufacturers. Have any of them defined code pages of their own? (For example understand that this is a problem with code pages designed for Greece.)

## KEYBOARDS

The customer's computer will have a keyboard appropriate to his country. (Compaq's DOS manuals have good pictures of keyboard layouts; so do the localization guides from Apple). The customer's computer will be set up to interpret keycodes from the keyboard according to a character set that is appropriate to that country. A German keyboard has characters like ä and ö. A French keyboard lacks square [] brackets. Greek keyboards switch between a Greek character set and an English set. Scandinavian keyboards let you type characters, such as œ, that are not defined in the character set closest to a general set for Western Europe (code page 850). The program you're testing might not support the Scandinavian keys, but it must do something reasonable when you type one of them.

There is no substitute for testing with the target country's keyboard, with your computer's system software (and your program) set for that country. Some keyboards support another Shift key, marked <Alt-Gr>. This provides access to the third character shown on the keycap. Non-US keyboards also support *dead keys*. When you hit a dead key (an accent symbol), nothing appears on screen until you hit the next letter. Then you see the letter, with the accent. Does the program recognize <Alt-Gr> and dead keys?

One last character set issue: the program should give the customer access to off-keyboard characters (otherwise how will an Italian address a letter to a German colleague?) Make sure that if the program displays the alternate (control, upper ASCII) characters, it displays the right ones, and you get the right ones when you select them.

## TEXT FILTERS

The program may accept only certain characters in a field, perhaps blocking upper ASCII and various control codes. This is appropriate for English but may exclude valid non-English characters.

Test how the program accepts and displays every character, in every place in which you can enter characters. Just because a program handles upper ASCII when you enter main body text doesn't mean that it will work well with footnotes, file names, search and replace strings, or macro names.

## LOADING, SAVING, IMPORTING, AND EXPORTING HIGH AND LOW ASCII

Create test files with all 255 characters, or with the subset of these that your program supports. Save the files. Load them under different code pages and see what you get. Display and print them to confirm that the characters are coming in correctly.

Save full character sets to every file format that the program supports, and read them from every file format the program supports. Programs often mishandle one or two formats out of a larger group.

Check that your program can import and export these characters. Pay attention to characters below 32 because they also have meanings as control codes. They might be taken as instructions rather than data by printers, file managers, other editors, or by your program when it imports a file with these characters in it.

When you test importing, make sure you test European versions of the programs you support, not just the American ones. For example, suppose you localize a product for the French market and that your program will import files from WordStar. Don't just test the English version. Test with a copy of the French version, if there is one. Similarly, if you expect PageMaker to be able to read your files, try to test with a French version of PageMaker.

## OPERATING SYSTEM LANGUAGE

Do wildcard symbols or file name delimiters vary from language to language? What about file naming conventions, file name filters, and names of common operating system commands?

## HOT KEYS

The hot key is an underlined, boldfaced or otherwise highlighted character in a menu item, such as X in eXit. Pressing that key selects the item, which is a touch faster than highlighting the choice and selecting it. Are the hot key choices reasonable in the translated product? Do they work? Are there any residuals: do any hot keys (e.g., X) from the original product have their old effect even though they no longer appear on the menu? Along with hot keys, think about *menu accelerator keys* and *predefined function keys*. Should they change across translations? Did they change? Are there residuals?

## GARBLED IN TRANSLATION

Messages might be built from fragments. Fragments might include commonly used groups of words that the program will reuse in many messages. Also there are file names and data values that the program inserts into an error message to make it more descriptive. The odds are good that you can't combine the same fragments successfully in the same ways from language to language. Look for nonsense combinations or bad orderings of text.

## ERROR MESSAGE IDENTIFIERS

No matter how well you structure technical support in other countries, they will have to pass some queries back to head office. Much gets lost in the translation and second-, third-, or fourth-hand description of the customer's problem. The program can help a little by adding a unique identifier to every error message and warning. Just tack a number in parentheses at the end of each message, like (23). Check that the same number stays with the same message in every language and update version of the product.

## HYPHENATION RULES

Hyphenation rules are not the same across languages and can differ across dialects (British versus U.S. dialects of English). In a few languages, spelling of a few words changes when you hyphenate the word. Does your program hyphenate these correctly? Does it unhyphenate correctly?

## SPELLING RULES

Spelling rules vary across dialects of the same language. If your product includes a spell checker, does it check spelling correctly?

## SORTING RULES

Character sorting rules vary from country to country. Sorts by internal code values (e.g., ASCII sorts) make absolutely no sense in many languages. A good sorting routine groups letters with the same accents together, such as all î's before ì's. And some languages treat two letters as one for sorting purposes. For example, the ll in llama is treated as one letter in Spanish. Also, rules for sorting names vary across countries. d'Allessio may be sorted as Allessio, van Essen as Essen, del Zoppo as Zoppo.

## UPPERCASE AND LOWERCASE CONVERSION

Only in English is case conversion correctly done by adding or subtracting 32 to the letter. Beware of case conversion errors in search dialogs and any other text pattern matching.

## UNDERSCORING RULES

Underlining conventions differ from country to country. It can be poor form to underscore punctuation, spaces, and other characters.

## PRINTERS

Many printers sold in Europe are essentially the same as printers in the U.S. Relative market shares differ, so some important machines in Europe don't matter in the U.S. (and vice versa). There are also European-made printers.

Printers have character sets in ROM and some printers accept downloaded characters. Lasers and laser-like inkjets are more flexible this way than dot matrix and dot matrix-like inkjets. If you are planning to support a certain printer, check what character sets it supports when (if) sold in Europe. The same model of printer may have different character ROMs in different countries.

If the printer does not directly support the standard code pages, how will your program print, on that printer, in the character set the customer wants? As a tester, you don't have to design the answer to this, but you do have to get the answer from the project manager and make sure it works.

## SIZES OF PAPER

Europe generally uses DIN standard sizes, especially A3 and A4. Note that the single-sheet and tractor-fed versions of these paper sizes are slightly different. Test with both. By the way, are your default margins correct for each paper for each country?

## CPU'S AND VIDEO

We think that anyone selling in the MS-DOS market in Europe should test on Olivetti and Amstrad equipment. Don't write your test schedule assuming that the program will pass configuration testing on these machines the first time through. Check for video cards and modes that don't have perfect American analogs.

## RODENTS

In the MS-DOS market, the mouse driver is a separate product. When you buy a pointing device and driver in the U.S., are you getting the same driver that is sold in Europe?

## DATA FORMATS AND SETUP OPTIONS

The customer should be able to set defaults for basic variables such as time display format, date display format, language in use (i.e., French, not COBOL), money formats, etc.

- *Time format* can be 12- or 24-hour clock, with colon or other separators. Dates may be displayed using different combinations of separators (dashes, spaces, slashes) and the order of the day, month, and year varies.

- *Numeric separator* usages differ from country to country. Where Americans put a comma, others put a decimal point or a space. Where we put the decimal point, others put a decimal comma. Expect to find many bugs in this code. Many subroutines that your programmers automatically link into their code will treat commas as separators between items in a list.

- *The # symbol* is not a universal symbol for "number." N° is also common, for example.

- *A negative number* isn't preceded by a dash in all languages. Bracketing conventions for negative numbers vary, too.

- *Money symbols* might go before or after (or in the middle) of the amount of money, and you might use a graphic symbol or a character string of up to three letters.

## RULERS AND MEASUREMENTS

No more measuring everything in inches. Metric measures (centimeters) are important. Picas are also appreciated. Rulers, tab dialogs, grids, and every other measure of length or height that is measured and displayed in any unit must be displayable in all of the program's units.

## CULTURE-BOUND GRAPHICS

Clip art, tool icons, the opening screen, the tutorial, manual, sample data files, packaging, and the marketing literature may all contain culture-bound graphics.

## CULTURE-BOUND OUTPUT

Non-Americans don't necessarily like their output printed in the same ways Americans do. Calendar formats vary. The appearance of a "standard" invoice varies. Address formats differ; so does the way people write them in their address books. Lots of things vary across cultures. Your European customer doesn't want her output to shout "Printed by an American Program!"

## EUROPEAN PRODUCT COMPATIBILITY

Not all software is designed and developed in the United States. If your product imports data from databases or spreadsheets or word processors, maybe you should check what locally developed products sell well in the target market. Is your localized product compatible with them?

## MEMORY AVAILABILITY

On DOS machines, international support steals memory. Programs that ran fine under the standard U.S. configuration (no code pages, no keyboard driver, no country.sys, no NLSFUNC program in the background) might not fit on a European-configured machine. At least on the first localized version of your product, test memory and out-of-memory handling very carefully.

## DO GUIS SOLVE THE PROBLEM?

Don't be naive. Just because the program is on a Macintosh or a Windows machine doesn't mean that it self-localizes. These environments make localization much easier. They take care of many of the issues raised here. But they don't do everything. Make your own list of localization requirements that is independent of the particular GUI's technical literature and the project specification (which was probably based on the technical literature). This chapter and the references at the start of it are good starting points for the list. Check the program against the list. Flag a bug every time you find a localization issue missed in the localized product.

## AUTOMATED TESTING

The localized program has essentially the same functionality and user interface as the American version. Most of the tests you can use on the American version are appropriate for European versions too, except for a difference in the text strings. This makes it very tempting to develop a large suite of automated regression tests while developing the American version, with the idea of using these tests for the localized versions.

Test automation *can* work under these circumstances, and if it works you'll be able to do more thorough testing than you otherwise might have been able to afford.

Microsoft (1990) recommends that when you use output comparison programs, you should capture and compare only the essential parts of the output. This restriction is necessary because the screen changes (different language) across versions. You want to spend as little time as you can updating your test scripts or analyzing test outputs flagged "bad" only because part of one screen was in English whereas part of the other was (correctly so) in Italian. However, anything you don't automatically compare between products must be independently tested.

Microsoft (1990), while recommending automated testing, also cautions:

- Your test developer probably has to know more about testing and localization issues than someone who tests manually and can learn subtleties on the job.

- Your test scripts can be sources of apparent bugs. You must check and carefully debug them before relying on them for testing a new language.

We strongly recommend automated testing whenever you are testing non-UI aspects of the program. For example, you can write an easy conversion utility to switch decimal points and decimal commas, and then check numeric output files. You can also set up automated comparisons of the saved and exported character set test files. Think creatively about tasks like these and you can save yourself significant amounts of time, especially if you plan to develop and test localized versions of your product for more than one language or country.

# TESTING USER MANUALS

**10**

## EFFECTIVE DOCUMENTATION

Documentation is fully effective when it provides the following benefits:

- *Improves usability.* A well-documented product is easier to use. Schneiderman (1987) reviews evidence that better documentation leads to faster learning, fewer errors, and better throughput (i.e., people get more work done).

- *Lowers customer support costs.* When one of your customers can't figure out how to use the product, she'll call for help (or for a refund). Telephone-based technical support is an expensive service. A good manual prevents many unnecessary support calls.

- *Improves reliability.* Unclear and inaccurate documentation makes the product less reliable because the people who use it make errors. Excellent documentation helps reduce the number of user errors, even (or especially) when the program's design is awkward.

- *Increases maintainability.* Much time and money is spent tracking down problems that turn out to be user errors. Many product changes merely repackage the same capabilities. They're made in the hope that people will finally understand how to use these capabilities and quit complaining that they aren't there or don't work. Better manuals reduce these problems substantially; poor documentation contributes to them (see Martin and McClure, 1983).

- *Improves installability.* Customers have to install software products on their computers. They may have to copy the software onto their systems, then customize it or load a special database that reflects their needs and equipment. Installation software is written last. Developers take it less seriously than other parts of the product because customers will install the product only once or twice. These routines get the least amount of testing and development support. However, your customer's first experience with the product is installation. Difficulties will lead to refunds and expensive technical support demands. Clear, correct installation instructions are among the most important parts of the documentation.

  Installation of some types of products (such as telephone systems) is so complex that customers hire an installer. As a rule, installers work with many different products. Don't expect them to be expert users or installers of your product. Expect them to have to look things up in the manual. The harder it is for them to find information, the more they have to charge the customer. Some vendors refuse to carry products that cost too much to install.

  Installation software also needs re-installation instructions. The manual must explain how to change options and how to upgrade from a previous version

- *Enhances salability.* Documentation quality is often a selling feature. It helps retail salespeople explain and demonstrate the product. It also plays a major role in many software reviews.

- *Reduces liability.* Your company makes a false claim about the program's capabilities when the manual says that the program does something that it doesn't. Your company misleads the reader when the manual says to do something in a way that doesn't work. Incorrect instructions cost the reader unnecessary time, effort, and mental anguish.

---

*It will not go over well if the company's attorney has to argue that the court shouldn't take the manuals seriously because no one in the company did.*

---

Engineering and marketing teams who don't take liability and honest advertising seriously are working on borrowed time.

## THE DOCUMENTATION TESTER'S OBJECTIVES

Reviewers of documentation are concerned with improving its accuracy, completeness, clarity, ease of use, and the degree to which it captures the spirit of the design. The documentation will have problems in all of these areas. Plan to test the manual, online help, and any other documentation many times.

As a tester working with the manual (or help), you are responsible for checking the technical accuracy of every word. There is no substitute for a thorough, thoughtful comparison between the claims and implications in the manual and the actual behavior of the running program. This is what you do. (As a side benefit, you find lots of bugs this way too.)

Be on the lookout for confusions in the writing. Many of them stem from confusions and complexities inherent in the product's design. The writers must describe the product as it is. You can help them substantially by pressing for changes that make the program more documentable (and more usable).

Look out, too, for missing features. Writers work from specifications, notes, and rumors. Developers try to keep writers up to date, but sometimes they forget to mention recently added features. You often discover changes much sooner than the writer—make sure these get into the manual. And don't assume that they got into the help text just because they got into the manual. These are probably being written by different people; updating information can easily get lost.

Realize that you are a reviewer, not the writer. Most testers who think they know more about writing than the writer are wrong. You have no more right to demand changes in the manual than in the program. It is your responsibility to find and identify problems, but after giving them a fair hearing, writer and programmer alike can choose not to follow your suggestions.

In particular, you have no authority to *demand* stylistic changes. The writer can reject stylistic suggestions without justifying her decisions to you. Making decisions about style is what she (not you) is paid to do.

You probably won't use a formal problem reporting system with the writer. Most comments will be on a marked up copy of the manual. Keep a copy of your comments and compare the next draft's changes to them. Talk with the writer about editing and commenting conventions. What can you adopt easily that would be helpful to her? For example, some proofreader's marks are useful. It also pays to ask for feedback about the comments you've made. Were they useful?

## HOW TESTING DOCUMENTATION CONTRIBUTES TO SOFTWARE RELIABILITY

Many testers skimp on documentation testing because they think it somehow detracts from their "real" job, which is testing the program. They are sorely mistaken.

- *You'll find more bugs than you expect.* Surprisingly many bugs show up when a competent tester thoroughly checks the manual (or help) against the program. The writer looks at the program from a different angle than the programmer and the tester, so the manual will reveal different problems than the ones programmers and testers look for. We've seen this happen on so many projects that we now take it for granted that tests of the manual will reveal many serious errors that other testing has not yet turned up.

  Documentation testing doesn't *always* reveal significant new problems. Testers who don't do a thorough job don't find many problems. A full test of the manual takes about an hour per three to five pages. Testers who speed through the material more quickly find much less in the book and in the program. We make a point of monitoring for this problem and retraining or reassigning staff to deal with it.

- *It's an important source of real world combination test cases.* You can't hope to test all the combinations of features or other options in the product; there are just too many. But you can test every combination that the manual describes as interesting or useful. Any time the manual even hints that two aspects of the program work well together, test them together.

- ***Bug reports arising out of documentation testing are particularly credible.*** The manual is your company's instruction to the customer on how to use the product. It's hard to dismiss a bug as "esoteric" when you report that the program failed while you were following the manual's instructions or suggestions, or were checking one of its statements of fact. These are mainstream tests. These are things many people will do. These are errors that magazine reviewers can publish without fear of correction. These bugs are hard to defer—either the manual will change or the program will change.

We've often seen previously deferred bugs reconsidered and fixed when they showed up again during testing of the manual.

In your main test of the manual, you should sit with it at the computer and:

- ***Use the program exactly as the manual says.*** Enter every keystroke in every example.

Customers make mistakes when they try to follow instructions. Feel free to make mistakes too. How does the computer respond? Bad error handling in the program will look worse when you show that it happens in response to an obvious, common mistake that several people will make when they try to follow the manual's instructions.

- ***Try every suggestion***, even if the suggestions aren't fully spelled out, step by step. Do what a reasonable customer would do who was trying to follow the suggestion.

- ***Check every statement of fact*** and every obvious inference from the stated facts, instructions, and suggestions. The manual is the product's final specification, and the customer's first place to check whether the program is working correctly.

It also pays to retest the documentation when you add a tester to the project. This keeps the manual current while the software is changing, and it educates new testers about the program. Consider assigning every new tester to work through the most recent draft of the manual as his first task.

## BECOME THE TECHNICAL EDITOR

If possible, the Testing Group should assign *one* person to the manual as technical editor. He might play other roles too, but in this role he is *the* primary technical reviewer, even if many other people also review the manual.

It is very common when two or more people check a product for none of them to take ownership of the task. Rather than improving the thoroughness of the review by adding another tester, thoroughness declines because everyone expects the other person to do the job (Deming, 1982). The technical editor should be encouraged to feel ownership of the technical accuracy of the book.

## WORKING WITH THE MANUAL THROUGH ITS DEVELOPMENT STAGES

Read McGehee (1984) for a good description of the components of a user manual.

The manual is developed in stages. The four major stages are:

- *Conceptualization and initial design:* The writer makes decisions about the scope, target audience, degree of coverage, and general organization of the manual.

- *Preparation:* The manual is written, reviewed, rewritten, etc. The manual is in the preparation stage until its content is in final form.

- *Production:* The manual is laid out for publication. This might involve typesetting or making revisions to make the manual look as good as possible when printed by a laser printer or a daisy wheel. Typefaces are chosen, page style (margins, etc.) is designed, final artwork is prepared, and so forth. See McGehee (1984) and Brockmann (1990) for more discussion.

- *Publication:* The manual is printed or copied and bound, ready for circulation.

Testing is concentrated in the preparation stage, with some spillover into production. You review the manual's content, not the layout, unless you have expertise in layout. You probably won't be involved in the initial design of the manual. You will rarely be involved in publication: the writer checks that the printed manual contains all the pages, none upside down, and so forth. Brockmann (1990), Hastings and King (1986), and Price (1984) are thoughtful discussions of documentation development and offer insights into documentation reviewing and revision.

Some comments are more welcome at some times than others. Sometimes the writer wants to work on accuracy, sometimes on style, sometimes on organization. The following sections look at the value and appropriateness of different types of comments across various preparation and production stages. These notes describe the needs of the "typical" writer; there are many individual differences. Talk with the person you work with about her needs and schedule.

### THE FIRST DRAFT

You will *rarely* see the first draft of the manual. Excellent writers often write a horrid first draft. It might be badly written and full of spelling mistakes and factual errors. It might be badly and inconsistently organized—writers often experiment in this draft. Think of it as a set of personal notes.

If you are freshly assigned to a project, you don't know how the software should work and can't find any specifications, or if you are desperate, you might beg the writer for any documentation she has, even if it is first draft material. If she gives it to you, realize that it is for your use only. It is not for review, circulation, or criticism. It is not ready. Breach this trust and you will embarrass the writer and ensure that you never get first draft material again.

The writer will find some comments helpful. Correct factual errors. If you think the writer doesn't understand something, volunteer to share your understanding. Treat this as a shared learning experience, not as a set of comments and criticisms. Finally, make no comments about the manuscript's style, structure, or organization unless you are explicitly asked for them. Even then, make them cautiously.

## THE SECOND DRAFT

This might really be the twenty-third draft but it's the first one circulated for review. It goes to the programmers, managers, and you. It is not ready for review by the user community, except for users who have been explicitly assigned to the development team. Do the following:

- *Make your structural comments early.* If you don't like the order of chapters, or think that material should be combined into one chapter or split into two, say so early. You can wait a little longer (not much) before saying that the order of topics within a chapter is wrong. The longer you wait, the harder it is to change the book's structure.

  Some documentation groups review a document plan before they write the first line of text. A good document plan names each chapter and each section within each chapter. It gives an estimated page count for each section, and breaks sections longer than 10 pages into subsections. You might be invited to a meeting to review this document plan. This is the best time to make structural comments.

  If you think that some aspect of the program's design *should be* difficult to explain, but the document plan doesn't assign many pages to it, ask why not. The writer probably doesn't realize what she's in for. Explain the complexity in a factual, non-judgmental, non-sarcastic way. On hearing your explanation, the project manager may revise the design to eliminate excess options or to make it more consistent with the rest of the program.

- *Do a general review.* Read the manual with an eye to improving its accuracy, clarity, usability, and completeness. Don't be afraid to make comments like "I had to read this three times to understand it." Even if you can't say why it was difficult, the writer wants to know that a careful reader found a section, paragraph, or sentence difficult.

- *Look for areas that need discussion.* Some features have not yet been described in the manual. The writer may not know that a new feature has finally made it into the program and is ready to be examined, and described, carefully.

- *Look for violations of the spirit of the design.* The writer might miss a simple conceptual relationship between features, and describe each independently. Carefully devised large-scale consistencies are lost. The writer might imply disapproval of a program's restrictions. While some restrictions are arbitrary, designers *choose* others, often to simplify the user interface. The writer might approve if she understood the reasoning. The manual might suggest inefficient strategies for some tasks—they work, but a user who understood the program well would do things differently. In cases like these, the writer has missed something fundamental. Once she gains understanding, she may make significant changes, redoing not only this material but also discussions of related topics. These might be big revisions. The writer must understand the need for them as soon as possible.

- *Look for things that mislead.* Some examples and feature descriptions aren't incorrect, but a reasonable reader might generalize incorrectly from them. She might expect the program to be more capable than it is. She might believe she can do something under more general circumstances than she can. Or she might imagine restrictions that don't exist on the use of a feature. It is particularly important to flag misleading material early because the writer might believe those incorrect generalizations. She might make significant changes if she understood the product differently.

- *Check the error messages.* The writer will probably include a list of error messages in an appendix, with notes on how the reader probably got to this message and what to do about it. If you've been keeping a list of every way you've found to get each message, this is invaluable for the writer. The writer will base her explanations on your list and on information from the project manager and the technical support staff (who rely on these explanations to help keep customers from flooding the company with phone calls). It pays to test every message as it's explained in the book— you'll find more bugs. After you've tested a message, give the writer your additional notes about other message meanings, ways to get the message, or things the customer must do or avoid doing as soon as he gets the message.

**TESTING USER MANUALS**

- *Look for confusions that reflect on the program.* If the writer can't describe some aspect of the program in a clear and consistent way, evaluate the program before condemning the manual. If the program has many inconsistent options, it's a mess and so will be the documentation. Suggest improvements to the writer (if you can). Don't spend hours rewriting sections of the manual, but if you can do it quickly, do provide a description that you think is clear and acceptable. Also, write Problem Reports if you think confusion in the program is the cause of confusion in the manual.

---

*It's easy and common to condemn writers for documentation that accurately describes an incompetent design. We find it more profitable to start with the assumption that the writer is competent and that bad text is telling us something about the program.*

---

## THE REVISED SECOND DRAFT(S)

Keep looking at the accuracy and effectiveness of the manual, as you did in the second draft. You will often be aware of program changes long before the writer—flag these for her in the manual.

There may be many revised second drafts, tuned to different types of changes. In one of these, the writer will polish the manuscript, cleaning up its style and doing the final organizational tweaking. You don't have to comment on the style and organization of the manual—your comments on accuracy and the design's spirit are more important. If you do have comments on style, they will be most effective just before the polishing draft. After polishing, the writer wants to get rid of inaccuracies and finish up. She may ignore further comments on style and organization.

## THE BETA TEST DRAFT

This draft, or a revision addressing comments to this draft, will be the last one you'll see before production. (In companies that don't rely heavily on beta tests, the final circulating draft is the *user interface freeze draft*, circulated after the software's design has frozen.)

---

Beta testers don't work for your company. They use the product in the same ways they would have had they bought it in finished form. They report their difficulties with the product, their suggestions for improvement, and any bugs they find. You should review their reports about the software and about the documentation.

Up to this point the marketers, programmers, writers, and you have been making assumptions about how people will react to the product and about what they'll understand. Some of those assumptions are wrong. Some seemingly obvious aspects of the program may be incomprehensible to beta testers. Many changes to the manual come from user testing.

Users often complain if the documentation is not task-oriented. (Sohr, 1983; Schneiderman, 1987). A *task-oriented manual* anticipates what users want to do with the product and explains how to do each task. It describes features in the context of using them to get specific tasks done. In contrast, a *feature-oriented manual* describes features individually, maybe in alphabetical order. Each section includes everything you ever wanted to know about one feature. Brockmann (1990) notes that task-oriented manuals are much longer, but reviews some further evidence that they are more effective.

If the product is so widely useful that people could do thousands of different types of tasks with it, the writer could never finish a task-oriented manual. As a compromise, writers often write a task-oriented tutorial that covers the most popular tasks. Beta test comments may convince the writer to improve the task orientation with more examples, more illustrations, a different index, or a different organization.

Customers will raise many other issues about the documentation. As always, ask yourself whether their confusion is really due to poor documentation. We repeat this point because it's so often missed. The manual is often blamed for the faults of a poorly designed program, but no accurate description of a fundamentally confused program can be clear. Complaints about documentation should often lead you to file Problem Reports about the program's user interface.

## PRODUCTION

*Your main concern during production is that the document stay accurate.*

Someone in the documentation group, the writer or an editor or editorial assistant, will do the main proofreading of the laid out or typeset manuscript. You too can note spelling mistakes, misaligned headers. etc., and these notes will be welcome, but if that's all you can provide at this point, you're wasting your time.

*If the company wants to release the product as soon as the software is complete and tested, documentation production must start 8 to 14 weeks before the program is finished.*

The program will change over those many weeks. Some parts of the manual will no longer be correct. Further, some bugs that everyone expected to be fixed will not be. Sections of the manual that assumed that a given bug would be fixed, in good faith and on good authority, have to be revised.

Not all desirable changes can be made during production. The writer will (should) change as little as she can get away with. You can get her to make more changes, and help keep the cost of the changes down, by designing the changes to match production constraints.

As soon as a manual enters production, it stops being an organized collection of words. It is now a bunch of pages. There happen to be words and pictures on the pages, but each page is separate from all others. Each was carefully laid out; each will be photographed on its own.

The writer will not make changes that affect more than one page unless they are essential.

At the other extreme, it is easy to make a change that affects only one line, without moving words down to the next line or needing words from the line above. If you can keep a change within a line, a paragraph, or a page, you have some hope of convincing the writer to make it. It is your responsibility to convince her that the change will stay within those limits. Be prepared to provide a suggested wording, and to show how the words fit on the lines. The wording must be stylistically acceptable to the writer.

To make a change fit within a paragraph or a page, you will often have to cut out other words. We recommend Cheney (1983) and Judd (1990) as sources of advice.

This degree of editing is beyond the formal scope of your job. You can be asked to stop doing it. You don't have to do it and you shouldn't try unless you can do it well without taking too long. If you don't do it, you should send the writer a memo describing your problems with the manual. She will save it and incorporate your comments in revisions made for the next printing of the manual, or in the manual for the next version of the product. Also, if she thinks that one of the problems you raise is *critical*, she will work on the wording and get it to fit.

Another area to test during production is the index. The earlier you can get your hands on a draft index the better. You can improve the index's completeness by working with the draft manual and constantly trying to look things up in the index as you use the manual. Many words you expect in the index won't be there. Report them to the writer. You (or an editorial staff member) must also check the index when everything is finished, just before the book goes to the printer. The "final" index may miss entries from one chapter, or it may still be based on a previous version of one chapter. At a minimum, check at least two index entries in each five pages of the book. (That is, look up two items that the index says should be in pages 1 to 5; look up another two in pages 6 to 10, etc.)

## POST-PRODUCTION

Some companies don't print the manual until after the software is finished. In these cases, there are no post-production tasks. (The writer still has some tasks, such as checking *bluelines,* a first print run from the printer, but you probably won't have to check bluelines.)

If your company does send the manual to print before the software goes to the duplicator, the writers probably have to write two further documents. One is a printed *supplement* that includes corrections, troubleshooting notes, and discussion of additional features. The typical supplement goes to print a few days before the disks go to the duplicator. Later-breaking information must go into a README file on the disk.

Apart from checking the accuracy of material in the supplement and README, your most valuable contribution during this period is identifying troubleshooting tips and explaining them to the writer. Every deferred bug is a potential idea for a troubleshooting tip. If you (or the writer) can describe the bug in a positive tone, and tell the customer something useful, it's a good candidate for the troubleshooting section.

## ONLINE HELP

Most of what we've said about the manual is equally true for help. Here are a few additional notes.

- *Accuracy:* You must check the accuracy of help at least as closely as the manual. Help text is generally not well done, not well tested, and not well respected by customers. A customer will probably quit using the help immediately if she finds factual errors.

- *Good reading:* The best book we've read (or seen) on online help is Horton (1990).

- *Help is a combination of writing and programming:* You have to check the accuracy of the text and the reliability of the code. If the programmers implement help using special system-provided tools (common in GUI environments), it will pay to read the system's instructions to the writer and to the programmer. You will find bugs that stem from the writer and programmer not understanding each other's job well enough to cooperate perfectly.

- *Test hypertext links:* If the program includes hypertext links (cross-references that will take you directly to other topics), you have to check each link. Suppose the writer cross-references to "Keyboard layout" in two different places. In most systems, she could have the program jump to one help message if you select the first "Keyboard layout" and to a different message if you select the second "Keyboard layout." What you see doesn't necessary identify correctly where you will go. You have to check it in each case.

- *Test the index:* If the program includes an index or a list of topics, and lets you jump from the index to the topics, you must check each one.

- *More on the index:* If the program includes an index, or hypertext links, you should note whether the index entries or the list of linked topics (per topic) are sensible. Some help topics never appear in the index or appear only under odd names. Customers will back away from the system if they can't quickly find information they need.

- *Watch the style:* Few customers take a leisurely read through help. They come to help with a specific question, or specific task they have to do, or error state they have to attend to. Help readers are often nervous or distracted, and they are often impatient. Expect the help text to be much more concise than the manual. Its style should also be much simpler (grade 5 reading level is sometimes recommended). Good help text is also very task- or action-oriented. It must say something useful, which the customer can do right away. If you find anything confusing or drawn out in help, report it as a problem.

# TESTING TOOLS

## FUNDAMENTAL TOOLS

Your fundamental tools are:

- *A personal computer, terminal, or workstation at your desk*. You should have use of the computer any time you feel the need. You shouldn't have to leave your desk to use it.

> *Your efficiency will improve significantly if you run two computers at your desk. Use one to run the software, the other to report problems and to update the test plan.*

- **A good word processing program.** You need something that was created for manuals, test plans, reports, memos, and letters. Find a word processor that you like. You'll use it so much that it will pay to get one that suits you.

- **An outline processor.** A good one is much better at making, reorganizing, and maintaining outlines than a word processor. It will help you make test plans, function lists, detailed status reports, and checklists. We prefer stand-alone outline processors to the limited versions included in some word processors. When you're comparison shopping, look for features that make it easy to group, sort, and reorganize your information.

- **A spreadsheet.** You need this for making test matrices.

- **File comparison utilities.** These compare two files, tell you whether they're the same or different, and list any differences. The best of these programs can show what changes must be made to one comparison file in order to produce the other.

  Simple programs often come with your computer's operating system. If better versions are available, you will use them often, and it will pay to buy them. Binary comparison utilities are useful for comparing object code, graphics, and compressed data files. Text comparison programs show difference between two text files.

- **File viewers.** These programs let you look at the data in disk files, from many different file formats.

- **File format converters.** These let you convert data files, text files, or graphic files, from one format to another (such as one word processor's text format to another).

- **Memory utilities.** Get a utility that lets you block access to specified amounts of memory. With this tool you can run low memory tests easily, in reasonably fine increments.

- **Screen capture utilities.** These utilities dump the contents of the screen, or the current window, to a printer or file. You'll probably need a few different ones, because some screen capture programs are incompatible with some programs or operating environments. These are very handy for capturing the look of the screen when you find a bug. Garbled messages or odd object placements are much easier to point to than to describe.

- **String-finding utilities.** These utilities scan the program's object code files for ASCII text. The simplest ones read a single compiled program file and print or save to disk a list of all the ASCII strings contained in the file. Use this utility to get an accurate list of all the program text and error messages. You might be told that this type of work is unnecessary because the programmers store all text in resource files. However, even in these environments, individual programmers will often embed some text into the code files, especially messages used for critical error handling.

- **A VCR.** You can videotape the screen output from most microcomputers using special video cards, or using an RGB output from the computer. (Note that NTSC cards will *not* save a full screen of

VGA to tape.) If you're testing a flaky program, there is no VCR substitute. It makes reproducing complex steps to a bug easier. It gives you proof of a bug that you cannot make recur. It often gives the programmer enough information to tell him what needs fixing. But be warned: even though the VCR is indispensable when the program is full of hard-to-recreate bugs, it can be turned into a disaster. Some project managers (or test managers or their managers) will want a video record submitted with every bug report. Others will ask for a video record for every deferred bug, to be shown during bug review meetings. Making these records can take so much time that they distract you from other needed testing. So remember, this is a sharp sword, but it's double-edged.

- *Hardware and configuration diagnostics.* These utilities tell you what devices have been successfully connected to the computer, and how well they, and the other components of the computer, are working. It's handy to know that you have a bad block of memory (fix it before running any more code tests or reporting any more bugs) or that your video card is not running in the mode you think it's running in.

- *Software diagnostics.* Load these in memory before loading the program under test to obtain information on specific types of errors. One common type of diagnostic utility saves memory and stack information when the program crashes. Another saves program and memory status information when the program reads or writes data in an inappropriate area of memory. The programmers use the output from these tools to fix the bugs. Ask them which tools to use. Programmers are often glad to supply you with the specific software.

- *Stopwatch.* It should count in tenths or, preferably, hundredths of a second. You must be able to start and stop it easily and very quickly. Most wristwatch stopwatches are unacceptable because they are too clumsy to use accurately. You'll use it to measure time-out intervals, delays between events, and timing parameters in race conditions. You may not use it often, but if you test interactive programs, you will need it.

- *Bug tracking system.* This is so important that we discuss it in its own chapter.

- *The programmer.* If you can't reproduce a bug or you don't know what the boundaries are supposed to be or you don't understand how to test something, go ask the programmer. Don't be a dummy about this—don't expect that you're always going to get the right answer, or even a good faith attempt at an accurate answer. Some programmers may even deliberately mislead you. So critically analyze what you hear. But the programmer can save you hours or days of wasted time. The programmer can also write special diagnostic code for you (memory tests, screen dumps, printer dumps, whatever) and may be able to suggest other tools that can make your work more effective.

## AUTOMATED ACCEPTANCE AND REGRESSION TESTS

Many test groups run an acceptance test each time they receive a new version of the program. A typical test runs less than a day. It includes mainstream (rather than boundary or other hard to pass). tests of all features, The point of the test is to flag serious problems in the basic functionality of the program. Some test groups publish the acceptance test suite, making it easy for the project manager to ensure that the program will pass this first round of testing.

- In some companies, a program that fails an acceptance test is withdrawn from (or kicked out of) testing. This is most common late in the project, after the program has passed the acceptance test a few times. Failure probably indicates a source control error, a compiler error, or some other basic mistake that can be quickly corrected.

- In other companies, acceptance test results are used to highlight this version's most obvious problems. This tells testers what problem areas to focus on, or what areas to avoid because they are not yet ready to test.

- The key practical problem of the acceptance test is that it's boring and time consuming. To keep the test's time cost down, the acceptance test suite must be restricted to a relatively small number of tests, no matter how large the program is.

You run regression tests every time the program changes. If the program didn't fail them last time, it probably won't fail this time either. These tests can feel like a major waste of time, but you have to run them just in case.

It would be so nice to have the computer run acceptance and regression tests. It should be possible. The tests are the same each time and the results should be too. All you have to do is teach the computer how to execute the test, collect the results, compare them with known good results, and report the results to you. We'll consider automation of the regression tests here. The same practical considerations apply to acceptance tests.

For a discussion of automated printer testing, read Chapter 8, "Some tips on automated testing." Much of what we say here applies to printer testing, and some of the points made there are also generally applicable in this chapter.

## WHERE REGRESSION TEST CASES COME FROM

When a programmer fixes a bug, there's a good chance that he'll either get the fix wrong or break something else. Regression tests retest the particular bug and recheck the integrity of the program as a whole. The regression suite includes the difficult tests, the ones the program will probably fail if it's broken. Here are the common sources of regression tests:

- *Boundary tests and other preplanned tests:* From the tests in your test plan, choose the ones most likely to reveal an error.

- *Tests that revealed bugs in the program:* What was once fixed is often rebroken; the problem is that special code added to fix an error is often confusingly written. Mistakes are especially likely when the programmer fixing the current bug isn't the one who fixed the previous ones.

- *Customer-reported bugs:* Bugs reported by customers, tech support staff, or other non-testers indicate holes in the test plan. Some test groups add every one of these reports to their regression test suite.

- **Batteries of randomly generated test data:** We introduced the random number generator in Chapter 7, "Function equivalence testing." Random data shouldn't replace your boundary tests but they will exercise the program with many different inputs. Run these tests at night, or any other time that the computer won't be busy.

## FEEDING INPUT TO THE PROGRAM

The practical problem of regression testing is that there are too many candidate tests. There isn't enough time to rerun them all every time the program must be retested. In the discussion of Regression Testing in Chapter 7, we suggested ways to eliminate regression test cases from a large suite. Here we consider ways to automate, or partially automate, regression testing, so that we aren't forced to eliminate as many tests.

Here are some of the ways to feed test data to the program:

**TESTING TOOLS**

- **Data files:** The program can load much of your test data from disk files. Tests using disk-based data don't test the program's user interface, but they can test its core functionality in detail. Use prepared data files to test all programs' file loading, import, and export routines. If you put the right data in the test files, you can put the program right at the edge of many boundary conditions (almost too many records, almost too large numbers, etc.) For each program, there will also be unique things you can test, and tests that you can do 90% of the preparation for, just by loading the right set of data values from the disk.

    It sometimes pays to enter test data into a database manager. Have it create appropriately formatted test files. When the program's input format changes, the database manager can rewrite the test files in the new format. Even if input format is only a minor issue, a database manager can provide more convenient entry and editing facilities and a place for comments in each test record.

- **Batch files:** Some programs (such as compilers and linkers and many mathematical programs) can read all of their inputs, including commands, from a set of disk files. Some programs, designed to work in batch processing environments, are designed to always read their commands and data from disk. You can test all or almost all aspects of these programs with test files.

- **Input redirection:** If the program expects some commands via keyboard input, you may still be able to control it from a disk file. If the operating system lets you redirect input and output, you can make statements stored on disk appear to come from the *standard input device* (normally the keyboard). The operating system handles the details of doing this.

    Input redirection doesn't always do what you need. Can you build a 3.2-second delay between two keystrokes into your data file? Such delays may be essential.

- **Serial input:** Another trick is to use a second computer and a serial link (such as a modem). You can run programs on many computers from a terminal, and you can easily emulate a terminal with a computer. On personal computers that don't rely much on terminals, there are still lots of utilities that let you control an office computer while you're on the road. Just dial it up with the modem on your portable computer and type.

    Once you're connected with a second computer, you can control the first one (and the program under test) with your own test program. Inserting delays of a few seconds between characters is easy. The program could also capture the first computer's outputs and choose its responses to them.

High-powered, expensive systems along these general lines are available for testing personal computers. These are improving quickly—check computer shows to see what's new.

- *Keyboard capture and replay:* With the keyboard capture/replay program you run a test once with the capture program on. It records your keystrokes, mouse position, and mouse clicks. Thereafter, it can replay the steps you took, recreating the test.

Keyboard capture reduces the boredom of entering repetitive keystrokes. It helps you stay alert while testing and it guarantees that you run each test the same way each time. But this convenience comes at a price. First, you should immediately rerun any test you record, using the capture program's output. Make sure you recorded what you think you recorded. Second, you have to document the files of saved keystrokes. We take three to ten times as long to capture, check, identify, and save a test's keystrokes as to run the test manually.

Keyboard capture methods are sensitive to program changes that rearrange the order of steps. In a mouse-driven program, the program may be sensitive to the location of menu commands.

Before you buy a capture/replay program, make sure you can enter delays between keystrokes or mouse clicks. And make sure it handles mouse input correctly across the different screen resolutions that your product must support. Check into its reliability too. Testing tools are sold to a small market and they aren't necessarily well tested. Along with simple bugs, be aware that the capture program sits in memory along with the program you're testing. We all know of badly designed memory resident programs that misbehave and trigger often-deferred crashes in other programs. We have wasted so much time on problem reports induced by capture/replay programs that we've given up on automating all but the simplest tests in the MS-DOS environment.

A stripped down program with minimal functionality is useful for controlling tests in memory-bound environments. For example, you might use keyboard replay to automate a long series of printer tests. In this case it may not matter whether the tool provides timing, mice, screen resolutions, or even high reliability. As long as the replay program will fit into memory with the program you're testing, you can probably get it to make the program print the right files to the right printers in the right order.

## CAPTURING THE PROGRAM'S OUTPUT

Capturing the program's output into a useful format can be much harder than feeding it canned input. The capture itself is fairly easy in most environments. You typically have some of the following choices:

- *Data file output:* Whatever the program can save or export to disk is usable for testing.

- *Redirected output:* For example, redirect output intended for the printer to a disk file. It's better to do it this way if you can, rather than having the program use a built-in print-to-disk function. This way, you know that you're capturing all the control characters being sent to the printer.

In a text-based program, you can often also redirect the program's screen output to a disk file.

- ***Output down a serial link:*** If you can control the computer remotely, using a terminal or a second computer and a remote control utility, you can have the program send its output down the modem link to the second computer. This computer captures the output to disk for later analysis.

- ***Screen capture:*** Lots of programs let you take snapshots of the whole screen or the active window. Earlier in this chapter, we noted that screen capture programs are among your fundamental tools.

- ***Output capture using an input/output test program:*** A capture program designed for testing will give you more freedom to select and manipulate your data than any of the other methods. These (good ones) let you capture just part of the screen or mask out areas of the screen (like the date) that will always change from test to test.

## EVALUATING THE OUTPUT

Once your testing system captures the program's output, it must determine whether the output is correct. How does it do that? Here are some traditional approaches:

- ***Find a reference program*** that already does what your program does, and compare the outputs of each.

- ***Create a parallel program*** which should give the same outputs as the one under test. Compare the outputs of the two programs. In practice, it is easier to create a few dozen special purpose parallel programs, one for each class of tests that you're going to run. These should be shorter and easier to code and check than the program under test.

- ***Build a library of correct outputs.*** Add a new set as you create each new test case. This can be slow, especially if you create the reference files by entering data yourself. You will have to catch and correct many entry errors. However, the process is incremental—you don't have to do all the work at the start. You can automate test cases one by one, as you have time.

- ***Capture the program's output.*** Keep the results, bad and good, from every test you run. Keep them in separate files (one per test case) for later comparison. The first time through, inspect as many results as you can and mark each file correct or incorrect. If you don't have time to inspect every output this time, inspect as many more as you can during the next cycle of testing.

  Next time you run the test series, have the system flag differences between the previous test results and the new ones. Mismatches against previously correct results indicate either new bugs or a specification change. Mismatches against old files that contain errors indicate a fix or new bugs. If the new results are good, keep them and discard the old file. Results that match known good outputs are still good. Results that match known bad outputs show that the bug is still there. You can usually ignore both cases.

  This is another incremental strategy. Eventually, you should have a large library of inspected test results, with one file per test, most containing correct results.

Output comparison, especially screen comparison, is not a risk-free testing strategy. How do you tell the comparison program to ignore differences in the date? What if the screen's title changes? What if output data are printed to a different level of precision, in a different order, or in a slightly different place on the screen? Small changes in a program have made magnetic trash out of many carefully built comparison files.

Some capture/compare programs let you capture or compare only selected parts of a screen. You can have the program ignore the rest. Another neat trick in some of the newer test software is that the program will display both screens (old and new) and white out everything that matches. You get to examine the differences and decide whether you're looking at a bug or not.

We've seen capture/compare software for Macintosh and Microsoft Windows environments that looks quite good. Other test managers have told us they rely heavily on these programs, especially for acceptance testing. We haven't yet applied these tools to a significant project, so we're hesitant to endorse or criticize any of them. Here are a few points to consider:

- *Time cost:* It takes a long time to create automated tests. According to the *Microsoft Test User's Guide* (Microsoft, 1992, p. 15) automated tests require careful planning and organizing, and this "is often the most time-consuming part of testing."

  Suppose it takes ten times as long to design, create, and document an automated test as it does to design an execute the test once by hand. The automation pays for itself the tenth or eleventh time you run the test. Any repetitions of the automated test beyond an eleventh are essentially free (as long as you don't have to modify the automated test itself), but any tests you run only a few times are excessively expensive to automate.

- *Testing delay:* If you delay doing significant testing until you have an automated test battery, you may be doing the project a disservice. Programmers need fast feedback on the reliability of their work. Perhaps you should plan to have extra staff near the start of the project, with some people creating automated tests and others doing traditional black box testing to give feedback as quickly as possible.

- *Inertia:* Once you've created a test suite, you've made a big investment. If the programmers now change the user interface (or the data file format) in a way you hadn't anticipated, you're going to have to redo or discard many automated tests. This problem is made worse if you create tests early in the project, because there will be more opportunity for the program to change between the time you created the test and the time the program is finished.

  Design changes don't (usually) happen by whim. The project manager agrees to change the user interface to make the program easier to use or more consistent. She changes the data file format to improve some type of compatibility or to eliminate errors. These are important improvements to the product's quality, and you should be there cheering when the project manager decides to make them. But if your automated tests rely on the old interface or file format, you might be a source of inertia rather than a support for change.

- *Risk of missed bugs:* Microsoft (1990, p. 7.33) cautions that automated "tests must be planned and organized meticulously since their execution is not monitored as closely as manual test cases." This corresponds well with our experience. We've seen testers working with automated test output miss serious, obvious, embarrassing bugs. Myers (1979) mentions research showing that testers don't inspect test output carefully enough and miss significant numbers of errors.

You must plan your output from automated tests. Never let a system bury you in printouts of the results. You won't read all the printouts.

In terms of printouts, we think you need a slim summary report. Perhaps you want a one-line log of each test that was run, to make it easy to check that every test was executed. Beyond that, concentrate on program failures. Which tests did the program fail? For each failure, the report should also show all bad data.

It might also be wise to have an automated test program sound an alarm (beep beep), display a message, and wait for tester inspection before progressing beyond an erroneous test result. This makes sure that a person catches every error. However, it will drive your staff mad if the test comparison files are slightly out of date, triggering false alarms.

- *Partial automation:* You don't have to fully automate your tests. You can run some tests manually and others by machine. Perhaps you should automate the easiest ones first. Or the ones you know you'll run 40 times. Or the ones that are hardest or most annoying to key in by hand.

You can also partially automate individual test cases. For instance, it often pays to capture and replay your keystrokes, but to analyze the program's output visually. This saves you the time and bother of retyping the test data each time, but it doesn't force you to make and maintain comparison files for the output.

## AUTOMATING ACCEPTANCE TESTS

Some test managers spend most of their automation budget on acceptance test suites. Here are some reasons:

- *These are the tests run most often:* If the project manager submits an updated version into testing every week, plus a few correction versions when particularly bad versions bounce out of testing, you might run the acceptance test suite fifty or a hundred times.

- *There aren't many tests of any individual area of the program:* The acceptance test skips quickly through the program. Nothing is covered in detail. If one area of the program changes, it's no big deal to change the associated tests.

- *Boredom-induced missed bugs:* Repeating the same tests so many times tempts every tester to skip most of the acceptance test or to run through it like an automaton, not paying careful attention to the results. By the time they repeat the same test the tenth time, testers working manually are likely to miss obvious errors. A well designed automated test might miss fewer errors than a small group of bored human testers.

## STANDARDS

Your company might have signed a contract that specifies that the product will conform to certain programming standards. If so, you should test whether these standards have been met. *Standards compliance-checking programs* analyze the product's source code. Standards compliance checkers are often home grown or heavily modified in-house. They might complain about any of the following:

- ***Lack of portability.*** The program will detect such things as enhanced language features that won't work with a different compiler, direct reads or writes to specific memory locations, or assumptions about advanced capabilities of some I/O devices.

- ***Recursion.*** A program is recursive if it contains subroutines that call themselves. Recursion is forbidden by some standards.

- ***Levels of nesting.*** The main routine calls a subroutine, which calls a subroutine, which calls a subroutine, etc. This continues until we finally reach the routine that does the work. How many calls does it take to reach worker routines? Is this acceptable? Similarly, is there a limit to the degree to which we can have loops nested inside loops or IF statements nested inside IFs? Finally, if the language allows you to create custom data types, to what degree is it tolerable to have a variable defined in terms of a type that is defined in terms of another type that is defined in terms of some other type? How deeply do you have to dig to figure out what type of data are really stored in this variable?

- ***Embedded constants.*** Suppose the program checks whether input values are less than 6. Some programmers will make a symbol, such as MAX_VAL make its value 6, and compare inputs to it. Other programmers just write the 6s into the code. These 6s and any other numbers written directly into the program are embedded constants. If the legal input values change, it's easy to change the definition of MAX_VAL. It's harder to find all the right 6s. Embedded constants are often forbidden.

- ***Module size.*** How many lines of code are there per subroutine or function? Is any routine too long? Too short? How about the number of routines per code file?

- ***Comments.*** The standard might call for an average of one comment per three lines of source code. It might specify comments' format, length, location in the file, and other characteristics.

- ***Naming conventions.*** The standard might specify how variables, functions, files, and statements are to be named.

- ***Formatting.*** The standard might specify such things as indentation, the location of brackets that mark the start and end of blocks of code, and the number of characters of text per line.

- ***Prohibited constructs.*** For example, the standard might disallow GOTO, or subroutine calls to addresses stored in pointer variables, statements such as EXIT, that halt execution midstream, or certain types of error logging or other I/O commands.

- ***Prohibited actions.*** For example, a branch forward might be okay, but the programmer might not be allowed to GOTO a line that appeared earlier in the code. (Backward branches are more error-prone than forward ones.)

- *Aliasing.* If two different names refer to the same variable (or the same storage locations in memory) at the same time, they are aliases. This might not be allowed.

- *Consistent data typing.* In some languages it is easy to switch data types across a subroutine or function call. For example, the programmer might send an integer array as a function parameter, but treat it as a string inside the function. The standard might disallow this.

If the standards compliance checker can catch all these problems, maybe it can look for a few errors. Such programs often catch:

- *Invalid syntax.* A compiler will catch this, but a syntax error might not show up in an interpreted language until run-time, perhaps not until a customer uses that part of the program.

- *Mixed mode calculations.* If A = 5 and B = 2, then A/B is 2.5 if A and B are both floating point variables. A/B is 2 if they're both integers. The quotient might be 2 or 2.5 if one is an integer and the other is floating point. Most languages allow calculations that involve variables of different types, but they don't always produce the results the programmer expects. Often, the programmer doesn't even realize he's mixing modes (types) in a calculation.

- *Variable defined in the code but never used.* The program sets A = 5, but never uses the value of A. Maybe the programmer planned to use A but forgot. This might be harmless, but it will confuse a maintenance programmer later.

- *Variable used before it's initialized.* The program sets B = A, then gives A an initial value. What's the value of B?

- *Read a file that hasn't been opened, or after it's closed.* This can catch some attempts to read or write to I/O devices in the wrong state.

- *Unreachable code.* A subroutine is never called, or some lines are always branched around and can't be executed. Why?

- *Obviously infinite loops.* Several loops are too subtle (e.g., data-dependant) to catch.

The list can go on. The point is that the program can be checked for style, format, adherence to various rules, and freedom from many types of errors. Most of this information is of more interest to the programmer, who can tell quickly whether something is an error or a deliberately unusual construction in his code. It's of interest to you if you have to enforce compliance to certain coding standards. If a contract specifies standards that must be met, you have to test whether the specified rules were followed.

Consider carefully whether standards enforcement is appropriate on other projects. The idea is fine in principle but it can pose real problems in practice:

- Programmers may do dumb or undesirable things to get better scores on your group's tests and get you off their back (Kearney, et al., 1986; Weinberg, 1971)

- The more attention you focus on standards, the less time, staff, and energy left to focus on other issues like, does the program do something useful, how easy is it to use, is it riddled with bugs, and is it, despite its intricacies, a surprisingly successful solution to a difficult problem?

We've heard *quality* defined as measured *conformity with a set of standards*. Many people want to apply that definition to software quality. Unfortunately, we can only measure the easy things now. To the degree that we focus attention on these, at the expense of the harder questions of functionality and feel, we are shooting ourselves in the feet.

Glass (1992, p. 92) states a conclusion we strongly agree with: "Efforts to measure quality in terms of standards conformance are doomed to letting poor quality software slip through undetected." We suggest that you keep out of the standards compliance business. Help programmers write or evaluate compliance checking tools, but let them define and enforce their own standards.

## TRANSLUCENT-BOX TESTING

In glass box testing, you look inside the program and test from the source code. In black box testing, the subject of most of this book, you analyze the program strictly from the outside.

Sometimes the programmer, or a separate test tool, can provide test support code that you can use when doing black box testing. Some examples are:

- Instrumenting the code, for coverage monitoring
- Assertion checks
- Memory validity and usage checks

If you're interested in this type of work, Glass (1992) will probably help you think about other types of testing support you can negotiate with the programmers.

### INSTRUMENTING THE CODE, FOR COVERAGE MONITORING

The impossible dream of path testing is to test every path through the program. A more practical objective is to exercise every line of code, and every branch from one line to another (see "Path testing: coverage criteria" in Chapter 3, "Glass box testing"). The obvious glass box approach is to sit at the computer with a source code listing in hand and try test after test to force the program down every branch you see in the code.

Some programmers add special debugging code during development. When the program reaches a given point, the program prints a "Kilroy was here" message. Each message is slightly different (usually they're numbered), so it's easy to tell where in the program the printout came from. Programmers put many of these messages in the code, at "interesting" places. At the end of a test series, they check the printout (or a message log file on disk) to see if every message was printed at least once. If any are missing, that part of the program wasn't tested. Further testing is needed.

Once the programmer has added these messages, he doesn't have to run these tests. You can do it. You don't need a listing of the source code. Just run your tests and the program will print its messages as you drive it through its different parts.

Also, there are tools to add these special messages to the code. You feed source code to the tool. It analyses the control structures in the code and adds *probes* (lines of code that say that the program has reached a certain place). It adds a probe for each branch in the program. Inserting these probes into the code is called *instrumenting* the program. You know that you've pushed the program down every branch when all probes have been printed.

Along with instrumenting the code, a good *coverage monitor* captures probe outputs, analyzes, and summarizes them. It counts the different probe messages, reports the percentage of probes triggered so far and so reports on thoroughness of testing done so far. It might also report untriggered branches. Create tests to exercise those parts of the program.

Coverage monitors are designed for glass box testing, but you can use one without knowing the internals of the program under test. It helps to have a listing of the program, but even without one, you can find out your level of coverage of the program, which can be important feedback.

Many coverage monitors are available commercially. To encourage the programming staff to use one, build a good file on what's available. However, the programmers may raise honest and considerable objections:

- ***These monitors insert code into the program:*** The shipping program won't include this test code. It is risky to test a program that significantly differs in its control flow (as these do, because they pass through the monitor routines all the time) from the one you will release.

- ***The monitoring software makes the program run more slowly:*** It might create race conditions that can't arise in real use of the final product, and it might hide race conditions and other performance problems that will arise in the real product.

- ***The instrumented program is much larger than the final product:*** It might very well not fit on test machines of interest, and its size might disguise the fact that the non-instrumented program has also grown to be too big.

- ***Some of this software is full of bugs:*** Programmers get upset when they spend two days tracking down a bug in the program only to find that it's just another bug in the test tool. Before buying and using a coverage monitor, ask the monitor's developer for a list of its known bugs. Since this program is designed to help find bugs, a request for the product's known bugs is not unreasonable.

## ASSERTION CHECKS

The programmer often knows that something must be true at a certain point in the program. At this point, many programmers will test an assertion that this something is in fact true. This is an *assertion check*. The typical program does nothing visible if the assertion is correct, but prints or displays an error message if the assertion is false. Other programs print nothing, but silently execute error recovery code.

To make the internal testing visible in the program, have the programmer log a message to the screen or printer whenever an assertion (or a particularly interesting assertion) is tested. Assertion checking is most often made visible to the tester to help track down bugs that are hard to reproduce or that the programmer doesn't understand how to solve. To keep the noise level down, usually the only assertions made visible are those in the suspected area of the program.

## MEMORY VALIDITY AND USAGE CHECKS

The running program uses memory in the following ways:

- *Some memory is used by the code itself:* Except for (very unfashionable) self-modifying programs, no programs can write to the code area.

- *Some memory is used for data:* The program can read from and write to this area of memory, but it shouldn't point the CPU to execute its next instruction from a data area.

- *Some memory is hardware related:* The program can talk to an external device by reading from or writing to these memory addresses. However, many programs talk to these areas indirectly, relying on the BIOS (basic input/output system) or even higher-level device handlers supplied with the system to talk to the hardware. In these cases, the program is behaving incorrectly (probably wildly) if it accesses a hardware address.

- *Some memory is out of bounds:* The operating system allocates a certain memory area to each program. In multi-tasking systems, the program is forbidden from accessing most of the computer's memory. In all systems, the program can't access memory that the computer doesn't have.

A memory-usage checking program will report suspicious memory accesses. Depending on the program and the options you use, it might stop and dump status data, it might jump into a debugger mode, or it might just flag the event and move on.

A different type of memory report that testers often find useful states how much free memory is available and reports the size of the largest block (or few blocks) of free memory. It's also handy to (optionally) get a more detailed listing for all of memory (or all memory in use by the program). This listing shows what areas of memory are free and what routines are using the rest, block by block. This report is handy because memory usage problems often don't result in visible misbehavior until long after they've occurred. You can use this tool to discover:

- How much memory each feature or option takes.

- Whether the program cleans up after a given graphic, feature, or dialog (frees up the memory it was using) when you are done with it. If not, the program will eventually run out of memory.

This tool often presents a cleaner picture because it has to do some cleanup in the process of getting the data for the report. Sometimes, using the tool will block you from reproducing the bug. However, that information is often useful and significant to the programmer in its own right.

In our experience, the memory usage report is the single most valuable tool the programmer can build into the code for the benefit of the tester.

# TEST PLANNING AND TEST DOCUMENTATION

## THE REASON FOR THIS CHAPTER

Chapter 7 explains how to create and evaluate individual test cases. Chapter 8 is an illustration of test planning, in that case for printer testing. Chapter 9 provides the key background material for creating a localization test plan. Chapter 11 describes tools you can use to automate parts of your test plan.

This chapter ties these previous chapters together and discusses the general strategy and objectives of test planning. We regard this chapter as the technical centerpiece of this book.

We see test planning as an ongoing process. During this process, you do the following:

- *Use analytical tools to develop test cases:* Test planners rely on various types of charts to identify separately testable aspects of a program and to find harsh test cases (such as boundary tests) for each aspect.

- *Adopt and apply a testing strategy:* Here and in Chapter 13, we suggest ways to decide what order to explore and test areas of the program, and when to deepen testing in an area.

- *Create tools to control the testing:* Create checklists, matrices, automated tests, and other materials to direct the tester to do particular tests in particular orders, using particular data. These simple tools build thoroughness and accountability into your process.

- *Communicate:* Create test planning documents that will help others understand your strategy and reasoning, your specific tests, and your test data files.

## OVERVIEW

The chapter proceeds as follows:

- The overall objective of the test plan.
- Detailed objectives of test planning and test documentation.
- What types of (black box) tests to cover in test planning documents.
- A strategy for creating test plans and their components: evolutionary development.
- Components of test plans: Lists, tables, outlines, and matrices.
- How to document test materials.

The *ANSI/IEEE Standard 829-1983 for Software Test Documentation* defines a *test plan* as

> A document describing the scope, approach, resources, and schedule of intended testing activities.
> It identifies test items, the features to be tested, the testing tasks, who will do each task, and any
> risks requiring contingency planning.

Test plans are broad documents, sometimes huge documents, usually made up of many smaller documents grouped together. This chapter considers the objectives and content of the test plan and the various other documents we create in the process of testing a product.

## TEST PLANNING AND TEST DOCUMENTATION

The amount of effort and attention paid to test documentation varies widely among testing groups. Some are satisfied with a few pages of notes. Others generate multi-volume tomes. The variation isn't explained simply in terms of comparative professionalism of the groups (although that certainly is a factor). In large part, the groups have different objectives for test planning and they create documents appropriately for their objectives.

## THE OVERALL OBJECTIVE OF THE TEST PLAN: PRODUCT OR TOOL?

We write test plans for two very different purposes. Sometimes the test plan is a product; sometimes it's a tool. It's too easy, but also too expensive, to confuse these goals. The product is much more expensive than the tool.

### THE TEST PLAN AS A PRODUCT

A good test plan helps organize and manage the testing effort. Many test plans are carried beyond this important role. They are developed as products in themselves. Their structure, format, and level of detail are determined not only by what's best for the effectiveness of the testing effort but also by what a customer or regulating agency wants. Here are some examples:

- Suppose your company makes a software-intense product for resale by a telephone company. (Call accounting programs and PBX phone systems are examples of such products.) Telephone companies know that they must support products they sell for many years. Therefore, they will scrutinize your test plan. They will demand assurance that your product was thoroughly tested and that, if they need to take over maintenance of the software (e.g., if you go bankrupt), they'll be able to rapidly figure out how to retest their fixes. The test plan's clarity, format, and impressiveness are important sales features.

- If you sell software to the military, you also sell them (and charge them for) Mil Spec test plans. Otherwise, they won't buy your code.

- If you develop a medical product that requires FDA inspection, you'll create a test plan that meets very detailed FDA specifications. Otherwise, they won't approve your product.

- A software developer might choose to leverage the expertise of your independent test agency by having you develop a test plan, which the developer's test group will then execute without further help. You must write a document that is very organized and detailed, or your customer won't know how to use it.

Each of the above test plans is useful for finding bugs. However, it's important to note that in each case, if you could find more bugs in the time available by spending more time thinking and testing and less time writing an impressively formatted test plan, you would still opt for the fancy document (test plan) because the customer or the regulating agency requires it.

## THE TEST PLAN AS A TOOL

The literature and culture of the traditional software quality community prepare readers and students to create huge, impressive, massively detailed test planning documents. Our major disagreement with the traditional literature is that we don't believe that creating such detailed documents is the best use of your limited time—unless you are creating them as products in their own right.

Look through standards like ANSI/IEEE 829 on test plan documentation. You'll see requests for test design specifications, test case specifications, test logs, test-various-identifiers, test procedure specifications, test item transmittal reports, input/output specifications, special procedure requirements specifications, intercase dependency notes, test deliverables lists, test schedules, staff plans, written lists of responsibilities per staffer, test suspension and resumption criteria, and masses of other paper.

Listen carefully when people tell you that standards help you generate the masses of paper more quickly. They do, but so what? It still takes a tremendous amount of time to do all this paperwork, and how much of this more-quickly generated paper will help you find more bugs more quickly?

Customers of consumer software ask for something that adds the right numbers correctly, makes the right sounds, draws the right pictures, and types the text in the right places at the right times. They don't care how it was tested. They just care that it works. For these customers and many others, your test plan is not a product. It is an invisible tool that helps you generate test cases, which in turn help improve the product.

When you are developing a test plan as a tool, and not as a product, the criterion that we recommend for test planning is this:

**12**

> *A test plan is a valuable tool to the extent that it helps you manage your
> testing project and find bugs. Beyond that, it is a diversion of resources.*

As we'll see next, this narrowed view of test planning still leaves a wide range of functions that good testing documentation can serve.

## DETAILED OBJECTIVES OF TEST PLANNING AND DOCUMENTATION

Good test documentation provides three major benefits, which we will explore in this section. The benefits are:

- Test documentation facilitates the technical tasks of testing.
- Test documentation improves communication about testing tasks and process.
- Test documentation provides structure for organizing, scheduling, and managing the testing project.

Few organizations achieve all potential benefits of their test plans. Certainly, anyone who writes a test plan gains at least some education about the test-relevant details of the product. But not every test group reviews test plans effectively or uses other project members' review feedback effectively. And many consult test plans only as technical documents, never using one to control a testing project or monitor project progress.

As a tester, you will spend many, many hours developing test plans. Given the investment, it's worth considering the potential benefits of your work in more detail. You may as well make the most of it.

(See Hetzel, 1988, for a different, but very useful, analysis of the objectives of test plans.)

## TEST DOCUMENTATION FACILITATES THE TECHNICAL TASKS OF TESTING

To create a good test plan, you must investigate the program in a systematic way as you develop the plan. Your treatment of the program becomes clearer, more thorough, and more efficient. The lists and charts that you can create during test planning (see "A strategy for developing components of test planning documents" later in this chapter) will improve your ability to test the program in the following ways:

- *Improve testing coverage.* Test plans require a list of the program's features. To make the list, you must find out what all the features are. If you use the list when you test, you won't miss features. It's common and useful to list all reports created by the program, all error messages, all supported printers, all menu choices, all dialog boxes, all options in each dialog box, and so forth. The more thorough you are in making each list, the fewer things you'll miss just because you didn't know about them.

- *Avoid unnecessary repetition, and don't forget items.* When you check off items on lists or charts as you test them, you can easily see what you have and haven't already tested.

- *Analyze the program and spot good test cases quickly.* For example, Figures 12.15 and similar figures in Chapter 7 ("Equivalence classes and boundary values") analyze data entry fields for equivalence classes and boundary conditions. Each boundary value is a good test case, i.e., one more likely to find a bug than non-boundary values.

- *Provide structure for the final test.* When all the coding is done, and everything seems to work together, final testing begins. There is tremendous pressure to release the product now, and little time to plan the final test. Good notes from prior testing will help you make sure to run the important tests that one last time. Without the notes, you'd have to remember which tests should be rerun.

- *Improve test efficiency* by reducing the number of tests without substantially increasing the number of missed bugs. The trick is to identify test cases that are similar enough that you'd expect the same result in each case. Then just use one of these tests, not all of them. Here are some examples:

  - **Boundary condition analysis**. See "Equivalence classes and boundary values" in Chapter 7 and "Components of test planning documents: Tables: Boundary chart" later in this chapter.

  - **The configuration testing strategy.** See Figure 8.1 and "The overall strategy for testing printers" in Chapter 8. For example, with one or a few carefully chosen printers, test all printer features in all areas of the program. Then, on all similar printers, test each printer feature only once per printer, not in each area of the program.

    To follow this strategy well, list all printers and group them into classes, choosing one printer for full testing from each class list. To test the chosen printers, use a table showing each printer, each printer feature and each area of the program that printer features can be set. The printer test matrix of Figure 8.4 illustrates this. To test the rest of the printers, create a simpler test matrix, showing only the printers and the printer features to test, without repeating tests in each program area.

- **Sample from a group of equivalent actions**. For example, in a graphical user interface (GUI), error messages appear in message boxes. The only valid response is an acknowledgment, by mouse-clicking on <OK> or by pressing <Enter>. Mouse clicks in other places and other keystrokes are typically invalid and ignored. You don't have enough time to check every possible keystroke with every message box, but a keystroke that has no effect in one message box may crash another. The most effective way we've found to test message box handling of invalid keystrokes is driven by a test matrix. Each row is a message. Each column represents a group of keys that we class as equivalent, such as all lowercase letters. For each row (message), try one or a few keys from each column. We examine this matrix in more detail later in this chapter, in "Error message and keyboard matrix.".

- *Check your completeness.* The test plan is incomplete to the degree that it will miss bugs in the program. Test plans often have holes for the following reasons:

  - **Overlooked area of the program**. A detailed written description of what you have tested or plan to test provides an easy reference here. If you aren't sure whether you've tested some part of a program (a common problem in large programs and programs undergoing constant design change), check your list.

  - **Overlooked class of bugs**. People rarely cover predictable bugs in an organized way. The Appendix lists about 500 kinds of errors often found in programs. You can probably add many others to develop your own list. Use this bug list to check if a test plan is adequate. To check your plan, pick a bug in the Appendix and ask whether it *could* be in the program. If so, the test plan should include at least one test capable of detecting the problem.

**12**

TEST PLANNING &

DOCUMENTATION

We often discover, this way, that a test plan will miss whole classes of bugs. For example, it may have no race condition tests or no error recovery tests.

Our test plans often contain a special catch-all section that lists bugs we think we might find in the program. As we evolve the test plan, we create tests for the bugs and move the tests into specific appropriate sections. But we create the catch-all section first, and start recording our hunches about likely bugs right away.

  - **Overlooked class of test**. Some examples of classes of tests are volume tests, load tests, tests of what happens when a background task (like printing) is going on, boundary tests on input data just greater than the largest acceptable value, and mainstream tests. Does the test plan include some of each type of test? If not, why not? Is this by design or by oversight?

  - **Simple oversight**. A generally complete test plan might still miss the occasional boundary condition test, and thus the occasional bug. A few oversights are normal. A detailed outline of the testing done to date will expose significant inconsistencies in testing depth and strategy.

## TEST DOCUMENTATION IMPROVES COMMUNICATION ABOUT TESTING TASKS AND PROCESS

A tester is only one member of a product development team. Other testers rely on your work; so do programmers, manual writers, and managers. Clearly written materials help them understand your level, scope, and types of testing. Here are some examples of the communication benefits of the test plan:

- *Communicate the thinking behind the tester's strategy.*

- *Elicit feedback about testing accuracy and coverage.* Readers of your testing materials will draw your attention to areas of the program you're forgetting to test, your misunderstandings of some aspects of the program, and recent changes in the product that aren't yet reflected in your notes.

- *Communicate the size of the testing job.* The test plan shows what work is being done, and thus how much is being done. This helps managers and others understand why your test team is so large and will take so long to get done. A project manager interested in doing the project faster or less expensively will consider simplifying or eliminating the hardest-to-test areas of the program.

- *Elicit feedback about testing depth and timing.* Some test plans generate a lot of controversy about the amount of testing. Some project managers argue (and sometimes they're absolutely right) that the test plan calls for far too much testing and thus for unnecessary schedule delays. Managers of other projects may protest that there is too little testing, and will work with you to increase the amount of testing by lengthening the schedule or increasing your testing staff.

  Another issue is insufficient time budgeted for specific kinds of tests. Project and marketing managers, for example, often request much more testing that simulates actual customer usage of the program.

  These issues will surface whether or not there's test documentation. The test plan helps focus the discussions and makes it easier to reach specific agreements. In our experience, these discussions are much more rational, realistic and useful when a clear, detailed test plan is available for reference.

- *Divide the work.* It is much easier to delegate and supervise the testing of part of the product if you can pass the next tester a written, detailed set of instructions.

## TEST DOCUMENTATION PROVIDES STRUCTURE FOR ORGANIZING, SCHEDULING, AND MANAGING THE TESTING PROJECT.

The testing of a product is a project in and of itself, and it must be managed. The management load is less with one tester than with twenty, but in both cases the work must fit into an organized, time-sensitive structure. As a project management support tool, the test plan provides the following benefits:

- *Reach agreement about the testing tasks.* The test plan unambiguously identifies what will (and what won't) be done by testing staff. Let other people review the plan, including the project manager, any other interested managers, programmers, testers, marketers, and anyone else who might make further (or other) testing demands during the project. Use the reviews to bring out disagreements early, discuss them, and resolve them.

- *Identify the tasks.* Once you know what has to be done, you can estimate and justify the resources needed (money, time, people, equipment).

- *Structure.* As you identify the tasks, you see many that are conceptually related and many others that would be convenient to do together. Make groups of these clustered tasks. Assign all the tasks of a group to the same person or small team. Focus on the tests (plan them in more detail, execute the tests) group by group.

- **Organize.** A fully developed test plan will identify who will do what tests, how they'll do them, where, when, and with what resources, and why these particular tests or lines of testing will be done.

- **Coordinate.** As a test manager or a project's lead tester, use the test plan as your basis for delegating work and for telling others what work someone has been assigned. Keep track of what's being done on time and what tests are taking longer than expected. Juggle people and equipment across assignments as needed.

- **Improve individual accountability.**

  - **The tester understands what she is accountable for.** When you delegate work, the tester will understand you better and take the assignment more seriously if you describe the tasks and explain your expectations. For example, if you give her a checklist, she'll understand that you want her to do everything on the list before reporting that the job is complete.

  - **Identify a significant staff or test plan problem.** Suppose you assigned an area of the program to a tester, she reported back that she'd tested it, and then someone else found a horrible bug in that area. This happens often. A detailed test plan will help you determine whether there's a problem with the plan (and perhaps the planning process), the individual tester, both, or neither (you will *always* miss some bugs).

Do the materials that you assigned include a specific test that would have caught this bug? Did the tester say she ran this test? If so, make sure that the version she tested had the bug before drawing *any* conclusions or making *any* negative comments. The reason you run regression tests is that when programmers make changes, they break parts of the program that used to work. Maybe this is an example of that problem, not anything to do with your tester.

More testers than you'd like to imagine will skip tests, especially tests that feel uselessly repetitive. They will say they did the full test series even if they only executed half or a quarter of the tests on a checklist. Some of these people are irresponsible, but some very talented, responsible, quality-conscious testers have been caught at this too. Always make it very clear to the offending tester that this is unacceptable. However, we think you should also look closely at the test plan and working conditions. Some conditions that tend to drag this problem with them are: unnecessarily redundant tests, a heavy overtime workload (especially overtime demanded of the tester rather than volunteered by her), constant reminders of schedule pressure, and an unusually boring task.

We suggest that you deal with redundant tests by eliminating many of them. Quit wasting this time. If the tests are absolutely necessary, consider instructing the tester to sample from them during individual passes test through the plan. Tell the tester to run only odd-numbered tests (first, third, etc.) the first time through this section, then even-numbered tests next time. Organize the list of test cases to make this sampling as balanced and effective as possible.

We suggest that you reduce boredom by eliminating redundant and wasteful testing and by rotating testers across tasks. Why make the same tester conduct exactly the same series of tests every week?

- **Identify a significant test plan design problem**. If the tester didn't find a particularly embarrassing bug because there was no test for it in the test plan, is there a problem in the test plan? We stress again that your test plan will often miss problems, that this is an unfortunate but normal state of affairs. Don't go changing procedures or looking for scapegoats just because a particular bug that was missed was embarrassing. Ask first whether the plan was designed and checked in your department's usual way. If not, fix the plan by making it more thorough; bring it up to departmental standards and retrain the test planner. But if the plan already meets departmental standards, putting lots more effort in this area will take away effort from some other area. If you make big changes just because this aspect of testing is politically visible this week, your overall effort will suffer (Deming, 1986).

If your staff and test plans often miss embarrassing bugs, or if they miss a few bugs that you know in your heart they should have found, it's time to rethink your test planning process. Updating this particular test plan will only solve a small fraction of your problem.

- *Measure project status and improve project accountability.* Reports of progress in constructing and executing test plans can provide useful measures of the pace of the testing effort so far, and of predicted progress.

If you write the full test plan at the start of the project, you can predict (with some level of error) how long each pass through the test plan will take, how many times you expect to run through it (or through a regression test subset of it) before the project is finished, and when each cycle of testing will start. At any point during the project, you should be able to report your progress and compare this to your initial expectations.

If you develop test materials gradually throughout the project, you can still report the number of areas you've divided the test effort into, the number that you've taken through unstructured stress testing (guerilla tests), and the number subjected to fully planned testing.

In either case, you should set progress goals at the start of testing and report your status against these goals. These reports provide feedback about the pace of testing and important reality checks on the alleged progress of the project as a whole. Status reports like these can play a significant role in your ability to justify (for a budget) a necessary project staffing level.

## WHAT TYPES OF TESTS TO COVER IN TEST PLANNING DOCUMENTS

Good programmers are responsible people. They did lots of testing when they wrote the code. They just didn't do the testing you're going to do. The reason that you'll find bugs they missed is that you'll approach testing from a different angle than the programmers.

The programmers test and analyze the program from the inside (glass box testing). They are the ones responsible for path and branch testing, for making sure they can execute every module from every other module that can call it, for checking the integrity of data flow across each pair of communicating modules. Glass box testing is important work. We discussed some of its benefits in Chapter 3, "Glass box testing is part of the coding stage."

You might be called on to help the programmers do glass box testing. If so, we recommend Myers (1979), Hetzel (1988), Beizer (1984, 1990), Glass (1992), and Miller & Howden (1981) as useful guides. We also recommend that you use coverage monitors, testing tools that keep track of which program paths, branches, or modules you've executed.

There is a mystique about glass box testing. It seems more scientific, more logical, more skilled, more academic, more prestigious. Some testers feel as though they're just not doing real testing unless they do glass box testing.

Two experiments, by very credible researchers, have failed to find any difference in error-finding effectiveness between glass box and black box testing. The first was Hetzel's dissertation (1976), the second by Glenford Myers (1978).

In our experience, mystique aside, the two methods turn up different problems. They are complementary.

## WHAT GLASS BOX TESTING MISSES

Here are three examples of bugs in MS-DOS systems that would not be detected by path and branch tests.

- Dig up some early (pre-1984) PC programs. Hit the space bar while you boot the program. In surprisingly many cases, you'll have to turn off the computer because interrupts weren't disabled during the disk I/O. The interrupt is clearly an unexpected event, so no branch in the code was written to cope with it. You won't find the absence of a needed branch by testing the branches that are there.

- Attach a color monitor and a monochrome monitor to the same PC and try running some of the early PC games under an early version of MS-DOS. In the dual monitor configuration, many of these destroy the monochrome monitor (smoke, mess, a spectacular bug).

- Connect a printer to a PC, turn it on, and switch it off line. Now have a program try to print to it. If the program doesn't hang this time, try again with a different version of MS-DOS (different release number or one slightly customized for a particular computer). Programs (the identical code, same paths, same branches) often crash when tested on configurations other than those the programmer(s) used for development.

**12**

TEST PLANNING &
DOCUMENTATION

**Figure 12.1 What code paths don't tell you**

1. Timing-related bugs

2. Unanticipated error conditions

3. Special data conditions

4. Invalidity of onscreen information

5. User interface inconsistency

6. User interface everything-else

7. Interaction with background tasks

8. Configuration/compatibility failures

9. Can't cope with volume, load, hardware faults

It's hard to find these bugs because they aren't evident in the code. There are no paths and branches for them. You won't find them by executing every line in the code. You won't find them until you step away from the code and look at the program from the outside, asking how customers will use it, on what types of equipment.

In general, glass box testing is weak at finding faults like those listed in Figure 12.1.

> *This book is concerned with testing the running code, from the outside, working and stressing it in all the many ways that your customers might. This approach complements the programmers' approach. Using it, you will run tests they rarely run.*

## IMPORTANT TYPES OF BLACK BOX TESTS

Figure 12.2 lists some of the areas covered in a good test plan or, more likely, in a good group of test plans. There's no need to put all of these areas into one document.

We've described most of these areas elsewhere (mainly Chapter 3, but see Chapter 13's "Beta: Outside beta tests.") Here are a few further notes.

**Figure 12.2 Important areas of black box test plans**

- *Acceptance tests (into testing):* When project managers compete to pump products through your group, you need acceptance tests. The problem is that project managers have an incentive to get their code into your group, and lock up your resources, as soon as possible. On the other hand, if you're tight on staff, you must push back and insist that the program be reasonably stable before you can commit staff to it.

  Publish acceptance tests for each program. Be clear about your criteria so the programmers can run the tests themselves and know they pass before submitting the code to you. Many project managers will run the test (especially if they understand that you'll kick the program out of testing if it doesn't pass), and will make sure the product's most obvious bugs are fixed before you see it.

| | |
|---|---|
| 1. | Acceptance test (into testing) |
| 2. | Control flow |
| 3. | Data flow and integrity |
| 4. | Configuration/compatibility |
| 5. | Stress tests |
| 6. | User interface |
| 7. | Regression |
| 8. | Performance |
| 9. | Potential bugs |
| 10. | Beta tests |
| 11. | Release tests |
| 12. | Utility |

This brief test should cover only the essential behavior of the program. It should last a few hours—a few days at most in a particularly complex system. It is often a candidate for automation.

- **Control flow:** When you ask about control flow, you're asking how to get the program from one state to another. You're going to test the visible control flow, rather than the internal flow. Ask what are the different ways that you can get to a dialog box? What different menu paths can you take to get to the printer? What parameters can you give with commands to force the program into other states?

- **Utility:** A utility test asks whether the program will satisfy the customer's overall expectations. In gaming, this is called playability testing. A game may have a perfectly clear and usable interface, it may be bug free, it may perform quickly and have great sound and graphics, but if it's not fun to play, it's not worth shipping.

## A STRATEGY FOR DEVELOPING COMPONENTS OF TEST PLANNING DOCUMENTS

We recommend Evans (1984) and Hetzel (1988) for further reference: they look at test planning strategies from a different, but still practical, perspective.

### EVOLUTIONARY DEVELOPMENT OF TEST MATERIALS

Traditional software development books say that "real development teams" follow the *waterfall method*. Under the waterfall, one works in phases, from requirements analysis to various types of design and specification, to coding, final testing, and release.

In software design and development as a whole, there are very serious problems with the waterfall method. For details, see Tom Gilb's excellent book (*Principles of Software Engineering Management, Addison-Wesley, 1988*) and his references. (See also Gould & Lewis, 1985, and Chapter 11 of Baecker & Buxton, 1987.)

As an alternative, Gilb says to deliver a small piece, test it, fix it, get to like it eventually, then add another small piece that adds significant functionality. Test that as a system. Then add the next piece and see what it does to the system. Note how much low-cost opportunity you have to reappraise requirements and refine the design as you understand the application better. Also, note that you are constantly delivering a working, useful product. If you add functionality in priority order, you could stop development at any time and know that the most important work has been done. Over time, the product evolves into a rich, reliable, useful product. This is the *evolutionary method*.

We discuss product development methodologies in more detail in the next chapter. In this chapter we consider the methodology of developing test plans. In testing, and especially in test planning, you can be evolutionary whether or not the program was developed in an evolutionary way. Rather than trying to develop one huge test plan, you can start small. Build a piece of what will become part of the large, final test plan, and use it to find bugs. Add new sections to the test plan, or go into depth in new areas, and use each one. Develop new sections in priority order, so that on the day the executives declare an end to testing and ship the product (an event that could happen at any time), you'll know that you've run the best test set in the time available.

In our opinion, the evolutionary approach to test plan development and testing is typically more effective than the waterfall, even when the rest of the development team follows something like a waterfall. Be warned that this is a controversial opinion:

- Kaner and Falk take the extreme position that the evolutionary approach is always better for consumer software testing.

- Nguyen recommends the waterfall (write a complete test plan up front, get it approved, then start testing) when the rest of development truly follows the waterfall. Under a "true waterfall," the event that triggers the start of test plan development is delivery of a signed off, complete, accurate, detailed specification that is subject to a formal change control and notification process for the rest of the project. This circumstance is rare in consumer software but not in larger projects. When the specification is not so detailed or is more likely to change without notice, Nguyen also recommends the evolutionary approach for test development.

Our impression of the traditional view is that it says testers should always follow the waterfall, unless the entire project is organized in some other way (like evolutionary development). Under this view, no one should ever ask testers to start testing a marginally working product against a largely incomplete or outdated specification. To preserve product quality, testers should demand a complete specification before starting serious work on the test plan.

Unfortunately, the traditional view misses what we see as the reality of consumer software development. That reality includes two important facts:

- Consumer software products are developed quickly and in relatively unstructured ways. Development and testing begin before a full specification is complete, there may never be a full specification, and all aspects of the program are subject to change as market requirements change. There is no point in releasing a program that can't compete with the features and design of a just-released competitor.

- As a tester or test manager, you cannot change your company's overall development philosophy.

You must learn to test as effectively as possible under the existing conditions. In our opinion, an evolutionary approach to testing and test plan development can make you very effective.

We also note here two significant advantages to evolutionary test plan development:

- In waterfall-based testing, you do your thinking and test planning early and you execute the tests later. As organized as this looks on paper, you actually learn the most about the product and how to make it fail when you test it. Do you really want to schedule the bulk of thinking before the bulk of your learning? The evolutionary method lets you design as you learn.

- Suppose you do receive a complete specification, written at the start of development. (This is when such things are written, under the waterfall method.) You start writing your test plan in parallel with programming, so that you can start testing as soon as coding is finished. Unfortunately, during the next year of implementation the specification changes significantly in response to technical problems and new market conditions. We are aware of disasters along these lines—in one case, by the time the programming was complete and before any testing had started, the project's entire test budget had been spent revising the test plan. Under the evolutionary method, you design tests as you need them.

The ability to complete a project quickly is an important component of the quality of the development process underlying that project. (See Juran, 1989, p. 49, for a discussion of this point.) The evolutionary approach to testing and test plan development is often the fastest and least expensive way to get good testing started at a time when the code is ready to be tested.

## INITIAL DEVELOPMENT OF TEST MATERIALS

Our approach requires parallel work on testing and on the test plan. You never let one get far ahead of the other. When you set aside a day for test planning, allow an hour or two to try your ideas at the keyboard. When you focus on test execution, keep a notepad handy for recording new ideas for the test plan. (Or, better, test on one computer while you update the test plan on another computer sitting beside it.) You will eventually get an excellent test plan, because you've preserved your best creative ideas. Beware that the test plan starts out sketchy. It will be fleshed out over time. Meanwhile, you test a lot, find lots of bugs, and learn a lot about the program.

Figure 12.3 describes the first steps for developing the test plan. Start by going through the entire program at a superficial level. Try to maintain a uniform, superficial, level of coverage across the whole program. Find out what problems people will have in the first two hours of use, and get them fixed early.

- **Test against the documentation:** Start by comparing the program's behavior and whatever draft of the user documentation you get. If you also have a specification, test against that too. Compare the manual and the product line by line and keystroke by keystroke. You'll find plenty of problems and provide lots of help to the programmers and the manual writers.

- **Begin creating test documentation that's organized for efficient testing, such as a function list**. Such a list includes everything the program's supposed to be able to do. Make the list, and try everything out. Your list won't be complete at first—there will be undocumented features, and it will lack depth—but it'll grow into a complete list over time. We'll discuss the gradual refinement of the function list later (see "Components of test planning documents: Outlines—the function list" later in this chapter.)

**Figure 12.3 Tactics of evolution (1)**

**Start broad**

1. Full review of (user) documentation

2. Superficial function list

3. Analyze inputs, limits, ignoring most interactions

- **Do a simple analysis of limits.** Try reasonable limits everywhere that you can enter data. If the program doesn't crash, try broader limits. User manual drafts rarely indicate boundary conditions. Specifications (if you have such things) too often describe what was planned before the developers started coding and changed everything. In your testing, find out what the real limits are. Write them down. Then circulate your notes for the programmers and writers to look at, use, and add to.

In sum, start by building a foundation. Use an outline processor so you can reorganize and restructure the foundation easily. In laying the foundation, you test the whole program, albeit not very thoroughly. This lets you catch the most obvious problems right away. As you add depth, you add detail to a centrally organized set of test documentation.

## WHERE TO FOCUS NEXT, WHERE TO ADD DEPTH

Once you finish the superficial scan of the program, what next? What are the most important areas to test? What's the best area of focus? There's no magic formula. It depends on what you know and what your instincts suggest will be most fruitful this time, but it will probably be in one of the six areas listed in Figure 12.4.

- *Most likely errors:* If you know where there are lots of bugs, go there first and report them. Bugs live in colonies inside the program. In a study cited by Myers (1979), 47% of the errors were found in 4% of the system's modules. This is one example of a common finding—the more errors already found in an area of the program, the more you can expect to find there in the future. Fixes to them will also be error prone. The weakest areas during initial testing will be the least reliable now. Start detailed work on these areas early.

- *Most visible errors*: Alternatively, start where customers will notice errors first, where customers look soonest or most carefully. Look in the most often used program areas, the most publicized areas, and the places that really make your program distinct from the others, or make it critically functional for the user. Features that are nice to have but you can live without are tested later. If they don't work, that's bad. But it's worse if the core functionality doesn't work.

**Figure 12.4 Tactics of evolution (2)**

Targets for focus

1. Most likely errors
2. Most visible errors
3. Most often used program areas
4. Distinguishing areas of the program
5. Hardest areas to fix
6. Most understood by you

- *Most often used program areas:* Errors in these areas are repeatedly encountered, so very annoying.

- *Distinguishing area of the program*: If you're selling a database and you claim that it sorts 48 times faster than your competitor, you better test sorting because that's why people are buying your program. If your sorting is very fast but it doesn't work, customers will get grumpy. It's important to do early testing on heavily optimized areas that distinguish your program because heavily optimized code is often hard to fix. You want to report these bugs early to give the programmers a fighting chance to fix them.

- *Hardest areas to fix*: Sit with the programmer and ask, "If I found bugs in the most horrible areas that you don't ever want to think about, what areas would those be?" Some programmers will tell you. Go right to those areas and beat on them. Do it now, when it's four months before the program will ship, to give the staff a chance to fix what you find. If you find these bugs a week before the scheduled ship date, the programmer will have a heart attack or quit and you'll never get them fixed.

- *Most understood by you*: Maybe you've read the code or you understand something about applications of this kind. Here's an area you understand, that you can test well right away. As to the rest, you're learning how to test the program while you test it. If you're an expert in one area, test it first and test how it interacts with the other areas. Even if it's not a critical area, you'll gain good experience with the program and find bugs too. This will be a base: it will help you go much more effectively, and much more quickly, into the next area.

## THE MECHANICS OF ADDING DEPTH TO THE TEST PLAN

Add depth to the test plan by creating and expanding the various test plan components: lists, decision trees, function lists, boundary charts, test matrices, and so on. These are your tools for analyzing the program and for identifying the tests to run:

- In the next section, "Components of Test Planning Documents," we describe these components and explain how to develop them. We also shows how to apply an evolutionary approach to their development.

- After the components discussion, "Documenting Test Materials" explains how to combine the components into the various types of test planning documents.

- We continue the larger discussion—how to organize the testing project and how to prioritize tasks—in Chapter 13. Further discussion of test plan evolution starts in "Testing activities after alpha" and runs through several sections.

**TEST PLANNING & DOCUMENTATION**

## COMPONENTS OF TEST PLANNING DOCUMENTS

Note: This section uses the Problem Tracking System as an example of a program that you might test. (We also use a simple billing system. We have to use some program, to get sample data for Figures 12.5 through 12.11. We prefer the tracking system to a freshly invented program because you already know it from Chapters 5 and 6.)

Throughout this chapter, rather than thinking about the Problem Tracking System from the viewpoint of someone who may design and use it, imagine that someone else wrote the system and wants you to test it.

Please don't be put off by any details of the Tracking System that weren't specified in Chapter 6. We invented details here for the sake of illustration. These details will vary from company to company.

This section describes the building blocks of testing documents. We organize our test planning around the development of four main types of charts (Figure 12.5 gives examples of each type).

- lists
- tables
- outlines
- matrices

**Figure 12.5 Examples of components of test planning documents**

| Lists | List of reports |
|---|---|
| | List of input and output variables |
| | List of features and functions |
| | Bill of materials |
| | List of program's files |
| | List of error messages |
| | List of compatible hardware |
| | List of compatible software |
| | List of compatible operating environments |
| | List of public documents |
| Tables | Table of reports |
| | Table of input values and output values |
| | Input/output table |
| | Decision table |
| | Keyboard convention table |
| | Printer compatibility table |
| | Boundary chart |
| Outlines | Function list |
| Matrices | Hardware and feature compatibility matrix |
| | Hardware combination matrix |
| | Environment matrix |
| | Input combination matrix |
| | Error message and keyboard matrix |

These are concise documents. They show only what you need to know to test the program. They organize your work quickly. They also help you identify information you don't have or don't understand.

In theory, you should be able to construct all the charts we describe from a full specification. If anyone ever asks you to review a specification for thoroughness, these charts provide your best tools for identifying the specification's holes.

In practice, few consumer software specifications are detailed enough to let you create test planning charts without significant further research. As a result, we spend most of our test planning time creating these charts. We find this extremely valuable, and we recommend it as good practice.

Unfortunately, it's easy to get so immersed in chart creation that you run out of testing time. To avoid this, we evolve our charts over time. We create skeleton charts first, then fill in unknown facts and new levels of detail as we progress through testing. We will illustrate this evolutionary approach with a few examples.

Much of the information that goes into these charts comes from developers' specifications or notes, from drafts of the user manual, and from your interviews of the programmers and project manager. But another large portion of the information, sometimes as much as 75%, comes from experimenting with the program. This is a fact of life—you will run test cases, find boundary conditions, combine inputs, and create new report formats in ways that the project manager never considered. Some, but not all, project managers will check your results and tell you whether the program is behaving correctly in their view. You will often simply have to decide for yourself whether the program's behavior is reasonable or not. If it appears unreasonable, file a Problem Report. If you're not sure, file a Problem Report marked as a `Query`.

A final note: as you develop these charts, pass them to the people writing the user and technical support manuals. They need the same information. They'll often return the favor by giving your their charts and by keeping you up to date on their discoveries of undocumented program changes.

## LISTS

Lists are simple enough to make. The only problem is making sure that you've included everything in the list that belongs there. Once you've made a list, you don't have to remember anything that's on the list any more. If your list is complete, you can stop worrying about whether you're missing anything. Just check the list.

**Figure 12.6 Reports available in the Problem**

**Tracking System**

- Problem Report (Figure 5.1)

- Summary of New Problems (Figure 6.1)

- Project Status (Figure 6.3)

- Test Cycle Complete (Figure 6.4)

- Unresolved Problems, Sorted by Severity (Figure 6.5)

- Unresolved Problems, Sorted by Development Group (Figure 6.6)

- Deferred Problems (Firgure 6.7)

- Weekly Totals (Figure 6.8)

- Release Report (Figure 6.9)

- Patches (Figure 6.10)

## Lists of reports and data entry screens

Two of the first lists to make are the list of reports the program can print or display and the list of data entry screens (including dialog boxes). From these, you can list all the individual variables that the program will display or print and all the variables that the user can type into the program.

As an example, if you were testing the Problem Tracking System, you would list its reports, as in Figure 12.6.

You gain a lot from a simple list like this. If you were testing the tracking system, then during most testing cycles, you would want to check each report. This list tells you every report the program generates. You can use it as a reminder for yourself, or you can ask another tester to generate the reports. You know she won't miss any reports, even if she doesn't know the program well, because she's working from a complete list.

## Lists of input and output variables

List every variable that you can enter at any data entry screen or dialog box. An example of a *variable* is PROBLEM REPORT NUMBER. The number will be different on each bug report, but each report will have a number. Each field in the Problem Report is a variable that you or the computer will fill in when you enter a bug report.

If you were testing the tracking system, you would list all of its variables, starting with every variable on the Problem Report form (Figure 5.1). Figure 12.7 lists the first few variables on that form.

According to the design of the report, some of the variables call for simple numbers, such as PROBLEM REPORT NUMBER. Others call for many lines of text, such as the field named PROBLEM AND HOW TO REPRODUCE IT.

If the program reads data from disk, find out the file's data structure from the project manager. List every variable that you retrieve from the file. As your testing gets more thorough, you should consider writing a test program to read the data file directly, to check whether the project manager's list is always correct. Data files often vary in format under special circumstances that project managers forget to mention or don't know about. These special cases are excellent opportunities to find new bugs.

**Figure 12.7 Some variables entered on the Problem Report form**

Problem Report Number

Program Name

Release (number or letter)

Version (number or letter or date)

Report type

Severity

Attachments (Y/N)

Attachments Description

Problem Summary

Problem and How to Reproduce it

You should also list every variable printed in reports, displayed in response to queries, or sent as output to another computer.

Taken together, these lists identify all the variables that you can directly test. In themselves, these simple lists leave out much information:

- They don't tell you where to find the variables (such as which dialog box or report). You'll record that information in a table, such as the ones in Figures 12.11 through 12.13.

- They also don't tell you what values, for each variable, are valid or invalid. For that, make a boundary chart (see Figure 12.17).

- They don't identify relationships between input and output variables. (As an example of a relationship, the PROBLEM SUMMARY in a summary report comes directly from the PROBLEM SUMMARY entered into each Problem Report. An output variable can have a different name from the input variable, but still take the input variable's value.)

  Output variables are often direct copies of input variables, but the relationships can be more complex. For example, imagine a mail order billing system. One report is a customer invoice. Its input variables, entered by the order taker, include the items ordered and their price. These are also output variables—they'll appear on the report (customer invoice) sent to the customer. Another variable is total purchase price, calculated from the purchase prices of the individual items bought. Another output variable, sales tax (multiply the total purchase price by some percentage), doesn't directly involve any of the input variables even though it is based on their values. A third output variable might be total balance due, including the total purchase price, the tax, and any balance owing from previous purchases. Note that the balance is retrieved from a data file, rather than from entry of the customer's current order.

  To describe relationships between input and output variables, build a data input/output table (Figures 12.12 and 12.13 are examples).

Simple lists of variables are extremely useful even though they skip important, detailed information. First, they are the basis for more detailed tables, such as the three just noted. Second, during the first few rounds of testing, you won't have time to build these detailed tables. Instead, use these lists as pointers to the variables. Invent test cases on the fly for each variable to check its handling of extreme values and its effect on reports. These tests won't be as thorough or as elegant as more carefully planned ones, but they are a strong start.

Finally, in your first round of test planning, don't expect to have time or knowledge of the program to successfully make a complete list of variables. You will discover new dialog boxes, new reports, new associated data files, and newly programmed changes to old boxes, reports, and files.

## List of features and functions

List all the user-visible functions. Include commands, menu choices, pulldowns, command line options, and any other significant capabilities that you know are present in the program. This is your list of top-level functions.

**Figure 12.8 First draft function list for the**

**Problem Tracking System**

1. Display sign-on screen (date, copyright, etc.)

2. Enter user ID

3. Enter new problem reports

4. Edit old problem reports

5. Work with a holding file

6. Work with a reference file

7. Generate a summary report

8. System utilities

9. Create new forms or reports

10. Help

Later you will list the subfunctions and the subsubfunctions. Eventually you will develop a detailed, structured listing of the program's capabilities. We recommend using an outline processor to manage this list, and we will discuss the full development of the function list, as an outline, later in this chapter ("Components of test planning documents: Outlines—the function list"). That outline will become an invaluable map of your knowledge of the program.

Through all stages of its development, the function list serves as a useful checklist of the program features that you should check during each full cycle of testing.

As an illustration, if you were testing the Problem Tracking System, your first draft of the feature list might look like the one in Figure 12.8. There are few details. Later drafts will be more complete.

**List of error messages**

List every error message the program can generate. If you can't get the list directly from the project manager, use a utility program that will help you pull the messages out of the code and resource files. If you can't do this either (because the text has been compressed or encrypted), push the project manager harder to give you copies of the source files that contain the messages.

You must put the program into every state that can result in an error message. Test the program's production of an error message in each state. Does the program give the right message? Is the message appropriate for the circumstances that led up to it? How well does the program recover after displaying the message?

The program's error handling will be one of your most consistent sources of bugs. You will often find it worthwhile to expand this list into a detailed test matrix, to check error recovery. We discuss one example of such a matrix in "Error message and keyboard matrix" (under "Components of test planning documents: Matrices," later in this chapter).

**List of program's files**

Compare time and date stamps of the just-submitted version's files with the previous version's. The project manager will probably give you a list of every change he thinks was made in the new version, but many managers' lists are incomplete. If you know what data or functional areas are involved with which files, then comparing the old and new versions gives you some hints about unmentioned changes.

Sometimes the documentation lists all the files too. Compare that list to your list, and pass on your corrections to the writers.

---

***Before you release the program, you MUST check that the release disks contain the most recent version of every file.***

---

*So many companies* have shipped—and had to replace or recall—disks with the wrong files. It is *so embarrasing.* It's plenty expensive too. When you get a set of (alleged) release disks at the last minute, it's *so tempting* to send them to the duplicator after a brief check, or no check at all. *Don't take this shortcut.* Check the disks carefully.

### List of compatible hardware

List the computers, printers, displays, and other types of devices that the program is supposed to be compatible with. See Chapter 8 for notes on hardware compatibility testing.

### List of compatible software

List the programs that this program is supposed to work with. Check each program for compatibility. Eventually, you'll expand this list into a table that shows not only the programs but also the area of compatibility. Is this program compatible with another one in the sense that:

- both can reside in memory simultaneously?
- one can read the other's data files?
- the two can pass messages to each other?
- both store data in the same file format?
- both follow the same keyboard conventions?
- both follow the same user interface conventions?

### List of compatible operating environments

What operating system does this program run under? Which versions? If some versions of the operating system have been customized for specific hardware, which ones should the program be tested with? If a second company makes an operating system that it claims is compatible with one of the systems you are testing, should you test this compatible system too?

On top of the operating system are resident utilities. These might include additional programs that manage a network or memory or the hard disk or that superimpose a graphical interface on top of a command-driven system, or a richer interface on top of a more basic graphical interface.

List all the different systems, utilities, interfaces, and drivers that your program must be compatible with. When you have time, organize these into tables that show relationships, such as which interfaces should be tested in the context of which operating system versions.

**12**

TEST PLANNING &
DOCUMENTATION

## Bill of materials

The bill of materials lists everything that goes to the customer in the box. It lists all the disks, advertising leaflets, stickers on the box, manuals, reference cards, loose correction pages, and anything else that is part of the product. You *must* test (for example, check for accuracy), *everything* listed in the bill of materials. The list helps you make sure you don't miss reviewing any component of the product.

## List of public documents

List every document about this program that anyone outside of the company will see or have read to them. This includes user documentation, advertisements, leaflets, technical support answer sheets, mail-out product literature, technicians' installation, diagnostic and maintenance guides, box copy, sticker copy, disk label copy, press releases, and perhaps others.

Prior to release (of the product, or of the document), check every document for accuracy.

## TABLES

The limitation of a list is that it doesn't organize information; it just lists it. Tables are better for showing relationships.

### Figure 12.9 Reports printed by the Problem Tracking System

| *Which report* | *When it's printed* | *How many copies* |
|---|---|---|
| Problem Report (Figure 5.1) | When it's entered | 4 |
| Summary of New Problems (Figure 6.1) | Weekly | 6 |
| Project Status (Figure 6.3) | Weekly | 12 |
| Test Cycle Complete (Figure 6.4) | End of this cycle of testing | 12 |
| Unresolved Bugs, Sorted by Severity Level (Figure 6.5) | Weekly | 6 |
| Unresolved Bugs, Sorted by Development Group (Figure 6.6) | On request only | 2 |
| Deferred Problems (Figure 6.7) | Monthly | 12 |
| Weekly Totals (Figure 6.8) | Product ready to be released | 12 |
| Release (Figure 6.9) | Product ready to be released | 12 |
| Patches (Figure 6.10) | Start of testing | 4 |

To illustrate the development and use of tables, suppose the Problem Tracking System developer modifies the system to print its reports automatically, on appropriate days. To test this enhancement, you would check whether the right reports are printed at the right times. A table is the natural chart for listing reports and the printing times for each.

## Table of reports

The table in Figure 12.9 shows the same reports as the list in Figure 12.6. These are the reports generated by the Problem Tracking system.The table also has room for further information—it shows when the system prints each report and how many copies of each it prints.

Tables organize information into rows and columns. The rows and columns are usually *labeled*:

- The top row usually shows what goes in each column. According to the top row of Figure 12.9, the first column lists reports, the second column shows how often each report is printed, and the third column shows how many copies of each report are printed.

- The first column usually shows what information belongs in each row. Figure 12.9 lists the type of summary report in the first column. Everything else in that report's row is about that report.

Figure 12.9 lists the reports in the order they appear in Chapter 6. This is a good start because it helps you check that you haven't missed anything. A more useful organization would list together all reports printed on the same day, as in Figure 12.10. This is better, because you'll probably want to test the printing of same day reports at the same time.

**12**

TEST PLANNING &
DOCUMENTATION

**Figure 12.10 Reports printed by the Problem Tracking System: Organized by when they are printed**

| *When* | *Which report* | *How many copies* |
|---|---|---|
| Start of testing | Patches (Figure 6.10) | 4 |
| On entry of problem | Problem Report (Figure 5.1) | 4 |
| Weekly | Summary of New Problem (Figure 6.1) | 6 |
|  | Project Status (Figure 6.3) | 12 |
|  | Unresolved Bugs, Sorted by Severity Level (Figure 6.5) | 6 |
| Monthly | Deferred Problems (Figure 6.7) | 12 |
| End of this cycle of testing | Test Cycle Complete (Figure 6.4) | 12 |
| Product ready to release | Weekly Totals (Figure 6.8) | 12 |
|  | Release (Figure 6.9) | 12 |
| On request only | Unresolved Bugs, Sorted by Development Group (Figure 6.6) | 2 |

## Tables of input variables and output variables

Here's an example of a table of input variables: in the first column, list the input variables, such as the variables listed in Figure 12.7. Label this column VARIABLES. In the second column, beside each variable, name the data entry screen or dialog box that the variable comes from. Where does the customer enter this data? Label the second column SOURCES. If the same variable appears in more than one place in the program, write down this source (entry screen) below the first one on a new line. If the customer can enter or modify many variables in more than one data entry screen, add a second SOURCE column. Figure 12.11 illustrates the layout:

### Figure 12.11 Table of input variables

| Variables | Source | 2nd source |
|---|---|---|
| Problem Report Number | Report Form | -- none -- |
| Report Type | Report Form | Modify Report |
| Problem and How to Reproduce It | Report Form | Modify Report |

  Organize a table of output variables in the same way as the input variables, except that instead of showing where the variable comes from (source), you want to show where the variable is displayed or printed. Just replace SOURCE with REPORT in the table headings. If different variables are saved to different files, then here (or in another similar table), you would add another column, headed FILE, listing the data file(s) in which this variable is saved.

### Figure 12.12 An input/output table

| Input variable | Output variables | Relationship |
|---|---|---|
| Item_price | Billed_item_price | Same as Item_price |
| | Total_purchase | Sum of prices of all items purchased |
| | Sales_tax | 7% of Total_purchase |
| | Total_balance_due | Total_purchase + Sales_tax + Previous_balance_due |

## Input/Output Table

Each piece of information entered in the program is used somewhere. It may appear in reports, or be used in calculations, or it may be used to point the program toward some other piece of information.

You should know how each input variable is used. If you change the value of a variable, what output variables will be affected and why?

You should know how each output variable was obtained. How does the program decide to print this value instead of that? Is the decision based on a calculation, a search, or something else? What other variables are involved in this?

List input variables in the first column. In the second column, list an output variable whose value depends in some way on the input variable. Beside or under the output variable, describe the relationship. We don't have a good example of this in the problem tracking system, so we'll use the billing system and customer invoice described earlier in this chapter, in "Components of test planning documents: Lists: Lists of input And output variables." One input variable is the price of an item that was ordered. This variable is associated with the following output variables:

Two of the four output variables listed in Figure 12.12 are based on `Total_purchase`, which is in turn based on `Item_price`. Along with being an output variable in its own right, `Total_purchase` is an *intermediate variable*, i.e., a variable that sits between input and output variables. Its value is determined by the inputs, and its value in turn determines the outputs.

It's often convenient to reorganize an input/output chart to show intermediate variables. In this chart, you would list output variable `Sales_tax`, that depends directly on the intermediate variable (`Total_purchase`) and only indirectly on the input variable (`Item_price`), beside the intermediate variable and not beside the input variable. The chart might look like this:

### Figure 12.13 Another input/output table

| Input variable | Intermediate variable | Output variables | Relationship |
|---|---|---|---|
| Item_price | | Billed_item_priced | Same as Item_price |
| | | Total_purchase | Sum of prices of all items purchased |
| | Total_purchase | Sales_tax | 7% of Total_purchase |
| | | Total_balance_due | Total_purchase + Sales_tax + Previous_balance_due |

Why is this second chart a refinement over the first? Because it will save you testing time. In both charts, you should run at least one test case per pair of variables. Usually you'll run a few tests to check for boundary effects (such as, what is the effect on the output variable if you enter the largest possible value for the input variable). If an intermediate variable's value is based on many inputs, and this intermediate variable in turn affects many output (or other intermediate) variables, it will require far fewer tests to check the relationships between the inputs and the intermediate, and between the intermediate and its outputs than to check all the relationships between the many inputs and the many outputs.

To test your understanding of this, try creating two further charts like those in Figures 12.12 and 12.13. The input variables are Price_1, Price_2, Price_3, and Price_4. The output variables are Billed_price, Total_purchase (the sum of the four prices), Sales_tax, and Total_balance_due.

Your first chart, the one structured like Figure 12.12, should have sixteen lines, showing sixteen pairs of variables. There are four lines in the table for Price_1, which is paired with Billed_price, Total_purchase, Sales_tax, and Total_balance_due. There are four similar lines for Price_2, another four for Price_3, and a final four for Price_4.

Your second chart will have only ten lines. Price_1 will pair with Billed_price and Total_purchase, as will Price_2, Price_3 and Price_4. This makes eight lines. Then Total_purchase, as an intermediate variable, is paired with Sales_tax and Total_balance_due (two more lines, plus the eight).

The difference in strategies is that, in the second case, you never test directly the relationship between the input variables (the prices) and the remote output variables (tax and total due).

You can extend and deepen your analysis of the flow of data through the program by subdividing the program into processing stages. Each stage gets input data from the stage before. Each stage passes its outputs on to the next. Some outputs are just copies of the inputs while others are totally different variables. In either case, these are intermediate results. Checking intermediate values helps you pin down where the program fails, when it fails. Thinking about them helps you find new boundaries, and imagine things that can go wrong, expanding your list of possible tests.

There are thus three types of tables:

- One shows *all input variables*, how they're used, where they appear as intermediate results, and how they affect intermediate and final output values. For each input variable, list all relevant processing stages and intermediate and final outputs.

- One shows *all output variables*, and where their values come from. For each output, list all relevant input and intermediate variables and processing stages.

- One shows *all visible processing stages*. A stage is visible if you can look at its input or output data. For each stage, list all input and output variables.

These three tables are redundant. You could show everything you need to know in any one of them. But each list will force you to look at the program in a little different way. If you make all three and compare them, you'll find information in each that you missed in the others.

We often supplement lists with *data flow diagrams*, noting how the program gets or generates each piece of information, where it uses each, what it will output (print, save to disk, etc.) and when. It takes a lot of pages to describe these diagrams. Read Gane and Sarson (1979). For more detail (about 125 very readable pages) read De Marco (1979).

### Decision tables and trees

A decision table shows the program's logic. Each entry in the table, shows Y (yes) or N (no) (or T or F). The program will do one thing or another. The table shows which it will do under what circumstances.

Figure 12.14 illustrates a decision table. The system will print two summary reports. The first lists all problems deferred this month (July). The second lists all problems deferred to date. For each Problem Report, the program has to decide whether to include it in either summary.

The top three rows of the table show the questions the program must ask to make the decision:

- Did the programmer defer the problem? (If so, RESOLUTION CODE is 3.)
- Did the tester say Yes in the TREAT AS DEFERRED field?
- Was the resolution entered in July?

The bottom two rows of the table show the decisions.

Note that Figure 12.14 includes every possible combination of Yes's and No's for these three conditions. Decision tables always show what the program will do under any combination of relevant events. They always list all relevant events.

Any decision table can be redrawn as a decision tree. Many people initially understand decision trees more readily than decision tables. Figure 12.15 is a decision tree that shows the same information as Figure 12.14's decision table. For more examples of decision tables and trees, we recommend Gane and Sarson (1979).

**12**

TEST PLANNING &
DOCUMENTATION

### Figure 12.14 A decision table

Two summary reports are to be printed. The first only includes problems deferred in July. The second includes all deferred problems. A problem is considered deferred if it is resolved as deferred (code = 3) or if the tester said Yes in the Treat As Deferred field. The table shows the rule in deciding whether to include a Problem Report in either summary.

| IF | Resolution Code = 3 | Y | Y | Y | Y | N | N | N | N |
| | Marked "Treat As Deferred" | Y | Y | N | N | Y | Y | N | N |
| | Resolved During July | Y | N | Y | N | Y | N | Y | N |
| THEN | Include it in July Report | Y | N | Y | N | Y | N | N | N |
| | Include in Overall Report | Y | Y | Y | Y | Y | Y | N | N |

**Figure 12.15  A decision tree**

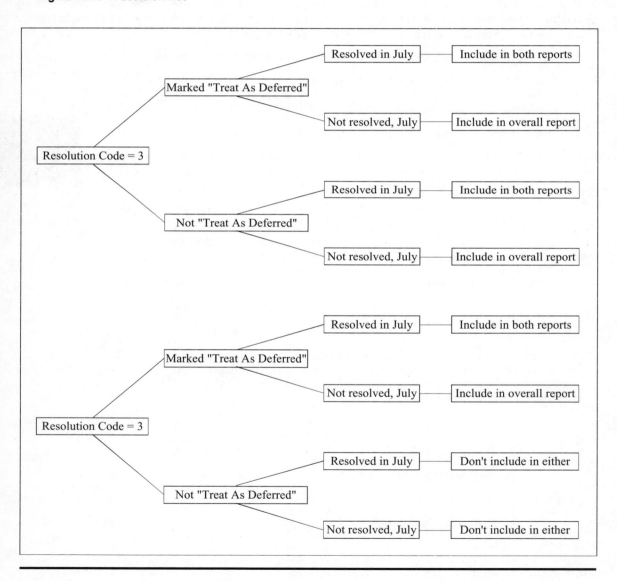

## Keyboard convention table

The keyboard convention table is quite large. Use a spreadsheet to make it. In the form we describe here, the table shows the program's response to each character, in each program state.

The keyboard convention table reveals inconsistencies in the user interface (e.g., F1 means different things at different places in the program). Some inconsistencies are there by design (or by lack of design); others are coding errors. In creating the table you'll also discover undocumented behavior including half-finished discarded ideas (oops, crash), back doors into the debugger, strange messages, exotic animated image sequences, and once-planned features that the development team decided to drop but someone coded them and tossed them in anyway without telling anyone.

Each row in this table is devoted to a single character. A, a, B, b, *, &, -, É, and • are all individual characters. So are <Alt-A>, <Command-D>, <Option-B>, <Open-Amiga-C>, <F1>, <Ctrl-Shift-F1>, and the various dead keys on non-English keyboards.

The first column in the table lists the individual characters (one per line). Succeeding columns list the effects of entering the characters in the various states, dialog boxes, and entry screens of the program. For example, at a data entry screen, if you press A, the computer will echo the A in the appropriate field on the screen. On the row for A, in the column for this screen, enter an A. Now suppose that at error message boxes, the computer requires you to press <Escape> to continue. It ignores all other characters at the message box. On the row for A, in the column for error messages, enter Ignored.

In practice, you will condense the keyboard table by grouping equivalent keys together. For example, you might group together all lowercase letters. You have to exercise judgment when you condense the keyboard table; your results will vary across programs and operating systems. Even after condensing the table, though, it is big—you (and the program's spec writer) will reserve rows for many groups and for many individual special characters. We describe some keyboard groupings later in this chapter, in "Components of test planning documents: Matrices: Error message and keyboard matrix."

It takes a few days to create this chart. After you've made it, print it out, mark the inconsistencies with a highlighter, perhaps suggest effective ways to use unused function or command keys, and pass your work to the project manager. If this work is done reasonably early, it often results in a signficant user interface cleanup.

The manual and help writers will also find this chart extremely useful.

### Figure 12.16 A printer compatibility matrix

| *Printer* | *Mode* | *Compatibility source* | *Tested* | *Notes* |
|---|---|---|---|---|
| HP LaserJet III | Native | LJ III (self) | | |
| HP LaserJet III compatible | Postscript | Postscript | Full test | 100% |
| | | | | |

## Figure 12.17 Sample analysis of data entry field

| Field | Valid Equivalence Classes | Invalid Equivalence Classes | Boundary & Special Cases | Notes |
|-------|---------------------------|------------------------------|---------------------------|-------|
| Problem Report # | 0 - 999999 | 1. < 0<br><br>2. > 999999<br><br>3. Duplicate any other report #<br><br><br><br>4. Any non-digits | 1. 0<br><br>2. 999999<br><br>3. Enter a record after 999999<br><br><br><br>4. -00001 | Default automatically entered but you can edit the number<br><br>Can you enter a smaller number than the default? If so, what happens to the default next time? |
| Program | Up to 36 printable chars. <Return>, <Tab>, leading <Space> not OK. Must match a name in reference file PROGRAMS.DAT | 1. Contains non-printing chars (like control chars)<br><br>2. No matching name in reference file | | Required field |
| Version | 12 printable characters "UNKNOWN" OK | | | 1. Your company standard will be more precise<br><br>2. Required field |
| Report Type | 1 digit, range 1 - 6 | 1. < 1<br><br>2. > 6<br><br>3. Not number | 1. 0<br><br>2. 7<br><br>3. /<br><br>4. : | Required field |
| Attachments | Y, y, N, n.<br><br>Blank field is treated as equivalent to OK | 1. Any other letters<br><br>2. Non-letters | 1. M, m<br><br>2. O, o<br><br>3. W, w<br><br>4. Z, z | All input converted to upper case |
| Attachments Text | Up to 80 printable characters | | | 1. Automatic word wrap to the next line<br><br>2. Cursor reaches this field only if Attachments is Y<br><br>3. Field is erased if Attachments reset to 0 |

## Printer compatibility table

There are over 1000 printers on the market, and most of them *emulate* (work just like) other printers. If 50 printers all emulate the Hewlett Packard LaserJet II, don't test all 50 printers.

We've found it useful to create charts, along the lines of Figure 12.16, that show what printers are compatible with what others. (You can create similar charts for other devices but here, as in Chapter 8, we'll stick with printers as our model device.) Formats vary widely. All charts contain some of the following columns:

- *Printer:* make and model.

- *Mode:* some printers can be set in their own native mode, or to emulate a few other, different, printers.

- *Compatibility:* make and model of the printer this one emulates.

- *Source:* how do you know this printer emulates that one? Name the magazine article, the person, the advertisement. Some reports are much more trustworthy than others.

- *Tested:* indicate whether your lab has tested this printer's compatibility and what test was used. Have you confirmed graphic mode compatibility? Escape sequence command compatibility? Character set compatibility?

- *Notes:* list incompatibilities, doubts, customer reports, etc.

## Boundary Chart

See "Equivalence classes and boundary values" in Chapter 7 for a detailed discussion of equivalence class and boundary chart development. Figure 12.17 illustrates a boundary analysis of some of the input variables used in the Problem tracking system.

**12**

Don't expect to complete this chart early in testing. It takes a long time to do this chart well. Start by listing every input field (use the input variable list if you made one). Identify their functions. Assign limit values and further information as you learn more, but let yourself experiment with the variables from a full list from as early a time as you can.

## OUTLINES—THE FUNCTION LIST

Function lists outline what the program can do. They express *your* organization of the program's functions. Organize them in a way that you'll find convenient for testing and test planning. We use a function list as the core of our notes.

You can develop these lists to almost any level of completeness and detail. We suggest an incremental approach. Start simple; add detail as you go. Figure 12.18 summarizes our approach.

You'll find it much easier and faster to add items and reorganize the list if you use an outline processor, rather than a word processor.

Figure 12.8 shows a basic, first draft, top-level list of the problem tracking system's functions. It shows everything the program is supposed to do. This first step toward a more thorough outline is valuable in its own right. Keep a copy at your desk while testing the program; check it as you go to make sure that you've tested each function on the list. You can summarize the stability of different parts of the program by highlighting working functions in one color and failing ones in another.

Make your next draft more organized. Choose an organization that seems natural and easy to work with. Try an alphabetic listing for a command language that invokes each function with a separate command. Try a hierarchical layout for menu-driven programs. Alternatively, you could organize around the program's conceptual structure, grouping all functions that do related work, rely on related input data, or generate related outputs.

Figure 12.19 expands the first draft list of Figure 12.8. Many of the main functions have been left alone. The figure breaks one function, `5. Work with a holding file`, into two subfunctions. It explores one of these, `5.1 Read data from a file`, in further detail.

You can keep adding detail to a function list. For example, you can expand `5.1.3.6 (Optional) Print record` to show that the program will (should) check whether the printer is online and ready to print. Expand the list gradually. If you try to make a full list before starting to test, you may never have time to start testing.

Figure 12.20 magnifies section `3. Enter new Problem Reports` from Figure 12.19. You can call a list that's as detailed as this a *function* or *program outline*. This list is so detailed that in many cases, if you do the operation listed, the computer will do exactly one thing. This is a test case. Expected results belong here.

Include the following types of information as you add detail to the outline:

- *Every function* of the program.

- *Every visible subfunction*.

- *Every command* you can issue to the program.

- *The effect of pressing each command key* at each place that the program accepts input.

**Figure 12.18 Evolving the function list**

1.  List the top level, user-visible functions (commands, actions, menu options).

2.  Deepen the list with subfunctions (all available options or menu choices from a main function).

3.  Show subfunctions to their deepest level. (Each line at this level represents a fully parameterized choice -- something that will actually be executed.)

4.  List entry and exit conditions for each function and subfunction.

5.  List all keyboard and other input device effects on dialogues in this function.

    *Eventually, make each line a test case.*

**Figure 12.19 Second draft of a function list**

1. Display sign-on screen (date, copyright, etc.)
2. Enter user ID
3. Enter new problem reports
4. Edit old problem reports
5. Work with a holding file
5.1   Read data from a file
5.1.1     Get drive and file name
5.1.2     Check whether this file has already been appended to database
5.1.3     For each record in the file:
5.1.3.1       Read the record
5.1.3.2       Skip to next record if this one is marked as appended already
5.1.3.3       Fill "Problem Report #" with next available number
5.1.3.4       If any required fields are empty, display record and get data
5.1.3.5       (Optional) Display record and get OK before adding to database
5.1.3.6       (Optional) Print record
5.1.3.7       Add record to database
5.1.3.8       Mark record as appended to database
5.1.4     Mark file as having been appended to database
5.1.5     Return to "Work with a holding file" menu
5.1.6     Error handling while reading/editing holding file records
5.1.6.1       Invalid file or disk file name
5.1.6.2       File not on disk
5.1.6.3       Disk I/O error
5.1.6.4       File has been read and appended to database already
5.1.6.5       Attempt to save a record with blank required fields
5.1.6.6       Enter field value that doesn't match reference file
5.1.6.7       Printer not ready
5.2   Write data to a file
6. Work with a reference file
7. Generate a summary report
8. System utilities
9. Create new forms or reports
10 Help

**Figure 12.20 Detailed function outline of section 3: Enter new problem reports**

| | | |
|---|---|---|
| 3.1 | Display top 24 lines of report form (or less of the form, plus a keystroke menu) | |
| 3.1.1 | Automatically fill in "Problem Report #" | |
| 3.1.2 | (Optional) If this is the 2nd (or later) report entered during this session, fill "Program," Version," "Your Name," and "Date" with value entered into the last report. | |
| 3.1.3 | Position cursor in "Report Type" field. | |
| 3.2 | Keystroke assignments while entering/editing data in a field | |
| 3.2.1 | F1 | Display help menu |
| 3.2.2 | F2 | Repaint screen |
| 3.2.3 | F3 | Print this report |
| 3.2.3.1 | | Check if printer on or online |
| 3.2.3.2 | | (Optional) Form feed to top of next page |
| 3.2.3.3 | | Print copy(s) of Problem Report |
| 3.2.4 | Up-Arrow | Move cursor to field closest to directly above this one. Ignore if cursor on top line. |
| 3.2.5 | Right-Arrow | Move cursor back one character |
| 3.2.5.1 | | Move to last character of previous field if on first character of a field. |
| 3.2.5.2 | | Ignore if at first character of first field of form. |
| 3.2.6 | Ctrl-A | Ignored |
| 3.2.7 | Ctrl-B | Move cursor to previous field. Ignore if in "Problem Report #" |
| 3.2.8 | Ctrl-C | "Clear all fields and start over?" |
| 3.2.9 | Ctrl-D | If all required fields completed: |
| | | "Done entry?" |
| | | Else |
| | | "Incomplete entry: Need more information" |
| | | Move cursor to required field |
| 3.3 | Exit from form without saving data | |
| 3.3.1 | Ctrl-Q | Asks do you really want to quit without saving record (Y/N) |
| 3.3.2 | Reset | |
| 3.3.3 | Power-down | |
| 3.4 | Error handling | |
| 3.4.1 | Value out of range | |
| 3.4.2 | No match for entry in a reference file | |
| 3.4.3 | Can't find reference file | |
| 3.4.4 | Disk full when trying to save form data | |
| 3.4.5 | Other disk errors | |

- ***Every menu and every choice on every menu.*** Testers often create *menu maps* to show this information. These are free-form diagrams. Show where each menu choice leads. It often helps to name each menu or screen, showing the names on the map. The names should directly reflect the menu or screen as displayed.

- ***Every entry to each part of the program.*** How can you get there? Does how you got there make any difference or does the program behave in the same way no matter what menu, prompt screen, etc., you came from?

- ***Every exit from each part of the program.*** How do you go to the next menu, dialog, form, state, whatever? How do you quit entering data? How do you get back to where you came from? How do you halt the program from here?

- ***Every data entry screen, dialog box, and message box.*** Analyze the data values in a boundary chart. Here, show how to get to each screen, any sequence-dependencies (such as different behavior the first and second times you reach the screen), special commands, how to exit with and (if possible) without saving the data you entered, and where you get to from here.

- ***Error handling*** in this part of the program. We often find it easier to treat error handling as a separate section rather than trying to show it under each topic.

## MATRICES

A matrix is like a table. Both have rows and columns. The top row of each (the heading), shows what belongs in each column. The first column of many tables, and of all matrices, shows what belongs in each row.

As we use the terms, a table and a matrix differ in the following ways:

- The ***table's*** main function is descriptive. It summarizes the behavior of the program or (as in Figure 12.16) of hardware. A person with a complete enough specification could completely fill in the table without doing any testing. The tester would then compare the program's behavior against the information in the table.

- The ***matrix's*** main function is data collection. It provides a structure for testing the effect of combining two or more variables, circumstances, types of hardware, or events. The row and column headings identify test conditions. After she runs the test, the tester enters the result into the corresponding cell of the matrix. (For example if she combines the condition listed in the third row with the one listed in the fifth column, she'd enter the result in the matrix cell 3 rows down and 5 columns across.) Often, the cell entry is just a checkmark, indicating that the program behaved correctly.

### Disk input/output matrix

The disk I/O matrix is a classic example of a widely used test matrix. Suppose that your program can use the following functions to send data to the disk:

- ***Save:*** a copy of the data in memory to the disk.
- ***Save As:*** save a fresh copy of the data in memory under a new name.

- *Print to disk (ASCII):* format the output as if you were going to send it to an ASCII printer (no formatting codes fancier than tabs, line feeds, or carriage returns), but direct the output to a disk file rather than to a printer.
- *Print to disk (formatted):* format the output as if you were going to send it to your current printer. Include all formatting codes for that printer. Direct the output to a disk file rather than to a printer.

Suppose it can use the following functions to read data from the disk:

- *Open:* erase what's in memory (perhaps after saving it), then load this file into memory.
- *Append:* load the contents of this file into memory, placing them at the end of the data already in memory.
- *Insert:* load the contents of this file into memory, placing them at the current cursor position.
- *Import text:* open a text file that was created by some other application and is not in this program's native file format. Bring the text, and perhaps some of its formatting, into memory.
- *Import graphics:* load a picture into memory.

Suppose you're trying to save or read one of the following types of files:

- *A very small file* (one or two bytes).
- *A typical file.*
- *A large file* (more bytes in the file than available in RAM).

Suppose the program can run on computers that can use any of the following types of disks:

- *Low density floppy.*
- *High density floppy.*
- *Hard disk.*
- *Network volume.*
- *Optical disk.*
- *RAM drive.*

And finally, suppose any of the following events can happen:

- *Disk already full* when you try to write to it (via Save, Save as, or Print to disk).
- *Disk almost full,* fills during the attempted write or when creating a temporary file during the attempted read.
- *Disk is write-protected.*
- *Time-out:* the disk (probably the network) takes too long to respond.
- *Power failure* or power turned off.

- *Keyboard entry:* hit keys during the read or write.
- *Mouse activity:* move the mouse or click its buttons during the read or write.

There are lots more possibilities in each of these categories, but these cases illustrate the four categories involved in an I/O matrix analysis:

- *File operation* (such as Save As or Open).
- *File characteristics*, such as type, format, and size.
- *Hardware,* such as disk drive types, but also including individually listed computers if compatibility with specific models is suspect.
- *Failure condition,* such as a full disk or a hardware failure.

There are many ways to organize these categories into one or more I/O matrices. Figure 12.21 shows part of one possible matrix.

Using the matrix as a guide, you would run such tests as attempting to save a medium-size file (2nd row) to a write-protected low-density floppy disk (3rd column). If the program responded with a write-protected disk error message, and behaved reasonably thereafter, you would put a checkmark in the cell that at the intersection of the 2nd row and 3rd column. This is the starred (***) cell in Figure 12.21.

The disk I/O matrix is one of your most important testing charts. We recommend that you fill out the four category lists to match your application, and then make an input table and an output table.

**12**

## Other hardware-related matrices

Figure 8.4 is a test matrix that varies the type of printer across columns and the print features across rows.

Another printer matrix would show the types of printer across columns (such as LaserJet II, LaserJet III, LBP-8, etc.) and the amount of printer memory down the rows (such as 0.5, 1.0, 1.5, 2.0, and 2.5 megabytes). Perhaps the test case is a three-quarter-page graphic image. The program passes the test if it can print the image without running the printer out of memory.

## Figure 12.21 A disk I/O matrix

| | Low Density Floppy Disk | | | | | | |
|---|---|---|---|---|---|---|---|
| *Operation* | *Disk full* | *Almost full* | *Write-protected* | *Timeout* | *Power* | *Keyboard* | *Mouse* |
| Save | | | | | | | |
| Save As | | | *** | | | | |
| Print to Disk | | | | | | | |

**Figure 12.22 Character groupings, for keyboard testing**

| | |
|---|---|
| *Low ASCII* | These are the Ctrl keys. Interesting ones include 000-null, 007-beep, 008-BS, 009-Tab, 010-LF, 011-VT/home, 012-FF, 013-CR, 026-EOF (end of file, very nasty sometimes), 027-Esc |
| *Non-alphanumeric, standard, printing ASCII characters. We often lump these together even though they are in four distinct groups* | Low non-alphanumeric (ASCII codes 32-47) <space> ! " # $ % & ' ( ) * + , - . / <br><br> Intermediate non-alphanumeric (ASCII codes 58-64) : ; < = > ? @ <br><br> Further intermediate non-alphanumeric (ASCII codes 91-96) [ \ ] ^ _ ' <br><br> Top of standard ASCII (ASCII codes 123-127) { | } ~ <Del> |
| *Digits* | (ASCII 48-57)    0 1 2 3 4 5 6 7 8 9 |
| *Upper and lower case alpha* | (ASCII 65-90)    A B C D E F G H I J K L M N O P Q R S T U V W X Y Z <br> (ASCII 97-122)  a b c d e f g h i j k l m n o p q r s t u v w x y z |
| *Upper ASCII* | (ASCII 128-254) These might subdivide further depending on the application. |
| *Modifier keys* | These keys include (depending on the keyboard) <Alt>,< Shift>, <Control>, <Command>, <Option>, <Left-Amiga>, <Right-Amiga.> They generally have no effect when pressed alone, but when pressed in conjunction with some other key, they create a special keystroke such as  a command. Check your program, windowing environment, and operating system for lists of functions assigned to modified keys. <br><br> It often pays to test all the "interesting" standard values and a sample of others. <br><br> It is often best to assign a separate chart column to each modifier key, i.e., one column for <Ctrl>, one for <Shift>, one for <Alt>, etc. |
| *Function keys* | Test them alone and in combination with the modifier keys. |
| *Cursor keys* | Test them alone and in combination with the modifier keys. It's common for every modifier key to have a different effect on cursor keys. |
| *Numeric keypad keys* | These are not necessarily equivalent to number keys elsewhere on the keyboard |
| *European keyboards* | The left and right <Alt> keys often have different effects on non-English keyboards. Also these keyboards provide dead keys -- you press a dead key to specify an accent, then press a letter key, and (if it's a valid character) the computer displays that letter with that accent. |

### Environment matrix

In this case the rows (or columns) show environment variables, such as type or version of windowing environment, type or version of memory manager, operating system version, language, or country.

The columns (or rows) could also show environment variables, or they might list individual features, types of hardware, error states, or anything else you want to test in combination with a set of environment alternatives.

### Input combination matrix

Some bugs are triggered by a combination of events. If the program crashes only when you type a 60 character string on the third line of the screen, then press the up-arrow (this was a real bug), you won't find the problem by testing single actions or variables. Unfortunately, in most programs, the number of combinations of actions and variables' values is nearly infinite. Therefore, the question is not how to test all combinations of inputs (you can't). The question is, how to find a few interesting combinations.

Myers (1979) describes one powerful but complex approach called *Cause-Effect Graphing*. We will not describe it here, but we recommend it for further study.

Our approach is more experiential. We learn a lot about input combinations as we test. We learn about natural combinations of these variables, and about variables that seem totally independent. We also go to the programmers with the list of variables and ask which ones are supposed to be totally independent. Their memories aren't perfect, and some programmers think it's funny to throw in the odd falsehood, so check a few combinations of allegedly independent variables just to reassure yourself.

Once we develop a feel for the relatedness among variables, we test different combinations of values of related variables.

### Error message and keyboard matrix

Earlier in this chapter, we described a keyboard convention table that showed all the program's responses to all possible keyboard inputs. Here we also look at program responses to keystrokes, but in a more tightly focused matrix.

In a graphical user interface (GUI), error messages appear in message boxes. The only valid response is an acknowledgment, by mouse-clicking on <OK> or by pressing <Enter>. Mouse clicks in other places and other keystrokes are (supposedly) invalid and ignored. In practice, even on systems with extensive, standardized message box building support, programmers often add special case diagnostics or other responses to specific keys in individual message boxes.

We often hear the claim that all message boxes in a given Macintosh application always work the same way, so if you test one message box thoroughly, you've tested them all. This is pablum, not suitable for real testers. We've found message-specific ways to crash Macintosh applications, Amiga applications, Windows applications, and DOS applications.

You don't have enough time to check every possible keystroke with every message box, but a keystroke that has no effect in one message box may crash another. We drive this testing with a test matrix that lists messages on rows and groups of related keys in columns. For each row (message), we try a few keys from each column.

Figure 12.22 shows some of the ways that we group characters.

## DOCUMENTING TEST MATERIALS

This section discusses documents that describe the testing process. It's good to record what you did, why, when, the results, and what should be done next.

Previous sections of this chapter have described the objectives underlying these documents and the development of their components. Here we look at the types of complete test planning documents that you might create and distribute.

Test documentation is not a monolithic concept. There are many different types of documents. Some are more useful than others, some cheaper to write, some more fundamental. You have to decide which ones to write. This section describes the different needs for testing documents, and many types of documents that have been proposed to satisfy these needs.

### WHO WILL USE THIS DOCUMENTATION?

A key to the document's cost and value is that the reader must understand it. How much time and effort you have to invest to make the document understandable depends on the intended reader's sophistication—the more knowledgeable she is, the less you have to explain. It also depends on what she'll use the document for. The more thorough an understanding she needs, the more time you must spend writing.

This section describes seven possible users of your documentation and their needs. You don't have time to write documents that will be good for everyone. You have to decide who'll read a document and adjust your writing to meet their sophistication and needs.

Time estimates in the sections below are based on clocking of our own work under variable circumstances and are very rough.

### Personal notes

These are the simplest documents. Write them so that if you read them a month from now you'll know what testing was done, why each test was done, and what the results were. All you need is enough detail to accurately jog your memory. It should take you between one-half and three times as long to make these notes as it took to design the tests and execute them once.

You'll use these notes to:

- ***Describe tests that you'll run again.*** Why recreate each test from scratch when you can consult your notes for details instead? Your description may include complex details. If you use a fancy test file with lots of boundary conditions and other special values, note what they are and why. When the program changes, you must understand what to modify.

- ***Remind yourself of what's been done.*** It's surprisingly easy to run virtually the same test ten times over the course of a few days. Sometimes you forget you've run the test. Other times you're not sure, so you rerun it just to be safe. You can eliminate this waste by keeping a log of the tests you conduct.

- *Remind yourself of what has not yet been done.* Jot down ideas for further testing. Refer to them later, when you have time to create new tests.

- *Answer programmers' questions.* If you report a bug that the programmer finds hard to reproduce, he'll probably ask you about other tests he thinks are related. Did you run those tests? Exactly those tests? What happened?

## Notes for another team member

This person is experienced in testing this product, and you are available to answer her questions. It should take you between one and five times as long to describe each test as you spent developing it.

These notes should tell her:

- *How to run each test.* This can be brief because she's so knowledgeable.

- *The expected results of each test.* Sometimes they should also describe likely failure conditions.

- *The significance of each data value.* When the program changes, either the next tester can modify these tests appropriately or she'll have to ask you what to change. To know what to change, she has to understand the significance of what's there. In many cases, you don't have to write much about significance because the reader can deduce it from expected results.

- *Any other special instructions,* such as how long to wait or how quickly to press keys during timing tests.

- *Which tests should be conducted regularly* (regression tests), which were really one-shots (maybe you don't even need to describe these), and what ideas you have for further testing.

- *What these tests are looking for.* What area of the program is being studied? What types of problems are likely to be found? If you run many related tests, describe them that way. Perhaps you should describe a general theme for the group, describe one test in step-by-step detail, then describe the rest as variations on the prototype. This is faster to write and often easier to understand.

## Notes for another experienced tester

The difference between this case and the last (in "Notes for another team member") is that this time you assume that you won't be around to answer questions. If you're developing these materials under contract, for example, you'll leave when the contract is complete. Plan to spend three to ten times as long describing each test as you took to develop it and execute it once.

You should provide:

- *Everything you would provide to a teammate* but usually in more detail. Be especially careful to describe which results indicate success or failure. If you think some instructions are hard to understand (as notes on timing-related tests so often are), get someone in the group to read the notes and run the test in front of you. Does she understand what you wrote? If not, rewrite that section with her.

- *More overview material,* more about why each test is there, more on the relationship between tests, and more discussion of groups of related tests as such, rather than descriptions of them in isolation.

TEST PLANNING &
DOCUMENTATION

- ***Dependency flags.*** For example, if the program can read only 80 bytes of data at a time, you'll test it with 80 and 81 bytes. If the program is enhanced to deal with 256 bytes, the old tests are obsolete. Now you want to try 256- and 257-byte streams. State explicitly that the test assumes that the program processes only 80 bytes, perhaps in a special section called "Dependencies" or "Assumptions." You don't have to say what to do when the specification changes. You're writing for an experienced tester who can figure this out. You do have to alert her that when the program changes in a certain way, she'll have to change this test.

### Notes to be used in the next release (a year from now)

After testing is finished and the program is released, work will start on the next version. These testers may be new to the product, and you might not be available to guide them. They may find it hard to understand your current test materials. Try to prepare a set of notes to make their work easier. These are similar to those you'd write for a distant but experienced tester (discussed in the previous section).

In preparing this documentation, imagine the future testers as archaeologists. They're going to sift through your long-boxed notes and disks looking for useful material. They will probably throw out anything they don't understand. Worse, they might use it anyway and miss all sorts of bugs. They will probably have to modify anything they do keep—after all, the program has changed since you worked with it.

You should provide:

- ***The details of each test.*** How to conduct it and the exact results expected.

- ***A history of program failures.*** What problems did each test catch, what did they look like and what kinds of changes in the program might resurrect them?

- ***Even more stress on the thinking behind the tests*** and the dependencies of each test case on the details of the program's behavior or specification.

### Test script for the inexperienced tester

This person might be experienced with computers (a programmer, manager, or hardware or software support technician) or he might be a computer novice. In either case, he has no testing experience and probably not much familiarity with the program being tested. A test script will guide him through each test, step by step. You give him the script and, after spending a minimum of time on instruction, leave. He follows the directions in the script, fills in the blanks beside each of its questions, and returns it to you when he's done.

A script offers some important advantages:

- ***It helps keep down the size of the Testing Group.*** Under a crunch, you can hire outside staff and train them quickly. They need a minimum of training since they need only follow the script. Also, you probably don't have to pay these people as much as you pay full-time testers.

- *It can relieve the testing staff of the most boring work.* After you test the same feature for the umpteenth time, using the same test, you will get bored and sloppy. How pleasant it would be to pass the most repetitive tests to temporary staff!

- *It provides a standardized set of tests* for each testing cycle. This can be a good baseline of regression tests, but make sure to supplement it with more sophisticated testing (e.g., timing), by experienced testers.

- *A well laid out script looks impressive to management.* Don't underestimate the value of this.

Unfortunately, there are also some problems:

- *Inexperienced testers (including many experienced programmers) are not very good.* For example, one of us studied the performance of some bright software support technicians. These people deal with customers' post-purchase complaints. They were highly motivated to find problems. They used a detailed and carefully prepared script to test some easily understood programs. Unbeknownst to them, experienced testers also tested the same versions of the same programs, using the same scripts. The testers found many more problems including many that we still don't understand how the technicians missed.

  Inexperienced testers often fail to report timing-related or transient bugs, including junk that flashes on the screen and then goes away. They rarely report problems they can't quickly replicate. They don't report problems that they think might be attributable to their misunderstanding of the program. They don't report problems that they think the reader of the report might consider minor. They don't report lots of other problems either.

- *A good script takes a long time to write.* You'll spend from 5 to 15 times as long writing the script and preparing support materials (screen dumps, disk files, etc.) as you spend developing the original tests and executing them once.

- *The script must be kept up to date.* These testers don't have the background or the skills to recover from errors in the script. Further, if they realize that the script has errors, they won't report some problems, blaming discrepancies on the script rather than the program.

Another point to keep in mind about scripts is that they include different information than notes written for experienced testers. You may have to write both types of documents. Test scripts do not discuss the reasons behind each test case or the special significance of input data items. Such discussions would distract and confuse the inexperienced tester. Instead, the script focuses on the nuts and bolts of getting the testing done. It includes:

- *A clear, step by step description of how to run the test.* Very little is left to the reader's imagination or discretion.

- *An exact statement of the expected test results,* including what the tester should see at each stage in the test. It helps to provide printouts or photos showing exactly what's on the display. Show where the tester should look by highlighting the printout with a colored marker.

- *A description of the ways the program might fail the test.* Don't go into internal program mechanics. Just give examples of things the tester might see or hear if the program doesn't work. You might put these in fine print to avoid distracting her.

- *Boxes for the tester to check off when he completes each test* or test section. Organized the script as a checklist, or as questionnaire with fill-in-the-blank questions about what the tester saw. If you want him to pay attention to some aspect of the program, you must include specific questions about it in the script.

Layout is important. Line up the boxes for checkmarks in a column down the page. Keep instructions separate from descriptions: WHAT TO DO should be in a separate column, beside WHAT YOU WILL SEE. The order of tasks should make sense. The tester shouldn't bounce between classes of tasks. Nor should he feel that he's wastefully repeating steps. Have an experienced tester try the script before inflicting it on the temporary help.

## Notes for your manager

Your manager is probably a fine tester and, if he has time to read them, he'll probably find all your test materials interesting. For the moment, though, ignore his technical skills. Think of him as an administrator. He needs to know the progress of testing and how well tested each area of the program is. He may also need to know when a given test was last run or whether any test was run that should have detected a problem just reported from the field.

The ideal set of management support notes would be in a database. Perhaps there would be one record per test case, and each record would include:

- *A name or number that uniquely identifies the test.*

- *A set of classification identifiers.* Taken together, these fields might indicate that a given test checks retrieval of information from the disk, sorting, selection of an option from the main menu, and display of sorted data. In effect, you are indexing this test in many ways, so that if a problem is found later, it will be easy to find every test relevant to it.

- *A list of test results.* For each cycle of testing in which this test was used, the list would identify the cycle and the tester, and describe the results as `pass` or `fail` (with a cross-reference to the Problem Report.)

Along with this database, you should broadly divide the program into a set of functional areas. For each area, you should roughly estimate how many test cases are needed for an "adequate" level of testing. Over time (for example, as you refine your function list for the program) you can break this down more finely. If you classify tests by the functional area(s) and sub-area(s) of the program they test, you can easily generate reports of how many tests there are for each area and how many are still needed.

## Legal audit trail

If your company is sued over a flaw in the program, your attorney will want to prove that design and evaluation were done in a thorough and professional manner.

If you are doing a careful and professional job of testing, and if failures of the program could be expensive or dangerous to the customer, keep records. Ask your company's attorney what records she would find most useful if there were a liability suit, and provide them.

We discuss these issues in more detail in Chapter 14.

## TYPES OF TEST DOCUMENTS

This section describes some types of documents that you can develop for test materials. Many of these descriptions summarize *IEEE Standard 829-1983 for Software Test Documentation*, which attempts to define a common set of test documents, to be used across the industry. Schulmeyer (1987) summarizes many other test documentation specifications.

You can order Standard 829-1983, which includes examples and much more detailed definitions, for a few dollars from:

> Computer Society of the IEEE
> P.O. Box 80452
> Worldway Postal Center
> Los Angeles, CA 90080

Or call the IEEE Standards Sales office in New Jersey: 201-981-0060.

Standard 829 does not specify which documents you should write for each project. We won't either, except to say that you probably don't want to write one of each. Also, you might choose to omit some of the detail required by the Standard. We urge you not to feel bound to make your documents conform to the IEEE standard. We describe the Standard because it provides a background of careful thought, which you should adapt to your needs. Finally, don't feel compelled to write everything at the start of testing. Try to publish your qualifying acceptance test before testing begins. It also helps to write the first draft of the test plan up front. Write and refine the rest as you go.

**12**

TEST PLANNING &
DOCUMENTATION

### Test plan

The test plan provides an overview of the testing effort for the product. You can put everything into this one document (some people do), but it's more common to write many documents and reference them in the appropriate sections. Here are the sections of the test plan, as defined by IEEE Standard 829:

- *Test plan identifier.* A unique name or number, useful if you store all documents in a database.

- *Introduction.* Include references to all relevant policy and standards documents, and high level product plans.

- *Test items.* A test item is a software item (function, module, feature, whatever) that is to be tested. List them all, or refer to a document that lists them all. Include references to specifications (e.g., requirements and design) and manuals (e.g., user, operations, and installation).

- *Features to be tested.* Cross-reference them to test design specifications.

- *Features not to be tested.* Which ones and why not.

- *Approach.* Describe the overall approach to testing: who does it, main activities, techniques, and tools used for each major group of features. How will you decide that a group of features is adequately tested? The Standard also says that this section, not the Schedule section, is the place to identify constraints, including deadlines and the availability of people and test items.

- *Item pass/fail criteria.* How does a tester decide whether the program passed or failed a given test?

- *Suspension criteria and resumption requirements.* List anything that would cause you to stop testing until it's fixed. What would have to be done to get you to restart testing? What tests should be redone at this point?

- *Test deliverables.* List all of the testing documents that will be written for this product.

- *Testing tasks.* List all tasks necessary to prepare for and do testing. Show dependencies between tasks, special skills (or people) needed to do them, who does each, how much effort is involved, and when each will be done.

- *Environmental needs.* Describe the necessary hardware, software, testing tools, lab facilities, etc.

- *Responsibilities.* Name the groups (or people) responsible for managing, designing, preparing, executing, witnessing, checking, fixing, resolving, getting you the equipment, etc.

- *Staffing and training needs.* How many people you need at each skill level, and what training they need.

- *Schedule.* List all milestones with dates, and when all resources (people, machines, tools, and facilities) will be needed.

- *Risks and contingencies.* What are the highest risk assumptions in the test plan? What can go sufficiently wrong to delay the schedule, and what will you do about it?

- *Approvals.* Who has to approve this plan? Provide space for their signatures.

### Function list

IEEE Standard 829 does not discuss this document. For its details, see "Components of test planning documents: Outlines—the function list" in this chapter. You could include a function list in the test plan's section on test items, or treat it as a separate document.

### Criteria for acceptance into testing

IEEE Standard 829 does not discuss this document.

This acceptance test is a brief test that the program must pass when submitted for testing. If it passes, the Testing Group runs the item through a full test cycle. Otherwise they reject it as too unstable for testing. Such tests should take less than half an hour—never more than two hours.

If you use an acceptance test, write a document that describes it *exactly*. Circulate it to programmers, preferably before the first cycle of testing. Make the document detailed enough for programmers to run the tests themselves before submitting the product for testing. Let them catch their most obvious blunders in private.

## Test design specification

This specifies how a feature or group of features will be tested. According to Standard 829, it includes the following sections:

- *Test design specification identifier.* This is a unique name or number.

- *Features to be tested.* Describe the scope of this specification.

- *Approach refinements.* Expand on the approach section of the test plan. Describe the specific test techniques. How will you analyze results (e.g., visually or with a comparison program)? Describe boundary or other conditions that lead to selection of specific test cases. Describe any constraints or requirements common to all (most) tests.

- *Test identification.* List and briefly describe each test associated with this design. You may list a test case under many different designs if it tests many different types of features.

- *Feature pass/fail criteria.* How can the tester decide whether the feature or combination of features has passed the test?

## Test case specification

This defines a test case. According to Standard 829, the test case specification includes the following sections:

- *Test case specification identifier.* A unique name or number.

- *Test items.* What features, modules, etc., are being tested? References to specifications and manuals are in order.

- *Input specifications.* List all inputs by value, by range of values, or by name if they are files. Identify anything else that's relevant, including memory-resident areas, values passed by the operating system, supporting programs or databases, prompt messages displayed, and relationships between the inputs.

  Describe any timing considerations. For example, if the tester should enter data while the disk light is flashing, or within half a second after a certain message, say so. For very short intervals, describing the rhythm can be more effective than describing the exact times involved.

- *Output specifications.* List all output values and messages. Consider including response times.

- *Environmental needs.* List special requirements, including hardware, software, facilities, and staff.

- *Special procedural requirements.* List anything unusual in the setup, tester's actions, or analysis to be done of the output.

- *Inter-case dependencies.* What tests have to be executed before this one, why, and what if the program fails them?

**Test procedure specification**

This describes the steps for executing a set of test cases and analyzing their results. According to Standard 829, it includes the following sections:

- *Test procedure specification identifier.*

- *Purpose.* What is this procedure for? Cross-reference all test cases that use this procedure.

- *Special requirements.* List any prerequisite procedures, special tester skills, and special environmental needs.

- *Procedure steps.* Include the following steps as applicable:

  - **Log:** any special methods or formats for logging results or observations.

  - **Setup:** preparations for execution of the procedure.

  - **Start:** how to begin execution of the procedure.

  - **Proceed:** any actions necessary during procedure execution.

  - **Measure:** how test measurements (e.g., response times) are made.

  - **Shut down:** how to suspend testing in the face of unscheduled events (or when the tester goes home for the night).

  - **Restart:** where to restart and how, after a shut down.

  - **Stop:** how to bring execution to an orderly halt.

  - **Wrap up:** how to restore the environment to its original state.

  - **Contingencies:** what to do when it all goes wrong.

**Test item transmittal report**

This report accompanies anything submitted to you for testing. The report tells you what you're getting. According to Standard 829, it includes the following sections:

- *Transmittal report identifier.*

- *Transmitted items.* Names the submitted program or modules, along with their version identifiers or revision levels. Names the people responsible for this submission.

- *Location.* Where is the submitted material—on a disk or tape, in a shared directory, in a binder? How is it labeled?

- *Status.* How has this changed since the last time you tested it? Which Problem Reports were resolved? Did the specification or visible program behavior change? What invisible changes were made and how might they affect program reliability? How does this material differ from the published specification or manual and which is correct? What significant changes are yet to come?

- *Approvals.* The people who have to agree that this material is ready to test should sign the transmittal before you accept it for testing.

## Test script

IEEE Standard 829 does not discuss this document. It is described above, in "Test script for the inexperienced tester." It should include the following components:

- *General Instructions.* These tell the tester how to read and use the script, how and when to fill out Problem Reports, where to find them, etc. You might provide this material in a separate binder, rather than pad the script with it, but you must provide it to the inexperienced tester.

- *Getting started.* Setup information.

- *Step by step procedural description for each test.*

- *Check-off boxes for each step and result.*

- *Ample room to describe behavior that was odd or just not understood,* and questions that prompt these descriptions. An experienced tester should review these answers later, examine the behavior herself, and probably file many new Problem Reports on the basis of them.

## Test log

This is a chronological record of the test executions and events that happened during testing. According to Standard 829, it includes the following sections:

- *Test log identifier.*

- *Description.* What's being tested, including Version ID, where testing is being done, what hardware (printer, amount of available memory, type of computer, etc.), and all other configuration information (for example, operating system revision level).

- *Activity and event entries.* What happened, including:

  - **Execution description:** The procedure used, who witnessed the test, and their role in testing.

  - **Procedure results:** What happened. What did you see, and where did you store the output?

  - **Environmental information:** Any changes (e.g., hardware substitutions) made specifically for this test.

  - **Anomalous events:** Unexpected events (usually due to bugs). What happened before and after they occurred.

  - **Incident report identifiers:** Problem Report numbers.

### Test incident report

This is a Problem Report. The IEEE Standard report has different fields from the report in this book. The IEEE report has these fields: test incident report identifier, summary, inputs, expected results, actual results, anomalies, date and time, procedure step, environment, attempts to repeat, testers, observers, and impact on test plans and specifications.

### Test summary report

This is a summary of a series of tests, of the type that you might issue after completing a cycle of testing. It briefly describes the testing done and evaluates the results. According to Standard 829, it includes the following sections:

- *Test summary report identifier.*
- *Summary.* Say what was tested (including Version ID), in what environment, and summarize your evaluation of it. Refer to test case specifications.
- *Variances.* Report any deviation of test procedures from the specified ones, and explain why.
- *Comprehensiveness assessment.* Was testing as comprehensive as the test plan called for? What modules, features, or feature combinations weren't tested enough, and why?
- *Summary of results.* What problems were reported, which were resolved, and what were the resolutions? Which are still outstanding?
- *Evaluation.* Overall evaluation of each item (program or module) tested, based on the test results. Optionally, estimate the risk and probability of failure of the item in actual use.
- *Summary of activities.* Summarize such things as the number of staff who worked on the tests summarized in this report, the total machine time used, total elapsed time, and any special events or other resource uses that deserve mention.
- *Approvals.*

### Documentation embedded in data and control files

When you create a file of input data for a test, if you can, embed comments in these files to explain why you chose each data value.

Control files execute a test. If comments are possible in the file, use them to explain each step in the file.

During a test, it pays to show the expected results onscreen or in a printout. The tester can compare these to the obtained results. This is convenient, since she has to make this comparison anyway. Don't display explanations of why you chose certain procedure or data values. These take space and distract from the test results. If the tester has the file, she can look at these comments with an editor.

There are problems with embedded comments. They're less likely to be standardized than descriptions in printed documents. They will vary more from author to author. Some test file creators will do incompetent or careless jobs of commenting their files. And they're rarely as detailed as printed comments.

The key advantage to embedded comments is that they're easy to update. When data or procedures change, the comments are right there. Embedded comments are also easier to find and duplicate than printed documents. Anyone who works with the test files gets the comments automatically when she gets the test data or procedures.

## A CLOSING THOUGHT

Many testers generate too much paper. Remember your primary task—finding bugs and getting them fixed—not designing or filling out forms. We've described several types of documents in this chapter, but we certainly don't use them all. Pick carefully.

**12**

TEST PLANNING &
DOCUMENTATION

# TYING IT TOGETHER

By now you know how to test, how to plan your testing, and how to communicate your plans, designs, and results. This chapter is less concerned with "how to" and more concerned with "when" and "how much." Chapter 12 was the technical center of this book; this chapter ties together the organizational and strategic issues.

In the real world, you will never be able to do all the testing you want to do, not even all the testing that you honestly believe you *must* do. (This was the lesson of Chapter 2.) The real world project manager must constantly make tradeoffs among four types of factors: reliability, feature set, project cost, and release date. Further (as discussed in Chapter 4), even if the project manager wants to maximize product quality, he still has to trade off between reliability and richness of the feature set. You must understand the project manager's tradeoff factors and be able to speak to them appropriately.

In the real world, your work is an expense. To be worth funding, your work must improve customer satisfaction and increase your company's profits. You can probably get funding for almost all the work you can cost-justify. The cost of testing is part of a larger pattern of quality-related costs, often categorized into four groups: prevention costs, appraisal (including testing) costs, internal failure costs, and external failure costs. Consciously or (more often, somewhat) unconsciously, your company will trade off expenditures in each area, hoping to minimize overall quality-related costs. The most effective way to cost-justify your work is to show how much it reduces other quality-related costs.

Early in the project, a great project manager thinks through his approach to making the necessary tradeoffs and adopts a development model that provides the right mix of structure and flexibility. He might use one of the published models (such as waterfall or evolution) or he might use his own variation. A less thoughtful manager will adopt someone else's development model without thinking through its consequences. In either case, the model determines when different types of work get done, when tested, when fixed. You must understand the project manager's model—otherwise you'll make mistakes like scheduling the bulk of usability testing for the month after the program's user interface is frozen. We call these "mistakes" because of the typical results: most Problem Reports are deferred because it's too late to make the changes, and most changes that are made disrupt other project plans. Everyone loses.

**13**

You are at your most effective when you understand the project manager's development tradeoffs, the company's quality cost tradeoffs, and the constraints of the project manager's development model. This understanding lets you explain, in terms that the project manager and his management will appreciate, when during the project money should be spent on what type of testing, how much must be done, and what types of risk the project manager will face if he doesn't take your advice.

The majority of this chapter breaks a project into stages and notes the different types of testing work that can be done at each stage. This breakdown reflects our (and our colleagues') combined experiences with many projects in several software publishing companies. We do NOT recommend this as the One True Way to structure a project. On the contrary, it has many problems. But the odds are good that you'll face something like it. Our goal is to help you anticipate and justify the types of testing you should propose and conduct as the project moves forward.

## OVERVIEW

The chapter considers the following topics:

- Software development tradeoffs
- Software development models
- Quality-related costs
- The development time line
- Product design
- Analyze customer data
- First functionality
- Almost alpha
- Alpha
- Depth vs. breadth of testing
- Pre-beta
- Beta
- Outside beta tests
- User interface freeze
- Pre-final
- Reliability ratings
- Final integrity test
- Product release
- Project post-mortem reviews

### Useful Reading

The American Society for Quality Control's best selling book is *Principles of Quality Costs* (Campanella, 1990). It's very useful for anyone setting up a quality cost tracking system. So is Juran and Gryna's (1980) chapter on Quality Costs. This book is a respected introduction to the broad field of quality control. Feigenbaum (1991) is another interesting discussion of quality costs.

Chapter 3 also discusses product development stages, and many concepts used here are defined there. Glass (1992) looks at development stages from the point of view of the project manager helping programmers improve product quality.

## SOFTWARE DEVELOPMENT TRADEOFFS

The project manager's job is to ship a high quality product on time and within budget. This is often impossible. Software projects commonly run late and over budget. To bring the project under control (months or days before product release), the project manager must make tradeoffs among the following:

- reliability of the released product
- the number and depth of features
- dollar cost of further work on the project
- release date

The project's development methodology has a big effect on his flexibility when dealing with late products. When we discuss development models, we'll note the effects they have on the options available to management. Here are a few constraints common to all methodologies:

- *Reliability.* The project manager can always ship the product sooner, at a lower development cost, by cutting back on testing and shipping it with lots of bugs. There is no end to the testing you can do on a product, *and this means* that *every* decision to ship a product is a decision to ship the product with bugs that could have been found with more testing. (If this isn't obvious to you, reread Chapter 2.)

- *Features.* One way to shorten a project is to simplify it. When a feature has been badly designed or coded, or when the technical complexity of a feature was underestimated, the project manager can save time by cutting the feature out of the product, perhaps substituting a scaled down version. However, if the feature is important, dropping it will hurt customer satisfaction. So will revisions that make the feature more awkward to use.

- *Dollars.* The project manager can try to rush the project by spending money. He might spend money on new tools, on high level consultants to answer specific questions, or on additional staff. Adding staff is common but not always successful. The more people, the more communication problems and costs. Senior staff are distracted from their work by having to support and supervise the newcomers. Toward the end of the project, adding staff might even delay it. (See Brooks, 1975.) This is just as true for adding testers as for adding programmers. You can ruin the effectiveness of a testing team by adding a flock of junior contractors in the project's last few months or weeks.

- *Release date.* If the project is running behind schedule, the project manager can always delay the release date. However, the costs of finishing the product late can be enormous:

  - **Direct cost of continuing development.** Estimate this by adding up the weekly (gross) pay of every person working on the project, including project managers, programmers, testers, writers, etc. Multiply by two or three to include the cost of benefits, facilities, and of other staff managing these staff, reviewing project progress, planning how to install or support the project, etc.

  - **Window of opportunity cost:** There may be late penalties in the contract (or large bonuses for timely completion). Products developed for retail sale might be released too late to sell during the fall, Christmas, and early January selling seasons. A product that would have been highly profitable might be a dismal failure if it is not released in time for this year's peak selling season (your target computer might be obsolete by next year) or because it was released after a competitor's product. (You *must* understand that in new product categories, the first product or two to market will outsell much higher quality products that are released later. Delaying the schedule to improve the product could kill the product.)

- **Wasted marketing costs:** Advertising expenses and pre-release publicity efforts are wasted if the product isn't ready for release soon after the ads and articles have run.

- **Alternative opportunity cost:** Everyone who works an extra week on a late project is unavailable to work on other projects. The other projects fall behind schedule or don't get done.

- **Absence of current revenue:** If your company needs this product's cash this quarter, and it's not going to get it, you have a big problem.

## SOFTWARE DEVELOPMENT MODELS

The project manager's plan for ordering tasks is his development model. These models are discussed at length in the literature. Some good sources are DeGrace & Stahl (1991), Evans & Marciniak (1987), Gause & Weinberg (1989), and Ould (1989). We discussed these models in Chapter 12 ("Evolutionary Development of Test Materials"). Chapter 3's ordering of tasks follows the waterfall model, and we will consider the waterfall from a different angle in Chapter 14 ("Of Contracts and Waterfalls").

Each model offers a different balance among the development tradeoffs. The project manager is best served by a development model that allows him flexibility in the areas he is most likely to want to change. For example, if the product he delivers absolutely must provide every feature in the list, he won't use a method whose primary benefit is that it minimizes the cost of eliminating features.

Testers sometimes develop strong opinions about the relative merits of the different models. We want to discourage you from believing that you have The Right Answer. The three of us, for example, have strong, long considered, and carefully reasoned opinions—but we disagree with each other. Be especially careful about criticizing the project manager for choosing (or being stuck with) The Wrong Development Model. If you don't choose the time and tone of your comments carefully, you may sound more pompous than informed.

The next two sections examine some risks and tradeoffs inherent in the waterfall and evolutionary development models. In presenting these, our goal is illustrate our approach to analyzing a development model's implications. We encourage you to try a similar analysis of the methodologies in use in your company.

### THE TRADITIONAL WATERFALL METHOD

The waterfall method is the classic approach to project management, especially to the management of large projects. It envisions projects progressing in stages from requirements analysis to internal and external top-level design to internal and external deeper design, then to coding, then to testing, then to release. One class of tasks is largely finished before the next one begins. The functional requirements document is finished, then the specifications (external and internal are started). Coding begins after the specs are written.

The waterfall method looks reasonable on paper. It is the standard approach. It is the approach most testing groups ask programming groups to use. It gets specifications into the hands of testers before testing begins. It focuses and defines the project. It limits the number of late changes in the design or vision of the project. It makes test scheduling, planning, budgeting and staffing much easier.

The waterfall originated in an environment of custom software development contracts. The buyer specified the requirements and had to do so early in order to control project costs. The customer also had to examine and approve the external design, many data flow specifications, report definitions, and other design details as early as these could be written. Then the programming organization would code to these contract specifications. When customer requirements changed, the programming company would adopt the changes but bill for work already done. This is a useful legal model, but no one ever claimed that lawyers are good engineers.

Unfortunately, the waterfall forces everyone to make their design and functionality decisions at the start of the project, when they understand the product least well. They don't yet know what things will be outrageously hard to implement or test, or what other things might turn out to be easy to tack on. They probably don't know as much as they'll know later about competitive products. They don't have their understanding of this product's strengths and character that they'll have after a working version has been developed.

What do the tradeoffs look like near the end of a waterfall project that runs late?

- **Features.** By this point, all the requirements planning and specifying of each feature has been done. If the product is in testing, then each feature has also been coded. Eliminating features offers little benefit to the schedule or to costs.

  If a feature has been so badly designed or implemented that all the work must be redone, cutting it will reduce programming and design time. However, if everyone else on the project team has relied on the specification, cutting or changing the feature may trigger added work and delay for documentation and marketing staff.

# 13

- **Dollars.** It might be easier to add programmers because the specifications have all been written and reviewed already. The new programmers can follow written design instructions.

- **Release date.** So much preparatory work has already been done that it rarely seems to make sense, toward the end of the project, to drop anything. If all the features are coded, the typical decision is to struggle through testing and fixing them, no matter how long it takes.

- **Reliability.** If all the features are coded and management has added as much staff as it makes sense to add, the only way to release the product in a hurry is to stop testing and release it, bugs and all. Under these circumstances there is tremendous pressure on testing to prove that a product is not ready to ship. The product will ship as soon as testing fails to find horrible bugs for a few days.

The traditional waterfall model often yields projects that are horribly behind schedule, with every task so far along that there is no alternative to adding staff at high cost, delaying the release date, and reducing quality.

However, advocates of the waterfall can point to many project disasters that could have been prevented if the programmers had taken the time at the start to thoroughly analyze the requirements, design the product, and schedule every task. If you don't do the work up front, you might assume tremendous risk when you try to add it later in the project. Early, detailed approval and planning are especially important when the product is being written for a single customer or when a major part of the product is hardware, which would be tremendously expensive to re-engineer.

## THE EVOLUTIONARY METHOD

The evolutionary method is characterized by incremental feature additions to a core product.

For any product concept, there is a range of possible implementations: at one extreme is the minimally acceptable feature set. At the other is the dream product that has every feature the programmer would like to include. The evolutionist starts by gaining an understanding of the product range.

The programmer then builds a core product that is designed flexibly, to make it easy to add the many desired features later. The core itself has very few features—just enough for it to be considered an independent program that can go through some testing. The test group (or someone else) tests the core as if it were a final product; testing and fixing continue until the core appears stable.

From here, the programmer adds single features or small groups of features. Each time a new feature or group goes into the program, the program goes through another round of testing and fixing until it stabilizes.

The programming and testing team continue to add features and retest the system until they have built the minimally acceptable product. They now have something that the company can sell or deliver, if it must. There are dozens of further features that they still want to add to the program, and it might need many of these to be a competitive product. But it is now a useful program that at least some customers would find acceptable.

The programming team continues to add features to the minimally acceptable product, one at a time, retesting the system each time before adding the next piece. The team is constantly delivering a working, useful product. If they add functionality in priority order, they can stop programming at any time and know that the most important work has been done. Over time, the product evolves into a rich, reliable, useful product. This is the evolutionary method.

Waterfall projects are often plagued with huge testing schedule uncertainty. No one knows how many bugs there are or long will it take to find and fix them. Evolutionary development addresses this uncertainty much earlier. Each new version of the program is tested and debugged before new features are added. The project's rate of progress is much easier to track.

A final benefit that we'll note is that this approach provides good opportunity to reappraise requirements and refine the design as the team understands the application better.

Here are some tradeoffs for an evolutionary project that runs behind schedule:

- *Features.* It is easy to drop features once the minimally acceptable product is done. Because programmers don't specify, design, or code features until they're ready to start adding them, all work done is directly reflected in the product. There is little wasted planning time on features that never made it into the shipping version.

- *Dollars.* Management can try to add features more quickly, rather than dropping them, by spending money. However, because new features haven't yet been fully specified or designed, the project's designers may become bottlenecks.

- *Release date.* The power of the evolutionary approach is best seen in the degree of schedule control that it gives management. The project manager can always postpone the release date. Often, though, he will choose to ship the product on time rather than adding those last 15 features.

  Because the program is always stabilized before the next wave of features is added, a project manager who decides to stop adding features can probably finish the project within a few weeks.

- *Reliability.* The reliability of evolutionary products is high. Because the product is tested and stabilized as each new piece is added, most of the project's testing budget is spent before the end of the schedule. If management says stop adding features and get the thing ready to ship, it won't take much additional final testing before the product is ready for release. The incentive to skimp on testing and release something buggy is gone.

The testing cost under the evolutionary model threatens to be large because testing starts early. However, much of that cost is recouped because there isn't so much testing at the end. Further, all those features that weren't specified or coded weren't the subject of test plans or tests either.

One way to make a mess of an evolutionary project is to have the programmers keep writing fresh code rather than fixing the problems discovered during testing. This is very tempting when the project is running behind schedule, but the appearance of progress is deceiving. The problems will take longer to fix and retest later. The project manager will face last minute tradeoffs between reliability and release date.

Another risk of adopting an evolutionary approach is that an inexperienced project manager may imagine that he doesn't have to do much initial planning, because the product will evolve over time. This is a big mistake. If the core is built inflexibly, it will need extensive reworking before key features can be added. Fundamental work might have to be redone many times. Also, at what should be the end of the project, the marketing group might realize that they forgot to identify some features as critical, so others were done instead. Now the product has to wait until those features are added.

**13**

TYING IT
TOGETHER

Marketing and sales staff sometimes don't understand this approach well enough to realize that when the project manager says that some features might be in the product or they might not, no one should sell the product as if it has a given feature, until that feature has been added.

The test manager has another way to ruin the project. If he doesn't assign test resources to the project early (perhaps because they're still assigned to some other project that's behind schedule), then the core program doesn't go through the full test cycle, nor do the incremental changes. No one sees this slippage on the schedule until the testing staff are finally assigned, perhaps near what should be the very end of the project. At that point, the testers are in the traditional system test situation, with a big pile of untested code and very little remaining testing time left in the schedule. The result is something that looks like a badly managed waterfall project—testing costs more, the schedule falls apart, and lots of bugs are missed.

The Testing Group probably has more ability to destroy an evolutionary project than anyone else. Be considerate of this risk.

## A DEVELOPMENT MODEL'S IMPLICATIONS FOR TESTING

Once you understand the project manager's development model from his point of view, think about its implications for the testing effort. Here are some implications of the waterfall method:

- *Review the user interface early,* perhaps by testing prototypes. If the user interface is specified and approved before the code is written, usability tests near the end of the project won't have much effect.

- *Start writing the test plan as early as possible* because this will force you to critically analyze the specifications (or drafts of them). Any risks they pose for testability of the project must be raised early.

**Figure 13.1  The product development cycle (?)**

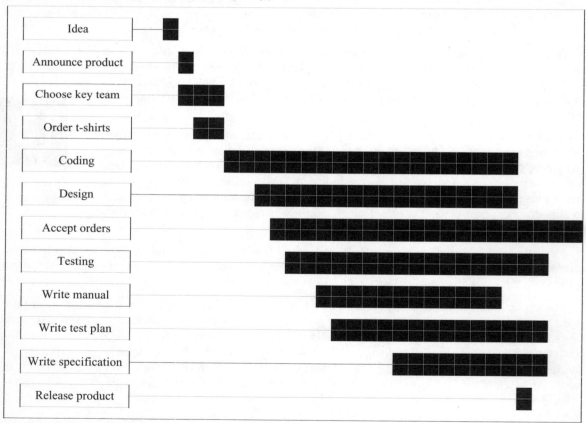

**Theoretical models are important, but you must also be effective when managers throw out the rule book. Think about this Figure as you read the tidy sequence of tasks in this chapter.**

- *You cannot start testing until late in the project.* The odds are that you will start later than the initial schedule projects because design and coding will fall behind schedule. Plan to spend extra time crafting your staffing plan. For example, you want to unleash a trained group of testers as soon as the product is ready for testing, but what should they do if the program is so unstable that you kick it back to the programmers for rework almost immediately? You should anticipate this and have alternate work ready—perhaps you can use the time to automate some tests or create additional test data files. As another example, develop a strategy for incorporating new people at the last minute. You can delegate many simple but time-consuming tasks to new staff, making maximum use of your experienced testers during the limited time available. You and your testing team can make it easy to hand off these tasks by identifying them and organizing your work accordingly. If you don't do this planning in advance, you'll find it much harder to incorporate new testers at the end of a behind-schedule project, when no one has time to think.

- *By the time you start testing, your work is on the critical path.* Coding is complete, or nearly so. As soon as you stop finding bugs, the program ships. On a project large enough for a few testers, consider dedicating one to guerrilla raids and other relatively unstructured testing. This person's goal is to find one or two bugs each week that are so obviously bad that no one would ship the project with these problems in it. The time it takes to fix these bugs is time the rest of the test group can use to plod through the program more systematically. Projects that need this tactic for buying testing time are no fun, but this tactic might buy you several months of testing time, slipping the schedule week after week, one week at a time. (Warning: *never* delay reporting a critical bug. It might be tempting to keep a bug in reserve, to be reported when you can't find anything else that week. This buys you that one last week of testing (the week needed to fix this bug). Don't try this unless you like the idea of being hated, fired, and blacklisted. Don't do it. Don't think about it. And never, never joke about it.)

In contrast, consider these (quite different) implications of the evolutionary method:

- *Plan to staff the project with testers very early,* starting reliability testing as soon as the program reaches its first level of functionality.

- *Plan waves of usability tests as the project grows more complex.* You can probably argue successfully for design changes in recently added code.

- *Plan to write the test plan as you go,* rather than as a big effort before testing.

- *Plan to do your most powerful testing as early as possible.* Be careful about gambling that you'll have time later to conduct tests that you know are critical. The project manager might stop development at any time. We don't mean "any time after the planned release date." We mean *any time*—for example, two of us shipped a product three months early by stopping adding features earlier than planned.

## QUALITY-RELATED COSTS

Quality-related costs include the costs of preventing, searching for, and coping with product errors and failures. From a business point of view, you have a testing budget because the cost of testing is lower than the cost of dealing with customer complaints about undiscovered bugs. If you can show that the company will save money if you conduct a certain type of test at a certain point in the project, you'll probably get funding to do that work.

As you envision ways to tailor your team's work to the project manager's development model, you'll want to propose testing assignments that might be unusual in your company. For example, your company might not be used to assigning testers to review the product's external design—or to giving them enough time to do the job competently. Other tasks that might require justification include analyzing customer support call records, automating test cases, delegating some types of last minute work to newly added junior testers or administrative staff, testing compatibility with a broader range of printers, or conducting an outside beta test. In each case, you can dramatically strengthen your argument with data that shows that this work will prevent significantly larger expenses later.

**Figure 13.2 Quality-Related Costs**

| *Prevention* | *Appraisal* |
|---|---|
| Design reviews | Glass box testing |
| Requirements verification | Black box testing |
| Specification reviews | Testing by tech support |
| Training programmers to make or miss fewer bugs | Training testers how to find more bugs |
| Defensive programming (including assertion check, fault tolerance, etc.) | Beta testing: in-house users and tests of representative (or important) customers |
| | Acceptance testing by the customer |
| *Internal Failure* | *External Failure* |
| Bug fixes | Technical support calls |
| Regression tests of fixed bugs | Prepare technical support answer books |
| Delaying tester's access to areas of the code | Refunds |
| Wasting in-house user time | Replacement with updated product |
| Slowing down the writers | PR work to soften drafts of harsh reviews |
| Rewriting sections of the manual | Litigation |
| Cost of shipping the product late | |
| Opportunity cost to other products due to shipping this product late. | |

The more you know about your company's quality-related expenditures, the better you'll do at evaluating and advocating new testing procedures.

Quality-related costs are normally discussed in terms of four categories (Campanella, 1990):

- *Prevention costs:* everything the company spends to prevent software and documentation errors.
- *Appraisal costs:* all testing costs and the costs of everything else the company does to look for errors.
- *Internal failure costs:* all costs of coping with errors discovered during development and testing.
- *External failure costs:* all costs of coping with errors discovered, typically by your customers, after the product is released.

Figure 13.2 shows examples of the different types of costs. Feigenbaum (1991) estimates that the typical company spends 5 to 10 cents of every quality cost dollar on prevention, another 20 to 25 cents on appraisal, and the remaining 65 to 75 cents on internal and external failure costs.

Quality Assurance (QA) groups often systematically collect quality-related cost information. The typical software testing group has a narrower focus and mandate than a QA group. You will probably find much information hard to obtain. Don't despair. Even if you can't learn everything, you can often learn a lot just by pooling data with your company's technical support group. As to the rest of the data, make (but be ready to explain) educated guesses as needed. What you collect or reasonably estimate will often be sufficient to justify a proposal to reduce failure costs by increasing prevention or testing costs.

## Figure 13.3 The development time line

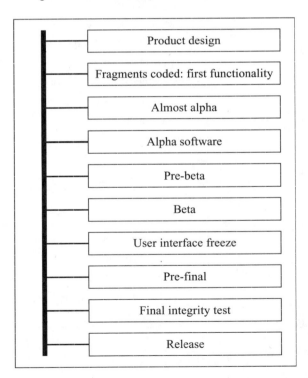

| Product design |
| Fragments coded: first functionality |
| Almost alpha |
| Alpha software |
| Pre-beta |
| Beta |
| User interface freeze |
| Pre-final |
| Final integrity test |
| Release |

## THE DEVELOPMENT TIME LINE

The typical project manager will publish schedules that contain a series of milestones, the most common of which are called "alpha" and "beta." The exact definitions vary (widely) from company to company, but in essence, alpha software is preliminary, buggy, but usable, while beta software is almost complete. Figure 13.3 is an example of a project time line, showing the milestones.

**13**

TYING IT
TOGETHER

This milestone-based approach is pragmatic. It recognizes that programming, testing, manual writing, and many other activities are done in parallel, and it maps them all onto the same time line. In some companies, requirements writing, prototyping, specifying, etc., might be mapped in parallel with all of these tasks (e.g., under an evolutionary model) whereas in others, this work might be considered preliminary and be put earlier on the line. But however the work is to be done in theory, the approach in practice involves a set of agreements—

**Figure 13.4a  Milestone Chart**

| Milestone | Development Activity | Marketing Activities | Documentation Activities | Testing Activities |
|---|---|---|---|---|
| *Product Design* | · Requirements<br>· Specifications<br>· Proposals<br>· Contracts<br>· Internal design<br>· External design | Market research including:<br>· Focus groups<br>· Customer surveys<br>· Analyze competing products | · Help draft the specifications | · Learn about the product<br>· Review specs, design, proposal<br>· Ask for testing support code:<br>  - printer automation<br>  - memory meter<br>  - cheat keys<br>  - screen dump<br>· Write contractual acceptance test<br>· Analyze stability of acquisitions<br>· Analyze customer data<br>· Review the UI for consistency<br>· Negotiate early testing structure<br>· Start setting up relationships with equipment vendors<br>· Review competitors' products<br>· Start looking for beta testers |
| *Fragments Coded: First Functionality* | · Specifying<br>· Designing<br>· Programming<br>· Unit (glass box) testing | | | · Initial informal testing<br>· (Evolutionary model) Start formal tests of the product core<br>· First informed estimates of tasks, resources, time & budget |

these people will get this work done by this time and these people will be doing these things with the results of that work.

Figures 13.4 (13.4a, 13.4b, 13.4c, and 13.4d) are our rendition of a milestone chart. We stress that this is only an example, and that no company that we know of conforms exactly to this illustration. Every company defines its milestones its own way and organizes the work in its own way, but these ways are often reasonably close to what we show here. We think this is a useful way to think about the ordering of the tasks.

For the rest of this chapter, we will explore this table and map your testing and test planning strategy and priorities onto the time line. (Note: many of these terms were defined and discussed in Chapter 3.)

## PRODUCT DESIGN

This is the start of the project, when all parties concerned figure out what this product should be. This phase includes requirements analysis and internal and external design. For thoughtful discussions, see DeMarco (1979), Gause & Weinberg (1989), Gilb (1988), Gould & Lewis (1985), Ould (1990), Weinberg (1982), Yourdon (1975), and Yourdon & Constantine (1979).

### PROGRAMMING ACTIVITIES DURING PRODUCT DESIGN

If requirements documents, proposals, and contracts are written, they are written during this phase. Coding begins at the end of this phase. In waterfall projects, the internal and external specifications are written during this phase. Detailed internal and external design might be done in this phase or later.

**13**

### MARKETING ACTIVITIES DURING PRODUCT DESIGN

The marketing department does research during this phase, to help define the product and to communicate the vision of the product to management and to the programmers.

TYING IT
TOGETHER

Marketing might run ideas or very early prototypes through small groups of customers, in focus groups. They might also survey customers of this product (or competitors), asking what features these people like in this type of product, how they perceive competitors' quality (and why), and how much they would pay for a product they liked in this category. You may be asked to help with some of these early consumer tests.

### DOCUMENTATION ACTIVITIES DURING PRODUCT DESIGN

Some documentation groups help draft specifications during this phase.

### TESTING ACTIVITIES DURING PRODUCT DESIGN

If you're lucky, you might be asked to review the product design documents as they are written. This way, you'll learn about the product and be prepared for some early test planning.

See Chapter 3, "Testing during the design stages" for thoughts on design flaws that you can find in the various specifying documents. In practice, many testers don't make many useful comments during this review.

**Figure 13.4b  Milestone chart (continued)**

| Milestone | Development Activity | Marketing Activities | Documentation Activities | Testing Activities |
|---|---|---|---|---|
| **Almost Alpha** | • Specifying<br>• Designing<br>• Coding<br>• Bug Fixing<br>• Unit testing | | • Documentation plan·<br>• Review the manual plan & the help plan | • Order equipment for testing<br>• Borrow equipment for testing<br>• Set test objectives, tasks, time and resources required, & budget<br>• Write first draft of test plan.<br>• Identify testing risks<br>• Do mainstream testing: find bugs<br>• Waterfallers review final spec. |
| **Alpha** | • Coding<br>• Unit testing<br>• Bug fixing<br>• Revise design<br>• Device drivers<br>• Start sample art | • Packaging<br>• Collaterals | • First drafts of the manual and help (but simple help systems may start later) | • Find lots of bugs; test all areas<br>• Mainstream testing<br>• Guerrilla tests on selected areas<br>• Plan & run detailed tests on selected areas<br>• Review the test plan<br>• Test the manual<br>• Raise design issues<br>• Estimate probable number of bugs<br>• Get final list of supported devices<br>• Start device testing<br>• Begin adding regression tests<br>• Review & publish resource needs<br>• Begin developing acceptance test<br>• Start automating tests |

In many companies, these reviews are not high priorities for testers. If you are invited into this process, read Gause & Weinberg (1989) and Freedman & Weinberg (1982).

Under a strict waterfall model, user interface design reviews might be your only effective opportunity to challenge the design. In this case, you need time to study the design before the review. Look to customer support for statistics on the costs of user interface inconsistencies in previously shipped products and use these to justify setting aside the time you need.

### Prepare for test automation

Often, the most important thing you can do during the design period is to identify testing support code that you want in the program (or with it). You might not get this support, but if you ask early, and explain the value of the individual tools clearly, you stand a good chance of getting some of them. Here are some examples for your wish list:

- *Printer automation.* you want command line control for test automation. The program will probably need the following parameters: name of the input file that the program is to print, name of the output file if printing is to be redirected to a file, name of the printer (possibly including the printer driver), and setup information such as the initial font or printer output resolution. The program should exit after printing. Given this facility, you can build a batch file that feeds a file to the program, selects the printer, tells it to print the file to disk, compares the file to one saved previously and prints the result, then starts the next test. See "Some Tips On Automated Testing" in Chapter 8 for further discussion.

- *Memory meter.* You want to be able to press a key at any point in the program and get a display or printout of the program's memory usage. Something as simple as the number of bytes free is handy. This might be more useful if it also lists the sizes of the five or ten largest contiguous blocks of memory. It is amazing (testers never believe it until they try it) how many new tests you will invent and how many hard to reproduce bugs become easily reproducible once you know how much memory is available before you do something, while you're doing it, and after you stop (or after you erase what you did).

- *Cheat keys.* These take you to a specific place in the program. This is essential for testing arcade games and role playing games and it might be handy in other programs.

- *Screen dump.* You need an easy way to copy everything on the screen to a printer or file (or serial port if you analyze the data in real time on another machine). The screen dump utility should capture cursor and mouse position. The tester will want to capture the screen put up by the program as it crashed, so the screen dump utility should be available even when the program under test crashes. If the computer you test on doesn't have excellent programs for this, ask the programmers to make one.

**13**

TYING IT
TOGETHER

### Create contractual acceptance tests

If your company is custom developing a product, it is extremely important to include an acceptance test in the sales contract. You and your company's customer should define a set of tests that the customer will run when development is complete. The customer must agree that if the program passes the tests, the contract has been fulfilled and any further changes or bug fixes are to be paid for separately. The test must be so clearly stated that you can execute the test, and confirm that the product is ready for delivery, before sending the product to the customer. It is important that you (Testing) work with the customer to define this test. The risk is too high

**Figure 13.4c  Milestone chart (continued)**

| Milestone | Development Activity | Marketing Activities | Documentation Activities | Testing Activities |
|---|---|---|---|---|
| **Pre-Beta** | • Fix bugs | (see beta) | (see beta) | • Check whether software meets beta stability and completeness requirements |
| **Beta** | • Finish features<br>• Fix bugs<br>• Revise UI<br>• Installation code<br>• Device drivers<br>• Sample art<br>• Customize disks for beta testers | • Packaging<br>• Collaterals<br>• Disk labels<br>• Support beta sites<br>• Send beta copies to reviewers | • Multiple drafts and reviews of manual & help<br>• Screen shots<br>• Technical tables<br>• Troubleshooting<br>• First draft index<br>• Late-starting help starts now | • Get approval of final test plan<br>• Continue executing & deepening the test plan (keep automating)<br>• Review marketing materials<br>• Review documentation<br>• Retest fixed bugs quickly<br>• Full round of device testing<br>• Publish formal test summaries<br>• Deferred bug meetings<br>• Review UI, prepare for UI freeze<br>• In-house and outside beta tests<br>• Measure and publish testing progress against milestones |
| **User Interface Freeze** | • No more visible changes<br>• Bug fixes<br>• Improve speed<br>• Final data<br>• Final installation<br>• Final disk config | • Promoting and selling<br>• Stickers to cover up errors on the box | • Fix help text<br>• Screen shots<br>• Lay out and print the manual | • Prune and run regression tests<br>• Execute test plan<br>• No more design issues<br>• Look for show stoppers, data corruption, memory allocation<br>• Push for resolution of open bugs<br>• Extensive device testing |

that a non-tester will agree to something that is too vague, takes much too long to run, or guarantees too high a level of quality, given the contract price. Talk to your company's lawyer about this.

### Analyze the stability of acquisitions

If your company is considering acquiring someone else's product, you should conduct an initial stability test (Chapter 3, "Black box testing: The usual black box sequence of events") before anyone signs the papers. So many disasters could have been avoided by companies if they had only done some preliminary testing before a bad acquisition.

### Analyze customer data

*Quality* is complex concept. A high quality product has the features that customers want and is also free from deficiencies (e.g., bugs) (Juran, 1989). Customer feedback will give you insight into a product's quality.

If this is a second or later release of a product, start analyzing customer data as early as possible during development. Customer data comes from the following sources:

- *Product reviews* in newspapers, magazines, and user group newsletters.

- *Letters* from customers. Read every letter, or a large sample of them.

- *Phone calls* from customers. If your company is so large that there are many, many calls, ask your technical support group to track the types of complaints coming in, and the number of calls associated with each. Unless you're working with an exceptionally sophisticated group, the phone support staff won't be able to track more than about 15 categories of complaints. Work with them to develop the 15 most useful categories.

- *Focus groups* and other interviews of selected customers. Marketing Departments often interview small groups of customers. They use some of these meetings to get reactions to new ideas, and other meetings to get feedback on the current product. If possible, attend all meetings in which customers describe their (positive and negative) experiences with the current version of the product. Comparable information often comes when you meet with user groups.

- *Telephone surveys.* Marketing might call 50 or 100 customers to determine what they'd like in a next version and what disappointed them about the current version. You might call some registered customers and some complaining customers to ask similar questions, but with an emphasis on the product's reliability.

Each of these sources will give you different, but important, indications of the product's quality. For example, reviewers complain about missing features that few of your current customers care about. Don't dismiss this: a year from now your customers might care a lot about these features. Reviewers also miss (or don't mention) egregious bugs. (Most reviewers mention relatively few bugs.) In contrast, callers and letter writers will point out many bugs but far fewer absent capabilities.

You have the following objectives in collecting these data:

- *Identify bugs that you missed.* You couldn't find every bug when you tested the last program. Customer data will reveal bugs you missed. Use these to help enhance your test plan.

**13**

TYING IT
TOGETHER

**Figure 13.4d  Milestone chart (continued)**

| Milestone | Development Activity | Marketing Activities | Documentation Activities | Testing Activities |
|---|---|---|---|---|
| **Pre-Final** | • Fix bugs | • Promote & sell | • Manual supplement <br> • Final help fixes | • Flag problems for the supplement <br> • Regression tests on many software versions <br> • Try to complete one full round of the test plan on the last version <br> • One more round of device testing <br> • Retest old bug fixes <br> • Tie up project's loose ends <br> • Circulate final deferred bug list <br> • Evaluate program's reliability |
| **Final (Integrity) Test** | • Fix bugs <br> • Code the demo <br> • Archive source code | • Promote & sell | • Supplement to the printer <br> • Last tweaks to on-disk READ ME file. | • Evaluate first day of use reliability <br> • Predict reviewer comments <br> • Mainstream tests <br> • Audit test plan and bugs <br> • Make the disk masters <br> • Check for viruses <br>  Archive everything <br>  Check manufactured masters |
| **Release** | • Party, then sleep | • Sell, sell, sell | • Party, then sleep | • If necessary, keep testing during manufacturing <br>  Check manufactured product <br>  Sleep, then party, then sleep. |

- *Assess the severity of the bugs you missed or that were deferred.* Identify the 10 or 15 problems that cost the most customer support time and money. If you can attach a support cost to each problem, all the better. Project managers will schedule and fix old, expensive, problems. Executives will supplement the programming budget, if necessary, to get rid of these problems.

- *Develop an empirical basis for evaluating deferred bugs.* Many programs include dozens of deferred bugs that no one ever complains about. By comparing your knowledge of the deferred bug list and the customer complaint list, you can predict which bugs will cause customer reaction. When the project manager defers a bug that you think will generate customer calls, approach her with the customer call records and explain the costs of similar deferrals last time.

- *Justify the expense of necessary further testing.* For example, suppose it would cost $20,000 to equip your lab with three particularly suspect brands of computers, so that you can expand your compatibility testing. If no one complains of incompatibility with these brands, don't bother setting up this lab. But if your technical support group spends $40,000 per year answering calls from irate owners of these machines, you fully justify the lab and testing expense by holding out the promise of eliminating this customer service expense.

Project managers and marketing staff are also interested in these data and may have further uses for them. They may be looking for design or feature suggestions, or for information about the changing demographics of the user base. We aren't considering these types of uses here, but in practice you may be able to do your research as part of a joint study.

We recommend that you set up a detailed, multi-page table of problems and customer requests. Count how many times each complaint or request is made. Keep a separate table for each type of data (reviewer, letter, call, etc.). In setting up the tables, make a fast pass through the letters, reviews, and printed survey results to identify problems to list on the tables and leave room on them for things you missed. For design issues, track how often people said that they liked the way a feature works, along with the number of people who said they didn't.

You'll almost certainly find that most of the complaints come from a relatively small number of problems. This is the well known *Pareto Principle* (Gryna, 1988; McCabe & Schulmeyer, 1987). After you've collected the data, sort the individual complaints in frequency order, from most often to least often mentioned. (Don't be surprised if ordering differs significantly across data sources. Reviewers complain about different things than letter writers and both complain about different things than randomly sampled customers.) A table showing the most frequent complaints, in order, is an effective way to present the information. Or, more classically, use a *Pareto Chart* (Walton's 1986 explanation is the simplest we've seen). If possible, also show each problem's support cost (cost of reading and answering letters, average cost per call, average customer call length for each type of problem, etc.).

### Review the user interface for consistency

Some, but not all, testers are talented at spotting user interface inconsistencies early in a product's design. (Similarly for some technical writers.) If your test group includes someone with this skill, get that person into the design reviews as early as possible and give her enough time to review the product to be able to do this task well. This is a very valuable skill.

**PRODUCT DESIGN**
   TESTING ACTIVITIES DURING PRODUCT DESIGN
     **Negotiate early testing milestones**

### Negotiate early testing milestones

A good development team will want you to start testing before all the code is written. A disorganized team will waste a tremendous amount of your time in early testing. Negotiate some structure with the project manager.

A project manager is often delighted to prioritize programming tasks in order to make your early testing effective. With just a little encouragement from you, she may reorganize tasks in order to finish the highest risk tasks, or the tasks that will take the most testing, first.

For example, if printing quality and multi-printer compatibility are high risk areas for a particular product, decide with the project manager how to get this into Testing early and what parts of the printer code (which printers, which reports or other types of output) will be finished when the first versions come in.

### Other early preparation for testing

Start setting up relationships with vendors of equipment that your program must be compatible with (see Chapter 8, "Printer testing: Setting up a printer test lab"). The sooner you start, the easier it will be to get loaners or free equipment.

Think about reviewing competitors' products. The lead tester for this project should be familiar with the competition and the types of bugs common to this category of software, on this type of hardware. When will she get this expertise?

Start looking for beta testers. Good ones are hard to find. Beware that some capable volunteers will also be beta testers of competitive products. If you use them, they will tell your competitors about your products' strengths and progress months in advance. Others will give copies of the beta software to their friends or post a copy on public bulletin boards. We are speaking from experience and are not kidding about these risks. You must allow lead time to appraise potential beta testers.

## FRAGMENTS CODED: FIRST FUNCTIONALITY

The program may work in only one video mode. It may print to only one type of printer. It lacks most features. It's full of bugs. In an evolutionary development group, the first functionality milestone is reached when the program's core functionality (with almost no features) is complete.

### PROGRAMMING ACTIVITIES AFTER FIRST FUNCTIONALITY

The programmers keep specifying, designing (unless they're waterfallers who've done all this already, or programmer-anarchists who code first and specify later), and programming.

## TESTING ACTIVITIES AFTER FIRST FUNCTIONALITY

Somebody starts testing at this point. The programmer does unit testing. Someone (programmer, tester, programmer's assistant, someone) should start testing the program from the outside. This might merely involve playing with the program. In an evolutionary environment, the goal is to make this core software as reliable as a finished product, so formal testing starts here.

Start setting testing objectives. Make a rough list of the key testing tasks, the people who might do them, and how long they will take. This is the first draft of your schedule and budget. These are rough figures, and you should present them as such, but they are very important.

As soon as the product is capable of doing something useful, someone should start using it. In some companies, testers do most of this; others leave this work for the project or product manager's staff. Perhaps it doesn't matter who does the work as long as testers monitor it and report bugs. When you try to use the program to do things that a customer would do with it, you will find errors in the design that you would never notice otherwise. Also, some bugs that looked deferrable in theory turn out to be very annoying in practice. Some companies start this type of testing late, after the program is almost fully functional (perhaps at beta). This is unwise—the most likely result is last minute discovery of new bugs and renewed controversy over old bugs.

## ALMOST ALPHA

More of the program is finished—enough that you can know its character and style.

Some companies use the alpha milestone as an activity trigger. For example, test planning and execution, and manual writing may not start until alpha. For these companies, we recommend spending a few weeks before alpha on verification tasks. The lead tester (you) should work with the program to determine which problems and missing features are significant enough to keep the program from being honestly called "alpha." This becomes a period of intense negotiation with the project manager. You must also allow lots of time for retesting, to check whether the agreed changes and fixes were successfully made. Given pre-alpha verification, the declaration that a program has reached the alpha stage is usually made jointly by the project manager and tester.

**13**

TYING IT
TOGETHER

The alternative to pre-alpha verification, when alpha is an important milestone, is post-alpha friction. In the common case, the project manager declares a program alpha. We think that most (but definitely not all) project managers believe it when they say that the program has met alpha requirements. Then, *after* the project manager has publicly committed herself, you begin testing and discover enough missing features or serious problems that you don't think the program has reached alpha. Now what?

### PROGRAMMING ACTIVITIES WHEN ALMOST ALPHA

Specifying, designing, coding, bug fixing, and glass box testing.

### DOCUMENTATION ACTIVITIES WHEN ALMOST ALPHA

The documentation plan is probably ready for review by now. Some companies invite testers to documentation plan reviews; others don't. There are probably separate reviews for the manual, the online help, the tutorial, and any significant amounts of collateral material (such as libraries of sample files). Each review probably discusses the schedule for that type of document. Be ready to ask for a schedule modification if you're going to be asked to edit or check a long document during a critical week of testing.

Typical manual plan reviews work from a detailed outline of the book, with estimated page counts for each section or topic. You help the writer significantly by pointing out underestimated areas, explaining why a particular discussion will have to be longer than planned. You might also help the software design when long explanations are needed for a particularly complex group of features. When the manual plan review makes a project manager (also attending the review) realize how complicated a design will be for customers, the result is often a reworked, simplified design.

Typical help plan reviews cover the structure of online help, including the ways that the reader can jump from one topic to another. Some systems get very elaborate and provide many different types of cross-references and other ways to move through the help file. How will you test them all? Do you have to test every jump from every topic to every other topic? Are there any tools available to make testing easier (there often are). A simplified and testable help system design is better than a more elaborate but error-ridden one.

## TESTING ACTIVITIES WHEN ALMOST ALPHA

Order the equipment that you will buy for in-house testing. Locate the equipment that you will rent for in-house testing.

Start pestering equipment manufacturers to send you the loaners or free machines. You should have started talking with these companies already and completed their paperwork. On longer term testing projects you may still have lots of time, but if you have only four months left until the release date, hurry up or you won't get what you need.

If you haven't done so yet, start setting testing objectives. List the key testing tasks and estimate staff and time requirements. Hopefully this is your second draft.

Prepare the first draft of your test plan. Include the obvious things here. Leave fine details for later, partially because they're subject to change and partially because the information you need will probably be easier to get later. You might include the following:

- *List supported devices* (such as printers) and a first draft list of the features you'll want to test on them.

- *List the main features*, commands, menu options, i.e., start preparing the function list.

- *Prepare a structure for the test plan*, sections for you to put in other information. For example, don't list boundary conditions yet, but make a place for them in your document.

We stress again, as in the chapter on test planning, that you should be wary of creating too much test documentation. Write only what you need. Use what you write as a tool for thinking about testing, while you write. Always test while you write: it keeps your test notes accurate and it keeps you testing while you're doing your best thinking about tests. Don't give in to the temptation to spend days writing about how to test the program, instead of testing it. The objective is to find errors, not to make notes.

Do *mainstream testing*. Do the obvious tests, don't spend too long on every area of the program, and make sure to cover *every* area of the program that you can reach. Test every obvious choice point. If you can answer a question Yes, No, or Sometimes, try it all three ways. But only try a few if there are dozens of different answers. Don't try to check all combinations of inputs. Keep it simple for now; deal with things one at a time. Enter data everywhere you can, but don't go out of your way to stress the program. Check boundaries if you know them, but feel free to use less extreme values if you don't. Ask how the program fares under normal or even gentle use. If you have time after this, guess what might crash the program and try those tests.

You will find plenty of errors with these gentle tests, without wasting time on subtleties that don't work simply because the programmer hasn't gotten around to coding them yet.

## ALPHA

Definitions of alpha vary widely. Here are a few. Take your pick, or make up one of your own (everyone else does).

- At alpha, most of the functionality is present, but a few functions may be missing or untestable. The program clearly demonstrates its nature and style. Background music, some video modes, and many printers probably do not work.

- At alpha, all functions are coded, even though some may have serious bugs. All types of devices work (e.g., printing works), but perhaps only a few devices of each type work. The specification and design are substantially complete and there are no significant coding risks left. (This definition of alpha is so stringent that under it, further software development costs can be capitalized rather than expensed, according to the criteria laid out in FASB (Financial Accounting Standards Board) Statement No. 86. See Miller, 1990, Chapter 35. Normally capitalization starts no sooner than beta.)

- At alpha (evolutionary model), the core routines are complete. All critical added features are in: the minimal acceptable product is complete. You can use the product, and know its look and feel, but many features are yet to come.

### PROGRAMMING ACTIVITIES AFTER ALPHA

The programmers finish features, fix bugs, revise the external design (and perhaps the spec) in response to user or tester comments, and rework the internal design to improve performance. Work begins or continues on data files (such as templates, sample data, clip art, and translation tables for device drivers).

Note that if your company starts testing at alpha, and has a relatively short cycle from alpha to product release, then project managers will often lie about being at alpha just to gain access to testers. Don't get angry when this happens. Understand that they see this as the only way to defend their project under this development model. The model sets their project up for serious lateness by putting off testing until the last minute.

## MARKETING ACTIVITIES AFTER ALPHA

Work begins on the package design and marketing literature. This could begin sooner or later than alpha, as long as it's done in time for the release. Perhaps to get the best price from the printer, the package must be ready to print 10 or 15 weeks before the product ships.

You will (should) review the package design and all marketing literature for technical accuracy (but not for tone, style, or market positioning).

Many project dates, especially marketing dates, are calculated backwards from the expected ship date rather than forward from the status of the product. Package design, ad layouts, sell sheets, and other marketing collaterals are set to be finished as late as possible to maximize the probability that what they say matches the finished product. The same usually goes for user manuals because of long printing lead times.

Because marketing and documentation dates are driven by the expected product ship date, rather than by the state of the program, it is important to update the expected ship date as soon as possible when the programming or testing effort falls behind schedule. The project manager updates these dates; you should give her timely, clear, written testing status reports and should interpret their schedule implications.

## DOCUMENTATION ACTIVITIES AFTER ALPHA

The first drafts of the manual and help are probably finished shortly after alpha, so expect to review drafts a few weeks after alpha. (If the help system is quite simple, its first draft will come later.)

## TESTING ACTIVITIES AFTER ALPHA

In many companies, testing starts at alpha. We recommend that you start sooner, and continue your early testing during alpha. Remember the bug fixing cost curve. The cost of finding and fixing a bug rises exponentially as the project progresses. The sooner you find a bug, the easier it is to fix and the fewer implications that fix will have for other parts of the program. Your goal in early testing is to find all easily found problems in every area of the program. Your testing continues to be broad, shallow, mainstream testing.

As soon as you can get a draft of it, stroke the manual. Try everything in the manual at the computer. Try every program path it describes plus any other obvious ones. Check every example in the manual, keystroke by keystroke. Verify every claim. Check obvious implications.

During the first cycle or two of testing, the program may be so unstable that you can't get through much of the manual. Eventually you will. In the interim, you'll report lots of problems and have lots of time for thinking. By the end of the first *complete* cycle of testing, you should accomplish the following:

- *Start with a bang.* You will write dozens or hundreds of Problem Reports covering most aspects of the program and its documentation. Your reports probably cover the work of every programmer and writer on the project. Make your work visible and your productivity obvious, and keep everybody busy fixing bugs.

- *Learn the product.* You won't be an expert user, but you'll try every feature once or twice.

- *Make the test plan complete enough for review* by the test group manager. That draft or the next, developed not much later, should also go to the project manager for review. (The test plan grows during the first test cycles, and forever after, because you expand and correct the test plan as you test. Don't be talked into treating test planning and testing as separate activities.

- *Raise Design Issues.* Include usability observations. Your initial impressions can be invaluable.

- *Test the manual.* Check every fact and implication. Give a marked up copy of it back to the writer. (Keep a copy for reference. You'll need it until you get the next draft of the manual.)

- *Assess the product's overall quality*.

    - **Form an impression of the stability** of every major area of the program. Identify and comment on weak areas that are not ready to test.

    - **Estimate the probable reliability** of the program. How many cycles of testing do you expect to need? How many bugs do you expect to find? (Yes, the first time you come up with these numbers you'll be way off. But keep a private track of your estimates as you move from project to project. Eventually you'll develop a very good feel for the number of bugs likely in a program, and the number of test cycles it will take before they are eliminated.

Shortly after alpha:

- *Get signoff on the final list of supported devices* from the project manager. Put this list in the test plan.

- *Start the first round of device testing.* You should complete at least one full pass of device testing (all printers, modems, etc.) by the end of alpha.

- *Begin adding regression tests to the test plan.* These are tests that you will execute every time you test this area of the program. You should periodically reappraise this collection of tests. Some program areas are problem areas: the programmer fixes a bug, then breaks the fix, then fixes the fixes, etc. Keep testing problem areas heavily until they definitely and reliably settle down.

**13**

TYING IT

TOGETHER

- *Review your resource needs and publish testing milestones.* List the testing tasks carefully and estimate how many people each will take for how long. You may have published a draft of this list already, but now you have more details and more test experience. This is draft you will (should) be held to. The list should be complete, in the sense that if everything on it is done, and nothing else is done, you would agree that adequate testing was done. Individual tasks on the list should require more than half a day but less than a week. Map the list onto a time line, showing when the tasks will be done. This is hard work, but it is essential. This list is the tool that you and the project manager will use to review testing progress against the testing schedule.

As alpha progresses, you will expand the test plan and deepen the level of testing.

- *If you need it, develop and publish an acceptance test.* (An *acceptance test* is a test suite each version of the program must pass before being subjected to more detailed testing. See Chapter 3, "Black box testing: The usual black box sequence of events: Acceptance testing" and Chapter 12, "Documenting test materials: Types of test documents: Criteria for acceptance into testing.") By the way, most testing groups don't expect the program to pass the acceptance test until beta, so they don't start kicking a nonpassing version of the program out of testing until after beta (or some other date negotiated with the project manager). Publish the test early, but don't enforce it early.

- *Lay out and fill in your test planning lists and charts.* These include:

  - **Your list of lists, charts, matrices,** and so forth. What kinds of testing notes are you going to create? What kinds of tests are you going to run, or bugs are you going to find, that don't fit in any of these notes? Use the Appendix as a source of bugs, to check your coverage.

    This list helps you meet a critical early objective. You must develop a list of tasks, such that if you complete all the tasks, you'll be satisfied that you tested the program as much as you think it should be tested. You need this for scheduling, resource planning, and budgeting.

  - **Input boundary charts.**

  - **Output boundary charts.**

  - **The function list,** including strategies for finding control flow problems, such as initial state errors, the effects of going back and forth between a group of states, entering a state a second time, or leaving a state without supplying the requested input

  - **List of all error messages.**

  - **Printer (and other device) configuration test matrices.**

  - **Benchmarks for performance testing** across test versions and against competitors' products.

  - **Descriptions of load and stress tests.**

  - **Strategies for data flow tests** and for tracking consequences of any changes of existing data.

  - **Charts identifying the function of every key** in every area of the program. (If the keys work the same way everywhere in the program, this is an easy chart, but make sure to test many areas of the program against it, because many project managers and programmers erroneously claim that the keys work the same way everywhere.)

  - **Strategies for finding race conditions,** problems with messaging, shared data, interrupts, and other issues that won't show up in a simple linear analysis of the program.

  - **Matrices showing interactions** between input values or feature settings.

  - **Memory/activity charts,** showing the amount of memory used up by different activities, commands, etc., in different places in the program. These are investigative tools, and you probably won't fill them with data until you decide that you need to explore memory usage to track an irreproducible bug. But keep the data as you collect it. It comes in handy.

- **And so on.** The Appendix is a long list of bugs. Read it to find bugs to look for or areas to consider that aren't yet in the test plan.

• Again, don't try to do all of this at once. Always leave time for finding and reporting bugs, no matter what else you're doing. Don't try finish everything even by the end of alpha. Structure these lists, then add to them gradually as you come to understand the program, especially as you decide to investigate and thoroughly test some part of the program. On the other hand, do make progress on these materials as you go. These are your notes—if they're shallow and incomplete, what does that say about your testing?

Finally, during alpha, you should start laying out your automated tests. Automated tests are regression tests that the computer either runs for you or helps you run. They hold out the promise of saved testing time. The less time you spend re-executing old tests, the more time you'll have to create new ones.

• *Archive non-trivial data files* as you create them for testing purposes. Make sure to note what the files contain. Your notes might be terse but they must be sufficient to remind you of the file's contents, in detail. Don't force yourself to figure out what a given file contains every time you use it. You'd be as well off recreating the thing from scratch. If your main notes are comments in the files, prepare external documentation (such as an index and explanatory text) to help the reader locate test cases in these files.

• *Archive any reusable batch files, test drivers, data files, and captured series of keystrokes.* Organize these into two groups. Fully document the most critical and the most easily documented. Make these readily available to other testers. Lightly document other test files. Treat these as private materials since no one else will be able to understand them.

• *Prepare the printer test files.* Start preparing a standard group of input files that you will use to test every printer. Test with them, printing the output to disk as well as on paper. Construct the batch files to execute these tests automatically next time, comparing one program version's output through a given printer driver to the next version's.

• *Prepare the configuration tests.* List the environments under which you will test the program. Get the necessary versions of each operating system, memory manager, desktop manager, font display manager, etc. How will you combine these into a manageably small set of tests? Obtain the necessary models of other devices (modems, mice, video cards, etc.—you should get these from manufacturers in the same way, and on the same schedule as printers) and start preparing test files that will check program compatibility with each.

• *Automate the acceptance test.* If you really will run a brief, standard series of tests every time the program comes in for testing, and boot the version out of testing if it fails the series, you will run these tests many, many times. You must be able to replay keystrokes and mouse strokes, to capture all output (to all video modes supported by your program), and to mask off date and version information on the screen. Then you can compare known good behavior with the current version's behavior. Beware of commercial tools for this that are full of bugs or marketed with inflated claims: make sure to buy yours from a vendor offering a 30 day money-back guarantee.

There is a difficult tradeoff in automation. It can take ten times as long to automate and document tests as it takes to create them and run them once. Because of this:

- *You should automate as early as possible* or you will not recoup the cost of automation.

- *You should not automate early* because that reduces available testing time during early testing. This delays discovery and correction of many errors. It inflates management's confidence in the product's stability, which is exactly what you don't want.

- *You should automate early* because automating later will lower testing productivity during the peak bug finding period

- *You should not automate early* because the program will change too much. The program is unstable and subject to significant design change. Many painstakingly documented control or comparison files can quickly become so much magnetic pollution.

- *You should automate early* to create a standard acceptance test, because you'll run that test so many times that every minute you spend running it manually is wasted.

- *You should not automate early* because it will cause political problems. If you spend ten times as long creating an automated test case as you would spend recreating and running it once, the automation won't pay for itself for ten cycles of testing. Some project managers insist that their bug-free wonder needs only two or three testing cycles. They are probably wrong (*always budget for at least eight cycles*) but they can be offended by too much visibly long-term work. Automate some tests, but not so many that you're chastised for delaying testing. Even managers who expect many testing cycles may question your judgment over a heavy initial investment in test automation.

You get the idea. You'll have to rely on your own good judgment on this issue.

## DEPTH VS. BREADTH IN TESTING

You must specialize to test thoroughly. You must focus on one feature, one module, or one type of problem, and spend significant time and thought with it.

Unfortunately, specialization carries its own serious risk. When the product is released, will you have tested some areas of the program much more thoroughly than others? What about the weakly tested ones?

> *During each testing cycle, be conscious of the tradeoff between depth and breadth of testing.*

Think of the program as a collection of many areas of concern. List and test each of them. We don't want to define "area" too rigidly. You might focus on a class of problems, a feature, a module, a function, a menu, or something else. If you can think of it separately from the rest of the program, it's an "area of concern."

- **When you focus on a class of problems,** ask where a problem of this type could possibly arise in the program. Run tests for this problem everywhere reasonable in the program. For example, when you focus on configuration problems, try to imagine every aspect of the program that system hardware or operating software could affect. Test each of these as you change configurations.

- **When you focus on a module, a function, or a feature,** ask what types of problems it could possibly have. Look for them all. For example, you might test for every possible failure in the routines that display or print graphs.

Try to test every area of concern during every testing cycle. During any given cycle, though, plan to test some areas more thoroughly than others. You might test at any of the following levels:

- **Mainstream testing:** relatively gentle tests, which ask how the program fares under "normal" use.

- **Guerrilla raids:** a short series of the nastiest tests you can quickly imagine.

- **Intense planned testing:** a longer series that includes your best ideas for exposing problems in this area of concern.

- **Regression testing:** a series that you run each cycle. The ideal series checks every aspect of the area of concern in a minimum amount of time.

## Mainstream testing

During the early stages, the program constantly changes in response to the many Problem Reports and user interface criticisms. These changes will be error-prone (perhaps one error per three changes). Some of the new errors will be in the new code. Many others will be disruptions of code that used to work. Because of this, even mainstream-level tests will keep exposing errors.

Test each area of the program in each cycle of testing. Use the strongest tests that you've created. If you haven't tested an area rigorously before and don't have time during this cycle, use the mainstream tests that you used before. If you discover new boundaries or think of any interesting tests, add them to the test plan. Even without formal planning this will gradually improve the level of testing of this area.

## Guerrilla raids

Decide which areas of the program you will soon focus on and start testing them now. Spend up to a day finding as many problems in one area of the program as possible. Make the tests as tough as you can in the time available. Try to do something real (i.e., something that a customer would want to do) that uses these features. Then use boundary values when you know them, try to set up race conditions, etc. Follow your hunches about ways to expose errors. Your objectives are:

- **Clear away bugs early. Let the dust settle before starting formal planning.** It takes a long time to search for the best test cases, make notes, and document tests. Much of it will be wasted if horrible bugs force significant redesign. Rather than risk the investment when you focus on this area in a few weeks, bash it early. Try to find the worst problems and trigger the major redesign before detailed testing begins.

- *Give yourself thinking time.* Read and think about this area of the program now. Take just enough time to develop an appreciation of the possible problems and types of tests needed. Test the area enough to expose its worst problems. This buys you a week or two to mull over the problems before further testing. Many of your best intuitions will come almost effortlessly over those weeks.

- *Start fixing problems early.* The earlier you report a problem, the more likely it will be fixed.

- *Even up the level of testing.* What if management halts testing tomorrow? How many weakly tested areas will there be? Guerrilla raids are brief and informal, but much stronger than mainstream tests. They are much faster than the more focused tests, so you can test more areas of the program to this level. Test as many areas of the program as possible at this level before testing is halted.

## Intense planned testing

Choose an area of the program and concentrate on it. As testing continues, you'll spend more time on guerrilla raids and focused, planned testing. It will be a gradual transition. Start now by spending a little time thoroughly testing one area.

It's hard to decide where to specialize first. Chapter 12 ("Where To Focus Next, Where To Add Depth") described six reasonable choices:

- The area that looked weakest during initial testing, i.e., the area most likely to have errors.
- The area in which errors would be most visible.
- The most often used area of the program.
- An area that distinguishes the program from its competition or will be especially interesting to customers or reviewers.
- The area that will be hardest to fix if it's broken.
- The area you understand best.

Where you start is a matter of preference. Instead of writing detailed test plans for the weakest parts of the program, we often do early guerrilla testing, hoping that the stack of Problem Reports will get the mess cleaned up. We shift attention to these unreliable areas within a cycle or two of submitting the reports.

You may not have enough time to plan and conduct all of an area's tests during one cycle of testing. Take as much time for planning, documenting, and executing planned tests as seems reasonable. Spend the rest of the time available to this area by testing it on the fly. In the next cycle, you might take the time to finish planning and documenting tests in this area or you might postpone completion until Later. Use your judgment.

## Regression testing

After you've thoroughly tested an area of the program, you must retest it regularly. There will be new problems and old ones will reappear. The goal of regression testing is to provide coverage comparable to the focused work but without the cost in time.

Your regression test series always includes tests of recent bug fixes. However, these particular regression tests come and go. You'll use most only once or twice throughout testing. Along with these retests is a core regression test suite.

A regression test suite should be the minimum possible set of tests that covers an area of the program. It should cover as many aspects (sub-functions, boundary conditions, etc.) of the area as possible, with values the program is least likely to pass. It should use as few tests and as little execution time as possible.

In practice, few regression suites are this elegant. Yours should include the most interesting or useful retests of fixed bugs and the best other tests run so far. Add them to your test notes during mainstream and guerrilla testing. Add more tests while doing the more detailed test planning. Spend up to half of that time creating tests that you'll want to use again.

Consider structuring your regression test series so that you run some tests every time there's a new version, some every second or third version, and some much less frequently. To cope with waves of new versions (common near the very end of testing), make it easy to sample the reliability of each area by using a different subset of regression tests each time.

## A NOTE ON TESTING CYCLES

The ideal cycle of testing includes a complete round of tests of one version of the product. In practice, the amount of testing varies from version to version. We still call the testing of Version 1.20b a cycle of testing, and the testing of 1.20c another cycle, even if we skipped many tests in each.

**13**

TYING IT
TOGETHER

In many companies, programmers submit a new version of the product for testing with the understanding that it will go through a complete test cycle. When the *Testing Group* decides they've tested this version sufficiently, they close this cycle of testing and accept the next version for testing.

In many other companies, programmers submit a new version for testing after they've made so many changes to the program that they (and you) feel that it's wiser to test the new code than the old. Early in testing, expect delays of two to six weeks between new versions (this varies widely across companies). Later versions arrive once per week, then once every few days.

Beware of turning versions around so quickly that you spend most of your time on acceptance tests, acceptance paperwork, the same old regression tests, and end of cycle paperwork. This is no way to find errors. Some programming teams will try to make you test a new version each day, and to make the point, some even refuse to read new reports of bugs found in old versions. In our experience these people are usually acting in good faith. However, some project managers know full well that they can cripple your test efficiency by churning versions, and if they're trying to meet a tight schedule with a bad product, and they don't care if it ships with bugs, this is an important trick they can and will use to limit your ability to find new errors.

Try to set a schedule that allows you to spend between 25% and 50% of your time planning and executing new tests. These tests are the most likely to expose problems. This is easy during the first few cycles but once you have a large regression test battery, it's hard to dedicate 25% of your time to new tests. You must keep the regression test battery lean enough and the test cycle long enough that you're not just re-running regression tests from cycle to cycle.

## PRE-BETA

If your company use the beta milestone as an activity trigger, or makes significant decisions or commitments based on the day the product goes beta, we recommend spending two to three weeks before beta on verification tasks. Work with the program to determine which problems and incomplete features are significant enough to keep the program from being honestly called "beta." Given pre-beta verification, the declaration that a program has reached the beta stage is usually made jointly by the project manager and tester.

Some companies sequence alpha and pre-beta, and call this the "beta submission phase." In this case, the testing (often, and writing) planned for the alpha phase are complete. Therefore the project manager can declare "beta" as soon as the program meets the beta requirements. The project manager submits the program for beta evaluation, and, after much negotiating, fixing, and retesting, Testing certifies the program as "beta."

In other companies, the pre-beta review is not publicly seen but is done during the last few weeks of alpha testing.

As with pre-alpha testing, expect to receive a flurry of releases containing changes and fixes to the specific problems you've reported. Budget your time so that you can check these changes and fixes quickly, and report the results quickly.

## BETA

As with alpha, definitions of beta vary widely. Here are some examples of the variety of meanings of this milestone:

- At beta, the program is ready to send to *beta testers*, people who don't work for your company, who will use the product and tell you about their experiences. The product must be customer-usable, useful, and not embarrassing. Most devices are supported. There are few serious known bugs and you can warn people away from any areas that are bad. Most *in-development* design issues are resolved. However, since the beta testers are representative of your customer base, they may open new design issue debates with their feedback.

Note that under some development models, all features were coded by alpha, but under others, some features may still not be coded. Beta means the product is ready to be appraised by outsiders, but it doesn't necessarily mean that product implementation is finished.

- At beta (typical waterfall definition), all features are complete and tested, there are no fatal errors and few serious ones, non-essential data files (sample art, tutorials, templates, etc.) are at least 50% complete, device data files (such as printer translation tables) are almost complete, the design and specification are complete (if they exist), and the product meets its initial requirements. Even the most conservative accountant would agree that further development costs can be capitalized under FASB-86.

- At beta (evolutionary model), the core product is complete, all essential features for the minimally acceptable product are present and fully tested. Some other desirable features have (probably) been added.

The product reaches this milestone very early under evolutionary development. This lets you send early versions of the product to outside beta testers after the program becomes useful but long before all features are implemented.

Your company might want to create a third milestone (*gamma?*), more similar to the other definitions of beta. Under this definition, lots of features have been added, no others are critical to the marketability of the program, very few others will be added, none that can't be easily backed out. The focus is on finishing up.

From beta on, most project managers submit disks in their final shipping configuration. By now there's a list of what files will ship on which disks and whether they'll be compressed or not. The project manager will submit versions with all the files on the right disks, including blank dummy files with the names of those yet to come, in the right compressed or uncompressed format.

**13**

## PROGRAMMING ACTIVITIES AFTER BETA

The programmers finish features if there are any left to do. Primarily they are fixing bugs, finishing any data files, writing installation software, and adding any final device support.

The amount of attention to design issues depends on your definition of beta. This may be a key time to polish the design, based on user feedback, or it may be too late for anything but serious errors and problems that are trivial to fix.

The programmers, or customer support, or marketing, or you in testing, support beta testers (if there are any). Even if the programmers don't usually support beta testers, they may be called in to write utilities to salvage lost data from a customer's hard disk or to recover from some other horrible failure. Also, the programmers may be adding protection code to the beta disks, to guard against widespread piracy of a pre-release version. Typical approaches include:

- *Time bombs,* which crash or even erase the program after a given date.

- *Personalized versions,* with the beta tester's name embedded in many places in the code, probably even encrypted in the code. The personalized copy will flash the tester's name on screen (everyone will know she was the original pirate). If she modifies the name that displays, and modifies the other copies that the program compares against the name that displays, and modifies the other copies that don't do anything but sit in the code file, she will still miss the encrypted copies of her name. That way, if she posts the thing on CompuServe and the whole world downloads it and makes the product totally unmarketable, you can still prove in court that she's the one who did it, and sue her for everything she's got. (Unfortunately, few beta testers have much money, so you won't get much in court. But the threat is sobering. . . .)

- *Copy protection:* not much in favor today, but its future is unpredictable.

- *Other proprietary (trade secret) tricks.*

This special coding is important because it affects beta testers' comments and it may add bugs. Errors reported by beta testers might be irreproducible unless you test with their customized version.

## MARKETING ACTIVITIES AFTER BETA

If work on the package and collaterals isn't done yet, it continues. Disk label design often begins at beta (and finishes soon after). Expect to review final drafts of these on a very fast turnaround basis.

Marketing may be supporting beta testers and reporting large numbers of design complaints. Similarly, they may send beta copies to reviewers and ask for changes to placate them. There is often an air of crisis associated with these requests. Last minute design changes will perturb the schedule and may significantly improve or weaken the product.

## DOCUMENTATION ACTIVITIES AFTER BETA

Manual development continues through multiple drafts and reviews. The writers add technical tables (printer compatibility lists, keystroke summaries, etc.), and troubleshooting tips for hardware problems, bugs, design wobblies, and normal user errors and problems.

Now or right after UI freeze, the writers take screen shots (pictures of the program's display) and prepare the first draft index—it will probably have index entries (the words), but no page numbers until after final layout. The writers add boilerplate license agreement, copyright notice, trademarks, etc., to make a final draft manual.

If help hasn't been written yet, it starts now.

The writers also almost-finalize other product aids like keyboard templates and quick reference cards.

## TESTING ACTIVITIES AFTER BETA

On entry to beta, have the project manager sign off on the test plan. He has probably reviewed the plan already, but it has been evolving throughout alpha testing. The plan will continue to evolve, but to a lesser degree. Make sure there is no remaining controversy over the scope or adequacy of its coverage.

Review the marketing materials before they go to production.

If you haven't already done so, you *must* start *real-use testing*. Use the product as a tool, to do things that it should be able to do. If you're testing a word processor or desktop publisher, start using it to write memos and lay out reports. If you're testing a presentation manager, start preparing slides with it—not test slides but real slides that you need for real meetings. This testing is entirely independent of the functional test plan. Even though function testing is behind schedule, don't give in to the temptation to postpone this work until final testing. Real-use testing will reveal dozens of errors that inexplicably evade other types of tests, and it will reveal them in a compelling context—normal use of the product.

Continue executing the test plan, deepening your coverage of individual areas of the program, and doing unstructured guerrilla testing.

- This is the time to *be as truly nasty to the program as you possibly can*. Now you know the program well and you're gaining expertise in finding its bugs. Later will be too late, because the project manager will have to defer too many of your best finds. This is the time, right after beta, to do your best testing:

    - Retest all significant fixed bugs.

    - Exploit what you learned from old bugs to find new ones.

    - Analyze, retest, and resubmit hard-to-reproduce bugs that haven't yet been fixed.

    - Test at boundaries, test quickly on slow machines, test combinations of extreme cases, test error handling, test where you think you can make the program fail.

    - In a multi-tester project, consider specializing one person. Make her a full-time error guesser, whose only job is to find and exploit promising new test areas. Leave regression testing, test planning, and documentation to everyone else. Her role gains importance through final. If you choose her well, she'll find much more than her share of the last minute show stoppers, buying the rest of your group the time to find the rest.

- Make sure to *check code fixes very soon after you receive a new version*. This is a good general rule, but it's even more important as the project nears completion. Make a special effort to tell the programmers within very few days whether each fix worked or didn't.

- *Complete a full round of testing of all devices,* under all configurations. You tried to do this during alpha but didn't get all the way through, for every device, because you kept finding bugs. Now you can do the job properly. If you were able to test every device during alpha, and the program passed with them all, you should still redo device testing sometime after beta to confirm that everything still works (or prove that it doesn't). Some people wonder why they shouldn't start device testing during beta, since they have to redo it then. The answer is that you'll probably find many, many device-related errors. If you wait until beta to find them, you'll have to retest them all during final testing.

- *Continue automating some tests,* even if automation *might* no longer be economical. Some programs need many more cycles of testing than anyone expects. The more quickly you can regression test during these latter cycles, the better. Stop automating only when you're *certain* that the last cycle of testing is near. But ask skeptically about each test that you could automate, why it's so important to run exactly this test time and time again. Be sure that each test is worthy of the time you invest in it.

- *Test all data files*, including clip art, templates, tutorials, samples, etc. Testers almost always underestimate the time this takes. Try a small, representative group of files and clock your time. Work out the average and multiply it by the number of files to check. This gives you the time required for one cycle of testing of these files. You must also estimate the time required to retest revised files.

Make the testing status clear and get Problem Report issues resolved:

- *Circulate summary and status reports* that summarize open problems and provide various project statistics. You have probably already been circulating reports like these, but as the project progresses there are probably more reports, prepared more formally, and circulated to more senior people in the company.

- *Use good sense with statistics.* Don't treat the number of open reports and newly reported problems as meaningful and important without further interpretation. This late in the schedule, senior management will believe you (or act as if they believe you to put pressure on the project manager). These numbers convey false impressions. For more discussion, see Chapter 6, "Users of the tracking system: Senior managers."

- *Be careful when you add testers near the end of the project.* A new tester who writes a stack of reports that essentially say, "this Amiga program should follow Macintosh user interface rules" is wasting valuable last minute time. Late-joining testers who combine enthusiasm, poor judgment, and obstinacy can cost a project much more than they benefit it.

- *Circulate lists of deferred problems* and call or participate in meetings to review the deferrals. By beta, or soon after, these meetings should be weekly. Later they might be every few days. It's important to get these decisions considered now, rather than a day or two before shipping the product. Highlight any reports you want reconsidered—pick your appeals carefully.

- *Circulate a list of open user interface design issues* and call or join in a review meeting before the UI freeze. You have no business asking for reconsideration of design decisions after the freeze if you had the opportunity to ask before the freeze.

Review the manuals thoroughly as you get them. For drafts issued before beta, do all this testing before beta too. For more discussion of documentation testing, read Chapter 9:

- You are probably more familiar with detail changes and late design changes than the writer, so *make a point of checking that the manual is up to date*.

- *Warn the writer of impending probable changes* to the program.

- *Look for features that aren't explained, or not explained clearly enough*, or not in enough detail.

- *On a multi-tester project, have each new tester stroke the latest version of the manual* (check every word of it against the program). This should usually be their first testing task. In the best case, on a moderately large project, new testers join the project from mid-alpha until just before the UI freeze. If so, each draft of the manual will be reviewed in depth by a tester who has never read it before, as well as by someone familiar with it.

Continue measuring progress against the testing milestones you published at alpha. Check your progress every week. Is your testing team running ahead or behind? What new tasks have you taken on, how much time are they taking, and how do they affect the work you planned to get done? If you are running behind, or if you've added lots of new work, what are you going to do? Can you eliminate or reduce some tasks? Do you need more staff? Or is the programming schedule slipping so far anyway that your slippage doesn't matter?

Beware of the excuse that the programmers are so far behind that they're driving the schedule delays, not you. Every tester and test manager believes this about their projects, when the schedule goes bad, but that doesn't mean they're right:

- If you fall behind in testing, you will find bugs later that you could have found sooner. If you keep finding errors that were in the program many versions ago, which could have been found and fixed many versions ago, then part of the reason the program isn't ready to ship is that you're taking too long to find the bugs.

- If you push yourself and your test team too hard, your reports will be harder to read and reproduce, they'll include less investigation and simplification, and they'll take the programmers longer to fix.

- Bugs that live on and on in a project may reflect poor test reporting. If they do, it's partially your fault when there's a late delay when the project manager finally realizes that what you're talking about is a serious problem, and the programmer finally figures out (or you finally show him) how to reproduce the problem, so you all take time out to fix and retest it.

Make sure that you're covering the program at a pace you should consider reasonable, and reporting problems in a way you should consider responsible.

## OUTSIDE BETA TESTS

We need feedback from customers before shipping a product. But we often try to get too much from too few people at the wrong times, using the wrong type of test. The common problem of beta testing is that the test planners don't think through their objectives precisely enough. What is the point of running the test if you won't have time to respond to what you learn? What types of information do you expect from this test and why can't you get them just as well from in-house testing? How will you know whether these outsiders have done the testing you wanted them to do?

One reason behind the confusion is that there are at least seven distinct classes of end user tests that we call beta tests. Figure 3.5 shows the objectives that drive these seven classes.

**Figure 13.5  Seven objectives of outside beta tests**

1. Expert consulting

2. (Marketing) Testimonial/magazine reviews

3. (Marketing) Profile customer uses

4. Polish the design

5. Find bugs

6. Check performance or compatibility with specific equipment

7. Feature feedback for next release

- *Expert consulting*: early in development, marketing or the project manager may talk with experts about the product vision and perhaps about a functional prototype. The goal is to determine how they like the overall product concept, what they think it needs, and what changes will make it more usable or competitive.

Some companies get caught up in an idea that they shouldn't show outsiders anything until "beta", some late stage in development. After beta, the experts are consulted. By then it's too late to make the kinds of fundamental changes they request, so everybody gets frustrated.

---

*If you're going to use experts, use them early.*

---

- *Magazine reviewers*: some reviewers love to suggest changes and save their best reviews for products they were successful in changing. To them, you have to send early copies of the program. To others, who want to evaluate final product without changing it, you want to send very late copies. You won't expect feedback from them, apart from last-minute bug discoveries, and no one should expect the programmers to make late design changes in response to design feedback from these late version reviewers. There's no time in the schedule to even evaluate their design feedback.

The marketing department must decide, on a case-by-case basis, who gets early code and who gets it late.

- *Testimonials* might also be important for advertising. Again, marketing manages the flow of product to these people. Some get code early and get to feel that they contributed to the design. Others get almost-final code and can't contribute to the design.

- *Profiling customer uses and polishing the design*: it might be important to put almost-final product in the hands of representative customers and see how they actually use it. Their experience might influence the positioning of the product in initial advertising. Or their feedback might be needed to seek and smooth out rough edges in the product's design. To be of value, this type of test might leave preliminary product in customer hands for a month or more, to let them gain experience with the program. To allow time for polish to be implemented, in response to these customer results, you might need another month (or more).

People often say that they do beta testing to find out how customers will use the product and to respond to the problems these sample customers raise. If you want any hope of success of this type of testing, budget at least 10 weeks, preferably more, between the start of this testing and the release of final product to manufacturing.

- *Finding bugs:* Rather than using outside beta testers to look for functionality issues, argue for bringing in members of your target market to evaluate the program and its documentation. You can watch these people. You're paying them for this, so you can make sure they test for the desired number of hours. You can replicate their problems with them instead of trying to interpret an incoherent description over the phone. You can see what they're trying to do and gain a much clearer understanding of where the program failed or why they're confused or disappointed.

- *Checking performance and compatibility with specific equipment:* You can't have one of every interesting type of printer, modem, computer, mouse, sound card, video card, etc., in the lab. Sending the program to someone (customer or manufacturer) who owns an interesting device might be the best (or only) way to test compatibility with that equipment. You must be organized about this or you'll waste time and get less feedback than you want:

  - **Write a test plan for these testers**—make it simple, direct, obvious, short, easy, and whenever possible, have them print things out or save them to disk so that you can see the results instead of taking their word for it.

  - **Call to confirm that they received the materials.**

  - **Call again a week later** for feedback and to see how they're progressing. You are probably doing this testing at the last minute. You are dealing with people who probably don't care whether your product ships on time. Do everything that you reasonably and politely can to get their feedback.

  - **Consider using redundant beta testers**—two for each type of equipment, or each other type of special test you want run. (Don't tell your testers about their alternates.) This doubles the number of packages you send and the number of people you call, but if one tester delays, you can still get the results from the other one.

  - **Plan your resources carefully for beta test support.** When you add up all the time it takes to find these people, have them sign nondisclosure agreements, maybe customize the program for them, write the beta test plan, make copies of the product, stuff and address the envelopes, call the testers, play telephone tag with them, answer their questions and deal with their problems and complaints, and get the test results back and evaluate them, you'll probably spend a total of six or eight hours of your staff's time per beta tester, for a simple test of a simple product. Adding complexity to the test or product adds further time.

**13**

TYING IT
TOGETHER

## USER INTERFACE (UI) FREEZE

After this milestone is met, no changes are made to the visible product. Exceptions are always made for disasters, but invisible fixes will be preferred to visible ones, even if the visible ones are better. New error messages are normally allowed after the freeze, even though they're visible, especially when added to help avoid a more noticeable change.

In some companies, UI freeze and final software are the same milestone. The design keeps changing until the code is frozen for release to manufacturing. This is not necessarily unreasonable. For example, the visual appeal and playability of an arcade style game are much more important than the accuracy of every detail in the manual. Late design changes can make a big difference in customer satisfaction.

Other companies freeze the user interface well before the beta milestone. This is good for test automation and makes the manual and help writers' jobs easier, but it keeps the company from using beta test results to improve the design.

## USER INTERFACE (UI) FREEZE

In the following sections, we treat UI freeze as a milestone that occurs a few weeks after beta, and several weeks before final software.

### PROGRAMMING ACTIVITIES AFTER UI FREEZE

The programmers make internal (invisible) bug fixes and, maybe, essential performance enhancements. They may have to finish creating sample data files and must do so in a way that exactly conforms to the manual's description. The installation software probably needs some final tweaks. Knowing this, the documentation writers probably didn't say much about installation. The programmers may do anything that wouldn't surprise a reasonable reader of the installation documentation.

If your company will create a demo version of the program to give away, it will probably start developing the demo code now, perhaps on a very tight release schedule.

### MARKETING ACTIVITIES AFTER UI FREEZE

Magazine reviewers' demands for design changes can no longer be satisfied because the design is frozen.

Marketing is busy showing the product, preparing a mailing of demo copies, and designing stickers and other kludges to deal with the design change that no one quite realized would contradict what's on the box and in the sales literature.

Marketing and Sales are doing *much* more than this—they're now in full gear, but what they do is not relevant to testing (except inasmuch as the promotion and sales effort will be badly hurt if the project falls seriously behind its current schedule).

### DOCUMENTATION ACTIVITIES AFTER UI FREEZE

Help text might be frozen at this point or the writer might have a few days or weeks left. Some companies schedule most of the help text writing after UI freeze.

This is the best time for taking screen shots. Some companies postpone all screen shots until UI freeze.

This is the best time for a final review of the accuracy of the manual.

The manual goes to page layout and will go to the printer soon. Some companies hold the manual until after the software goes final. In others, final blue lines will be back for proofreading just before final test begins.

### TESTING ACTIVITIES AFTER UI FREEZE

Plan to spend time checking the accuracy of the manual. If you've already done a thorough review you can move more quickly this time, just checking detailed procedures, descriptions of the screen or the order of events, and screen shots. This may take an hour per ten pages, or maybe a bit longer.

By now you've explored every area of the program. You will probably spend the majority of your remaining time on regression testing. Follow your test plan.

Prune your list of regression tests, especially in the areas of the program that seem the most solid:

- *If two tests are similar, get rid of the weaker one.* You may archive the details of the discarded test. The point is that you want to quit using it and quit seeing it.

- *Reconsider ineffective tests.* Archive tests that the program consistently passes. Select some for retesting during each cycle of testing, but don't use them all in each cycle.

You will probably still be testing a few printers, modems, terminals or other devices during this period, even though the program should have been modified to work correctly with them all already.

Stop looking for design issues. Look mainly for serious functional errors. Add significant or interesting tests to the test plan—as to the others, run them without spending much time documenting them.

Now that you understand the program even better than before, look for ways to corrupt data by changing it. Make small changes and big changes, change data and their output format separately or together. Trace the effects of your changes on program memory, looking for problems.

Reconsider the open bug reports. Why are they still open?

- *Retest all open reports.* Have any been left open that were actually fixed? Don't assume a fix just because you can't recreate the problem. Make sure you can recreate the error in the version in which it was reported, then talk with the project manager about it.

- *Look for ways to simplify these reports* or for more serious consequences of them.

- *Deal effectively with ignored bugs.* Near the end of the project, new Problem Reports may be ignored. Reports are lost en masse. Others are deferred en masse. A new distribution schemes unexpectedly delays delivery of reports to programmers by days or weeks. Consciously or unconsciously, the programming team, including the project manager, find ways to make these reports go away. Take this as a signal that they are bone tired of the project and demoralized by the delays.

13

It will be hard, but try to react professionally. Emotions are running high enough already. Showing your annoyance will hurt your effectiveness.

Use the problem tracking system to fight this battle. Issue weekly reports summarizing deferred and unresolved problems. If the circulation list doesn't include middle managers, broaden it. If you're challenged, say it's standard procedure to send summary reports to middle or senior managers when the product is so near to release. (If this isn't standard policy, change your standard policy.) These regular reports constantly remind people that sticking their heads in the sand won't make the bugs go away. This tactic usually succeeds in gently forcing attention back to the bugs.

If this tactic doesn't work, document the problem and ask your manager how to proceed. Good luck.

## PRE-FINAL

This milestone might be the same as UI freeze. Any data files or installation routines or anything else that wasn't done before is complete now. On entry to pre-final, there are no more open bugs. The program would be in final test if company policy didn't require a few days or a week of surprise-free testing after pre-final before allowing the program into final test.

You will probably find a few more serious bugs during pre-final. After the programmers fix them, and you don't find serious enough new ones, the program moves into final testing.

## PROGRAMMING ACTIVITIES DURING PRE-FINAL

The programmers fix only the errors they are told to fix by the project manager. Many others might be found, and could perhaps be easily fixed, but are deferred because of the risk that fixing a bug will break something else in the program, in a way that might go unnoticed.

## DOCUMENTATION ACTIVITIES DURING PRE-FINAL

The writers create supplements, i.e., pamphlets or text files for the disk, if they are needed. You have to check these for accuracy.

You'll probably be a key source of information for the supplement. Tell writers about changes made to the program since the manual went to the printer. The writers will be particularly interested in design changes (such as revised dialog boxes, menus, or command names), new warnings and error messages, and modifications to the capability of the program (new limits on the number of objects the program can handle, for example).

## TESTING ACTIVITIES DURING PRE-FINAL

*Software products are never released—they escape!*

This is your last chance to find shipment-stopping bugs. You have three challenges during pre-final testing:

- *Keep looking for terrible problems,* to keep the test effort alive. The product will go into final testing (and ship soon after that) as soon as you fail to find anything bad enough in time. You are most likely to find release-stopping problems by playing your hunches. Work with areas of the program that you feel are most promising; try whatever tests seem most likely to pay off.

- *Make sure that new bug fixes didn't break anything.* This is a challenge when you get three versions per day and the test plan takes two person-weeks to execute. You can't get through the whole plan on any version, so just keep working through it as you get new versions. That is, when you get a new version, test the error that was allegedly fixed. Then start testing from the test plan, at the place you left off in the previous version. If you get all the way to the end in this version, start again at the front.

- **Tie up loose ends.** You can probably find a few tests that your staff didn't quite finish, a printer that wasn't fully tested, and other tasks that weren't quite completed, or were forgotten altogether. This is your last chance to make sure that every critical test has been run at some point(s) during the project.

This is a high stress, exhausting phase of testing, even though it seems simple on paper. The problem is that you will find a few serious bugs, which must be fixed. As soon as you find one, it will be fixed and you'll get a new version of the program immediately. If the programmers aren't on site, they'll be sending fixes by electronic mail, modem, or, at worst, next day courier.

You might get a new version of the program every day, or even twice or three times in the same day. This isn't a matter of *churning versions,* feeding you new versions of the program too frequently. Instead, the program is finished except for the one change necessitated by your undeferrable Problem Report. After the programmer makes that one change, all parties agree that as far as they know, there is nothing else to be done. Therefore, the fixed program goes into testing immediately. There's no point testing the old version further, and there's no point delaying the new version. But this repeats each time you find a new undeferrable problem.

Project managers sometimes forget to tell you about some of the last minute changes. Whenever a new version comes in for testing, it's wise to compare all files with those of the old version. When you notice a change in a file that has nothing to do with the program areas on the project manager's list of changes, ask what changes are missing from the list.

Do one last round of device testing; make sure that every device in every menu or program list has been selected in every supported mode and resolution. If you have time, resurrect some archived tests during what appears to be the last cycle of testing. The program probably still passes them, but this is your last chance to make sure.

If you have time, retest every fixed bug.

Circulate the final deferred bug list. The development team (or senior management, or whoever has been coming to the bug review meetings) has evaluated all of these before, so this last review is pro forma. But give management one last chance to reconsider the quality of the product before releasing it.

**13**

## RATING THE RELIABILITY OF THE PRODUCT

Once you finish pre-final testing, the product will either be mastered and shipped or it will leave your hands for final acceptance testing by someone else, perhaps by some other group, such as customer support.

Before the product leaves, you will be asked to evaluate the quality of the program. Is it ready for release? Your opinion may be ignored, but it will be solicited.

The quality of a product is its fitness for use. The product's design, functional capabilities, usability, and reliability all contribute to the product's quality. Don't get caught up in this when management asks you for a rating of the program's quality at the end of the project. They don't want a rehash of the design issues—all they want (probably) is information about the program's reliability. When asked for pre-release quality ratings, provide pre-release reliability ratings, possibly supplemented by some design comments.

Reliability is high if customers probably won't find a bug in the product. Reliability is low if the customer is likely to find a bug, especially a serious one. We don't know how to make a good numerical estimate of reliability. Many managers are satisfied with four rating levels:

- *Low reliability:* the product has serious bugs which the customer will probably find. These are known, deferred, problems.

- *Medium reliability:* somewhere between low and high.

- *High reliability:* the product has been well tested and you can no longer find any serious problems. You may have missed a few problems but you doubt that many customers will find them.

- *Unknown reliability:* you haven't adequately tested the program, or you've tested it as well as you can, haven't found anything horrible, but are certain there are still serious problems. The second case isn't worth raising unless you can explain why you're concerned and outline a reasonable plan to expose the problems you think might exist. (A reasonable plan might include short term help from an outside consultant or a short term lease on special testing hardware.)

### Minimum reliability

Your company won't ship products that don't meet its minimum reliability standards. You might not know your company's minimum standards—these are often not written down. Your company probably requires *at least* the following:

- *All input data boundaries have been checked.* If the program treats any good values as if they were out of bounds, it rejects them gracefully.

- *The final version of the manual has been stroked.* It accurately describes the program's behavior. You can issue all commands, you've tried all menu choices, taken all obvious branches, answered all yes or no questions both ways. It all works, at least if you don't try any fancy combinations.

- *All primary configurations have been tested.* The program works with the most common combinations of hardware and system software that it is supposed to work with.

- *Editing commands, repetitions, and other sequences that the customer can enter don't drive the program wild.*

- *The system can tolerate all errors the customer can make.*

Your company's minimum standards should be, and probably are, much higher than this. As a valuable exercise, try to add your company's other criteria to this list. For the sake of illustration, though, suppose these are your standards.

The company will not ship the product if you say that it doesn't meet one of these criteria.

The company won't ship the product if you justifiably give any of these criteria "unknown" reliability ratings. You might be scolded for not running the necessary tests already, but you (or your replacement) will get time for them now.

Many released programs haven't met these criteria. We blame tester disorganization for most of these. We suspect that many of the most obvious and embarrassing errors reached the field because the testers didn't keep track of how carefully they'd tested basic program areas. Had they flagged a basic area's reliability as unknown, they would have gotten an extension to check it.

### Reliability estimates for each area of the product

It pays to estimate the reliability of every area of the program. How likely is a failure? If you've followed the recommendations in this chapter, this information is available to you. You should know which areas have been tested to what level, and how the tests went. You might even publish a regular status report that lists all functional areas and problem classes and shows the estimated reliability for each.

If you rate an area's reliability as low, list every problem that led to this conclusion. If you believe that many more problems are yet to be found, say so. Estimate how long you need to confirm or reject this opinion. Be prepared to describe how you would check it.

If an area of the program hasn't been intensely tested, its reliability is unknown. Don't just describe it as unknown. Tell the people how long it would take to run a guerrilla raid on it to estimate the reliability. Give examples of bugs you might find. If you can't think of any candidates, look in the Appendix. Describe a serious problem that you are sure the tests run so far could not have caught. Don't say the bug is there. Say that you don't yet know whether it's there or not.

### The final decision

It's management's job to balance risks and costs. They have to decide whether it's better to ship a slightly imperfect product today or an immaculate one next year. The answer is different for different applications and price ranges. It's their job to understand the market and the position they want to the company to occupy in it.

**13**

It's your job to make sure that management understands the risks. They already understand the costs—they know how much opportunity they lose for each week that the product's not on the market. They know the project team's salaries. What they don't know is the probability that the program will fail in embarrassing or costly ways. They don't necessarily want to hear about these risks if the product is way behind schedule. You have to make sure that, like it or not, the decision makers have information about quality immediately at hand, in a format they can easily understand, couched in calm, authoritative tones that give no grounds for doubt.

TYING IT

TOGETHER

The final decision to ship the product belongs to management, not to you. You might not respect their quality standards (battle them directly, or leave), but if you've followed the strategy of this chapter you should be satisfied that you've done as well as possible within the constraints imposed by those standards.

## FINAL INTEGRITY TESTING

The product is finished. It goes through one last round of release testing, the disk masters are made, and they go to manufacturing.

### PROGRAMMING ACTIVITIES DURING FINAL TEST

The programmers stand by to fix undeferred problems found during final testing. Perhaps they're working on the demo version of the program. Or they're archiving everything, making final notes on the source code, and generally tidying up.

## TESTING ACTIVITIES DURING FINAL TEST

Many companies stop testing at the end of what we've labelled pre-final testing. Those companies probably split what we've described as pre-final work into a pre-final test phase and a final phase that includes the mastering tasks we mention here.

Other companies do one last wave of tests before mastering the disks. This is often called integrity testing. It might be done by a customer service or marketing group or by a different test group. Here are the objectives:

- *Evaluate first day of use reliability.* Use the product in ways that typical customers will use it during their first day. Carefully check the manual, tutorials, and other training aids. What problems will new users likely have?

- *Predict reviewer comments.* This is the company's last chance to change the program before reviewers jump on some obvious (but not necessarily easy to fix) shortcoming or flaw.

This testing is mainstream, not stress testing. The tester does things she'd expect of typical buyers and reviewers, not typical testers. However, this tester might be required to independently inspect your work, appraise its completeness, and look for holes and unfixed errors. Prepare a test materials kit that summarizes the testing process, includes the test plans, the Problem Reports, the data files, the printer test outputs, etc. (An integrity tester can check for holes in your testing by using our Appendix. She will take a sample of potential errors, then ask whether a tester with these test materials would have caught these errors if they were in the program .)

Once the integrity test is complete (if there was one), it's time to make the disk masters and check them. The files are copied to fresh, never-before-used, freshly formatted disks. The date stamps on the master disks' files are reset to the release date. The disks are checked for viruses and for bad sectors. The amount of free space on each disk is checked. If a disk is completely full, manufacturing errors are much more likely, so last minute file transfers might be made from one disk to another.

After the master disks are made, they are checked by installing the software on a computer (might fail if files were moved from one disk to another) and running a very brief, simple test of the program. The individual files on the final master are also compared against a known good set, just in case there was a copying error.

Other components of the release procedure:

- Check the disks for viruses.

- Archive the master disks.

- Archive the source code.

- Circulate a final addendum (if needed) to the final deferred bug list and get everyone's signature on the final release paperwork.

- When the first few sets of disks come back from the duplicator (have a few sets made before manufacturing in quantity), compare them against copies of the masters that were sent to the duplicator. Install the program from these masters onto one machine. Copy every file from the master disks to another set of disks, to check for I/O errors. And look again for viruses.

## RELEASE

The duplicator copied the master disks correctly and is now duplicating them in quantity. Following that, they go to an assembler to be boxed with the manual and other in-box goodies.

If you have any doubts, by all means, keep testing! It will be days or weeks before the product is manufactured and available to customers. If you find anything really nasty, maybe you can justify a recall. This will be expensive, but much cheaper than a recall after the program starts selling.

Your company might plan to issue a maintenance release almost immediately. This will let them ship the buggy product now and fix it soon. Don't be satisfied with the fixes they're working on. Find more problems for them.

Don't automate any more tests unless you can't run them any other way. Spend almost no time planning or documenting tests.

Along with testing, spend significant time tidying up. Organize your testing materials with the next release in mind. Even a maintenance release won't be ready to test for a few months. You'll move to another project within a few weeks. Even if you do test the maintenance release, you'll have had plenty of time to forget what you know now. Take a week or two now, document the most important materials, write notes to yourself or the next tester, print listings of the test files and scribble comments on them, whatever.

## 13

Your objective is to make testing of the next release easier and more effective than this release. You are now an expert in the testing of this product, at the peak of your knowledge. You should be able to do a great deal to make the next tester's job easier, even in just a week or two. Do it.

## PROJECT POST-MORTEMS

Some companies (or some individual test managers) like project post-mortems. You might be asked to prepare a final summary report on everything that happened, what went well, what needed improvement, what was a true disaster, what just never got done. You might be asked for a summary on paper, or verbally in a meeting.

The post-mortem document or meeting may be your most politically charged product, and you are often asked to prepare it when you are at your most exhausted. These can be very useful, or very destructive, or both. Watch out:

- Be constructive. Say what can be done better, more than what was not done well.

- Praise what was done well. Point to what worked, what others did that made your life easier or your work more effective.

- Don't pretend that problems didn't exist. If the programmer constantly made slipshod bug fixes, don't say that bug fixing went well or that he did a good job. You might choose to not say anything about this, or you might raise the problem in a gentle and impersonal way, but you should not deny the problem or deliberately mislead people about it. Don't praise people for things they didn't do, or that they did badly.

- Whatever you do, don't be a complainer. Don't point fingers. Don't make excuses. Don't be defensive.

- Never say or imply that someone else should be fired.

- Don't criticize the design or resurrect old bugs.

- Talk (or write) about problems in a neutral, factual manner.

- If you believe the released product is no good, think carefully about whether you want to say so at this meeting, or in this report. A good tester's opinion of a product is at its lowest at release—this is part of the psychology of harsh testing—you want that program to fail. Don't say something today that you might not feel is correct next month. And even if the program is a real stinker, think twice about saying it. If you did your job, they know it's a stinker. If their quality standards are so extremely different from yours, maybe you should smile and work on getting a good reference while you look for a new job.

  "Think carefully" doesn't mean "never say it." If you think that you can raise quality issues or process issues (or maybe even personnel issues, but think another time before doing it) in an honest, straightforward way that can improve the way the company operates, go for it.

- Beware of volunteering an opinion that you did a bad job. You might be at your most self-critical at this point, and if so, you'll do yourself a disservice. If you choose to criticize your own performance, raise the issues boldly and confidently. Explain what needs to be changed for these types of projects to be successful next time.

- Have a trusted friend (who might or might not be your manager) review your report or your notes, before you circulate them (speak them) to anyone else.

# LEGAL CONSEQUENCES OF DEFECTIVE SOFTWARE

## THE REASON FOR THIS CHAPTER

Most Quality Control (QC) staff get some training in products liability law[1] for two reasons:

- QC should recognize product defects that are so serious that the company will be sued over them.
- QC should be able to use the law as ammunition, in an argument to get a serious defect fixed.

Software testers are rarely trained in products liability, because few lawsuits have involved consumer software products. The situation is changing, however. For example:

- A Small Claims Court judge ruled that TENpointO perpetrated fraud when it continued to market *Focal Point II* and *Reports* after a number of users had reported bugs (see Taylor, 1991).
- In 1990, the Federal Trade Commission fined Commodore Business Machines $250,000 for advertising vaporware (Commerce Clearing House, 1990).
- In 1990, NEC was held liable for falsely advertising that its original Multisync monitor is VGA-compatible (*Princeton Graphics v. NEC*, 1990).

Magazines like *Byte, Communications of the Association for Computing Machinery, PC Week, PC Magazine*, and *InfoWorld* regularly describe serious bugs in shipping software products. Some of these bugs have caused so much loss of time, work, and data, and publishers have handled complaints about them so ineptly, that it is surprising the publishers have not been sued. In a few cases, lawsuits would probably have been successful, and could have cost the publishers hundreds of thousands, or millions, of dollars.

There hasn't yet been a precedent-setting lawsuit against a consumer software publisher.[2] Lawsuits are expensive, so the typical lawyer will be cautious about bringing this type of suit until someone else wins a significant award. There seem to be deserving candidate products for suit every year, so one of these years the trendsetting suit will happen. After that, the floodgates will open.

The American law of products liability is quite strict. Learn it now, and help steer your company's products away from liability.

## NOTE

This chapter is by Kaner alone—at time of writing, I am a fourth year law student at Golden Gate University, not a lawyer. Direct, practical experience with the law is essential for accurately interpreting the law, and I don't have that yet. I write this chapter to raise issues, not to provide legal advice. If I succeed in raising legal issues in your mind about the products you build, talk with your company's attorney about them.

**14**

[1]The American Society for Quality Control (ASQC) is the main professional society for Quality Assurance specialists. You can be certified by ASQC as a Certified Quality Engineer (CQE) if you have appropriate work experience and pass their certification exam. Products liability law is one of the areas covered on the exam.

[2]The TENpointO case is not a precedent setter because other courts are not bound by Small Claims Court rulings like the one made against TENpointO.

Software law will evolve significantly over the next ten years. Some points made in this chapter will be obvious in a few years; others will be flat wrong. To make it easier for you (or your legal advisor) to check the state of the law when you need to, I've included detailed references in this chapter.

*It's OK to Skip the Footnotes.*

A few points of law are still unsettled in the courts and have raised eyebrows when I've discussed them with interested engineers. I cover these in more depth in the footnotes, mainly identifying the controversy and pointing to key references. It's OK to skip these footnotes. If you're not planning to do further reading, you'll probably enjoy the chapter more if you do skip the footnotes.

## OVERVIEW

This chapter considers seven general areas of law, or *legal theories*, under which a consumer can sue a software company:

1. Breach of contract

2. Breach of warranty

3. Breach of implied warranty

4. Strict liability in tort for injury to a person or damage to property

5. Negligence liability for injury to a person or damage to property

6. Malpractice liability (negligence liability for professional services)

7. Fraud and misrepresentation

In each case, the key questions of interest are:

- What does this legal theory involve?

- Under what circumstances can someone bring a lawsuit under this theory (such as a contract theory or a negligence theory)?

- What types of product failures could lead to a lawsuit of this type?

- If a consumer or user of the software brings a lawsuit under this theory and wins, what is a court likely to give her or to do to the losing company?

- How can your company protect itself from having to face a lawsuit of this type?

The chapter concludes with a brief discussion of trade secret law and engineering ethics.

People acquire computer software in different ways, with different legal implications. Consider the following spectrum of possibilities.

- *Assigning an employee to create or modify a program.* An employer generally can't sue an employee for writing bad code. If the employee's work is directly responsible for a successful negligence suit against the employer, the employer can probably sue the employee to recover the damages. This is a rare type of suit and it is outside the scope of this chapter.

- *Hiring a consultant to create or modify a program.* A customer can argue that the consultant provides professional services. Professionals can be sued for malpractice. Malpractice is briefly discussed toward the end of the chapter.

- *Buying a program that is written or customized to match the buyer's specifications.* This is the classic example of software purchased for a large computer system.

- *Buying a program off the shelf, from a retailer.* This is the normal case for consumer software.

- *Copying a shareware program.* This is just like buying a program off the shelf. The programmer wrote it for sale and is selling it in a finished form. The only difference between this and retail sale is marketing technique.

- *Copying (illegally) a program bought by someone else.* There is no contract, express or implied, between the seller and the copier of this program. Even so, the seller may be liable for injuring the copier or causing property damage.

- *Copying a public domain program from a bulletin board.* There is no contract. What about personal injury or property damage?

LEGAL

CONSEQUENCES

## BREACH OF CONTRACT

A contract is an agreement between two or more people (or companies) that creates obligations to do or to provide particular things. A software contract can involve goods (such as a program bought at a store) or services (such as custom programming), or some mix of the two (such as a program that comes with a promise of free updates or bug fixes). Contract law comes into play when software is developed under contract by a consultant, when custom software is written by a software developer, and when the customer buys the software at retail.

Levy & Bell (1990), Boss, Weinberg, & Woodware (1989), Salter (1989), Schneider (1985), and Harris (1983) are good discussions of the application of contract law to retail and custom software development.

## THE U.C.C. AND SOFTWARE CONTRACTS

This chapter is primarily concerned with goods: software products. These are covered by the law of sales, including the *Uniform Commercial Code (U.C.C.)*. The U.C.C. is the law in all American states.

The U.C.C. is important because it revises the general law of contracts in significant ways. Under the U.C.C.:

- The express warranty rules are quite strict.

- Two types of implied warranty apply to software. These are the implied warranty of merchantability and the implied warranty of fitness.

- The Code defines three types of damages: breach of bargain, incidental, and consequential.

- Software publishers can disclaim some warranties and types of remedy.

The U.C.C. applies only to goods, *not* to contracts for services. Are computer programs goods or services? This has been the central question in many lawsuits, and the law is fairly well settled:

- If the customer contracts for development of a program, and pays by the hour for the programming and testing work, the customer has bought services (programming and testing), not goods. Therefore the U.C.C.'s rules don't apply. *Micro-Managers, Inc. v. Gregory* (1988) is typical of this type of case.

  When you do contract testing for so much per hour, you're selling a service.

- Suppose you sign a contract to supply a bug tracking database system. The customer will pay a fixed rate of $10,000. Is your database application program goods or a service? It depends. If you have to write the program from scratch, and especially if you're developing it exclusively for this one customer according to her specifications, you're selling a service. But if you've already written most of the database and just have to customize it for this customer, you're probably selling goods. If the customer is primarily paying for the product you've already developed, you're selling *goods*. If the customer is paying primarily for your programming, you're selling a *service*. *RRX Industries, Inc. v. Lab-Con, Inc.* (1985) is probably the most cited case along these lines. *Systems Design & Mgmt. Info., Inc. v. Kansas City Post Office Employees Credit Union* (1990) is another good example.

- Programs that are published (many copies are made, packaged, and sold) are goods, covered by the rules of the U.C.C. *Advent Systems, Ltd. v. Unisys Corp.* (1991) and *Step-Saver Data Systems v. Wyse Technology* (1991) make this point clearly.

  Rodau (1986) and Levy & Bell (1990) contain excellent discussions of this issue. White & Summers (1988, § 9-2) provides a good general distinction between goods and services.

## BREACH OF WARRANTY

In a contract case, the buyer sues because she didn't get what she paid for. The seller breaches the contract by failing to deliver the product on time, or by delivering a product that doesn't live up to his promises. The program must do everything he promised it could do and it must not do anything (bugs) that he promised it would not do. For example:

- A seller who promises a program that will fail no more than once per hour breaches the contract by delivering one that crashes once every 59 minutes. However, a program that crashes once every 61 minutes satisfies this contract.

- If the seller promises a program that lets the buyer load, edit, and print text files, he is not in breach if the program does these tasks but doesn't let the buyer save the edited text files. (Some companies actually sold programs like this a few years ago.) There's no breach if the program can't do what the seller didn't promise it could do.

Promises about the quality and capability of a product are *warranties*.

## EXPRESS WARRANTY

The Uniform Commercial Code defines three ways of creating an express warranty:

§ 2-313 (a) Any affirmation of fact or promise made by the seller to the buyer which relates to the goods and becomes part of the basis of the bargain creates an express warranty that the goods shall conform to the affirmation or promise.

§ 2-313 (b) Any description of the goods which is made part of the basis of the bargain creates an express warranty that the goods shall conform to the description.

§ 2-313 (c) Any sample or model which is made part of the basis of the bargain creates an express warranty that the whole of the goods shall conform to the sample or model.

A warranty doesn't have to be in writing, and it definitely doesn't have to say "warranty or guarantee." (See U.C.C. § 2-313 (2) and the section's Official Comment 3.):

**14**

LEGAL
CONSEQUENCES

- *Sales brochures are warranties.*

- *Specifications are warranties.* This general rule is reflected in *Northern States Power Co. v. ITT Meyer Industries* (1985) and *Consolidated Data Terminals v. Applied Digital Data Systems* (1983). However, see *Hoover Universal, Inc. v. Brockway Imco, Inc.* (1987) for a case in which the seller avoided warranty liability by using a disclaimer in the contract.

- *User manuals are warranties.* Any statement in the manual about how the program works is a warranty that the program will work that way. The manual is a warranty even if the customer never reads the manual.

To show that a statement of fact in the manual is not a warranty, the seller must prove that the statement wasn't part of the *basis of the bargain*, that is, that it had absolutely nothing to do, directly or indirectly, with the buyer's decision to purchase the program. To show this "requires clear, affirmative proof" (U.C.C. Official Comment 3 to § 2-313; see White & Summers 1988, p. 402). If a buyer heard about a feature of the program from a friend who'd read about it in a newspaper article that summarized a claim in the manual about that feature, a seller could find it impossible to provide "clear, affirmative proof" that the manual's statement had nothing to do with the buyer's purchase decision, even if the buyer never read the manual.

- ***The box is a warranty.*** Some software test groups don't check product packaging carefully enough. If the box says "compatible with Epson printers," the program must be compatible with every model of Epson printer. If the box's only comment about memory is "requires 2 megs of memory," every feature described on the box must be available to the customer who has only 2 megs on her machine.

  Software publishers sometimes mock up sample output for the box. One reason for this is that photography and printing can distort images. A carefully designed mockup might yield a box cover that looks more like the actual output or screen than a photo of the real thing. Another reason for mockups is the long manufacturing time to cost-effectively produce the box. Sometimes, the package has to go to press before the program is stable. But whatever the reason for the mockup, sample output on the box is a warranty that the program can precisely reproduce every detail of that output.

Express warranties are hard to disclaim. For example, in *Fundin v. Chicago Pneumatic Tool Co.* (1984, p. 794), Chicago Pneumatic published specifications in a sales brochure, along with a disclaimer saying that "We reserve the right to amend these specifications at any time without notice. The only warranty applicable is our standard written warranty. We make no other warranty expressed or implied and particularly make no warranty for any particular purpose." The court held that the specifications constituted a warranty anyway, and Chicago Pneumatic couldn't disclaim it because a disclaimer won't work against affirmations of specific facts.

If an advertisement promises that a program is error free, no disclaimer on a warranty card can negate that promise. The program is warranted error free, period. (See, for example, *Redmac, Inc. v. Computerland,* 1986.)

Read Ackerman (1989) for a readable and very detailed discussion of warranties and consumer software.

## IMPLIED WARRANTY OF MERCHANTABILITY

The Uniform Commercial Code writes implied warranties into every contract, and the seller is liable for breaching them for any reason, even if he doesn't realize he's breaching them (Salter, 1989, p. 473). Here is the implied warranty of merchantability:

§ 2-314 (1) Unless excluded or modified (Section 2-316), a warranty that the goods shall be merchantable is implied in a contract for their sale if the seller is a merchant ...

§ 2-314 (2) Goods to be merchantable must be at least such as

(a) pass without objection in the trade under the contract description; and ...

(c) are fit for the ordinary purposes for which such goods are used; and ...

(f) conform to the promise or affirmations of fact made on the container or label if any.

In other words, the program must do what a reasonable customer would expect it to do. A word processing program must accept text, display it on screen in an understandable way, and print the text, all in an easy enough to use manner that a reasonably tolerant person wouldn't despise the program. A spreadsheet must handle numbers immaculately. This implied warranty doesn't require that the program be bug free, but under clause (a) the program can't be significantly less reliable than comparable products and under (c) the bugs mustn't stop the customer from successfully using the program in a normal way.

## IMPLIED WARRANTY OF FITNESS FOR A PARTICULAR PURPOSE

The Uniform Commercial Code defines the implied warranty of fitness as follows:

> § 2-315 Where the seller at the time of contracting has reason to know any particular purpose for which the goods are required and that the buyer is relying on the seller's skill or judgment to select or furnish suitable goods, there is unless excluded or modified under the next section [§ 2-316] an implied warranty that the goods shall be fit for such purpose.

In *Barazzotto v. Intelligent Systems, Inc.* (1987), a retailer was held liable for selling software incompatible with the buyer's computer when he knew the machine involved and the application intended. (See also *Hollingsworth Enters. v. Software House, Inc.*, 1986.) However, the manufacturer can't be held liable for the retailer's promises of fitness because the manufacturer doesn't know, at time of its sale to the retailer, whom the retailer will sell the program to or what the retailer's customers want to use the program for. (See *Professional Lens Plan v. Polaris Leasing*, 1985.)

## OF CONTRACTS AND WATERFALLS

You now know enough about contract law to appreciate the waterfall method of software development. In Chapters 12 and 13, we discussed this strictly from an engineering viewpoint, but to appreciate its strengths and liabilities you should understand its legal implications.

Years ago, most software development was done on contract. Large projects, and many intermediate ones, are still done on contract today. The waterfall method protects the contractor (the software developer) from the ignorance or sharp practices of the buyer. Here's how:

# 14

LEGAL

CONSEQUENCES

- The process starts when the buyer and the contractor sign a preliminary agreement to research the product requirements. The buyer often pays for this research, but some software companies will do it for free.

- After research, the buyer and contractor list the requirements that the final product must meet. These can include functional capabilities, reliability levels, hardware requirements, hardware compatibility, and performance requirements. These requirements are now "signed off" and the contractor will charge extra to change them.

- The contractor and customer next contract to develop specifications for the full job. The specifications define every feature of the program. During specification, the customer and contractor will often realize that the requirements should change. The contractor will revise them (at a price), and will then revise the relevant specifications. In making these revisions, the contractor is writing specs to match requirements that didn't exist at the time the specification-writing contract was signed, so the contractor gets to charge extra for this work.

- After the customer reviews the specifications and signs that she approves them, the contractor can make a reasonably accurate estimate of the time and cost to develop this product. The next contract tells the contractor to build exactly this product as specified. The contractor will charge extra for any changes to the requirements or specifications and for any coding that must be redone as a consequence of the changes.

- The warranties in this situation are quite limited. The customer has already agreed that a program that meets the listed specifications will meet the requirements, so all the contractor has to do is write a program that meets the specifications. For any changes, pay extra. If the program is too hard to use, too bad (or pay extra). If the program doesn't do basic things that any reasonable person would expect (but they weren't listed in the requirements), too bad (to change it, pay extra). If the specification says 2+2=5, so the program computes that way, too bad (to fix spec-induced bugs, pay extra).

The waterfall method is essential when dealing with customers who often change their minds, change requirements, add lots of new requirements and expect the project to still cost the old price, or who don't review specifications until after all the code's written and then say they hate everything. Too many customers, especially people without computing experience, are like this.

As I see it, the key advantage of the waterfall method to the contractor is that it transfers so much of the risk to the customer. If the customer approved the design but doesn't like the end product, the customer must still pay for it, or pay to fix it. Another advantage is that it controls changes. Because the customer pays for every change, she thinks carefully about what she asks for. A final advantage is that the late-change penalty is high enough to encourage many customers to review requirements and specifications rather than to wait and complain about the finished product.

Roetzheim's (1991) first few chapters illustrate how the waterfall approach helps structure software development work done under government contracts. This is the best description that I've read of the waterfall as a practical methodology.

Anyone who has worked with retail software developers knows that some software marketing people are like customers from hell. They read no specs, they add, drop, or revise features almost daily, and they whine incessantly that the project isn't finished yet. It's tempting (and sometimes essential) to impose a waterfall method just to control the marketeers or the executives, but be wary. In the contracting world the customer accepts the risk of a bad product. But retail customers won't accept this risk. If they don't like your product, they'll buy someone else's.

## DAMAGES

Suppose someone buys a communications program, but along with controlling her modem, it erases her hard disk. Suppose she sues the program's publisher and wins. Now what? The judge can't wave a magic wand and fix the disk. Instead, the judge will order the publisher to pay the buyer some money. The awarded money is called *damages*. The buyer's lawyer will try to prove different types of injuries or losses in court, and ask for separate damages for each. The totals can be huge.

This section defines the main damages-related terms that I'll use in the rest of this chapter. See Calamari & Perillo (1987) and White & Summers (1988) for good discussions. See Black's Law Dictionary (1990) for many more definitions and examples. I assume in each case that the buyer won the lawsuit and is entitled to damages. More general definitions would substitute "prevailing party" for "buyer."

First are the three types of damages defined by the Uniform Commercial Code:

- ***Benefit of the bargain damages:*** The difference between the purchase price (or the value of the product as stated by the seller, if this is higher than the purchase price) and the actual value of the defective product. (U.C.C. § 2-714.)

- ***Incidental damages:*** These cover costs like handling and processing expenses that the buyer had to pay because of the seller's breach of contract. For example, the buyer's cost of returning (mailing or delivering) the communications program to the seller is an incidental expense. So is the cost of shopping for a new program. (See U.C.C. § 2-715.)

- ***Consequential damages:*** These include (a) economic losses and (b) injuries to the person or damage to property.

  § 2-715 (2) (a) describes the economic loss: "any loss resulting from general or particular requirements and needs of which the seller at the time of contracting had reason to know…"

  Suppose the buyer bought a $100 communications program so she could exchange draft contracts quickly with an important customer. But the program crashed, destroyed her disk files, and as a result the buyer lost the deal. If this lost deal was worth $1,000,000 to the buyer's company, this $1,000,000 loss is a consequence of the program's failure.

  The U.C.C. says that the court should award this $1,000,000 in consequential damages to the buyer if the seller had reason to know that the buyer was purchasing the program in order to negotiate million dollar deals. ("Dear Seller: I need a communications program to set up multi-million dollar deals with European customers. The program must be super-reliable or I'll lose a fortune. I hear that your AcmeCom program fits the bill. Here's my $100. Please send AcmeCom right away so I can start making those deals.")

**14**

LEGAL
CONSEQUENCES

  On the other hand, if no one told the seller that the buyer was buying the software in order to make huge deals, the seller would not be responsible for the $1,000,000 loss. When it comes to consequential economic losses, the U.C.C. holds the seller responsible only for the risks he realized he was taking when he made the sale.

  § 2-715(2)(b) covers "injury to person or property proximately resulting from any breach of warranty."

  Think of "proximately resulting from" as meaning "caused by." If the buyer's smooth-talking lawyer convinces the judge that erasing a hard disk is "property damage," the seller will have to pay to reload the programs and data onto the disk, and to recreate data that were on the disk but weren't yet backed up.

Next is an important distinction between contract and tort damages:

- *Compensatory damages:* These damages make good the loss, without giving the buyer any profit. The only damages available in lawsuits involving breach of contract are compensatory damages. In tort suits (discussed later), compensatory damages can include payment for non-economic losses such as pain and suffering.

- *Punitive damages:* These damages are awarded in order to punish the defendant, not to compensate the plaintiff. The buyer can't collect punitive damages in a breach-of-contract lawsuit. She can collect them in a tort lawsuit (discussed later). Punitive damages are rarely awarded. They are available only when the seller's conduct was oppressive, fraudulent, or otherwise very blameworthy.

Finally, an important set of distinctions among losses. I'll discuss later a general rule that if the only losses are economic losses, the buyer must sue on a contract theory. However, if there's property damage or personal injury, the buyer can sue on a tort theory and collect compensatory damages to cover all direct and indirect economic losses, plus the cost to replace or repair the damaged property, plus medical expenses, lost wages and other direct results of the personal injury, plus any provable non-economic damages, plus punitive damages if appropriate.

- *Direct Economic Loss:* This includes benefit of the bargain damages, plus repair cost, plus any direct incidental expenditures in replacing a defective item that cannot be repaired. (For a thorough discussion, see *Continental Insurance v. Page Engineering Co.*, 1989, dissenting opinion, p. 667.)

- *Indirect economic loss:* "is down time and the loss of use which includes loss of profits during repair or replacement." (*Continental Insurance v. Page Engineering Co.*, 1989, dissenting opinion, p. 667.) This includes indirect, consequential economic losses, including loss of future business profits and business opportunities.

- *Property damage (to other property):* "If A manufactures paste which it sells to B who uses it to cement shoes which he sells to C, *a failure of the paste to properly adhere causes economic loss if it does not physically damage the shoes but merely renders them unsalable; on the other hand, a defect in the paste which physically damages the shoes causes property loss.*" (*Continental Insurance v. Page Engineering Co.*, 1989, dissenting opinion, p.668. Italics added.)

- *Non-economic damages:* These include payment for suffering, such as physical pain, mental distress, and loss of consortium (the companionship of one's spouse). Maybe no amount of money can truly repay someone for these types of suffering, but in tort cases the judge and jury usually have to figure out an appropriate award for non-economic damages. Non-economic damages are not available in breach-of-contract lawsuits.

## THE SHRINK-WRAP WARRANTY DISCLAIMER

All these types of possible damages make software publishers (and their liability insurers) uncomfortable. Consequential damages can mount up quickly, for example. In response, publishers try legal techniques to limit their liability.

A sales *contract* is an agreement between a buyer and a seller. They are free to put in whatever terms they want, subject to limited judicial tinkering. Shortly, we'll look at twelve terms that sellers often try to include in their contracts.

### Validity of the disclaimer

In the case of consumer software, there is no detailed written contract between the consumer and the software publisher or retailer. To achieve the same liability limitations as the sales contract, the publisher of consumer software will include carefully chosen contract language in a warranty disclaimer, as if this was a sales contract. This warranty disclaimer is not a contract. It is not a voluntary, negotiated agreement. The manufacturer wrote it and put it in the box. The buyer gets it. There is no bargaining over the terms, which strongly favor the manufacturer. Therefore, many courts and commentators have expressed strong feelings that shrink-wrapped warranties are not or should not be enforceable.[3]

No one knows whether warranty disclaimers in consumer software are valid or not. Software publishers will to continue include them with products until and unless they are rejected by the courts. However, when planning its product quality levels, a wise company will take into account the possibility that some (or many) judges will probably throw the disclaimers out.

---

[3] Cases in which courts have expressed reservations about shrink-wrap licenses include *Horizons, Inc. v. Avco Corp.* (1982), *Pawelec v. Digitcom, Inc.* (1984), *Barazzotto v. Intelligent Systems, Inc.* (1987), *Vault Corp. v. Quaid Software Ltd.* (1987), and *Step-Saver Data Systems, Inc. v. Wyse Technology and The Software Link* (1991). Einhorn (1985) and Kemp (1987) are representative commentators.

The United States Supreme Court recently affirmed the validity of a liability-limiting clause that was in small print on the back of a ticket stub (much the same thing as a shrink-wrapped disclaimer) under harsh circumstances. The particular clause, called a *forum selection clause,* stated that lawsuits against Carnival Cruise Line had to be pursued in its home state of Florida. An elderly passenger was injured on a ship she boarded in California. There was evidence that she was physically and financially unable to pursue litigation in Florida.

In *Shute v. Carnival Cruise Lines, Inc.* (1990), the Ninth Circuit Court of Appeals refused to enforce this clause. It noted that buyers had no opportunity to negotiate or even discuss the forum selection clause when they bought tickets for the cruise, and that highly restrictive take-it-or-leave-it clauses in form contracts are generally ruled invalid. (Mullenix, 1992, discusses this general rule as it applies to this case.) The court concluded that a decision to enforce the clause would be grossly unfair to the injured passenger.

The Supreme Court overruled the Ninth Circuit decision, in *Carnival Cruise Lines, Inc. v. Shute* (1991). It declared the clause valid and enforceable even though the passenger couldn't negotiate it and even if it did deprive her of her day in court. Very similar reasoning would support validity of shrink-wrap warranty disclaimers.

**14**

LEGAL
CONSEQUENCES

## Terms contained in the typical disclaimer

Here's an example of a software warranty disclaimer (the company name is fictitious). You've probably seen one just like it a dozen times:

> NoName Software warrants the diskettes on which the programs are furnished to be free from defects in the materials and workmanship under normal use for a period of ninety (90) days from the date of delivery to you as evidenced by your proof of purchase.

> The entire liability of NoName Software and your exclusive remedy shall be replacement of any diskette which does not meet the Limited Warranty and which is returned freight prepaid, to NoName Software. NoName Software does not warrant that the functions contained in the programs will meet your requirements or that the operation of the programs will be uninterrupted or error-free. THE PROGRAMS CONTAINED IN THIS PACKAGE ARE PROVIDED "AS IS" WITHOUT WARRANTY OF ANY KIND, EITHER EXPRESSED OR IMPLIED, INCLUDING, BUT NOT LIMITED TO, THE IMPLIED WARRANTIES OF MERCHANTABILITY AND FITNESS FOR A PARTICULAR PURPOSE. THE ENTIRE RISK RELATED TO THE QUALITY AND PERFORMANCE OF THE PROGRAMS IS ON YOU. IN THE EVENT THERE IS ANY DEFECT, YOU ASSUME THE ENTIRE COST OF ALL NECESSARY SERVICING, REPAIR, OR CORRECTION. SOME STATES DO NOT ALLOW THE EXCLUSION OF IMPLIED WARRANTIES, SO THE ABOVE EXCLUSION MAY NOT APPLY TO YOU. THIS WARRANTY GIVES YOU SPECIFIC LEGAL RIGHTS AND YOU MAY HAVE OTHER RIGHTS WHICH VARY FROM STATE TO STATE.

> This agreement constitutes the complete and exclusive statement of the terms of the agreement between you and NoName Software. It supersedes and replaces any previous written or oral agreements and communications relating to this software. No oral or written information or advice given by NoName Software, its dealers, distributors, agents or employees will create any warranty or in any way increase the scope of the warranty provided in this agreement, and you may not rely on any such information or advice.

Let's look at this legalese in more detail. Here are terms that a seller can put into a contract to limit its liability. Look for examples of these in the warranty disclaimer above:

1. *Disclaimer of all express warranties.* The Uniform Commercial Code § 2-316 lets the seller state that the goods have no warranty and are being sold "as is." If the buyer accepts them "as is," she has no cause to complain if they aren't any good. However, as discussed earlier in this chapter ("Express Warranties"), once the seller has made an express warranty, a disclaimer won't release him from it.

2. *Exclusion of implied warranties.* Each state passes its own version of the U.C.C. In most states, the contracting parties can agree to exclude the warranties of merchantability and fitness, so long as these exclusions aren't "unconscionable."

   The court in *Meeting Makers, Inc. v. American Airlines* (1987) held that a disclaimer of implied warranties wasn't unconscionable because Meeting Makers had a real voice in setting the contract terms. In *Hunter v. Texas Instruments, Inc.* (1986) the court said a warranty disclaimers wasn't unconscionable because the customer was an accountant, who knew enough about business to understand the terms. The court in *Office Supply Co., Inc. v. Basic/Four Corp.* (1982) states the general rule: damage and warranty limitation clauses are not unconscionable between businesses.

3. ***Limit the duration of an express warranty (and any surviving implied warranties),*** for example to 30, 60 or 90 days. The Magnuson-Moss Warranty—Federal Trade Commission Improvement Act (15 U.S.C. § 2308) allows warrantors to limit implied warranties to the same duration as express warranties as long as the duration is reasonable and not unconscionable.

4. ***Restrict the remedy for a defective product to repair, replacement, or refund.*** For example, in *Southwest Forest Industries, Inc. v. Westinghouse Electric Corp.* (1970), the court held that between commercial parties, warranty limitations that limit remedies to repair and replacement are not unconscionable, so other (consequential) damages were not available.

The Magnuson-Moss Act (15 U.S.C. § 2301)gives consumers a right to repair or replacement. The publisher can't simply "elect a refund unless (i) the warrantor is unable to provide replacement and repair is not commercially practicable or cannot be timely made, or (ii) the consumer is willing to accept such refund." Customers who complain about bugs sometimes refuse refunds and demand bug fixes instead. Development and support staff often perceive these people as unreasonable. Understand that these customers are completely within their rights.

5. ***Limit liability to direct damages,*** excluding consequential damages.

> U.C.C. § 2-719(c) Consequential damages may be limited or excluded unless the limitation or exclusion is unconscionable. Limitation of consequential damages for injury to the person in the case of consumer goods is prima facie unconscionable but limitation of damages where the loss is commercial is not.

In *RRX Industries, Inc. v. Lab-Con, Inc.* (1985), software developer Lab-Con limited remedies to fixing bugs, and limited damages (if it couldn't fix the bugs) to no more than the contract price. Lab-Con never got the system to work. The court held that Lab-Con had so fundamentally breached the contract that the damages limitation clause was oppressive and invalid. Therefore it overrode the consequential damages exclusion. The dissenting opinion in this case analyses this issue intensely.

**14**

*Ritchie Enterprises v. Honeywell Bull, Inc.*, (1990) and *Office Supply Co., Inc. v. Basic/Four Corp* (1982) are good examples of cases upholding liability limitations between businesses.

LEGAL
CONSEQUENCES

Here's a rule of thumb: if a judge thinks this is a normal business deal, she'll probably uphold the liability limitation. But a judge who suspects that a sale was fraudulent might not let a seller hide behind *any* limitations on remedies. This is another reason for checking the software against the manual, the box, publicity releases, and the software development contract (if there is one). To an outsider, like a judge, mismatches between these and the software can look like fraud.

6. ***Minimize the seller's exposure to fraud liability*** by including an integration clause. An integration clause says that buyer and seller agree that the only enforceable claims and promises made about this product are the ones in the contract. The buyer cannot hold the seller responsible for claims made in advertisements or by the salesperson, or for statements in the manual or on the box. (See the U.C.C. § 2-202 and White & Summers, 1988, Chapter 2.)

Sometimes (but don't count on it) this can even beat an express warranty. For example, in *Kalil Bottling Co. v. Burroughs Corp.* (1980), Burroughs included an integration clause in its sales contract, which Kalil signed. Kalil later sued claiming that statements about the computer's and software's capabilities made to it during the sale were fraudulent. The court held these claims not actionable because of the integration clause.

7. *Specify that the litigation forum (where the lawsuit takes place) must be in the seller's home state.* (*Carnival Cruise Lines, Inc. v. Shute*, 1991). The NoName warranty missed this one. The effect is that a Florida consumer has to come to California to sue a Silicon Valley software publisher.

8. *Specify that the applicable law will be that of the seller's home state.* This is a benefit if the home state doesn't ban disclaimers and exclusions and doesn't allow tort claims for economic loss. The court in *Vault Corp. v. Quaid Software Ltd.* (1987) noted that choice of law provisions in consumer contracts are usually respected unless they result in substantial injustice to the person who didn't draft the contract.

9. *Specify that litigation will be by arbitration* rather than in court. This agreement is generally favored and enforced by the courts. (See *Southland Corp. v. Keating*, 1984.)

10. *Specify acceptance criteria.* If the program meets the acceptance test, the vendor has satisfied the contract. (See, for example, Harris, 1983.) Understand what this means: any bugs not covered by the contract aren't bugs (pay extra to fix them). These clauses are common in large contract software projects, such as government projects.

11. *Award reasonable attorneys' fees* to the winner of any litigation between the parties. This is common in contracts, but not in warranty disclaimers.

12. *Allocate risk of tort loss* if the parties are of comparable bargaining power and if tort waiver was actually negotiated. U.C.C. § 2-719 (3) declares it unconscionable to include a contract term that limits consequential damages arising from personal injury to a consumer. The law lets two *companies* agree that one should accept the risk of torts by another—without that, we couldn't have general liability insurance or malpractice insurance. In *Salt River Project Agricultural Improvement and Power District v. Westinghouse Electric Corp.* (1984), the court held that a manufacturer and a large corporate customer can agree that the customer will accept liability for any damages caused by the manufacturer's product.

Restrictive warranty disclaimers like the one above have resulted in a lot of customer dissatisfaction. Attorneys have strongly recommended giving consumers more warranty rights, rather than forcing consumers to sue on a non-contract theory such as fraud, personal injury, or property damage (Boss, Weinberg, & Woodware, 1989). Even though few of these suits will succeed, the successful ones will set precedents that the software industry will not enjoy.

ADAPSO, a major software industry association, has published guidelines on Packaged Microcomputer Software Warranties in the Absence of Negotiated Agreements (April 1986) (available from ADAPSO, Arlington, VA). ADAPSO recommends easily readable specifications, express warranties that the program will perform as described in the manual and advertisements, longer warranty periods, and repair, replace, or refund warranties. "These guidelines have prompted at least forty software companies to improve their warranties." Levin (1986, p. 2126).

## TORTS: LAWSUITS INVOLVING FAULT

The core of a breach-of-contract lawsuit is a broken agreement. Because agreements can fail for many reasons that don't involve any fault or dishonesty on either side, the breach-of-contract lawsuit focuses on the agreement itself rather than on the blameworthiness of the people involved. Judges award limited damages in contract lawsuits. For example, within contract law, the natural award for a product that doesn't work as advertised is a refund.

Imagine that a customer buys a $100 program, and its bugs then cost her $20,000 in lost business records, lost sales, lost work, tax penalties, or investment losses. A customer who loses $20,000 wants more than a $100 refund. She will probably not recover most of this $20,000 in a breach-of-contract lawsuit.

Rather than bring a contract suit, the buyer's lawyer will look for some way to sue in tort, because tort law would let the buyer recover:

- the cost of the program, plus
- any incidental expenses, plus
- consequential economic damages ($20,000 for a $100 program), plus
- consequential non-economic damages, such as pain and suffering, plus
- punitive damages.

The core of a tort lawsuit is fault, either blameworthy behavior that causes property damage, money loss, or personal injury, or a defective product that causes property damage or personal injury. The requirements to win a tort lawsuit are quite strict: Conley (1987) reviewed the history of computer tort cases and concluded that tort suits have so far been largely unsuccessful and will continue to fail because plaintiffs suffer mainly economic damage, more suited for litigation on contract principles. Levy & Bell (1990) made the same point three years later. Many other reviewers agree.

**14**

LEGAL
CONSEQUENCES

This chapter considers five types of tort lawsuits that some customers will someday win:

- *Conversion:* the software publisher intentionally designed the software to steal from the customer or destroy her property.
- *Negligence:* the publisher failed to take steps (e.g., adequate testing) that a reasonable publisher would have taken. Because of this failure, the software injured the customer or damaged her property.
- *Strict products liability:* the program caused an injury or property damage because it is dangerously defective.
- *Malpractice:* the program's authors (or the program itself) provided unreasonably poor professional services.
- *Fraud:* the publisher (or reseller) knowingly misrepresented the capabilities of the product.

## CONVERSION

*Conversion* is an "intentional exercise of dominion or control over a chattel which so seriously interferes with the right of another to control it that the actor may justly be required to pay the other the full value of the chattel" (Restatement (Second) of Torts (1965) § 222A(1)). *A chattel* is a tangible piece of property, such as a car or stereo. Theft is an example of conversion. If someone steals something from you, the government can prosecute her for theft. You can sue for conversion. Deliberate destruction of personal property is also conversion.

The law of conversion applies only to chattels (tangible personal property). It doesn't apply to intangible property, such as a patent or a copyright. For example, suppose you buy a book at a bookstore. The book is *tangible*—you can touch it. If someone steals the book from you, sue her for conversion. Now suppose instead that you write a book. Before you publish it, someone borrows your manuscript with your permission, photocopies it, and returns the manuscript to you. Then she publishes your book under her name. In this case, she has stolen your words and your ideas. This is breach of copyright, not conversion. (For further discussion, read Keeton, Dobbs, Keeton, & Owen, 1984, which is the most influential book on tort law.)

No American court has determined if material stored on a disk, such as software, memos, pictures, financial information, and research data, are chattels. I expect the courts to rule that disk-based materials are chattels. My argument for this is fairly detailed, so I've put it into a footnote.[4]

---

[4] **PROPERTY DAMAGE**

No American court has determined if material stored on a disk, such as software, memos, pictures, financial information, and research data, are *chattels*, i.e., tangible personal property as distinguished from intangibles and services. This is an important issue, not only for conversion but also for negligence and strict liability lawsuits, described in the next sections of this chapter.

I expect the courts to rule that disk-based materials are chattels. Here are my reasons:

1. The Uniform Commercial Code treats disk-based materials as "goods" (i.e., chattels).

2. The Copyright Act treats disks as "tangible media of expression," just like books. If books are chattels (they are), so are program- or data-filled disks.

3. Court cases involving conversion of documents indicate that the physical documents themselves are chattels, and taking the documents or doing

anything else that deprives their owner of the contents of the documents is conversion.

*1. U.C.C. Goods:*

The starting inquiry is whether programs and data on disks are goods within the meaning of the Uniform Commercial Code (U.C.C.). According to the U.C.C. § 2-105(1), "*Goods* means all things … which are movable at time of identification to the contract for sale." While the U.C.C. does not use the word "chattels" (Official Comment 1 to § 2-105), the concepts of goods and chattels are almost the same. For example, *Black's Law Dictionary* defines "Personal Chattel" as "Movable things. Personal property which has no connection with real estate."

I discussed the applicability of the U.C.C. above. Judges interpreting the Uniform Commercial Code treat non-custom software, including disk-based consumer software, as goods rather than as services or intangibles. By their reasoning, disks of clip art or data are also goods since they can be (and are) packaged, like programs, and sold in

Under what circumstances could a software publisher be held liable for conversion? Answer: whenever the publisher releases a product that is designed to steal from the customer, to destroy the customer's hardware, or to destroy the customer's disk-based materials. Here are two hypothetical examples:

- **Embezzlement:** With the rise in financial communications programs that help customers write checks, trade stocks, or buy (and pay for) things, someone will create a program that includes an embezzlement scheme. This is conversion.

- **Practical joke:** Imagine a program that sends music to external speakers. Under the right (wrong) conditions, the program is designed to make abrupt large changes in the pitch and loudness of the music. The goal is to blow out the connected speaker. (Ha, ha.) Practical jokes are part of the culture of some programming teams. You might not be able to stop the mid-development follies, but you can certainly test to see that the games have been taken out of the software before the product ships.

Here's a real example of something that I would expect a court to class as conversion.

- **Copy protection, worms:** To protect their rights, some software publishers use copy protection routines that make it difficult to use copies in place of the original program. (See Joyce, 1990, for some history.) Some companies are expert developers of copy protection methods, which they sell to software publishers. However, because it's legal to publish and sell techniques and programs to circumvent copy protection (*Vault Corp. v. Quaid Software Ltd.*, 1988), developers of protection software are under constant pressure to invent tougher protection schemes.

  In 1984, Vault Corporation announced "Killer Prolok" (Howitt, 1984). According to Vault's president, "we had requests from customers who wanted a stronger form of copy protection, so we came up with a method that built in retribution" (Ruby, 1986). When Killer Prolok detects an unauthorized copy, it displays a warning message telling the user to turn off the computer. If the user doesn't turn off the computer quickly, Killer Prolok may erase the computer's hard disk or copy a worm to the computer that will destroy data and programs over time (Bermant, 1984).

---

stores. Voorhees (1991) bolsters this U.C.C. interpretation with tax-law based arguments that packaged software is a commodity. Sprague (1992) argues that the U.C.C. classification alone is enough to support the tangible property requirements of tort lawsuits.

### 2. The Copyright Act of 1976:

§ 102 (a) Copyright protection subsists, in accordance with this title, in original works of authorship fixed in any tangible medium of expression …. Works of authorship include the following categories: (1) literary works

§ 101 'Literary works' are works, other than audiovisual works, expressed in words, numbers, or other verbal or numerical symbols or indicia, regardless of the nature of the material objects, such as books, periodicals, manuscripts, phonorecords, film, tapes, disks, or cards, in which they may be embodied.

The statute lists both disks and paper as tangible media of expression. Copyright attaches to a literary work as soon as it is stored on a disk or written on a page.

Intellectual property on a disk is equivalent to intellectual property written on pieces of paper. Erasing the disk (done by having the computer write over it) is equivalent to damaging a manuscript by blacking out all the text on each page.

Therefore, if it is conversion to destroy another's manuscript by blacking out each page (of course it is), it is conversion to erase files from her disk.

### 3. Document conversion cases:

Start with *R.A. Weaver and Associates, Inc., v. Haas & Haynie Corp.* (1980). Here, a contractor (Blake) gave shop drawings prepared by one subcontractor (Weaver) to another subcontractor (Haas & Haynie) in return for a $13,000 credit on the contract price from Hass & Haynie. Blake then cancelled the contract with Weaver and gave it to Haas & Haynie. These drawings were Weaver's, not

**14**

LEGAL

CONSEQUENCES

Defendisk, a competitor of Vault, also announced a new copy protection scheme. According to their vice president, "[o]ur booby traps will make Vietnam look like a birthday party" (Howitt, 1984).

In 1985, Sheldon Richman, a columnist for the Washington Times, reported that he encountered the following message while using Microsoft Access, a telecommunications program: "Internal security violation. The tree of evil bears bitter fruit. Crime does not pay. The Shadow knows. Trashing program disk" (Mace, 1985). Richman claimed that several files were erased from his disk. Customers also reported the message in Microsoft Word, a popular word processor (Mace, 1985).

Microsoft claimed that it had no knowledge of this message (Mace, 1985), and that it had been placed in the code by a summer intern (Schuyler, 1991). Microsoft also denied that its programs would erase files when they gave this message. They merely moved the disk drive head back and forth, audibly but harmlessly (Mace, 1985). Interestingly, Richman was using an authorized copy of Access. As Microsoft acknowledged, Richman got the message because of an error in the copy protection code, not because of anything he did wrong (Mace, 1985).

After the firestorm in the trade press, Vault did not ship Killer Prolok. As far as I know, Defendisk didn't ship its product. Microsoft and most other PC software developers dropped on-disk copy protection (Ruby, 1986).

---

Blake's, so this was akin to stealing Weaver's work and selling it to Haas & Haynie. The jury awarded Weaver $17,000 in compensatory damages (mainly, the value of the drawings), plus $100,000 in punitive damages.

Note that the tangible stuff in *R.A. Weaver* is paper and ink, maybe worth $25. But once the court (or jury) decides that there was a conversion, the damages awarded include the full value of the ideas expressed in the converted drawings (worth $17,000) along with the cost of the paper. Similarly, the award from a converted disk would be the cost of the disk ($1) plus the value of the code or data on the disk (could be $1,000,000).

Next case: *Pearson v. Dodd* (1969). An employee of Senator Dodd's photocopied some of Dodd's documents and gave them to Drew Pearson and Jack Anderson, newspaper columnists. The information was published, and was unflattering. Dodd sued. He argued that this information was valuable when it was secret. Now that it was public, it wasn't worth anything any more. Thus, he argued, the photocopying staff and the press had converted

his information. The court held that ideas and information are not generally subject to legal protection under a conversion theory, but that they could be if they were gathered or arranged at some cost and sold on the market as a commodity. In this particular case, though, Dodd hadn't spent money gathering this information about himself, nor was he willing to sell it on the market. Further, the court noted that Dodd hadn't been deprived of his papers. They'd been taken out of his office for a few minutes when he wasn't there anyway, and then (after some copying) were put back. The court decided that this wasn't a serious enough interference with Dodd's right to possess the papers to be called conversion.

In *Harper & Row, Publishers, Inc. v. Nation Enterprises* (1983, p. 201), the court echoed *Pearson*, holding that "[c]onversion requires not merely temporary interference with property rights, but the exercise of unauthorized dominion and control to the complete exclusion of the rightful possessor. Merely removing one of a number of copies of a manuscript (with or without permission) for a

If the material on a disk are chattels, then it is conversion to deliberately destroy the contents of that disk without the consent of the owner. (Under the new anti-virus and anti-worm laws—see e.g., Branscomb, 1990—in some states this might also be a crime.)

Here's a trap that your company can fall into too easily:

- **Cleanup of too many files:** Suppose your company makes Program X. You release Version 2 with an auto-installation routine that checks whether there's already a Program X directory (for Version 1) on the computer's hard disk. If so then, without notifying the customer, it erases everything in that directory except for a few specially named data files that it specifically preserves. Then it copies over the new Version 2 software.

  The motivation behind erasing the old files is good. This gets rid of superseded code, frees up space on the disk and avoids bug-causing interactions between old code and new code. But what if the customer stored other things in that directory too? The auto-installer might erase the only copies of valuable work. This is probably conversion, though the programmer's good intentions would save the company from punitive damages.

  Your company's lawyer and the customer's lawyer can run up a big bill arguing about whether this is really conversion. Maybe it's just negligence. But even if your company wins that argument, this lawsuit will be costly, monetarily and in bad press.

It's your job to keep your company out of messes like this. Your company risks a conversion suit whenever it releases a program that will erase files (other than program-created temporary files) from a customer's disk without first getting the customer's permission. If you report a problem like this and are told that's how the program should work, don't drop the report until you've drawn it to your company's lawyer's attention.

---

short time, copying parts of it, and returning it undamaged, constitutes far too insubstantial an interference with property rights to demonstrate conversion." The Supreme Court didn't disturb this analysis of conversion, but did rule that the publication of parts of the manuscript (Gerald Ford's memoirs) was a breach of copyright. (*Harper & Row, Publishers, Inc. v. Nation Enterprises*, 1985.)

Note the distinction between these three cases. In *Pearson* and *Harper & Row*, the defendants borrowed the documents, copied them, and published them. In *R.A. Weaver*, the defendant took the documents (the drawings) and kept them. The distinction will be important for software. Merely making a copy of the contents of a computer disk would not be conversion. It might be breach of copyright but that's a separate issue. But according to *R.A. Weaver*, taking the disk, or doing anything else that permanently deprives the owner of the disk of it, such as damaging or destroying the disk, would be conversion.

A further case, *FMC Corporation v. Capital Cities/ABC, Inc.* (1990), continues this analysis. Someone gave copies (or the originals) of FMC documents dealing with the Bradley Fighting Vehicle to ABC. The originals disappeared, FMC had no other copies, and it needed them to fulfill contract obligations. The court ordered ABC to give FMC copies of FMC's documents. The court stated that:

> [T]he receipt of copies of documents, rather than the documents themselves, should not ordinarily give rise to a claim for conversion. The reason for this rule is that the possession of copies of documents—as opposed to the documents themselves—does not amount to an interference with the owner's property sufficient to constitute conversion. In cases where the alleged converter has only a copy of the owner's property and the owner still possesses the property itself, the owner is in no way being deprived of the use of his property. The only rub is

**14**

LEGAL
CONSEQUENCES

A final note on conversion: punitive damages awards are appropriate because the misbehavior is intentional. Punitive damages are intended to punish the person or company who committed the tort. They are awarded over and above compensatory damages, and the amounts are often much larger. Punitive damages are awarded when the defendant flagrantly, outrageously, recklessly or deliberately violates the victim's rights. The more outrageous the defendant's behavior, the more likely that the jury will award punitive damages and the court (and appellate court) will let large awards stand (*Pacific Mutual Life Insurance Company v. Haslip*, 1991). While punitive damages have certainly been awarded in negligence and strict liability cases, intentional torts are the paradigmatic cases for punitive damages. (For example, read the discussion of *Roginsky v. Richardson-Merrell, Inc.*, 1967, in Lawyer's Co-operative Publishing, Annotation 2.) One of the conversion cases described in Footnote 4, *R.A. Weaver and Associates, Inc., v. Haas & Haynie Corp.* (1980), yielded $100,000 in punitive damages.

## NEGLIGENCE

There are four aspects to any negligence lawsuit: duty, negligent breach of the duty, causation, and damages (see Keeton, et al., 1984). The definitions often confuse people, so I draw parenthetical analogies to driving cars, which is also subject to negligence law:

- **Duty:** Software publishers (and all other manufacturers) have a public duty to make products that don't create an unreasonable risk of injury or property damage. (Drivers have a public duty to drive in a way that doesn't create an unreasonable risk of injury or property damage.)

- **Negligent breach of the duty:** A publisher who doesn't take reasonable precautions to make sure that it satisfies its duty is acting negligently. (A driver who doesn't drive in a reasonably cautious manner is driving negligently.)

- **Causation:** The negligent publisher might make a lot of product without injuring anyone, but if its negligence does cause injury or property damage, it is liable to the victim. (People can drive

---

that someone else is using it as well... The gravamen of the tort of conversion is the deprivation of the possession or use of one's property.

The court held that ABC's refusal to turn over copies was conversion because it deprived FMC of all use of FMC property, the material contained in these documents. Similarly, it would be conversion to intentionally erase programs or data from a disk without the owner's consent because this would deprive the owner of her property.

One small complication: what if the owner has backed up her hard disk? Is it still conversion to erase the disk if she can recover everything from the backup? As I read *FMC*, maybe not. But so what? As testers, we know that Murphy's Law always applies in these situations: the program will erase the materials that weren't backed up, not the materials that were.

In conclusion, erasing the contents of a disk is like erasing every page of a book. Both are conversion. Both damage personal property. Going forward, I will simply assert that destroying data on disk is property damage.

unsafely without getting into accidents for a while, and you can't sue them until they cause an accident. But when a person's negligent driving causes an accident, everyone else involved the accident gets to sue the bad driver.)

- *Damages:* Once the publisher negligently causes harm, the victim can sue for compensatory and (sometimes) punitive damages. (For normal bad driving, a driver pays only compensatory damages. For reckless driving, a driver might have to pay punitive damages.)

## Negligence: duty defined

*Tort duty* is a matter of public policy. It's imposed by operation of law, not by any contract. It's the duty to behave in a way that doesn't reduce public safety.

---

*In products negligence law, the manufacturer's duty is to make products that do not create an unreasonable risk of personal injury or property damage.*

---

### Duty: unreasonable risk

Tort duty is *not* the duty to make things perfectly safe. Accidents happen. When you sell someone a product, you *aren't* selling insurance that the product will never hurt them or their property under any circumstances.

For example, no one expects cars to be perfectly safe. We expect cars to be *reasonably* safe. No one should expect to buy software that is perfectly bug free because, as we saw in Chapter 2, you can't find all the bugs in any non-trivial program. However, tort law demands that software safety be reasonable, that the program be unlikely to cause injury or property damage.

Under the most common view of *reasonable* safety, it is reasonable to stop testing before finding or fixing a certain bug in a product if the cost to find and fix the bug would outweigh the cost of all the damage that this bug will ever wreak (Keenan, et al.., 1984; Landes & Posner, 1987).

**14**

LEGAL
CONSEQUENCES

### Tort duty compared to contract duty

When you sell someone something, the law of contracts says that it's your duty to give them what they paid for. If you promise top quality, you have to deliver top quality. But if you promise junk, and they buy it, junk they get.

---

*Contract law covers quality; tort law covers safety.*

---

Tort law is not the way for unhappy (or unethical) buyers to get top quality for the price of junk. (This point is particularly well made in *Seely v. White Motor Co.*, 1965.) Tort duty is a duty owed to the public to make things that are reasonably safe, not a duty to any individual buyer to make things reasonably well. The purchaser of bug-ridden code can sue for breach of contract (breach of express or implied warranty) but she can't bring a tort lawsuit just because the program doesn't work well. To bring a tort lawsuit, she must be able to prove that the program breached its tort duty, i.e., that it caused injury to a person or damage to property.

TORTS: LAWSUITS INVOLVING FAULT
NEGLIGENCE
Negligence: duty defined
Tort duty compared to contract duty

After 30 years of intense litigation over the distinction between tort and contract law, the general rule is that there is no tort liability for purely economic losses. Everybody is still arguing over the definition of *purely economic losses* but the general idea is that something is a purely economic loss if it costs the customer money but doesn't hurt her or damage any of her property. As mentioned earlier in this chapter ("Damages"), economic losses can be direct (e.g., the program doesn't work) or consequential (indirect) (e.g., the customer loses a major contract because the program wouldn't print the sales proposal).

The most difficult question is how to classify it when a product destroys itself without injuring anyone or damaging any other property. Is this property damage (the product is property) or pure economic loss (you no longer have what you paid for)? The general rule of thumb, good in most states (and in the European Community) most of the time, is that product self-destruction is economic loss, not property damage.

The legislation and court decisions on product self-destruction will be very relevant to software law. For references and more discussion, read the footnote.[5]

### Tort duty: examples

This section gives some examples of software errors that might result in tort liability. The next one gives examples of errors more likely to result only in contract liability.

---

[5] *Seely v. White Motor Co.* (1965, California) contains the classic, readable, and convincing argument that courts and customers should treat quality as a contract issue, not a tort issue. *Santor v. A.M. Karagheusian, Inc.* (1965, New Jersey) is the classic case on the other side. It holds, and argues well, that consumers should be able to sue in tort when they receive substantially lower quality merchandise than they paid for. Most states followed the California policy; New Jersey restricted *Santor's* reach in 1985 (*Spring Motors Distributors, Inc. v. Ford Motor Company*) so that only consumers, not businesses, can sue for low quality in tort. Read Brown & Feinman (1991) for background on this case.

*Seely* and *Spring Motors* (as applied to businesses) illustrate the general rule in the United States. If the product simply doesn't work, the customer has to sue on the basis of an express or implied warranty, not on a negligence or strict liability (discussed later in this chapter) theory. The customer has to sue in contract even if she can prove that the product's failure is due to "negligent" (unjustifiably careless) behavior by the seller or manufacturer. Under some circumstances this is still controversial (read Powers & Niver, 1992, and Raitt, 1991), but for our purposes take it as settled. *Affiliates for Evaluation and Therapy, Inc. v. Viasyn Corp.* (1987) is a typical computer case along these lines.

The self-destruction issue is much more complex. In general, a product that ruins itself is just a defective product and the problem is governed by contract law. But what about the Consumer Reports (1989) claim that some Ford Escorts will catch fire if you leave them running idle for too long (maybe for as little as 10 minutes)? If no one's in the car and no other property gets damaged, the loss is purely economic: you used to have a car, now you need a new one. But since this type of self-destruction poses real risks to public safety, should you be able to sue in tort anyway? (You want to sue in tort in order to recover full consequential damages, not just the resale value of the

I predict that courts will hold software publishers liable in tort for a program that:

- *Corrupts or loses data:* Data that the customer entered or generated using some other program is property. If your program corrupts this data, it has caused property damage.

  As programs share more data, you must increase the amount and subtlety of testing done to detect data corruption by any one program in the chain. Any program that can write to the disk could potentially corrupt other files or data.

- *Makes data unreadable:* Suppose that the customer uses an encryption program that (because of a flaw in the program) never lets her reread the encrypted data. The data are lost, so this is like property damage. But the failure arose because the program almost but didn't quite work: this is also a breach of contract.

- *Damages connected peripherals:* Almost anything that controls hardware can overwork or burn out the hardware. This includes monitors, disk drives, speakers, printers, synthesizers, and any other attached devices. If the program ruins the hardware, that's property damage. If the hardware catches fire and someone gets hurt, that's personal injury.

  In the early days of the IBM PC, if you attached both a color monitor and a monochrome monitor to the same computer, some programs (mainly games) would fry one of the monitors.

---

car, minus lawyer's fees, that you'll get from a contract suit.)

Some courts will allow you to sue manufacturers of self-destructive products, even in the face of statutes that bar tort suits for economic losses, if the product destroyed itself suddenly and accidentally, or in a way that poses risks to public safety. (Read *Washington Water Power Company v. Graybar Electric Company*, 1989.)

If you would not allow the owner of the flaming Escort to sue in tort, because the losses are still just economic, you are in good company. The court in *American Universal Insurance Group v. General Motors Corp.* (1991; and many other courts) would probably agree with you. But suppose you left your teddy bear in the car and when the car burned up, so did Teddy. Now there's property damage so you can sue in tort. Does this distinction make sense?

In the case of *East River Steamship Corp. v. Transamerica Delaval, Inc.* (1986), the United States

Supreme Court ruled that contract law, not tort law, would govern federal (admiralty) cases of product self-destruction. Many states' supreme courts have followed this rule. As I read the literature, it appears that the large majority of states have adopted this rule. However, the dissenting opinions in some cases argue vigorously that the number of states who actually follow the rule is much lower than it appears.

The following court opinions are particularly interesting or instructive. Pay particular attention to dissenting opinions because they highlight the controversial issues: *East River Steamship Corp. v. Transamerica Delaval Inc.* (1986), *Waggoner v. Town & Country Mobile Homes, Inc.* (1990), *Hapka v. Paquin Farms* (1990), *Continental Insurance v. Page Engineering Co.* (1989), *Chemtrol Adhesives, Inc. v. American Manufacturers Mutual*

**14**

LEGAL

CONSEQUENCES

## TORTS: LAWSUITS INVOLVING FAULT
### NEGLIGENCE
#### Negligence: duty defined
##### *Tort duty: examples*

Another example: a few years ago, one control code made a certain dot matrix printer slam its printhead to the right repeatedly, until someone turned off the printer. People often start long print jobs on their way home, so a slamming printhead might continue overnight or over a weekend. Eventually this will ruin the printer (and maybe cause a fire?). What if a software publisher knew of this risk but chose not to design the program to filter out this control code when working with this printer?

- *Injures the listener:* Some computer games or music programs send output to external speakers. If the game is normally quiet, a loud enough explosion in the game could injure someone wearing headphones.

- *Induces an epileptic attack:* Some products that claim to induce relaxation pulse red lights at the viewer. Is there a risk to an epileptic viewer? I also noticed a warning to epileptics at a virtual reality demonstration. As this type of product gains popularity, what are the risks? What other risks are there like this?

- *Induces a cumulative trauma disorder:* These are sometimes called repetitive motion disorders. Carpal tunnel syndrome is a well known example. Another is tendinitis. (See Putz-Anderson, 1988.) Programs that are designed to make you do identical movements, rapidly, repeatedly, for a long time, might induce carpal tunnel syndrome. Suits have been filed against some computer game makers on these grounds.

- *Injures the customer who follows its directions:* A publisher of aeronautical charts is liable for accidents caused by inaccuracies in the charts (see *Brocklesby v. United States*, 1985; *Saloomey v. Jeppesen & Co.*, 1983; *Aetna Casualty & Surety Co. v. Jeppeson & Co.*, 1981). The basis of liability is that the chartmaker knows that people will rely on the charts for navigation. (This is garden variety products liability, having nothing to do with special F.A.A. regulations.) Some programs draw maps and recommend driving routes for car drivers. What if one of these routes unnecessarily takes a driver through a dangerous neighborhood and she is injured there?

- *Injures the customer who follows its recipes or instructions:* In *Winter v. G.P. Putnam's Sons* (1991), two people were poisoned by mushrooms that a mushroom encyclopedia led them to believe were safe. The Ninth Circuit of the federal Court of Appeals ruled that consumers can't hold book publishers liable for errors in the books. This is different from aeronautical charts, which are "technical tools." People are supposed to be able to rely on the information they get from these

---

*Insurance Company, Inc.* (1989), *Washington Water Power Company v. Graybar Electric Company* (1989), and *Consumers Power Co. v. Curtiss-Wright Corp.* (1986).

If you are testing localized software, for export to Europe, read Bungert (1992) for an instructive comparison of American, German, and European Community law and policy. Similar issues are controversial in Europe. The general rule there, as here, is to look to contract law for economic loss, but this is not always considered appropriate for product self-destruction.

charts. The court suggested that computer programs were tools like the charts. This court is a very influential on computer-related issues. Consider some possible implications:[6]

- What if a person follows a diet from a nutritional advice program, and gets sick?
- What about a person who has an accident because she learned terrible driving habits while playing realistic car or motorcycle simulations?
- What about children who "learn" from a simulation that it's OK to run red lights?
- What about a child who "learns" from a computer game that it's safe to jump off a roof?
- What about a computer-assisted electronic design package that does an ineffective consistency check and lets the user build something that shorts out immediately?
- What about a home design program that helps the user design modifications to her house that are dangerous or not permissible according to the local building codes?
- What about the physician who misdiagnoses or mistreats a patient because of incorrect advice from an expert system?

• ***Program loses data that it's supposed to manipulate:*** For example, suppose a disk utility corrupts the data on the disk? Or a database program designed to read and modify data collected by a different product, that corrupts the data in the process. In these cases, the program damages property, other data, that it had no role in creating.

However, one can argue that data corruption is a *contract* issue whenever a program corrupts data that it is *designed to manipulate*. This is defective program operation, and that's what breach of contract is all about. In *Professional Lens Plan v. Polaris Leasing* (1984), a hard disk corrupted the customer's data. The court ruled that this was pure economic damage, not property damage, and therefore not subject to tort liability. Note that the damage done by the hard disk—lost data—is exactly what you'd expect from a shoddy hard disk.

This might be treated as right on the border between torts and contracts. If so, the blameworthiness of the software developer's conduct might make an even larger difference than usual.

## Contract (not tort) duty: examples

If the program doesn't do what it's supposed to do, or does it badly, the dissatisfied customer sues for breach of contract. This is a failure to deliver what was paid for, not a tort. Here are some of the typical consequences of normal program failure, which I would expect courts to restrict to contract suits:

• ***Program loses its own data:*** Suppose your word processor corrupts its copy of a book that you're writing. You have to retype or rewrite what was lost. This is property damage, but the property (the book) is something you're using the word processor to create, and the damage (lost data) is what you'd expect from a defective word processor. Probably a court would rule that this is like a product damaging itself—contract suit yes, tort suit no.

**14**

LEGAL

CONSEQUENCES

---

[6] I haven't read enough on expert systems law to confidently elaborate on this issue. Cole (1990), Gemignani (1987), Mortimer (1989), Nimmer (1986), and Schwartz, Patil, & Szolovits (1987) are interesting papers.

---

**TORTS: LAWSUITS INVOLVING FAULT**
NEGLIGENCE
  Negligence: duty defined
    *Contract (not tort) duty: examples*

There are several published lawsuits in which plaintiffs complain that they bought a computer and a program, the system didn't work, and they wasted vast amounts of time reentering data. (See Nimmer, 1985, and Mundel, 1984, for many references.) *Louisiana AFL-CIO v. Lanier Business Products* (1986) is typical. Courts treat these complaints as breach-of-contract complaints.

- ***Program loses data as it collects the data:*** For example, a voice messaging program answers incoming calls and takes messages. What if it loses the messages?

- ***Program generates erroneous financial reports:*** Suppose that a spreadsheet or database prints incomplete or inaccurate reports and that a buyer relies on them and loses money. The loss is purely economic (money) so this is a contract action.

- ***Program has bugs that waste time:*** For example, the buyer of a compiler with bugs will waste time and payroll on excessive debugging. Similarly if the program is annoying, confusing, inefficient, and unpleasant to use. In *Louisiana AFL-CIO v. Lanier Business Products* (1986), the word processing and desktop publishing program lost data and didn't provide all the claimed functions. In determining the award (a partial refund), the court also considered the buyer's inconvenience. However, when the buyer's sole complaint was that the system was too hard to use (no lost data, no missing functions, just lots of wasted time), the court in *Family Drug Stores of New Iberia v. Gulf States Computer Services* (1990) awarded the buyer nothing.

- ***Promised compatibility feature doesn't work:*** For example, a program advertises an ability to import data from other products or to export data in a format other named products understand. The customer spends weeks creating graphics, page layouts, or a database with this product, only to discover that it is not compatible with a key program after all. All that time was wasted.

- ***Promised cost-reduction feature doesn't work:*** For example, a program controls the buyer's phone system and is supposed to deliver least-cost routing. That is, whenever the buyer or her staff make a long distance call, the computer should decide which phone company to use to pay the lowest rate. But the program selects companies poorly, and the buyer pays too much in phone service.

- ***Promised security features don't work:*** The program promises security of access for computers connected to telephone lines or networks. Hackers get to the buyer's computer anyway. They read trade secret information, then destroy the files.

This is another example of a borderline issue. The natural result of buying a low quality security program is poor security; therefore this is a contract issue. But the result of the program's failure is property damage, not just lost time or money; therefore this might be a tort issue as well.

### Two final notes on tort duty

- *Sometimes no good design can eliminate a given risk.* For example, maybe it's not possible to create a great arcade game that doesn't create a risk of carpal tunnel syndrome if the customer plays it too often. If the software developer can identify a specific risk that the buyer is exposed to, and can explain it in a way that can help the buyer protect herself, the developer has a duty to warn about the risk. (Read Bass, 1986, and Henderson & Twerski, 1987.)

- *The fact that an error is someone else's bug is no excuse* if it appears in your company's product. You must test everything that goes into your product's box, including software developed by others. (See Kellett's Annotation.)

### Negligence: breach of the tort duty

Your company's duty is to make products that do not create an unreasonable risk of personal injury or property damage. This does not mean that you must eliminate every error in the program. (You can't.) Nor does it mean that every person whose person or property is damaged by your software can recover against you. Your duty is to take reasonable steps to minimize the customer's risk, not to deliver an absolutely safe product. The law recognizes that absolutely safe products often cost far too much for any individual to afford.

In legal terms, all software errors are *design defects* as distinct from *manufacturing defects*. A software error exists in every copy of the program, not just on a few bad disks. Judges are cautious about ruling that a design is defective, because this can put a company out of business quickly, and perhaps unfairly. They are very aware that design decisions are subject to tradeoffs. Sometimes it's reasonable to trade away some safety or reliability in return for significant cost savings and functionality gains. (How would you feel if a judge banned cars because they don't withstand collisions well enough; instead we should all buy tanks?) Therefore judges look at the design alternatives, the state of the art, and the research and testing done by the manufacturer. This is a very difficult task for people who are acutely aware that they are not themselves design engineers. See Henderson (1973, 1976) and Henderson & Twerski (1987) for thorough discussions.

If your company is hauled into court it will be because someone using your product suffered a personal injury or a significant loss of property. Your company either failed to find the problem that hurt this customer, or you deferred it. In trying to evaluate whether a software publisher acted reasonably when it released a program to the public, judge and jury will consider issues like the following:

**14**

LEGAL

CONSEQUENCES

1. *Standard methodology* In designing and implementing the product, did the publisher follow a standard methodology?

   The issue here isn't whether the publisher followed the "right" method. There's too much controversy (See, e.g., DeGrace & Stahl, 1990) for judge or jury to choose the One True Method. But they can ask how systematic your company was, and check your company's story against its design, planning, and scheduling documents. Courts have held that a company's failure to follow its own procedures is evidence of negligence. See *Kushner v. Dravco Corp.* (1959) and *Kelly v. Boston & Maine R.R.* (1946).

   Your company will fare better if the judge or jury decide that you missed a problem despite a thorough, systematic, reputable approach to designing and testing the program.

2. *Industry standards:* To what degree did the developers and testers follow industry standards?

Many courts look to normal practice in an industry (especially published standards documents) for evidence of negligence. Failure to follow a standard practice is evidence of negligence (Fishbein, 1980). In design defect cases, conformity with industry standards can be evidence of reasonable practice (Urban, 1990).

Roetzheim (1991) says there are over 1000 government and industry software standards, covering design, development methods, testing, documentation, etc. He discusses fifty of them. The American National Standards Institute (ANSI) has adopted many software standards, including such test-relevant standards as *ANSI/IEEE Standard 730 for Software Quality Assurance Plans*, *ANSI/IEEE Standard 1008 for Software Unit Testing*, and *ANSI/IEEE Standard 1012 for Software Verification and Validation Plans*. Juran & Gyrna (1988) provide a long list of general product development standards. See also Andriole (1986) and DeMillo, et al. (1987). Brown (1991) provides a good overview of standards development.

ANSI recently revised its "Green Book," which explains ANSI procedures for development of American national standards. You can order it from ANSI headquarters (call 212-642-4900, or write ANSI Sales Department at 11 West 42nd Street, New York, NY, 10036). *IEEE Computer* and ACM's *SIGCHI* magazines regularly publish descriptions of software standards work in progress.

The ANSI/IEEE standards should apply to consumer software testing, but very few consumer software test groups (I know of none) find these standards relevant to their work. Few consumer software testers have read these standards, and of those testers, very few (I know of none) consider the standards useful. To my eyes, these documents assume or call for an excessive level of administrative overhead without providing useful guidance for prioritizing tasks and eliminating less essential test cases.[7] I assume that these standards are more applicable to larger projects.

If you work in the industry, you have a right to comment on standards under development. ANSI's rules are very strict about this. You can write ANSI directly to review final circulating drafts. (for this, write American National Standards Institute, at 1430 Broadway, New York, NY 10018.) Or you can join committees of the American Society for Quality Control, the Association for Computing Machinery, the IEEE Computer Society, the Human Factors Society, or other professional societies that develop standards.

---

[7] About that administrative overhead: In *DynaLantic Corp. v. The United States* (1991), the Air Force refused to accept a bid to write a 10,000 line program because DynaLantic bid to complete the job at a rate of 10 (ten) lines of code per programmer per day. The Air Force's Source Selection Authority believed this was a "low ball" bid—to write good code that conforms to Mil Spec, programmers can't go faster than 3 (three) lines per day. For consumer software, even thirteen (10+3) lines per day would be too slow to yield affordable products.

Standards committees often meet four times per year, in four different parts of the country. It's easy to attend these meetings if you work for a big company that will pay to send you there. It's a cost of doing business if you're a consultant who makes a living in the area covered by a given standard. But budget-conscious startups, small companies, and individuals often can't pay for travel. Companies on a tight budget have as much interest in industry standards as companies that can afford large travel bills. If you want to work on one of the standards under development, *and are willing to spend the time to review documents quickly*, you should insist on being allowed to review and comment by mail. Some committee chairs may give you a hard time over this, but remember that these are America's industry standards, not their committee's private memos. If you can't get onto a committee because you can't afford their travel requirements, complain to ANSI.

If your company ends up in court, the judge and jury will take industry standards seriously. Your lawyer's job will be much easier if you are doing development in compliance with realistic standards than if you are ignoring non-useful standards.

3. **Safety committee:** Did the publisher's safety committee evaluate and approve this product?

   The wrong answer is, "Safety committee? What safety committee?"

   Lawyers (and judges) are trained that reasonable manufacturers have safety committees. (For example, see Henderson & Twerski, 1987, p. 509-512. This is a leading law school textbook on products liability, written by two of the most influential people in the field.) The safety committee includes enough people with enough different perspectives that, together, they understand who will use the product and how they'll use it, how they can make mistakes with the product, how the product can fail, how it can interact with other products, etc. Given this knowledge, the committee evaluates the initial design and reevaluates the product as it develops. They decide whether the product is suitable for sale, and they may specify the design changes necessary to make the product suitable.

   Many software publishers use development teams to create products. The team members work together informally and come to meetings. A typical team meeting might include the marketing product manager, project manager, lead writer, lead programmer, lead tester, and lead customer support technician. This group is often the appeals committee for the project manager's bug deferrals (see Chapter 6). In practice, this group is the safety committee even though that's not its name.

   14

   LEGAL
   CONSEQUENCES

   You can enhance the appearance of a safety committee, and maybe also significantly improve the quality of the product and of your test plan, by arranging a few team meetings that focus exclusively on safety issues. Invite a few extra people to these meetings, who are skilled at assessing the risk of personal injury or property damage from a product (i.e., safety risks). Your head of Human Resources might be good at recognizing some of these risks. Similarly for your lawyer, accounting staff, etc. Don't invite too many people. More than seven will make the meeting unwieldy. Run the meeting formally (Doyle & Straus, 1976; Freedman & Weinberg, 1982). Keep a written record of all the safety issues raised and make sure that the project manager (or the team) responds to each.

4. **Hazard analysis:** How thoroughly did the publisher conduct the hazard analysis?

   A hazard is a risk of harm; in our case it is a risk that the product will hurt the user by causing personal injury or property damage. Hazard analysis tasks include:

- Identify all potential product hazards, i.e., all the ways the product could possibly cause injury or property damage.

- If a potential hazard may or may not be in the product, depending on whether there's a certain type of bug in the product, identify how you will test for the bug. Also estimate the probability that the program has the bug.

- If the hazard is built into the product's design (or is due to a deferred bug), estimate the probability that the customer will encounter this software problem, and the probability that this problem will harm the customer rather than doing something less terrible (such as a clean crash).

Start this analysis by dedicating a specific part of your test plan to hazards, and fill in every hazard that you can think of. Next, in a company that works with project teams (or that has a safety committee), brainstorm with them about further hazards and about the probabilities. Make this a formal technical review meeting if possible. Keep records of the discussion and make sure that your test plan identifies and addresses each potential hazard. Report actual hazards (the bug is there; the program can cause the injury) as fatal bugs.

If you're writing and testing this product yourself, you can still do a hazard analysis. Create the draft document yourself and walk through it with a friend.

Leveson (1991) introduces software hazard (safety) analysis. Bass (1986) provides a good general description of hazard analysis, and discusses software hazard analysis in Chapter 7 of the book's supplement. Also read Bohan (1988), and Juran & Gryna (1988, Chapter. 13) for an overview.

Leveson points out that it is hard to evaluate software system safety, especially the probabilities, because we don't have enough data and empirical models available to generate reliable failure probability estimates. Instead (p. 43), she suggests qualitative analyses to highlight system risk, and design heuristics to reduce risk:

> It is foolhardy to design process-control systems that rely solely on the proper functioning of software to maintain safety. Unfortunately, systems of this sort are being built. For example, the software controlling a radiation therapy device (... Therac 25) has been involved in several accidents. These accidents might have been prevented if the standard hardware interlocks used in the previous noncomputerized models had not been left off when the computer was introduced. After several deaths due to software errors, a hardware interlock was finally installed.

The problem with this much-discussed medical machine was a simple user interface design error. Bass (1986; supplement section § 7.35), Massingale & Borthick (1988), and Lawrence (1987) discuss the Therac-25 in more detail.

5. **Bug tracking system:** Is there a bug tracking system? Were all reports examined and carefully considered? Were they kept for future reference? Were they considered during the design of the next release? Was the decision to leave a flaw in the product made by one person or by a review board? Was there an appeal procedure for deferred bugs and design issues?

Weinstein (1980), Walker (1984), Williams (1984), and Bass (1986, and supplement), make numerous suggestions for writing and handling bug reports in ways that will look good in court. I'll summarize these below, with my thoughts on their ideas in *italics*.

- **Avoid judgmental phrases in bug reports:** For example, never use the word "defect" because lawyers treat "defect" as a special word. Using it is like signing a confession. Say "flaw" or "anomaly" instead.

  *Similarly your attorney would advise you to never, never use a word like "fatal" to describe the severity of a bug. In real life, though, testers have their own meanings for these words, which don't correspond perfectly to the lawyers' meanings. Maybe someday you'll find the following two statements useful. I (Kaner) would testify to both in court:*

  *(a) In my experience, testers use the word "defect" interchangeably with "flaw," "error," and "bug." They do not express a legal conclusion with this word, they simply mean that they think something is wrong with the program.*

  *(b) In 1983, I started my first job in the California software industry, at MicroPro (now called WordStar), as a supervisor in the software test group. On my first day, my boss explained how to write bug reports. He said I should classify an error as **fatal** if I consider it serious enough to stop the release of the program. Here's one of his examples: It's a fatal bug if "WordStar" is spelled wrong on one of the product's main screens. (In a discussion with him on September 24, 1992, this person repeated that he would class a bug like this as fatal.) "Fatal" means "fatal to the release" not "dangerous." In this industry, "fatal" is used this way routinely.*

- **One person should be responsible for handling**, routing, and tracking the most critical bug reports.

  *In the practice recommended in Chapter 6, a senior tester tracks the reports but the project manager routes and prioritizes them. If the project manager doesn't accept responsibility for carefully reviewing, routing, and checking the status of all critical bugs, then the lead tester should make sure they are visible in testing status reports.*

- **Responses and comments on the report should be attached directly to the original document.**

  *Most modern reports are online. There is no "original" document. But followup information can and should be entered as commentary on the report record. Every comment paragraph should include the date and initials of the person making it.*

- **Sensitive documents should never be copied.** They should be routed from person to person and initialed.

  *I disagree. Yes, this limits the possibility of leaks, but it means that the most serious bugs can't go into the bug database. A multi-user database probably provides open comment*

**14**

*fields where different members of the team can brainstorm toward a solution. This helps the bug get fixed, so giving it up is a bad thing.*

*Also, when there's only one copy of the report, the company will be tempted to destroy it when sued. This would be illegal and unethical, but it happens. However, other reports or memos will refer to this one. And someone may have made copies of the reports, which he's willing to bring to the trial. Or someone might remember some of the destroyed reports even if he doesn't have them, and be willing to testify about them. In each case, the judge and jury learn that the company has destroyed incriminating evidence. Down that path lie punitive damages.*

- **Keep records of the evaluation of critical bugs.** ("Even a negligent response by a concerned manufacturer will probably eliminate the possibility of an award for punitive damages" Bass 1986, supplement § 20.19B.)

- **Treat every complaint from the field** (customers, press) **seriously.** Make sure that every complaint is analyzed. ("[D]o not have a bare-faced complaint saying this product is not functioning properly with no evidence that any action was taken. Make certain that you provide some basis for answering the unfortunate report, even when no action is taken." Weinstein, 1988, p. 134).

  *I'm not sure that we should spend much effort on reports of minor problems, especially known minor problems. But I've seen some very embarrassing cases in which customer complaints of data corruption or system crashing bugs never made it through the bureaucracy to the right engineering manager. As a result, no one fixed them. This is bad for business, and it would look very bad in court.*

6. *Effect of customer complaints on subsequent designs:* When upgrading an existing product, how much did the publisher consider customer complaints from past versions?

   It makes good sense to seriously consider customer-reported problems. Reasonable manufacturers read their mail and take remedial steps based on what they've learned. We discussed Pareto analysis of customer reports in Chapter 13.

7. *Test plan:* Is the test plan structured for accountability? Can a supervisor or manager determine what has been tested and what has not? Did the testers follow the plan? Can we tell what was tested?

8. *Test plan design audits:* Have you tested the coverage of the test plan? The issue here is whether the test plan is likely to catch the critical problems in the program. As the test plan expands, it's worth reviewing again.

   Someone other than the tester who wrote the plan should check the plan. For example, this checker might sample from the hypothetical error conditions from the Appendix and determine whether the test plan would have detected them. (See the discussion in the introduction to the Appendix.) You can also audit a test plan using technical review meetings (Freedman & Weinberg, 1982).

9. ***Test plan execution audits:*** Did anyone actually *follow* the test plan? How do you know?

Test plans are sometimes written and then set aside, without ever being executed. Others are followed early in testing, but discarded as testing progresses. It might be entirely reasonable to *choose* to stop using a test plan. Perhaps the program has changed too much. If so, write a memo documenting your decision and summarizing what you'll use instead.

The more serious problem is that one of your staff may decide to abandon the test plan without telling you. This is a real problem, and you should be prepared for it when you supervise any test team. I've seen the discovery of serious bugs delayed until far too late in the project because a junior tester decided the test plan was boring, or too detailed, or took too much time. Have your staff mark up a copy of the test plan as they test, and review their notes with them.

When bugs are discovered by people outside the test group (such as beta testers or customers), check the test plan. If the problem is indeed part of a class that the test plan would miss, you've found a hole in your test design. On the other hand, if a tester following the test plan should have found this problem, you have a test plan execution problem.

10. ***Virus:*** How did the publisher check for viruses on the disk at time of mastering?

A few products have been released with viruses. There's rarely an excuse for this any more. We all know the risk. There are lots of good virus detection programs around. Since it's a crime in many states to release a virus deliberately (Branscomb, 1990; for example, California Penal Code § 502), a reasonable manufacturer will take steps to avoid releasing one accidentally.

11. ***Boundary testing:*** Were boundary and out-of-bounds data entry conditions and other likely failure conditions identified and tested?

I break out boundary tests separately because products liability lawyers are so keenly aware of the importance of tolerance limits tests. They'll ask about these.

We all know that programs are likely to fail at their boundary conditions. Every book and article on software testing worth reading (and many others) stresses that we should look for bugs at boundary points. Some testers give in to project managers who demand testing of mainstream values rather than boundary values. If the program causes harm at a garden variety boundary, reasonable testing was not done.

**14**

LEGAL
CONSEQUENCES

12. ***Documentation:*** Was every assertion in the manual and on the box verified against the software?

13. ***User errors:*** Does the system contain adequate safeguards to cope with user errors? (Read Lewis & Norman, 1986).

Don't be steered away from a serious problem by a programmer who dismisses it as a "user error." According to Dhillon (1986), writing about industrial accidents in general, "about 90% of accidents are related to unsafe acts, and only about 10% are due to unsafe physical or mechanical conditions." Senders & Moray (1991) cite the same 90% figure, and continue (p. 2):

> Those who have studied the impact of error on complex human-machine systems generally believe that between 30% and 80% of serious incidents are due, in some way, to human error.

Courts are used to classifying designs as defective when they lack adequate safeguards to protect against user errors. The most commonly applied legal doctrine is *comparative negligence*. Under this approach, the judge or jury divide responsibility for a failure between the software publisher and the customer. If a program caused $10,000 of property damage, and the jury found the publisher 50% at fault, the publisher would pay $5000 and the customer would lose the other $5000 (see Keeton et al., 1984).

For a flavor of the general legal attitude toward user errors of products, see Bass (1986), especially Chapters 3, 8, 9, 11, and Table 11-3 of "Unacceptable Product Design Criteria."

For further discussion of the responsibilities of the reasonable manufacturer, read Brown's (1991) Chapter 4, *Guidelines for Manufacturers*. This is written for makers of hardware (such as ladders or cars), but much of his thinking can be applied to software products as well, especially those whose failure can result in injury or property damage.

### Negligence: causation

Causation is the third component of a negligence lawsuit. It is a technical legal issue, beyond the scope of this book. Use common sense. If a customer is injured or suffers property damage *because* of a bug in the program, and that bug is in the program *because* you missed it (and it was reasonably possible to find) or *because* your company deferred it, then the causation requirement in a torts lawsuit is satisfied. For more discussion, read Keeton et al. (1984), Chapter 7.

### Negligence: damages

If your company is found liable, the judge or jury will assess damages: money that your company must pay. Damages have been discussed a few times already in this chapter. Here is one final point to bear in mind.

Judges and juries don't often award punitive damages in products liability cases, but they can under the right circumstances. Suppose that you learn, through testing or through customer feedback, that one of your products does cause personal injury or property damage. If you continue to sell it, without warnings, you risk punitive damages. (See *Wangen v. Ford Motor Co.*, 1980, for example, and read Owen, 1976, and Walker, 1984.) If you learn that your program trashes customers' hard disks, consider putting a hold on advertising and sales and recalling unsold copies from retailers. Free upgrades later to a fixed version won't undestroy a customer's lost data. Nor save your company from a large punitive damages claim.

## STRICT PRODUCTS LIABILITY

It takes a lot of research to prove that a company acted negligently when it designed a product. It's not easy to evaluate the quality of a company's testing effort, or to discover how much they knew about the flaws in a product, and when.

Under the right circumstances, a customer can bring a strict products liability lawsuit instead. In this case, a company is liable if it sells a product that (Restatement of Torts § 402A):

- is defective;
- is unreasonably dangerous; and
- causes personal injury or property damage.

In theory, an expert can tell these things by analyzing the product itself, without ever investigating the internal practices of the manufacturer. This can make the lawsuit much easier to win. However, when dealing with design errors (as opposed to manufacturing errors), arguments about design defectiveness are largely the same as the negligence arguments, so I won't spend much time on the strategy of the strict liability lawsuit here. (See Henderson & Twerski, 1987, for a thorough discussion.)

There is one aspect of strict liability that you should be aware of, however. Suppose a manufacturer releases a product and publishes its specification, but the product's design doesn't match the specification. This is an example of an *inadvertent design defect*. If it causes injury or property damage, a court might treat this defect as equivalent to a manufacturing defect—in both cases, the product fails to meet the manufacturer's own specifications (see Henderson, 1973, 1976, and Walkowiak, 1980).

How does this apply to software? It applies most directly to your evaluation of the manual. Some writers gloss over serious bugs or design problems, even ones the project manager asks be documented. In the extreme (and rare) case, a writer insists on documenting a product as it "should" work, challenging the programmers to change the software because she won't change the manual. In the more common case, a significant problem feels too embarrassing or hard to describe, or the writer just misses it.

The manual is a specification of the product. If you ship a product that doesn't match the manual, and the mismatch results in injury or property damage, the customer's lawyer will argue persuasively that this is enough evidence, in and of itself, to justify an almost immediate ruling against your company.

## MALPRACTICE

When a company or individual sells services, rather than a product, the Uniform Commercial Code does not apply. Nor does products liability law. Instead, a dissatisfied customer can sue for malpractice. Malpractice is the failure "to exercise the skill and knowledge normally possessed by members of that profession or trade" (Restatement (Second) of Torts § 299A, 1965).

**14**

LEGAL
CONSEQUENCES

Malpractice is a tort, akin to negligence. The person who files the suit, if successful, will recover full compensatory and consequential damages. Further, malpractice is not restricted to personal injury and property damage. Accountants and lawyers are subject to malpractice suits, even when the damage they do is purely economic. Someone whose business is destroyed by a computer will want to bring a malpractice suit because this may be the only way she can recover full damages.

Claims of malpractice can arise in three types of situations:

- *Purchase of a defective product.* The claim is that anything having to do with software should be subject to malpractice liability.

    It's largely settled that defective products are covered by the Uniform Commercial Code (see my discussion at the start of the chapter), and not by malpractice law. The leading case denying malpractice liability is *Chatlos Systems v. Nat'l Cash Register Corp.* (1979). However, some law review articles, such as Kraemer (1984, 1988) and MacKinnon (1983), make a case for sometimes allowing product-related malpractice claims.

- *Purchase of programming services.* The customer buys programming services, paid for by the hour, either on their own or in conjunction with the purchase of a computer system. These are more clearly services. The question is, are they subject to the same level of regulation as the legally recognized professions and trades?

A few courts have accepted the idea that programming services are subject to malpractice claims (e.g., *Invacare Corp. v. Sperry Corp.,* 1984, and *Data Processing Services, Inc. v. L.H. Smith Oil Corp.,* 1986). Kraemer (1984, 1988) and MacKinnon (1983) also argue for this position.

Conley (1987) and Graziano (1991) cite contrary cases, arguing that there is very little precedent for computer malpractice liability, and that until the profession develops uniform minimum standards, it will be too hard for courts to determine the required minimum level of professional skill.

Two recent cases offer contradictory messages about the liability of professional accountants who provide computer consulting. In *Diversified Graphics, Ltd. v. Groves* (1989), the federal Second Circuit Court of Appeals held that Ernst & Whinney (now called Ernst & Young) could be held accountable for malpractice for acting as a consultant for its client's purchase and implementation of an in-house data processing system. But the Appellate Division of New York's Supreme Court came to precisely the opposite conclusion in *RKB Enterprises Inc. v. Ernst & Young.* Condo (1991) discusses *Diversified Graphics* in detail.

- *The software provides a professional service.* The Internal Revenue Service has decided that a tax preparation program can be held to the same standards as a professional tax preparer (*Rev. Rul.* 85-189, 1985-2 C.B. 341, and IR-86-62 5/5/86; see Journal of Taxation, 1986). A well-researched student comment (Kraemer, 1988) argues that some programs are practicing law, and should be held to the same standards as attorneys. Mortimer (1989) suggests a negligence/malpractice standard for medical software. Programs also provide accounting advice, nutritional advice, and various other types of professional services.

Should programs that provide what appears to be professional services be held to the same standards as the professionals (lawyers, accountants, nutritionists, doctors, etc.)? I don't know the answer, and I haven't found much in the literature that helps me think about it more clearly. But here's one suggestion if your company is developing expert system software or other advisory software:

> *The more your advertising, documentation, and online instructions make the customer think she can replace a professional with your product, the better her chances of success in a malpractice suit if your program gives her bad advice.*

## FRAUD

When a software publisher releases a product that does not meet advertised claims, the publisher has breached the warranty created by the advertisement (giving rise to a contract suit). The publisher has also misrepresented the product's capabilities. If the publisher knew the claims were false when it made them, the publisher has also committed fraud.

Fraud and misrepresentation are torts. A defrauded or misled consumer can collect the traditional tort damages, including incidental and consequential damages, and, in the case of fraud, punitive damages.

The typical computer-related fraud lawsuits have involved negotiated contracts for large system software, and assurances by the developer that the software was already complete. *Schroders, Inc. v. Hogan Systems, Inc.* (1987) and *Clements Auto Company v. Service Bureau Corp.* (1971) are good examples of this type of suit. Kraemer (1988) lists and briefly summarizes many such cases. One variation: in *Ritchie Enterprises v. Honeywell Bull, Inc.* (1990), Honeywell Bull committed fraud after the sale, making false statements to the keep the customer from rejecting the system within the acceptance test period. Post-sale fraud is actionable if it causes a person to forego or refrain from asserting an existing right or to change position in some other way. You might want to mention this to technical support staff who think they're supposed to lie if necessary to keep a customer from returning a product.

Sherman (1981) provides a concise overview of fraud and misrepresentation. As usual, Keeton et al. (1984, Chapter. 25) provide the classic treatment.

I often hear a very narrow definition of fraud from salespeople and other imperfectly informed managers. They think it's not fraud unless they deliberately tell a bald lie. They're mistaken—read this, from the *Restatement of Torts (Second)* (1965):

§ 526 A misrepresentation is fraudulent if the maker

(a) knows or believes that the matter is not as he represents it to be,

(b) does not have the confidence in the accuracy of his representation that he states or implies, or

(c) knows that he does not have the basis for his representation that he states or implies.

A misrepresentation can be of fact, opinion, or intention (Restatement § 525). "Ambiguous statements ... will amount to misrepresentation if the false meaning is ... intended to be accepted." (Keeton, et al., 1984, p. 736.) Further, "misrepresentation may be found in statements which are literally true but which create a false impression in the mind of the hearer." (Keeton, et al., 1984, p. 736-737).

A software publisher advertises fraudulently when it claims that a program is capable of doing something after it learns from internal tests or dissatisfied customers that this aspect of the program doesn't work.

**14**

LEGAL
CONSEQUENCES

## WHISTLE BLOWING

Some day, after a project manager defers a particularly annoying bug, you will feel so angry that you'll want to describe it to one of the computer magazines' gossip columnists. Some testers make these calls. Should you?

The answer to that question depends on the specific facts of your situation. Let's consider garden variety (non-life-threatening) bugs first.

In general, you have a responsibility to your company to keep its products' bugs secret.

- When you joined the company, you agreed to not reveal its trade secrets. Most software companies make you sign an agreement to protect the secrets (Marzouk, 1988), but you have that duty whether you signed a paper or not. I'll consider whether bugs are trade secrets in a moment. But if they are secrets, you've agreed to keep them. (See also Ortner, 1985.)

- When you interview for a job and the interviewer asks about bugs in products you tested, make it clear that you'll only describe problems that were completely fixed. Explain that you have to protect your past employers' secrets, just like you will protect your new employers' secrets. (By the way, most interviewers who ask about shipping bugs ask to hear how you think, and to pick up gossip. However, some of us ask in order to see whether you'll give away secrets. If you do, we don't hire you.)

Is a bug report a trade secret? Under the *Uniform Trade Secrets Act of 1979*, a trade secret is information that:

§ 1.(4)(i) derives independent economic value, actual or potential, from not being generally known to, and not being readily ascertainable by proper means by, other persons who can obtain economic value from its disclosure or use, and

(4)(ii) is the subject of efforts that are reasonable under the circumstances to maintain its secrecy.

I haven't found any court decisions that decided whether bug reports are trade secrets or not. In an informal setting, I did ask an experienced trade secret attorney his opinion and he said "of course."

- Bug reports satisfy the economic value criterion for trade secrets because (a) the competition can gain advantage by publicizing your bugs, and (b) it would cost them a lot of money to find these bugs on their own.

- It is more questionable whether bug reports satisfy the criterion of reasonable efforts to preserve secrecy. (Marzouk, 1988, provides a list of common measures.) Most bug report forms don't have "Confidential" stamped on them. Many (maybe most or all) employment agreements that list trade secrets don't include bug reports in the long list of things that have to be kept secret. But you know that your management would be absolutely scandalized and outraged if they discovered that you were reporting deferred bugs to the press. If you know that management expects you to keep this information secret, what other measures are needed?

Professional societies' codes of ethics are slightly instructive on this issue.

- The American Society for Quality Control (ASQC) and the Association for Computing Machinery's (ACM) codes both require the member to protect the employer's confidential information. As I interpret these Codes, if a bug doesn't threaten life, limb, or significant property damage, the tester has no business publicizing it.

- However, the Codes of the ASQC, ACM, and Human Factors Society all obligate the member to protect the public's safety. The ACM's published comments on its codes (Association for Computing Machinery, 1992, p. 96) explicitly note that the member must blow the whistle (warn the public) if a bug might "result in serious personal or social damage" and the member's employers won't rectify the situation.

I agree with the ACM's requirement of "serious personal or social damage." If the bug will merely lose data, by all means tell your boss about the bug, tell the project manager, and make sure that someone in senior management knows about it. But if the company defers it, I think you have to respect the company's ownership of the secret.

On the other hand, if a bug does threaten "serious personal or social damage," you will face a difficult, personal decision.

Understand that when you publicize errors in your employer's products, you risk your career. As Goldberg (1987, p. 159) put it in an article about the space shuttle explosion,

> Whistleblowers get fired. Put more cautiously, there are inadequate mechanisms in place to protect private sector whistleblowers from retaliatory discharge. A government whistleblower has said, "If you have God, the law, the press and the facts on your side, you have a 50-50 chance of winning." For an engineer in the private sector, these odds are optimistic.

Mundel (1991) gives further examples of professionals whose careers were destroyed when they reported extremely serious problems to responsible people outside of the professional's company.

Many states have statutes that protect whistleblowers from being fired, but these are very restrictive laws. To be protected, you might have to be a government employee or you might have to be reporting criminal activity by your company that threatens public safety. Don't expect these laws to protect you if you work for a private employer and publicize a bug that has not yet resulted in any injuries.

# 14

**LEGAL
CONSEQUENCES**

One possibility to consider if you ever run into this situation. If the problem is *that* serious, your company is going to get sued for a lot of money some day if it releases this product. Rather than going public with the bug (or before going public), consider raising the issue with your company's lawyer:

- You can't do this very often, and you had better have a very serious (lawsuit-worthy) bug to discuss or you will lose credibility.

- Let your manager know that you want to talk with the lawyer *before* you arrange the meeting. Don't let your manager feel that you're going behind her back. (Besides, in most companies you'll want your manager's help in getting the meeting approved.)

- Mark any summary reports you prepare for the lawyer "Confidential—For the Attorney" and don't show them to anyone outside your company or to most people inside it. Ask your lawyer how he wants you to protect the confidentiality of these reports.

- Describe the bug fairly. Don't exaggerate. Explain its likely consequences as well as the worst case. Explain how often you expect it to arise in real use, and why.

If the problem is serious enough, the odds are good that the lawyer will successfully advise the company's president to hold up or stop shipment of the product.

# MANAGING A TESTING GROUP

## THE REASON FOR THIS CHAPTER

This chapter discusses selected issues of specific interest to test managers. It describes techniques and attitudes that have worked for us, and a few problems we think you can avoid. This is not a general chapter on management.

Modern thinking about quality starts from the position that senior managers must take responsibility for the quality of their companies' products. Deming (1982), Feigenbaum (1991), Ishikawa (1985), and Juran (1989) are solid presentations of this view. We encourage you to learn and advocate their views. However, we write this book from a different premise.

Everywhere in this chapter, we assume that you are not part of a company-wide quality improvement system, and that "Total Quality Management" (TQM) is something that your executives don't talk about or just pay lip service to. We assume that the mandate of your group is no broader than you make it and that your group's primary role in the company is to test code. The TQM vision of your role is broader than this. If you work in a TQM-oriented shop, don't let your thinking be constrained by this book.

If you don't work in a TQM shop, don't let yourself or your staff be demoralized by books and courses that stress top management's leadership role. If you run a typical software test group in a typical American software company, you won't have TQM, but you can adopt a workable, narrower vision and provide tremendous value to the company.

## OVERVIEW

We start by considering the mission of the Testing Group. What role does it play in the company? A traditional view is that Testing should strive for the power and influence of a Quality Assurance Group. We disagree. Instead we suggest that Testing is best conceived as a group that provides technical services and information.

Independent test labs are often described as good supplements or alternatives to in-house testing. Good supplements, probably. A good alternative to the in-house lab? No. The test group's mission should include doing or supervising the testing of all the company's products, including close supervision of independent labs' work.

Next, we consider scheduling and performance measurement. Can you reliably estimate how long it will take to test a product? How do you protect your staff from late project nightmares, in which they either work extensive, unpaid, overtime, or they seem disloyal to the company in its time of need?

Finally, we consider staffing. Who should you hire? What skills does a tester need? How do you keep staff morale high in an inherently frustrating job? It is possible.

## USEFUL READINGS

If you're new to management, read Drucker (1966).

We think that understanding the progress in quality management in mainstream industries is more urgent for most test managers than further reading of software test books. Deming (1982), Feigenbaum (1991), Ishikawa (1985), and Juran (1989) are important books. Join the American Society for Quality Control, P.O. Box 3005, Milwaukee, Wisconsin, 53201-3005, 800-248-1946, or order the ASQC Quality Press book catalog (800-952-6587).

Pick up meeting management techniques from Doyle & Straus (1976) and Freedman & Weinberg (1982). And learn about negotiating—you're going to do a lot of it. We like Fisher & Ury (1981) and Karrass (1986).

**15**

MANAGING A
TESTING GROUP

# MANAGING A TESTING GROUP

The Testing Group's prime task is to search out and report bad news. Your findings can convince management to cancel a project. You can force schedule rewrites and delay a product's release by months or even years. Such delays have cost programmers and managers their jobs and start-up companies their independence.

Management of the Testing Group offers high pressure. Plus headaches from dealing with your inexperienced and underpaid staff. And little glory.

Your company puts up with you and your staff because you provide cost-effective ways to help improve the company's products. A well run group provides the company with:

- *Competence:* Testers specialize in testing. They train together and criticize each other (usually constructively). They develop a shared sense of professionalism: testing is what they do, and they try to excel at *that* rather than at programming, writing, or managing.

- *Testing time:* The testers are assigned to do testing. The schedule calls for them to finish testing tasks, not programming or writing tasks. They won't be distracted, as are so many programmers and writers who try to test in their spare time.

- *Independence:* The testers report to you, not the project manager. If they miss or cover up important problems, you'll chastise them. If they report too many problems or find serious new problems at the last minute, you'll give them a raise. They can afford to do their best work, no matter how bad it makes the project manager look or how much he wishes they'd be quiet.

But make no mistake—you have your job on sufferance. Turnover of test managers is extremely high. One factor is that the unusual stress of the job drives many test managers to seek transfers and promotions. Another large factor, though, is self-inflicted. Test managers who play annoying political roles in their companies detract from overall product quality, and from the quality of life of everyone they work with. They are working on borrowed time.

You can create an extremely effective test group that plays a big role in improving the quality of your company's products, without driving everyone crazy with politics, and without abusing or overworking your staff. The challenge of your job is to make your group effective without sacrificing your sense of integrity, your professionalism, your ethics, or your appreciation of the human worth of the people around you.

Here is the most important lesson of this chapter:

> *Integrity, professionalism, and humanistic management will always*
> *reinforce each other and your overall effectiveness as a test manager.*

# THE ROLE OF THE TESTING GROUP

We've seen four basic types of Testing Groups. Each has a different charter from the company and a different self-concept.

- *Quality Control* groups enforce standards.

- *Quality Assurance* groups assure quality (somehow). (Or, at least, they try to assure quality.)

- *Testing Services* groups provide a specific technical service to the project manager (and thus the company): they find and report bugs.

- *Development Services* groups provide a variety of technical services to the project manager, including testing.

## THE QUALITY CONTROL (QC) GROUP[1]

In theory, the QC group is powerful. QC inspectors can refuse to ship the product until procedures are followed, standards met, and designated problems are fixed. Members of testing and development services groups often wish they had this power, but what power there actually is comes at a high price.

A Software QC Inspector isn't just taking a few cans of tomatoes off a long production line. She is stopping the line, maybe the company's only line, for days, weeks, or months. Senior managers respond quickly to a QC refusal to release a program. Often they respond by releasing it, as recommended by the project manager, over the objections of QC.

---

**Management is the real quality control group in any company.**

---

[1] Our definition of *Quality Control* is narrow. We highlight two features of the QC group: they do a lot of inspection and they have the power to remove defective goods from production or to stop production. Popular descriptions of QC groups stop here, as does our treatment of the group in this chapter.

The role of many QC groups is broader. In the right company, any aspect of design, development, manufacturing, or provision of services that can be measured is fair game for a QC group. Based on reports from these groups, management can change the (design, development, manufacturing, or service delivery) process in ways that yield more customer satisfaction, fewer failures, higher production, or greater product consistency.

In companies that practice top-down quality management, the QC group provides important information gathering services to a management-driven, multi-departmental, quality improvement team. As we noted in the Introduction, this is a broader, more modern approach than the situation we address in this chapter.

We continue to recommend extreme caution about expanding your role to report more than just software and documentation errors, if you work in a company that doesn't practice top-down quality management. It's too easy to become embroiled in political messes between departments without leading to useful change. Read Deming (1982). You can't solve the company-wide problems he identifies, but you can too easily get caught up in them. If management isn't trying to solve these problems, then reporting on the productivity, work practices, design practices, competence, or general effectiveness of other groups than your own will all too often cause more harm than good.

A Testing Group is a management assistant. It informs management of product problems and their severity. Ultimately, management decides. The real power of the QC group is that it can hold a questionable product until management makes a deliberated decision. However, developers and QC inspectors rarely look at QC's role in this way. Instead, when management overrides a QC refusal to ship the product, QC loses face.

Further, because QC appears to have tremendous power, many developers fear and mistrust it. Here are the words of one project manager:

> I had feared that Product Integrity was run along similar principles to Marine boot camp, with you guys as the drill instructors and my precious [product name] in the role of defenseless recruit.

As a result, project managers pressure the QC group to be "fair." "Fairness" is not well defined. Is it unfair to add new tests during each cycle of testing? Is it unfair to test the program at its limits, where real customers might never be? Is it unfair to deliberately feed the program bad data? What about creating test cases on the spot? Should programmers have the right to see every test case in advance? Is it unfair to report minor problems or to challenge the design, especially in minor ways? Is it unfair to use a Problem Report form to suggest an improvement or to note a mismatch of the program against incorrect documentation? Finally, is it unfair to refuse to test a program that fails a published set of acceptance test cases? But what if it fails only one of these tests, seems fully functional and ready for testing otherwise, and it will take a long time to fix that one error?

Some project managers call anything unfair that makes them or their product look bad. Some QC managers refuse to change practices that are blatantly unfair and unreasonable. Whether you are fair or unreasonable, if you run a QC group, expect to spend a lot of time discussing fairness.

We rate a Quality Control group high on the heartburn scale, high in potential for adversarial relations, low in probable staff satisfaction, and only medium in testing quality. Its power is more limited than it seems, and more easily overridden.

## QUALITY ASSURANCE (QA)

*Quality Assurance* groups "assure quality." *You can't do that by testing.* A low grade program that goes through extensive testing and bug fixing comes out the other end as an extensively tested lousy program.

A true Quality Assurance group must be involved at every stage of development. It must set standards, introduce review procedures, and educate people into better ways to design and develop products. The big payoff from Quality Assurance is that it helps the company prevent defects. It *also* does testing, but this is just one part of its job. Bryan and Siegel's (1984) description of the full mandate of the software QA group illustrates the breadth of work of QA.

Beware that true QA staff must be *extremely* senior. They must be unquestionably competent programmers, writers, managers, designers, and analysts. Otherwise they won't be credible.

> *It seems to us that every company already has a proper group to set standards, evaluate and train staff, and generally monitor and work to improve every phase of product development. That group is called Management. Management is the real quality assurance group in every company.*

Naming a group "Quality Assurance" carries a dangerous message. If this is *the* group that assures quality, the rest of the company does not assure quality. Juran (1989, p. 6) points this out and notes that the idea of separate Quality Assurance groups predates World War II. It doesn't work. If you've worked in software testing for any length of time, you've heard project managers say "It's my job to get the product out on time. It's QA's job (not mine) to make sure the product has quality."

Delegating responsibility for product quality to a centralized non-management group is a recipe for failure. The whole company, especially management, must share ownership of quality. This is the lesson of our competition with Japan (Deming, 1982), and the lesson that underlies the Total Quality Management movement.

> *Quality flows from the top, not from "QA."*

In practice, many groups who call themselves QA don't do anything like quality assurance. They just do testing. But this confuses everyone, especially the testers. To the degree that testers understand that a real QA group does more than just testing, members of a "QA" group that just does testing will feel that they aren't being allowed to do their full job. Perfectly good testers become demoralized because they can't fulfill their inflated titles and job descriptions.

## TESTING SERVICES

*Testing Services* provides testing services to the project manager. Your mandate is to find code-roaches, describe them carefully, and make sure that everyone who needs to know about them finds out. You do not have the authority to release a product, or to refuse to release it. You describe the program's problems, the level of testing done so far, and your estimate of the program's quality. Management decides.

Your staff might not test all areas of the product, especially not during every cycle of testing. The company might even declare that the programmers are the primary product testers. In that environment, your group is a skilled supplement.

Members of a Testing Services group should create detailed function lists, document their work, automate tests when it makes sense, and so forth. Your group is responsible for the technical tasks of testing: analysis, design, creation, execution, and documentation. Encourage your staff to take professional pride in their technical prowess.

Some project managers prefer to shift quality management responsibility to Testing Services. They try to force you into a QC mold. They may announce that you're responsible for all testing and tell their programmers to do none, not even glass box testing. They may say that any bugs you don't find, they don't have to fix, and then blame you for not finding bugs. Understand that they are trying to avoid accountabil-

**15**

MANAGING A
TESTING GROUP

ity for their products' quality. When they pull adversarial stunts that make you want to take charge and force quality on them, resist the temptation. If you take the challenge, you'll enter into a classic adversarial *QC versus The World* environment. Instead, have your management restate your mandate.

> *The Project Manager is the head of quality assurance on his project. You provide him with technical information, and your interpretation of that information, to help him make quality-related decisions.*

Characterizing your group this way is *not* a way to avoid responsibility. Your staff is responsible for delivering high quality testing, test documentation, and test result interpretation, and for delivering it in a timely manner. Giving up the pretense of control doesn't free you from the reality that the company depends on your group as testing experts.

Giving up the pretense of control also doesn't take away any of your real power. You still have the authority to argue with the project manager and to present information to senior management. Your power lies in the data you collect and the skill with which you present it. You will achieve more by persuasion than by stopping a production line or mandating a new procedure.

The main problem with Testing Services is its narrowness. This isn't as much a problem for staff whose primary career interests lie in testing and test management, because you can expose them to new standards, new tools, and new techniques, such as new approaches to scheduling, automation, and test case selection. But what about members of your staff who have goals outside of testing? What is their career path? How can they stay in your group and grow?

## DEVELOPMENT SERVICES

*Development Services* extends the concept behind Testing Services. We see Testing Services as a service provider. It's technical, nonadministrative, noncontrolling and, as much as possible, apolitical. The staff help improve products (programs) developed by others (programmers) by applying a specialized skill (testing) that the developers don't necessarily have. Development Services is a service group that provides other quality-enhancing skills as well. Its objectives are to improve the product, help developers, and provide room for its members to grow professionally.

Development Services offers a range of services. Testing is your primary service: you always provide that. The others are optional; different companies will have different needs. Some of the services you can provide, with the right staff, include:

- Debugging
- Technical (customer) support, especially in the first few weeks after product release
- Copy editing of the manuals

- Technical editing of the manuals (technical verification, with greater authority than usual for testers to make changes)
- Usability testing
- Comparative product evaluations
- Customer Satisfaction studies

Different members of your staff have different skills and interests. These tasks are career growth opportunities for some people, and drudge work for others. Ask your people what they want to do, beyond testing, and assign them to these supplemental tasks appropriately.

Beware of spending so much time on these additional tasks that you don't test effectively.

## RECOMMENDATIONS

We strongly recommend the service group concept over the traditional QA and QC groups. We like the idea of Development Services, but we haven't tried a full version of it yet. Testing Services groups work, but you have to pay careful attention to the career paths of your staff or you will suffer turnover.

## A TEST GROUP IS NOT AN UNMIXED BLESSING

In a software department that doesn't have a Testing Group, the programmers know that it's up to them to make sure that the code works correctly. Once a test group enters the picture, programmers know they can afford to relax a little bit, and let some errors slip by. (After all, that's what all those testers are paid for, right?)

You *want* programmers to do their own testing, and to worry about the stability of their own code. You want this because they're good at it and they can do it more cheaply.

Programmers find the vast majority of their own errors. They understand the internals of their code better than anyone else, so they know where most of the problems are most likely to be. While testers can always find errors that the programmers missed, programmers testing their own code can find problems that testers will miss too.

Programmers find bugs comparatively cheaply. Remember Figure 3.1—the earlier a problem is found, the lower the cost to find and fix it. Here are some of the reasons:

- The programmer may not need to replicate her tests to figure out what's wrong. If she sees the problem once, she can look directly in the code for the error. She can also fix it as soon as she finds it.

- The programmer doesn't have to explain the problem to anyone else.

- The programmer doesn't have to spend time asking how the program is supposed to work, then write Problem Reports, keep track of any responses, and print summaries and status reports. She can skip the paperwork and just fix the problem.

**15**

MANAGING A

TESTING GROUP

The reduction in testing done by programmers can evolve gradually. Often it evolves at the urging of a particularly ambitious manager. He recognizes that testing takes time, and orders his group to do less of it. Let the testers do it. Now he can meet those milestones so much more easily. At the extreme, which is all too often realized, programmers test so little of their own code that it crashes immediately when your staff start working with it.

Keep this in mind if you are just forming a Testing Group. You'll have to do a lot of testing just to catch up with the company's old standards. This is one of the reasons that we recommend that you have a staff (counting yourself) of at least four testers.

## AN ALTERNATIVE? INDEPENDENT TEST AGENCIES

Your company doesn't have to do all of its own testing, or any of the testing that a test group would do. Instead, you can take the draft manuals and program to a company that specializes in testing. They can go through it for a few cycles (or for many) until the program is satisfactory.

> *The testing literature reflects and promotes a strongly held belief that product reliability will be better if testing is done by a fully independent test agency.*

In theory, these are professional testers, who are independent of any internal political pressures that could be brought to bear on an in-house Testing Group.

Our experience with independent test agencies has been limited, but not positive. Here are some problems to watch out for:

- *Testing agencies are less independent than they seem.* They have no job or contract security with you. They want to continue testing this product, and win a contract from you for the next. Some may be more anxious to please and more willing to overlook problems than an in-house group.

- *Agency standards might not be as high as yours*. In particular, they are less prone to criticizing the design, more willing to agree that a badly designed program is correct if it meets its specification and matches the manual's description. Who's going to help polish the design if an outside agency does your testing?

- *Agency staff may not be very senior.* The worst agency we know used untrained high school students. The project leader had a programming background and testing experience but had never read a book on testing. We're still not sure she understood what a boundary condition was, or why it was important to test at boundaries. Most test organizations are more senior than this group, but as far as we know, this group is still in business. Don't be shy about thoroughly interviewing agency staff before signing up the agency.

The good agencies still have to charge you a premium to cover their overhead. Consulting firms often bill you triple their labor costs, so if you pay a testing agency $24 per hour for the work of a junior tester, they pay the tester $8 per hour. We wouldn't want to hire anyone so unskilled that we could get her for $8 per hour. Your better junior testers might compare with their intermediates, and your intermediates with their expensive seniors.

We've waded through a lot of poorly written and poorly thought out Problem Reports from independent agencies. At least with in-house staff, we can train them.

- *Agencies miss significant test areas, just like your staff does.* For example, we've never seen an agency-designed test for a race condition. We've seen some horrible race bugs that testing agencies have missed or misreported. Another example: an agency that received about $250,000 to test a medium complexity product to be sold to the public apparently spent almost no time testing the output routines. They made sure that the program calculated the right numbers, but they missed many blemishes and downright errors in the graphs.

- *Agencies may not provide enough supervision and support.* Don't count on the agency for 100% of the testing work. Don't reassign all your testers to other projects as soon as you hire a testing agency. No matter how good the agency is, its work will suffer if you don't assign someone to monitor their work, teach them your standards, follow up on their findings, and verify that reasonable fixes are being made to the problems they report.

- *Agencies don't necessarily help you budget realistically.* Don't expect an agency to test the product in fewer cycles than your group can. Don't budget for only two cycles of testing unless you have a clear plan for the third cycle and onward.

- *Agencies don't generally have product knowledge.* They don't know what you know about how a product like this should work and what benefit it should provide, or what compromises the better competition have *(or have not)* been willing to make, or the kinds of ways real customers will probably push the limits of the program.

Decide what you want from an agency. Realize that it will cost time and money to get it. Prioritize. Do you want fully documented reusable test materials? Automated tests? Or are a few solid rounds of testing adequate, without detailed support materials? If you don't decide what you want, and communicate it clearly and consistently, you'll get what you don't want instead.

Overall, we rate the results of independent test agency testing as mediocre. This is a lot better than bad. Many companies would do well to hire independent agencies.

On the positive side, an agency's work can provide an excellent baseline, a starting point from which your group can take off. You can approach agencies from that perspective. Instead of buying repeated testing, ask for a test plan, test cases, and suggestions for further work. They'll put more senior people on this, and charge you for it, but they'll do it. One important benefit to you is that the testing experience of these people is probably broader than yours or your staff's. They're bound to test for some problems you've never considered, or test for difficult problems in interestingly new ways. Combine their work with yours and your staff might do much better testing and learn something in the process.

## 15

**MANAGING A**
**TESTING GROUP**

One final recommendation: if you do contract with a testing agency, assign in-house testing staff to the project as well:

- *Replicate every bug reported by agency staff.* When needed, your staff should append explanations or descriptions of replication conditions to the report.

- *Look for related problems.* This is not redundant—your staff know more about the product, and about the people who write it. They'll find related problems that the agency staff would never have looked for.

- *Criticize the program's user interface*, whether or not the outside testers do so. Your staff understand the company's style better than the outsiders. If they miss a violation of style or standards, it will be due to carelessness, not ignorance.

- *Evaluate the testing coverage.* Are the agency staff testing everything important? Are they looking for every plausible type of error? Sometimes your staff should point out weaknesses to the agency's testers, other times they should just create and run the tests themselves. Use your judgment.

In sum, a testing agency does not solve your testing problems. They supplement your group's work. They may do a little or a lot for you, but you have to take responsibility for the overall quality of testing and you have to devote knowledgeable staff to monitoring and extending their work.

## SCHEDULING TIPS

As test manager, you are accountable for part of an overall project schedule. Testing schedules are difficult to estimate because they depend on someone else's work. Testing will take longer when coding falls behind schedule, when there are more bugs than expected, and when the user interface keeps changing. These are real difficulties, but you can't hide behind them. Don't use them as excuses for not managing your own schedules.

You have four key scheduling objectives:

- *Provide predictability to the project manager:* The project manager needs to know what testing tasks must be accomplished and how long they take.

- *Identify opportunities to pull in or protect the project schedule:* Identify points on the schedule where extra help will make a difference. Identify in advance programming or documentation tasks that must be finished at critical dates, or it will hurt the testing schedule. Many project managers can find money to meet these needs, especially temporary needs for extra testers. If your company can ship a product a week sooner if it invests in an extra person-month of tester or programmer time, it should invest. After all, it saves a week of everyone else's time (other testers, project manager, product manager, programmers, etc.) when a product ships a week sooner.

- *Be fair to your staff:* A project or marketing manager may be perfectly willing to burn out your people in an effort to ship a product a few days sooner. If they can convince or bully your staff into a few hours (days, weeks, months) of unpaid overtime, they get to ship the product sooner "for free." You and the company pay a price, in dealing with higher turnover, lower morale, and lower quality work from tired staff, but the exploiting manager is a hero.

- *Maximize productivity:* People will work hard to meet a schedule that is tight but achievable. Don't demand that they meet impossible schedules. After a burst of overtime, people set limits under impossible schedules. They work 40-hour weeks, period. They stop suggesting improvements to the product because those will slip the schedule even further. They become cautious, boring, uncaring. Some quit, including some of your most dedicated employees.

You serve all these objectives when you provide honest, reliable estimates of testing times. The next sections provide some tips toward achieving good estimates.

## MEASURE PERFORMANCE AND PRODUCTIVITY

In Chapter 6, we warned emphatically against using the bug tracking system to measure the performance of programmers. Here we do advocate measuring the performance of your staff. The difference is that programmers aren't your staff. Your measures of them would be public and taken as adversarial. On the other hand, measuring your staff's performance can help them, you, and your company, without creating any adversarial overtones.

We gave an example of a performance measure in Chapter 10. When a tester thoroughly reviews a program's user guide, and checks every statement at the keyboard, she completes about four pages per hour. Rates of three to five pages per hour are normal. Rates faster than five pages per hour, in our experience, result from incomplete testing.

Deming (1982) passionately advocates performance measurement as an essential part of quality improvement. He describes many benefits. Here are a few that we see for testers of software:

- You can find out how long, on average, a given task or process takes. When you understand how long things take, you can predict them.

- If you do similar tasks many times, you won't spend the same amount of time on each. There's variability. Perhaps (we have no empirical basis for this number, but imagine for the sake of illustration that) a typical tester reports an average of eight bugs per day for the first four weeks after a typical program is declared "beta." If you counted the number of bugs actually reported per day, per tester, during these weeks, you might find that testers typically report between 1 and 25 bugs per day, but the average is 8. If so, you wouldn't be alarmed if someone reported 24 bugs one day, but you would be alarmed if she reported 120.

  When you understand the normal amount of variability in a task, you can predict realistically. You can say that a task will probably take about six weeks and that it won't take longer than eight weeks unless something is wrong.

- When you know what is average, and how much variability there is around the average, you can interpret the results of your efforts to improve productivity. Does a certain type of training help? Does it help to capture and replay your keystrokes and mousestrokes?

**15**

MANAGING A
TESTING GROUP

*You must understand your baseline so you can recognize improvement.*

Here are a few examples of things you can measure:

- *Average number of cycles of testing:* Our educated guess is that a typical program completes eight full cycles of testing before it reaches commercial quality. There's a wide range: some products require dozens of cycles of testing, and some require fewer than eight.

- *Duration of the typical cycle of testing:* This is a meaningful measure if you test the same proportion of the program (such as a full pass against the program) during each testing cycle. It's not a useful measure if you receive a new version for testing every week, independent of the progress made over the week.

- *Bugs reported per tester-day:* If the average tester reports 5 bugs a day, and you expect to find 1000 bugs before releasing the product, you need 200 tester-days to find and report them.

- *Hours per printer-test:* Measure setup time separately from testing time.

- *Pages reviewed per hour:* Of course, this depends on the type of documentation, and on the objectives of the review.

- *Number of error messages tested per hour:* How long does it take to test and retest error handling?

- *Pages of the test plan completed per hour:* How long does it take to execute the test plan?

You can think of plenty of other examples. Jones (1991) provides many examples of measures of software productivity.

Once you have data like this, you can make strong scheduling arguments. When a project manager tells you to just plan for two cycles of testing, explain that your company's average is eight cycles. Show how long an average cycle of testing takes. Explain why. You'll get more time to do your job properly.

The risk of staff abuse is still present when you collect statistics on your own staff's performance. If you use these to prod individuals, telling them that they aren't testing fast enough, you will create a big mess. Deming (1982) argues as passionately against using performance measures as bases for quotas as he argues for taking the measures in the first place.

*If you work in a company that will use performance measures against individual testers, don't collect the data.*

## IDENTIFY AND ESTIMATE EVERY TASK

When you estimate the amount of testing a product needs, list every testing task that this project will require. Leave nothing out.

Here's a good way to come up with the list. Reserve a conference room for a day or two, and bring a few flip charts. Meet with the product's lead tester and her staff. If there's only one tester, try to bring in a third person knowledgeable about testing and about the product, perhaps the person who tested the previous release of this product. Bring in the specification, test plan, last release's test plan, user manuals, notes, anything you think might help you identify tasks.

On one piece of flip chart paper, list the main testing tasks. Do this as a group. Perhaps you'll identify the 5 or 10 or 20 big jobs. Tape this page to the wall, then make a new page for each of the main tasks, and list every subtask on these pages. Tape these pages to the wall. Some subtasks are complex enough that you'll split them into sub-subtasks, with a page each. When you identify a new main task (you'll keep thinking of new ones), mark it on the main task page, make a new page, and fill it in.

A meeting like this often has periods in which every person goes, individually, from list to list adding items. A tester might walk around the room two or three times, adding new items to each page each time she passes it—seeing what other people write will give her further ideas.

This listing task is brainstorming. Don't criticize the ideas (yet). Let them all go on the pages. You can filter them out later.

After making the lists, come back together to work as a group. Go through each list of individual tasks and ask how long each should take. Whenever possible, break a task down more finely, and estimate its components. Add them up to estimate the whole task. Estimate ranges: we like to generate a short estimate, a medium estimate, and a long estimate for tasks.

Many of your group's estimates will feel too long. This is normal. Encourage it. Push staff members to include every minute that they think a job will take. But do make people explain their estimates. You're looking for reality, not sandbags.

> *Never make someone feel guilty or stupid when she tells you it will take two weeks to do something you'd rather see done in one. Help her try to prove her estimate. Maybe it's correct. If not, soon after the discussion, she'll be much more comfortable with a shorter estimate.*

**15**

Estimate how many times you'll do individual tasks or groups of tasks.

Your total time estimate, across tasks, will be outrageous. Totaled across your 20 or 30 flip chart pages, you'll probably have enough work to run 5 or 10 (or more) times longer than the maximum possible length of the project. This is normal. Be concerned if you haven't listed way more work than you have time to do.

MANAGING A

TESTING GROUP

From here, given a comprehensive list of tasks, you can make explicit decisions:

- You can decide which tasks you simply cannot do.

- You can prioritize the rest.

- You can decide which tasks to do only partially, and how to decide which parts to do. (Perhaps you'll make deliberate decisions about test cases, perhaps you'll randomly sample.)

- You can identify important tasks that you must speed up (perhaps automate tasks that repeat often).

- You can write a detailed and convincing memo explaining why you can't finish testing within the schedule, or why you need more testers, and what you can achieve with how much more time, money, or people.

Also at the end of this day or two of work, you'll have a thorough outline that can serve as the basis of a very effective test plan.

## CLASSIFY THE PROJECT

You'll often have to guess about the testing cost for a project long before you have enough information. You can use a chart of estimates to come up with a ballpark first guess.

- *Start by classifying the complexity of the product.* Use a three-point or five-point scale, ranging from the simplest program or utility your company has ever tested to your company's most feature-rich, hardest-to-use, hardest-to-understand product.

- *Next, guess the reliability of this program during testing.* Use a three-point or five-point scale. Guess how many bugs you expect to find by the end of testing this program. You know the factors. Some project managers' products always have many more or many fewer bugs than the others. Some programmers' bug rates are well known to be high or low. A single fix to a mature program won't result in many bugs, but a release 1.0 of a high complexity program will be full of bugs.

Figure 15.1 A hypothetical scheduling estimation table

|  |  | Anticipated Reliability | | |
|---|---|---|---|---|
|  |  | High | Medium | Low |
|  | Low | 1 | 4 | 16 |
| Project Complexity | Medium | 4 | 16 | 64 |
|  | High | 16 | 64 | 256 |

- From here, build a table: Enter time and cost results (and estimates) in the table. For example, you might estimate one tester week for simple programs that you expect few bugs in. You might estimate 64 tester weeks for small modifications to a moderate complexity program that you expect lots of bugs in.

The estimation table will get more accurate over time, but it will never be more than a structured way to come up with a quick rough estimate. Still, this might be much better than an estimate you'd come up with on the fly, and it will look more rational to someone who questions your estimate.

Figure 15.1 is an example of an estimation table, to show its structure. The numbers are entirely hypothetical.

Read this table as saying that a small (low complexity) change would take a week if it was made to a highly reliable program by a very reliable programmer. According to the table, a more complicated change (medium complexity) would take 64 weeks if the program and/or programmer were not very reliable.

## IDENTIFY TASKS AS FIXED VERSUS RECURRING

A testing project involves two types of tasks, fixed and recurring.

- *Fixed tasks:* You do most fixed tasks once. For example, you will review the first draft of the manual once. It doesn't matter how many versions of the software go through testing, you will still review the first draft of the manual only once.

  Some fixed tasks are done more than once, but a fixed number of times. For example, some groups test installation instructions once when they're first written, a second time just before the manual goes to the printer, and a third time during final testing of the software. It doesn't matter how many changes are made to the program, or how long the project stretches, these groups test the manual's installation instructions three times.

  Writing the test plan is a fixed task. The integrity test is a fixed task. The initial acceptance test, certification that the program is alpha, certification that it's beta, and many devices tests are fixed tasks. Many boundary and limit tests are almost fixed tasks—they're run very rarely.

- *Recurring tasks:* Many recurring tasks are done every cycle of testing. For example, some groups run a quick functionality test every time they receive a new version of the program, before they begin thorough testing.

- You might run many regression tests every second or third cycle of testing. These are still recurring tests. If the program requires 30 cycles of testing, you run these regression tests 10 or 15 times.

The amount of time required to test the program is the amount of time to perform each fixed task, plus:

- the average amount of time per cycle of testing spent on recurring tasks,
  *multiplied by*
- the number of cycles of testing.

About halfway through a project you can make these types of divisions and calculations reasonably well. From there, based on the rate of bug fixing and bug finding, you can estimate the amount of testing time left in the project.

Miscellaneous tips

Here are a few more items, easily overlooked:

- *One person testing two products:* If someone is assigned to parallel projects, allow extra time for each. It will take her time to switch attention, to remember where she left off and what has to be done next.

- *Allow time for overhead:* List this as a separate item. How much time is lost to such things as meetings, reports, and time sheet accounting varies from company to company. Find out how much time your staff actually spend on these things. (Talk with them. Spend a day in a coffee house, away from the judgmental, restrictive atmosphere of the office, and figure it out with them. Make a list that you can explain to your management.)

You are doing pretty well if your staff spend six hours per day doing testing.

- *Recognize the individuality of your people:* Some are faster than others. Some work more overtime. Some are better testers, others better planners or writers. Some want training in new things. Reflect this in your time estimates and task assignments. You can't always give everybody the tasks they want, but you can always be aware of their desires.

- *Beware of hiring late in the schedule:* Budget time for hiring and training. Budget more time for communication each time you add a new person. You might lose more time to interviewing, hiring, training, and talking with the new people than they give back in productive work (see Brooks, 1975).

- *If you have to take shortcuts, choose them deliberately:* Call another scheduling meeting, go back to the list of tasks, update it now that everyone understands the project better. Choose the jobs that won't be done, the areas that won't be as well tested, the documents that won't be written. Minimize the risk to the product's quality. Leave the meeting knowing that you'll make the best use of the time available.

- *Meetings:* Be careful about spending too much time in meetings, and be especially careful of wasting time in them. To testers working unpaid overtime to meet a tight schedule, each hour wasted in an unproductive meeting represents an hour less sleep or an hour less with their families.

  Avoid status meetings. There is nothing more dulling than sitting around a table for an hour hearing what everyone did last week. If your company requires status meetings, tell people they're welcome to bring work to the meeting. During the periods that they don't have to pay attention, they can get work done.

## YOUR STAFF

We have a few suggestions on three staffing issues:

- Who to hire
- Morale
- Career growth

### WHO TO HIRE

Programmers are not necessarily good testers.

---

*Lousy programmers are usually lousy testers. Don't accept rejects from other departments.*

---

Here are some attributes and skills that we believe are useful to a good tester:

- *Integrity, and a commitment to quality.*

- *An empirical frame of reference, rather than a theoretical one:* Tests are miniature experiments. A tester must be able to refuse to take on faith anything about the program. She must translate claims about the program into testable assertions about how it will behave under known conditions, then check its behavior. Also, programmers may ignore design comments until the tester backs them with data, such as the number of calls to support staff that this problem caused in the last released version of the product. The tester must look for such data, and she needs a nose for sources of it.

- *Education:* More is better. University training is valuable. Training in research sciences, including human factors, is at least as valuable as training in computing.

- *Some programming background:* This is very useful, but it is not essential—we've known excellent testers who couldn't code. However, at least one of your staff, preferably more, should be a very competent programmer who other testers can turn to for advice.

- *Experience using many computers and many software packages.*

- *Knowledge of combinatorics:* Testers should be able to approximate or exactly compute the number of test cases required to fully evaluate some aspect of a program. This helps in many ways. As one example, it saves them from drastically underestimating the number of tests involved.

- *Excellent spoken and written communication:* Every tester makes verbal and written reports about controversial problems. Also, every tester should be able to anticipate misunderstandings and other problems that the documentation and screens will pose for customers.

- *Good at error guessing:* A good error guesser comes up with raw hunches that a program will fail some class of tests, ignores the formal test plan's limited testing in that area, kicks hard, and knocks over a can of worms. This is an invaluable talent.

**15**

MANAGING A
TESTING GROUP

- *Fast abstraction skills.*

- *Good with puzzles.*

- *Very conscious of efficiency:* A good time manager: If not good now, the person must be trainable.

- *Able to juggle many tasks:* This is more urgent in some groups than others, but it's a typical need.

- *Good at scheduling:* or trainable.

- *Careful observer, patient, attends to detail.*

- *Role-playing imagination:* The tester should be able to imagine herself in a different role. For example, she should be able to ask "How could I get in trouble here if I'd never used a computer before?"

- *Able to read and write specifications.*

In sum, the ideal tester is bright, articulate, attentive to detail but able to appreciate a larger picture, assertive without being obnoxious, creative, and possessed of a blend of management and technical skills. This is a different set than the mix needed by programmers.

Some great testers are also excellent programmers and some excellent programmers are also great testers, but you can be very good at one and poor at the other.


## MORALE

When we described how to report problems in Chapter 5, we said to make every effort to spare the programmer's feelings. But programmers and many others in the company are not so careful about testers' feelings. Many abuse testers, scream at them, call them stupid or liars. People who are otherwise quite reasonable become obnoxious when dealing with testers. Your staff have feelings too.

We told testers to describe problems with great care, lest the programmer find an excuse for ignoring it. This costs a lot of tester time, often to save not very much programmer time. Looked at that way, rather than in terms of probability that a problem will be fixed, it is a waste of tester time. Your staff will resent this, especially if they're working lots of overtime.

Your staff need moral support. Giving it to them is one of your major responsibilities.

Praise good work privately and publicly. Reward particularly good work with recognition at group meetings, lunches, and memos to their personnel file. Get testers' names in the company newspaper. If executive bonuses are awarded for excellent work, nominate deserving testers for them.

Don't just notice that a task was done on schedule. Spend the time to look beyond administrative details. Look over the work itself, and praise quality. Show that you value it when one of your staff:

- is particularly diplomatic.
- writes an especially detailed or understandable function list.
- finds a particularly interesting bug.
- holds up well and keeps testing under pressure to ease off.
- submits a particularly well written or researched set of Problem Reports.
- does a good job of training someone else.
- works overtime.
- takes care of some annoying group chore that everyone wants to avoid.
- tries something a little differently, shows some creativity, even if it didn't work out this time. Praise the initiative and the gamble.

Another morale booster is a group culture that values testing as a professional activity. Build a group that says "Great!" to each other, in counterpoint to the project manager's "Oh, damn," when someone finds a particularly nasty bug. Every tester needs support from coworkers who can assure her that finding new bugs is desirable, healthy, and important. Every tester needs someone else she can discuss new ideas with, ask for help, complain to, laugh about the job with. You can't provide all of these things; you're the manager.

Give your staff colleagues. You need at least four people (counting yourself) in the Testing Group to build a group culture. Don't try to form a Testing Group with less than four people.

It's also important to shield your staff. Don't repeat every unfair or unreasonable complaint that you hear about a tester. Don't talk about wild fluctuations in the schedule until they've settled down. Don't force your staff to talk with abusive people or with people who change their minds all of the time.

Make a policy that requests for staff overtime should go through you. Never let a project manager bully one of your staff into working late into the night to meet an impossible deadline. Have the manager ask you. You ask the tester, and make her know that it's okay to refuse. If there is bad news, you deliver it to the manager. Don't say that the refusal was the tester's choice. Let any bad feelings be between you and that manager. Keep your employee out of it.

You can make similar policies about schedule changes, standards changes, reassignment of tasks among different members of the same testing team, whatever someone else might try to impose on your staff that they might want to reject. Don't announce the policies until they're needed, but don't hesitate about stopping anyone who tries to run your people or make them to agree to unreasonable requests.

**15**

Finally, stand behind your staff, and let them see that. Testers say some of the stupidest, rudest, most embarrassing things. They'll say them in writing, in memos and in Problem Reports, where everyone can see them, again and again. Say what you want about these to your staff in private. In public, smooth the ruffled feathers, agree that it was a mistake, but stand behind your people. Defend their jobs, their salary, their status, and their reputation. They'll learn that you do this, and they'll trust you more for it. Your fellow and superior managers will learn to respect you for it.

Be willing to review particularly controversial memos before they're distributed. Suggest changes. If (and only if) the tester will make them, be willing to cosign the memo. If you agree with her work, set yourself up to take the flak for it.

If a tester says she dreads going to a particular meeting, be willing to go with her. If you can't make it, send a supervisor or a senior tester with her. If she needs company, or a fellow witness to help interpret what's going on, give this to her.

If you value their loyalty, make your staff feel that you're behind them in what they do, that it's okay for them to take risks, that you'll support them when they make mistakes, that you'll help them when they need it.

## CAREER GROWTH

Your staff want to progress professionally. They want to learn new things, become stronger technically or more skilled interpersonally. You can help them move forward, or you can hold them back. Help them move forward.

Testing is an entry point into the software industry for many people. They want to become programmers, writers, managers, consultants, whatever. Rather than fighting this, use it. Very skilled people with unusual backgrounds, or who are just reentering the work force, need time and an opportunity to prove themselves. They often need further technical training. You can often provide that. If you're willing to consciously accept staff who will leave your group in 18 months or 2 years, you can hire some exceptionally bright, hardworking, good people.

When you interview a testing candidate, ask why she wants to work in testing. If testing is a transitional job for her, ask yourself whether eighteen months or two years in your organization will be good for her. Will she keep learning things she needs to learn, throughout that period? If so, and if you believe she'd test exceptionally well during this period, hire her. Don't worry that she doesn't plan to make a career in testing. Few people do. Few people who are long-term professional testers planned it that way.

For each individual in your group, look for tasks that can teach them things they want to learn or give them experience they need. Sometimes, lend a tester to another group so she can broaden her experience and exposure.

Some people will leave your group sooner because they've grown quickly, but others will stay much longer. All will work more enthusiastically, because they're working for themselves as well as the company.

And, you'll make friends for life.

# APPENDIX: COMMON SOFTWARE ERRORS

## THE REASON FOR THIS APPENDIX

This Appendix describes over 400 bugs. The descriptions are short, including only what we considered the most interesting information. It's worthwhile reading this list, even though you may find it boring. On first reading it provides a frame of reference—details, and background about problems you should look for while testing. Its greater value is as an organized list of program problems for future reference. A good list, built up with time and experience, can be a powerful tool.

> *A set of test materials is nothing more than a list of possible problems in a program and a set of procedures for determining whether the problems are actually there or not.*

Generating reference lists of bugs on the fly is risky and inefficient. It takes too long to dredge up old insights, and you're too likely to get stuck on one or a few themes. We prefer to check a comprehensive "standard" list to get further ideas for testing a program. This Appendix is an example of a standard list.

Whenever you test a new program, you'll think of new entries for this list. Add them to it. We recommend that you enter this list onto your computer and manage it with an outline processor.

Here are examples of ways you should use this list:

1. Evaluate test materials developed for you by someone else.

   When you contract out the development of test materials you're likely to get back many thick binders of test cases. They look impressive, but they're incomplete. The author has blind spots, which you have to find. For example, in stacks of test materials that we've seen developed by contract testing agencies, we've yet to see an explicit race condition test. Unfortunately, it's easier to see what an author had in mind than to step back and see what's missing.

   We recommend evaluating the coverage of test materials against a checklist. Include a few examples of each class of error that you can imagine existing in the program. It doesn't matter whether the program *has* these problems — it only matters that they *could* be there. Once the list is complete, check the test materials to see which problems they would expose. If these tests wouldn't expose some errors in your list, look for tests for similar problems. This can quickly expose large classes of missing tests.

   It's easy to make a checklist from a large error list like the one in this Appendix. Just look for classes of errors that are relevant to your testing project and find a few good examples of each. Add any other problems that you think of that seem important for the program under test.

**A**

APPENDIX

363

**2. Developing your own tests.**

Write your own list of errors that you think the program could have. Then look here for more ideas. Consider each problem in this Appendix: if you're sure it's irrelevant to the program, forget it. Otherwise write a test case (or a few) to see if the program has the problem. When in doubt, ask the programmer whether a given type of error is possible in the program and how to test for it.

We also recommend this list for testing "on the fly." If you don't have time to plan and document a set of tests for a program, test from a list of candidate problems.

**3. Irreproducible bugs.**

A bug is hard to replicate because you don't know what triggered the failure, what the program did or displayed, or what could cause such a problem. You give up because you run out of hypotheses.

*Use this Appendix before giving up.*

Try to match reported symptoms with problems listed in this Appendix. Be creative: the matches won't be perfect because the reports are incomplete and incorrect. (If they weren't, you could reproduce the bug.) Even so, the list can help you break out of your current line of thinking. If you didn't need to refocus on other possibilities, you wouldn't be so close to giving up.

**4. Unexpected Bugs.**

When you discover a bug accidentally, or when one surfaces in a shipping product, look for others like it. You probably missed running a group of tests to detect the lot. This section can help you generate a list of possible related problems and tests.

# OUTLINE OF COMMON SOFTWARE ERRORS

USER INTERFACE ERRORS
> FUNCTIONALITY
>> Excessive functionality
>> Inflated impression of functionality
>> Inadequacy for the task at hand
>> Missing function
>> Wrong function
>> Functionality must be created by the user
>> Doesn't do what the user expects
> COMMUNICATION
>> Missing information
>>> *No onscreen instructions*
>>> *Assuming printed documentation is readily available*
>>> *Undocumented features*
>>> *States that appear impossible to exit*
>>> *No cursor*
>>> *Failure to acknowledge input*
>>> *Failure to show activity during long delays*
>>> *Failure to advise when a change will take effect*
>>> *Failure to check for the same document being opened more than once*
>> Wrong, misleading, or confusing information
>>> *Simple factual errors*
>>> *Spelling errors*
>>> *Inaccurate simplifications*
>>> *Invalid metaphors*
>>> *Confusing feature names*
>>> *More than one name for the same feature*
>>> *Information overload*
>>> *When are data saved?*
>>> *Poor external modularity*
>> Help text and error messages
>>> *Inappropriate reading level*
>>> *Verbosity*
>>> *Inappropriate emotional tone*
>>> *Factual errors*
>>> *Context errors*
>>> *Failure to identify the source of an error*
>>> *Hex dumps are not error messages*
>>> *Forbidding a resource without saying why*
>>> *Reporting non-errors*
>> Display bugs
>>> *Two cursors*

**A**

**USER INTERFACE ERRORS**
  COMMUNICATION
    **Display bugs**
      *Disappearing cursor*

      *Disappearing cursor*
      *Cursor displayed in the wrong place*
      *Cursor moves out of data entry area*
      *Writing to the wrong screen segment*
      *Failure to clear part of the screen*
      *Failure to highlight part of the screen*
      *Failure to clear highlighting*
      *Wrong or partial string displayed*
      *Messages displayed for too long or not long enough*
    Display layout
      *Poor aesthetics in the screen layout*
      *Menu layout errors*
      *Dialog box layout errors*
      *Obscured instructions*
      *Misuse of flash*
      *Misuse of color*
      *Heavy reliance on color*
      *Inconsistent with the style of the environment*
      *Cannot get rid of onscreen information*
  COMMAND STRUCTURE AND ENTRY
    Inconsistencies
      *"Optimizations"*
      *Inconsistent syntax*
      *Inconsistent command entry style*
      *Inconsistent abbreviations*
      *Inconsistent termination rule*
      *Inconsistent command options*
      *Similarly named commands*
      *Inconsistent capitalization*
      *Inconsistent menu position*
      *Inconsistent function key usage*
      *Inconsistent error handling rules*
      *Inconsistent editing rules*
      *Inconsistent data saving rules*
    Time-wasters
      *Garden paths*
      *Choices that can't be taken*
      *Are you really, really sure?*

**APPENDIX**

PROGRAM RIGIDITY
  User tailorability
      *Can't turn off the noise*
      *Can't turn off case sensitivity*
      *Can't tailor to hardware at hand*
      *Can't change device initialization*
      *Can't turn off automatic saves*
      *Can't slow down (speed up) scrolling*
      *Can't do what you did last time*
      *Can't find out what you did last time*
      *Failure to execute a customization command*
      *Failure to save customization commands*
      *Side-effects of feature changes*
      *Infinite tailorability*
  Who's in control
      *Unnecessary imposition of a conceptual style*
      *Novice-friendly, experienced-hostile*
      *Artificial intelligence and automated stupidity*
      *Superfluous or redundant information required*
      *Unnecessary repetition of steps*
      *Unnecessary limits*
PERFORMANCE
  Slow program
  Slow echoing
  How to reduce user throughput
  Poor responsiveness
  No type-ahead
  No warning that an operation will take a long time
  No progress reports
  Problems with time-outs
  Program pesters you
  Do you really want help and graphics at 300 baud?
OUTPUT
  Can't output certain data
  Can't redirect output
  Format incompatible with a follow-up process
  Must output too little or too much
  Can't control output layout
  Absurd printed level of precision

Can't control labeling of tables or figures
Can't control scaling of graphs

## ERROR HANDLING

### ERROR PREVENTION
Inadequate initial state validation
Inadequate tests of user input
Inadequate protection against corrupted data
Inadequate tests of passed parameters
Inadequate protection against operating system bugs
Inadequate version control
Inadequate protection against malicious use

### ERROR DETECTION
Ignores overflow
Ignores impossible values
Ignores implausible values
Ignores error flag
Ignores hardware fault or error conditions
Data comparisons

### ERROR RECOVERY
Automatic error correction
Failure to report an error
Failure to set an error flag
Where does the program go back to?
Aborting errors
Recovery from hardware problems
No escape from missing disk

## BOUNDARY-RELATED ERRORS

### NUMERIC BOUNDARIES
### EQUALITY AS A BOUNDARY
### BOUNDARIES ON NUMEROSITY
### BOUNDARIES IN SPACE
### BOUNDARIES IN TIME
### BOUNDARIES IN LOOPS
### BOUNDARIES IN MEMORY
### BOUNDARIES WITHIN DATA STRUCTURES
### HARDWARE-RELATED BOUNDARIES
### INVISIBLE BOUNDARIES

## CALCULATION ERRORS

### OUTDATED CONSTANTS
### CALCULATION ERRORS
### IMPOSSIBLE PARENTHESES
### WRONG ORDER OF OPERATORS
### BAD UNDERLYING FUNCTION
### OVERFLOW AND UNDERFLOW
### TRUNCATION AND ROUNDOFF ERROR

**APPENDIX**

CONFUSION ABOUT THE REPRESENTATION OF THE DATA
INCORRECT CONVERSION FROM ONE DATA REPRESENTATION TO ANOTHER
WRONG FORMULA
INCORRECT APPROXIMATION

INITIAL AND LATER STATES
FAILURE TO SET A DATA ITEM TO 0
FAILURE TO INITIALIZE A LOOP-CONTROL VARIABLE
FAILURE TO INITIALIZE (OR REINITIALIZE) A POINTER
FAILURE TO CLEAR A STRING
FAILURE TO INITIALIZE (OR REINITIALIZE) REGISTERS
FAILURE TO CLEAR A FLAG
DATA WERE SUPPOSED TO BE INITIALIZED ELSEWHERE
FAILURE TO REINITIALIZE
ASSUMPTION THAT DATA WERE NOT REINITIALIZED
CONFUSION BETWEEN STATIC AND DYNAMIC STORAGE
DATA MODIFICATION BY SIDE-EFFECT
INCORRECT INITIALIZATION
RELIANCE ON TOOLS THE CUSTOMER MAY NOT HAVE OR UNDERSTAND

CONTROL FLOW ERRORS
PROGRAM RUNS AMOK
  GOTO somewhere
  Come-from logic errors
  Problems in table-driven programs
  Executing data
  Jumping to a routine that isn't resident
  Re-entrance
  Variables contain embedded command names
  Wrong returning state assumed
  Exception-handling based exits
  Return to wrong place
    *Corrupted stack*
    *Stack under/overflow*
    *GOTO rather than RETURN from a subroutine*
  Interrupts
    *Wrong interrupt vector*
    *Failure to restore or update interrupt vector*
    *Failure to block or unblock interrupts*
    *Invalid restart after an interrupt*

PROGRAM STOPS
  Dead crash
  Syntax errors reported at run-time
  Waits for impossible condition, or combination of conditions
  Wrong user or process priority
LOOPS
  Infinite loop
  Wrong starting value for the loop control variable
  Accidental change of the loop control variable
  Wrong criterion for ending the loop
  Commands that do or don't belong inside the loop
  Improper loop nesting
IF, THEN, ELSE, OR MAYBE NOT
  Wrong inequalities (e.g., > instead of >=)
  Comparison sometimes yields wrong result
  Not equal versus equal when there are three cases
  Testing floating point values for equality
  Confusing inclusive and exclusive OR
  Incorrectly negating a logical expression
  Assignment-equal instead of test-equal
  Commands belong inside the THEN or ELSE clause
  Commands that don't belong inside either clause
  Failure to test a flag
  Failure to clear a flag
MULTIPLE CASES
  Missing default
  Wrong default
  Missing cases
  Case should be subdivided
  Overlapping cases
  Invalid or impossible cases
ERRORS IN HANDLING OR INTERPRETING DATA
  PROBLEMS WHEN PASSING DATA BETWEEN ROUTINES
    Parameter list variables out of order or missing
    Data type errors
    Aliases and shifting interpretations of the same area of memory
    Misunderstood data values
    Inadequate error information
    Failure to clean up data on exception-handling exit
    Outdated copies of data
    Related variables get out of synch
    Local setting of global data
    Global use of local variables
    Wrong mask in bit field
    Wrong value from a table

**APPENDIX**

DATA BOUNDARIES
  Unterminated null terminated strings
  Early end of string
  Read/write past end of a data structure, or an element in it
READ OUTSIDE THE LIMITS OF A MESSAGE BUFFER
  Compiler padding to word boundaries
  Value stack under/overflow
  Trampling another process' code or data
MESSAGING PROBLEMS
  Messages sent to wrong process or port
  Failure to validate an incoming message
  Lost or out of synch messages
  Message sent to only N of N+1 processes
DATA STORAGE CORRUPTION
  Overwritten changes
  Data entry not saved
  Too much data for receiving process to handle
  Overwriting a file after an error exit or user abort
RACE CONDITIONS
  RACES IN UPDATING DATA
  ASSUMPTION THAT ONE EVENT OR TASK HAS FINISHED BEFORE ANOTHER BEGINS
  ASSUMPTION THAT INPUT WON'T OCCUR DURING A BRIEF PROCESSING INTERVAL
  ASSUMPTION THAT INTERRUPTS WON'T OCCUR DURING A BRIEF INTERVAL
  RESOURCE RACES: THE RESOURCE HAS JUST BECOME UNAVAILABLE
  ASSUMPTION THAT A PERSON, DEVICE, OR PROCESS WILL RESPOND QUICKLY
  OPTIONS OUT OF SYNCH DURING A DISPLAY CHANGE
  TASK STARTS BEFORE ITS PREREQUISITES ARE MET
  MESSAGES CROSS OR DON'T ARRIVE IN THE ORDER SENT
LOAD CONDITIONS
  REQUIRED RESOURCE NOT AVAILABLE
  DOESN'T RETURN A RESOURCE
    Doesn't indicate that it's done with a device
    Doesn't erase old files from mass storage
    Doesn't return unused memory
    Wastes computer time
  NO AVAILABLE LARGE MEMORY AREAS
  INPUT BUFFER OR QUEUE NOT DEEP ENOUGH
  DOESN'T CLEAR ITEMS FROM QUEUE, BUFFER, OR STACK
  LOST MESSAGES

PERFORMANCE COSTS
RACE CONDITION WINDOWS EXPAND
DOESN'T ABBREVIATE UNDER LOAD
DOESN'T RECOGNIZE THAT ANOTHER PROCESS ABBREVIATES OUTPUT UNDER LOAD
LOW PRIORITY TASKS NOT PUT OFF
LOW PRIORITY TASKS NEVER DONE

## HARDWARE
WRONG DEVICE
WRONG DEVICE ADDRESS
DEVICE UNAVAILABLE
DEVICE RETURNED TO WRONG TYPE OF POOL
DEVICE USE FORBIDDEN TO CALLER
SPECIFIES WRONG PRIVILEGE LEVEL FOR A DEVICE
NOISY CHANNEL
CHANNEL GOES DOWN
TIME-OUT PROBLEMS
WRONG STORAGE DEVICE
DOESN'T CHECK DIRECTORY OF CURRENT DISK
DOESN'T CLOSE A FILE
UNEXPECTED END OF FILE
DISK SECTOR BUGS AND OTHER LENGTH-DEPENDENT ERRORS
WRONG OPERATION OR INSTRUCTION CODES
MISUNDERSTOOD STATUS OR RETURN CODE
DEVICE PROTOCOL ERROR
UNDERUTILIZES DEVICE INTELLIGENCE
PAGING MECHANISM IGNORED OR MISUNDERSTOOD
IGNORES CHANNEL THROUGHPUT LIMITS
ASSUMES DEVICE IS OR ISN'T, OR SHOULD BE OR SHOULDN'T BE INITIALIZED
ASSUMES PROGRAMMABLE FUNCTION KEYS ARE PROGRAMMED CORRECTLY

## SOURCE, VERSION, AND ID CONTROL
OLD BUGS MYSTERIOUSLY REAPPEAR
FAILURE TO UPDATE MULTIPLE COPIES OF DATA OR PROGRAM FILES
NO TITLE
NO VERSION ID
WRONG VERSION NUMBER ON THE TITLE SCREEN
NO COPYRIGHT MESSAGE OR A BAD ONE
ARCHIVED SOURCE DOESN'T COMPILE INTO A MATCH FOR SHIPPING CODE
MANUFACTURED DISKS DON'T WORK OR CONTAIN WRONG CODE OR DATA

## TESTING ERRORS
MISSING BUGS IN THE PROGRAM
   Failure to notice a problem
   Misreading the screen
   Failure to report a problem
   Failure to execute a planned test
   Failure to use the most "promising" test cases

**A**

APPENDIX

**TESTING ERRORS**
  Missing bugs in the program
    Ignoring programmers' suggestions

Ignoring programmers' suggestions
Finding "bugs" that aren't in the program
  Errors in testing programs
  Corrupted data file
  Misinterpreted specifications or documentation
Poor reporting
  Illegible reports
  Failure to make it clear how to reproduce the problem
  Failure to say that you can't reproduce a problem
  Failure to check your report
  Failure to report timing dependencies
  Failure to simplify conditions
  Concentration on trivia
  Abusive language
Poor tracking or follow-up
  Failure to provide summary reports
  Failure to re-report serious bugs
  Failure to verify fixes
  Failure to check for unresolved problems just before release

# USER INTERFACE ERRORS

The *user interface* (UI) includes all aspects of the product that involve the user. The UI designer tries to strike a balance between

- functionality
- time to learn how to use the program
- how well the user remembers how to use the program
- speed of performance
- rate of user errors
- the user's satisfaction with the program

In seeking a good balance, the designer weighs the experience and needs of the people she expects to use the program against the capabilities of the equipment and available software technology. An error in the UI results in a suboptimal match between the user and the program.

Because tradeoffs are unavoidable in UI design, a good designer might deliberately make any of many of the "errors" listed below. Don't take this list as gospel. If you are at all unsure, listen to the designer's reasoning before condemning one of her choices. See Baecker & Buxton (1987), Helander (1991), Laurel (1990, 1991), Rubenstein & Hersh, (1984), Schneiderman (1987), and Smith and Mosier (1984) for excellent introductions to user interface design, including extended discussion of many of the issues raised in this Appendix.

Throughout this Appendix we write as if you were the user of the program. As a tester of it, you will certainly use it heavily. Realize that other people will also use the program and they will have different problems from you. Try to be empathetic.

## FUNCTIONALITY

A program has a *functionality error* if something that you reasonably expect it to do is hard, awkward, confusing, or impossible.

### Excessive functionality

This is an error (see Brooks, 1975). It is the hardest one to convince people not to make. Systems that try to do too much are hard to learn and easy to forget how to use. They lack conceptual unity. They require too much documentation, too many help screens, and too much information per topic. Performance is poor. User errors are likely but the error messages are too general. Here's our rule of thumb: A system's level of functionality is out of control if the presence of rarely used features significantly complicates the use of basic features.

### Inflated impression of functionality

Manuals and marketing literature should never lead you to believe the program can do more than it can.

### Inadequacy for the task at hand

Because a key feature isn't there, is too restricted or too slow, you can't use the program for real work. For example, a database management system that takes 8 hours to sort 1000 records can claim sorting ability but you wouldn't want to use it.

### Missing function

A function was not implemented even though it was in the external specification or is "obviously" desirable.

## Wrong function

A function that should do one thing (perhaps defined in a specification) does something else.

## Functionality must be created by the user

"Systems that supply all the capabilities the user could want but that also require the user to assemble them to make the product work are kits, not finished products." (Rubenstein & Hersh, 1984, p. 45.)

## Doesn't do what the user expects

For example, few people would expect a program written to sort a list of names to sort them in ASCII order. They wouldn't expect it to count leading blanks or distinguish between uppercase and lowercase letters. If the programmers insist that the function should work this way, get them to change its name or add the expected behavior as an option.

## COMMUNICATION

This section describes errors that occur in communication from the program to the user. Our model is an interactive program, with the person sitting at a computer or terminal. However, batch programs also give information, such as error messages.

## Missing information

Anything you must know should be available onscreen. Onscreen access to any other information that the average user would find useful is also desirable.

### No onscreen instructions

How do you find out the name of the program, how to exit it, and what key(s) to press for Help? If it uses a command language, how do you find the list of commands? The program might display this information only when it starts. However it does it, you should not have to look in a manual to find the answers to questions like these.

### Assuming printed documentation is readily available

Can you use the program after losing your manual? An experienced user should not have to rely on printed documentation.

### Undocumented features

If most features or commands are documented onscreen, all should be. Skipping only a few causes much confusion. Similarly, if the program describes "special case" behavior for many commands, it should document them all.

### States that appear impossible to exit

How do you cancel a command or back up in a deep menu tree? Programs should allow you to escape from undesired states. Failure to tell you how to escape is almost as bad as not providing an escape path.

### No cursor

People rely on the cursor. It points to the place on the screen where they should focus attention. It can also show that the computer is still active and "listening." Every interactive program should show the cursor and display a salient message when turning the cursor off.

### Failure to acknowledge input

An interactive program should acknowledge every keystroke by echoing it immediately on the screen. A few exceptions are not errors:

- When choosing a menu item, you are not confused if your keystroke is not echoed, as long as the next screen appears immediately and the words in the screen's title are identical to those of the menu choice.
- If the program ignores erroneous commands or keystrokes, it should not echo them.
- The program should honor your choice if you can tell it not to echo input.
- When you input your password or security code, the program should not echo it on the screen.

### Failure to show activity during long delays

When a program is doing a long task (two seconds), it must show you that it's still working, it's not in an infinite loop, and you don't have to reset the computer.

### Failure to advise when a change will take effect

A program may execute a command much sooner or later than you expect. For example, it may continue to display erased data until you exit. If it's unclear when the program will do something, customers will perceive it as having bugs and will make many errors.

### Failure to check for the same document being opened more than once

Program that allows user to open multiple documents must check for the same document being opened more than once. Otherwise, the user will not be able to keep track of the changes made to the documents since they all have the same name. For example, the file My_Doc is open, if the user attempts to open My_Doc again, there must be the way for users to identify the first My_Doc versus the second one. A typical method for keeping track is to append a number after the file name such as My_Doc:1 and My_Doc:2 for the first and second file respectively. An alternative method is not to allow the same file to be opened twice.

## Wrong, misleading, or confusing information

Every error trains you to mistrust everything else displayed by the program. Subtle errors that lead readers to make false generalizations, such as missing qualifications and bad analogies, annoy testers more than clear factual errors because it's harder to get them fixed.

### Simple factual errors

After a program changes, updating screen displays is a low priority task. The result is that much onscreen information becomes obsolete. Whenever the program changes visibly, check every message that might say anything about that aspect of the program.

### Spelling errors

Programers dont woory much abuot they're speling misteaks but customers do. Get them fixed.

### Inaccurate simplifications

In the desire to keep a feature description as simple as possible, the author of a message may cover only the simplest aspects of the feature's behavior, omitting important qualifications. When she tries to eliminate jargon, she may paraphrase technical terminology inaccurately. Look for these errors. As the tester, you may be the only technically knowledgeable person who carefully reviews the screens.

### Invalid metaphors

Metaphors make the computer system seem similar to something you already know. They are good if they help you predict the behavior of the computer and bad if they lead you to incorrect predictions. For example, the trash can icon can be a bad metaphor (Heckel, 1984). If you can take a discarded file out of the trash can, the metaphor is correct. If the file is gone forever once moved to trash, a paper shredder is a better icon.

### Confusing feature names

A command named SAVE shouldn't erase a file; nor should it sort one. If a command name has a standard meaning, in the computer community or in the English language, the command must be compatible with its name.

### More than one name for the same feature

The program shouldn't refer to the same feature by different names. Customers will waste much time trying to figure out the difference between shadow and drop shadow when the programmer uses both to mean the same thing.

### Information overload

Some documents and help screens swamp you with technical detail, to the point of hiding the information or confusing the answers you're looking for. If you think these details are useful, ask whether they are more appropriately located in an appendix in the manual.

Some (not all) detailed discussions of program functioning are disguised apologies from the programmer or complaints from a writer over a poor design. Do users need this information? Also, is there a solution to the problem the programmer is claiming to be insoluble?

### When are data saved?

Suppose you enter information that the program will save. Does it save data as you type, when you exit, when you ask for a save, every few minutes, when? You should always be able to find this out. If you get confused answers, look for bugs immediately. Two modules probably make different assumptions about when the same data will be saved. You can probably get one of them to claim that outdated data are up to date. You may find one module erasing or overwriting data that another has just saved.

### Poor external modularity

External modularity refers to how modular the product appears from the outside. How easily can you understand any one piece of it? Poor external modularity increases learning time and scares away new users. Information should be presented as independently as possible. The less you need to know in order to do any particular task the better.

## Help text and error messages

Help text and error messages are often considered minor pieces of the product. They may be written by junior programmers or writers. Updating them may be given low priority.

You ask for help or run into error handlers when confused or in trouble. You may be upset or impatient. You will not suffer bad messages gladly. The product will build credibility with you as you use it. If some messages mislead you, the rest may as well not be there.

### Inappropriate reading level

People don't read as well at computer terminals (see Schneiderman, 1987). When given their choice of reading levels for onscreen tutorials, experimental subjects preferred Grade 5 (Roehmer and Chapanis, 1982). People reading help or error messages may be distressed: these messages should never be more complicated than tutorial text. Messages should be phrased simply, in short, active voice sentences, using few technical terms even if the readers are computer-experienced.

### Verbosity

Messages must be short and simple. Harried readers are infuriated by chatty technobabble. When some users need much more information than others, it's common to give access to further information by a menu. Let people choose where and how much further they want to investigate (Houghton, 1984).

### Inappropriate emotional tone

People feel bad enough when they make an error or have to ask for help. They don't need their noses rubbed in it. Look for messages that might make some people feel bad.

Exclamation marks can be interpreted as scolding, so they should not be in error messages. Violent words like "abort," "crash," and "kill" may be frightening or distasteful. Even the word "error" is suspect: many "errors" wouldn't be if the program (or the programmer) were more intelligent. As a final note, many actions may be invalid or unexpected at a computer, but few are truly "illegal."

### Factual errors

Help and error messages often give incorrect examples of how to do something "correctly." Some are outdated. Others were never right. Every message should be (re)checked in one of the last testing cycles.

### Context errors

Context-sensitive help and error handlers check what you've been doing. They base their messages (recommendations, menu lists, etc.) on that context. This is excellent when it works, but the message makes no sense when they get the context wrong.

### Failure to identify the source of an error

At a minimum, an error message should say what's wrong, and unless it's immediately obvious, repeat or point to the erroneous input (data, program line, whatever). A good error message will also say why something is wrong and what to do about it.

### Hex dumps are not error messages

An error message that merely says `Error 010` or dumps one or more lines of hexadecimal (octal, even decimal) data is acceptable only if the cost of printing a message is outrageous, the computer doesn't have enough time to print a real message before it crashes, or the programmer is the only person who will ever read it.

**USER INTERFACE ERRORS**
  FUNCTIONALITY
    **Help text and error messages**
      *Forbidding a resource without saying why*

### Forbidding a resource without saying why

If a program tries to use a printer, modem, more memory, or other resource, and can't, the error message should not only announce the failure but should also say why. You need this information because you'll respond differently to Printer already in use versus Printer not connected.

### Reporting non-errors

Error messages should only be triggered by error states. You will ignore all error messages if most are normal-case debug messages or reports of events that are rare but not necessarily due to a bug.

### Display bugs

Display bugs are visible. If you see many, you are less likely to buy or trust the program. Unfortunately, display bugs are often considered minor and not even investigated. This is risky. They may be symptoms of more serious underlying errors.

### Two cursors

It is a nuisance if the programmer forgets to erase the old cursor when he jumps to another part of the screen. Worse, a second cursor might reflect confusion in the code about which area of the screen is active. The program may misinterpret inputs even it echoes them correctly. If the cursor misbehaves during a test, save and examine any data that you enter.

### Disappearing cursor

The cursor usually disappears because the programmer displayed a character on top of it or moved it and forgot to redisplay it. However, a program's pointer to the cursor can be corrupted. If it is, then when it points to a memory location used for data or program storage rather than to screen memory, you won't see the cursor. The program will overwrite information in memory whenever it tries to display the cursor.

### Cursor displayed in the wrong place

The program shows the cursor in one place but echoes inputs, etc., in another. This is annoying because it leads you to focus on the wrong part of the screen. A slightly misplaced cursor may warn that the program will truncate entered character strings or pad them with garbage. As with dual cursors, entered text may be echoed correctly but saved incorrectly.

### Cursor moves out of data entry area

The cursor should never move out of data entry areas. This is usually a coding error but some programmers deliberately let you move the cursor anywhere on the screen, then beep and display an error message that says you can't enter anything here. This is a design error.

### Writing to the wrong screen segment

The cursor is in the right location, but data are displayed in the wrong place on the screen.

### Failure to clear part of the screen

A message is displayed for a few seconds, then only partially erased. Or your response to a previous question is left onscreen. It is confusing and annoying to have to type over prompts or irrelevant responses in order to enter something new.

### Failure to highlight part of the screen

If a program usually highlights a particular class of items, such as prompts or all text in the active window, it must always do so.

### Failure to clear highlighting

This is common when attributes of screen positions are stored separately from displayed text. The programmer removes highlighted text but forgets to clear highlighting from that area of the screen. The error is most confusing when the program highlights with double intensity or boldfacing (as opposed to inverse video, for example). The blank screen area looks fine. The problem only becomes evident when new text is displayed: it is always highlighted.

### Wrong or partial string displayed

The displayed message might be garbage text, a segment of a longer message, or a complete message that should appear some other time. Any of these might reflect errors in the program logic, the values of the pointers used to find message text, or the stored copies of the text. They might indicate minor problems or severe ones.

### Messages displayed for too long or not long enough

Many messages are displayed for a fixed time, then erased automatically. The message should be onscreen long enough to be noticed and then read. Unimportant messages can be cleared sooner than critical ones. Short messages can go sooner than long ones. Messages that come up frequently and are easily recognized can be displayed for less time than rare ones.

Be suspicious when the same message sometimes displays briefly and sometimes lasts longer. This may reflect unanticipated race conditions. Try to figure out how to obtain which delays, then get this looked into carefully by the programmer.

### Display layout

The screen should look organized. It should not be cluttered. Different classes of objects should be displayed separately, in predictable areas. There are many guidelines for display layout, but they boil down to this: it should be easy to find what you want on the screen.

### Poor aesthetics in the screen layout

The screen may be unbalanced, rows or columns may not be aligned, or it might just look "bad." Use your good taste. If you're not confident, get a second opinion. If it looks badly laid out to you, something is probably wrong even if you can't articulate the problem yet.

### Menu layout errors

Schneiderman (1987) and Smith and Mosier (1984) cover this area well. Their discussions run to many more pages than are available here. Here are a few points that we want to emphasize:

APPENDIX

- Similar or conceptually related menu choices should be grouped. Groups should be clearly separated.
- The action required to select a menu item should be obvious or should be stated onscreen.

- Menu selections should generally be independent. To achieve a single result, the customer shouldn't have to make two or more different selections on different menus.

- Selecting a menu item by typing its first letter is usually better than selecting it by a number. However, all items have to start with different letters for this to work well. Watch out for assignments of odd names to menu items.

### Dialog box layout errors

For further reference in this area, we recommend IBM's *SAA Advanced Interface Design Guide* (1989), and *SAA Basic Interface Design Guide* (1989), and Apple's *Human Interface Guidelines* (1987).

- Dialog boxes should operate consistently. For example, they should use consistent capitalization, spelling, and text justification rules.Dialog box titles should occupy a consistent place and match the name of the command used to call up the dialog. The same shortcut keys should work from dialog to dialog—<Escape> shouldn't cancel out of some dialogs (no changes made) but complete (all changes accepted) others.

- Controls in the dialog box must be arranged logically. Group related controls together, and separate groups by using proper spacing.

- Selection and entry fields should be aligned vertically and horizontally so users can navigate the cursor movement in a straight-line pattern.

- Watch out for interdependencies across dialogs. It is confusing when a selection in one dialog box determines which options are available in another box.

### Obscured instructions

You should always know where to look to find out what to do next. If the screen is at all crowded, an area should be reserved for commands and messages. Once you understand this convention, you'll know where to focus attention. It may also be good to blaze *critical* information across the center of the screen, no matter what used to be there.

### Misuse of flash

Flashing pictures or text are noticeable; lots of flashing is confusing and intimidating. You should be able to tell immediately why an object is flashing. Excessive or ambiguous flashing is an eyesore, not a good alert.

### Misuse of color

Too much color can be distracting, make the text harder to read, and increase eye strain. Color shouldn't make the screen look busy or distracting. Programs like word processors, spreadsheets, and databases should use highlighting colors sparingly. Most text should be one color. You should also complain if the program's combinations of colors looks ugly.

### Heavy reliance on color

Programs limit their audience severely if they use color as the only differentiator between items. What happens to a colorblind person or someone with a monochrome monitor? A few applications may not be worth running in monochrome, but many others (including drawing programs and many games) don't need color.

### Inconsistent with the style of the environment

If the style associated with a computer offers certain consistencies and conveniences, you'll notice their absence from any one program. Even if the programmer thinks he can replace them with "better" ones, many people will resent having to learn a new series of conventions. For example, if the operating system and most applications are mouse and icon-based, an application that requires typed command words will feel inappropriate. New programs should also follow the lead when most others display error messages in a certain way, on a certain place onscreen.

### Cannot get rid of onscreen information

It's great (often essential) to have a menu of command choices available on part of the screen. However, once you become proficient with the program, the menu is a waste of screen space. You should be able to issue a command to get rid of it, and another to call it back as needed.

## COMMAND STRUCTURE AND ENTRY

This section deals with the way the program organizes commands and presents them to you, and with how you enter those commands. Schneiderman (1987) considers how to choose among the different command entry styles. There are many choices. This section assumes that the programmer's choice of style was reasonable. It deals only with flaws in the implementation.

### Inconsistencies

Increasing the number of always-true rules shortens learning time and documentation and makes the program more professional-looking. Inconsistencies are so common because it takes planning and agony to choose a rule of operation that can always be followed. It is so tempting to do things differently now and again. Each minor inconsistency seems insignificant, but together they quickly make an otherwise well conceived product hard to use. It is good testing practice to flag all inconsistencies, no matter how minor.

### "Optimizations"

Programmers deliberately introduce inconsistencies to optimize a program. Optimizations are tempting since they tailor the program to your most likely present need. But each new inconsistency brings complexity with it. Make the programmer aware of the tradeoff in each case. Is saving a keystroke or two worth the increase in learning time or the decrease in trust? Usually not.

### Inconsistent syntax

Syntactic details should be easily learned. You should be able to stop thinking about them. Syntax of all commands should be consistent throughout the program. Syntax includes such things as:

- the order in which you specify source and destination locations (copy from source to destination or copy to destination from source)
- the type of separators used (spaces, commas, semicolons, slashes, etc.)
- the location of operators (infix (A+B), prefix (+AB), postfix (AB+)).

### Inconsistent command entry style

You can select a command by pointing to it, pressing a function key, or typing its name, abbreviation, or number. A program should use one command style. If the program offers alternative styles for doing the same task, it should offer the same alternatives everywhere. If the program must switch styles across different parts of the program, it must make it clear when to use which.

**A**

APPENDIX

### Inconsistent abbreviations

Without clear-cut abbreviation rules, abbreviations can't be easily remembered. Abbreviating `delete` to `del` but `list` to `ls` and `grep` to `grep` makes no sense. Each choice is fine individually, but the collection is an ill-conceived mess of special cases.

### Inconsistent termination rule

Fill-in-the-blanks forms only allow so much room for a command name or data item. Suppose an entry can be eight characters long. When you enter seven characters or less, you have to say you're done by pressing <ENTER> or some other terminator (<Space>, <Comma>, <Tab>, etc.). If you enter an eight-character name, some programs act on it without waiting for the terminator. This is confusing.

The program should require terminators for multi-key entries. People rarely remember commands (or data) in terms of how many letters they are. They will habitually enter the eighth character then press <ENTER>. If the program has already supplied its own <ENTER>, the extra one typed by the user is an annoying input "error."

### Inconsistent command options

If an option makes sense for two commands, it should be available with both (or neither), should have the same name, and should be invoked in the same sequence in both cases.

### Similarly named commands

It is easier to confuse two different commands if their names are similar.

### Inconsistent capitalization

If command entry is case sensitive, first letters of all commands should all be capitalized or none should be. First letters of embedded words in commands should always or never be capitalized.

### Inconsistent menu position

It's hard to keep the same command in the same position on different menus if it occurs in many submenus, but with work and care the programmer can frequently achieve this.

### Inconsistent function key usage

The meaning of function keys should remain constant across the program. Reversals (sometimes <F1> saves data and <F2> deletes, other times <F1> deletes and <F2> saves) are unacceptable.

### Inconsistent error handling rules

When the program detects an error, it may announce it or attempt to correct it. After handling the error, the program may stop, restart, or return to its last state. The error handler may change data on disk or save new information. Error handlers can vary a great deal. The behavior of any one program's should be completely predictable.

### Inconsistent editing rules

The same keys and commands should be available to change any datum as you entered it or examined it later.

### Inconsistent data saving rules

The program should save data in the same way everywhere, with the same timing and scope. It shouldn't sometimes save data as each field is entered, but other times save at the end of a record, a group of records, or just before exit.

### Time-wasters

Programs that seem designed to waste your time infuriate people.

### Garden paths

A program leads you down the garden path if you must make choice after choice to get to a desired command, only finding at the end that it's not there, wasn't implemented, or can't be used unless you do something else (down a different path) first. Look for these problems in complex menu trees.

### Choices that can't be taken

There is no excuse for including choices in a menu that cannot be made. How can you view, save or erase the data if there are no data? How can you print the document if there is no printer? How dare the programmer say, `Press <Alt-F1> for Help,` then when you press it say, `Sorry, Help Not Available at this Level` (whatever that means)?

### Are you really, really sure?

Programs should ask you to confirm critically destructive commands. You should have to tell the computer twice to reformat a data-filled disk. The program should not pester you for confirmation of every little deletion. You become annoyed; you'll learn to answer Yes automatically, even in the critical cases when you should think first.

### Obscurely or idiosyncratically named commands

Command names should be informative. You should not have to constantly look up the definition of a command name in the manual, until you eventually memorize it. There is no excuse for names like `grep`, `finger`, and `timehog` in products released to the public.

### Menus

Menus should be simple, but they become complex when there are poor icons or command names and when choices hide under nonobvious topic headings. The more commands a menu covers, the more complex it will be no matter how well planned it is. But without planning, complex menus can become disasters.

### Excessively complex menu hierarchy

**APPENDIX**

If you have to wade through menu after menu before finally reaching the command you want, you'll probably want to use another program. Programmers who create deep menu trees cite the design rule that says no menu should have more than seven choices. This may be best for novices. Experienced users prefer many more choices per menu level, make fewer errors and respond more quickly, so long as the choices are well organized, neatly formatted, and not ridiculously crowded or abbreviated. Paap & Roske-Hostrand (1986) and MacGregor, Lee, & Lam (1986) provide some interesting discussion.

### *Inadequate menu navigation options*

In even a modestly deep menu structure, you must be able to move back to the previous menu, move to the top of the menu structure, and leave the program at any time. If there are hundreds of topics, you should also be able to jump directly to any topic by entering its name or number.

### *Too many paths to the same place*

The program needs reorganization if many commands reappear in many menus. It can be handy to have a command repeated in different places, but there are limits. You should worry about the program's internal structure and reliability if it feels like you can get anywhere from anywhere.

### *You can't get there from here*

Some programs lock you out of one set of commands once you've taken a different path. You have to restart to regain access to them. This is usually unnecessary.

### *Related commands relegated to unrelated menus*

Grouping commands or topics in a complex menu is not easy. It is easy to overlook what should be an obvious relationship between two items, and to arbitrarily assign them to separate menus. When you report these, explain the relationship between the two items, and suggest which menu both belong in.

### *Unrelated commands tossed under the same menu*

Some commands are dumped under a totally unrelated heading because someone thought it would take too much work to put them where they belong, which may involve adding a new higher level heading and reorganizing.

### Command lines

It is harder to type the command name without a hint than to recognize it in a menu, but experienced users prefer command line entry when there are many commands and many options. The menu system feels too bulky to them. Anything that makes it easier to remember the command names and options correctly is good. Anything that makes errors more likely is bad.

### *Forced distinction between uppercase and lowercase*

Some programs won't recognize a correctly spelled command name if it isn't capitalized "correctly." This is more often a nuisance than a feature.

### *Reversed parameters*

The most common example is the distinction between source and destination files. Does COPY FILE1 FILE2 mean copy from FILE1 to FILE2 or from FILE2 to FILE1? The order doesn't matter (people can get used to anything) as long as it stays consistent across all commands that use a source and a destination file. Application programs must follow the operating system's ordering conventions.

### Full command names not allowed

Abbreviations are fine, but you should always be able to type `delete`, not just `del`. The full name of a command is much more reliably remembered than the abbreviation, especially if there are no consistent abbreviating rules.

### Abbreviations not allowed

You should be able to enter `del` instead of having to type `delete` in full. Enough systems don't allow abbreviations that we can't class their absence a design error, but, implemented properly, it sure is a nice feature.

### Demands complex input on one line

Some programs require complicated command specifications (Do X for all cases in which A or B and C is true unless D is false). You will make many mistakes if you have to specify compound logical operators as part of a one-line command. Fill-in-the-blank choices, sequential prompting, and query by example, are all more appropriate than command line entry with compound logical scope definition.

### No batch input

You should be able to type and correct a list of commands using an editor, then tell the computer to treat this list as if you had typed each command freshly at the keyboard.

### Can't edit commands

You should be able to backspace while typing a command. If you try to execute an incorrectly typed command, you should be able to call it back, change the erroneous piece, and re-execute it.

### Inappropriate use of the keyboard

If a computer comes with a standard keyboard, with labeled function keys that have standard meanings, new programs should meet that standard.

### Failure to use cursor, edit, or function keys

It doesn't matter if a program was ported from some other machine that doesn't have these keys. Users of this machine will expect their keys to work.

### Non-standard use of cursor and edit keys

The keys should work the way they usually work on this machine, not the way they usually work on some other machine, and definitely not in some totally new way.

### Non-standard use of function keys

If most other programs use <F1> as the Help key, defining it as Delete-File-And-Exit in this program is crazy or vicious.

### Failure to filter invalid keys

The program should trap and discard invalid characters, such as letters if it adds numbers. It should not echo or acknowledge them. Ignoring them is less distracting than error messages.

### Failure to indicate keyboard state changes

Lights on the keyboard or messages on the screen should tell you when `Caps Lock` and other such state changing features are on.

**APPENDIX**

USER INTERFACE ERRORS
COMMAND STRUCTURE AND ENTRY
Inappropriate use of the keyboard
Failure to scan for function or control keys

### Failure to scan for function or control keys

You should be able to tell the computer to quit what it's doing (<Ctrl-C>, for example). The program should also always recognize any other system-specific keys, such as <PrintScreen>, that programs on this machine usually recognize quickly.

## MISSING COMMANDS

This section discusses commands or features that some programs don't, but should, include.

### State transitions

Most programs move from state to state. The program is in one state before you choose a menu item or issue a command. It moves into another state in response to your choice. Programmers usually test their code well enough to confirm that you can reach any state that you should be able to reach. They don't always let you change your mind, once you've chosen a state.

### Can't do nothing and leave

You should be able to tell an interactive program that you made your last choice by mistake, and go back to its previous state.

### Can't quit mid-program

You should be able to quit while using a program without adversely affecting stored data. You should be able to stop editing or sorting a file, and revert to the version that was on disk when you started.

### Can't stop mid-command

It should be easy to tell the program to stop executing a command. It shouldn't be hard to return to your starting point, to make a correction or choose a different command.

### Can't pause

Some programs limit the time you have to enter data. When the time is up, the program changes state. It might display help text or accept a displayed "default" value, or it may log you off. Although time limits can be useful, people do get interrupted. You should be able to tell it that you are taking a break, and when you get back you'll want it in the same state it's in now.

### Disaster prevention

System failures and user errors happen. Programs should minimize the consequences of them.

### No backup facility

It should be easy to make an extra copy of a file. If you're changing a file, the computer should keep a copy of the original (or make it easy for you to tell it to keep it) so you have a known good version to return to if your changes go awry.

### No undo

*Undo* lets you retract a command, typically any command, or a group of them. *Undelete* is a restricted case of undo that lets you recover data deleted in error. Undo is desirable. Undelete is essential.

### No "Are you sure?"

If you issue a command that will wipe out a lot of work, or that wipes out less but is easy to issue in error, the program should stop you and ask whether you want the command executed.

### No incremental saves

When entering large amounts of text or data, you should be able to tell the program to save your work at regular intervals. This ensures that most of your work will have been saved if the power fails. Several programs automatically save your work in progress at regular intervals. This is an excellent feature, so long as the customer who is bothered by the delay during saving can turn it off.

## Error handling by the user

People can catch their own errors and recognize from experience that they are prone to others. They should be able to fix their work and, as much as possible, build in their own error checks.

### No user-specifiable filters

When designing data entry forms, spreadsheet templates, etc., you should be able to specify, for each field, what types of data are valid and what the program should ignore or reject. As examples, you might have the program reject anything that isn't a digit, a letter, a number within a certain range, a valid date, or an entry that matches an item in a list stored on disk.

### Awkward error correction

It should be easy to fix a mistake. You should never have to stop and restart a program just to return to a data entry screen where you made an error. You should always be able to back up the cursor to a field on the same screen in which you entered, or could have entered, data. When entering a list of numbers, you should be able to correct one without redoing the rest.

### Can't include comments

When designing data entry forms, spreadsheet templates, expert systems—anything in which you are, in effect, writing a program—you should be able to enter notes for future reference and debugging.

### Can't display relationships between variables

Variables in entry forms, spreadsheet templates, etc., are related. It should be easy to examine the dependence of any variable on the values of others.

## Miscellaneous nuisances

### Inadequate privacy or security

How much security is needed for a program or its data varies with the application and the market. On multi-user systems you should be able to hide your files so no one else can see them, and encrypt them so no one else—not even the system administrator—can read them. You should also be able to lock files so no one else can change (or delete) them. Beizer (1984) discusses security in more detail.

**APPENDIX**

### Obsession with security

The security controls of a program should be as unobtrusive as possible. If you are working at your own personal computer at home, you should be able to stop a program from pestering you for passwords.

### Can't hide menus

Many programs display a menu at the top, bottom, or side of the screen. They use the rest of the screen for data entry and manipulation. The menus are memory aids. Once you know all the commands you need, you should be able to remove the menus and use the full screen for entry and editing.

### Doesn't support standard O/S features

For example, if the operating system uses subdirectories, program commands should be able to reference files in other subdirectories. If the O/S defines "wildcard" characters (such as * to match any group of characters), the program should recognize them.

### Doesn't allow long names

Years ago, when memory was scarce and compilers were sluggish, it was necessary to limit the length of file and variable names to six or eight characters. We're past those days. Meaningful names are among the best possible forms of documentation. They should be allowed.

## PROGRAM RIGIDITY

Some programs are very flexible. You can change minor aspects of their functioning easily. You can do tasks in any order you want. Other programs are utterly inflexible. Rigidity isn't always bad. The fewer choices and the more structured the task, the more easily (usually) you'll learn the program. And you won't be confused by aspects of a program's operation that can't be changed without affecting the others. On the other hand, different people will like different aspects of the program and dislike others. If you change these to suit your taste, you'll like the program more.

### User tailorability

You should be able to change minor and arbitrary aspects of the program's user interface with a minimum of fuss and bother.

### Can't turn off the noise

Many programs beep when you make errors and provide a loud key click that sounds every time you touch the keyboard. Auditory feedback is useful but in shared work areas, computer noises can be annoying. There must be a way to turn them off.

### Can't turn off case sensitivity

A system that can distinguish between uppercase and lowercase should allow you to tell it to ignore cases.

### Can't tailor to hardware at hand

Some programs are locked to input/output devices that have specific, limited capabilities. People who upgrade their equipment either can't use these programs or can't take advantage of the new devices' features. Experienced users should be able to tailor a program to the hardware. You should be able to change control codes sent to a printer and copy a program onto any mass storage device. It should not be impossible to use a mouse with any interactive program.

### Can't change device initialization

An application program should either be able to send user-defined initializers or it should leave well enough alone. Suppose you want to send control codes to a printer to switch to condensed characters. If the program that prints the data doesn't let you initialize the printer, you have to change the printer mode from the device, then run the program. Some programs, however, defeat your printer setup by always sending the printer their own, inflexible, set of control codes. This is a design error.

### Can't turn off automatic saves

Some programs protect you against power failures by automatically saving entered data to disk periodically. In principle this is great but in practice the pauses while it saves the data can be disruptive. Also, the program assumes that you always want to save your data. This assumption might not be true. You should be able to turn this off.

### Can't slow down (speed up) scrolling

You should be able to slow down the screen display rate so you can read text as it scrolls by.

### Can't do what you did last time

### Can't find out what you did last time

You should be able to re-issue a command, examine it, or edit it.

### Failure to execute a customization command

If the program lets you change how it interacts with you, your changes should take effect immediately. If a restart is unavoidable, the program should say so. You should not have to wonder why a command wasn't executed.

### Failure to save customization commands

You should not only be able to tell the computer to turn off its beeps and clicks now, but should also be able to tell it to turn them off and keep them off forever.

### Side-effects of feature changes

Changing how one feature operates should not affect another. When there are side effects, they should be well documented when you change the feature setting, in the manual and onscreen.

### Infinite tailorability

You can change virtually all aspects of some programs. This flexibility can be good, but you have to step back from the program to figure out how it should work. To make the decisions intelligently you have to develop an expert user's view of the program itself along with learning the command language.

**APPENDIX**

Programs this flexible usually have horrid user interfaces. The developers spent their energy making the program adjustable, and didn't bother making the uncustomized product any good. Since everyone will change it, they reason, its initial command set doesn't mean anything anyway. Such a program is terrible for novices and occasional users. It isn't worth their time (sometimes weeks or months) to figure out how to tune the program to their needs, but without the tuning, the program is only marginally usable.

The user interface of customizable products should be fully usable without modification. You should subject it to the same rigorous criticism applied to less flexible ones. Many people will use the uncustomized version for a long time.

### Who's in control

Some programs are high-handed. Their error and help messages are condescending. Their style is unforgiving—you can't abort commands or change data after entering them. None of this is acceptable. Programs should make it easier and more pleasant for you to get a task done as quickly as possible. They should not second-guess you, force a style on you, or waste your time.

### *Unnecessary imposition of a conceptual style*

Some programs demand that you enter data in a certain order, that you complete each task before moving to the next, that you make decisions before looking at their potential consequences. Examples:

- When designing a data entry form, why must you specify a field's name, type, width, or calculation order, before drawing it onscreen? As you see how the different fields look together, won't you change some fields, move them around, even get rid of a few? You may have to enter field specifications before using the form, but subject to that restriction, you should decide when to fill in the details.

- When describing tasks to a project management system, why must you list all tasks first, all available people second, then completely map the work assigned to one individual before entering any data for the next? Since you're probably trying to figure out what to assign to whom, won't you want to change these data as you see their consequences?

A surprising number of limits exist because some programmer decided that people should organize their work in a certain way. For "their own good" he won't let them deviate from this "optimal" approach. He is typically wrong.

### *Novice-friendly, experienced-hostile*

Programs optimized for novices break tasks into many small, easily understood steps. This can be good for the newcomer, but anyone experienced with the system will be frustrated if they can't get around it.

### *Artificial intelligence and automated stupidity*

In the names of "artificial intelligence" and "convenience" some programs guess what you want next and execute those guesses as if they were user-issued commands. This is fine unless you don't want them done. Similarly, the program that automatically corrects errors is great until it "corrects" correct data. People make enough of their own mistakes without having to put up with ones made by a program that's trying to second-guess them.

Better than automatic execution, especially of something that takes noticeable time or changes data, the program should give you a choice. You should be able to set it to wait until you type Y (yes) before executing its suggestions. If you say No the program should abandon its suggestion and ask for new input.

### Superfluous or redundant information required

Some programs ask for information they'll never use, or that they'll only use to display onscreen once, or ask you to re-enter data you've already entered—not to check it against the old copy, just to get it again. This is a surprisingly common waste of time.

### Unnecessary repetition of steps

Some programs make you re-enter the works if you make one mistake in a long sequence of command steps or data. Others force you to re-enter or confirm any command that might be in error. To do something "unusual" you may have to confirm every step. Repetitions or confirmations that are not essential are a waste of your time.

### Unnecessary limits

Why restrict a database to so many fields or records, a spreadsheet cell to digits only, a project manager to so many tasks, a word processor to so many characters? Limits that aren't essential for performance or reliability shouldn't be limits.

## PERFORMANCE

Many experienced users consider performance the most important aspect of usability: with a fast program, they feel more able to concentrate and more in control. Errors are less important because they can be dealt with quickly. With few exceptions, reviewed by Schneiderman (1987), the faster the better.

Performance has different definitions, such as:

- *Program Speed:* how quickly the program does standard tasks. For example, how quickly does a word processor move to the end of the file?
- *User Throughput:* how quickly you can do standard tasks with the program. These are larger scale tasks. For example, how long does it take to enter and print a letter?
- *Perceived Performance:* How quick does the program *seem* to you?

Program speed is a big factor no matter how you define performance, but a fast program with a poorly designed user interface will seem much slower than it should.

### Slow program

Many design and code errors can slow a program. The program might do unnecessary work, such as initializing an area of memory that will be overwritten before being read. It might repeat work unnecessarily, such as doing something inside a loop that could be done outside of it. Design decisions also slow the program, often more than the obvious errors.

Whatever the reason for the program being slow, if it is, it's a problem. Delays as short as a quarter of a second can break your concentration, and substantially increase your time to finish a task.

### Slow echoing

The program should display inputs immediately. If you notice a lag between the time you type a letter and the time you see it, the program is too slow. You will be much more likely to make mistakes. Fast feedback is essential for any input event, including moving mice, trackballs, and light pens.

### How to reduce user throughput

A lightning quick program will be molasses for getting things done if it slows the person working with it. This includes:

- anything that makes user errors more likely.
- slow error recovery, such as making you re-enter everything if you make a mistake when entering a long series of numbers or a complicated command.
- anything that gets you so confused that you have to ask for help or look in the manual.
- making you type too much to do too little: no abbreviations, breaking a task into tiny subtasks, requiring confirmation of everything, and so on.

Other sections of the Appendix describe specific errors along these lines. One tactic for applying pressure to fix user interface errors involves a comparative test of user throughput. Compare the product under development with a few competitors. If people take longer to do things with your program, and if much of the delay can be attributed to user interface design errors, these errors take on a new significance.

### Poor responsiveness

A responsive program doesn't force you to wait before issuing your next command. It constantly scans for keyboard (or other) input, acknowledges commands quickly, and assigns them high priority. For example, type a few lines of text while your word processor is reformatting the screen. It should stop formatting, echo the input, format the display of these lines as you enter them, and execute your editing commands. It should keep the area of the screen near the cursor up to date. The rest is lower priority since you aren't working with it at this instant. The program can update the rest of the display when you stop typing. Responsive programs *feel* faster.

### No type-ahead

A program that allows type-ahead lets you keep typing while it goes about other business. It remembers what you typed and displays and executes it later. You should not have to wait to enter the next command.

### No warning that an operation will take a long time

The program should tell you if it needs more than a few seconds to do something. You should be able to cancel the command. For long jobs, it should tell you how long so you can use the time rather than waste it waiting.

### No progress reports

For long tasks or delays, it is very desirable to indicate how much has been done and how much longer the machine will be tied up (Myers, 1985).

### Problems with time-outs

Some programs limit the time you have to enter data. When the time's up, the program changes state. Except for arcade games, you should not have to race against a short time-out to stop the program from executing an undesired command.

Time-outs can also be too long. For example, you might have a short interval before a program does something reasonable but time consuming. If you respond during the interval, you shortcut the task (e.g., a menu isn't displayed unnecessarily). Program speed will suffer if this isn't kept short.

Time-out intervals can simultaneously be too long for people who wait them out and too short for others who try to enter data during them.

## Program pesters you

```
BEEP! Are you sure?
BEEP! Your disk is now 85% full. Please swap disks shortly.
BEEP! Are you really sure?
BEEP! You haven't saved your text for the last hour.
BEEP! Your disk is now 86% full. Please swap disks shortly.
BEEP! Please re-enter your security code.
BEEP! You haven't entered anything for 10 minutes. Please log off.
BEEP! Your disk is now 86% full. Please swap disks shortly.
BEEP! 14 messages still unanswered.
```

Reminders, alerts, and queries can be useful but if they are frequent they can be annoying.

## Do you really want help and graphics at 300 baud?

On a slow terminal, help text, long menus, and pretty pictures are usually irritating. You should be able to use a terse command language instead. Similarly, programs that format output in a beautiful but time-consuming way on a printer should have a "fast and ugly" mode for drafts.

## OUTPUT

Program output should be as complete as desired and intelligible to the human or program that must read it. It should include whatever you want, in whatever format you want. It should go to whatever device you want it to go. These requirements are real, but too general to (usually) achieve. You'll probably add many other annoyances and limitations to the following list.

### Can't output certain data

You should be able to print any information you enter, including technical entries like formulas in spreadsheets and field definitions. If it's important enough to enter, it's important enough for you to be able to print and desk check it.

### Can't redirect output

You should be able to redirect output. In particular, you should be able to send a long "printout" to the disk and print this disk file later. This gives you the opportunity to polish the output file with a word processor or print it with a program that can print files more quickly or as a background task.

The program should not stop you from sending output to unexpected devices, such as plotters, laser printers, and cassette tapes.

### Format incompatible with a follow-up process

If one program is supposed to be able to save data in a format that a second can understand, you must test that it does. This means buying or borrowing a copy of the second program, saving the data with the first, reading it with the second, and looking at what the second program tells you it got. This test is all too often forgotten, especially when the second program was not made by the company that developed the first.

**APPENDIX**

### Must output too little or too much

You should be able to modify reports to present only the information you need. Having to dig through pages of printouts that contain just a few lines of useful information is nearly as bad as not getting the information.

### Can't control output layout

You should be able to emphasize information by changing fonts, boldfacing, underlining, etc. You should also be able to control the spacing of information; that is, you should be able to group some sections of information and keep others separate. At a minimum, the program should be able to print reports to a disk file, in a format suitable for touchups by a word processor.

### Absurd printed level of precision

It is silly to say that $4.2 + 3.9$ is $8.100000$ or that the product of $4.234$ and $3.987$ is $16.880958$. In final printouts, the program should round results to the precision of the original data, unless you tell it to do otherwise.

### Can't control labeling of tables or figures

You should be able to change the typeface, wording, and position of any caption, heading, or other text included in a table, graph or chart.

### Can't control scaling of graphs

Graphing programs should provide default vertical and horizontal scales, but you should be able to override the defaults.

## ERROR HANDLING

Errors in dealing with errors are among the most common bugs. Error handling errors include failure to anticipate the possibility of errors and protect against them, failure to notice error conditions, and failure to deal with detected errors in a reasonable way. Note that error messages were discussed above.

## ERROR PREVENTION

Yourdon's (1975) chapter on Antibugging is a good introduction to defensive programming. The program should defend itself against bad input and bad treatment by other parts of the system. If the program might be working with bad data, it should check them before it does something terrible.

### Inadequate initial state validation

If a region of memory *must* start with all zeros in it, maybe the program should run a spot check rather than assuming that zeros are there.

### Inadequate tests of user input

It is *not* enough to tell people only to enter one- to three-digit numbers. Some will enter letters or ten-digit numbers and others will press <Enter> five times to see what happen. If you can enter it, the program must be able to cope with it.

### Inadequate protection against corrupted data

There's no guarantee that data stored on disk are any good. Maybe someone edited the file, or there was a hardware failure. Even if the programmer is sure that the file was validated before it was saved, he should include checks (like a checksum) that this is the same file coming back.

### Inadequate tests of passed parameters

A subroutine should not assume that it was called correctly. It should make sure that data passed to it are within its operating range.

### Inadequate protection against operating system bugs

The operating system has bugs. Application programs can trigger some of them. If the application programmer knows, for example, that the system will crash if he sends data to the printer too soon after sending it to the disk drive, he should make sure that his program can't do that under any circumstances.

### Inadequate version control

If the executable code is in more than one file, someone will try to use a new version of one file with an old version of another. Customers upgrading their software make this mistake frequently enough, then don't understand what's wrong unless the program tells them. The new version should include code that checks that all code files are up to date.

### Inadequate protection against malicious use

People will deliberately feed a program bad input or try to trigger error conditions. Some will do it out of anger, others because they think it's fun. Saying that "no reasonable person would do this" provides no defense against the unreasonable person.

## ERROR DETECTION

Programs often have ample information available to detect an error in the data or in their operation. For the information to be useful, they have to read and act on it. A few commonly ignored symptoms or pieces of diagnostic information are described below. There are many others.

### Ignores overflow

An *overflow condition* occurs when the result of a numerical calculation is too big for the program to handle. Overflows arise from adding and multiplying large numbers and from dividing by zero or by tiny fractions. Overflows are easy to detect, but the program does have to check for them, and some don't.

### Ignores impossible values

The program should check its variables to make sure that they are within reasonable limits. It should catch and reject a date like February 31. If the program does one thing when a variable is 0, something else when it is 1, and expects that all other values are "impossible," it must make sure that the variable's value is 0 or 1. Old assumptions are unsafe after a few years of maintenance programming.

### Ignores implausible values

Someone *might* withdraw $10,000,000 from their savings account but the program should probably ask a few different humans for confirmation before letting the transaction go through.

### Ignores error flag

The program calls a subroutine, which fails. It reports its failure in a special variable called an *error flag*. The program can either check the flag or, as often happens, ignore it and treat the garbage data coming back from the routine as if it was a real result.

APPENDIX

## Ignores hardware fault or error conditions

The program should assume that devices it can connect to will fail. Many devices can send back messages (set bits) that warn that something is wrong. If one does, the program should stop trying to interact with it and should report the problem to a human or to a higher level control program.

## Data comparisons

When you try to balance your checkbook, you have the number you think is your balance and the number the bank tells you is your balance. If they don't agree after you allow for service charges, recent checks, and so forth, there is an error in your records, the bank's, or both. Similar opportunities frequently arise to check two sets of data or two sets of calculations against each other. The program should take advantage of them.

## ERROR RECOVERY

There is an error, the program has detected it, and is now trying to deal with it. Much error recovery code is lightly tested, or not tested at all. Bugs in error recovery routines may be much more serious than the original problems.

## Automatic error correction

Sometimes the program can not only detect an error but correct it, without having to bother anyone about it, by checking other data or a set of rules. This is desirable, but only if the "correction" is correct.

## Failure to report an error

The program should report any detected internal error even if it can automatically correct the error's consequences. It might not detect the same error under slightly different circumstances. The program might report the error to the user, to the operator of a multi-user system, to an error log file on disk, or any combination of these, but it must be reported.

## Failure to set an error flag

A subroutine is called and fails. It is supposed to set an error flag when it does fail. It returns control to the calling routine without setting the flag. The caller will treat the garbage data passed back as if they were valid.

## Where does the program go back to?

A section of code fails. It logs the problem, sets an error flag, then what? Especially if the failing code can be reached from several GOTO statements, how does it know where in the program to return control to?

## Aborting errors

You stop the program, or it stops itself when it detects an error. Does it close any open output files? Does it log the cause of the exit on its way down? In the most general terms, does it tidy up before dying or does it just die and maybe leave a big mess?

### Recovery from hardware problems

The program should deal with hardware failures gracefully. If the disk or its directory is full, you should be able to put in a new one, not just lose all your data. If a device is unready for input for a long time, the program should assume that it's off line or disconnected. It shouldn't sit waiting forever.

### No escape from missing disk

Suppose your program asks you to insert a disk that has files it needs. If the inserted disk is not the correct one, it will prompt you again until the correct disk is inserted. However, if the correct disk is not available, there is no way you can escape unless you reboot your system.

## BOUNDARY-RELATED ERRORS

A *boundary* describes a change-point for a program. The program is supposed to work one way for anything on one side of the boundary. It does something different for anything on the other side.

The classic "things" on opposite sides of boundaries are data values. There are three standard boundary bugs:

- *Mishandling of the boundary case*: If a program adds any two numbers that are less than 100, and rejects any greater than 100, what does it do when you enter exactly 100? What is it supposed to do?
- *Wrong boundary:* The specification says the program should add any two numbers less than 100 but it rejects anything greater than 95.
- *Mishandling of cases outside the boundary:* Values on one side of the boundary are impossible, unlikely, unacceptable, unwanted. No code was written for them. Does the program successfully reject values greater than 100 or does it crash when it gets one?

We treat the concept of boundaries more broadly. Boundaries describe a way of thinking about a program and its behavior around its limits. There are many types of limits: largest, oldest, latest, longest, most recent, first time, etc. The same types of bugs can happen with any of them so why not think of them in the same terms?

### NUMERIC BOUNDARIES

Some numeric boundaries are arbitrary (bigger or less than 100) while others represent natural limits. A triangle has exactly three sides (not more, not less). Its angles sum to 180 degrees. A byte can store a (nonnegative) number between 0 and 255. If a character is a letter, its ASCII code is between 65 and 90 (capitals) or between 97 and 122 (lowercase).

### EQUALITY AS A BOUNDARY

Every element in a list might be the same. Every element might be different. What happens if you try to sort either list? If the list is made of numbers, what happens if you try to compute their mean, standard deviation, coefficient of symmetry or kurtosis? (All four are summary statistics. The last two would either compute to 0 or cause a divide by 0 error depending on the calculation algorithm.)

### BOUNDARIES ON NUMEROSITY

An input string can be up to 80 characters long? What if you type 79, 80 or 81? What does the program receiving your input do in each case? Can a list have one element? No elements? What is the standard deviation of a one-number list of numbers? (Answer: undefined or zero)

### BOUNDARIES IN SPACE

For example, if a graphing program draws a graph and a box around it, what to do with a dot that should properly be displayed outside the box?

## BOUNDARIES IN TIME

Suppose the program displays a prompt, waits 60 seconds for you to respond, then displays a menu if you haven't typed anything. What happens if you start typing just as it's starting to display the menu?

Suppose you have 30 seconds to answer a ringing telephone. After that, your phone stops ringing and the call forwards to the operator. Do you lose the call if you reach it at the 30th second? What if you reach it after the 30th second but before the operator has answered it?

Suppose you press the Space Bar while the computer's still loading the program from the disk. What happens? Is <Space> sent to the operating system (which is loading the program), saved for the program being loaded, or is this just so unexpected that it crashes the computer?

---

*Race conditions reflect temporal boundaries.*

---

## BOUNDARIES IN LOOPS

Here's an example of a loop:

```
10 IF COUNT_VARIABLE is less than 45
THEN PRINT "This is a loop"
   SET COUNT_VARIABLE to COUNT_VARIABLE + 1
   GOTO 10
ELSE quit
```

The program keeps printing and adding 1 to COUNT_VARIABLE until the counter finally reaches 45. Then the program quits. 45 bounds the loop. Loops can have lower as well as upper bounds (IF COUNT_VARIABLE is less than 45 and greater than 10). Beizer (1990) discusses tests of loop boundaries.

## BOUNDARIES IN MEMORY

What are the largest and smallest amounts of memory that this program can cope with? (Yes, a few programs do crash if you give them access to too much memory.) Are data split across pages or segments of memory? Is the first or last byte of a segment lost or misread? (By the way, is that first byte numbered 0 or 1?) Are some of the data in RAM and some on disk, in virtual memory format? Suppose the program reads a value from RAM then a value from virtual memory, then the next value from what used to be in RAM, then back to what used to be (still is? is again?) virtual memory, etc. How seriously will this back-and-forth affect performance?

## BOUNDARIES WITHIN DATA STRUCTURES

Suppose the program keeps data in a record structure. Each record holds a person's name, followed by their employee number and salary. Then comes the next person's record (name, number, salary), etc. If it retrieves them from disk, does the program read the first record correctly? The last record? How does the program mark the end of a record or the beginning of the next? Does everything fit in this format? What if you have two employee numbers?

## HARDWARE-RELATED BOUNDARIES

If a mainframe can handle up to 100 terminals, what happens when you plug in the 99th, 100th, and 101st? What if you get 100 people to log on at the same time?

What happens when the disk is full? If a directory can hold 128 files, what happens when you try to save the 127th, 128th, and 129th? If your printer has a large input buffer, what happens if your program fills it but has more data to send? What happens when the printer runs out of paper or the ribbon runs out?

## INVISIBLE BOUNDARIES

Not all boundary conditions are visible from the outside. For example, a subroutine might approximate the value of a function, using one approximation formula when the function argument is less than 100 and a different approximation if the argument is 100 or greater. The first formula might be incalculable (e.g., divide by zero) when the function argument is 100 and its values might make no sense when arguments are greater than 100. 100 is clearly a boundary but you might never realize it.

## CALCULATION ERRORS

The program calculates a number and gets the wrong result. This can happen for one of three types of reasons:

- *Bad logic:* There can be a typing error, like A-A instead of A+A. Or the programmer might break a complex expression into a set of simpler ones, but get the simplification wrong. Or he might use an incorrect formula, or one inapplicable to the data at hand. This third case is a design error. The code does what the programmer intended—it's his conception of what the code should do that is wrong.

- *Bad arithmetic:* There might be an error in the coding of a basic function, such as addition, multiplication, or exponentiation. The error might show up whenever the function is used (2 + 2 = -5) or it might be restricted to rare special cases. In either case, any program that uses the function can fail.

- *Imprecise calculation:* If the program uses floating point arithmetic, it loses precision as it calculates, because of roundoff and truncation errors. After many intermediate errors, it may claim that 2 + 2 works out to -5 even though none of the steps in the program contains a logical error.

This area is huge and this section only begins to scratch its surface. For an introduction to the larger area, read Conte and deBoor (1980) and Knuth (1981). For a second source on topics in Conte and deBoor, try Carnahan, Luther & Wilkes (1969).

## OUTDATED CONSTANTS

Numbers are sometimes used directly in a program. The computer might be able to connect to a maximum of 64 terminals. The length of the configuration file might be 706 bytes. The first two digits in the year are 19 (as in 1987). When these values change, the program has to change too. Often, they are changed in a few places but not everywhere. Any calculations based on the old values are now out of date, and thus wrong.

## CALCULATION ERRORS

Some errors are as simple as typing a minus sign instead of a plus, or subtracting B from A instead of A from B. These usually show up easily if you exercise reasonable care in testing. If the program asks for input data, then prints a number calculated from these, do the same calculation yourself. Does your number match the computer's?

## IMPOSSIBLE PARENTHESES

```
(A + (B + C) * (D + (A / C - B E / (B + (F + 18 / (A - F))))))
```

---

Formulas with many parentheses are hard to understand. It's easy to get one wrong, when writing the code in the first place and when trying to change it later.

## WRONG ORDER OF OPERATORS

The program will evaluate an expression in a certain order, but it might be a different order than the programmer expected. For example, if ** represents exponentiation, so 5 ** 3 is 5 cubed, is 2 * 5 ** 3 equal to 1000 (10 cubed) or 250 (twice 5 cubed)?

## BAD UNDERLYING FUNCTION

Commercially supplied programs and languages usually do the most basic functions, such as adding and multiplying, correctly. Of course, if your development group has written their own, these functions are as suspect as everything else. Slightly fancier functions, like exponentiation, sine, cosine, and hyperbolics, are not necessarily as trustworthy. Errors of this class may be deliberate. Some programmers use inaccurate approximation formulas because they evaluate quickly or are compact and easy to code.

## OVERFLOW AND UNDERFLOW

An *overflow condition* occurs when the result of a numerical calculation is too large for the program to handle. For example, suppose the program stores all numbers in fixed point format, with one byte per number. It works with numbers from 0 to 255. It can't add 255 + 255 because the result is too large to fit in one byte. Overflows also occur in floating point arithmetic, when the exponent is too large.

Underflows occur only in floating point calculations. In *floating point*, a number is represented by a pair of values, one for the exponent, the other for a fraction. For example, 255 is 0.255 times $10^3$. 255,000 is 0.255 times $10^6$. The exponent changes, but the fractional part (0.255) is the same in both cases. Now, suppose the program allocates a byte for the exponent, and stores values of 0 to 255. What happens if the exponent is -1 (0.255 * $10^{-1}$ is 0.0255)? This is too small to be stored (because the smallest exponent we can store in this scheme is 0), so we have an *underflow*. Underflows are usually converted to 0 (0.255 * $10^{-1}$ becomes 0), without an error message. This is usually appropriate, but it can lead to computational errors:

Is 100 * .255 * $10^{-1}$ zero or 2.55?

## TRUNCATION AND ROUNDOFF ERROR

Suppose the program stores only two digits per number. The number 5.19 has three digits. If the program truncates (drops) the 9, it stores 5.1. Instead, it could round 5.19 upwards to 5.2, which is much closer than 5.1.

If a programming language keeps two digits per floating point number, it works in *two-digit precision*. Calculations in this language would not be accurate. For example, $2.05^6$ is about 74. However, if you round 2.05 to 2.1, the calculated value of $2.05^6$ is nearly 86. If you truncate 2.05 to 2.0, you get 64 instead.

We don't know of any language that uses two-digit precision, but many keep only six digits in floating point calculations. Six-digit calculations are fine for simple computations but they can cause surprisingly large errors in more complicated calculations.

## CONFUSION ABOUT THE REPRESENTATION OF THE DATA

The same number can be represented in many different ways; they can be confused with each other. For example, suppose that the program asks you for a number between 0 and 9. You type 1. It might store this 1 in a byte, as fixed point number between 0 and 255. There are 8 bits in this byte: the bit pattern is 0000 0001. Or it might store the ASCII code of the character you typed. The ASCII code for 1 is 49, or 0011 0001 in binary. In both cases, the number fits in one byte. It is easy to get confused later and treat something stored in ASCII format as if it were as a fixed point integer, or vice versa. Your number might also be stored in some other format, such as floating point. Again, confusion between formats is possible. Some programming languages straighten this out themselves, others issue warnings during compilation, and others just let you get the wrong answer.

## INCORRECT CONVERSION FROM ONE DATA REPRESENTATION TO ANOTHER

The program asks for a number between 0 and 9. You type 1. This is a character, and the program receives the ASCII code 49. To convert your input to a number, it should subtract 48 from the code value. It subtracts 49 instead. You entered 1, but the program will treat your response as 0. Whenever a program does its own conversion from one data representation to another, it has plenty of opportunity to go wrong. ASCII to Integer is only one example of a conversion. Conversions are common between ASCII, floating point, integer, character (string), etc.

## WRONG FORMULA

Some programs use complicated formulas. It's easy to miscopy one, to read the wrong one from the book, or to make an error when deriving one.

## INCORRECT APPROXIMATION

Many formulas for approximating or estimating certain values were developed long before computers. They're great formulas in the sense that they don't require much computation, but lousy otherwise. Unfortunately, they are also traditional. They will keep appearing in text books and programs for years. As a common example, if you are graphing a set of data and want to fit a curve to them that has the form $Y = a\ X^b$, it is traditional to take logarithms of everything in sight, estimating $a$ and $b$ by fitting a line to the new function, $\log Y = \log a + b \log X$. This is easy to program, quick to run, and inaccurate. When you return from logarithms and plot $a\ X^b$, the curve fits data on the left of the figure (small values of $X$) better than data toward the right.

Many programs use bad approximation methods and other incorrect mathematical procedures. They might print impressive output, but it is wrong output. You can't test for these types of problems unless you understand a fair bit of the mathematics yourself. If you are testing a statistical package or other mathematical package, it is essential that you or another tester have a detailed understanding of the functions being programmed.

## INITIAL AND LATER STATES

Before you can use a function, the program may have to initialize it. Typical *initialization* steps include identifying the function's variables, defining their types, allocating memory for them, and setting them to default values (such as 0). The program may have to read a disk file that contains defaults and other configuration information. What happens when the file is not there? Initialization steps might be done when the program is loaded (data defaults can be loaded into memory along with the program), when it is started, when the function is first called, or each time the function is called.

Initialization needs and strategy vary widely across languages. For example:

- In many languages, a function's local variables keep their values from one call to the next. If a variable is supposed to keep the same value, the function can set the variable's value once and leave it alone thereafter. The function usually has to reset other variables to their starting values.

- In other languages, local variables are erased from memory on exit from the function. Whenever the program calls a function, it must redefine its variables, allocate memory for them, and assign starting values.
- Some languages allow the programmer to specify whether a variable should stay in memory or be erased after each function call.
- Some compilers provide initialization support. The programmer can specify a starting value for a variable; the compiler will make sure that this loads into memory with the program. If the programmer doesn't assign an initial value, the compiler sets it to 0. Other compilers, even for the same language, do not provide this support. The function must set each variable's value the first time it's called. To avoid resetting each variable every time it's called, the function must know whether it's been called before.

Initialization failures usually show up the first time the function is called or the second time, if it doesn't reinitialize variables correctly. Reinitialization failures may be path-dependent. If you reach a function in a "normal" way, it works fine. However, if you take an "abnormal" route, the program might branch into the function at some point after the initialization code. Programmers often treat backing up to modify data or redo calculations as abnormal.

## FAILURE TO SET A DATA ITEM TO 0

Since so many compilers, in so many languages, set data to 0 unless you tell them otherwise, many programmers don't bother specifying the starting value of a variable unless it is non-zero. Their coding style fails as soon as they use a compiler that doesn't automatically zero data.

## FAILURE TO INITIALIZE A LOOP-CONTROL VARIABLE

A *loop-control variable* determines how many times the program will run through a loop. For example, a function prints the first 10 lines of a text file. The program stores the number of the line reaches 11, printing stops. Next time, the function must reset LINE to 1 or it will never start printing because LINE's value is 11 already.

## FAILURE TO INITIALIZE (OR REINITIALIZE) A POINTER

A *pointer* variable stores an address, such as the location in memory where a given string starts. The value of the pointer can change—for example, it might point to the first character in a string, then be changed to point to the second, the third, and so on. If the programmer forgets to reset a pointer after changing it, it will point to the wrong part of the string or to the wrong string. If subsequent function calls keep changing the pointer without reinitializing it, the pointer may eventually point to code rather than data.

You should suspect pointer errors if you see string fragments or incorrect array elements displayed.

## FAILURE TO CLEAR A STRING

A *string* variable stores a set of characters. Whereas the value of a numeric variable might be 5, a string might have the value Hello, my name is John. Strings can vary in length. You can change the string from Hello, my name is John to the shorter string, Goodbye. Some routines assume that a string is empty (filled with zeroes) before they use it. A routine that writes Goodbye into the first 7 bytes of a string without terminating it with zeroes might yield Goodbye my name is John rather than Goodbye.

## FAILURE TO INITIALIZE (OR REINITIALIZE) REGISTERS

*Registers* are special memory areas usually found on the central processing unit itself. You can manipulate data stored in registers more quickly than those stored in normal memory. Because of this speed advantage, programs constantly use registers for temporary storage. They copy a few variables' values to registers, work with them, and copy the new values in the registers back. It's easy to forget to load the latest data into one of these registers.

## FAILURE TO CLEAR A FLAG

*Flags* are variables that indicate special conditions. A flag can be set (true, on, up, usually 1) or clear (false, off, down, usually 0 or -1). The flag's value is normally clear. It is set as a signal that a routine has failed, that its variables have been initialized, that the result of a calculation was an overflow or an underflow, that you've just pressed a key, etc. Less desirably, but also common, a flag might tell a routine that it was called from one place in the program rather than another, or that it should perform one type of calculation rather than another.

The flag must be kept current. For example, a routine should clear its error flag each time it's called, returning with a set flag only when it fails. A routine should clear its data-initialized flag whenever any of its variables change from default values that should be changed back the next time the routine is used. Some programs can set or clear the same flag in a dozen different places. It's hard to tell whether the flag's value is current or not.

## DATA WERE SUPPOSED TO BE INITIALIZED ELSEWHERE

A function may not initialize all of its data. For example, variables shared by different functions might be initialized together. Suppose that some functions are listed in the same menu, and their shared variables are initialized whenever that menu is displayed. This works as long as there's no other path to any of these functions, but can you reach one by a back door? Is any function an option on another menu? Might the program call it as part of another function's error recovery?

## FAILURE TO REINITIALIZE

Programmers may forget to make sure that a function's variables have the right values the second time around. Simple forgetfulness is especially common when dealing with languages that automatically initialize variables to 0. The programmer didn't have to set it to 0 for the first pass through the function. Why should she think about setting it back to 0 later?

The programmer might also fail to reinitialize a function's data when it's reached "by the back door," especially when you try to back up to change data. Imagine entering data on a form, displayed onscreen. The program initializes all relevant variables when it paints the form. You enter the wrong number, notice it after entering a few other values, move the cursor back, and fix it. Any calculations based on this number now have to be redone. Will the variables in those calculation sections be reinitialized? Moving backward in the program is risky as far as variable reinitialization is concerned. The risk is much higher if the programmer uses GOTOs to move back to lines in the middle of a block of code, rather than at the start of it.

## ASSUMPTION THAT DATA WERE NOT REINITIALIZED

Some programs initialize the same variables repeatedly, before they could have changed. This is harmless, except for the waste of computer time.

## CONFUSION BETWEEN STATIC AND DYNAMIC STORAGE

A local variable is called *dynamic* or *automatic* if it is erased from memory when the function that owns it exits. Each time the program calls the function, it has to redefine the variable, allocate memory for it, and assign starting values. A *static* variable stays in memory and keeps its value across function calls. In some languages, all local variables are dynamic, in others all locals are

**APPENDIX**

static, and in some, the programmer gets to choose which variables are static and which dynamic. When both types of variables exist, confusion is easy. The programmer might forget to reinitialize a static variable because she thinks it's dynamic, and so doesn't need initialization. Similarly, she might forget to update the value of an automatic variable because she forgets that it doesn't keep its value across function calls.

## DATA MODIFICATION BY SIDE-EFFECT

After initialization, a routine might use a variable without changing it. The programmer might consider reinitialization unnecessary, since the variable doesn't change, but even if she intends the variable to be local to that routine, the language she's writing in might not recognize the concept of local variables. Any other part of the program can change this variable; after much maintenance, any other part of the program might.

## INCORRECT INITIALIZATION

The programmer might assign the wrong value to a variable, or declare it integer instead of floating point, static instead of dynamic, global instead of local. Most of these errors are caught by the compiler, long before you see the program.

## RELIANCE ON TOOLS THE CUSTOMER MAY NOT HAVE OR UNDERSTAND

This is rare but it happens—it's surprisingly easy to miss. The programmer expects you to use some other program to modify this one or to set up some aspects of the program's environment. You must do this the first time you use the program, to get its memory limits or whatever into the right initial state. Thereafter, as the tester, you may forget that you ever did it.

# CONTROL FLOW ERRORS

The control flow of a program describes what it will do next, under what circumstances. A control flow error occurs when the program does the wrong thing next. Extreme control flow errors stop the program or cause it to run amok. Many simple errors lead to spectacular misbehavior.

## PROGRAM RUNS AMOK

The program displays garbage onscreen, saves garbage to disk, starts printing forever, or goes to some otherwise totally inappropriate routine. Eventually, it may stop dead. Whatever the exact behavior, the program's actions are out of your control. These are the most spectacular bugs, and are usually the easiest to find and fix.

From the outside, these bugs can look the same. They all make the program go out of control. The descriptions below are examples of the causes of programs running amok. You would not test specifically for one of these errors unless you knew something about the programming language, the programmer's style, or the internal design.

### GOTO somewhere

GOTO transfers control to another part of the program. The program jumps to the specified routine, but this is obviously the wrong place. The program may lock, the screen display may be inappropriate, etc.

The GOTO command is unfashionable. The structured programming movement is centered on a belief that GOTO encourages sloppy thinking and coding (Yourdon, 1976).

Errors involving GOTO are especially likely when:

- The program branches backward, going somewhere it's been before. For example, the GOTO may jump to a point just past validity checking or initialization of data or devices.

- The GOTO is indirect, going to an address stored in a variable. When the variable's value changes, the GOTO takes the program somewhere else. It's hard to tell, when reading the code, whether the variable has the right value at the right time.

### Come-from logic errors

A routine uses *come-from logic* if it changes what it does based on what routine called or jumped to it. Errors arise when the routine fails to correctly identify what called it or does the wrong thing after correctly identifying the caller. Calling routines often set flags or other variables to identify themselves, but a few different routines may use the same flag to mean different things, some may reset a flag when they're done with it while others don't, and some may give it values that the called routine doesn't expect. Come-from logic is fragile, and particularly prone to failure during maintenance programming.

### Problems in table-driven programs

A *table-driven program* uses a table (array) of addresses. Depending on the value of some variable(s), the program selects a table entry and jumps to the memory address stored there. The table may be a data file read from disk that can be changed without recompiling the program. Table-driven programming can make code easier to maintain, but it has risks:

- The numbers in the table might be wrong, especially if they were entered by hand. These incorrect addresses could send the program anywhere.

- If the table is long, it is easy to supply the wrong entry for a given case, and easy to miss this when desk-checking the code.

- Suppose the table has five entries, and the program selects one of the five based on the value of a state variable. What if the variable can take on six values? Where does the program go in the sixth case?

- It's easy to forget to update a jump table when modifying the code.

### Executing data

You can't tell from a byte's contents whether it holds a character, part of a number, part of a memory location, or a program instruction. The program keeps these different types of information in different places in memory to keep straight which byte holds what type of data. If the program interprets data as instructions, it will try to execute them and will probably lock. It may print odd things on the screen first. Some computers detect execution of "impossible" commands and stop the program with an error message (usually a hexadecimal message flagging program termination or reference to an illegal machine code.)

The program will treat data as if they were instructions under two conditions:

(a) *Data are copied into a memory area reserved for code. The code is overwritten. Examples of how to do this:*

- *Pointers* are variables which store memory addresses. A pointer might hold the starting address of an array; the programmer could put a value in the fourth element of the array by saying store it in the fourth location after the address stored in this pointer. If the address in the pointer is wrong, the data go to the wrong place. If the address is in the code space, the new data overwrite the program.

- Some languages don't check array limits. Suppose you have an array MYARRAY, with three elements, MYARRAY[1], MYARRAY[2], and MYARRAY[3]. What happens if the

**A**

APPENDIX

program tries to store a value in MYARRAY[2044]? If the language doesn't catch this error, the data will be stored in the spot that would have been MYARRAY[2044] if that MYARRAY element existed. This memory location is a few thousand bytes past the end address of MYARRAY. It might be reserved for code, data, or hardware I/O, but not for MYARRAY.

(b) *The program jumps to an area of memory that is reserved for data, and treats it like an area containing code.*

- A bad table entry in a table-driven program can lead the program to jump into a data area.
- Some computers divide memory into *segments*. The computer interprets anything in a code segment as instructions, and anything in a data segment as numbers or characters. If the program misstates a segment's starting address, what the computer interprets as a code segment will probably be a combination of code and data.

### Jumping to a routine that isn't resident

To save room, computers may swap pieces of large programs in and out of memory. These pieces are called *overlays*: when one is in memory, the others aren't. When another is needed, the computer reads it from disk and stores it in the same area of memory used by the first overlay. When routines in the first overlay are again needed, they are again read into the shared area of memory. The routine in memory right now is *resident* in memory.

Before using a routine that is part of an overlay, the program must check that the right overlay is resident. Otherwise, when it jumps to what should be the starting address of the routine, it may be jumping into the middle of some other routine.

Overlays can also cause performance problems. The programmer might ensure that a routine is resident by always loading it from disk before jumping to it. This wastes a lot of computer time if he calls the routine many times. The program will also waste time if it alternates between routines that are part of two different overlays. This is called *thrashing*: the program loads the first overlay, executes the first routine, then overwrites it with the second overlay to execute the second routine, reloads the first overlay, etc. It spends most of its time loading overlays rather than getting work done.

### Re-entrance

A *re-entrant program* can be used concurrently by two or more processes. A *re-entrant subroutine* can call itself or be called by any other routine while it's executing. Some languages don't support re-entrant subroutine calls: if a routine tries to call itself, the program crashes. Even if the language allows re-entrance, a given program or routine might not be. If a routine is serving two processes, how does it keep its data separate, so that what it does for one process doesn't corrupt what it does for the other?

### Variables contain embedded command names

Some language dialects ignore spaces. A phrase like PRINTMYNAME would be interpreted by the language as PRINT MYNAME. The program would attempt to print the value of variable MYNAME. This is an error if the user was trying to define a variable named PRINTMYNAME. This type of error is usually caught by the programmer, but occasional ones do survive.

## Wrong returning state assumed

Imagine a subroutine that's supposed to set a device's baud rate. The program calls this routine and *assumes* that the routine did its job successfully. It starts transmitting through the device as soon as possible. This time, the routine failed. The transmission fails and the program hangs waiting for acknowledgment of the data.

As another example, suppose a routine usually scales the data passed to it, passing back numbers that lie between 1 and 10. Under exceptional circumstances, the routine will scale from 0 to 10 instead. Because the calling program assumes that it will never receive a 0, it crashes on a divide by 0 error.

## Exception-handling based exits

Suppose that a routine designed to calculate square roots sets an error flag but does no computations when asked to take the square root of a negative number. The idea behind error flags is that the calling program can decide how to deal with the problem. One might print an error message, another display a help screen, and a third might send the number to a slower routine built for complex numbers. Subroutines that flag and reject exceptional conditions can be used under more conditions. However, each time one is called, the caller must check that it did what the programmer expected it to do. If the exit-producing conditions are rare, he may miss them. During testing, they may show up as "irreproducible" bugs.

## Return to wrong place

The key difference between a subroutine and a GOTO is that when the subroutine ends, it returns to the part of the program that called it, whereas GOTO never returns. Occasionally, a subroutine can return to the wrong place in a program. The next few sections are examples.

### Corrupted stack

When a subroutine finishes, program control returns to the command following the call to the subroutine. The address of that command is stored in a data structure called a *stack*. The top of the stack holds the address most recently pushed onto it. The subroutine returns to the address stored at the top of the stack. If the stack is only used to hold return addresses, it is called a *Call/Return Stack*. Most stacks are also used as a temporary spot to stash data.

If a subroutine puts data on the stack and doesn't remove them before finishing, the computer will treat the number(s) at the top of the stack as a return address. The subroutine might "return" anywhere in memory.

### Stack under/overflow

The stack might only be able to hold 16, 32, 64, or 128 addresses. Imagine a stack that can only hold 2 return addresses. When the program calls Subroutine 1, it stores a return address on the stack. When Subroutine 1 calls Subroutine 2, another return address goes on the stack. When Routine 2 ends, control goes back to Routine 1, and when Routine 1 ends, control returns to the main body of the program.

What if Subroutine 2 calls Subroutine 3? The stack is storing 2 return addresses already, so it cannot also hold the return address for Subroutine 3. This is a stack overflow condition. Programs (or central processing chips) often compound a stack overflow problem by replacing the oldest stored return addresses with the new one. The program will now return to Subroutine 2 when Subroutine 3 is done. From Subroutine 2 it returns to Subroutine 1. From Subroutine 1 it returns to...???...there is no return address for Subroutine 1. This is a *stack underflow*.

### GOTO *rather than* RETURN *from a subroutine*

Subroutine 1 calls routine 2. Routine 2 GOTOs back to 1, rather than returning normally. The return address from routine 2 to 1 is still on the stack. When subroutine 1 finishes, the program will return to the address stored on the stack, which takes it back to subroutine 1. This is rarely intentional.

APPENDIX

## CONTROL FLOW ERRORS
### PROGRAM RUNS AMOK
#### Return to wrong place
##### *GOTO rather than RETURN from a subroutine*

To avoid this error, subroutine 2 might POP (remove) its return address from the stack when it does its GOTO back to routine 1. Used incorrectly, this can cause stack underflows, returns to the wrong calling routine, and attempts to return to data values stored on the stack with the return addresses.

## Interrupts

An *interrupt* is a special signal that causes the computer to stop the program in progress and branch to an interrupt handling routine. Later, the program restarts from where it was interrupted. Input/output events, including signals from the clock that a specified interval of time has passed, are typical causes of interrupts.

### *Wrong interrupt vector*

When an interrupt signal is generated, the computer has to find the interrupt handling routine, then branch to it. The address of the interrupt handler is stored in a dedicated location in memory. The computer jumps to the address stored in that location. If the computer can distinguish between several different types of interrupts, it finds a given interrupt's handler in a list of addresses stored in a dedicated section of memory. This list is called the *interrupt vector*.

If wrong addresses are stored in the interrupt vector, any error might be possible in response to an interrupt-generating event. If the addresses are merely out of order, the program is less likely to run amok but it might try to echo characters onscreen in response to a clock signal, or treat keyboard inputs as if they flagged time-outs.

### *Failure to restore or update interrupt vector*

A program can change the interrupt vector by writing new addresses into the appropriate memory locations. If a module temporarily changes the interrupt vector, it might not restore the old address list on exit. Another might fail to make a permanent (or temporary) change to the vector. In either case, the computer will branch to the wrong place after the next interrupt.

### *Failure to block or unblock interrupts*

Programs can *block* most interrupts, instructing the computer to ignore blockable interrupts. For example, it's traditional to block interrupts just before starting to write data to a disk and to unblock immediately after output to the disk is complete. This prevents many data transmission errors.

### *Invalid restart after an interrupt*

The program is interrupted, then restarted. In some systems, at restart time, the program gets a message or other indication that it was interrupted. The message usually identifies the type of interrupting event (keyboard I/O, time-out, modem I/O, etc.). This is useful. For example, if a program knows it was interrupted, it can repaint the screen with information it was showing before the interrupt. The programmer might easily specify the wrong action or a branch to the wrong location in response to a signal that a certain type of interrupt has been executed. Programmers are as unlikely to catch these errors as error-handling errors.

## PROGRAM STOPS

Some languages will stop a program when certain types of errors are detected. Some programs aren't designed to stop, nor are the languages designed to stop them, but they do anyway.

Not all halts are control flow errors. If the program code says "If this happens, halt," the program is supposed to stop. It is a user interface error, but not a control flow error, if this program stops unexpectedly, without a message.

### Dead crash

In a *dead crash*, the computer stops responding to keyboard input, stops printing, and leaves lights on or off (but doesn't change them). It usually locks without issuing any warnings that it's about to crash. The only way to regain control is to turn off the machine or press the reset key.

Dead crashes are usually due to infinite loops. One common loop keeps looking for acknowledgment or data from another device (printer, another computer, disk, etc.). If the program missed the acknowledgment, or never gets one, it may stay in this wait loop forever.

### Syntax errors reported at run-time

An interpreted language may not check syntax until run-time. When the language finds a command that it can't interpret, it prints an error message and stops the program. Any line of code that the programmer didn't test may have a syntax error.

### Waits for impossible condition, or combination of conditions

The program stops (usually a dead crash) waiting for an event that cannot occur. Common examples:

- *I/O failure:* The computer sends data to a broken output device, then waits forever for the device to acknowledge receipt. A similar problem arises between processes in a multi-processing system. One process sends a request or data to another, then waits forever for a response that never arrives.

- *Deadly embrace:* This is a classic multi-processing problem. Two programs run simultaneously. Each needs the same two resources (say, a printer and extra memory for a printer buffer). Each grabs one resource, then waits forever for the other program to finish with the other resource.

- *Simple logic errors:* For example, a program is supposed to wait for a number between 1 and 5, discarding all other input. However, the code testing the input reads: IF INPUT > 5 AND INPUT < 1. No number can meet this condition so the program waits forever.

Similarly, in multi-processing systems, one process may wait forever for another to send it an impossible value.

### Wrong user or process priority

A computer that runs many programs at once switches between them. It runs one program for a while, then switches to a second, to a third, eventually returning to the first. Multi-processing systems run smoothly because a scheduling program switches back to programs when events like keyboard input happen or when a program has been suspended for too long.

If two programs have been waiting equally long to run, or if the same type of event happens to trigger each, the scheduler must decide which program to run first. It uses a priority system: priorities might be assigned to users or programs. The program being run by a higher priority user will run first.

Some programs run at such low priorities, they may be suspended for hours before being restarted. This may be appropriate. In other cases, priorities were incorrectly assigned or interpreted. Less extreme priority errors are more common but harder to detect unless they trigger race conditions.

**A**

## Loops

There are many ways to code a loop, but they all have some things in common. Here's one example:

```
1 SET LOOP_CONTROL = 1
2 REPEAT
3     SET VAR = 5
4     PRINT VAR * LOOP_CONTROL
5     SET LOOP_CONTROL = LOOP_CONTROL + 1
6 UNTIL LOOP_CONTROL > 5
7 PRINT VAR
```

The program sets LOOP_CONTROL to 1, sets VAR to 5, prints the product of VAR and LOOP_CONTROL, adds 1 to LOOP_CONTROL then checks whether LOOP_CONTROL is greater than 5. Since LOOP_CONTROL is only 2, it repeats the code inside the loop (lines 3, 4, and 5). The loop keeps repeating until LOOP_CONTROL reaches 6. Then the program executes the next command after the loop, printing the value of VAR.

LOOP_CONTROL is called the *loop control variable*. Its value determines how many times the loop is executed. If the expression written after the UNTIL is complex, involving many different variables, it is a loop control expression, rather than a loop control variable. The same types of errors arise in both cases.

### Infinite loop

If the condition that terminates the loop is never met, the program will loop forever. Modify the example so that it loops until LOOP_CONTROL was less than 0 (never happens). It will loop forever.

### Wrong starting value for the loop control variable

Suppose that, later in the program, there is a GOTO to the start of the loop at line 2. LOOP_CONTROL could have any value. It probably isn't 1. If the programmer expects this loop to repeat five times (as it would if the GOTO was to line 1), he is in for a surprise.

### Accidental change of the loop control variable

In the example, the value of LOOP_CONTROL changed inside the loop. A bigger loop might change LOOP_CONTROL in more than one place (especially if it calls a subroutine that uses LOOP_CONTROL), and the program might repeat the loop more or less often than the programmer expects.

### Wrong criterion for ending the loop

Perhaps the loop should end when LOOP_CONTROL > 5 rather than when LOOP_CONTROL >_ 5. This is a common mistake. And, if the ending criterion is more complex, it is more prone to error.

### Commands that do or don't belong inside the loop

In the example, SET VAR = 5 is inside the loop. The value of VAR doesn't change inside the loop, so VAR is still 5 the second, third, fourth, and fifth times the loop executes. Resetting VAR to 5 each time is wasteful. Some loops repeat thousands of times: unnecessary repetition within them is significant.

Alternatively, suppose VAR did change inside the loop. If the programmer wants VAR to start at 5 each time the loop repeats, he has to say SET VAR = 5 at the head of the loop.

## Improper loop nesting

One loop can be *nested* (completely included) inside another. It is not possible (without error) for one loop to start inside another but to end outside of it.

## IF, THEN, ELSE, OR MAYBE NOT

An IF statement has the form:

```
IF This_Condition IS TRUE
   THEN DO Something
   ELSE DO Something_Else
```

For example:

```
IF VAR > 5
   THEN SET VAR_2 = 20
   ELSE SET VAR_2 = 10
```

The THEN clause (SET VAR_2 = 20) is only executed if the condition (VAR > 5) is met. If the condition is not met, the ELSE clause (SET VAR_2 = 10) is executed. Some IF statements only specify what to do if the condition is met. They don't include an ELSE clause. If the condition is not met (VAR =< 5) the program skips the THEN clause and moves on to the next line of code.

## Wrong inequalities (e.g., > instead of ≥)

The tested condition (VAR > 5) might be incorrect, or incorrectly stated. Programmers often forget to consider the case in which the two variables are equal.

## Comparison sometimes yields wrong result

The condition tested by the IF is usually the right one, but not always. Suppose the programmer wants to test whether three variables are the same. He might write IF (VAR + VAR_2 + VAR_3) / 3 = VAR.

If VAR, VAR_2, and VAR_3 are the same, the average of them will have the same value as any one of them. Further, for almost all values, if VAR, VAR_2, and VAR_3 are not the same, their average will not equal VAR. But suppose that VAR is 2, VAR_2 is 1, and VAR_3 is 3. (VAR+VAR_2+ VAR_3) / 3 = VAR, but VAR, VAR_2, and VAR_3 aren't equal. Shortcuts like this that try to combine a few comparisons into one regularly go awry.

## Not equal versus equal when there are three cases

The three-case problem often comes up during maintenance programming. The initial code may have restricted VAR's values to 0 and 1, but later changes allow it to be 2 as well. In the original program, an IF statement for VAR = 0 was fine. The THEN clause covered VAR = 0, and, since VAR could only be 0 or 1, the ELSE clause said what to do when VAR = 1. Now that VAR can also be 2, the ELSE clause is probably wrong.

It's risky to compare a variable to only one value (like VAR = 0), leaving all the others to the same ELSE clause. There are so many other possible values: some may arise as originally unanticipated special cases.

## Testing floating point values for equality

Floating point calculations are subject to truncation and round off errors. For example, rather than being exactly zero, a variable's value might be 0.000000008 because of small computational errors. This is close, but it wouldn't pass a test of equality (IF VAR = 0).

**APPENDIX**

413

### Confusing inclusive and exclusive OR

Many IF statements test whether one of a group of conditions is true (IF A OR B is true, THEN...) Unfortunately, "or" is ambiguous:

- *inclusive or*: satisfied if A is true, B is true or both A and B are true
- *exclusive or:* satisfied if A is true or B is true, but not if A and B are both true

### Incorrectly negating a logical expression

IF statements sometimes take the form, IF A is NOT true, THEN. Programmers often carry out the negation incorrectly or don't think through what the negation means. For example, IF NOT (A or B) THEN... means IF A is false AND B is false, THEN.... The THEN clause will not be taken if A or B is true, even if the other is false.

### Assignment-equal instead of test-equal

In the C language, if (VAR = 5) means SET VAR = 5, then test whether it's nonzero. Programmers often write this instead of if (VAR == 5), which means what some people think if (VAR = 5) should mean.

### Commands belong inside the THEN or ELSE clause

Here's a simple example of this type of error:

```
IF    VAR = VAR_2
      THEN SET VAR_2 = 10
      SET VAR_2 = 20
```

Clearly, SET VAR_2 = 20 belongs inside an ELSE clause. As it is now, VAR_2 is always set to 20. Setting VAR_2 to 10 first, when VAR = VAR_2, has no effect.

### Commands that don't belong inside either clause

Sometimes the programmer will include a command inside a THEN or an ELSE clause that should always be executed (i.e., in both cases). If he repeats the command inside both clauses, he wastes code space, but this usually doesn't matter. If he includes it only inside one clause, it will be missed whenever the other clause (ELSE or THEN) is executed.

### Failure to test a flag

For example, the program calls a subroutine, which is supposed to assign a value to a variable. The subroutine fails, sets its error flag, and leaves the variable alone. The program doesn't check the error flag. Instead, it does its usual IF test on the variable. Whatever code the program executes from here is wrong, or is right only by luck. The value stored in the variable is junk. That's what the subroutine means when it sets the flag.

### Failure to clear a flag

A subroutine set its error flag the last time it was called. The flag is still set. This time the subroutine does its task and leaves the error flag alone. The error flag is still set. The program will believe this error flag, ignore the subroutine's output, and do error recovery instead.

## MULTIPLE CASES

An IF statement considers only two cases: an expression is either true or false. Commands like CASE, SWITCH, SELECT, and computed GOTO are used when a variable might have many different values and the programmer wants to do one of many different things depending on the value.

The typical command of this type is equivalent to this:

```
IF VAR is 1 do TASK-1
IF VAR is 2 do TASK-2
IF VAR is 3 do TASK-3
IF VAR is anything else, do DEFAULT-TASK
```

If there is no default case, the program falls through to the commands following this multiple-choice block.

### Missing default

A programmer who thinks VAR can only take on the values listed may not write a default case. Because of a bug or later modifications to the code, VAR can take on other values. A default case could catch these, and print any unexpected value of VAR.

### Wrong default

Suppose the programmer expects VAR to have only four possible values. He explicitly deals with the first three possibilities, and buries the other one as the "default." Will this default be correct for VAR's unanticipated fifth and sixth values?

### Missing cases

VAR can take on five possible values but the programmer forgot to write a CASE statement covering the fifth case.

### Case should be subdivided

Some cases cover too much: perhaps one case covers all values of VAR below 30, but the program should do one thing if VAR is below 15 and something else for larger values. The most common example of this problem is the default case. The programmer doesn't think it matters what happens if VAR has certain values, so he covers them all with the default.

### Overlapping cases

The CASE statements are equivalent to this:

```
IF VAR > 5 then do TASK_1
IF VAR > 7 then do TASK_2
etc.
```

The first and second cases overlap. If VAR is 9, it fits in both cases. Which should be executed? The first task is the usual choice. Sometimes both are. Sometimes the second one is the correct choice.

### Invalid or impossible cases

The program executes TASK_16 only if VAR < 6 AND VAR > 18. TASK_16 can never run because VAR can't meet this condition. Similarly, the program might specify a value that VAR can't reach in practice, even though it's not an impossible number. You won't see this type of problem unless you look at the code, but it wastes code space and may reflect fuzzy thinking.

## ERRORS IN HANDLING OR INTERPRETING DATA

Data are passed from one part of a program to another, and from one program to another. In the process, the data might be misinterpreted or corrupted.

### PROBLEMS WHEN PASSING DATA BETWEEN ROUTINES

The program calls a subroutine and passes it data, perhaps like so:

```
DO SUB(VAR_1, VAR_2, VAR_3)
```

The three variables, VAR_1, VAR_2, and VAR_3 are *passed* from the program to the subroutine. They are called the subroutine's *parameters*. The subroutine itself might refer to these variables by different names. The statement at the start of the subroutine definition might look like this:

```
SUB(INPUT_1, INPUT_2, INPUT_3)
```

The subroutine receives the first variable in the list passed by the program (VAR_1) and calls it INPUT_1. It calls the second variable in the list (VAR_2) INPUT_2. INPUT_3 is its name for the last variable (VAR_3).

The program's and subroutine's definitions of these variables must match. If VAR_1 is an integer, INPUT_**1** should be as well. If VAR_2 is a floating point value for someone's temperature, that's what the subroutine had better expect to find in INPUT_2.

### Parameter list variables out of order or missing

If the program says DO SUB(VAR_2, VAR_1, VAR_3), the subroutine will associate INPUT_1 with VAR_2, and INPUT_2 with VAR_1. Programmers routinely type the variable names in the wrong order in these lists.

Missing parameters are less common in many, but not all, languages because their compilers catch this problem.

### Data type errors

Suppose the program defines VAR_1 and VAR_2 as two-byte integers but the subroutine defines INPUT_1 and INPUT_2 as one-byte integers. What happens is language dependent, but it would be no surprise if INPUT_1 got the first byte of VAR_1 and INPUT_2 got the second byte.

The *data type* specifies how the data are stored. Integers, floating points, and character strings are simple examples. Arrays, records (like a record in a database, with fields—see Chapter 12) and arrays of records are common examples of slightly more complex data structures. There are also stacks, trees, linked lists, and others. (See Elson, 1975, for descriptions of these.)

Sometimes a mismatch between the structure of data in the calling and called routines is deliberate. The calling program might pass a three-dimensional array which the subroutine treats as a bigger one-dimensional array. The calling routine might pass an array of characters to a subroutine that treats them as an array of numbers. Some languages ban this, but it is standard form in others. As you can imagine, it can lead to a big mess, especially when the variable(s) being reinterpreted are part of a larger list. If the calling and called routines differ in the amount of memory they expect these mismatched variables to use, anything that comes after these in the parameter list might be misread.

## Aliases and shifting interpretations of the same area of memory

If two different names refer to the same area of memory at the same time, they are aliases. If VAR_1 and FOO are aliases for each other, then if the program says SET FOO = 20, VAR_1 becomes 20. Some aliases are trickier. Suppose VAR_1 and VAR_2 are both one-byte integers and FOOVAR is a two-byte integer whose first (high order) byte just happens to be VAR_1 and whose second byte is VAR_2. In this case, SET FOOVAR = 20 sets VAR_2 to 20 and VAR_1 to 0.

It is easy to forget an alias. Expect maintenance programmers to miss it. In either case, the programmer will freely change one variable without realizing the effect on the "other." This can cause all sorts of unexpected results, even more so when the aliasing is more complex than two variables with the same name.

## Misunderstood data values

The program passes temperature in centigrade to a subroutine which interprets the value as fahrenheit. The subroutine puts a 1 into an error flag to indicate that the flag is clear. It uses –1 to indicate a set flag. The program expects 0 for a clear flag and any other value if the flag is set .

## Inadequate error information

The subroutine fails to set an error flag (maybe there is no error flag). Or it does signal an error but doesn't say enough else for the calling program to decide how to handle it.

## Failure to clean up data on exception-handling exit

The subroutine detects an error or a special case and exits quickly. Before it detected the problem, it changed the values of variables passed to it. If possible, it should reset these to their original values before returning to the calling program.

## Outdated copies of data

Two processes may keep their own copies of the same data. Two routines within the same process might do the same. When the data change, both (all) copies have to be updated. It's common to find one process or routine working with an outdated copy of the data, because another changed the data without indicating that it did so.

## Related variables get out of synch

One variable is usually a multiple of another, but one was changed and the other was not updated. In contrast to the outdated copy problem just described, which is more likely a problem between processes, this one is common within the same routine.

## Local setting of global data

*Global variables* are defined in the main program. Any subroutine can use them —read their values or change them. Subroutines' changes of a global variable are often accidental. The programmer thought that a second variable, local to the subroutine, had this name and that the change would be to that local variable.

## Global use of local variables

A variable is *local* to a subroutine if only that subroutine can use it. Most languages distinguish between global and local variables, but not all. In many BASICs, for example, all variables are global. In these, variables are kept local only by usage: they appear only in one subroutine. Especially if the variables are not carefully named, the programmer might unintentionally refer to a local variable in other places in the program.

**APPENDIX**

417

### Wrong mask in bit field

To save a few bytes and microseconds, some processes pass data in bit fields. Each byte might hold eight variables, with one bit assigned to each. Or, the processes might use the first two bits for one variable, the next three for a second, leaving one bit each for third, fourth, and fifth variables. A *mask* is a bit pattern that allows the programmer to focus only on the bits of interest. It has 0's in the other bit positions. The program refers to these to zero out the irrelevant bits in the bit field. If the mask has the wrong bits set, the program looks at the wrong "variable."

### Wrong value from a table

Data are often organized in tables (arrays or records). Pointer variables indicate where in the table a value should be stored or retrieved. The program might look in the wrong place (bad pointer) or it might look in the right place but find an incorrect value.

### DATA BOUNDARIES

The program may use the wrong starting or ending address of a set of data.

### Unterminated null terminated strings

STRING_VAR is a string variable. It can hold the string Hello or the string I am a string variable or a much longer string. The number of characters stored by a string variable isn't fixed, so there must be a way to indicate the end of the string. One approach puts a null character (all bits zero) after the last character. This is called the *string terminator*. In languages which use null terminators, all string handling routines look for the null. Occasionally, the null character is forgotten, overwritten, or just not copied with the rest of the string. A routine that works with this unterminated string, perhaps copying or printing it, will include the string and everything past what should be the string's end until it reaches a null or the end of the computer's memory. In copying the string to another variable, the routine might fill the new variable's data space plus hundreds of bytes past it, overwriting other variables or code.

### Early end of string

STRING_VAR is supposed to hold I am a string variable but a routine that operates on STRING_VAR (perhaps copying or printing it), behaves as if it held I am a str. Perhaps a null character was copied into the middle of the string. If string length is kept in a separate byte (the *length byte*), perhaps this value was miscalculated or overwritten.

### Read/write past end of a data structure, or an element in it

An array is a good enough example of a data structure for this description. The program might miscalculate the length of each element and so err when it tries to read the value of a specific element. In doing so, it might read a memory location well past the end of the array. The routine will probably also overshoot the end of the array if it expects the array to have more elements than it does. This kind of error usually happens when one routine sends the array to another, and their definitions of the data stored in it don't match.

### READ OUTSIDE THE LIMITS OF A MESSAGE BUFFER

A *buffer* is an area of memory used for temporary storage. Messages between processes often include buffers: the message includes a pointer to the start of the buffer and, in effect, says "for more details, read this. " When the process receiving the message is done with it, it "releases" the buffer which becomes "free memory" again, ready for other uses as needed by the operating system.

The receiving routine might get the address or the length of the message buffer wrong. It could start reading memory locations that precede the start of the buffer or it could keep reading data out of locations past the buffer's end.

### Compiler padding to word boundaries

Depending on the computer, a *word* might be 12 bits, 1, 2, 3, or 4 bytes long, or some other length. A word is a computer's most natural unit of storage. Some compilers "pad" all one-byte variables to make them a word long. For example, a variable whose value was 255 now has the value 00255: the leading zeros are padding. The variable takes more space but keeps the same value. Such a compiler might pad individual variables, individual elements of arrays, or the full array itself, to ensure that variables (or the array) have their first byte at the start of a word. Another compiler for the same language might not do this type of padding. Some routines calculate how many bytes a piece of data should be from the start of a data structure (perhaps the start of a message buffer). Such routines will fail when the programmer switches from a compiler that uses one set of padding rules to another compiler whose rules are different.

### Value stack under/overflow

Earlier in the Appendix ("Control flow errors") we described stack problems as they relate to subroutine calls. The programmer might also store data on the stack. A stack that holds data only, no—return addresses—is a *value stack*.

Suppose a stack can hold 256 bytes and the programmer tries to store 300 bytes on it. The stack overflows: the last 256 bytes stored are usually kept, and the first 44 values lost, overwritten by the others. When the program tries to retrieve these data from the stack, it can only get the last 256. When it tries to pop the 257th value off the stack (the 44th pushed onto the stack) there is an underflow condition—the program is trying to retrieve a value from a stack that is now empty.

### Trampling another process' code or data

This is especially common when processes share areas of memory, rather than passing data back and forth using messages. One process loses a null terminator from a string or miscalculates the length of a data structure or just runs amok. It writes junk into areas of memory that it shares with another process, or it writes into areas it can reach even though they should be private to that other process.

## MESSAGING PROBLEMS

The safest way for two processes to communicate is via messages. If they pass data through shared memory areas instead, a bug in one process can trash data used by both, no matter how defensively the other process was written. The most prevalent problems arising out of messaging architectures are race conditions, which are discussed in the next section. There are also errors in sending and receiving the data in a message.

### Messages sent to wrong process or port

A message can go to the wrong place. Even if it goes to the right process, that process may expect messages from this one to arrive only at certain ports (think of ports as virtual receiving areas). Even a message that goes to the right process and port may carry an invalid ID (such as the name of the communication protocol in use between the processes). In any of these cases, the message will be rejected.

### Failure to validate an incoming message

A process must check messages that it receives to make sure that they are intended for it, that they contain the right identifiers, etc. The process that sent this message may have sent it to the wrong place or it may be running amok. It is up to the receiving process to ensure that it accepts and acts on no garbage.

**APPENDIX**

## Lost or out of synch messages

One process may send many messages to another, in a predictable order. Sometimes, however, a process will send MESSAGE_2 before MESSAGE_1. It might send a request to write something to a disk file before sending a message that names the file and requests that it be opened. Messages can get out of order for hundreds of reasons; not all of them are bugs. The receiving program should be able to cope with this, perhaps by saving MESSAGE_2 until it gets MESSAGE_1, or by telling the other process that it discarded MESSAGE_2 because it came out of order.

Mismatching state information is a common symptom of a failure to cope with badly ordered messages. In the state table of one process, the disk file is open, the printer is initialized, the phone is offhook, etc. According to the other process, the disk file has not been opened, the printer is not ready, and the phone is on hook. It doesn't matter which process is right. The mismatch causes all sorts of confusion.

## Message sent to only N of N+1 processes

Suppose that many (N+1) processes keep private copies of the same data, and update their local databases when they get a message instructing them to do so. Or suppose that many people are at their terminals, a separate control and communications process is assigned to each terminal, and an urgent message is sent out, to be printed on each screen, saying that the system will go down in three minutes. Sometimes, one of the processes doesn't get the message. This is usually the most recently activated process or the one most recently coded.

## DATA STORAGE CORRUPTION

The data are stored on disk, tape, punch cards, whatever. The process corrupts stored data by putting bad values into these files.

## Overwritten changes

Imagine two processes working with the same data. Both read the data from disk at about the same time. One saves some changes. The second doesn't know anything about changes made by the first. When it saves its changes, it overwrites the data saved by the first process. Some programs use field, record, or file locking to prevent processes from changing fields, records, or files that another process is changing. These locks are not always present, and they don't always work.

## Data entry not saved

The program asks for data, which you enter. For some reason, maybe because the file is locked, it doesn't succeed in storing your entries on disk.

## Too much data for receiving process to handle

The receiving process might not be able to cope with messages beyond a certain length, or with more than so many messages per minute. It might discard the excess, crash, or print error messages. What it won't do is process the excess messages successfully.

## Overwriting a file after an error exit or user abort

You enter data but try to stop the program before it saves them. It saves the new (bad) data first, then stops.

# RACE CONDITIONS

In the classic race, there are two possible events, call them EVENT_A and EVENT_B. Both events will happen. The issue is which comes first. EVENT_A almost always precedes EVENT_B. There are logical grounds for expecting EVENT_A to precede EVENT_B. However, under rare and restricted conditions, EVENT_B can "win the race," and occur just before EVENT_A. We have a *race condition* whenever EVENT_B precedes EVENT_A. We have a *race condition bug* if the program fails when this happens. Usually the program fails because the programmer didn't anticipate the possibility of EVENT_B preceding EVENT_A, so he didn't write any code to deal with it.

Few testers look for race conditions. If they find an "irreproducible" bug, few think about timing issues (races) when trying to reproduce it. Many people find timing issues hard to conceptualize or hard to understand. We provide more than our usual amount of detail in the examples below, hoping that this will make the overall concept easier to understand.

## RACES IN UPDATING DATA

Imagine that one routine reads a credit card balance from the disk, adds the amount of the card holder's latest purchase, and writes the new balance back to the disk. A second routine reads the same balance, subtracts the latest payment, and saves the result to disk. A third routine adds foreign currency transactions. Each of these routines can run concurrently. Each runs quickly, and there are many different card holders, so the following scenario is most unlikely:

A credit card has a balance of $1000. The card holder has just made a purchase for $100 and a payment of $500. The correct balance is thus $600. However, the first routine reads the $1000 balance from the disk. While it adds the $100 purchase, the second routine reads the same card holder's balance (still $1000). Then the first routine stores the new balance ($1100) to disk. The second routine subtracts the $500 payment amount from the $1000 balance that it read from the disk. It saves the new balance ($500) to disk. The $100 addition made by the first routine has been completely lost because the second routine read the balance before the first routine had finished updating it.

This is a race condition: it should almost never happen that the second routine will read the balance after the first routine has started changing it but before the first routine finishes. However, it can happen and occasionally it will.

## ASSUMPTION THAT ONE EVENT OR TASK HAS FINISHED BEFORE ANOTHER BEGINS

The previous and the next sections provide examples of this type of problem.

## ASSUMPTION THAT INPUT WON'T OCCUR DURING A BRIEF PROCESSING INTERVAL

You type a character. The editing program you're testing receives it, moves other displayed characters around on the screen so it can display this one at the cursor location, echoes the received character, then looks for your next input. Naturally, since the computer is faster than the finger, the program should get everything done and be ready for the next input long before you're ready to type it. Accordingly, the program doesn't allow for the possibility that other characters will arrive before it's done with this one. However, a fast typist might enter two, three, or more characters before the editor is ready for them. The editor catches the last one typed and misses the others, which were typed while it was in the middle of dealing with the first one.

## ASSUMPTION THAT INTERRUPTS WON'T OCCUR DURING A BRIEF INTERVAL

The program is doing time-critical operations, such as:

- writing bits to the right place on a spinning disk or a moving cassette tape
- getting a pen to draw at the right place on a moving sheet of paper
- responding to a message or acknowledging input within a short time period

The programmer realizes that these operations take very little time. Since it's so unlikely for an interrupt-triggering event to happen in this brief interval, why take the time to block interrupts during it? Usually all goes well, but every now and again the program will be interrupted.

Failure to block interrupts was raised earlier ("Program runs amok: Interrupts"). There the focus was on the problems of interrupts. Here the point is one of timing. Even if part of a program is brief, if it lasts long enough that an interrupt-triggering event can happen during this interval, then some day an interrupt-triggering event will happen during the interval.

### RESOURCE RACES: THE RESOURCE HAS JUST BECOME UNAVAILABLE

Two processes both need the same printer. The one that takes control of the printer first gets it. The other has to wait. Even though there's a "race" here, this is not a race condition in concurrent systems. Programs are, or should be, written to expect the printer (or other sharable resources) to be temporarily unavailable.

Suppose, though, that one process checks whether a printer is available. If the printer is busy, the program does something else. If the printer is available, the program starts to use it. Since the program knows the printer is available, it doesn't consider the possibility that the printer is unavailable.

Unfortunately, there is a short *window of vulnerability* between the time that a process checks whether the printer is available and the time it takes the printer over. It takes a little time to examine the variable that says that the printer is free, call the right routine when the printer is available, find the data it's supposed to print, etc. During this short period, a second routine might take over the printer and start printing.

Some programmers would argue that this is a rare event. They're right. The window of vulnerability is so small that it is hard to set up a situation in which the second process can snatch away the printer just before the first one gets back to it. However, these processes maybe run by customers thousands or millions of times. Even unlikely race conditions will occur in use. If the consequences of a race condition bug are severe enough, it must be fixed even it will only happen once per million times that the program is used.

### ASSUMPTION THAT A PERSON, DEVICE, OR PROCESS WILL RESPOND QUICKLY

For example, the program puts a message on the screen and waits for a response for a few seconds. If you don't respond during this *time-out interval*, the program decides that you aren't there and halts. Similarly, another program trying to initialize a printer will wait only so long. The program will report that the printer is unavailable if it doesn't respond by the end of the time-out interval. Programs also impose time-outs while waiting for messages from other processes.

Very short time-out intervals cause races. If you have to press a key within a few tenths of a second after a program displays its message, you will often lose the race, the program will decide that you aren't there, and stop. If it gives you a few seconds, you will usually win the race, but sometimes the time-out interval will end just as you notice and respond to the message. If the program gives you minutes to respond, it is probably safe to assume that you are not there or are not going to respond. The intervals are different for device, or process responses, but the principle is the same. Some intervals are too short, some are just a little too short, and some are plenty long enough.

If the interval is too short, the programmer has probably anticipated that the program will time out before the person, device or process has had a chance to complete its response. Since this isn't an unusual case, he probably has good recovery code to deal with this. This isn't a classical race condition.

If the interval is just a little too short, the risks are higher. The programmer might believe that if the program doesn't receive a response within the specified period, it will never receive a response. What happens if the response arrives milliseconds after the time-out interval has ended? The program might interpret this as a response to some other message, or it might just crash. This is a classic race because it is unlikely, but not impossible, for the response to occur after the time-out period is over.

## OPTIONS OUT OF SYNCH DURING A DISPLAY CHANGE

The computer displays a menu and waits for your response. Triggered by a time-out or by another event (a message or a device input), the program switches to another menu. You press a key just as the program is writing the new menu. Here are two possible errors:

- Even though it's displaying the new options, the program will interpret your keypress as selecting a choice from the old menu if it hasn't yet updated its list of choices associated with keystrokes.
- Even though it's displaying the old options, the program will interpret your keypress as selecting a choice from the new menu, because it updated its key-to-option list before displaying the new values onscreen.

This is a real-user problem. Experienced users of a program know when the menu will change. Many make their responses as soon as possible, so they will frequently press a key just as the screen is being repainted.

## TASK STARTS BEFORE ITS PREREQUISITES ARE MET

The program starts sending data to the printer just before the printer is ready, starts trying to fill memory with data just before it's assigned a memory area to work with, etc. Perhaps the program is supposed to wait until it receives a specific message from another process before starting the task. But based on other information (such as other messages), the programmer knows that the trigger message will come soon. He starts this task early, to improve performance. The prerequisite tasks are usually completed in time, but occasionally the program is just barely ahead of them.

## MESSAGES CROSS OR DON'T ARRIVE IN THE ORDER SENT

Suppose you have $1000 in a bank account, and you try to do three things, in order:

(a) withdraw $1000

(b) deposit $500

(c) withdraw $100

The first withdrawal goes through. The deposit is accepted, but when you try withdraw the $100, you're told that your account's balance is zero, not $500. For some reason, your deposit has taken longer to process than your request for a withdrawal.

Problems of this class are common in message-passing systems: some messages are transmitted along circuitous routes, or their contents have to be verified, or for some other reason they don't arrive at their target process or aren't read by it before another message that was sent later. As a result, until the system catches up, you aren't (are) able to do something that you should (shouldn't) be able to do.

The most annoying version of this involves contradictory messages that cross each other's path. One process requests an action of another. The second process sends a message indicating that it can do that task (e.g., gives a receipt for the $500), but then sends a message saying that it can't (your balance is zero). The verification message that you deposited $500 reaches you and the central database at the same time, and just after your request for $100 reaches the database. To the database, it seemed that you asked for $100, then deposited $500, but because you received early verification, it seems to you that the database should have known about the $500 when it rejected the withdrawal.

## LOAD CONDITIONS

Programs misbehave when overloaded. A program may fail when working under high volume (lots of work over a long period) or under stress (maximum amount of work all at once). It may fail when

**A**

it runs out of memory, printers or other "resources." It may fail because it's required to do too much in too little time. All programs have limits. The issues are whether a program can meet its stated limits and how horribly it fails when those limits are exceeded.

Also, some programs create their own load problems, or, in multi-processing situations, make problems for others. They hog computer time or resources or create unnecessary extra work to such an extent that other processes (or themselves later) can't do their tasks.

## REQUIRED RESOURCE NOT AVAILABLE

The program tries to use a new device or store more data in memory, but can't. Run separate tests run for the program's handling of each of the conditions below, and similar tests for any other device you use (plotters, telephones, etc.). The following conditions should be self-explanatory:

- Full disk
- Full disk directory
- Full memory area
- Full print queue
- Full message queue
- Full stack
- Disk not in drive
- Disk drive out of service
- No disk drive
- Printer off line
- Printer out of paper
- Printer out of ribbon
- No printer
- Extended memory not present

## DOESN'T RETURN A RESOURCE

Systems may run out of resources because one or a few processes hog them all. Programmers are good at making sure that their programs get the resources they need. They are not as conscientious about returning resources they no longer need. Since the program won't crash (usually) if it hangs on to the printer or a memory buffer for too long, this type of problem seems less urgent.

The following sections are examples to consider when designing test cases.

### Doesn't indicate that it's done with a device

For example, a process uses the printer. All other processes have to wait until this one signals that it's done. The process fails to send that signal, and so prevents others from using an unused device.

### Doesn't erase old files from mass storage

The program doesn't erase outdated backups and internal-use temporary files. There are limits on how much erasure should be done automatically, but the process doesn't get rid of files that obviously should go.

### Doesn't return unused memory

In multi-processing systems, a memory management process can assign segments of memory to processes on a temporary basis (such as data and message buffers). The process is supposed to signal the memory manager when done with a segment. The manager takes back control of the segment and assigns it for use by other processes as needed. Failure to return buffers, especially message buffers, is *extremely* common.

### Wastes computer time

The process checks for events that are no longer possible or does other things that used to be necessary but now aren't.

## NO AVAILABLE LARGE MEMORY AREAS

In a message passing, multi-processing system, a pool of memory is available to be assigned as message buffers to any process. Some buffers are large, others just a few bytes. A large block of memory might be divided into many small buffers. What happens when the program needs a larger block of memory than any of these small ones?

Some memory management programs don't attempt to merge used buffers into the memory pool. Instead, they reuse these old buffers whenever a buffer their size is needed. As a result, there are few large areas of memory in the common pool.

## INPUT BUFFER OR QUEUE NOT DEEP ENOUGH

The process loses keystrokes, messages, or other data because too much comes at once and there's nowhere to put it all. When a process receives more individual data items (like keystrokes) than it can immediately handle, it usually stores the extras in an *input buffer*, reading them from the buffer and dealing with them when it has time. Similarly, it might store packets of information (like messages) in a *queue*, getting to them one at a time.

If the process' input buffer is 10 characters deep, what happens if you type 11 (or more) characters quickly? Does it signal that the buffer is full? What if the device sending input is a computer, connected to a modem? Does the program tell the sending program to stop for a while?

If the process' message queue is 256 messages deep, what happens when 256 messages are waiting, one is being processed, and the 257th arrives? Is it discarded or is it returned to the sender with an error code signaling that the message queue is full? If a few messages are discarded without notification, what is the most consequential message discarded? What important information has the receiving process lost that the sending process will assume was received?

## DOESN'T CLEAR ITEMS FROM QUEUE, BUFFER, OR STACK

Suppose the program receives messages, puts them in a queue, and reads them from the queue when it has time. It can store up to 256 messages in the queue. When it reads a message, the process should remove it from the queue, making room for a new one. However, programmers may forget to remove debugging messages, so the queue fills as soon as the program tries to use the queue for the 257th time.

In more subtle cases (similarly for failures to return buffers), messages are usually but not always removed from the queue. In one special case, the program doesn't discard old messages. It fails on the 257th time that this bug is triggered. It's because of these kinds of errors that you should occasionally test a program for a long time without rebooting it. Make sure that a minor problem, invisible over short periods, doesn't eventually devastate the system. A "long time" is defined in terms of your customers' needs. They will restart a word processor much more often than a telephone system. You might test the word processor for hours before rebooting, the telephones for weeks or months.

**A**

APPENDIX

## LOST MESSAGES

The operating system might lose some messages (presto, vanish). Or the receiving process might, if enough messages arrive at once. If a process is supposed to be able to handle a queue of 256 messages, what happens to the message it's working on, the message at the start of the queue, and the one at the end, when the 256th message arrives? What happens with the 257th, 258th, and 259th messages? Are they returned to the sending process with a "send-me-again-later" notification or are they just thrown away? Does the sending process need to know that the process it sent a message to was too busy to read it?

## PERFORMANCE COSTS

When the workload is high, everything slows down. Larger arrays have to be searched, more users or processes have to be served, etc. A program that must respond within a certain time or process so many events per second might fail because it's running under too busy a multi-processing system or because it's trying to juggle too many inputs itself. Other programs, expecting that this one will respond within a short interval, might also fail if this one responds too slowly.

## RACE CONDITION WINDOWS EXPAND

As performance gets worse, *race conditions* become more likely. In the classic race, two events can happen. One almost always precedes the other but sometimes the second will (or will appear to) precede the first by a tiny bit. As you slow the system down, it may take the computer longer to generate or detect the first event. If the second event is an input (keystroke or modem input), the person or machine that generates it may not be affected by the increased load. The second event will happen as quickly as usual even though the processing of the first has slowed. Thus there is more time for the second event to appear to beat the first.

## DOESN'T ABBREVIATE UNDER LOAD

Some processes make lots of output. Formatting all this information and sending it to the printer or screen takes lots of computer time. When the computer is operating under heavy load, an output-intensive process should try to send out less. It might express error messages more tersely, or abbreviate system log messages to short codes or send them to a buffer or disk file to be printed later. Only urgent messages should go to the printer or screen immediately.

Use your judgment before criticizing a program that doesn't abbreviate or run at lower priority. A word processing program that is about to print the agenda for a board meeting that starts in three minutes should neither delete items from the agenda nor wait till tomorrow before printing it.

## DOESN'T RECOGNIZE THAT ANOTHER PROCESS ABBREVIATES OUTPUT UNDER LOAD

Imagine a multi-user system in which all programs log failures and other "interesting" events to the system operator's console. Usually, the log messages include a few numbers plus English-language descriptions. Under heavy load, the messages are abbreviated to short numeric codes. No one can understand the codes without looking them up in a book, but at least the messages themselves don't further slow down the system.

Now suppose these logs are stored on disk. At the end of every day (week, month), a maintenance program reads the files and analyzes the system's failures, perhaps running hardware diagnostics in response to some of the messages. This maintenance program will have to be able to cope with the short code abbreviation system, or it will fail whenever it has to read a message that was saved when the system was under heavy load. A dismaying number of analysis programs do not know how to deal with abbreviated output.

## LOW PRIORITY TASKS NOT PUT OFF

Under heavy load, any task that doesn't have to be done immediately should be postponed. In a multi-processing system, programs or people are assigned priorities. Those with higher priorities should get a higher share of available machine time than those with lower priorities.

## LOW PRIORITY TASKS NEVER DONE

You can put off changing the oil in your car for a while, but eventually it must be done or else. Many low priority tasks are like this: you don't have to do them right away, but they must be done eventually. High priority tasks cannot be allowed to use all of the computer's time under prolonged periods of heavy load. Some time must be given to lower priority tasks.

## HARDWARE

Programs send bad data to devices, ignore error codes coming back, try to use devices that aren't there, and so on. Even if the problem is truly due to a hardware failure, there is also a software error if the software doesn't recognize that the hardware is no longer working correctly.

### WRONG DEVICE

For example, the program prints data on the screen instead of the printer.

### WRONG DEVICE ADDRESS

In many systems, a program writes data to a device by writing them to one or a few addresses in memory. The physical copying of data from these special memory locations to the devices themselves is taken care of by hardware. The program might write the data to the wrong memory location(s).

### DEVICE UNAVAILABLE

See "Required resource not available" earlier in this Appendix.

### DEVICE RETURNED TO WRONG TYPE OF POOL

For example, in a multi-processing system there might be many dot matrix printers and many laser printers. A program uses a dot matrix printer, then signals that it's done with it. On returning it to the pool of available devices, the resource manager erroneously marks it as an available laser printer.

### DEVICE USE FORBIDDEN TO CALLER

For example, you might not be allowed to use this expensive or delicate device. Programs running under your user ID can't use the device and must be able to recover from the refusal.

### SPECIFIES WRONG PRIVILEGE LEVEL FOR A DEVICE

To use a device (for example, to read a certain file or to place a long distance phone call), the program must supply a code that indicates its privilege level (often the privilege level of the person using the program.) If its privilege level (or priority) is high enough, the program gets the device.

## NOISY CHANNEL

The program starts using a device, such as a printer or a modem. A communication channel links the computer and the connected device. Electrical interference, timing problems or other oddities might cause imperfect transmission of information over the channel (we.e., the computer sends a 3 but the device receives a 1). How does the program detect transmission errors? What does it do to signal or correct them?

## CHANNEL GOES DOWN

The computer is sending data through one modem across a telephone line to another computer (and modem). One of the modems is unplugged halfway through the transmission. How do the sending and receiving computers recognize that they are no longer connected, how long does it take them, and what do they do about it? Similarly, how does a computer recognize that it's connected to a no-longer-printing printer, and what does it do about it?

## TIME-OUT PROBLEMS

The program sends a signal to a device and expects a response within a reasonable time. If it gets no response, eventually the program must give up, deciding perhaps that the connected device is broken. What if it just didn't wait long enough?

## WRONG STORAGE DEVICE

The program looks for data or a code overlay on the wrong floppy disk, removable hard disk, cartridge, or tape reel. Some programs announce that the information isn't there, then ask you to insert the right disk. Some look for the information on other drives first, then ask. Others just die. In one particularly feisty operating system, programs could destroy a floppy disk's directory while looking for a file that wasn't there.

## DOESN'T CHECK DIRECTORY OF CURRENT DISK

Insert one disk (hard disk pack, tape), work with it, then remove it and insert a different one into the same drive. Some operating systems don't detect the swap. They copy the directory of a disk into memory and don't read it again from the disk unless you explicitly tell them to. If you don't force a reboot or a directory reread, they'll use the old directory when trying to read or write to the new disk, reading gibberish and destroying the new disk's data when they write.

## DOESN'T CLOSE A FILE

When the program finishes with a file (especially if it's been writing to the file), it should close the file. Otherwise, changes made to the file during this session might not be saved on disk, or further changes may be added inadvertently. Open files can be destroyed or corrupted when you turn the machine off. Programs should close all open files as part of their exit procedures.

## UNEXPECTED END OF FILE

While reading a file, the program reaches the end-of-file marker. Suppose the program expects to find specific data later in the file. Does it ignore the end-of-file and try to keep reading? Does it crash?

## DISK SECTOR BUGS AND OTHER LENGTH-DEPENDENT ERRORS

Disk storage is done in chunks (sectors) of perhaps 256 or 512 bytes. Many other values, usually powers of 2, are common. Some programs fail when they try to save or read a file that is an exact multiple of a sector size. For example, if sectors are 1024 bytes, a program might be unable to save files that are 1024, 2048, 3072, etc., bytes long. (Similarly, a program that copies data to an output buffer of a fixed size might fail if the number of bytes to go is the same size as the buffer.)

The last character of each sector, or only the last character of the file, might be miscopied, copied twice, or dropped. In more extreme cases, the program corrupts the entire file or overwrites the next file on disk.

## WRONG OPERATION OR INSTRUCTION CODES

The program sends a command to the terminal that is supposed to reposition the cursor onscreen but it turns on inverse video display mode instead. The program sends a command to the printer to do a form feed, but the printer line feeds instead.

Devices are not standardized. Two printers probably require two different commands to do the same thing. Similarly for terminals, plotters, and A/D converters. The program must issue the right command for this device to get the right task done.

## MISUNDERSTOOD STATUS OR RETURN CODE

The program sends a command to the printer telling it to turn on boldfacing. The printer may respond, saying it can or can't do this. It may indicate why it can't carry out the command (e.g., no paper, no ribbon, no such command, option module not installed.). Many programs ignore these codes, or compare them against a list of codes written for the wrong machine or compiled years ago.

## DEVICE PROTOCOL ERROR

The communication protocol between the computer and a device or between two computers specifies such things as when the computer can send data, at what speed, and with what characteristics (parity, stop bits, etc.). It also specifies whether and how the receiving device will signal that it got the data, that it's ready for more, or that it can't take any more until it clears some of the buffer that it's working with.

A device might send data or respond out of turn, or it might send the data in the wrong format.

## UNDERUTILIZES DEVICE INTELLIGENCE

As a simple example, if the printer can print boldface text directly, why try to simulate boldface by printing on top of the same character three or four times? One possible answer is that the program was designed with less capable printers in mind, and has not been updated to take advantage of this printer's features.

A connected device might be able to define its own fonts, detect its own error states, etc., but the program using the device must recognize this or it won't make any use of these advanced capabilities.

This can be a touchy issue. Printers' control codes differ by so much that it is very expensive to try to support all the built-in features of every printer. Some printer manufacturers have made this problem even more complex by including certain control codes in one ROM version for a printer, but including different codes in other ROMS, plugged into the same (from appearance and model number) printer.

**A**

## PAGING MECHANISM IGNORED OR MISUNDERSTOOD

This is a memory storage issue. Memory might be divided into sections called *pages*. A program might not be able to read from all pages at once or switch pages (or memory *banks*) correctly.

Larger computers use disk storage as *virtual memory*. The program refers to data without knowing whether they reside in memory or on disk. If the program references a nonresident set of data or code, a *page fault* has occurred. The computer fetches the page containing this information from disk automatically, overwriting data that were resident. The operating system usually takes care of paging (swapping data and code between main memory and a disk), but a few programs try to do it themselves. A program might overwrite a memory area without first saving new data that were stored there.

A program that *thrashes* is constantly generating page faults: the computer spends more time moving data in and out of main memory than it does executing the program. With a little reorganization of the code or the data, many programs can avoid thrashing.

## IGNORES CHANNEL THROUGHPUT LIMITS

Examples:

- The program tries to send 100 characters per second across a connection that only supports transmission of up to 10 characters per second.
- The program can send data at a fast rate until the connected device's input buffer is full. Then it has to stop until the device makes more room in its input buffer. Some programs don't recognize signals that the device is no longer ready to receive more data.

## ASSUMES DEVICE IS OR ISN'T, OR SHOULD BE OR SHOULDN'T BE INITIALIZED

Before sending text to the printer, a word processing program sends an initialization message telling the printer to print ten characters per inch in a certain font, without making them bold or italicized. Should it have sent this message? This wastes time if the printer was already initialized. It is irritating if you deliberately initialized the printer to a different setting before trying to print the file. On the other hand, if the printer is set to an unsuitable font, the printout will be unsatisfactory and the failure to initialize will have wasted time and paper. Which error is more serious?

## ASSUMES PROGRAMMABLE FUNCTION KEYS ARE PROGRAMMED CORRECTLY

A programmable function key might be able to generate any code or any reasonably short sequence of codes when pressed. The program might expect these keys to generate specific codes, but if you can reprogram the keys, the program might be wrong. For example, suppose that function key `<PF-1>` normally generates `<Escape><r><Ctrl-D>`. A program says `Press PF-1 to Print`. It switches to its Print Menu when it receives `<Escape><r><Ctrl-D>`. What if you reprogram `<PF-1>` so that it generates `<Escape><Ctrl-Q>` instead? `Press PF-1 to Print` is no longer true.

If the program relies on the assignment of special values to programmable function keys, when it starts it has to make sure that those keys have been assigned those values.

## SOURCE, VERSION, AND ID CONTROL

If you're supposed to have Version 2.43 of the program, but some of the pieces you have are from 2.42 and others are advance bits of 2.44, you have a mess. You must know what you have, you must be able to tell from the code what you have, and what you have must be what you're supposed to have. If not, report a bug.

Some people calls these *Bureaucracy Bugs* because they reflect failures of labeling and procedure rather than operational failures. Only bureaucrats would worry about such things, right? Wrong. Or maybe right, but so what? They must be worried about—otherwise the products shipped to customers will not be what you think.

## OLD BUGS MYSTERIOUSLY REAPPEAR

Old problems can reappear simply because the programmer linked an old version of one subroutine with the latest version of the rest of the program. Many programs are split across dozens or hundreds of files: Programmers who don't purge old files frequently link old code with new by accident.

## FAILURE TO UPDATE MULTIPLE COPIES OF DATA OR PROGRAM FILES

Some programmers repeat the same code in many different program modules. When they have to change this code, they may update 20 of the 25 copies of it, forgetting the others. As a result, they might fix the same error 20 times, but you might still find 5 more just like it the next time you test.

## NO TITLE

The program should identify itself when it starts. You should know right away that you are now running Joe Blow's Super Spreadsheet, not Jane Doe's Deluxe Database.

## NO VERSION ID

The program should display its version identification when it starts or when you give it a display version command. Customers should be able to find this ID easily, so they can tell it to you when they call to complain about the program. You should be able to find the ID easily so that you can tell it to the programmer when you find bugs.

If the program is made of many independently developed pieces, it pays to be able to identify the version of each piece. These IDs may not display automatically—you may have to use a debugger or a special editor to find them. They are useful if they exist and if they are kept up to date by the programmers. However, unless you have firm management backing, do not insist that programmers compile separate version IDs for each module.

## WRONG VERSION NUMBER ON THE TITLE SCREEN

Programs usually display a version number on the title screen or in an *About* dialog box. Usually, the programmer can change the code much faster than she can keep the correct version number updated on the title screen. The result is you might be using software version 2.1 but the title screen still shows 2.0.

## NO COPYRIGHT MESSAGE OR A BAD ONE

The program should display a copyright message as soon as it starts. The message should include the copyright symbol (it is common to use (C)), the year(s) that the program was developed, copyrighted or shipped, your company's name and address, and the words *All Rights Reserved*. We use the following form:

Copyright © 1979, 1983, 1987, 1993
Cem Kaner, Human Interface Technologies
801 Foster City Blvd. #101, Foster City, CA 94404
All Rights Reserved

If an earlier version of the program showed a copyright year of 1979, you should still say 1979 in this notice, along with this year's date. For more details, ask your company's attorney.

## ARCHIVED SOURCE DOESN'T COMPILE INTO A MATCH FOR SHIPPING CODE

Before releasing a product to any customer, archive the source code. If the customer finds a bug, your company must be able to recompile this code and regenerate the product that the customer has. Without this starting point, you will have major problems addressing that customer's difficulties.

This should be obvious, but it seems not to be. I've been amazed at how many companies can't recreate products they sell. They may have archival copies of source code, but the code in their vaults is a bit different from the code in the product they shipped. This is begging for a disaster.

If you report that archives are not up to date with code that is about to be shipped, and are rebuffed, take it to a higher level. The president and the company lawyer might be much more concerned by this problem than mid-level engineering or marketing managers.

## MANUFACTURED DISKS DON'T WORK OR CONTAIN WRONG CODE OR DATA

When the disks have been duplicated and the product is ready to ship, check a few disks. We are not suggesting that you take over the role of manufacturing QA. We are suggesting that any error that occurs in all manufactured copies of the product is an error you should find.

Disk duplicators might crank out blank disks instead of the copies you expected them to make. It is embarrassing when you ship blanks as the product, and expensive to send customers replacement disks. This does happen. Over the last two years, I've received blank disks as a customer three times (three different companies). Similarly, the manufacturing group might duplicate the wrong version (Version 1.0 again instead of 2.0) or the wrong program (buy a database, get a spreadsheet instead), sometimes because you gave them the wrong disks to duplicate.

## TESTING ERRORS

This section deals with technical, procedural, and reporting errors made by testers and Testing Groups. Even though these aren't problems in the programs per se, you'll run into them when testing programs. Our focus is on suggestions for dealing with these problems, since they're under your control.

## MISSING BUGS IN THE PROGRAM

You will always miss bugs because you can't execute all possible tests. However, you'll probably miss more bugs than you have to. When a bug is discovered in the field or late in testing, ask why. Not to assign blame but to look for ways to strengthen your test procedures.

### Failure to notice a problem

You may miss a bug that a test exposes because:

- *You don't know what the correct test results are.* Whenever possible, include expected results in the test notes. In automated tests, display them beside test results on the screen and on printouts.

- *The error is buried in a massive printout.* People scan long outputs quickly. Keep printouts as short as you can, and make errors obvious at a glance. Patterned outputs are good. If possible, redirect long outputs to a disk file; have the computer check this against a known good file.

- *You don't expect to see it exposed by this test.* While a test may be designed to focus on one small part of a program it can still reveal other, unexpected, bugs. Beware of tunnel vision.

- *You are bored or inattentive.* Rotate tasks across testers. Try not to have the same person run the same test more than three times.

- *The mechanics of running the test are so complicated that you pay more attention to them than to the test outputs.* You will be distracted by files or printouts with erroneous comparison data, poorly organized checklists, procedures that require you to swap disks or tapes frequently, and tasks that you have to redo from the start if you make an entry error.

### Misreading the screen

You can easily miss errors like spelling mistakes, missing menu items, and misaligned text. Reserve some time exclusively for scrutinizing the screen. It's just like proofreading manuscripts: unless you're consciously looking for spelling and layout errors, you'll see what you expect to see, filling in gaps and correctly spelling mistakes unconsciously.

### Failure to report a problem

You may find a problem and not report it because:

- You keep poor notes
- You're not sure if it's a bug and are afraid to look silly
- You think it's too minor or you don't think it will be fixed
- You're told not to report bugs like this any more

These are not acceptable reasons. If you're not sure whether something is a problem, say so in the report. Appeal to higher management to relieve criticism for reporting minor or politically inconvenient bugs. It is your responsibility to report every problem you find. Deliberate suppression of bug reports leads to confusion, poorer tester morale, and a poorer product. It can also bring you into the middle of nasty office politics, possibly as a scapegoat.

### Failure to execute a planned test

You may not execute a planned test because:

- *Your test materials or notes are disorganized.* You've lost track of what has been tested.

- *You are bored.* The test series is repetitive. You take shortcuts by skipping tests that are similar to others. To reduce this, rotate tasks among testers. Reduce repetition by combining cases, cutting some out, or running some tests only on every second or third cycle of testing.

- *You have combined too much into one test.* If one test is buried inside another, or depends on another, then if that other test fails, this test probably won't be executed. Overly complex combinations of test cases can lead to missed tests because they confuse you.

### Failure to use the most "promising" test cases

If two test cases cover essentially the same code, you should use the one most likely to reveal an error (see Chapter 6).

### Ignoring programmers' suggestions

The programmer knows better than anyone else which areas of the program he tested least, and which ones proved least stable under his testing. He knows which areas he coded quickly. He knows which special types of tests have exposed bugs so far. Rigid test plans and bad politics are problems in their own right, but they are not excuses for ignoring programmers' tips.

### FINDING "BUGS" THAT AREN'T IN THE PROGRAM

You report an error. Eventually, the problem is traced to a flaw in your test procedure, a misunderstanding of the program, or to something else that you did. This wastes time and does your credibility no good.

## Errors in testing programs

When you automate tests, you write programs to drive test cases. Your test programs will have bugs. Some will abort your tests, or skip them. Others will make the program appear to fail tests that it can actually pass. It is common to compare test data against incorrect "known good" results. Your disk files and printed constants are no more likely correct than the program's output.

You should manually reproduce any automated tests that reveal errors. This doesn't take all that much time because you only redo tests that the program fails. Unless the program is in disastrously bad shape, it won't fail many tests.

## Corrupted data file

Some apparent bugs are due to a bad data file that you're using while testing. Programs will trash input, output, and comparison files. Your files may be corrupted at any time, even by program segments that, if they were error-free, wouldn't read or write these files. When a program is in testing, it doesn't matter that it *isn't supposed to* touch a file. If the program worked the way it was supposed to, you wouldn't have to test it.

It is wise to keep three backup copies of test files on separate disks or tapes. Before reporting an error, check your working copies of the input and comparison files against the backups.

## Misinterpreted specifications or documentation

You think the program works incorrectly because you've misunderstood the documentation. This is unavoidable. Specifications are outdated, and early versions of the documentation are rough. You rarely have much time to read before starting to test the program.

When you find an error, unless you're sure you understand what's happening in this part of the program, reread the relevant sections of the documentation and specifications. If you're not sure whether what you've got is an error, write your report as a Query. If the manual's unclear, file a Problem Report on that part of the manual too.

## POOR REPORTING

It's not enough to find a bug. You have to communicate it to someone who can fix it, in a way that makes it as easy as possible for that person to figure out what went wrong and what to do about it. How well you describe the problem will directly affect how easily it is resolved.

## Illegible reports

If the programmer finds it hard to read a report, he will ignore it for as long as possible. Many reports are hard to read because you pack too much information into them. Put separable problems on separate report forms. If a single problem requires a long description, type it on a separate page and attach it to the Problem Report.

## Failure to make it clear how to reproduce the problem

You report a problem without outlining, step by step, what the programmer must do to see it. *This is the most common error in problem reporting.* It saves time to skip the details, but realize that the first thing that the programmer is going to do with your report is sit at the machine and try to see the problem himself. If he can't reproduce the problem, he won't fix it.

For anything complicated, attach a copy of any data files you were using, a keystroke by keystroke list of things you did, a printed dump of the screen if your operating system supports this, or any other comments or materials that will make the programmer's job easier. The nearer you are to the development deadline, the more important this is.

### Failure to say that you can't reproduce a problem

If you can't consistently reproduce the problem, say so. This tips off the conscientious programmer that he should try variations on the conditions you describe. A non-conscientious programmer might ignore your report as soon as she sees that you can't replicate it, but she'd toss away the report anyway after trying exactly what you say you did and, like you, failing to see the bug.

### Failure to check your report

After writing a report, but before submitting it, follow it step by step to reproduce the problem. This costs a few moments but it catches transcription and other reporting errors that you make. It is all too easy to omit or misdescribe important details, especially if you're writing the report from notes or memory, long after seeing the bug.

### Failure to report timing dependencies

You might not notice that to reproduce a bug you have to press two keys within milliseconds of each other, or that you have to wait at least 5 minutes between keystrokes. Sometimes you will just not realize that you're dealing with a race condition or other time-dependent bug. If you do notice a time dependence, say so. Clock it as well as you can. If you didn't notice a time dependence, look for one when a report comes back to you as irreproducible.

### Failure to simplify conditions

You will often use complex test cases, combining many different tests into one, for speed of testing. If all goes well, you've gotten through many tests quickly. When a bug does show up, spend time looking for the simplest series of steps possible to reproduce it. Try not to lay out a long and complicated series that includes irrelevancies. Complex reports are disheartening to read and tempting to ignore.

### Concentration on trivia

Don't make big issues over small problems. Don't get too far drawn into long arguments over wording, or style of presentation. Don't exaggerate the severity of bugs. Be wary of getting a reputation as a nitpicker.

### Abusive language

If you refer to work as "unprofessional," "sloppy," or "incompetent," expect the programmer who did it to get angry. Don't bet that he'll fix the bug, even if it's serious. It can be useful to shock a programmer occasionally, but be conscious of what you're doing. Do it rarely (once a year).

## POOR TRACKING OR FOLLOW-UP

It's not enough to just report a bug. You've got to make sure that it's noticed and not forgotten. Otherwise, bugs will "slip through the cracks" and make it into the shipping product.

### Failure to provide summary reports

Don't assume that just because you gave it to a programmer, it's being dealt with. Some programmers lose reports. Other use them to make paper airplanes or wrap fish. Some also hide reports from their managers. Every week or two, you should circulate a brief description of unfixed bugs. Make this a standard procedure, for all bugs, to keep it impersonal and uncontroversial.

APPENDIX

### Failure to re-report serious bugs

If the bug is serious, don't automatically accept a response of `Deferred` or `Works to Spec`. Figure out a way to make it look a little worse and report it again. If it's an ugly, horrible bug, make it sound that way the second time. If that doesn't work, send a copy of the third report to a more senior manager.

### Failure to verify fixes

A programmer reports that he fixed a problem. Don't take his word for it without retesting. Up to a third of the fixes either won't work or will cause other problems. Further, some programmers only address the exact, reported symptoms. Instead of investigating the causes of a problem, they write special-case code to handle the precise circumstances reported. If you skimp on regression testing, you will assuredly miss bugs.

### Failure to check for unresolved problems just before release

Just before the product is released for use or sale, check for problems that are neither fixed nor deferred. It's good practice, which we recommend highly, to make sure that all Problem Reports are resolved one way or another before the product is released. At a minimum, make sure no one's sitting on anything serious. This is your last chance to remind people of serious bugs.

# REFERENCES

88open Consortium, Ltd. (1991). *The World of Standards: An Open Systems Reference Guide*. (Contact 88open at 408-436-6600).

Abramowitz, M. & Stegun, I. A. (Eds.) (1964). *Handbook of Mathematical Functions*. New York: Dover Publications.

Ackerman, P. (1989). Note: "Canned" Software Warranties: Concerns on Both Sides of the Transaction, *Santa Clara Computer & High Technology Law Journal, 5,* 163-198.

ADAPSO (1986). *Packaged Microcomputer Software Warranties in the Absence of Negotiated Agreements* (Available from ADAPSO, Arlington, VA).

*Advent Systems, Ltd. v. Unisys Corp.* (1991). Federal Reporter, Second Series, *925,* 670-682 (Third Circuit Court of Appeals).

*Aetna Casualty & Surety Co. v. Jeppesen & Co.* (1981). Federal Reporter, Second Series, *642,* 339-344 (Ninth Circuit Court of Appeals).

*Affiliates for Evaluation and Therapy v. Viasyn Corp.* (1967). Southern Reporter, Second Series, *500,* 688-693 (Florida District Court of Appeal).

American Society for Quality Control, *Code of Ethics*. These are published in many ASQC materials. Call ASQC at 1-800-248-1946 for a copy, or ask for their Certification Brochure for Certified Quality Engineers, which always contains a copy.

*American Universal Insurance Group v. General Motors Corp.* (1991). Southern Reporter, Second Series, *578,* 451-455 (Florida District Court of Appeal).

Andriole, S. J. (Ed.) (1986). *Software Validation, Verification, Testing and Documentation*. Princeton: Petrocelli Books.

*ANSI/IEEE Standard for Software Quality Assurance Plans*. ANSI/IEEE Std 730-1981.

*ANSI/IEEE Standard for Software Test Documentation*. ANSI/IEEE Std 829-1983.

*ANSI/IEEE Guide to Software Requirements Specifications*. ANSI/IEEE Std 830-1984.

*ANSI/IEEE Standard for Software Verification and Validation Plans*. ANSI/IEEE Std 1012-1986.

*ANSI/IEEE Standard for Software Unit Testing*. ANSI/IEEE Std 1008-1987.

Apple Computer, Inc. (1987). *Human Interface Guidelines: The Apple Desktop Interface*. Reading, MA: Addison-Wesley.

Apple Computer, Inc. (1992). *Guide to Macintosh Software Localization*. Reading, MA: Addison-Wesley.

Apple Computer, Inc. *Macintosh Worldwide Development: Guide to System Software* (M7047/A). Order from APDA, Apple Computer, 20525 Mariani Ave, MS 33-G, Cupertino, CA 95014-6299).

Apple Computer, Inc. *Software Development for International Markets* (A7G0016). Order from APDA, Apple Computer, 20525 Mariani Ave, MS 33-G, Cupertino, CA 95014-6299).

Association for Computing Machinery (1992) *ACM Proposed Code of Ethics and Professional Conduct (Draft, February 12, 1992)*. Reprinted in *Communications of the ACM, May, 1992*, p. 94-99.

Baecker, R. M. & Buxton, W. A. S. (Eds.) (1987). *Readings in Human Computer Interaction: A Multidisciplinary Approach.* San Mateo, CA: Morgan Kaufmann.

Bailey, R. W. (1989). *Human Performance Engineering: Using Human Factors / Ergonomics to Achieve Computer System Usability,* Second Edition. Englewood Cliffs, NJ: Prentice Hall.

Bard, Y. (1974). *Nonlinear Parameter Estimation.* New York: Academic Press.

*Barazzotto v. Intelligent Systems, Inc.* (1987). North Eastern Reporter, Second Series, *532,* 148-151 (Ohio Court of Appeals).

Bass, L. (1986; with 1991 Supplement). *Products Liability: Design and Manufacturing Defects.* Colorado Springs: Shepard's/McGraw-Hill.

Beck, J. V. & Arnold, K. J. (1977). *Parameter Estimation in Engineering and Science.* New York: John Wiley & Sons.

Beizer, B. (1984). *Software System Testing and Quality Assurance.* New York: Van Nostrand Reinhold.

Beizer, B. (1990). *Software Testing Techniques,* Second Edition. New York: Van Nostrand Reinhold.

Bergland G, D. (1981). A guided tour of program design methodologies. *Computer* (October issue), 18-37. Reprinted in Zelkowitz (1982).

Bergland G, D. & Gordon, R. D. (Eds.) (1979). *Tutorial: Software Design Strategies.* IEEE Computer Society. IEEE Catalog No. EHO149-5.

Bermant, C. (1984). Copy Protection: A Case of Overkill? Vault Corporation's Prolok Plus Causes Pirate Woes and Industry Debate, *InfoWorld*, *3*, Nov. 27, 54.

*Black's Law Dictionary* (1990). Sixth Edition. St. Paul, MN: West Publishing.

Boehm, B. W. (1976). Software Engineering. *IEEE Transactions on Computers, C-25.* Reprinted in Bergland & Gordon (1979).

Boehm, B.W. (1981). *Software Engineering Economics.* Englewood Cliffs, NJ: Prentice Hall.

Bohan, T.L. (1988). The Performance Audit: Minimizing Software Liability (Part II). *Idea, 29,* 134-152.

Boss, A.H., Weinberg, H.R., & Woodward, W.J. (1989). Survey: Scope of the Uniform Commercial Code: Advances in Technology and Survey of Computer Contracting Cases. *The Business Lawyer, 44,* 1671-1698.

Branscomb, A. (1990). Rogue Computer Programs and Computer Rogues: Tailoring the Punishment to Fit the Crime. *Rutgers Computer & Technology Law Journal, 16,* 1-61.

Branstad, J. C., Cherniavsky, J. C. & Adrion, W. R. (1980). Validation, Verification and Testing for the Individual Programmer. *NBS Special Publication 500-56,* National Bureau of Standards. Reprinted in McCabe (1983), p. 57 - 78.

*Brocklesby v. United States,* (1985). Federal Reporter, Second Series, *767,* 1288-1299 (9th Circuit Court of Appeals), *Certiorari denied,* (1986). United States Reports, *474,* 1101.

Brockmann, R.J. (1990). *Writing Better Computer User Documentation: From Paper to Hypertext.* New York: John Wiley & Sons.

Brooks, F. P. (1975). *The Mythical Man-Month: Essays on Software Engineering.* Reading, MA: Addison-Wesley.

Brooks, L. R. (1978). Nonanalytic concept formation and memory for instances. In Rosch & Lloyd (1978).

Brown, P.A. & Feinman, J.M. (1991). Economic loss, commpercial practices, and legal process: Spring Motors Distributors, Inc. v. Ford Motor Co. *Rutgers Law Journal, 22,* 301-320.

Brown, S. (Ed.) (1991). *The Product Liability Handbook*. New York: Van Nostrand Reinhold.

Bryan, W. L. & Siegel, S. G. (1984). Product assurance: Insurance against a software disaster. *Computer, 17* (April issue), p. 75-83.

Bungert, H. (1992). Compensating harm to the defective product itself—A comparative analysis of American and German products liability laws. *Tulane Law Review, 66,* 1179-1266.

Calamari, J. D. & Perillo, J. M. (1987). *The Law of Contracts,* Third Edition. St. Paul, MN: West Publishing.

California Penal Code. St. Paul, MN: West Publishing, 1988 & Supp. 1991.

Campanella, J. (Ed.) (1990). *Principles of Quality Costs: Principles, Implementation and Use,* Second Edition. Milwaukee, WI: ASQC Quality Press.

Card, S. K., Moran, T. P. & Newell, A. (1983). *The Psychology of Human-Computer Interaction*. Hillsdale, NJ: Lawrence Erlbaum Associates.

Carnahan, B., Luther, H. A., & Wilkes, J. O. (1969). *Applied Numerical Methods*. New York: John Wiley & Sons.

*Carnival Cruise Lines, Inc. v. Shute* (1991). United States Reports, *499,* —; Supreme Court Reporter, *111* S.Ct. 1522-1533.

Carroll, J.M. (1990). *The Nurnberg Funnel.* Cambridge, MA: The MIT Press.

Carter, D.R. (1991). *Writing Localizable Software for the Macintosh.* Reading, MA: Addison-Wesley.

Carterette, E.C. & Friedman, M. P. (Eds.) (1978) *Handbook of Perception, Volume IV*. New York: Academic Press.

Chambers, J. M. (1977). *Computational Methods for Data Analysis*. New York: John Wiley & Sons.

*Chatlos Systems v. National Cash Register Corp.* (1979). Federal Supplement, *479,* 738-749 (District of New Jersey).

*Chemtrol Adhesives, Inc. v. American Manufacturers Mutual Insurance Company, Inc.,* (1989). North Eastern Reporter, Second Series, *537,* 624-640 (Ohio Supreme Court).

Cheney, T. A. R. (1983). *Getting the Words Right: How to Revise, Edit & Rewrite*. Cincinnati, OH: Writer's Digest Books.

Churchman, C. W. & Ratoosh, P. (Eds.) (1959). *Measurement: Definitions and Theories*. New York: John Wiley & Sons.

Churilla, K. R. (1991). *The Computer Industry Directory*. San Jose, CA: Mentor Market Research.

*Clements Auto Company v. Service Bureau Corp.* (1971). Federal Reporter, Second Series, *444*, 169-191 (Eighth Circuit Court of Appeals).

Cole, G.S. (1990). Tort liability for artificial intelligence and expert systems. *Computer/Law Journal, 10,* 127-231.

Commerce Clearing House (1990). Computer Company Agrees Not to Advertise Unavailable Software. *CCH Guide to Computer Law*, 23 April 27.

Condo, J. (1991). Computer malpractice: Two alternatives to the traditional "professional negligence" standard. *Computer/Law Journal, 11,* 323-340.

Conley, J.M. (1987). Tort theories of recovery against vendors of defective software. *Rutgers Computer & Technology Law Journal, 13,* 1-32.

*Consolidated Data Terminals v. Applied Digital Data Systems* (1983). Federal Reporter, Second Series, *708,* 385 (Ninth Circuit Court of Appeals).

*Consumers Power Co. v. Curtiss-Wright Corp* (1986). Federal Reporter, Second Series *780,* 1093-1102 (Third Circuit Court of Appeals).

Consumers Union (1989). A breakdown in auto safety. *Consumer Reports* (February issue), 84.

Conte, S. D. & de Boor, D. (1980). *Elementary Numerical Analysis: An Algorithmic Approach*. New York: McGraw-Hill.

*Continental Insurance v. Page Engineering Co.,* (1989). Pacific Reporter, Second Series, *738* 641-685 (Wyoming Supreme Court).

Copyright Act of 1976, *United States Code*, Title 17, beginning at § 101.

Curtis, B. (1983). Software metrics: Guest editor's introduction. *IEEE Transactions on Software Engineering, SE-9,* p. 1044-1050.

Curtis, B. (Ed.) (1981). *Tutorial: Human Factors in Software Development*. Los Alamitos, CA: IEEE Computer Society.

*Data Processing Services, Inc. v. L.H. Smith Oil Corp.* (1986). North Eastern Reporter, Second Series, *492,* 314-323 (Indiana Court of Appeals).

DeGrace, P. & Stahl, L.H. (1991). *Wicked Problems, Righteous Solutions: A Catalogue of Modern Software Engineering Paradigms*. Englewood Cliffs, NJ: Yourdon Press.

DeMarco T. (1979). *Structured Analysis and System Specification*. Englewood Cliffs, NJ: Prentice Hall.

DeMillo, R. A., McCracken, W. M., Martin, R. J. & Passafiume, J. F. (1987). *Software Testing and Evaluation*. Menlo Park, CA: Benjamin/Cummings.

Deming, W. E. (1982). *Out of the Crisis*. Cambridge. MA: Massacusetts Institute of Technology.

Dhillon, B. S. (1986), *Human Reliability with Human Factors*. New York: Pergamon Press.

*Diversified Graphics, Ltd. v. Groves* (1989). Federal Reporter, Second Series, *868,* 293-297.

Doyle M. & Straus, D. (1976). *How to Make Meetings Work*. New York: Jove Books.

Draper, J.M. (Annotation). Third-Party Beneficiaries of Warranties Under UCC 2-318, *American Law Reports, Third Series, 100,* 743.

Drucker, P.F. (1966). *The Effective Executive*. New York: Harper & Row.

Dunn R. H. (1984). *Software Defect Removal*. New York: McGraw-Hill.

Duran, J. W. & Ntafos, S. C. (1984). An evaluation of random testing. *IEEE Transactions on Software Engineering, SE-10,* p. 438 - 444.

*Dynalantic Corp. v. The United States* (1991) (unpublished opinion). Reported as Table Case at Federal Reporter, Second Series, *945,* 416 (Federal Circuit Court of Appeals). Full text available on LEXIS (1991 U.S. App. 21110).

*East River Steamship Corp. v. Transamerica Delaval Inc.* (1986). United States Reports, *476,* 858-876.

Einhorn, D. (1985). Comment: The Enforceability of "Tear-Me-Open" Software License Agreements, *Journal of the Patent and Trademark Office Society, 67,* 509-529.

Elson, M. (1975). *Data Structures*. Chicago: Science Research Associates.

Endres, A. (1975). An analysis of errors and their causes in system programs. *IEEE Transactions of Software Engineering, 1,* p. 140-149. Reprinted in Jones (1981).

Epson Corporation (1985). *Epson FX-85 and FX-185 Printers User's Manual*.

Evans, M.W. (1984). *Productive Software Test Management*. New York: John Wiley & Sons.

Evans, M.W. & Marciniak, J.J. (1987). *Software Quality Assurance and Management*. New York: John Wiley & Sons.

Fagan M.E. (1976). Design and code inspections to reduce errors in program development. *IBM Systems Journal, 15,* p. 182-211. Reprinted in Miller & Howden (1981).

*Family Drug Store of New Iberia, Inc. v. Gulf States Computer Services, Inc.* (1990). Southern Reporter, Second Series, *563,* 1324 (Louisiana Court of Appeal).

Feigenbaum, A. V. (1991). *Total Quality Control,* Third Edition. New York: McGraw-Hill.

Feller, W. (1968). *An Introduction to Probability Theory and Its Applications,* Third Edition. New York: John Wiley & Sons.

Fernandez, E. B., Summers, R. C. & Wood, C. (1981). *Database Security and Integrity*. Reading, MA: Addison-Wesley.

Fishbein, J. I. (1980). Industry custom evidence: Its relevance in design defect products liability cases. *Journal of Products Liability, 11,* 341-358.

Fisher, R. & Ury, W. (1981). *Getting to Yes: Negotiating Agreement Without Giving In*. New York: Penguin Books.

*FMC Corporation v. Capital Cities/ABC, Inc.* (1990). Federal Reporter, Second Series, *915,* 300-306 (7th Circuit Court of Appeals).

Freedman, D. P. & Weinberg, G.M. (1982). *Handbook of Walkthroughs, Inspections and Technical Reviews. Evaluating Programs, Projects and Products,* Third Edition. Boston: Little, Brown and Company.

*Fundin v. Chicago Pneumatic Tool Co.* (1984). California Reporter, *199,* 789-795 (California Court of Appeal).

Gane, C. & Sarson, T. (1979). *Structured Systems Analysis: Tools and Techniques*. Englewood Cliffs: Prentice Hall.

Gause, D. C. & Weinberg, G. M. (1989). *Exploring Requirements: Quality Before Design*. New York: Dorset House.

Gemignani, M.C. (1981). Product liability and software. *Rutgers Computer & Technology Law Journal, 8,* 173-204.

Gemignani, M.C. (1987). More on the use of computers by professionals. *Rutgers Computer & Technology Law Journal, 13,* 317-339.

Glass, R.L. (1992). *Building Quality Software*. Englewood Cliffs, NJ: Prentice Hall.

Goldberg, S. (1987). The Space Shuttle Tragedy and the Ethics of Engineering. *Jurimetrics Journal, 27,* 155-159.

Goodenough, J. B. & Gerhart, S. L. (1975). Toward a theory of test data selection. *IEEE Transactions on Software Engineering* (June issue), 156-173. Reprinted in Miller & Howden (1981).

Gould, J. D. & Lewis, C. (1985). Designing for usability: Key principles and what designers think. *Communications of the ACM, 28,* 300-311. Reprinted in Baecker & Buxton (1987).

Graziano, S.G. (1991). Computer Malpractice—A New Tort on the Horizon? *Rutgers Computer & Technology Law Journal, 17,* 177-187.

Green, D. M. & Swets, J.A. (1966). *Signal Detection Theory and Psychophysics*. New York: John Wiley & Sons.

Griffiths, S. J. (1979). Design methodologies—A comparison. *Infotech State of the Art Report, Structured Analysis and Design*. Reprinted in Bergland & Gordon, (1979), p. 189-213.

Grimm, S. J. (1987). *How to Write Computer Documentation for Users,* Second Edition. New York: Van Nostrand Reinhold.

Gross, A.V. (Annotation). Computer Sales and Leases: Breach of Warranty, Misrepresentation, or Failure of Consideration as Defense or Ground for Affirmative Relief. *American Law Reports,* Fourth Series, *37,* 110.

*Hapka v. Paquin Farms* (1990). North Western Reporter, Second Series, 683- 690 (Minnesota Supreme Court).

*Harper & Row, Publishers, Inc. v. Nation Enterprises* (1983). Federal Reporter, Second Series, *723,* 195-217 (Second Circuit Court of Appeals 1983), *rev'd on other grounds* in *Harper & Row, Publishers, Inc. v Nation Enterprises,* (1985).

*Harper & Row, Publishers, Inc. v Nation Enterprises,* (1985). United States Reports, *471,* 539 (1985).

Harris, C.E. (1983). Complex Contract Issues in the Acquisition of Hardware and Software. *Computer/Law Journal, 4,* 77-100.

Hartson, H. R. (Ed.) (1985). *Advances in Human-Computer Interaction.* Norwood, NJ: Ablex Publishing.

Hastings, G. P. & King, K. J. (1986). *Creating Effective Documentation for Computer Programs.* Englewood Cliffs: Prentice Hall.

Heckel, P. (1982). *The Elements of Friendly Software Design.* New York: Warner Books.

Helander, M. (Ed.) (1991). *Handbook of Human-Computer Interaction,* Second Edition. Amsterdam: North-Holland.

Henderson, J.A. (1973). Judicial Review of Manufacturers' Conscious Design Choices: The Limits of Adjudication. *Columbia Law Review, 73,* 1531-1578.

Henderson, J.A. (1976), Design defect litigation revisited. *Cornell Law Review, 61,* 541-558.

Henderson, J.A. & Twerski, A.D. (1987). *Products Liability: Problems and Process.* Boston: Little, Brown & Co.

Hetzel, B. (1976). *An Experimental Analysis of Program Verification Methods.* Ph.D. dissertation, University of North Carolina at Chapel Hill.

Hetzel, B. (1988). *The Complete Guide to Software Testing,* Third Edition. Wellesley, MA: QED Information Services.

*Hoke, Inc. v. Cullinet Software, Inc.* (1992). Federal Supplement (to be published). Available on LEXIS 1992 U.S. Dist. 4616. (District of New Jersey).

*Hollingsworth Enterprises v. Software House, Inc.* (1986). North Eastern Reporter, Second Series, *513,* 1372-1378 (Ohio Court of Appeals).

*Hoover Universal, Inc. v. Brockway Imco, Inc.* (1987). Federal Reporter, Second Series, *809,* 1039-1044 (Fourth Circuit Court of Appeals).

*Horizons, Inc. v Avco Corp.* (1982). Federal Supplement, *551,* 771-783 (District of South Dakota).

Horton, W.K. (1990). *Designing and Writing Online Documentation: Help Files to Hypertext.* New York: John Wiley & Sons.

Houghton, R. C. (1984). Online help systems: A conspectus. *Computing Practices, 27,* p. 126-133.

Howden, W. E. (1985). The theory and practice of functional testing. *IEEE Software* (September issue), p. 6-17.

Howitt, D. (1984). Latest protection schemes promise to raise ire—and lawsuits. *InfoWorld,* Nov. 19, 45.

Human Factors Society (1989). *Code of Ethics.* Reprinted in *Human Factors Society Directory and Yearbook, 1992.* Contact the Society at P.O. Box 1369, Santa Monica, CA 90406-1369.

*Hunter v. Texas Instruments, Inc.* (1986). Federal Reporter, Second Series, *798,* 299-304 (Eighth Circuit Court of Appeals).

IBM National Language Technical Centre (1987). *National Language Information and Design Guide, Volume 1. Designing Enabled Products, Rules and Guidelines.* North York, Ontario, Canada: IBM Product SE09-8001. (Order these guides from any IBM office, not from North York.)

IBM National Language Technical Centre (1990). *National Language Design Guide, Volume 2. National Language Support Reference Manual*, Second Edition. North York, Ontario, Canada: IBM Product SE09-8002-01.

*Invacare Corp. v. Sperry Corp.* (1984). Federal Supplement, *612,* 448-454 (District of Central Ohio).

Irving, R.H., Higgins, C.A. & Safayeni, F.R. (1986). Computerized Performance Monitoring Systems: Use and Abuse. *Communications of the ACM, 29,* p. 794-801.

Ishikawa, K. (1985). *What is Total Quality Control? The Japanese Way.* Englewood Cliffs, NJ: Prentice Hall.

Jensen, K. & Wirth, N. (1982). *PASCAL—User Manual and Report.* New York: Springer-Verlag.

Jones, C. (1979). A survey of programming design and specification techniques. *Proceedings, Specifications of Reliable Software* (April issue), p. 91-103. Reprinted in Jones (1981).

Jones, C. (Ed.) (1981). *Tutorial: Programming Productivity: Issues for the Eighties.* Los Alamitos, CA: IEEE Computer Society.

Jones, C. (1991). *Applied Software Measurement: Assuring Productivity and Quality.* New York: McGraw Hill.

Jones, S., Kennelly, C., Mueller, C., Sweezy, M., Thomas, B., Velez, L. (1992). *Developing International User Information.* Bedford, MA: Digital Press. (See also the companion volume, *Digital Guide to Developing International Software.*)

Jones, W.K. (1990). Product defect causing commercial loss: The ascendancy of contract over tort. *University of Miami Law Review, 44*, 731.

Journal of Taxation (1986). Computer Service Bureau may be "preparer" under Section 6694. *Journal of Taxation, 64*, 122.

Joyce J.M. (1990). Comment: The battle against piracy: Hard times for software. *Saint Louis University Law Journal, 34,* 325-343.

Judd, K. (1990). *Copyediting: A Practical Guide.* Los Altos, CA: Crisp Publications.

Juliussen, E. & Juliussen, K. (1992). *The 1992 Computer Industry Almanac.* Available from the authors at 225 Allen Way, Incline Village, Lake Tahoe, NV, 89451. 702-831-2288.

Juran, J. M. (1988). *Juran on Planning for Quality.* New York: The Free Press.

Juran, J.M. (1989). *Juran on Leadership for Quality. An Executive Handbook.* New York: The Free Press.

Juran, J.M. & Gryna, F. M. (1980). *Quality Planning and Analysis,* Second Edition. New York: McGraw Hill.

Juran, J.M. & Gryna, F. M. (Eds) (1988). *Juran's Quality Control Handbook,* Fourth Edition. New York: McGraw Hill.

*Kalil Bottling Co. v. Burroughs Corp.* (1980). *Pacific Reporter, Second Series, 619,* 1055-1059 (Arizona Court of Appeals).

Kaner, H. C. & Vokey, J. R. (1984). A better random number generator. *Micro,* No. 72 (June issue), p. 26-35. *Errata:* July, 1984.

Karnezis, K.C. (Annotation). Products Liability: Modern Cases Determining Whether Product is Defectively Designed. *American Law Reports,* Third Series, *96, 22.*

Karrass, G. (1985). *Negotiate to Close: How to Make More Successful Deals.* New York: Simon and Schuster.

Kearney, J. K., Sedlmeyer, R. L., Thompson, W. B., Gray, M. A. & Adler, M. A. (1986). Software complexity measurement. *Communications of the ACM, 29,* p. 1044-1050.

Keeton, W. P., Dobbs, D. B., Keeton, R. E., & Owen, D. G. (1984; with 1988 Supplement). *Prosser and Keeton on The Law of Torts*. St. Paul, MN: West Publishing.

Kellett, E.L. (Annotation). Products Liability: Manufacturer's Responsiblity for Defective Component Supplied by Another and Incorporated in Product. *American Law Reports,* Third Series, *3,* 1016.

*Kelly v. Boston & Maine R.R.* (1946). North Eastern Reporter, Second Series, *66,* 807-814 (Massachusetts Supreme Court).

Kemp, D. (1990). Mass market software: The legality of the form license agreement. *Louisiana Law Review, 48,* 87.

Kernighan, B. W. & Plauger, P. J. (1974). *The Elements of Programming Style*. New York: McGraw-Hill.

Knuth, D. E. (1973). *The Art of Computer Programming. Volume 1 / Fundamental Algorithms*. Reading, MA: Addison-Wesley.

Knuth, D. E. (1981). *The Art of Computer Programming. Volume 2 / Seminumerical Algorithms*. Reading, MA: Addison-Wesley.

Kraemer, S. (1984). Note: Disclosure and the computer programmer, *Computer/Law Journal, 5,* 557-578.

Kraemer, S. (1988). Comment: "Computer Malpractice" and Other Legal Problems Posed by Computer "Vaporware," *Villanova Law Review, 33,* 835-893.

Krantz, D. H., Luce, R. D., Suppes, P., & Tversky, A. (1971). *Foundations of Measurement: Volume I: Additive and Polynomial Representations*. New York: Academic Press.

*Kushner v. Dravco Corp.* (1959) North Eastern Reporter, Second Series, *158,* 858-862 (Massachusetts Supreme Court, 1959).

Landes, W. M., & Posner, R. A. (1987). *The Economic Structure of Tort Law*. Cambridge, MA: Harvard University Press.

*La Rossa v. Scientific Design Co.* (1968). Federal Reporter, Second Series, *402,* 937-943 (Third Circuit Court of Appeals).

Laurel, B. (Ed.) (1990). *The Art of Human-Computer Interface Design*. Reading, MA: Addison-Wesley.

Laurel, B. (1991). *Computers as Theatre*. Reading, MA: Addison-Wesley.

Lawrence, (1987). Strict Liability, Computer Software and Medicine: Public Policy at the Crossroads. *Tort and Insurance Law Journal, 23,* 1-18.

Lawyer's Co-operative Publishing (Annotation 1). What Constitutes False, Misleading or Deceptive Advertising or Promotional Practices Subject to Action by Federal Trade Commission. *American Law Reports,* Second Series, *65,* 225.

Lawyer's Co-operative Publishing (Annotation 2). Allowance of Punitive Damages in Products Liability Case, *American Law Reports*. Fourth Series, *13,* 52.

Leveson, N.G. (1991). Software Safety in Embedded Computer Systems. *Communications of the ACM, 34* (February issue), 34. (Also, see her forthcoming book.)

Levin, S.J. (1986). Comment: Examining Restraints on Freedom to Contract as an Approach to Purchaser Dissatisfaction in the Computer Industry. *California Law Review, 74,* 2101-2141.

Levy, L.B. & Bell, S.Y. (1990). Software Product Liability: Understanding and Minimizing the Risks. *High Technology Law Journal, 5,* 1-27.

Lewis, C. & Norman, D.A. (1986). Designing for error. In Norman & Draper (1986), 411-432.

*Louisiana AFL-CIO v. Lanier Business Products* (1986). Federal Reporter, Second Series, *797,* 1364-1369 (Fifth Circuit Court of Appeals).

Mace, P. (1985). Microsoft Drops Some Protection. *InfoWorld,* Nov. 18, 8.

MacGregor, J., Lee, E. & Lam, N. (1986). Optimizing the structure of database menu indexes: A decision model of menu search. *Human Factors, 28,* p. 387-399.

MacKinnon, K.S. (1983). Comment: Computer Malpractice: Are Computer Manufacturers, Service Bureaus, and Programmers Really the Professionals They Claim to be? *Santa Clara Law Review, 23,* 1065-1093.

Magnuson-Moss Warranty - Federal Trade Commission Improvement Act. *United States Code,* Title 15, beginning at § 2301.

Mandell, (1984). *Computers, Data Processing and the Law: Text and Cases.* St. Paul, MN: West Publishing.

Martin, J. (1973). *Design of Man-Computer Dialogues.* Englewood Cliffs, NJ: Prentice Hall.

Martin, J. & McClure, C. (1983). *Software Maintenance: The Problem and Its Solutions.* Englewood Cliffs, NJ: Prentice Hall.

Marzouk, T.B. (1988). *Protecting Your Proprietary Rights in the Computer and High Technology Industries.* Washington: IEEE Computer Society Press.

Massingale, C.S. & Borthick, A.F. (1988). Risk allocation for injury due to defective medical software. *Journal of Products Liability, 11,* 181-198.

McCabe, T.J. (Ed.) (1983). *Structured Testing.* Los Alamitos, CA: IEEE Computer Society.

McCabe, T.J. & Schulmeyer, G.G. (1987). The Pareto principle applied to software quality assurance. In Schulmeyer & McManus (1987), p. 178-210.

McGehee, B.M. (1984). *The Complete Guide to Writing Software User Manuals.* Cincinatti: Writer's Digest Books.

*Meeting Makers, Inc. v American Airlines* (1987). Southern Reporter, Second Series, *513,* 700-701 (Florida District Court of Appeal).

*Micro-Managers, Inc. v. Gregory,* (1988). North Western Reporter, Second Series, *434,* 97-104 (Wisconsin Court of Appeals).

Microsoft Corporation (1990). *Microsoft Windows: International Handbook for Software Design.* (This book has no Microsoft part number; we understand that you may have difficulty obtaining it from Microsoft.)

Microsoft Corporation (1991). *Microsoft Mouse Programmer's Reference,* Second Edition. Redmond, WA: Microsoft Press.

Microsoft Corporation (1992). *Microsoft Test User's Guide.* (Sold with the Microsoft Test program.)

Miller, E. (1981). Introduction to software testing technology. In Miller & Howden (1981), p. 4 - 16.

Miller, E. & Howden, W. E. (Eds.) (1981). *Tutorial: Software Testing & Validation Techniques,* Second Edition. Los Alamitos, CA: IEEE Computer Society.

Miller, J.D. (1978). Effects of Noise on People, in Carterette & Friedman (1978), 609-640.

Mills, H.D. (1970). On the statistical validation of computer programs. Reprinted in Mills (1988), p. 71-81.

Mills, H.D. (1988). *Software Productivity.* New York: Dorset House.

Mortimer, H. (1989). Computer-aided medicine: Present and future issues of liability. *Computer/Law Journal, 9,* 177-203.

Mosteller, W. S. (1981). *System Programmer's Problem Solver*. Cambridge, MA: Winthrop Publishers.

Mundel, A.B. (1991). *Ethics in Quality*. New York: ASQC Quality Press / Marcel Dekker.

Mullenix, L.S. (1992). Another easy case, some more bad law: Carnival Cruise Lines and contractual personal jurisdiction. *Texas International Law Journal, 27,* 323-370.

Myers, B. H. (1985). The importance of percent-done progress indicators for computer-human interfaces. In *Proceedings of CHI '85: Human Factors in Computing Systems* (San Francisco, April 14-18). ACM No. 608850, p. 11-17.

Myers, G. J. (1976). *Software Reliability: Principles & Practices*. New York: John Wiley & Sons.

Myers, G. J. (1978). A controlled experiment in program testing and code walkthroughs/inspections. *Communications of the ACM* (September issue), p. 760-768. Reprinted in Curtis (1981).

Myers, G. J. (1979). *The Art of Software Testing*. New York: John Wiley & Sons.

Neisser, U. (1967). *Cognitive Psychology*. New York: Appleton-Century Crofts.

Nimmer, R. (1985; supplemented 1990). *The Law of Computer Technology.* Warren, Gorham & Lamont.

Nimmer, R. & Krauthaus, P.A. (1986). Computer error and user liability risk. *Jurimetrics Journal* (Winter issue), 121-137.

Norman, D. A. (1988). *The Design of Everyday Things*. New York: Doubleday.

Norman, D. A. & Draper, S.W. (1986). *User Centered System Design: New Perspectives on Human-Computer Interaction.*Hillsdale, NJ: Lawrence Erlbaum Associates.

Mortimer, H. (1989). Note: Computer-Aided Medicine: Present and Future Issues of Liability. *Computer/Law Journal, 9,* 177-203.

*Office Supply Co., Inc. v. Basic/Four Corp.* (1982). Federal Supplement, *538,* 776-793 (Eastern District of Wisconsin).

Open Software Foundation (1990). *OSF/Motif Style Guide,* Revision 1.1. Englewood Cliffs, NJ: Prentice-Hall.

*Orthopedic & Sports Injury Clinic v. Wang Laboratories, Inc.* (1991). Federal Reporter, Second Series, *922,* 220-228.

Ortner, C.B. (1985). Current trends in software protection—A litigation perspective. *Jurimetrics Journal,* (Spring issue) 319-332.

*Ostalkiewicz v. Guardian Alarm* (1987). Atlantic Reporter, Second Series, *520,* 563 (Rhode Island Supreme Court).

Ould, M. A. (1990). *Strategies for Software Engineering: The Management of Risk and Quality*. New York: John Wiley & Sons.

Owen, D. (1976). Punitive damages in products liability litigation. *Michigan Law Review, 74,* 1257.

Paap, K.R. & Roske-Hofstrand, R. J. (1986). The optimal number of menu options per panel. *Human Factors, 28,* p. 377-385.

*Pacific Mutual Life Insurance Company v. Haslip* (1991). United States Reports, *499,* —; Supreme Court Reporter, *111,* 1032-1067.

Parikh, G. & Zvegintzov, N. (Eds.) (1983). *Tutorial on Software Maintenance*. Los Alamitos, CA: IEEE Computer Society.

*Pawelec v. Digitcom, Inc.* (1984). Atlantic Reporter, Second Series, *471,* 60-63 (New Jersey Superior Court, Appellate Division).

*Pearson v. Dodd* (1969). Federal Reporter, Second Series, *410,* 701-709 (District of Columbia Circuit Court of Appeals).

Perlis, A. J., Sayward, F. G. & Shaw, M. (Eds.) (1983). *Software Metrics.* Cambridge, MA, MIT Press.

Perry, W. E. (1986). *How to Test Software Packages.* New York: John Wiley & Sons.

Perry, W. E. (1988). *A Structured Approach to System Testing,* Second Edition. Wellesley, MA: QED.

Petschenik, N. H. (1985). Practical priorities in system testing. *IEEE Software* (September issue), p. 18-23.

Pfanzagl, J. (1971). *Theories of Measurement.* Wurzburg-Wien: Physica-Verlag.

Popper, K. R. (1965). *Conjectures and Refutations: The Growth of Scientific Knowledge,* Second Edition. New York: Harper & Row.

Poston, R.M. (1984). When does more documentation mean less work? *IEEE Software* (October issue), 98-99.

Powers, W. & Niven, M. (1992). Negligence, breach of contract, and the "economic loss" rule. *Texas Tech Law Review, 23,* 477-523.

Price, J. (1984). *How to Write a Computer Manual. A Handbook of Software Documentation.* Menlo Park, CA: Benjamin/Cummings.

*Princeton Graphics Operating L.P. v. NEC Home Electronics (U.S.A.), Inc.* (1990). Federal Supplement, *732,* 1258-1267 (Southern District of New York).

*Professional Lens Plan v. Polaris Leasing* (1984). Pacific Reporter, Second Series, *675,* 887-901 (Kansas Supreme Court).

*Professional Lens Plan v. Polaris Leasing* (1985). Pacific Reporter, Second Series, *710,* 1297-1304 (Kansas Supreme Court).

Putz-Anderson, V. (Ed.) (1988). *Cumulative Trauma Disorders: A Manual for Musculoskeletal Diseases of the Upper Limbs.* London: Taylor & Francis.

Rapps, S. & Weyuker, E. J. (1985). Selecting software test data using data flow information. *IEEE Transactions on Software Engineering, SE-11,* p. 367-375.

*R.A. Weaver & Associates, Inc. v. Haas & Haynie Corp.* (1980). Federal Reporter, Second Series, *663,* 168-277.

*Redmac, Inc. v. Computerland of Peoria* (1986). North Eastern Reporter, Second Series, *489,* 380-384 (Appellate Court of Illinois).

Reifer, D. J. & Trattner, S. (1977). A glossary of software tools and techniques. *Computer* (July issue), p. 52-60. Reprinted in Jones (1981).

*Restatement (Second) of Torts* (1965). St. Paul, MN: American Law Institute.

*Ritchie Enterprises v. Honeywell Bull, Inc.* (1990). Federal Supplement, *730,* 1041-1055 (District of Kansas).

*RKB Enterprises, Inc. v. Ernst Young* (1992). New York Supplement, *582,* 814-817 (New York Supreme Court, Appellate Division).

Rodau, A. (1986). Computer Software: Does Article 2 of the Uniform Commercial Code Apply? *Emory Law Journal, 35,* 853-920.

Roehmer, J. M. & Chapanis, A. (1982). Learning performance and attitudes as a function of the reading grade level of a computer-presented tutorial. In *Proceedings of the Conference on Human Factors in Computer Systems* (Gaithersburg, Maryland, March 15-17). ACM (Washington D.C. Chapter), p. 239-244.

Roetzheim, W. R. (1991). *Developing Software to Government Standards.* Englewood Cliffs, NJ: Prentice Hall.

*Roginsky v. Richardson-Merrell, Inc.* (1967). Federal Reporter, Second Series, *378,* 832-854 (Second Circuit Court of Appeals).

Rosch, E. & Lloyd, B. B. (1978). *Cognition and Categorization.* Hillsdale, NJ: Lawrence Erlbaum Associates.

Rosenthal, R. (1966). *Experimenter Effects in Behavioral Research.* New York: Appleton-Century Crofts.

*RRX Industries, Inc. v. Lab-Con, Inc.* (1985) Federal Reporter, Second Series, *772,* 543-552 (Ninth Circuit Court of Appeals).

Rubenstein, R. & Hersh H. (1984). *The Human Factor: Designing Computer Systems for People.* Burlington, Massachusetts: Digital Press.

Ruby, D. (1986). Breaking the copy protection barriers. *PC Week, 3* (April 8 issue), 45.

*Saloomey v. Jeppesen & Co.* (1983). Federal Reporter, Second Series, *707,* 671-680 (Second Circuit Court of Appeals).

Salter, J.H. (1989). Software Performance Standards Under Article 2 of the Uniform Commercial Code. *Computer/Law Journal, 9,* 465-489.

*Salt River Project Agricultural Improvement & Power District v. Westinghouse Electric Corp.* (1984). Pacific Reporter, Second Series, *694,* 198-215. (Arizona Supreme Court).

*Santor v. A. & M. Karagheusian, Inc.* (1965). Atlantic Reporter, Second Series, *207,* 305-314 (Supreme Court of New Jersey).

Schneider, N. (1985). Taking the "byte" out of warranty disclaimers. *Computer/Law Journal, 5,* 531-555.

Schneiderman, B. (1980). *Software Psychology: Human Factors in Computer and Information Systems.* Cambridge, Massachusetts: Winthrop Publishers.

Schneiderman, B. (1987). *Designing the User Interface: Strategies for Effective Human-Computer Interaction.* Reading, MA: Addison-Wesley.

Schneiderman, B. & Kearsley, G. (1989). *Hypertext Hands-On!: An Introduction to a New Way of Organizing and Accessing Information.* Reading, MA: Addison-Wesley.

*Schroders, Inc. v. Hogan Systems, Inc.* (1987). New York Supplement, Second Series, *522,* 404-407 (New York Supreme Court).

Schulmeyer, G. (1987). Standardization of software quality assurance. In Schulmeyer & McManus (1987), p. 79-103.

Schulmeyer, G. & McManus, J. I. (Eds.) (1987). *Handbook of Software Quality Assurance.* New York: Van Nostrand Reinhold.

Schuyler, M. (1991). Systems Librarian and Automation Review. *Small Computers in Libraries, 11,* N° 1, 12.

Schwartz, M. & Schwartz, N.F. (1987 and 1991 Supplement). *Engineering Evidence,* Second Edition. Colorado Springs: Shepard's / McGraw-Hill.

Schwartz, W.B., Patil, R.S., & Szolovits, P. (1987). Artificial intellgence in medicine: Where do we stand? *Jurimetrics Journal* (Summer issue), 362-369.

*Seely v. White Motor Co.* (1965). *Pacific Reporter, Second Series, 403,* 145-158 (California Supreme Court).

Senders, J. W. & Moray, N. P. (1991). *Human Error: Cause, Prediction, and Reduction.* Hillsdale, NJ: Lawrence Erlbaum.

Sheldon & Mak (1991). *California Intellectual Property Handbook.* Oakland, CA: Matthew Bender.

Shell, G.R. (1988). Substituting Ethical Standards for Common Law Rules in Commercial Cases: An Emerging Statutory Trend. *Northwestern University Law Review, 82,* 1198-1254.

Sherman, P. (1981, and 1991 Supplement). *Products Liability for the General Practitioner.* Colorado Springs: Shepard's / McGraw-Hill.

*Shute v. Carnival Cruise Lines, Inc.* (1990). Federal Reporter, Second Series, *897,* 377-389 (Ninth Circuit Court of Appeals 1990). *Overruled* by *Carnival Cruise Lines, Inc. v. Shute (1991).*

Silver, N.C., Leonard, D.C., Ponsi K.A., & Wogalter, M.S. (1991). Warnings and Purchase Intentions for Pest-Control Products. *Forensic Reports, 4,* 17-33.

Smith, S.L. & Mosier, J.N. (1984). *Design Guidelines for User-System Interface Software.* Bedford, MA: Mitre Corporation. Report prepared for the USAF, MTR-9420, ESD-TR-84-190.

Sohr, D. (1983). Better software manuals. *Byte, 8* (May issue), p. 286-294.

*Southland Corp. v. Keating* (1984). United States Reports, *465,* 1.

*Southwest Forest Industries, Inc. v. Westinghouse Electric Corp.* (1970). Federal Reporter, Second Series, *422,* 1013-1021 (Ninth Circuit Court of Appeals).

Spilker, J. & Strudwick, K. (1992). *Northwest High Tech: A Guide to North America's Fastest Growing Computer Region,* Fourth Edition. Bellevue, Washington: Resolution Business Press.

*Spring Motors Distributors, Inc. v. Ford Motor Company* (1985). Atlantic Reporter, Second Series, *489,* 660-681.

*Step-Saver Data Systems, Inc. v. Wyse Technology and The Software Link, Inc.* (1991). Federal Reporter, Second Series, *939,* 91-107.

*Systems Design & Management Information, Inc. v. Kansas City Post Office Employees Credit Union* (1990). Pacific Reporter, Second Series, *788,* 878-882 (Kansas Court of Appeals).

Taylor, W. (1991). Stung by bum software? Consider legal action. *PC Computing, 4* (April issue), p. 218.

Torgerson, W. S. (1958). *Theory and Methods of Scaling.* New York: John Wiley & Sons.

Trollip, S. R. & Sales, G. (1986). Readability of computer-generated fill-justified text. *Human Factors, 28,* p. 159-163.

*Uniform Commercial Code.* Official 1990 Text. Reprinted in *Selected Commercial Statutes* (1992), St. Paul, MN: West Publishing Co.

*Uniform Trade Secrets Act of 1979* as quoted in Annotation, What is Computer Trade Secret Under State Law? *American Law Reports,* Fourth Series, *53,* 1046

*United States v. May* (1980). Federal Reporter, Second Series, *625,* 186-195 (Eighth Circuit Court of Appeals).

Urban, D.A. (1990). Custom's proper role in strict products liability actions based on design defect. *UCLA Law Review, 38,* 439-487.

Uren, E., Howard, R. & Perinotti, T. (*in press,* 1993). *An Introduction to Software Internationalization and Localization.* New York: Van Nostrand Reinhold.

*Vault Corp. v. Quaid Software Ltd.* (1987). Federal Supplement, *655,* 750-763 (Eastern District of Louisiana), *affirmed* in *Vault Corp. v. Quaid Software Ltd,* (1988).

*Vault Corp. v. Quaid Software Ltd,* (1988). Federal Reporter, Second Series, *847,* 255-270 (Fifth Circuit Court of Appeals).

Vincenti, R.D. (1988). Comment: Self-help legal software and the unauthorized practice of law. *Computer/ Law Journal, 8,* 185-226.

Voorhees, J.J. (1991). Note: Price discrimination and software licensing: Does the Robinson-Patman Act fail to accommodate modern technology? *Washington University Law Quarterly, 69,* 317-336.

*Waggoner v. Town & Country Mobile Homes, Inc.* (1990). Pacific Reporter, Second Series, *808,* 649-661 (Oklahoma Supreme Court).

Walker, G.T. (1984). Defending punitive claims in products cases, in *Product Liability of Manufacturers Prevention and Defense* 497-529, Practicing Law Institute.

Walkowiak, V.S. (1980). Reconsidering plaintiff's fault in product liability litigation: The proposed conscious design choice exception. *Vanderbilt Law Review, 33,* 651-679.

Walton, M. (1986). *The Deming Management Method.* New York: Putnam Publishing.

*Wangen v. Ford Motor Co.* (1980). North Western Reporter, Second Series, *294,* 437-473.

Wasserman, A. I. & Shewmake, D. T. (1985). The role of prototypes in the User Software Engineering (USE) methodology. In Hartson (1985), p. 191-210.

Weinberg, G. M. (1971). *The Psychology of Computer Programming.* New York: Van Nostrand Reinhold.

Weinstein, A.S. (1988). The Performance Audit: Minimizing Software Liability (Part I). *Idea, 29,* 127-135.

White, J. J. & Summers, R. S. (1988). *Uniform Commerical Code,* Third Edition. St. Paul, MN: West Publishing.

Whitten, N. (1990). *Managing Software Development Projects.* New York: John Wiley & Sons.

Williams, R.D. (1984) Corporate Policies for Creation & Retention of Documents and Their Application to the Defense of a Product Liability Case, in *Product Liability of Manufacturers Prevention and Defense* 325-360, Practicing Law Institute.

*Williams v. Chittenden Trust Co.* Atlantic Reporter, Second Series, *484,* 911-915 (Vermont Supreme Court).

Winkler, R. L. & Hays, W. L. (1975). *Statistics: Probability, Inference, and Decision,* Second Edition. New York: Holt, Rinehart and Winston.

Winston, P. H. (1977). *Artifical Intelligence.* Reading, MA: Addison-Wesley.

*Winter v. G.P. Putnam's Sons,* (1991). Federal Reporter, Second Series, *938,* 1033-1038 (Ninth Circuit Court of Appeals).

Wogalter, M.S., Allison, S.T. & McKenna, N.A. (1989). Effects of Cost and Social Influence on Warning Compliance. *Human Factors, 31,* 133-140.

Wolverton, R.W. (1974). The cost of developing large-scale software. *IEEE Transactions on Computers* (June issue), p. 282-303. Reprinted in Jones (1981).

Yourdon, E. (1975). *Techniques of Program Structure and Design.* Englewood Cliffs: Prentice Hall.

Yourdon, E. & Constantine, L.L. (1978). *Structured Design: Fundamentals of a Discipline of Computer Program and Systems Design..* Englewood Cliffs: Prentice Hall.

Zelkowitz, M. (Ed.) (1982). *Selected Reprints in Software.* Los Alamitos, CA: IEEE Computer Society.

Zitter, J.M. (Annotation). Strict products liability: Recovery for damage to product alone. *American Law Reports,* Fourth Series, *72,* 12.

Zupanec, D.M. (Annotation). Practices forbidden by state deceptive trade practice and consumer protection acts. *American Law Reports,* Third Series, *89,* 449.

# INDEX

## A

abbreviations   171, 384, 387, 394
acceptance testing   29, 51, 191-197, 212, 266, 268, 269, 279, 281, 285, 316
   not rigidly enforced until beta milestone   280
access to data   37
acquired products.   *See* initial stability assessment
advertisements   53, 224, 303, 307, 315, 339
algorithm-specific testing   42
almost-alpha milestone   265, 268, 275–277
alpha milestone.   *See also* milestones
   -generally   265, 268, 277–286
   as an activity trigger   275
   defined   277
   report all bugs found after alpha   116
Alternate Graphics Mode   154.   *See also* printer testing
American Society for Quality Control   330, 341, 343
analysis of bugs.   *See* Problem Reports: analyzing reproducible bugs before reporting them
analysis of the program   37.   *See also* boundaries
   into equivalence classes.   *See* equivalence classes
Annoyance.   *See* Problem Reports, fields: Severity
anomaly reports.   *See* Problem Reports
ANSI Standard terminals   57
appeal meeting.   *See* review meetings: for deferred bugs
appeal process.   *See* deferring bugs: review process
application (database)   121
architects   29
archives   272, 431
archiving test materials   281, 301
area of concern in the program   283
arithmetic errors.   *See* errors (calculation)
arrays   37, 404, 407, 416, 418, 419, 426
As designed.   *See* Problem Reports, fields: Resolution
ASCII code   9–11, 171–172, 173, 376, 399, 403
assertion checks   201
Assigned To.   *See* Problem Reports, fields
Association for Computing
   Machinery   ix, 169, 303, 330, 341
Attachments.   *See* Problem Reports, fields
auditing the test plan   207, 272, 300, 334–335, 363
automatic variables   405
automation
   automated acceptance testing   191–197, 268, 281, 282
      why this is the best area to automate   197
   automated regression testing   50, 177, 191–197, 281, 282, 289
      easier when UI freeze comes early   293
      regression test library   140–141, 177, 192
   capturing output   139, 162, 177, 194–195, 281
   compare costs of manual and automated tests   136, 282
   costs   136, 160, 177, 194, 196, 282, 434

automation (continued)
   coverage monitors   200–201
   disincentives to polish the design   196
   early automation vs. early testing   196, 263
   function equivalence testing   135–138, 195
      costs and advantages   135, 136
      generalized beyond mathematical comparisons   139
      using sensitivity analysis to get good test cases   136–137
   international issues   177
   printer testing   155, 159–164, 194, 266, 269
   random generation of input data   137–138, 193
   simulating keyboard input   136
   sophistication of the automating tester   177
   timing issues; need to insert delays   193, 194
   using comparison files   135, 162, 163, 177, 195–197
   ways to feed test data to the program   193

## B

base code   170
batch processing   193
battery of tests.   *See* test series
bebugging   49
benchmark tests   49
benefit of the bargain damages   311.   *See also* contracts
beta milestone   185, 265, 270, 286–293
   defined   287
   start enforcing the acceptance test   280
   submit disks in final, shipping configuration   287
   time for your nastiest testing   289
beta testing   52–53, 71, 185–186, 270, 286, 291–294
   beta testers   266, 274, 287
   costs   52–53, 293
   documentation   185
   guarding against piracy of beta code   287–288
   Problem Reports   71
big bang testing   44–46
bill of materials   224
bit fields   418
black box testing
   -generally   23–25, 41, 50–57, 123–141, 212–213
   acceptance testing   51, 191–197, 212, 266, 268, 269, 279, 280, 285
   assertion checks   201
   automated regression testing   50, 177, 191–197, 270, 281, 282
   beta testing   52, 54, 71, 185, 266, 270, 274
   boundary testing   5, 7–11, 54, 131–132, 215, 233, 289
   certification   54
   combination tests   237, 241, 433
   compatibility testing   56, 273, 328
   computations   54, 135
   configuration testing   56, 131, 134, 143–167, 206, 223, 238, 270, 272, 279, 281, 293, 297
   contrasted with glass box   42
      no more effective than glass box testing   211
   control flow testing   213
   conversion testing   56
   coverage monitoring   200
   data file format testing   56

**costs (continued)**
  of reporting errors  117
  of software development  31–32, 257, 259, 261
  of technical support calls  154, 179, 263, 264, 269, 273
  of test planning  204, 205, 208, 242, 243, 245
  of testers vs. programmers  92
  of testing  23–25, 31, 255, 261, 268, 273,
    282, 294, 350, 351
  of videotaping bugs  191
**coverage criteria  43–44**
**coverage monitors  41, 44, 200, 201, 211**
**crashed.** *See* locked (program)
**critical error messages  171, 190**
**critical path.** *See* schedules
**cross-referencing bugs  118**
**cursor  2, 269, 380**
**custom development of software  54, 204, 259, 266,**
  **269–271, 305, 309–310, 316, 338–339**
**customer (final acceptance) testing  54, 266, 269–**
  **271.** *See also* beta testing
**customer complaints  30, 154, 263, 264, 265, 269,**
  **271–273, 334**
  become regression test cases  192
  legal issues  334
**customer expectations  60, 61, 204, 213, 216**
**customer feedback  271–273, 291, 292**
**cycle of testing  51, 108, 285**

**D**

**damages  310–312, 316, 322, 323, 336, 339.** *See also*
  contracts; torts
**data, access to  37**
**data communication  29**
**data design  36, 37.** *See also* design: data
**data entry fields  123.** *See also* field
**data entry form (defined)  121**
**data entry screens (may be state dependent)  133**
**data file format testing  56**
**data files (contents) testing  290, 295, 434**
**data flow  228, 229, 259.** *See also* test planning documents
**data integrity: tested during glass box testing  41**
**data sharing  29**
**data storage  37**
**data structures  29, 37, 400, 409, 416, 418, 419**
**data types  9, 416**
**data-handling errors.** *See* errors (handlng data); errors
  (interpreting data)
**Database Management System (DBMS)  121**
**Date.** *See* **Problem Reports, fields**
**date of discovery of a bug.** *See* Problem Reports, fields: Date
**dead keys  172**
**deadly embrace  411**
**debugging.** *See also* tools: source code debuggers
  -generally  41, 80, 270, 272
  done by testers  92
  sometimes aided by comparison output  139

**debugging (continued)**
  tester's analysis of the bug simplifies debugging  78, 83
  under incremental and big bang test models  45
**decision tables and trees  229**
**decomposition (of a program)  36**
**defect  333**
**Deferred.** *See* Problem Reports, fields: Resolution;  Problem
  Reports, fields: Treat as deferred
**deferring bugs**
  -generally  69, 73, 74, 77–78
  later consequences  273
  reopening them for the next release  113–114
  review process  95–96, 109–111, 119, 270, 272, 333
  timing (of deferral) issues  103
**Deming management method  87, 343, 347, 353**
**demo version of the program  272**
**dependency flags  244**
**design**
  data  36, 37
  external  35–36, 38, 52, 54, 267, 277, 375
  internal  29, 35, 36–38, 267, 277
  logic  38–51
  polishing  292
  specifications.  *See* specifications
  structural  36–38
  top-down  38, 39
**design defects (legal term)  329, 337**
**design documents  32–41.** *See also* documents (development)
**design errors  103.** *See also* errors (user interface)
**design goals  32**
**Design issue.** *See* Problem Reports, fields: Report Type
**design stages.** *See* software development stages
**designers  29, 33**
**desk checking  47**
**destructive attitude.** *See* harsh testing -- why
**development complete milestone  112.** *See also* milestones
**development model.** *See* evolutionary development;  waterfall
  method
**Development Services groups  345**
**development stages.** *See* software development stages
**development team  29–30, 71**
  and Problem Reports  71
  and the printer compatibility database  159
  and the problem tracking system  88, 95–96
  reviews deferred bugs  95–96, 112–113, 119, 270
  reviews the test plan  208, 270
  use the test plan  207
**development time line.** *See* milestones
**device testing.** *See* configuration testing;  printer testing
**device-class-specific errors.** *See* configuration testing
**diagnostics  191.** *See also* tools
**dialog boxes  171, 382**
**digits, testing.** *See* numbers
**DIP switches  154.** *See also* printer testing: printer features
**direct damages  315**
**Disagree with suggestion.** *See* Problem Reports, fields:
  Resolution

file comparison utilities   190.  *See also* tools
file format converters   190.  *See also* tools
file format testing   56, 173
file viewers   190.  *See also* tools
files (defined)   121
    index file   121
    main data file   121
    reference file   121
filters   172
final acceptance testing   54
final integrity test milestone   265, 272, 299–301
final testing milestone
    you might report only serious bugs this late   116
Financial Accounting Standards Board (FASB)   277,  287
finding strings embedded in code files   190
first functionality milestone   265, 274–275
first hours of use testing   215, 216, 272, 300
first-time errors.  *See* errors (initial and later states)
Fixed.  *See* Problem Reports, fields: Resolution
fixing bugs
    probability of success   50
    regression testing   50, 270, 272
    side effects   50
    unmask other bugs   50
flags   397, 398, 405, 407, 409, 414, 417
fleas.  *See* Problem Reports, fields: Severity: Minor
floating point numbers   138, 401–403, 406, 413, 416
focus groups   33, 34, 266, 267
form (defined)   121
fraud   303, 315, 317, 339.  *See also* torts

friction between testers and project managers
    how to reduce it   119
front panel switches   154.  *See also* printer testing: printer
    features
full testing.  *See* complete testing (impossible)
function equivalence testing   135–139, 195
    automation   135–138
        advantages   135
    generalized beyond mathematical comparisons   139
    reference functions   135
    test functions   135
    using sensitivity analysis to get good test cases   136–137
function list.  *See* test planning documents: outlines: function
    lists
function testing   42, 52
Functional Area.  *See* Problem Reports, fields
functional definition   32–33, 33–35
functionality errors   375.  *See also* errors (user interface)
functions   36.  *See also* modules

## G

gamma milestone   287
generalized equivalence testing   139.  *See also* function
    equivalence testing
glass box testing.  *See also* path testing;  software metrics
    -generally   41–49, 210–212, 266, 347
    analyzing pseudocode   40–41
    automated regression testing   50
    benefits of glass box approach
        can analyze code's control flow   41
        can focus on individual modules   41
        easier to force memory overflow   42
        easier to force race condition   42
        internal boundaries more visible   42
        makes algorithm-specific testing possible   42
        testing coverage can be tracked   41
    code reviews   47
    contrasted with black box   42
        no more effective than black box testing   211
    contrasted with translucent box   200
    coverage
        branch coverage   43
        complete coverage   43
        condition coverage   44
        coverage criteria   43
        coverage monitors   41, 44, 211
        line coverage   43
        logic coverage criteria   43
    debugging   41, 45, 78, 83
    desk checking   47
    drivers   45
    dynamic testing   46
    element testing   44
    integration testing   45–46
    module testing   44
    mystique: it looks scientific   211
    path testing   20–22, 43–44, 210
    software metrics   47–48
    standards compliance   47

managers, marketing. *See* product managers
managers, project. *See* project managers
managers, senior. *See* senior managers
manuals. *See* documentation; errors (documentation)
manufacturing masters   272, 432
market analysis   34, 266
   printers   146–147
market requirements   30. *See also* requirements analysis
marketing staff. *See* product managers
marketing support materials   53, 176, 224, 268, 270, 278, 288, 289, 308, 315
masked bugs   50
masks   418
master disks   272, 300
matrices. *See* test planning documents
matrix inversion   42
meeting managers   40. *See also* technical reviews
memory
   -generally   83, 144
   available memory   83, 269, 400, 425
   debugger can show memory-related problems   80
   equivalence classes on amount available   131
   fragmented memory   83
   insufficient   176
   memory banks   429
   memory hogs   80, 425
   memory locking utilities   190
   pages of memory   429
   screen memory   380
   testing utilities   202, 266, 269
   virtual memory   400, 430
memory meter. *See* tools
menus   381, 384, 385–386
   -generally   130, 171, 173
   accelerator keys   173
   and state transition analysis   132–133
      same testing problems as path testing   133
   hot keys and menu accelerator keys   173
   menu maps   133, 237
merchantability   308–309. *See also* contracts: warranties
messages   80, 173–174, 418–420, 422, 423–425, 426
metrics. *See* software metrics
middle-of-the-road tests. *See* mainstream usage testing
Mild (bugs). *See* Problem Reports, fields: Severity: Minor
milestones. *See also* software development stages
   -generally   265–302
   almost alpha   116, 265, 268, 275–277
   alpha   116, 265, 268, 275, 277–286
   beta   185–186, 265, 286–293
   development is complete   112–113
   development time line   265
   final integrity test   265, 272, 299–301
   final testing   116
   first functionality   265, 266, 274–275
   gamma   287
   negotiating acceptance criteria for milestones   275, 286
   pre-beta   265, 286
   pre-final   265, 272, 295–299

milestones (continued)
   pre-milestone negotiations about bug fixes   96
   product design   265, 266, 267–274
   product release (ship it)   113–114, 265, 272, 299, 301
   short alpha-to-final time sets up conflicts   277
   testing milestones   279, 291
   user interface freeze   185, 265, 293–295
minimally acceptable product. *See* evolutionary development
minor bugs. *See* Problem Reports, fields: Severity: Minor
mismanagement (by the project manager)   24
misrepresentation. *See* fraud
missing commands. *See* errors (user interface)
missing errors. *See* errors, missed
mission of testing. *See* purpose of testing
model-specific errors. *See* configuration testing
models. *See* prototypes
modems   136, 143, 293
modular decomposition   36
modular design   37
modular testing
   -defined   44
   bottom-up vs top-down   46
   stubs and drivers   45
modules   36, 63, 120, 210, 216, 283
morale. *See* testers
More info needed on bug report. *See* Problem Reports, fields: Resolution: Need more info
mouse   144, 175, 269, 293
multi-processing systems   63, 85, 411, 424–427
mutation (variant of bebugging)   49

## N

Need more info. *See* Problem Reports, fields: Resolution
negative numbers. *See* numbers
negligence   317, 322–336, 337. *See also* torts
networks   163
non-economic damages   312
nondisclosure agreements. *See* trade secrets (and nondisclosure agreements)
"Not a bug" responses to bug reports. *See* Problem Reports, fields: Resolution: Disagree with suggestion
nuisances. *See* Problem Reports, fields: Severity: Minor
numbers
   integer vs. floating point   138, 402
   numeric separators   175
   positive vs. negative   8–9, 176
   storage of   8–11, 402, 403. *See also* storage units
   testing entry of   7–11
   testing statistics. *See* problem tracking system: statistics
numerical analysis   42, 62

## O

objectives of testing. *See* purpose of testing
objectives statement. *See* documents (development)
OEM testing. *See* port testing
online help. *See* documentation; help

# ABOUT THE AUTHORS

**Cem Kaner** has a broad background in software development. He has worked as a human factors analyst, programmer, tester, test manager, documentation manager, and project manager at Electronic Arts, Power Up Software, Telenova, and WordStar. He'll shortly take on new responsibilities, as an attorney. The unifying theme of Kaner's work is improvement of product usability, reliability, and safety. Kaner specialized in Mathematics & Philosophy as an undergraduate at Brock University and the University of Windsor (Canada). His Ph.D. (McMaster University, Canada) is in Psychology, with an emphasis on Engineering Psychology. He is certified as a Quality Engineer by the American Society for Quality Control. In about 3 weeks (May, 1993), he expects to receive a J.D. from Golden Gate University in San Francisco.

**Jack Falk** is an Associate Producer (project manager) at Electronic Arts, developing consumer entertainment and creativity software. Before this, Jack managed a software test group, and then all of product development operations. He has also been a Director of Operations for some well-known retail chains, managing up to 112 employees. In these positions, cost control and efficiency were critical issues. Jack studied Business Administration at Golden Gate University.

**Hung Quoc Nguyen** is a Software Development Manager (project manager) at Power Up Software, developing business organization and productivity software. He was the founding manager of Power Up's software testing group, and a Software Analyst at Electronic Arts, where he also managed the development of two music software products. Hung started his career in the electronics industry in *hardware* engineering and quality assurance— he was a Group Manager of Engineering and Quality Assurance at Energy Transformation Systems, where he also founded its QA organization. Hung has also been a part-time instructor and professional musician. He is certified as a Quality Engineer (ASQC-CQE) by the American Society for Quality Control, and he holds a B.Sc. in Quality Assurance from Cogswell Polytechnical College in Cupertino, California.